Duties of the Heart
by Rabeinu Bahya ibn Paquda
with commentaries

translated by Yosef Sebag

VOLUME 1

OTHER WORKS BY YOSEF SEBAG

Ethics of the Fathers   www.dafyomireview.com/489

Path of the Just   - www.dafyomireview.com/447

Gates of Holiness   - www.dafyomireview.com/442

Vilna Gaon on Yonah   - www.dafyomireview.com/259

Torah Numerology   - www.dafyomireview.com/543

Marks of Divine Wisdom - www.dafyomireview.com/427

Torah Authenticity   - www.dafyomireview.com/430

yosefsebag@gmail.com

Dafyomi Advancement Forum

Produced by Kollel Iyun Hadaf • Rosh Kollel: Rabbi Mordecai Kornfeld

'Your Chavrusa in Yerushalayim'

בס"ד

Rosh Kollel:
Rabbi Mordecai Kornfeld

Chairman of the Board:
Rabbi Gedalya Rabinowitz
Manostrishtcher Rebbe

Advisory Board:
Rabbi Berel Eichenstein
Rabbi Aharon Feldman
Rabbi Emanuel Feldman
Rabbi Yaakov I. Homnick
Rabbi Zecharyah Greenwald
Rabbi Elimelech Kornfeld
Rabbi Joseph Pearlman
Rabbi Fabian Schonfeld
Rabbi Berel Wein
Rabbi Chaim Wilschanski
Dr. Moshe Snow
Dr. Eli Turkel
Avi Berger
Samson Krupnick ז"ל
Andrew Neff
Mordechai Rabin, LLM
Kenneth Spetner ז"ל
Uri Wolfson

Talmud-study publications:
In English:
Insights to the Daf
Background to the Daf
Dafyomi Review Q & A
Outlines of the Daf
Halachah Outlines for the Daf
Ask the Kollel (email/fax)
Weekly In-Depth Video Lectures
Daily Quizzes on the Daf
Mishnah Yomis Review Q & A
Revach I'Daf

בעברית:
יוסף דעת (הערות)
יוסף דעת (שאלות לחזרה)
גלי מסכתא (סיכומי סוגיות)
טבלאות לכל דף
חידוני חזרה

Bookmarks & Calendars

Leather-bound 12th-cycle calendar
Yearly Dafyomi-schedule bookmarks
Dafyomi-cycle bookmarks
Rishonim-on-the-Shas bookmarks
Hadran cards

Chovos ha'Levavos, the monumental work of Rabeinu Bachye ben Yosef Ibn Pakuda, a judge in Islamic Spain (circa 1040), is one of the earliest works on Jewish philosophy and beliefs. It remains one of the fundamental works of Musar and Hashkafah. Even the great Rambam (Maimonides) bases a large part of his treatises in these fields on the revered words of the Chovos ha'Levavos. (It has been suggested that Rav Shlomo Ibn Gevirol took ideas from the Chovos ha'Levavos as well.)

Originally written in Arabic, this classic was translated into Hebrew not longer after its original publication, and more recently to many other languages. Among works of Jewish philosophy, its prominence in even the most traditional houses of learning makes it unique. The Chovos ha'Levavos' methodical and systematic analyses or every aspect of the human character makes reading it an experience in growth through introspection.

We owe a debt of gratitude to Rabbi Yosef Sebag for his exceptionally readable English translation of this important work. By adding translations of classic commentaries on the text, he has made the depth of the work available to all. Rabbi Sebag's investment of time and effort is evident in every part of the work, but especially in the Sha'ar ha'Yichud, the somewhat "controversial" section dealing with philosophical proofs of G-d.

I have known Rabbi Sebag for many years, and I have witnessed firsthand his overwhelming dedication to Torah-study and to raising a family on Torah-true ideals. His careful adherence to the instructions of our Torah giants, coupled with his strong will to teach others the timeless lessons of the Torah, has made him a true "Ben Aliyah."

May his investment bear the dividends of allowing him to help many of our brethren improve their faith and strength of character!

With Torah blessings,

Mordecai Kornfeld

Rabbi Mordecai Kornfeld

Israel office: P.O.B. 43087, Jerusalem 91430, Israel • US office: 140-32 69 Ave., Flushing, NY 11367
Tel. - Israel: (02) 651-5004 • Fax - Israel: (02) 591-6024 • email: daff@dafyomi.co.il
http://www.dafyomi.co.il • http://dafyomi.shemayisrael.co.il/
U.S. tax ID: 11-3354586   580-28-908-0 עמותה מס' ע"ר

*** INTRODUCTION ***

Blessed be the L-ord, G-d of Israel, to Whom true Unity can be fittingly ascribed, whose existence is Eternal, whose beneficence is unceasing, who created all that is found as a sign of His Unity, who formed beings to serve as witnesses of His power and brought new things into existence to testify to His wisdom and great benevolence, as written *"one generation shall praise your works to another, and shall declare Your mighty acts"* (Ps. 145:4), and *"all Your works shall give thanks to You, O L-ord; and Your saints shall bless You; they shall speak of the glory of Your kingdom, and talk of Your power; To make known to the sons of men His mighty acts, etc"* (Ps.145:10-12).

(*Marpe Lenefesh*: *"true Unity"* - i.e. He alone is truly One and there is no other unity like His. For all the things which we call "one" are only one in a borrowed and relative sense as will be explained in the Gate of Unity. *"whose existence is Eternal"* - (1) His existence always was and always will be, therefore (2) He preceded everything, and therefore (3) He must also be the true Unity. For each of these three conditions imply the other two as will be explained in the Gate of Unity. See there and you will understand.

"who created all that is found as a sign of His Unity" - for all the creations are testimony and proof that He who created them is the true Unity, since behold, the entire creation is like one man and one house, where each part needs the other. If there were more than one creator, then there would need to be some non-uniformity and conflict in the creations, and it would not be interdependent as will be explained in Gate 1 ch.7

Pas Lechem: *"one generation shall praise your works to another"* - from this verse alone, we can only deduce that the wise must make known to the ignorant. But how do we know that even if all of us were wise men, we must still thank G-d? For this he brought the second verse, *"all Your works shall give thanks to You (yoducha)"*. The word "yoducha" (give thanks to You) is a combination of two words, "yodu" and "lecha". For the matter of thanks, is for the beneficiary to tell his benefactor that he recognizes his good, as written "give thanks to the L-ord for He is good" (Ps.107:1). Afterwards, he explained the matter of thanks, in saying *"they shall speak of the glory of Your kingdom"*, namely that the honor of Your sovereignty is different from that of flesh and blood, because a flesh and blood king has pleasure and benefit from his people, unlike G-d who needs nothing as mentioned earlier. Hence, we do not yet know if He wants that we examine His beneficence and thank Him for them. Therefore, he brought this verse *"to make known to the sons of man"*, i.e. G-d's intent in creation was to make known to the sons of man, etc. And like the verse (Prov. 16:4) "the L-ord made everything for His praise" [Rashi there: "To testify concerning Him. i.e. that His work testifies concerning Him, about His mighty deeds"])

The greatest gift which the Creator bestowed on His servants, human beings, after bringing them out to full perception and complete (mature) understanding - is wisdom, which is the life of their spirit and the candle of their intellect; It brings them to the favor of G-d and saves them from His wrath in this world and the next, as Scripture says *"for the L-ord gives wisdom: out of His mouth comes knowledge and understanding"* (Prov.2:6); And Elihu said: *"but there is a spirit in man, and the breath of the Almighty that gives them understanding"* (Job 32:8); And Daniel said: *"He gives wisdom unto the wise, and knowledge to them that know understanding"* (Daniel 2:21), and *"I am the L-ord your G-d who teaches you for your benefit, who leads you by the way that you should go"* (Isaiah 48:17).

(*Manoach Halevavos*: *"wisdom"* - i.e. the intellectual soul. At first it is only a faculty and potential, to perceive and understand. But when a man strives to bring out his intellect from potential to actual, then his perception is complete and his understanding is perfect - only then G-d will impart on him a spirit from above, to enlighten and illuminate him with wisdom. This is what the author meant *"after bringing them out.."* i.e. then G-d grants him the wisdom, for *"for the L-ord gives wisdom.."* (Prov. 2:6). And in tractate Berachot (55a): "Rabbi Yochanan says, G-d grants wisdom only to one who has wisdom, as written 'He gives wisdom unto the wise' (Daniel 2:21)... Rabbi Avahu says: I learn this from the verse: (Ex. 31:6) 'and in the hearts of all that are wise hearted I have put wisdom' ". This is the greatest good, that G-d shines on him the radiance of wisdom and understanding provided he strove to bring out his intellect from potential to actual, using the faculties and powers with which he was endowed at birth. [*Translator*: for more on this see Derech Etz Chaim by Rabbi Luzatto])

alternative explanation (applies to all human beings)
Marpe Lenefesh: that G-d endowed man in this structure and form, after he has grown up with mature faculties of perception and comprehension - with wisdom and understanding. Through wisdom, his spirit will vivify and the light of his intellect will illuminate him, but the fool walks in darkness. The Manoach Halevavos explained this differently. Let the chooser choose [which explanation fits better].)

Wisdom falls into three divisions.
The first division is the science of nature, called in Arabic, *"Al-Ilm al-tibi"*. This branch of knowledge deals with the essential and incidental properties

of material bodies.

The second division consists of the practical sciences, called in Arabic, *"Al-Ilm al-riazi"*. These comprise arithmetic, engineering, astronomy, and music.

> (*Pas Lechem*: such as mathematics for business, measurements, engineering. Astronomy is useful for navigating the sea. Music is also used to bring joy to human beings and dispel sadness. Unlike, the first division, namely, the wisdom of created things and the wisdom of theology which has no use for material matters. Their purpose is only for knowledge. And even though the wisdom of created things is needed for healing purposes, this is only a part of it...)

The third division, called in Arabic, *"Al-Ilm al-ilahi"*. is the science of theology, which deals with the knowledge of G-d, knowledge of His torah, and other [spiritual] things, such as the soul, the intellect, and spiritual beings.

All these divisions of wisdom, and their respective branches, are gates which the Creator has opened for men through which they may attain [a comprehension] of religion and of the world. Only that some sciences are more needed for religious matters while others are more needed for secular interests.

The sciences whose use is closest to worldly matters is the science of nature, which is the lowest science (in worth and importance - *LT*) and the practical science, which is second (in quality and importance - *LT*). These two sciences instruct on all the secrets of the physical world, its uses and benefits, its industries and trades and is conducive to physical and material well-being.

The science which is most needed for religion is the highest science - Theology. We are under duty to study it in order to understand and obtain a knowledge of our religion. But to study it in order to attain worldly benefits is forbidden. Our teachers said (Nedarim 62a): "[expounding the verse:] 'to love the L-rd your G-d, to hearken to His voice, and to cleave to Him' [This means] that one should not say, 'I will read Scripture that I may be called a scholar.' I will study [mishna], that I may be called Rabbi, I will study [Talmud], to be an Elder, and sit in the assembly [of elders]; but learn out of love, and honor will come in the end.". And "Do [good] deeds for the sake of their Maker, and speak of them [words of torah] for their own sake. Make not of them a crown wherewith to magnify yourself, nor a spade to dig with" (ibid). And *"Fortunate is the man that fears the L-ord, that delights greatly in His commandments' (Ps. 112:1), R. Eleazar expounds thus: 'In His commandments' but not in the reward of His commandments. This is just what we have learnt. 'He used to say, Be not like servants who serve the master on the condition of receiving a reward; but be like servants who serve the master without the condition of receiving a reward.'"* (Avodah Zara 19a).

(*Marpe Lenefesh*: *"learn out of love"* - out of love of G-d only. But other intents that a man intends in his service, be it material reward or even for [reward] in the next world - it will not be accepted, for he is serving for his own benefit not for G-d, as will be explained in this book.

Manoach Halevavos: some want to explain this that it is not proper to have intent to receive reward in this world immediately after one did a mitzva (precept), like slaves who minister their master in order to receive immediate benefits, namely, daily food and drink, as a reward for their work. But if the master does not give this to them, they will not work for him. Likewise, some slaves are contracted for a fixed period and seek their reward immediately after the time period has passed. And if the master does not give it to them right away, they rebel against him. Rather, one should have intent to receive reward in the next world.
Alternatively, others want to explain that one should serve G-d out of pure love, and not have intent for any reward, not even for reward in the next world, and the honor will come indirectly, out of kindness from G-d. For, in truth, a man does not deserve anything on his own merits, because he already received reward [for his service] through the many benefits which G-d continually bestowed on him. This likewise seems to be the author's view based on his words in Gate 4 ch.4 and in Gate 10, and other places in this book.)

The avenues which the Creator has opened for the knowledge of His law and religion are three.

The first is a [sound] intellect which is free of any damage.

(*Marpe Lenefesh*: G-d graced man with knowledge and understanding to know and understand His torah and to do His will, provided that his intellect is free from serious damage, namely, that it has not become erroneous or that it has not become ruined due to some brain damage. alternatively,
Lev Tov: that the intellect is free of any damage due to error or due to tending towards the lusts of this world (since "a bribe blinds the eyes of the

wise" Exodus 23:8, hence the bribe of personal desire twists a man's mind until he sees only what he wants to see - Translator).
Pas Lechem: the intellect (which is rooted in the spiritual) is not something which can be harmed like physical things, which grow and decay. Hence, "free" means "removed and separated" (from desire) as the Onkelos renders the verse in Gen. 31:9)

The second, the book of His law revealed to Moses His prophet.

(*Marpe Lenefesh*: this was explained in the Kuzari (maamer sheni ot 25,48,50). The summary of his words is as follows: a man cannot attain the favor of G-d or come close to Him except through His commandments. For He [alone] knows the measure, amount, time, and place of each commandment. Therefore, if we perform them as G-d commanded Moses, the divine presence will rest on our handiwork as was the case in the building of the Tabernacle despite that we do not understand their reasons and effects and that they are beyond our human logic... so too by the torah, we must listen and carefully follow that prescribed quantity and quality, how and with what we can do His will, namely, His law and religion. For otherwise, as with all the nations of the world which also strive, each man trying to come close to G-d in his own way, but he does not succeed. For no prophet, seer, or [man with] divine spirit (ruach hakodesh) has appeared to them as is the case with the Jewish people when they would follow the torah and commandments properly as is known. Therefore, a man should not become "smart" against the word of G-d, as written (Prov. 21:30) "there is no wisdom nor understanding nor counsel [that can succeed] against the L-ord". See also Gate 8 ch.3 part 4 where the author wrote similar words there.)

The third, the tradition which we have received from our ancient Sages who in turn received them from the prophets, peace be unto them. The great Rabbi Saadia of blessed memory already discussed on this avenue to a sufficient extent.

(*Marpe Lenefesh*: i.e. the oral law, which was received from generation to generation until Moses, as our Sages said (Pirkei Avot 1:1) "Moses received the torah at Sinai and transmitted it to Joshua..." Because every commandment G-d gave to Moses was accompanied with an oral explanation and clarification. This is the oral law. And thus Moses transmitted it to Joshua, and Joshua to the elders, etc. For without an explanation we would not know how to do even one precept fully, i.e. to do it completely, such as Tzitzit, Tefilin, and likewise for all of the others. Then each person would explain the precepts in the torah according to his knowledge and understanding, and every Jew would have a different torah and a different religion. Therefore, our torah depends on the transmitted oral law which Moses received at Sinai and which was transmitted until it reached the place G-d chose [for His temple]. For there [in Jerusalem] are the true receivers of the oral tradition, the great Sanhedrin and the Kohanim (priests). Therefore, the torah says (Deut. 17:10-12) "you shall do according to the torah which they [the Sanhedrin] teach you. Be careful to do everything they instruct you to do...and the man which does not hearken unto the priest that stands to minister there before the L-ord your G-d, or unto the judge [of the Sanhedrin] - that man shall die"... And they also received from Moses all the great secrets which are known to true Kabalists, and the amazing allusions, for it is all hinted in the torah. The torah is expounded in 4 ways (Pardes) as explained in the Zohar, Ramban, and the Alshich. The author was brief here for he relied on the words of Rabbi Saadia Gaon.)

Furthermore, the science of the torah falls into two divisions.
The first aims at the knowledge of the duties of the limbs (practical duties) and is the science of external conducts.

(*Tov Halevanon*: i.e. knowledge of the laws in the torah and its halacha, generally and specifically, and to learn the forbidden and the permitted, and the actions which are obligatory.)

The second deals with the duties of the heart, namely, its sentiments and thoughts, and is the science of the inner life.

(*Tov Halevanon*: Their fulfillment or transgression are not known [to other people] for they depend solely on the heart and mind. None but G-d can observe them.)

The duties of the limbs likewise fall into two divisions.
The first consists of precepts which reason would have dictated even if the torah had not made them obligatory.
The second, precepts received on the authority of Revelation which reason neither obligates nor rejects such as the prohibition of milk with meat, shaatnez (garments woven of wool and flax), kilaim (sowing diverse seeds together), and similar precepts whose reason for being prohibited or obligatory is unknown to us.

The duties of the heart, however, are all rooted in rational principles, as I will explain with G-d's help.

All the precepts are either positive commandments or negative commandments. We do not need to explain this for the duties of the limbs because these are universally known. I will, however, with G-d's help, mention of the positive and negative commandments of the duties of the heart to serve as examples of those not cited.

Among the positive commandments of the duties of the heart: to believe that the world had a Creator who created it from naught, that there is none like Him, that we acknowledge His Unity, that we serve Him in our hearts, that we reflect on the wonders of His works, that these may serve as evidences of Him, that we place our trust in Him, that we humble ourselves before Him, that we revere Him, that we fear and feel abashed when we consider that He observes our outer and inner being, that we long to do His will (alternatively, "that we yearn for His favor" - *PL*), that we devote our acts to His Name, that we love Him and those that love Him in order to come close to Him, that we hate His enemies, and similar duties which are not visible by the senses.

> (*Pas Lechem*: "*that we devote our acts to His Name*" - that our deeds be devoted solely to G-d - to not mix them with some ulterior motive such as to aggrandize oneself through this or some other motive.
> "*in order to come closer to Him*" - i.e. not with intent to receive some benefit from Him due to this.
> *Translator*: We often use the term "His Name" instead of just Him because He is too beyond for us to talk about. But we can talk about His Name which means how He manifests Himself to us. This is explained in Gate 1)

Negative commandments of the duties of the heart are the converse of those just mentioned. Also included among them: to not covet, avenge, nor bear a grudge; as written "*you shall not avenge nor bear a grudge*" (Levit. 19:18).

> (*Pas Lechem*: On coveting he did not bring a verse because it is a precept of Reason (i.e. it can be derived from reason) and therefore does not need a proof [from Scripture]. Unlike revenge and bearing a grudge which are not precepts of Reason. On the contrary, the Understanding resists them, and dictates that it is proper to be crooked with the crooked, and to return his evil to his head (Ps. 7:16). Therefore, he brought verses to show they are decrees of the King.)

Among them, that our minds not muse on [doing] transgressions, nor desire them, nor resolve to do them and other similar things which are hidden in a man and observed by none but the Creator, as written "*I the L-ord search the heart, I test the mind*" (Jer. 17:10) and "*the candle of G-d is the spirit of man, searching all the inner depths of the heart*" (Prov. 20:27).

(*Tov Halevanon*: even though technically only thoughts of avodah zara (idol worship) are punishable for dwelling about in one's mind, nevertheless, even for other sins, they are extremely damaging to the intellect and to the neshama (higher soul), as our Sages said (Yoma 29a): "thoughts of sin are worse than sin".

Pas Lechem: "*muse, desire, resolve*" - he outlined the preparation steps which lead to an act [of sin]. At first it is just thinking about the matter. And even though our Sages counted "thought" as one of the things which are not in a man's control, since thoughts pop up on their own in a man's mind. Nevertheless, there are two answers to this. Firstly, this was stated regarding the beginning of the thought's entering one's mind. Then it is only like a tiny spark that a man can easily extinguish. Hence, immediately, when he senses it, he can dismiss it and remove it from his mind and turn his mind to other things. However, if he does not dismiss it right away, then that spark will be fanned by a man's ruach (spirit) and will prolong for some time. This prolongation is called "hirhur" (musing) in the words of the Sages.
The second answer is that a man has the ability to not leave any room for these thoughts to arise, namely, by not allowing his mind to go idle in the first place - through the study of torah or engaging in work, as the Rambam wrote (Isurei Bia 22:21): "thoughts of lusts do not strengthen except in a heart devoid of wisdom". Behold, after the thought is fanned and prolongs in his spirit, this will correspondingly arouse the force of lust. And after he has lusted for it, he will hesitate a bit and deliberate whether or not to do it. Afterwards, he resolves to do it, and the matter will be held and pending in his mind until the time of the actual committing of the act of sin.

Marpe Lenefesh: "*candle of G-d*" - ... here is an excerpt from the Moray Nevuchim (Part 3 ch. 51): "behold I have explained to you that the understanding which G-d bestows on us - it is the connection between us and G-d. You have been granted free will in this. If you want to strengthen this connection, you may do so. And if you want to weaken it little by little until it is severed completely, you may likewise do so. This connection will only be strengthened if you employ it for love of G-d, and that your intent is to Him, as we wrote, and its weakening occurs when you set your thoughts to other than Him. [And even if you were the wisest man in divine knowledge, when you turn your thoughts to necessary eating or some other necessary occupation - you have already severed that clinging between you and G-d. You are not with Him then, and likewise, He is not with you. Because the relationship between you and Him is severed at that time..." End quote. see there more powerful words])

As the science of the torah deals with two parts, external and inward commandments, I studied the books of our predecessors who lived after the [compilers of the] Talmud. They composed many works dealing with the precepts. In the expectation of learning from them the science of inward religion, I found, however, that all that they intended to explain and clarify fall into three categories.

The first, to explain the Torah and the books of the prophets, and this is in one of two ways, either explaining the words and subject matter, as did Rabeinu Saadya, of blessed memory, in his commentaries of most of the books on Scripture. Or to explain the language and grammar, grammatical forms and usages in all their varieties, as well as paying heed to accuracy of the text, like the books of Ibn Ganach, the Massorites, and their school.

The second, to compile the explanation of the commandments into summary form, such as the work of Rav Chefetz ben Yatzliach of blessed memory. Or of only the commandments which apply today such as Halachot Pesukot, Halachot Gedolot, and similar collections; or of special topics as the Geonim did in their Responsa on practical duties and in their decisions.

The third, to confirm our faith in the matters of torah in our hearts through logical proofs and refutation of heretics like the book of Emunot (of Rabbi Saadia), the Sharashei Hadat, the Sefer Mekametz and similar works.

> (*Pas Lechem*: *"mekametz"* - (literally: gatherer) the book is called by this name because its author gathered together all the heretical views found in their nonsense and disgusting words, and then refuted them, demonstrating their foolishness, and exposing their foul stench, until everyone realized they are but wild dogs. And the Sages already said (Ketuvot 77a) "what is a mekametz? [Answer:] One who gathers up dog excrement.")

I examined these writings but failed to find among them a book specially devoted to the inner wisdom. I found that this wisdom, which is the duties of the heart, had been entirely neglected. No work had been composed, systematically explaining its roots and branches.

I greatly wondered about this, and thought to myself, perhaps this class of duties is not obligatory from the torah but is only an ethical obligation the aim of which is to teach us the proper and just way. Possibly it belongs to the class of extra practices that are optional, for which we will not be held accountable for them nor will we be punished for neglecting them. And therefore, our predecessors omitted to write a special book on them. I investigated the Duties of the Heart from Reason, Scripture, and Tradition (talmud,midrash,etc.) to inquire whether or not they are obligatory and found that they form the foundation of all the precepts, and that if there is any deficiency in their observance, no external duties whatsoever can be properly fulfilled.

(*Tov Halevanon*: Just like when the powers of the heart cease, the powers of all the limbs will likewise cease, because the heart is the root and power of the entire body, and from it the life [force] flows to all the other powers. So too, if the duties of the heart cease, the duties of the limbs become null and void.)

First the arguments from Reason. It is already familiar that man consists of body and soul. Both are among the benefits G-d has bestowed on us. One of these elements of our being is visible and the other is invisible. Therefore, we are accordingly under duty to render the Creator visible and invisible service. The outward service is the observance of the duties of the limbs such as praying, fasting, giving charity, learning the torah and teaching it, making a Sukka, waving a willow branch (on the festival of Sukkot), Tzitzit, Mezuza, Maake, and similar precepts whose performance is completed by the physical limbs.

Inward service, however, consists of the fulfillment of the Duties of the Heart such as: to acknowledge the Unity of G-d in our hearts, believe in Him and His torah, to undertake His service, that we revere Him and humble ourselves before Him, that we love Him, trust in Him, and give over our lives to Him, that we abstain from what He hates, devote our actions to His Name, that we reflect on the benefits He bestows, and similar things which are performed by the thoughts and sentiments of the heart but do not associate with activity of the visible limbs of the body.

(*Pas Lechem*: *"humble ourselves before Him"* - that we constantly display signs of humility as explained in the Gate of Submission.
"that we trust in Him" - for our livelihood and [other] needs.
"that we give over our life to Him" - if at some time, a man is struck with a fear of death due to some cause - he should not be too alarmed on this thereby weakening in his service of G-d. Rather, let him holdfast to the pillar of strength of his service and remove dread and fright from his heart by giving himself over to G-d, and saying to himself: "G-d will do whatever is good in His eyes".
"that we abstain from what He hates" - his intent is not on things which are specifically commanded as sins, but rather on things which we know that He hates, as the Rambam wrote regarding those things which are called

also under duty of service according to its power and ability.

Marpe Lenefesh: One cannot do a religious deed until he first pictures in his mind and thinks in his heart that it is proper to do that religious deed, and [considers] how he will do it. Afterwards, he performs it with his limbs.

Pas Lechem: "(1) will of the heart, (2) longing of the soul, (3) desire of the heart" - first he mentioned plainly: "will of the heart", which means to resolve by one's will to do it. Afterwards, he specified two divisions. Corresponding to things which are "[physical] actions" such as building a Sukkah, [donning] Tzitzit, making a fence on one's roof, etc. he wrote *"longing of the soul to do them"*. Corresponding to things which are not really [physical] actions such as prayer or study of torah, he wrote *"perform them"* since this term is more proper. After either of these two, namely, after (1) resolve of one's will to do it, he should arouse in himself a strong yearning and great desire to attain and fulfill it, as Rabbi Akiva said (Berachot 61b) "when will it come to my hand that I may fulfill it?")

After their obligation has become clear to me from the grounds of Reason, I said to myself "perhaps this matter is not written in the torah, therefore they refrained from writing a book which instructs on it and demonstrates it."

(*Pas Lechem*. i.e. since they did not find it in the torah then it is not something obligatory. Either because G-d knows man's capabilities and this is impossible due to the great difficulty or perhaps due to some other reason. Hence, even though Reason obligates this, nevertheless, once the Torah was given we need only to follow what is written there.)

But when I searched in the torah, I found that it is mentioned frequently. For example (Deut. 6:5-6): *"you shall love the L-ord your G-d with all your heart, and with all your soul, and with all your might; And these words, which I command you this day, shall be on your heart"*, and *"so that you may love the L-ord your G-d, and that you may hearken to His voice, and that you may cling to Him"* (Deut. 30:20), and *"to love the L-ord your G-d and to serve Him with all your heart and with all your soul"* (Deut. 11:13), and *"You shall walk after the L-ord your G-d and fear Him"* (Deut. 13:5), and *"you shall love your fellow as yourself"* (Levit.19:18) (which our Sages said includes the whole torah [Talmud Shabbat 31a] - *TL*), and *"now, Israel, what does the L-ord your G-d ask of you, but to fear the L-ord your G-d"* (Deut. 10:12), and *"Therefore love the stranger, for you were strangers in the land of Egypt"* (Deut. 10:19). And reverence for G-d and love for Him are among the duties of the heart.

"hated [by G-d]" (Pirkei Avot 1:17). And in the words of the wise m
(Prov. 6:16) "six people G-d hates..".
"that we devote our actions to His Name" - that our activities are dev
only to Him, that there no other motives mixed in.
"reflect on the benefits He bestows" - to recognize them and their grea
value. So that we are not among the blind who "do not consider the w
G-d" (Isaiah 5:12) and who have no understanding in this, as he will
explain in the Gate of Examination. Alternatively, (*Tov Halevanon:*) tl
one constantly reflects on the benefits of G-d towards him, how He be
on him all good, in order that love and fear of G-d enter his heart.
"thoughts and sentiments (literally: put away in the heart)" - he specifi
two terms *"thoughts and sentiments"* since some of these things need t
greatly maintained in man's thoughts and contemplated in detail to the
of his ability and they need to be thought about constantly such as love,
fear, humility, and trust. Therefore, he used the word *"thought"*. Other
things don't need to maintain constant thought such as faith in His torah
For, once his outlook has been firmly established, it is enough that it is '
away in the heart". Likewise, for *"abstaining from what He hates"*, only
when the opportunity for these things occur does one need to think about
abstaining from them. But after this, why should he think about them? O
the contrary, it is better to forget about them. Therefore he wrote *"put
away"*, that they are put away in his heart by force. Understand this.)

I am certain that [even] the duties of the limbs cannot be performed
properly unless they are accompanied by will of the heart, longing of the
soul to do them, and desire of the heart to perform them. If it should enter
our mind that we are under no obligation to choose the service of G-d and
to yearn for it, then we would be exempt from the duties of the limbs for
no act can be complete without the agreement of the soul. And since it is
clear that the Creator has put us under obligation to perform the duties of
the limbs, it would not be reasonable for us to suppose that our soul and
heart, the choicest parts of our beings, should have been exempted from
serving Him according to the extent of their ability, because their
cooperation is required for the complete service of G-d. Therefore, it is
clear that we are under obligation to perform outward and inner duties so
that our service to the blessed Creator will be whole and complete,
including both our inner and outer being.

(*Tov Halevanon*: i.e. not only the inner duties depend on the heart, but even
for all the duties of the limbs - their start and fulfillment are primarily from
the heart... for one cannot do something with his limbs without first
resolving in his heart to do it... Therefore, since we see that the duties of the
limbs depend primarily on the heart, and hence the heart is the root of torah
and service. If so, obviously, the heart by itself, even without the limbs, is

(*Tov Halevanon*: *"with all your heart"* - behold the verse set torah and emuna (faith) as depending on the heart and soul. Once a man attains these, then it is possible for him to serve G-d *"with all his might"*. For without love of G-d fixed in his heart and soul, a man will not do any further service.)

Regarding the negative commandments [of the duties of the heart], the torah wrote: *"nor shall you covet etc"* (Deut. 5:18), *"You shall not avenge, nor bear any grudge"* (Levit. 19:18), *"You shall not hate your fellow in your heart"* (Levit. 19:17), *"and so that you do not seek after your own heart and your own eyes"* (Numbers 15:39), *"you shall not harden your heart nor shut your hand from your poor fellow"* (Deut. 15:7), and many other similar passages.

Afterwards, the Torah reduced all [religious] service to the service of the heart and tongue in saying *"For this commandment which I command you today is not hidden from you, neither is it far off; It is not in Heaven...But the matter is very near you, in your mouth and in your heart, that you may do it"* (Deut.30:11). And in the other books of the prophets, they spoke extensively on the matter and mentioned it in several places. I do not need to mention them because they are numerous and well-known.

(*Tov Halevanon*: *"on the heart and tongue"* - after the Torah repeatedly exhorted on the heart which is the cornerstone of the Torah, it added a commandment on the tongue which is secondary to the heart, and which depends on the work of the heart and soul, as our Sages said (Shabbat 33b): "the heart understands, the tongue articulates, and the mouth completes. And the well-being of the heart and soul depends on the tongue. If the heart and tongue are lacking perfection, the soul will likewise be lacking perfection, as Scripture says: "Do not allow your mouth to cause your flesh to sin" (Eccles. 5:5). It is also well demonstrated in the wisdom of truth (Kabala) how [sins of] the mouth and tongue damage the soul.

Pas Lechem: *"in your mouth and in your heart"* - After Moshe Rabeinu reviewed and taught all of the Torah and the commandments, then, near the end of the Torah, he went on to encapsulate the entire service into these two things.)

After it had become clear to me that the duties of the heart are obligatory from the Torah and from reason, I searched the matter in the writings of our Sages. I found it to be even more explicit in their words than what is explained in the Torah and derived from reason. Some of them are stated as general principles such as *"G-d wants the heart"* (Sanhedrin 106b), and *"the heart and the eyes are the two agents of sin"* (Yerushalmi Berachos 1:5). Some of them in Tractate Avos, which there is no need to elaborate. I also found many in their traits and habits when they were asked about them as written regarding *"to what do you attribute your long life?"* (Megila 27b).

I found in the Torah regarding one who kills someone unintentionally, no capital punishment is incurred. Likewise, one who performs a sin unintentionally which if intentional would incur either capital punishment or the penalty of Karet (excision), the person had only to bring for them a sin-offering or an asham offering (as derived by the Sages - *PL*). All this is a clear proof that the essential condition of liability for punishment is the association of mind and body in a forbidden act, the mind by its intention, and the body by its movement.

So too our wise men said: "whoever performs a religious duty but did not intend to do it for the sake of G-d - he will not receive reward for it."

(*Tov Halevanon*: even though they said (Sotah 22b) "one should always occupy himself in the Torah even shelo lishma (not devoted to G-d), since from shelo lishma (not devoted) comes lishma (devoted to G-d)". Perhaps it means that even so, one will not receive any reward for those mitzvot he did shelo lishma. Alternatively, perhaps, his reward is much less relative to the reward for doing a mitzva lishma, as our Sages said (Nazir 23b) "a sin lishma (devoted to G-d) is greater than a mitzva shelo lishma (not devoted)", which implies there is some reward for a mitzva shelo lishma. Hence, according to this the author's words are not literal.)

And since the hinge and pillar of all deeds rests on the foundation of intention and hidden sentiment of the heart, a system of the duties of the heart should precede, by nature, a system of the duties of the limbs.

(*Pas Lechem*: *"intention and sentiment"* - intention refers to a man's intention at the beginning of the performance of a mitzva, namely, that he does it with intent that he has been commanded [by G-d] to do the mitzva. And what he thinks about during its performance with regard to the mitzva and its details, and that he has joy in doing it, the author called here *"sentiment"* (matzpuno).

Tov Halevanon: *"precede, by nature"* - ...one of the 5 "precedences" as is known in the science of logic - is called "precedence by nature". This refers to something whose nature does not need the nature of something else nor vice versa, even though neither preceded the other in time. For example, plants precede creatures by nature because the plant, namely, the growing power is needed by creatures, for they also need a growing power. But the "conscious awareness power" which exists in the nature of conscious creatures is not needed by the nature of plants (see the book Shaarei Kedusha to understand this - translator). So too by deeds, the duties of the limbs necessarily require the duties of the heart but the duties of the heart do not require the duties of the limbs.)

After it had become clear to me through Reason, Scripture, and Tradition that the inner science is indeed an obligation, I said to myself, "perhaps this class of commandments are not obligatory at all times and at all places, (i.e. only in Israel and only when the temple existed - *PL*) similar to shmita, yovel (jubilee year), and [temple] offerings".

But when I delved deeper into the subject, I found that we are obligated in them constantly, without pause, throughout our lives, and that we have no claim (excuse) whatsoever for neglecting them. This applies to such duties, for example, as acknowledging the Unity of G-d in our hearts, to serve Him inwardly, to revere Him and to love Him, to yearn to fulfill the commandments obligatory upon us, as Scripture says *"O my hope is that my ways are directed to observe Your statutes"* (Ps. 119:5); to trust in Him and surrender ourselves to Him (i.e. to trust in Him in all matters - *ML*), as written *"trust in Him at all times, pour out your heart before Him"* (Ps.62:9); to remove hatred and jealousy from our hearts, to separate from the superfluous worldly matters which preoccupy us away from the service of G-d - we are under constant duty in all of these things, at all times and in all places, every hour, every second, and under all circumstances, as long as we have life and reason.

(*Pas Lechem*: *"we have no claim whatsoever for neglecting them"* - i.e. we have no answer or excuse if we are negligent from this and abandon it.
"to serve Him inwardly" - the "service" which the author intends here is submission and shame, as he mentioned earlier. These are also called service as our Sages said (Sotah 5b) "humility is greater than all the sacrifices... as written 'the sacrifices of G-d are a broken spirit; a broken and a contrite heart, O G-d, You will not despise' (Ps. 51:11).

Tov Halevanon: *"O my hope"* - David beseeched that he will be successful in his ways to guard G-d's statutes at all times. These are necessarily the duties of the heart.
"to separate from the superfluous" - these are the material possessions and bodily pleasures which are not necessary for health of the body, service of G-d, or necessary livelihood.

Manoach Halevavos: *"O my hope"* (achalay) - he is bringing a proof regarding "yearning to do the commandments". For *"achalay"* is from the word "tocheles", and tocheles means yearning.)

The analogy of this is to a slave whose master charged him with two jobs. One in the house and the other in the field. The latter consisted of cultivating the ground and its care at definite periods and times. When those times are past or if he is unable to work there due to some thing which impedes him, he is then to be relieved of his responsibility for the work in the field. But he is never exempt for the work which he is commanded to do in the house, provided there is no impediment or other matter he must tend to. Hence, he is constantly charged to work the house when he is free to do so.

(*Pas Lechem*: *"some thing which impedes him...no impediment or other matter"* - In the work of the field the impediment is due to some lacking in doing the work such as a flood, or bad weather, or a windy day where he cannot sow seeds, etc. But for the work in the house of the king, certainly all the necessary means for his work are prepared and before him, for there is nothing lacking in the palace of the king. Hence, the impediment inside the house refers to some human being which impedes him. Therefore, regarding the field, he wrote *"some thing which impedes him"* while for the house work he wrote *"no impediment"* (literally: not impeded by an impending agent) which refers to some human being which impedes him and does not let him do and toil in the work of his king. He wrote two expressions (1. no impediment or 2. other matter), referring to either a man which impedes him despite that he is free to work or alternatively that he is not free in the work of his king due to being busy with other matters he must tend to.)

Such too is the case for the duties of the heart which are always binding upon us. We have no excuse for their neglect, and there is nothing which impedes us in their fulfillment, except for love of this world, and lack of understanding in regard to our Creator, as written *"they do not consider the work of G-d"* (Isaiah 5:12).

(*Tov Halevanon*: *"love of this world"* - It is well known in the writings of chakira (rational inquiry) that love of this world and love of the next world are two opposites, and there is no possibility whatsoever for both to co-exist together.
"we don't understand the matter of our Creator" - due to the coarse physicality of the body which conceals the light of the intellect which shines from the soul.

alternatively,
Pas Lechem: we don't understand His greatness, His sovereignty over us, and His beneficences to His creations.)

I said to myself, "perhaps this class of commandments does not branch out to many commandments. Therefore, they abandoned them and did not compose a book specially devoted to them".

(*Pas Lechem*: i.e. there is not enough material for a whole book. It was enough for them to insert pieces parenthetically in their words. A bit here and a bit there.)

But when I investigated, on their number and derivatives, I found their derivatives to be exceedingly numerous until I thought that what David, peace be unto him, said *"I have seen a limit to all perfection, but Your commandment is exceedingly broad"* (Ps. 119:96) was referring to the Duties of the Heart. Because, the Duties of the Limbs are a known number, namely, 613. But the Duties of the Heart are exceedingly numerous until their derivative branches are countless.

(*Pas Lechem*: *"number and derivatives"* - "number" according to their names, as he wrote earlier such as "love", "fear", "trust", etc. The derivatives are the branches which branch out and offshoot, each to several branches and parts. It is like a Menorah (candelabrum), with parts and branches.

Tov Halevanon: *"countless"* - Everything physical is necessarily bounded in the three dimensions. Hence, necessarily it must be finite. For it is impossible to find in actual reality an infinite number of physical objects, as will be demonstrated through logical proofs (see Gate 1 ch.5). But *"your commandments are exceedingly broad"*. The term "broad" here means infinite. For the Duties of the Heart cannot be encircled by any edge or boundary. For, they can offshoot, widen, and branch out indefinitely. And even though it is impossible for an actual physical thing to be infinite, it can nevertheless, potentially branch out infinitely. So too, for the Duties of the Heart, even though they depend on physical powers, they can nevertheless potentially branch out infinitely, since their number is unlimited. Understand this.)

I further said: "perhaps they are so clear and familiar to everyone, and every person clings to them that a book on the subject is unnecessary". When, however, I studied the conduct of human beings throughout the ages as recorded in books, I found that they are far from [the knowledge or practice of] this class of commandments, with the exception of some zealous individuals, special elect of them, according to what is recorded about them. But as for the rest, how much were they so in need of exhortation and instruction! And all the more so, for most of the people in our generation, who neglect even the commandments of the limbs, not to mention the commandments of the heart. And if any one of them is roused to devote himself to the study of the Torah, his motive in this is to be called a "wise man" by the masses, and to gain for himself a name among the great. And thus he strays from the way of the Torah to things which will neither aid him in ascending spiritually, nor save him from spiritually stumbling. And he studies unnecessary things the ignorance of which he would not be punished, while he omits to investigate the roots of the religion and the foundations of the Torah, which he should not have ignored nor neglected and without the knowledge and practice of which, no commandment can be properly fulfilled. For example, regarding acknowledging the Unity of G-d, (the question arises) whether we are under duty to examine this by the light of reason or whether it is sufficient if we accept it by tradition alone, namely, that we declare like the simpleton and the fool that "G-d is One" without argument or proof. Or, if we are under duty to investigate through rational inquiry the distinction between true Unity versus relative unity, so as to distinguish [the Unity of G-d] from other existing unities which we call "one".

(*Marpe Lenefesh*: it seems the author's view is like that of Rabbi Saadia Gaon, that the Tradition is primary. And if one is of strong intellect, so that he can also delve into rational inquiry in order that his faith will be more firmly implanted in his heart through both tradition and rational proofs and together they will be perfect in his heart and mind - then he can tread this path [of rational inquiry], as will be explained in Gates 1 and 2. Here is an excerpt from the introduction of Sefer Emunot by R.Saadia Gaon: even though the Sages prevented us from this inquiry in saying "whoever inquires into four things, better had he not been born" (Chagiga 11b). Their intent was only if we abandon the books of the prophets and instead each person relies on his own intellect in trying to understand the first beginnings of time and space [first existence]. For whoever inquires in this way, perhaps he will find [truth], perhaps he will err. And until he finds [the truth], he will be without religion. And even if he finds [truth] it is possible that he will stray from it due to some doubt that will surface in his mind and he may lose his faith. Everyone agrees that one who goes in this manner is a sinner. But we, the congregation of Israel, investigate and rationally inquire what we received from the prophets, who were confirmed true prophets through signs and miracles, so that what we received from them in knowledge may become tangibly clear to us. Secondly, [we study this in order to know how to] refute those who come against us in Torah matters in the way of "know what to answer a heretic" (Pirkei Avot 2:14). See there at length.)

On this the believer is not permitted by our religion to remain in ignorance, for the Torah exhorts us on this in saying *"Therefore, know this day and consider within your heart, that the L-ord is G-d in Heaven above and on the earth below. There is none other"* (Deut. 4:39).

The same is the case for other commandments of the heart which we have mentioned already or will mention. The believer's faith will not be complete until he knows these duties and practices them. They are the inner science, the light of the heart, and the shining of the soul. On this Scripture says: *"make me to hear joy and gladness"* (Ps. 51:8).

(*Marpe Lenefesh*: ...here is an excerpt from the Ibn Ezra "...he concluded in the end, that the complete knowledge is for a man to set in his heart until he has clarified through logical proofs that G-d is one, therefore Moses said 'Therefore, know this day and consider within your heart, that the L-ord is G-d in Heaven above and on the earth beneath. There is no other' (Deut. 4:39), and David said: 'And you, Solomon my son, know the G-d of your father and serve Him with a perfect heart and with a willing soul' (Chron. I 28:9), and 'knowing' means in the heart not on the mouth". end quote.

Pas Lechem. *"the light of the heart, and the shining of the soul"* - light refers to something which is luminescent by itself, while *"shine"* (noga) refers to something which reflects light that it received from something else, like the moon which reflects light it received from the sun. Therefore it is written (Isaiah 60:19) "The sun will no more be your light by day, nor will the brightness of the moon shine on you"... So too here, the author's intent is that wisdom enlightens the heart, and from the heart, radiance will flow to the soul. Hence, he wrote the shine (noga) of the soul.)

It is said of a Sage who would pass the first half of the day in the company of other people. But when he was alone, he would call out "O for hidden light", by which he referred to duties of the heart.

One of the wise men was consulted regarding a strange case on the laws of divorce. He replied to the inquirer: "you are asking on what will not harm you if you do not know it. Do you already know all that you are under duty to know of the commandments, and that you are not allowed to neglect, and that you should not be negligent of, that you turn to speculate on remote questions which will not avail you of any advancement, nor fix any crookedness in your soul. Behold, I swear, it has been 35 years that I have occupied myself with what is essential to the knowledge and practice of the duties of my religion. You are aware of my great in-depth study and the great library of books I possess. And yet, I have never turned my mind to the matter to which you have directed your attention and about which you inquire." And he continued to rebuke and shame him concerning the matter.

(*Tov Halevanon*: i.e. the question was remote and uncommon. Even though in the words of our Sages we find such questions such as "one who made an animal into a grave stone" (Tosfos Kesuvos 4b). This is because our Sages were already complete in the duties of the heart, and they also had the ability to deduce from the answers to these questions other laws which are common. Unlike this student which the wise man rebuked who did not reach this level.

Marpe Lenefesh: It appears there were two problems here. The question itself was remote. It was unlikely such a thing would ever happen, and the questioner asked this only to show off his wisdom and cleverness to the Rabbi. Secondly, the questioner was not on the level to be dealing with questions of marriage and divorce documents. For one must first acquire what he needs of good traits, Torah, and emunot... But one who turns the plate over, such as those who study Choshen Mishpat or Yoreh Deah while in the practical day to day commandments they do not know between their right and left.. Likewise, for the youths who study Talmud before knowing the Torah (five books of Moses) and wind up knowing neither, as the Maharal spoke of at length in his book Kenei Chachma, for one must teach a youth according to his capacity as the mishna says (Pirkei Avot 5) "Five year old for Scripture, ten year old for Mishna..."

Chasam Sofer parsha Bechukosai: This is in disagreement with the words of the Chovos Halevavos who warned against busying ourselves with remote questions such as laws of Gitin or the like and that all of our toil should be in practical things, and when such a strange question comes we can deal with it. Behold, I ask forgiveness of the pious author, but I disagree. This is not the proper path which G-d wants. Our Sages have set, and paved in the talmud many strange questions, and most of the talmud consists of such back and forth questions. For the Sages knew that knowledge of these things is the true wealth. And this is what brings a man to burning enthusiasm in fear of G-d and clinging to His great Name, provided that his intent should first be for G-d and Torah lishma. For if he toils in the Torah in these matters, he will come to cling to G-d. For one who clings to the Torah, clings to G-d. The laws he should cherish so that he will be able to do them when he has the opportunity, without needing to look it up...

Translator: Perhaps there is no contradiction, for the Chovos Halevavos also advocates delving as deep as one's mind can go in the sea of the talmud as he wrote above "You are aware of my great in-depth study" and as he explains in Gate 8 ch.3 way 5 that this is a duty from reason, etc. only that he should first focus this in-depth study on the practical parts of Torah which he needs to know.)

Another Sage said "I learned to purify my deeds for 25 years."

(*Marpe Lenefesh*: i.e. For twenty five years, I studied how to reach this trait, to purify my actions to G-d alone, without any other motive. This was my primary study and toil.)

A third Sage said "there is wisdom which lies hidden in the hearts of the wise, like secret treasure. If they conceal it, man cannot discover it. If they reveal it, man cannot deny the correctness of their words regarding it. And this is as Scripture says *"wisdom in the heart of man is like deep water, but a man of understanding will draw it out"* (Prov. 20:5), i.e. wisdom is innate in a man's being, in his nature and faculties of perception, like water that is hidden in the depths of the earth. The intelligent and understanding individual will strive to investigate what is in his potential and inward faculties in order to discover and expose this wisdom, and will draw it forth from his heart, just as one searches for water that is in the depths of the earth.

(*Pas Lechem*: *"If they conceal it, man cannot discover it"* - if they will leave it thus, concealed in potential, a man cannot apprehend it. The intent is on a man himself. i.e. the matters of wisdom are not openly revealed in a man's heart, that he can apprehend them automatically, without contemplation, as is the case with that which is apprehended automatically by the senses. For example, something which is before him, he will apprehend it through his sense of sight automatically without effort. Likewise, for a sound which reaches his ears, it will be apprehended immediately by his sense of hearing. Wisdom, however, is concealed in potential, and will not be apprehended by him unless he strives to draw it out through the power of contemplation. This is what he meant, *"If they reveal it.."*, i.e. excavate it from its hidden place through the faculty of reason, until it floats up and is revealed - then it will no longer be concealed to that man, that they are indeed just and correct words, and victorious in bringing a man to perfection. He said this corresponding to the lazy people, that even if they are intelligent by nature, and they fool themselves saying perhaps the reason (the duties of the heart) are not revealed in their hearts is because they are not things needed for wholeness.

Therefore, he wrote, let them test for themselves, through contemplation, and they will find the correctness of these words.

Translator: for this reason it is so important to study this book slowly and thoughtfully with the commentaries. Reading it fast in order to finish quickly will not affect a person in the least.

"in his potential and inward faculties" - for things which are still completely concealed, and he did not yet have any start in them, he wrote *"potential"*. For things which he already had some knowledge and now they are absent from his mind until he recalls them, spreads them out, and expounds their parts, in order to derive wisdom and understanding from them - he wrote *"inward faculties"*.)

I once asked a man who was considered among the Torah Sages concerning some of the topics we mentioned regarding the inner wisdom and he replied that on this and similar things, the tradition is sufficient to stand in place of rational inquiry.

I said to him: "This applies only to those who lack the ability to inquire due to low powers of perception and weakness of understanding, such as women and children, or feeble minded persons (*Translator*: women used to be much less educated than in our times). But a man who has sufficient power of intellect and perception to attain certainty on the truth of (what he received from - *PL*) Tradition, and he neglected to investigate this due to laziness or due to holding in light esteem the commandments of G-d and His Torah - certainly he will be punished for this and he sins for having neglected them.

(*Pas Lechem*: i.e. for his laziness and light esteem he will be punished. In addition to this, he sins for neglecting to inquire into these things.)

This matter is similar to [the following illustration]. An officer was charged by the king to receive money from the officials of his kingdom. The king gave him special instructions to count the coins, weigh them, and verify their quality. The officer was sufficiently intelligent and skilled to fulfill all that the king had commanded him. But the royal servants cunningly befriended him with words until he trusted in them. They brought the money to him and assured him that it was correct in amount, weight, and quality. He believed them and was too lazy to verify for himself the truth of their words thereby transgressing the king's orders. When the matter reached the king, he ordered that the money be brought before him. When the king questioned the officer as to the total count and weight of the money, he could not answer. Though the amount of money may have been correct, the king condemned him for having been lax in his

command in relying on the words of the servant in something he could
have obtained certainty for himself. Only if he was not skilled enough to
make an accounting, would he not have been found guilty for relying on
the servants.

So too, if you were not capable of grasping this subject with your
reasoning faculties, as is the case regarding reasons for received
commandments (such as shatnez etc. - *PL*), then your excuse for refraining
from this inquiry would be valid. Likewise, if your mind falls short and
your perception is too weak to understand it, you would not be punished
for your neglect, and you would be considered like children and women,
who accept it from the Tradition. But if you are a man of intellect and
understanding, who is capable of obtaining certainty on what you have
received from the Sages and prophets regarding the roots of the religion
and the pivots of the deeds, you are then commanded to use your intellect
until you comprehend the matter so that it will be clear to you from both
tradition and Reason. But if you ignore this and are negligent in it, you will
be considered as falling short in your duties to the blessed Creator.

> (*Pas Lechem*: "*if your mind falls short and your perception is too weak*" -
> On matters of emuna (faith) such as the Unity or the Eternity, or the like, he
> wrote "*your mind falls short*", i.e. to grasp their logical proofs. On the other
> things of the inner duties such as placing one's trust in G-d, giving over
> oneself to Him, and devoting one's acts to Him, and the like, which stem
> from recognizing the greatness of G-d and of His beneficence, on this he
> wrote "*your perception is too weak*".
> "*the roots of the religion and the pivots of the deeds*" - I already explained
> earlier that His Unity, and His Eternity, and the faith in prophecy and the
> like, are the roots of the religion, and from them it sprouts. For the other
> things in the inner science such as love, fear, trust, giving over oneself to
> Him, it is correct to call them "*pivots of the deeds*". For on them all the
> deeds pivot around and the purpose of all the deeds is to love Him, fear
> Him, and give our lives over to Him.)

This will be explained in two ways.

> (*Tov Halevanon*: The author will now clarify from the Torah and prophets
> that one who refrains from rational inquiry on the roots of the Torah and
> instead relies solely on the tradition is negligent (poshea) and like one who
> is falling short in fulfilling the duties the Creator placed on him.)

Firstly, from what Scripture says "*if there arise a matter too hard for you
in judgment, between blood and blood, between plea and plea, between*

affliction and affliction...and you shall do according to the sentence which they declare to you" (Deut. 17:8-10). If you examine what subjects are included in the first verse, you will find they are things which need to be detailed, distinguished, and discussed by the method of Tradition, and not by that of logical demonstration from Reason alone. You can see, the verse does not include matters which can be attained through Reason. For he did not say, for example, "when you have a question on the Unity of G-d"; or regarding the Names and attributes of the Creator, or as to any of the roots of the religion, such as the service of G-d (i.e. whether or not it is proper to serve G-d - *PL*), trusting in Him, submission before Him, devoting activities to Him, purifying conduct from the damage of detrimental things, repentance from sins, fear and love of Him, being abashed before Him, making a spiritual accounting, and similar duties which can be fulfilled through reason and recognition. He did not say to accept them on the authority of the Torah Sages and to rely only on the Tradition. On the contrary, Scripture says in regard to these to reflect on them to your heart and to apply your intellect on them after having first accepted them from the Tradition, which covers all the commandments of the Torah, their roots and branches. You should investigate them with your intellect, understanding, and judgment, until you will sift the truth of it from the false [notions], as written *"therefore, know this day and consider it within your heart, that the L-ord, He is G-d"* (Deut. 4:39).

(*Marpe Lenefesh*: *"between blood and blood, between plea and plea, between affliction and affliction"* i.e. this verse mentions three things, which are things whose explanation we cannot know except through the Torah Sages who received their explanation from Sinai, as mentioned earlier. Therefore, the verse specified these three. But if the entire Torah were included in this statement, why did the Torah mention only these three? Let it say either a blanket statement [such as "a commandment"] or let it also include a precept of Reason.

Tov Halevanon: Even though among the commandments of the limbs, there are also some commandments which Reason accepts, and on these the Sages said (Eruvin 100b) "even if the Torah were not given, we could have learned modesty from the cat, honesty from the ant, chastity from the dove.." But this is not from logical proofs. Rather it is from the aspect of mussar (ethics). Likewise, the details of monetary pleas cannot be known through Reason alone. This is unlike the Duties of the Heart where all of them can be demonstrated by clear logical proofs, and there aren't any derivatives of them which cannot be demonstrated by logical proofs. And likewise we have been commanded to inquire specifically on them - not to rely [solely] on what the Sages will tell us from Tradition.

Pas Lechem: *"to return them to your heart"* - this means the entering of the matter in one's heart. Afterwards, on contemplation of it, he wrote *"and to apply your intellect in them"*.
"inquire with your intellect, understanding, and power of discernment" - inquire with your intellect on the general matters. Then use your understanding and power of discernment to discern the roots from the branches, and contemplate the roots to discern with your comprehension which branches stem out from them.)

Likewise, we will say regarding all that we are capable of grasping by Reason, as our Sages said (Rabbi Yishmael's 7th rule of expounding the Torah) "if anything included in a general proposition is made the subject of a special statement, whatever is proclaimed of that special statement is not to be understood as limited to itself, but is applied to the whole of the general proposition". Knowing the Unity of G-d is but one branch of the topics which can be understood by Reason. And as it is our duty to use this method on this topic (of G-d's Unity), it is equally our duty to do so with all of them.

(*Marpe Lenefesh*: i.e. just like G-d commanded us to inquire on the matter of the Unity, despite that we received it by tradition and that it is explained in the Torah.)

The second argument is drawn from Scripture says: *"Have you not known? Have you not heard, that the everlasting God"* (Isaiah 40:28). It says *"known"* which implies knowledge from rational proofs, and afterwards *"heard"* which implies from the Tradition. And likewise, *"Have you not known? Have you not heard? Has it not been told you from the beginning?"* (Isaiah 40:21). The prophet preceded mentioning knowledge from rational proof to knowledge which is from received tradition. And likewise Moses, our teacher, said: *"Do you thus requite the L-ord, Oh foolish and unwise people? Is He not your Father who acquired you? Has He not made you and established you? Remember the days of old; consider the years of many generations. Ask your father, and he will show you; your elders, and they will tell you."* (Deut. 32:6). This is a proof to what we mentioned, that despite that the Tradition should be preceded by nature, for the students must learn it first, nevertheless, it is not right to rely solely on it for one who is able to comprehend it by the method of rational demonstration. It is therefore proper, that everyone who is capable of this, is under duty to investigate with his intellect and to bring logical proofs of it by the demonstration which deliberate judgment would support.

(*Tov Halevanon*: "*the Tradition should be preceded by nature*" - i.e.
Rational inquiry requires the Tradition. For it is impossible to find without
the [guidance of the] Tradition. Without the Tradition, it is highly unlikely
that a man will grasp the roots of Judaism by reason alone. Tradition guides
a person on the intellectual journey - to which bend to turn in his rational
inquiry. But the tradition alone can be without inquiry for the weak minded
and women. Behold, the tradition on existence of G-d and His Unity, and
other fundamental principles precede by nature to the commandments of
the Heart, which are the bringing of rational proofs on their truth.

Pas Lechem: "*for the students must learn it first*" - i.e. in the days of youth
before their understanding becomes strong so that they do not remain in
those days without faith. Therefore, one must then rely on the Tradition.
Also, from a different reason, one must precede the Tradition and that it be
the foundation of his faith, whether or not he understands it and his reason
agrees with it. Because if one starts from his own understanding and makes
it his foundation, namely, that which he agrees with he accepts and that
which he disagrees with or cannot grasp, he rejects. G-d forbid for us to go
in this way, for this is the path which the philosophers tread, who wound up
ruining the world and themselves. And that which he wrote earlier that the
inner wisdom precedes by nature, the answer is that there he was referring
to [intent of] deeds while here he is referring to faith.)

After I had become convinced that the commandments of the heart are
indeed obligatory, and that, on grounds we mentioned, we are obligated in
them, I found that these duties had been neglected and that no book had
been composed specifically on them. I contemplated on the condition of
low observance of them from my contemporaries due to their inability to
comprehend them, and hence, all the more so, were they unable to perform
them or toil in them. I was stirred by the grace of G-d to inquire into the
inner science.

(*Pas Lechem*: "*toil in them*" - i.e. to make them one's business, namely, to
expound their topics and to speak of their roots and branches.)

I also noticed from the practice of our Sages, and from their sayings that
we have received, that they were more zealous and engaged in their
personal duties than in developing inferences of laws and remote, doubtful
questions.

(*Pas Lechem*: Doubtful because they are strange matters, not found in the
words of the Tradition, and therefore need many logical constructs,
premises and deductions. Therefore, a man cannot render a definitive

answer and say "accept my reasoning". In truth, we find many of the great Rabbis end off their responsa in a doubtful tone in saying 'thus it seems according to my humble opinion'.)

Their efforts were first spent on determining the general principles of judgment, to make clear what is permitted and what is forbidden.

(*Pas Lechem*: *"general principles of judgment"* - i.e. monetary cases. He preceded these to "permitted/forbidden" things because most questions can be derived from them, for they are the cornerstone of the Torah. Therefore, he used the term "general principles" by them, since their rulings are based on many general principles such as "hamotzi mechavero.." or the principles of "migo", and many similar things.)

Afterwards, they busied and strove to clarify their active obligations and inward duties. If a strange case came before them that belonged to the class of inferences from existing laws, they investigated it at the time it was presented to them, and deduced the law from the principles known to them. But they never troubled their minds for these things before this for they regarded secular matters lightly.

(*Tov Halevanon*: *"they regarded secular matters lightly"* - i.e. acquiring a name and seeking honor)

And when they needed to render a ruling on that matter, if the ruling was clear to them from the Tradition transmitted to them by the prophets, they would rule on that basis. If it was a question which required expounding the Tradition, they would investigate it with the light of reason. If they all agreed together, they would give a ruling. But if there was a disagreement on the ruling, they would rule according to the majority opinion, as written by the Sanhedrin (Talmud Sanhedrin 88b): "when a question was posed to them, if they had a tradition on it, they gave the decision right away. If they differed, they took a vote. If the majority ruled the thing was clean, it was declared clean. If the majority ruled it unclean, it was declared unclean. This was according to the principle they received 'the decision follows the majority'". They composed in Tractate Avot, the traditions of the moral principles and ethical standards of the Rabbis as taught by each of them in his time and place.

(*Tov Halevanon*: *"the moral principles and ethical standards"* - i.e. when they mentioned the chain of tradition from Sinai, they mentioned of each of the receivers what he innovated of moral principles. But they did not at all mention their chidushim (novel ideas) in questions of dinim (monetary laws) which they expounded in their rational inquiry.)

The reports of the men of the Talmud regarding their teachers, are enough to demonstrate the depth of their wisdom and great toil in purifying their deeds. For instance (Berachot 20a): "Said R. Papa to Abaye: How is it that for the former generations miracles were performed and for us miracles are not performed? It cannot be because of their [superiority in] study, because in the years of Rab Judah the whole of their studies was confined to Nezikin (the mishna order of monetary damages), while we study all six Orders...And yet when Rab Judah drew off one shoe, rain used to come, whereas we torment ourselves and cry loudly, and no notice is taken of us! He replied: The former generations used to be ready to sacrifice their lives for the sanctity of [G-d's] Name; we do not sacrifice our lives for the sanctity of [G-d's] Name", and (Avodah Zara 17b): *"he who only studies the Torah, is like a man who is without a G-d, as it is said (Chronicles II 15:3) 'Now for long seasons, Israel was without the true G-d'. Hence, Torah study must be combined with acts of kindness".*

(*Tov Halevanon*: they did not set their attention to investigate strange questions, before these would be needed practically. Only in monetary laws, since this is very common and relevant, and is very necessary for the welfare of the world, as they said (Avot 1:18) "on three things the world stands, on justice, truth, and peace". But for other orders, they would not investigate too much on derivative laws.

Marpe Lenefesh: *"the depth of their wisdom"* - that their primary wisdom and toiling was only in delving into and purifying their deeds - that all their deeds be l'shem shamayim [devoted to G-d].

Manoach Halevavos: *"offered up their lives"* - the explanation is not that they literally gave up their lives to die as martyrs, for we do not find that Rab Judah ever did so. Rather, the explanation is that all of their thoughts and aims in their minds and souls, and their trust in all matters - was only on G-d.

Tov Halevanon: they would cleave very much to love of G-d until they no longer cared about loss of money or personal honor in regard to things which touched on the honor of G-d ... as we see there on how Rabbi Ada bar Ahava could not restrain himself until he rose up and did what he did.

Pas Lechem: *"Hence, Torah study must be combined with acts of kindness"* - behold, even for practical Torah study one should not spend all of his time because one must also leave over time for actual good deeds. All the more so, one should not spend his time with strange questions which would never have any relevance.)

Thus it became clear to me that all the roots of deeds which one intends for His Name are founded on purity of heart and mind and singleness of mind. Where the motive is tainted, good deeds, however numerous and diligent, are not accepted; as Scripture says *"even when you make many prayers, I will not hear. Wash yourselves, make yourselves clean; put away the evil of your doings from before My eyes; cease to do evil"* (Isaiah 1:16). And, *"but the matter is very near to you, in your mouth and in your heart, that you may do it"* (Deut. 30:14), and *"give Me your heart, and let your eyes keep My ways"* (Prov. 23:26). And our wise men have said: *"if you give Me your eyes and heart, I know that you are Mine"* (Yerushalmi Berachos 1:5); and Scripture says *"you shall not wander after your hearts and after your eyes"* (Numbers 15:39), and *"with what shall I come before the L-ord and bow myself before G-d on high? Shall I come with Olah offerings?"* (Micha 6:6), and the answer given was *"He has told you, O man, what is good, and what the L-ord demands of you; but to do justice, to love kindness, and to walk humbly with your G-d"* (ibid 6:8); and *"but let him that glories glory in this, that he understands and knows Me, that I am the L-ord doing kindness, justice, and righteousness"* (Jer. 9:23). The explanation is that a man who glories should glory in comprehending G-d's ways, recognizing His beneficence, reflecting on His creation, realizing His might and wisdom, as manifested in His works. All these verses which I have brought are proofs on the obligatory character of the commandments of the heart and the discipline of the soul.

(*Tov Halevanon*: *"Wash yourselves, make yourselves clean"* - washing and cleaning is referring to cleanliness of heart and mind, namely, that he removes from his heart the lust for sin, and from his mind, the thinking of them, until he resolves in his heart to desist from them, as Scripture says "tear your hearts and not your garments,etc." (Yoel 2:13), which means renouncing sin and removing it from his heart. This is the main component of repentance as is known.

"but the matter is very near to you, in your mouth and in your heart" - hence, all deeds depend on the intent of heart.

"with what shall I come before the L-ord...Shall I come with Olah offerings?" - behold, certainly, the proper repentance for sins of the limbs is known, as our Sages said (Yoma 86a): "there are three types of atonement..." and the repentance of each type is explained. Likewise an Olah offering atones for [bad] musings of the heart as our Sages said (Vayikra Raba 7:3). The question here was with what can he bow his heart and straighten its crookedness. Should he come with Olah offerings? Can the Olah straighten his heart to the service of G-d from now on, just like it can atone for [bad] musings of the past? The answer was *"He has told you, O man, what is good, and what the L-ord demands of you; but to do justice,*

to love kindness, and to walk humbly with your G-d", i.e. That G-d desires
only wholeness of the heart, and wholeness of (temimus) sentiment and
mind to His service.)

You should realize that the aim and value of the duties of the heart is that
our exterior and interior be equal and consistent in the service of G-d, so
that the testimony of the heart, tongue, and limbs be alike, and that they
support and confirm each other instead of differing and contradicting each
other. This is what Scripture calls *"tamim"* (innocent/perfect), in saying:
"You shall be perfect with the L-ord your G-d" (Deut. 18:13), and *"Noah
was a righteous man and perfect in his generations"* (Gen. 6:9), and *"he
who walks uprightly, and works righteousness, and speaks the truth in his
heart"* (Ps. 15:2), and *"I will give heed unto the way of integrity..I will walk
within my house with a perfect heart"* (Ps. 101:2).

On the other hand, one whose inner [being] is not consistent with his outer
[life] is condemned by Scripture, as written: *"his heart was not whole with
the L-ord, his G-d"* (Kings 11:4), and *"but they flatter Him with their
mouths and lied with their tongues. For their heart was not steadfast with
Him"* (Ps. 78:36).

It is well known, that whoever exhibits conflicting or contradictory
behavior in word or deed - people do not believe in his integrity and have
no confidence in his truthfulness. Likewise, if our exterior conflicts with
our interior, if our heart's intent conflicts with our words, if our physical
activities are not consistent with the convictions of our soul - our service to
our G-d will not be whole, for He will not accept from us fraudulent
service, as written *"I cannot [bear] iniquity with assembly"* (Isaiah 1:13),
and *"For I am the L-ord, Who loves justice, hates robbery in a burnt
offering"* (Isaiah 61:8), and *"if you offer a blind [animal] for sacrifice, is it
not evil? And if you offer the lame and the sick, is it not evil? Bring it now
to your governor. Will he accept you, or lift up your face"* (Malachi 1:8),
and *"Behold, to obey is better than a peace-offering; to hearken (is better)
than the fat of rams"* (Samuel 15:22).

(*Marpe Lenefesh: "It is well known.."* - this matter also applies to human
beings. If a man tells his fellow one thing and does the opposite, or
sometimes like this and sometimes like that - the fellow will not trust his
integrity and word since he contradicts himself. All the more so, that G-d,
for who everything is revealed, will not accept fraudulent service, namely,
if one does the commandments with intent for personal gain or for any
other [improper] motive.)

Hence, one commandment, according to the heart and intent with which it is performed, can outweigh many commandments, and likewise one transgression can outweigh many transgressions. Even the thought to do a commandment and the yearning to do it out of reverence for G-d, despite that one was unable to actually perform it, may, nevertheless, outweigh many commandments performed without this reverence, as G-d said to David: *"because it was in your heart to build a house for My Name"* (Chronicles II 6:8), and *"then the G-d fearing men spoke to one another, and the L-ord hearkened and heard it. And a book of remembrance was written before Him for those who feared the L-ord and for those who thought upon His Name"* (Malachi 3:16), and our Sages expounded the last words (Shabbat 63a): "what is meant by 'thought upon His Name?' - [answer:] "if one intended to fulfill a commandment but was prevented from doing it, it is accounted to him as if he had done it."

> (*Pas Lechem*: *"according to the heart and intent"* - according to the joy of heart to do it and the intent to G-d. Likewise for sins, according to how much joy he has in doing it, as written "those who rejoice to do evil, and delight in the perversity of evil" (Prov. 2:14), and according to the intent, whether he does the sin due to lust or to anger G-d (rebel), r"l.
> *"thought upon His Name"* - according to the Sages, the intent of the words "thought upon His Name", is that he thought to do a commandment for His Name. Then, even if he was prevented from doing it, it is accounted as if he did it, for a pure thought to G-d also makes a [good] impact in one's soul.)

When these arguments from Reason, Scripture, and Tradition dawned on me, I began to train myself in them, and I undertook on myself the task of knowing and practicing them. The discovery of one principle revealed another related to it, which in turn led to a third, until the matter became broad and it was difficult for me to retain it always in mind. I feared that I might forget what I had already thought out, and that what had become solid shaped in my mind might dissolve, especially since in our times there are so few helping on this wisdom. I decided to compose a book on them which would include their roots and surrounding divisions, and much of their derivatives; and so I would always urge myself to know them and obligate myself to do them.

Where my practice was consistent with my words, I thank G-d who helped me in this, and taught me His ways. But where my practice was inconsistent with my words and fell short of attaining this, I blame and rebuke my soul, and argue with it, so that from the standard of righteousness set forth in this work, my soul might realize its own iniquity, and from its standard of justness, its own deviation, and from its uprightness, its own perverseness, and from the perfection there taught, its own short-comings.

> (*Marpe Lenefesh*: (an alternative interpretation is that the last sentence refers to G-d not to the book, hence) Man does iniquity but G-d does to him righteousness, man deviates from G-d, but G-d does to him good and uprightness, man perverts his ways, and G-d rectifies him, man falls short in his deeds, while G-d is perfect in His deeds. When a man puts these ideas to heart always, he will not run away from G-d.)

I saw proper to make the book one of permanent value, a hidden treasure, a lamp to illuminate men's paths and teach them the path in which they should go. I hoped that the book would be of still greater use to others than to myself, and of greater beneficial instruction to others than to my own benefit of fulfilling my wish.

I said to myself that I will compose a book on this subject that would be systematically divided according to the roots of the duties of the heart and the inner commandments; be comprehensive and adequate to the matters, point out the good and right way; serve as a guide to the customs of the earlier Sages and the discipline of the pious; awaken men from their senseless sleep; delve in detail into the depths of this wisdom; recall to men the knowledge of G-d and of His Torah, promote the salvation of the soul; encourage the observant, stir up the negligent, set the eager on the right road, straighten the early, guide beginners and show the way to the perplexed.

> (*Pas Lechem*: "straighten the early" - he who has strong enthusiasm and yearning to serve G-d, and due to this he mixes up the order, preceding things which must be done later. In truth, this is a major detriment in the service of G-d. This book will straighten him, i.e. direct him in the straight path and the proper order of steps.
> "show the way to the perplexed" - many people are confused in many matters of service, and they are not capable of clarifying and deciding which way to turn, and which road to take. This book will teach them which is the proper path to choose.)

But when I thought of proceeding to carry out my decision to write this book, I saw that a man like myself is not fit to compose a work like this. I estimated that my strength was insufficient to properly divide its parts, the subject appearing too vast to my eyes, my knowledge too inadequate, and my intellectual faculties too weak to grasp the topics. Furthermore, I am not proficient in the subtleties of the Arabic language which it would need to be in, due to this being the easiest language for most of my contemporaries to grasp. I feared that I would be toiling at a task which would only serve to demonstrate my deficiencies and that I would thus be exceeding proper bounds of discretion. I therefore, told my soul to retract the thought and to draw back from what it had resolved on.

> (*Pas Lechem*: *"to properly divide its parts"* - I do not have the strength to divide the matters of the inner wisdom, that the matter be properly presented. For this is the chief aim of [rational] inquiry into something - to clarify what is its nature, and on what pillars does it rest on, and what are its roots, branches, and derivatives, as mentioned earlier.
> *"I would thus be exceeding proper bounds of discretion"* - it is a proper trait for a man to recognize his place, and to restrain his desires from doing something beyond his power, for that would be like haughtiness.
> *"retract (lit:return) the thought..draw back"* - he doubled the expression for this is human nature. When something is fixed in a man's thoughts for a long time and afterwards he regrets and wishes to retract from this thing, the immediate decision to retract is called "return" (chozer). However, since the thing was fixed in his imagination faculty for so long, the thoughts overpower him. A thought seizes him every time it enters his heart to persuade him to do that thing. A man must then draw it back and remove it from his heart, and dismiss it from his mind by force. This is the meaning of the double expression "return...draw back". Understand this.)

When I then decided to relieve myself of the burden of this undertaking and give up my plan of composing this work, I again suspected my soul of having chosen tranquility, to dwell in the abode of laziness, in peace and quiet. I feared that perhaps this decision to abandon the project stemmed from the lust for pleasure, and that this is what had inclined me to the way of peace and tranquility, to decide to abandon this in order to sit in the company of laziness.

> (*Pas Lechem*: i.e. other things besides service [of G-d]. Since, by defeating me in this indolence, automatically the power of lust will lead me to laziness, similar to the principle (Pirkei Avot 4:2) "sin drags more sin")

I knew that many great works were lost due to fear, and many losses were caused by concern. I remembered the saying: "it is part of prudence not to be overly prudent". I told myself, if every person who ever composed a good work or who ever taught the upright and proper path had waited until all his wishes were fulfilled, no person would have ever uttered a word after the prophets, whom G-d had chosen as His agents and strengthened with His divine help. If every person who had wished to attain all good qualities but was unable to attain them, had abandoned whatever he could attain of them, then all human beings would be devoid of all good and lacking all excellencies. They would have been perpetually pursuing after false hopes, the paths of righteousness would have been desolate, and the abodes of kindliness would have been abandoned.

> (*Pas Lechem*: *"many losses were caused by concern"* - ... just like I also had
> *"the abodes of kindliness would have been abandoned"* - for according to this logic, a man would also abandon doing any acts of kindness towards his fellow and bestowing good according to his capacity. For he would say to himself: why should I do kindness to my fellow since I don't have the ability right now to do a full and complete kindness as is my wish. Therefore, I will wait and hope to when I will be very rich. Then, I will bestow great kindness on my fellow according to my wish to fully fulfill his desire.)

I understood that while men's souls lust greatly to attain evil ends (worldly pleasures and benefits - *TL*), they are sluggish to toil in the pursuit of what is noble. They are lazy in seeking the good, and always walk in the paths of laughter and rejoicing.

> (*Tov Halevanon*: *"laughter and rejoicing"* - to this man's nature tends, due to his composition and inherent lust which stems from his physicality (the body), as Scripture says: (Job 11:12) "man is born as wild donkey's colt".)

If a vision of lust appears to them and beckons to them, they invent falsehoods so that they may turn to it. They bolster up its arguments to make its deception seem upright, to strengthen its lies, to make firm its looseness. But when the light of truth invitingly shines before them, they make up idle pretexts to refrain from turning to it. They argue against it, declare its courses misleading and contradict its assertions, so as to make it appear inconsistent and thus have an excuse to part from it. Every man's enemy is between his own ribs. Unless, he has an aid from G-d, a rebuker always ready for [rebuking] his soul, a powerful governor, that will harness his soul with the saddle of service, and will muzzle it with the bridle of righteousness, strike it with the stick of discipline; and when he resolves to do good, he should not delay, and if his heart entices him to a different path, he should scold it and overpower it.

> (*Pas Lechem*: *"they invent falsehoods"* - i.e. even though at first appearance, its evil and bitter end is visible. Nevertheless, they invent for themselves false pretexts to embellish the thing they lust for and cover up its evil, such as in the eating of the Tree of Knowledge, whose evil was

apparent to them, since, behold, they were warned by the word of G-d of a punishment of death. But when the serpent (thoughts of evil - Rabbi Uziel Milevsky zt'l) showed them its beauty and desirableness, and then built up excuses and covered up its evil, as written "you will not die, for G-d knows..." (Gen. 3:4). Their hearts enticed them and they were seduced by his words.

"make firm its looseness" - it is the way of falsehood to join together things which in truth do not logically follow. It then tricks the person with imaginations and joins the false premises to draw spurious conclusions.

"enemy between ribs" - this the lusting soul (nefesh bahamit/animal soul/evil inclination), whose source is in the liver which rests in the abdomen, between his ribs.

"a rebuker always ready...powerful governor" - this is the Understanding, that it be standing and ready always to rebuke the soul. Corresponding to the excuses and false claims of the soul, he wrote that his Understanding should be *"ready"* to deduce and clarify the truth, for all rebuke means "clarification of the matter". Corresponding to the strengthening of the soul with its lusts, he wrote *"powerful governor"* which stands against it and overpowers it.

"harness his soul with the saddle of service" - *"saddle"* is the belt which one harnesses the load to the donkey.. corresponding to the soul's fleeing from the service in doing good, he wrote *"harness,etc"*. This splits to two parts. That which is between man and G-d, he wrote *"harness it with the saddle of service"*, while corresponding to that which is between man and his fellow, he wrote *"muzzle it with the bridle of righteousness"*, i.e. muzzles its mouth with the muzzle of righteousness to turn it to the good. On the aspect of refraining from evil, namely, the soul's tending to evil, he wrote "strike it with the stick of discipline".

"he should not delay" - for another [later] time, lest the soul will overpower him and topple him with laziness..

Marpe Lenefesh: (quoting the Alshich) Each and every believer has daily times when he is stirred from the sleep of his foolishness and wants to separate himself from now on from the vanities and lusts of the world, and to load on himself the yoke of Torah and mitzvot, day and night. But immediately, the yetzer (evil inclination) greets him telling him, "it's good. you see well, but why so fast? You will collapse. When will you take care of your home and your numerous business activities? First, work hard for a few days to finish your occupations then you can return to this... But this is just a ploy to wait until he has cooled down and eventually his motivation disappears altogether. Thus he acts all of his days. Therefore, Solomon wrote: "lazy one, until when will you lie down?" (Prov. 6:9). He did not write "[until when will you] sleep" [but rather "lie down"] for he already awoke from his sleep.. do not listen to him, rather hold fast to the service of G-d immediately. Do not slacken and be strong as a lion to do the will of your Father in heaven, and you will succeed in your business also.. see

there.
"and if his heart entices him to a different path he should scold it and overpower it" - i.e. if while he has an opportunity to do good, his heart entices him to turn to a different matter in order to distract his mind and detour him from that good activity, he should scold it, and if it strengthens over him, he should likewise strengthen himself against it and overpower it.)

Therefore, I found myself obligated to force my soul to bear the task of composing this book, and resolved to expound its topics with whatever language or analogy would make the matters readily understandable. Among all the duties of the heart, I will only mention those which suggest themselves to me, and will not trouble to expound all of them, so that the book will not be too long. I will, however, cite among the things necessary for the clarification of each of its roots in the section allocated to it. And from G-d, the true Unity, may I receive aid. On Him, I place my trust and to Him I ask to teach me the right path which He desires, and which is pleasing and acceptable to Him, in word and deed, in inner and outer conduct.

(*Pas Lechem*: i.e. according to what we said earlier, that the nature of the soul is to instill laziness in a man, and to prevent him from a good activity, therefore, I saw myself obligated to direct and force my soul against its will to bear the strain...etc.
"aid me...teach me" - I will receive aid from G-d in terms of strength and I place my trust on Him to enlighten my mind. These correspond to the two problems he mentioned earlier *"my strength was insufficient"* and *"my knowledge too inadequate, etc."*)

When my deliberation was complete, and I finally resolved to write it, I laid its foundations. I built it on a basis of ten principles, which cover all of the Duties of the Heart and accordingly divided the book into ten parts, each part designated for one principle, discussing its scope and divisions, the things it depends on, and the things detrimental to it.

I propose to take the most direct (easiest) method of arousing, teaching, and instructing, using language clear, direct, and familiar, so that my words will be more easily understood. I will refrain from deep language, unusual terms, and the arguments in the way of *"defeat"* (nitzuach), which the logicians call in arabic *"Algidal"*, and likewise for remote inquiries which cannot be resolved in this work, for I only brought such arguments as are satisfactory and convincing according to the methods proper to the science of theology.

(*Tov Halevanon*: *"defeat"* (nitzuach) - It is known that the science of logic divides into three methods nitzuach (defeat), raya (proof), and mofet (definitive proof). Nitzuach (defeat) is when one cannot decide on either of the two views definitively, only that one view has more and stronger questions and claims which can be raised against it than the other view. The view which has fewer and weaker questions against it will prevail over the other view, and it is proper to follow that view even though it may also have some questions which can be raised. The "proof" (raya) is where one view has many questions and claims which can be raised against it while the other view has no claims against it. Certainly, it is proper to uphold it. This is better than nitzuach (defeat). Because here there are no claims and questions against it from the aspect of rational inquiry, but nevertheless, perhaps his inquiry was somehow flawed [for example, due to lacking certain information]. The "mofet" (definitive proof) is that which is impossible to refute in almost any way whatsoever, similar to the miracles of the prophets which were openly visible to the senses [at that time]. Behold, science is divided into three divisions: theology, nature, mathematics. It is known that for most of the science of theology, it is impossible to bring a "raya" (proof), and all the more so, a mofet (definitive proof). For due to the enormous depth and awesomeness of this science, and the limitations of human intellect, it is almost impossible to establish a clear view which is without any doubts. But they can be clarified in the way of Nitzuach (defeat), and a few of its topics through "raya" (proof) which are close to being mofet (definitive proof). For the science of nature, on the other hand, which is not as deep, one can explain much of it in the way of raya (proof), and some even from mofet (definitive proof). But the science of limudit which is the science of mathematics and geometry, all of its matters are clarified through mofet (definitive proof). This is what the author wrote that not all rational inquiry is found as mofet (definitive proof), but as nitzuach (defeat) or rayah (proof).)

As the philosopher said "it is not proper to seek of every inquiry a conclusion in the way of mofet (irrefutable proof), since not every topic in rational inquiry can be demonstrated to this extent. Likewise, we should not be satisfied in the science of nature with the method of 'sufficient' (since a full "raya" proof can be achieved). Nor in the science of theology should we strive to apprehend with the senses or draw comparisons with physical phenomena."

(*Pas Lechem*: for it is impossible to explain things in theology using our physical senses or to explain it through a familiar analogy, because it is exalted above and beyond all [physical] senses and comparison. It has no connection whatsoever with these things.)

Nor should we require logical demonstration of the first principles in nature (i.e. why the nature of this is like this and the nature of that is different, for this is how G-d created them -LT). Nor should we require logical demonstration of the first demonstrations of the first principles (the axioms of logic such as that the all is greater than the part, or that the diagonal of a right triangle is longer than the side -LT).

If we carefully avoid these things, it will be easier for us to achieve our aims. I we do not do so, we will stray from our subject, and it will be difficult for us to achieve our intended purpose.

Since this work is of theological character, I have refrained from the methods of demonstration usual in the sciences of logic and mathematics except in the first gate, where possibly the subtlety of the inquiry compels resort to these methods.

I have drawn most of my proofs from propositions which are accepted as reasonable and these I have made clear by familiar examples about which there can be no doubt. I supported them with what I found written in Scripture and afterwards with the words of tradition received from our Sages. I quoted also the pious and wise of other nations whose words have come down to us, hoping that my readers' hearts would incline to them and give heed to their wisdom, as for example, the words of philosophers, the ethical teachings of the ascetics, and their praiseworthy customs. Our Rabbis have already said regarding this (Sanhedrin 39b):

"One verse says: 'after the ways of the surrounding nations you have done' (Ezek. 11:12), while in another verse it says [in contradiction] 'after the ways of the surrounding nations you have not done' (Ezek. 5:7). How can this be reconciled? As follows - their good ways you have not copied; their evil ones you have followed."

Likewise, the Rabbis said (Megila 16a): "whoever says a wise thing, even among the gentiles is considered a Sage". They also said regarding bringing analogies to make difficult concepts easier to understand: "he taught it by signs and explained it by analogies" (Eruvin 21b); and the wise man said: *"to understand a parable and figure, the words of the wise and their riddles"* (Prov. 1:6).

When I accepted to undertake the task of composing this book on the divisions of the duties of the heart, I set my mind to select those which were most comprehensive and which would lead to the rest.

I set their chief root, and great foundation to be the wholehearted acceptance of G-d's Unity. Afterwards, I examined which of the duties of the heart are most fitting to be joined to the [wholehearted acceptance of the] Unity of G-d. I fully realized that as the Creator is the true Unity, and is subject to neither essence nor incident (this will be explained in Gate 1 - *TL*), it is impossible for us to grasp Him from the aspect of His glorious essence (to contemplate what He is - *TL*). We are therefore forced to know and grasp Him from the aspect of His creations. This is the topic of the second treatise, the Gate of Examination of G-d's works. I therefore made this examination the second root of the general principles of the duties of the heart.

I then reflected on the sovereignty belonging to the true Unity, and what service is correspondingly due to Him from His creatures. I therefore set the assuming of His service as the third root of the general principles of the duties of the heart.

> (*Tov Halevanon*: "sovereignty" - in that He is our king, our Master, our Maker, and how can we greet His face and assume His service)

It then became clear to me, what is proper regarding the true Unity, that as He alone rules all things and all the benefits and harms we receive come from Him and are under His permission, we are in duty bound to put our trust in Him and to surrender ourselves over to Him. I therefore made Trust in G-d as the fourth root of the general principles of the duties of the heart.

> (*Pas Lechem*: "under His permission" - regarding the benefits, he wrote "*from Him*", while on the harm, he wrote "*under His permission*". For the harm does not come from Him. Therefore, it is only correct to say that it comes with His permission, namely, that He did not prevent it.)

Afterwards, I pondered on the conception of absolute Unity, that as G-d is unique in His glory, has nothing in common with anything, nor resembles anything else, we must therefore join to this that we serve Him alone, and that we devote all activities to Him, since He does not accept worship which is associated with other than Him. Therefore, I placed the devoting of acts to G-d as the fifth root of the general principles of the duties of the heart.

> (*Tov Halevanon*: "associated" - i.e. if in the service of G-d, a man has some other motive combined with serving G-d, G-d will not accept it.)

Afterwards, when my thoughts continued pondering as to what we owe to the true Unity regarding proclaiming His glory and greatness. Since there is none like Him, therefore we decided to join to this - humbling ourselves before Him to the utmost of our ability. Hence, I made Humility/Submission the sixth root of the general principles of the duties of the heart.

> (*Tov Halevanon*: *"humility"* - that we realize our petty worth compared to Him.
> *Marpe Lenefesh*: we are obligated to proclaim His exaltedness and greatness, and this entails humbling ourselves before Him.)

When I reflected on what happens to human beings, that they neglect and fall short of what service they owe to the blessed Creator, and the path with which they can rectify their crookedness and shortcomings, namely repentance and beseeching for forgiveness, I therefore placed Repentance as the seventh root of the general principles of the duties of the heart.

When I sought to grasp what our inner and outer duties to G-d truly are, and realized that it is impossible for us to fulfill them until we bring ourselves to an accounting on them before G-d and are meticulous in this, I made the spiritual accounting the eighth root of the general principles of the duties of the heart.

When I meditated on the matter of the true Unity, I saw that the wholehearted acknowledgement of His Unity cannot possibly endure even in the soul of the believer, if his heart is drunk with the wine of love of this world and he inclines to the material pleasures. But if he strives to empty his heart and liberate his mind from the superfluities of this world and separate himself from its luxuries, only then will he completely accept G-d's Unity and rise to its level. I therefore set Abstinence as the ninth root of the general principles of the duties of the heart.

Afterwards, I inquired on what we are obligated to the blessed Creator, who is the goal of all our desires and the purpose of all our hopes and with whom all things begin and end, and as to what is due to Him from us in regard to the love of His favor and fear of His retribution, the former being the highest good and the latter being the greatest evil, as Scripture says *"For His anger is only a moment; in His favor is life; Weeping may endure for a night, but joy comes in the morning"* (Ps. 30:6), I therefore placed love of G-d as the tenth root of the general principles of the duties of the heart.

(*Tov Halevanon*: *"all things begin and end"* - He made our soul, and when it will separate from the body, it will return to Him, like Scripture says: "[then the dust shall return to the earth as it was, and] the spirit shall return to G-d who gave it" (Ecles. 12:7). Then, from Him the good person will receive the greatest good and the bad person, who inclined to the corrupt ways, will receive the greatest evil.
Marpe Lenefesh: *"all things begin"* - with this intent [of love] - all the service of G-d begins.)

After I arrived at these principles by Reasoning, I searched our Scriptures and traditions and found them indicated in many places. I will explain each of them in their respective treatise with G-d's help. I named the book, with a title which reflects my aim in writing it. It is called the Instruction of the Duties of the Heart.

My goal in this book is to obtain wisdom for myself and at the same time, to stir the simple and the negligent among the followers of our Torah and those who have inherited the precepts of our religion, by bringing sufficient proofs which reason can testify as to their soundness and truth and which will only be disputed by the hypocritical and false people, because to such people truth is a burden on them (for the light of their intellect has been extinguished by the sea of their lusts and enjoyments - *TL*) and their desire is to make things easier on themselves. I will not trouble myself to answer them because my purpose in this book was not to refute those who dispute the fundamentals of our faith. My aim is rather to bring to light what is already fixed in our minds and embedded in our souls of the fundamentals of our religion and the cornerstones of the Torah. When we arouse our minds to ponder them, their truth becomes clear to us inwardly and their lights will illuminate even our exterior.

The following is an analogy for this: An astrologer entered the courtyard of his friend and divined that there is a hidden treasure in it. He searched for it and found masses of silver that had turned black due to a crust of rust which had formed on it. He took a small portion, scrubbed it with vinegar and salt, washed and polished it until it had regained its original luster, splendor and shine. Afterwards, the owner [of the courtyard] gave orders that the rest of the treasure should be treated so.

My intent is to do the same with the hidden treasures of the heart, namely, to reveal them, and demonstrate their shining excellence, in order that anyone who wishes to draw close to G-d and cling to Him may do the same.

When, my brother, you have read this book, and comprehended its theme, take it for a remembrance. Bring your soul to a true judgement. Ponder it over, develop its thoughts. Cling it to your heart and mind. If you find an error in it, correct it; any omission, complete it. Have intent [when reading it] to follow its instruction and guidance. Do not have the aim of acquiring a name or to gain glory through its wisdom. Judge me leniently if you find any mistake, flaw, or whatever other shortcoming in its topics and words. For I hurried to compose it and did not tarry because I feared that death would overcome me and prevent me from my goal of completing it. You know how weak is the power of flesh to attain anything, and how deficient is man from fully grasping (the depth of something - *PL*), as Scripture says: *"Surely the sons of men are vanity; the sons of men are a lie; if they go up in the scales; they are altogether lighter than vanity"* (Ps. 62:10). I have already confessed from the outset on my insufficient strength. Let this admission atone for the errors and flaws in it.

(*Tov Halevanon*: *"bring your soul to a true judgement"* - behold since a man is biased on himself, it is unlikely that he will admit his own flaws and lackings and therefore will not judge himself correctly, as our Sages said (Shabbat 119a): "a man cannot see a fault in himself" - unless he habituates himself in much in-depth analyses and separation from worldly matters.

Pas Lechem: Do not be enticed by the evil inclination which desires to impede you, so that you continue conducting yourself in the same way you have done until now. He tries to befriend you with all sorts of false excuses. Rather judge your soul a true judgment and confess to its error and perverseness.)

You should know that all the Duties of the Heart and all disciplines of the soul, whether positive or negative, fall within these ten roots which I have composed in this book, just like many of the commandments fall under the precepts of *"love your fellow as yourself"* (Levit. 19:18), and under *"he did no evil to his fellow"* (Ps. 15:3), and under *"turn from evil and do good"* (Ps. 34:15).

Fix them to your mind. Return them to your thoughts continuously. Their derivatives will be made known to you, with G-d's help, when He will see your heart desiring in them and inclining to them, as written: *"Who is the man who fears the L-ord? Him will he instruct in the way that he should choose"* (Ps. 25:12).

(*Pas Lechem*: *"return them to your thoughts"* - since, by human nature, it is impossible to keep them continuously clinging in his thoughts, without any interruption, therefore he concluded and said that nevertheless, return them to your thoughts continuously.)

I saw fitting to conclude the introduction of this book with a wondrous parable, which will stimulate you to study its content, and arouse you to realize the special importance of this class of commandments over the others, as well as the difference between the level of the physical, philosophical, and linguistic wisdoms to the level of the wisdom of the Torah. Try to understand this parable when you read it. Recall it to your thoughts. You will find what you seek with G-d's help.

A king distributed balls of silk to his servants to check their intelligence. The industrious and sensible one sorted from the balls of silk allotted to him and selected the best quality ones. He then did the same with the remaining ones until he divided all of his portion into three grades - fine, medium, and coarse. He then made from each grade the best that could be done with it and had the material done by skilled craftsmen into expensive garments of various colors and styles, which he wore in the presence of the king, selecting garments suitable to the occasion and place.

The foolish among the king's servants used all the balls of silk to make that which the wise servant had made with the worst sort. He sold it for whatever he could get for it, and hastily squandered the money in good food and drink or the like.

When the matter came to the king, he was pleased with the deeds of the industrious and sensible one, drew him closer, and promoted him to a position of one of his treasured servants. The deeds of the foolish servant were evil in his eyes, and the king banished him to the faraway desert lands of his kingdom to dwell among those who had incurred the king's anger.

Likewise, the blessed Al-mighty gave His Torah of truth to His servants to test them. The thinking, intelligent man, when he reads it and understands it clearly, will divide it into three divisions. The first is the knowledge of fine spiritual themes, namely, the inner wisdom, such as the duties of the heart, the discipline of the soul and will obligate his soul on them always. Afterwards, he will select the second portion, namely, the practical duties of the limbs, doing each one in its proper time and place. Afterwards, he will make use of the third division, the historical portions of Scripture, to know the various types of men and their happenings in historical order, and the events of past ages and their hidden messages. He will use every part according to its proper occasion, place, and need.

Just like the industrious servant provided skilled craftsmen's tools in order to carry out his intentions in the manufacture of the silk of the king, so too, in each of these divisions, the intelligent man will use the help of the practical sciences, the science of logic, the science of language, etc. which he will employ as introductory to the science of theology. For one who is not knowledgeable in them cannot recognize the wisdom of the Creator in nature, and will not know the physical workings of his own body, much less for what is outside himself.

The foolish and distracted person when he occupies himself with the Book of G-d, uses it to learn riddles of the ancients or the historical accounts. He hastens to apply it for worldly benefits and will bring arguments from it to justify pursuing worldly pleasures, abandoning the way of abstinence (from the superfluous), going in his own way, and following the views and wishes of each type of person he meets, as written *"he shall die without instruction; and in the greatness of his folly he shall go astray"* (Prov. 5:23).

(*Pas Lechem*: *"to justify pursuing worldly pleasures"* - such as the fools adducing proofs that it is proper to pursue wealth from the forefathers who were all wealthy. Or they bring proofs that the important ancients would pursue excessive sexual relations, as we find by David who had eighteen wives or Solomon who had a thousand wives. But these fools do not realize that we are blind, and we have no understanding whatsoever of the ancients and what was their true motives in their activities which appear strange to us. We must not adduce any proofs from them to be lenient but rather to be stringent.)

Examine, my brother, this analogy. Ponder it in your thoughts. Deduce from the Book of G-d what I have called to your attention. Seek help in this by reading the books of Rabeinu Saadiah Gaon (Emunot V'Deot -TL) which enlighten the mind, sharpen the understanding, instruct the ignorant, and arouse the lazy.

(*Translator*: *"Examine, my brother, this analogy"* - see the Marpe Lenefesh commentary for a mystical interpretation.)

May the Almighty teach us the way of His service, as His anointed one beseeched Him: *"You make known to me the path of life; in Your presence there is fullness of joy; in Your right hand bliss forevermore"* (Ps. 16:11).

*** Shaar HaYichud - Gate of Unity of G-d *** (with commentaries)

NOTE: It is recommended for most people to start from later gates as this gate is very difficult and highly error prone for one without proper guidance.

* Important Foreword

* Introduction

* Chapter 1 - definition of the wholehearted acceptance of G-d's unity

* Chapter 2 - how many divisions does the subject of unity divide into?

* Chapter 3 - whether or not it is our duty to intellectually investigate the matter.

* Chapter 4 - which introductions must we know before we investigate the unity?

* Chapter 5 - To clarify the premises which demonstrate that the world has a Creator who created it from nothing.

* Chapter 6 - how we apply them to establish the existence of the Creator

* Chapter 7 - to bring proofs that He is one
  Translator: I have included here a treatise on evolution.

* Chapter 8 - to clarify the matter of conventional unity versus true unity

* Chapter 9 - demonstration that G-d alone is the true Unity and that there is no true unity besides Him.

* Chapter 10 - the Divine attributes ascribed to G-d or denied to Him

*** Important Foreword ***

This treatise sets out to demonstrate through rational investigation that this world must have a Creator who created it from nothing and that it is impossible otherwise. In doing so, it also provides a fascinating introduction to G-d. Many of the philosophical arguments used have been revised and reformulated over the generations. Thus, the terminology and methodology of these proofs may seem antiquated or outdated even though they remain philosophically sound.

There is a difference of opinion among the Torah authorities as to whether this section should be studied by the typical student of the Torah. Many Torah luminaries maintain that one should not seek philosophical proofs of G-d's existence. Belief in Hash-m should be based on the Mesorah that we received from our elders and mentors, the study of Hash-m's wondrous Torah, and the many ways He manifests Himself in His creations and in our daily lives. Indeed as the Pas Lechem commentary writes at the start of the next gate: "In philosophical inquiry, a man is not assured from stumbling and erring in treading this path, as in truth, there are many, many casualties strewn along the path of philosophical inquiry..."

For this reason, I have tried to add commentaries to provide a basic, but probably insufficient amount of guidance. If something does not make sense, please investigate with a wise Rabbi first before drawing the wrong conclusions. Also keep in mind, that it is important to study it in its entirety as many concluding points in the end tie everything together.

I once heard Rabbi Zev Leff say in a lecture: "in the time of the Rambam people were really seeking, and bringing intellectual proofs was beneficial, but today the biggest question on people's minds is whether to put ketchup or mustard on their hotdogs". Tragically most people have become comfortable living superficially, content to spend their few dozen years of life without thinking of who they are and why they are here. It is my hope that this translation will arouse others and myself on these questions.

In translating this, I consulted with the classic hebrew commentaries and also the out of print translation by Rabbi Moses Hyamson which came to my possession in a miraculous way. The translator studied in various yeshivas under great Torah scholars such as Rabbi Dov Shwartzman zt'l

(~2 years), Rabbi Nachman Bulman zt'l, Rabbi Nissan Kaplan (~5 years). He also completed a degree in physics at the University of Massachusetts, Amherst and was a research associate in nuclear physics for some time before heading off to yeshiva.

- Yosef Sebag, Jerusalem, May 2015 - Iyar 5775

*** Shaar HaYichud - Gate of Unity of G-d ***

Abbreviations used in this translation:
MH - **Manoach HeLevavos commentary by Rabbi Manoach Hendel (1540-1611)**
TL - **Tov HaLevanon commentary by Rabbi Yisrael Halevi (1700-1777)**
PL - **Pas Lechem commentary by Rabbi Chaim Avraham Hacohen (1740-1815)**
ML - **Marpe Lenefesh commentary by Rabbi Refael Mendel (1825-1895)**

*** Shaar HaYichud - Gate of Unity of G-d *** (with commentaries)

from Chovos Halevavos - Duties of the Heart

by Rabeinu Bachye zt'l

*** INTRODUCTION ***

The author says:

After investigating after what is the most necessary of the cornerstones and fundamentals of our religion, we found that the wholehearted acceptance of the unity of G-d is the root and foundation of Judaism. It is the first of the gates of the Torah, and it differentiates between the believer and the heretic. It is the head and front of religious truth, and one who strays from it - will not be able to perform religious deeds and his faith will not endure.

> (some commentaries:
> even if he does good deeds, his acts will not be correct and built on a foundation, nor will they be whole and enduring and if there is no foundation, the entire building will eventually collapse - *Pas Lechem*
> "he will not have any merit for his religious deeds" - Tov Halevanon
> "he will not be able to perform the service of G-d, since if one does not believe in Him, that He created the world, and that He is alone in His world, and that it is befitting to serve Him, if so, one has no master that he should serve, and there's no greater non-believer than this" - *Manoach Levavos*)

Because of this, G-d's first words to us at Mount Sinai were: "I am the L-ord your G-d...you shall not have other gods before Me", and later on He exhorted us through His prophet saying: (Shema Yisrael..) *"Hear O Israel the L-ord, is our G-d, the L-ord is One"* (Deut. 6:4)

You should study this chapter of Shema Yisrael until its close, and you will see how its words move from one matter to another, encompassing 10 matters, that number corresponding to the Ten Commandments. The explanation is as follows:

First there is the command to believe in the Creator, when it says *"Hear O Israel the L-ord"*. His intent was not for hearing of the ear, but rather for belief and acceptance of the heart, as the verse says *"we will do and we will hear" (Ex. 24:7)*, and *"Hear therefore, O Israel, and observe to do it" (Deut. 6:3)*, and similarly for all other verses which come in this way using a term denoting "hearing", the intent is only to bring to belief and acceptance.

After He placed us under obligation to believe in the reality of His existence (through rational investigation for those capable as in ch.3), we are then called upon to believe that He is our G-d, as indicated in the word "our G-d", and afterwards He commanded us to believe that He [alone] is truly one, in saying: "G-d is one" .

> (*Marpe Lenefesh*: "G-d is one" - that only G-d is truly one, but nothing else is truly one under any circumstances, and even if we say on something that it is "one", it is not really one, except in passing (relatively), rather it is more than one as will be explained.
>
> *Tov Halevanon*: If the intent in saying "one" was merely to exclude multiple gods, it should have said "H-shem yachid" (which, in hebrew, connotes specifically one and not many)...
> "our G-d" - He granted us existence and formed us, and took us to be His people.
>
> *Marpe Lenefesh*: "our G-d" - this eternal Being, who reigns supreme over all worlds, even so, He is specifically "our G-d", for He chose us among all nations during the giving of the Torah to be His treasured nation, and He drew us near to His service, and we undertook His sovereignty over us.
>
> *Translator*: "After He placed us under obligation to believe in (1) the reality of His existence, we are then (2) called upon to believe that He is our G-d" - The two blessings before reciting the Shema also correspond to these two aspects. The theme of the first blessing is knowing G-d through His creating this vast universe and the mystical worlds, etc. While the theme of the second blessing is that He is our G-d in having chosen us and

| giving us the Torah, etc.)

After He bid us to believe and accept these three principles we mentioned, He proceeded to what is incumbent on us to follow them with, namely, to love G-d wholeheartedly, in private and in public, with our life and with our might, as He said: *"And you shall love the L-ord your G-d with all your heart, and with all your soul, and with all your might" (Deut. 6:5).* I intend to clarify this matter in the Gate of Love of G-d (Gate #10), with the Almighty's help.

Afterwards, He moved on to exhort on the duties of the heart, in saying: *"And these words, which I command you this day, shall be on your heart",* which means to cleave them to your heart, and believe them in your inner being.

Afterwards, He proceeded to the commandments of the limbs which require both thought and action, as He said: "you shall teach them to your sons".

> (this refers to Torah study, which requires understanding of the heart (mind) and also physical acts, namely moving of the lips and pronunciation of the tongue - *PL*
> He started with the commandments of the limbs which are most important and most central, namely those which employ the mouth and tongue combined with the heart - to learn and teach Torah and to recite the Shema.)

And so that if you don't have a son, you will not mistakenly think that the (commandment of) verbally reading depends on having a son, He said: "You shall speak in them".

> (that on oneself is the primary obligation to study Torah - *TL*, another commentary: Do not think that since the main purpose is understanding of the heart, if so, the need for verbally speaking it with one's mouth is only for making them known to the sons, therefore he said that even by oneself one needs to verbally pronounce them with one's mouth and tongue - *PL*)

Afterwards, He continued: *"and you shall speak in them when you sit in your house, and when you walk by the way, and when you lie down, and when you rise up",* because the heart and tongue are never prevented from fulfilling the duties which apply to them, unlike the other limbs (which depend on various times and circumstances). In the introduction of this book, we have already pointed out that the duties of the heart are a constant duty.

And the purpose of all of this is to exhort on what He said previously: *"And these words, which I command you this day, shall be on your heart"*, which means that habitually having them on one's tongue always, brings to remembrance of the heart, and to never turn one's heart away from always remembering G-d, and this is similar to what King David, peace be unto him, said: *"I have set the L-ord always before me" (Tehilim 16:8).* And scripture says: *"But the word is very near unto you, in your mouth, and in your heart, that you may do it" (Deut. 30:14).*

> (*Marpe Lenefesh:* because this is the primary goal of all the levels of the Tzadikim (righteous) and the Chasidim (pious) - to not empty one's heart from remembering G-d always, as the Rama says in the first halacha in the Shulchan Aruch, which are the words of the Morey Nevuchim (Maimonides' Guide for the Perplexed) part 3 chapter 52, see there, and see also later on, and the Sefer Chasidim siman 35.
>
> *Tov Halevanon*: The reason the Torah exhorted on doing this always even though it is not an obligation to do this always, on this the author answered that the intent of the verse is on habituating the tongue on them always...)

Afterwards, He proceeded to the duties of the limbs which consist of action only, and gave three examples, as He said: *"And you shall bind them for a sign upon your hand; And they shall be as Totafot between your eyes; And you shall write them upon the doorposts of your house, and on your gates"*, which refers to the Tefilin of the hand and of the head, and the Mezuza, all of whom cause one to remember the Creator, and to wholeheartedly love Him, and yearn to Him, and as scripture says regarding how lovers keep their love in mind: *"Set me as a seal upon your heart, as a seal upon your arm"* (Songs 8:6), and *"Behold, I have engraved you upon the palms of my hands"* (Isaiah 49:16), and *"In that day, says the L-ord of hosts, will I take you, O Zerubavel, my servant, the son of Shealtiel, says the L-ord, and will make you as a signet ring: for I have chosen you"* (Chagai 2:23), and *"A bundle of myrrh is my beloved unto me; it (the myrrh) shall lie between my breasts"* (Songs 1:13). G-d ordained three signs in order that they be stronger and more enduring, as the wise man said: *"a threefold cord is not quickly broken"* (Eccles. 4:12).

> (*Manoach Halevavos:* "he (the myrrh) shall lie between my breasts" - this hints to the heart, which is between the breasts. The author renders the verse as referring to the practice of a man's beloved to give him a bundle of myrrh to hang around his neck, until it reaches between his breasts. Thus he

remembers his beloved always since the fragrance continuously rises to his nostrils from between his breasts, and he keeps the beloved in mind. The hint is to the precepts, which were given to us in order to remember G-d always, such as Tefilin, Tzitzit etc.)

Hence, this chapter contains ten matters, five of them concern the spiritual (mind/heart), and five of them the physical (the body).

The 5 spiritual: (1) That the Creator exists. (2) He is our G-d. (3) He is the true Unity. (4) That we love Him with all our heart. (5) That we serve Him wholeheartedly.

The 5 physical: (1) You shall teach them to your children. (2) You shall speak in them (3) You shall bind them as a sign on your hand (4) They shall be as Totafot between your eyes. (5) You shall write them upon the doorposts of your house and upon your gates.

And our Rabbis taught: "why does the reciting of the chapter 'Hear O Israel' precede the reciting of the chapter "And it shall be..."? (i.e.the second chapter. answer:) To teach that one must first acknowledge the sovereignty of G-d and afterwards assume the duty to fulfill His commandments" (Berachot 13a). Therefore, I deemed it proper to precede the Gate of Unity to the other gates of this book.

It will now be necessary for me to clarify on the subject of wholeheartedly acknowledging the unity (of G-d) ten matters:
1. What is the definition of the wholehearted acceptance of G-d's unity?
2. how many divisions does the subject of unity divide into?
3. whether or not it is our duty to intellectually investigate the matter.
4. what is the manner of investigating it and which introductions must we know before we investigate the unity?
5. To clarify the premises which demonstrate that the world has a Creator who created it from nothing.
6. how we apply them to establish the existence of the Creator.
7. to bring proofs that He is one.
8. to clarify the matter of a conventional (relative) unity versus a true unity.
9. demonstration that G-d alone is the true Unity and that there is no true Unity besides Him.
10. the Divine attributes, those deduced by reason and those written in scripture and the ways in which these should be ascribed to G-d or denied to Him.

*** CHAPTER 1 ***

The definition of the wholehearted acceptance of the unity of G-d is that the heart and the tongue are equal in acknowledging the unity of G-d, after understanding, in the way of logical proofs, the certainty of His existence and the truth of His unity. For acknowledgement of the unity of G-d among men differs according to their level of intelligence and understanding.

> (*Marpe Lenefesh*: the meaning of the word "definition" is: "a correct and complete teaching on the thing that one wishes to explain what it is". Therefore one must call it with a name which is specific to it, so that the reader does not err that one's intent was for something else... for example, if we define a human being as a "speaking being" - this is a comprehensive teaching without breaches, but if you define him as an "alive being" - this is not a complete definition, and there is a breach in your words since animals are also called "alive". So too for all things similar to this. Understand this. Now, likewise for the matter of the unity of the Creator, when the tongue and the heart are equal, and a person understands by the ways of logical proofs, that which a person says of the Creator that He is "One", how He is One, then the person's unifying (G-d) in his heart is a complete teaching on G-d, but if the person cannot bring logical proofs, and he says on G-d that He is "one", this is not a complete teaching on G-d, and there is a breach in his words, because there are many things in the world which are also called "one", even though they are not truly one, since really they are more than one, as will be explained. With this introduction you will understand this chapter and the next.)

Among them: One who declares the unity (of G-d) with only his tongue, namely, that he hears people say something and he is drawn after them without understanding the meaning of what he is saying.

Among them: One who declares the unity of G-d with his heart and tongue, who understands the matter of what he is saying through the Tradition that he received from his ancestors, but he does not understand the clarification of what he received of this matter, and the truth of what he believes in this matter.

Among them: One who declares His unity after understanding through logical proofs the truth of the matter, but he will conceive G-d's Unity like other unities to be found, and he will come to form a material conception of the Creator and represent Him with a form and likeness because he does not understand the true nature of His Unity and the matter of His existence.

Among them: One who declares G-d's unity with his heart and with his tongue after understanding the concept of true unity versus relative unity, and he can bring proofs to demonstrate G-d's existence and true Unity - this class of men is the complete (unblemished) group regarding the matter of unity of G-d.

Therefore, I defined the wholehearted acknowledgement of the unity (of G-d) - that it is the equalizing of the tongue and the heart (mind)) in the unity of the Creator, after one knows how to bring proofs on it and understands the ways of His true Unity through rational investigation.

*** CHAPTER 2 ***

(*Marpe Lenefesh*: Now he will explain from where came these different outlooks regarding the unity of G-d mentioned in chapter 1, he answers: since this word became common language and became used in their other affairs and needs.)

The author says: Regarding how many ways the unity of the Creator is conceived, I will answer as follows: Since the word "unity" spread among men of the unity (Jews), they became accustomed to using it frequently in their tongue and speech, until it became an expression of amazement whether for good or for bad.

(when some unusual amazing matter occurs to them whether good or bad, they will say it is a singular and unique matter, with no equal in the way of exaggeration and singling out - *TL*)

And they use it to express their dread of great calamity, and to exaggerate it and to express amazement on it, and they don't put to heart to understand the true matter of what passes through their tongue (when reciting the Shema), due to ignorance and laziness. And they consider the matter of Unity is done for them when they finish (reciting) its words, and they do not sense that their heart is devoid of His truth and that their mind is empty of its meaning because they declare His unity with their tongue and in words. They will conceive Him in their hearts to be more than One (i.e. with forms of "plurality" as will be explained) and represent Him in their minds with the likeness of other "unities" to be found, and they will speak of His attributes in a way that cannot belong to the true Unity (such as women and the masses who attribute to G-d love, hate, and anger as they imagine it in human beings - *PL*), because they don't understand the matter of true Unity versus temporary unity, except for a treasured few who plumbed the depths of wisdom and understood the matter of the Creator versus the created, and the characteristics of true Unity and what G-d is singular in.

The philosopher spoke truth when he said: "no one can serve the Cause of causes and Beginning of beginnings except the prophet of the generation with his senses or the primary (perfect - TL) philosopher with the wisdom he acquired, but others serve other than Him, since they cannot conceive what exists (without beginning - *TL*), but rather can only conceive that which is composite (i.e. created things - *TL*).

> *Marpe Lenefesh*: It is known that the prophets see, hear, and apprehend with their supernatural spiritual eyes as if they saw and heard them with their physical senses - awesome things which the philosophers and Sages would squander most of their lives to try to grasp correctly, and it is possible that they never manage to grasp them correctly, as the Kuzari book spoke on this.
>
> *Translator*: Many people mistakenly think the proofs of G-d have been refuted in our times. But these "refutations" are mistakenly based on treating the Eternal with the same logic as the non-eternal. It is not at all obvious what is implied by Eternal, as we will see.

Because of this the acceptance of the Unity falls into four divisions, corresponding to the different levels of recognition and understanding in men:

(1) Unity of G-d in the tongue only. This level is reached by the child and the simpleton who does not understand the matter of (true) religion, and in whose heart its truth is not fixed.

(2) Unity of G-d in the mind and in the tongue through Tradition, because he believes those who he received from, but he does not understand the truth of the matter through his own intellect and understanding. He is like the blind man who follows the seeing man, and it is possible that the one he follows received the Tradition from a receiver like himself, whereby it would be like a procession of blind men where each one places his hands on the shoulders of the fellow before him until at the head is a seeing man who guides them all. If the seeing man fails them or neglects them and is not careful to guard them, or if one of the blind men in the chain stumbles or some other trouble happens - all of them will share the same fate, and will stray from the path; and it is possible they will fall in a pit or ditch, or they will stumble in something which blocks their progress.

> (*Tov Halevanon commentary*: Certainly for a blind man who leans on a seeing man, it is impossible that he will align his walking very straight like the seeing man, without straying a bit in his steps. And even though this is not perceivable in the first blind man who is close to the seeing man, nevertheless, if there are many blind men who follow the seeing man, then, when each of them strays a bit, the combined straying will accumulate until it is possible that one of them will stumble. Furthermore, all of them will deviate from the straight path. The analogy is that one who does not know

the truth of faith through his own intellect but instead relies on tradition, one man from another, for many generations up until the one who properly understood from his intellect, behold, most of the time, it is possible that each one strayed a bit from the truth, until eventually, it became a big straying...)

Similarly for one who proclaims the unity out of tradition, one cannot be sure he will not come to association (which is the opposite of unity - *PL*), that if he hears the words of the Meshanim and their claims, It is possible that he will change his outlook, and will err without noticing. Because of this our Sages said: *"Be eager to study the Torah and know what to respond to an apikoros (heretic)"* (Pirkei Avos 2:14).

(*Tov Halevanon*: there was a man called Mani, yimach shemo, who would claim there are two gods, one who does good and one who does evil, and those who went after him are called after his name with the term: Minim. The word "apikoros" refers to the name of a man who was called "apikoros", yimach shemo, who would completely deny the existence of G-d, the Moray (Maimonides' guide for the perplexed) mentions him in the end of the first chapter, those drawn after his views are called "apikorsim", this term was also borrowed to refer to those who denigrate the Sages, and falsely give misinterpretations of the Torah, or the like, as brought in tractate Sanhedrin)

(3) The third group: Unity of G-d with the mind and the tongue after one can bring logical proofs demonstrating the truth of His existence, but without understanding the matter of true Unity versus temporary unity. This is like a seeing man who is travelling along the road, wishing to reach a faraway land. Even though he knows the general direction, but the road splits to many uncertain roads, and he does not recognize the correct road which leads to the city he wishes to reach.

(*Marpe Lenefesh*: he knows without doubt through logical proofs that there is a Being who created the world and that there is no other G-d, but he does not know the difference between the Creator and His creations.

Translator: his awe of the greatness of G-d will be weak, therefore his worship will be mostly by rote and without zeal. Hence, he will not get far.)

He will greatly tire himself and will fail to reach his destination, because he does not know the (correct) road, as the verse says: "the toil of the fool will tire him who knows not to reach a city" (Eccles. 10:15).

(*Tov Halevanon*: The term "fool" applies to a man who is able to understand with his faculties, however, he does not want to toil but instead seeks comfort, as in *"the fool does not desire understanding"* (Mishlei 18:2), this is what the verse says:

"the toil of the fool" - meaning the toil that the fool fears from and instead chooses comfort for himself.

"will tire him" - Just the opposite, it will tire him even more.

"who knows not to reach a city" - Just like he is lazy to study the roads properly, thinking he will manage without knowing it well, he will tire himself even more, because he will bring himself to err on the road and will not reach any city.

Pas Lechem: he is called a fool because he did not investigate and inquire which roads to take before setting on the journey. He is the opposite of the wise man, who looks into the future, whose eyes are on the head of every matter to contemplate beforehand every matter [and its consequences].)

(4) The fourth group: Acknowledgement of the Unity of G-d with the mind and the tongue after one knows how to bring proofs on it, and to comprehend the truth of His Unity through intellectual derivation and correct, sound reasoning - this is the complete and important group, and this is the level which the prophet exhorted us in saying: "Know therefore this day, and set it in your heart, that the L-ord He is G-d" (Deut. 4:39).

*** Chapter 3 ***

Regarding whether or not it is our duty to rationally investigate on the unity of G-d, I will say as follows: For anyone who is capable of investigating on this and other similar matters through rational inquiry - it is his duty to do so according to his intelligence and perception.

I have already written in the introduction to this book sufficient arguments which demonstrate the obligation of this matter. Anyone who neglects to investigate into it is blameworthy and is considered as belonging to the class of men who fall short in wisdom and conduct (because there are things which touch on practical matters as clarified in the introduction - PL). He is like a sick man (a doctor) who is an expert on the nature of his disease and the correct healing method, but instead relies on another doctor to heal him who applies various healing methods, while he is lazy to inquire using his own wisdom and reasoning into the methods employed by the doctor, to see whether or not the doctor is dealing with him correctly or not, when he was easily able to do this without anything preventing him. The Torah has already obligated us on this, as written: "know therefore today, and lay it to your heart[, that the L-ord is G-d in heaven above and on the earth beneath; there is no other]" (Deut. 4:39).

The proof that "lay it to your heart" refers to intellectual investigation, is from what the following verse says: "And none lays it to his heart, neither is there knowledge nor understanding" (Isaiah 44:19). So too David urged his son: "And you, Solomon my son, *know you* the G-d of your father, and serve him with a perfect heart and with a willing soul; for the L-ord searches all hearts" (Chronicles 28:9).

> (*Pas Lechem*: Through knowing G-d with your intellect, your heart will be perfect and your soul will be willing in His service. This is the meaning of "and serve him with a perfect heart and with a willing soul".

And David said: "*Know you* that the L-ord He is G-d" (Ps. 100:3).

> (*Pas Lechem*: *"the L-ord He is G-d"* - this is the primary matter of the Unity - to know that even though He exhibits different actions such as mercy and justice, nevertheless, in His essence, He has no plurality, rather the L-ord (His Name of mercy) is G-d (Elokim, His Name of justice)...

And "Because he has set his love upon Me, therefore will I deliver him: I will set him on high, because he has *known* My Name" (Ps. 91:14), and "But let him that glories glory in this, that he understands and *knows* Me" (Yirmiya 9:23), and our Sages said: "be diligent in the study of Torah and know what to answer a heretic" (Avos 2:14), and the Torah says: "Keep therefore and do them; for this is your wisdom and your understanding in the sight of the nations.." (Deut. 4:6).

And it is impossible for the nations to admit to our claims of superior wisdom and understanding unless there are proofs and evidences which can testify for us along with the testimony of the intellect on the truth of our Torah and our faith. And our Maker has already promised us that He will remove the veil of ignorance from their minds, and show His magnificent glory as a sign to us on the truth of our Torah when He said: "And the nations shall walk by your light" (Isaiah 60:3), and "And many peoples shall go and say, Come you, and let us go up to the mountain of the L-ord, to the house of the G-d of Jacob.." (Isaiah 2:3).

> (*Marpe Lenefesh*: He wrote this point so that you would not wonder, "behold, here are all the proofs and evidences, and the testimony of the intellect and the tradition are faithfully in our hands, which they are not capable of refuting, and they still do not retract from their error??".. For this he said that the "veil of ignorance", which refers to the overpowering of the lusts of this world (over their intellect)..as explained in the Gate of Abstinence... it is what separates between them and the truth, that they will not recognize it until G-d removes from them the veil of ignorance from the face of their intellect)

It is now clear from logic, scripture, and tradition that it is our duty to investigate into this of what we are capable of clearly grasping with our minds.

*** Chapter 4 ***

Regarding what is the way to investigate on the truth of the unity, and what introductions we need to know before we investigate on this unity, I will say as follows.

Any matter which one would like to understand when one is in doubt of its very existence, must first ask "does it exist or not?" After one has established its existence, one must then enquire as to what it is, how it is, and why it is. But regarding the Creator, a man may only ask whether He exists. And when His existence is demonstrated through rational investigation, we may further enquire whether He is one or more than one. And when it is clear that He is one, we may enquire on the matter of unity, and on how many ways this term is used, and in this way we will establish for ourselves the complete recognition of the unity of G-d, as the verse says: *"Hear O Israel, the L-ord is our G-d, the L-ord is One"* (Deut. 6:4).

Therefore, we must first enquire whether or not this world has a Creator. When it becomes clear that the world has a Creator who created it as something new, we can then further enquire whether He is one or more than one. Then, when it will be established that He is one, we can investigate into the matter of true (absolute) Unity and temporary (relative) unity, and then consider what we can say of the Creator regarding His true matter, and through this we will have completed the matter of acknowledgement of the unity of G-d in our hearts and minds, with G-d's help.

*** Chapter 5 ***

INTRODUCTION TO LOGICAL PROOFS (excerpt from Gate 5)
Tov Halevanon: It is known that through two ways a [logical] proof is established. One, through true premises. Two, through conclusions that necessarily follow. i.e. if there is a foundation of premises which are undoubtedly true, then when the premises are combined with each other, the conclusions that are drawn from them must undoubtedly follow... a spurious and faulty proof is due to either one of the premises is not true or that the conclusion does not follow these premises on proper consideration.

Pas Lechem: For example, if we start with the premise that Reuven is taller than Shimon and Shimon is taller than Levi. Then the conclusion that necessarily follows is that Reuven is taller than Levi. However, it is possible that the premises are not true, that Reuven is not taller than Shimon or that Shimon is not taller than Levi, and the conclusions are automatically null and void. The second example, if we establish that Reuven loves Shimon and Shimon loves Levi, and we want to draw the conclusion that Reuven loves Levi. Even though the premises are true, the conclusion does not necessarily follow.

There are three premises which lead to the inference that this world has a Creator who created it from nothing:
1) A thing cannot make itself.
2) Beginnings (causes) are limited in number; therefore, they must have a First Beginning (First cause) which had no beginning (cause) before it.
3) Anything composite must have been brought into existence (cannot be eternal, i.e. without beginning).

When these three premises are established, the inference will be, for one who understands how to apply them and combine them - that the world has a Creator who created it from nothing, as we will demonstrate with G-d's help.

(*Tov Halevanon commentary*: Understand, that to clarify the roots of religion, there are many different ways, but the central pillar which everything depends on is the logical demonstration of the "chidush haolam" (this world was brought into existence from nothing). When this has been clarified, then automatically, it will be demonstrated the existence of G-d who created it. Many of our Sages already endeavored in this route such as Rabeinu Saadia Gaon, and Rambam (Maimonides). Behold, Rambam in part 1 chapter 73 of the Moray Nevuchim started to show the logical demonstration of the existence of G-d and that He is the absolute Unity and not physical, but he brought the proofs from the words of the philosophers, and he spoke at length denigrating their views and all of their proofs. He then returned at the beginning of part 2, after mentioning the words of Aristotle who believed in the existence of G-d while also believing in the eternal existence of the world, and along the same line of reasoning which Aristotle brought for the existence of G-d and that He is one and not physical. The Rambam rose to argue with him and refute his proofs on the eternity of the world, and to demonstrate that Aristotle has no proof on this, until just the opposite - one can prove the creation. However, the author here, of blessed memory, sifted the truth from the words of the philosophers, and added strength and pure hands to revive the proofs for creation and to mend their breaches, and automatically the existence of G-d will be demonstrated.

Regarding the necessity of all three premises, since the main proof stands on the "chidush haolam" (that this world was brought into existence from nothing), and from there we begin to clarify the existence of G-d, namely, from the visible to the invisible, therefore it was necessary to bring these three premises, because from the first premise alone, the non-believer can claim: "whatever created this world was itself created from another cause, and that cause also has a cause, and so on endlessly". Therefore, he added the second premise. And lest the non-believer refute saying that this world is without beginning (eternal), he added the third premise.)

The proof of these three premises is as follows.

PROOF OF FIRST PREMISE

Anything that exists, after it had not existed, cannot escape one of two possibilities: Either it created itself or something else created it.

If it created itself, then, also it cannot escape one of two possibilities: Either it created itself before it existed or after it existed.

Both are impossible, because if we suppose that it created itself after it existed, then it did nothing, since it was not necessary to make itself because it already existed before doing anything, therefore, it did nothing.

If we suppose it made itself before it existed - at that time it was *"efes v'ofes"* (absolutely nothing - TL), and that which is efes (nothing) cannot perform any action nor preparation (potential) for action, because nothingness cannot do anything. Therefore, it is impossible for something to make itself in any way.

The first premise has been clarified.

> (*Tov Halevanon commentary* on *"efes v'ofes"*: this means that which is absolutely nothing, with no potential nor any way that would leave a possibility of existence in it. He doubled the term merely to emphasize the matter.

> *Translator*: Modern Physicists have discovered that **transient "virtual particles"** appear and disappear in vacuum space for extremely brief time intervals (quantum fluctuations). Some prominent atheists claim this is a refutation to the premise that a thing cannot create itself and propose that it is possible for the universe to simply appear out of nothing. In the USA, The Discovery channel's first episode of the first season of Curiosity (entitled "Did God Create the Universe?" by professor Stephen Hawking) said the following:

>> "...you enter a world where conjuring something out of nothing is possible (at least, for a short while). That's because at this scale particles, behave according to the laws of nature we call 'quantum mechanics', and they really can appear at random, stick around for a while, and then vanish again to reappear somewhere else."

> Another example: Professor Lawrence Krauss, a high profile American theoretical physicist and cosmologist with a long list of important positions and best selling books, claims in his best selling book *A Universe from Nothing*:

>> "Just the known laws of quantum mechanics and relativity can produce 400 billion galaxies each containing 100 billion stars and then beyond that it turns out when you apply quantum mechanics to gravity, space itself can arise from nothing, as can time. It seems impossible but it's completely possible..."

> Answer: First of all, quantum mechanics allows, and even requires temporary violations of conservation of energy. The virtual particles are a well established and well understood consequence of quantum mechanics - not something out of nothing. They are not uncaused events in the vacuum but rather *properties* of the spacetime vacuum. The virtual particles "borrow" for a very short amount of time the ground energy that is already available from time/energy uncertainty principles and converts that to virtual particles with $E=mc^2$. Neither does this actually violate the conservation laws because the kinetic energy plus mass of the initial decaying particle and the final decay products is equal. To make these 'virtual particles' in the vacuum real (longer lasting than time-uncertainty permits), you have to put in energy.

Furthermore, they don't magically disappear into nothing, but rather fluctuate in and out of observable existence due to quantum mechanical uncertainty laws (without the uncertainty principle, electrons would collapse into protons thus destroying the world). In quantum mechanics there is an extremely tiny grey area of observable uncertainty. They merely fluctuate in and out of this grey area - not that they disappear and reappear from nothing. (In truth, nothing has ever been found to be lost. Even for black holes. When light falls in, the Black Hole increases in mass. When it radiates out (Hawking radiation), it decreases in mass. Everything always balances out.) Hence, the above claims are wild and misleading extrapolations.

To summarize, a spacetime vacuum governed by quantum mechanics is still something. It is not nothing. It has a curvature which varies in proportion to whatever matter and radiation is present as has been posited by Einstein's general relativity theory and confirmed by experiments. Vacuum space even has a positive mass resulting from the cosmological constant and a positive expansion rate. There can be no property associated with "nothing" for that would be a contradiction. Likewise, only a thing can have states, and only a thing can be described in terms of physical law.

The author already guarded from these types of wild claims in saying "efes v'ofes", the double language to emphasize "absolutely nothing", as the Tov Halevanon commentary pointed out. Hence, there is no way *whatsoever* to describe quantum fluctuations or the like in non-existent space-time.

This fallacy is well explained by the American philosopher Edward Feser, here's an excerpt:

> "This is, of course, a summary of the argument of Krauss's book. And the problem with it, as everybody on the planet knows except for Krauss himself and the very hackiest of his fellow New Atheist hacks, is that empty space governed by quantum mechanics (or any other laws of physics, or even just the laws of physics by themselves) is not nothing, and not even an "example" of nothing (whatever an "example of nothing" means), but something. And it remains something rather than nothing even if it is a "good first approximation" to nothing (which is what Krauss presumably meant by "good first example"). When people ask how something could arise from nothing, they don't mean "How could something arise from almost nothing?" They mean "How could something arise from nothing?" That is to say, from the absence of anything whatsoever -- including the absence of space (empty or otherwise), laws of physics, or anything else. And Krauss has absolutely nothing to say about that, despite it's being, you know, the question he was asked, and the question he pretended to be

answering in his book."

The full version can be read online at http://edwardfeser.blogspot.com /2013/02/forgetting-nothing-learning-nothing.html.

This is sufficient grounds to dismiss the "proofs" of the atheist professors (actually they call themselves "anti-theists") and no further proof is necessary. Other physicists invoke the framework of string theory which states that there are multiple universes and that what we call matter and energy is a product of the collision of two or more of these universes. this leads to a new universe with its own laws of physics. This, they propose, because the physics of our universe break down at the time of the "Big Bang", but of course this assumes the "multiverse" already exists and only leads to more questions... This is similar to the eminent scientists who upon realizing the enormous complexity of even the simplest possible living organism come to the conclusion that it could not possibly have arisen randomly. So they propose that aliens may have planted life on earth. Of course this just raises the question of where did those aliens come from? (besides being more science fiction than science)

Among other misleading claims one may come across is something like: "we have observed matter and antimatter collide (ex. positive charge electron with negative charge electron), annihilating each other and disappearing into nothing. Therefore, the opposite could also happen - that matter and antimatter could simply pop out of nothing." The trick in this claim is that matter and antimatter do not magically disappear into nothing like some kind of rabbit trick. Rather they transform into energy radiation (photons).

The bottom line is that no matter what the method of creation of the universe, "Something" must have always existed in some fashion. This fundamental reality is "G-d" as we will see. The physicists deny there is a G-d, and yet they spend their whole lives futilely trying to quantify who and what G-d is, whether or not they realize it. No matter what space, energy, and mass relationships are, and regardless of whether those quantities are finite or infinite, it follows logically that "something" must be eternal and un-caused. Scientific inquiry can take you to the border, to the edge of the physical realm. At that border, it is apparent that something lies beyond.

As we will see, that which is eternal is of a completely different "type" of existence than anything we are familiar with. It's not like it can be held in the hand or looked at under a microscope. The Eternal exists above time, and that which is above time is also above space since the two are inextricably intertwined. If so, then it must also be unchangeable at least in the way we understand change. Since change as we know it happens in spacetime. Hence that which is eternal is inherently unknowable, unreachable and unscientific. We cannot perceive it or examine it in any way and can only deduce its existence through rational investigation and through the effects it manifests in our world. i.e. the existence of our non-eternal world. And when we examine the universe and especially life forms, we come to know that the Eternal has the characteristics of wisdom and also ability. If we reflect more, we may come to see G-d's manifestation as an over-all Intelligence, an ever-present, all pervading Spirit - which creates and sustains everything and gives life to everything.

Tov Halevanon commentary on *"efes v'ofes"*: (continuation.)
Some want to explain his intent in doubling the term to refer to two types of nonexistence:
(1) that which is nonexistent in actuality but has the potential for the thing, such as a seed from the fruit of a tree, which is nonexistent from being a tree but is not nonexistent in potential, since it has the potential when placed in the soil to produce a tree.
(2) that which is nonexistent in potential and in actuality, such as a rock, which will never produce a tree.
For this he added the word: "ofes", but if so, we need to complete the proof of the author, because that which he went on to say: "because nothingness cannot do anything", even though it clarifies that something which is completely nonexistent cannot do anything, but we still don't know that the "ofes", which is something which is non-existing in actual but exists in potential cannot do anything. To clarify this, we need to bring the eighteenth introduction from the beginning of part 2 of the Moray (Rambam's Guide for the Perplexed): "anything which comes out from potential to actual must necessarily have been taken out by something else which is external to it (i.e. you cannot have something existing eternally in potential and then suddenly - "Big Bang" all by itself. Rather, there must be something external to it which took it out to actual - translator). [Proof:] because either way,(1) if the thing which took it out from potential to actual was internal to it, and also that there is nothing [external] preventing it from coming out to actual - then it would never be in a state of potential.

(*Translator*: Later on he explains that it is impossible for such a potential to not come to actual if an eternity of time passed over it since nothing is holding it back from coming to actual. Therefore, since the past extends infinitely back, (whether in time or if time is a creation then an infinite timeless eternity extending forever back), if so there is no point in the past where we can find it existing in potential, since any point you pick will always have infinite time or infinite timeless eternity forever preceding it.)

Tov Halevanon: (2) Alternatively, if the thing which took it out from potential to actual was internal to it and there is also something [external] preventing it and holding it back [from coming out to potential], there is no doubt that this external thing which is holding it back is what will bring it from potential to actual. Understand this. We will explain further later on.

(*Translator*: To summarize: "efes" - nothing, i.e. something with no potential to become anything whatsoever, namely, that which is absolutely nothing, can certainly not produce anything, as earlier. "ofes" - Not only that which is absolutely nothing, but even something which existed eternally as a potential for something - that also cannot produce anything on its own, namely, it cannot come out from potential to actual on its own, without something which is external to it taking out of its potential to its actual.)

Tov Halevanon: Now the proof of the author is established, that something cannot make itself, and even something which exists in potential needs something else to bring it out [to actual]. End of Tov Halevanon commentary.

Manoach Halevavos: That which a thing cannot make itself applies only to something created but that which is Kadmon (eternal, without beginning) and infinite, behold, in truth, it did not make itself. This is the reason why the question of "how did G-d make Himself?" is not relevant. (Translator: Once we have established that there must be something Eternal, otherwise nothing would exist in the present, then you cannot ask "well, what created this Eternal thing?" or "who designed this Eternal thing?". Both questions are irrelevant since the Eternal by definition always existed.)

PROOF OF SECOND PREMISE - (Beginnings are limited in number)
The proof of the second premise is as follows: (commentaries to follow) Whatever has a limit/end (i.e. is finite) must have a beginning, because it is evident that something which has no beginning (i.e. existed eternally) has no limit/end (i.e. is finite), since it is impossible for man to fathom the limits of that which is without beginning.

Therefore, that which was found to have a limit/end, we know that it must have had a first beginning which had no beginning before it, and a starting with no starting before it. And when we consider the finite character of all the beginnings found in the world, we must conclude that they had a first Beginning with no beginning before it and a first starting with no start before it, since there cannot be an infinite chain of (non-eternal) beginnings.

SECOND PROOF THAT BEGINNINGS/CAUSES MUST BE FINITE IN
NUMBER

(commentaries to follow)

Furthermore, it is evident that anything which has parts must have a whole,
since a whole is merely the sum of its parts. It is not conceivable for
something infinite to be comprised of parts, because a part, by definition, is
an amount separated from another amount, and through the part the whole
is measured, as Euclides mentioned in the fifth treatise of his book of
measures.

> *Pas Lechem : "through the part the whole is measured"* - through the part,
> one can know the amount of the whole. For example, if we know that one
> third of an object's length is 4 cubits, from this we know that it's whole
> length is 12 cubits.

If we consider in our thoughts something which is infinite in actuality, and
we take a part from it, the remainder will undoubtedly be less than what it
was before. And if the remainder is also infinite, then one infinite will be
greater than another infinite, which is impossible.

Alternatively, if the remainder (of the whole) is now finite, and we put
back the part that we took away - then the whole will be finite, but it was
originally infinite, if so the same thing is finite and infinite which is a
contradiction and impossible. And therefore, it is impossible to take out a
part from something which is infinite, since whatever is comprised of parts
is undoubtedly finite.

Now of all things (individuals) that have ever existed in the world, if we
take out a part of this total number, such as all the individual things that
came into existence from the days of Noah to the days of Moses. The total
number of individual things of this part is finite, therefore the whole
together is also finite. And since the whole of this world is finite in the
number of its individual things, it must also be that the number of its
beginnings (causes) is also finite, and perforce this world has a first Cause
which had no previous cause, and it is necessary because of this, that the
beginnings reach an end.

> *(some commentaries on this second premise)*
>
> THE PROOF OF THE SECOND PREMISE IS AS FOLLOWS:
> WHATEVER HAS AN END MUST HAVE A BEGINNING, BECAUSE
> IT IS EVIDENT THAT SOMETHING WHICH HAS NO BEGINNING

(i.e. existed eternally) HAS NO LIMIT/END (i.e. is infinite), SINCE IT IS IMPOSSIBLE FOR MAN TO FATHOM THE LIMITS OF THAT WHICH IS WITHOUT BEGINNING.

Manoach Halevavos: *"whatever has an end must have a beginning"* - "end" refers to some finiteness/limit, whether those two endpoints (beginning/end) are in time or in causes (that it appears as the definite effect of a cause). Likewise any physical thing has limits in 3 dimensions, namely, its physical dimensions. If so, it is obvious that whatever has limits must have a beginning (is not eternally existing) (more on this in ch.7).

"something which has no beginning has no limit/end" - it it evident and also explained in books of wisdom that any power which is without beginning has no limit/end (i.e. is infinite). Just like it existed forever, infinitely, eternally back, so too it will continue infinitely, forever. This is a sound deduction which the intellect accepts. An intelligent person cannot claim that something without beginning is bound, and that he can fathom its limits. This is what he meant by "since it is impossible for man to fathom the limits of that which is without beginning", i.e. for man's intellect to fathom it... It must be indestructible since it has no cause and behold a thing cannot make itself. (i.e. if a thing cannot make itself, and it has no cause, then how can it possibly exist? Therefore, its essence must be beyond the limits of our finite human logic.)

Pas Lechem: Since the thing is eternal, without beginning, therefore, its power is infinite, since whatever is finite ceases when its finite power ceases. Therefore, it would have already ceased if it were finite (and would never have reached the present). Hence that which is without beginning cannot be finite, and since it is infinite, therefore it will never cease to exist forever, just like it did not cease eternally. And this is the meaning of "since it is impossible for man to grasp...", i.e. it is impossible for man's [finite] intellect and understanding to grasp the limit of its power and to investigate and consider how much longer it will continue to exist and when it will cease, according to the limit of its power - since it must be that its power is completely without limit.

Translator's note: If you ask: "it does not consume energy for something to exist. A rock can exist forever in the past and still not be infinite in power". Answer: A rock can theoretically exist forever as a rock but at some point it must have not existed as a rock since a rock cannot make itself, therefore something else caused its existence, such as energy, and that energy also cannot make itself and so forth until you reach a totally different "kind" of existence, of infinite power, and without beginning.

Furthermore, a rock cannot really exist forever on its own power but exists through the power of a higher Force as the Manoach Halevavos commentary points out: "some claim that even though the world is created, nevertheless, it is possible that it will exist forever, and will never cease. This is incorrect since that which the world would never cease to exist forever is not "in actual", but rather "in practice" (i.e. caused by something else), and that if the will of G-d is that it continues to exist, obviously it will continue just like He created it by His will, and if His will is not for this, it is impossible for it to continue to exist by itself. See the Moray Nevuchim part 2 introductions 1,2,3 with the commentary of Rav Shem Tov for a clearer explanation of this)

Similarly, regarding the "virtual particles" mentioned earlier, even if they did appear out of "nowhere" in space (which they don't), but even if they did, it would still not necessarily prove that they are uncaused events like some scientists claim. It just means we cannot see any cause. But the cause could well be there, we just don't see it. Indeed, all the strangeness and contradictions one encounters in quantum mechanics goes away once one realizes the physical does not have any independent existence - they is a higher Force pulling the strings and keeping track of everything. To quote Max Planck, one of the most important physicists of the twentieth century:

"As a man who has devoted his whole life to the most clear headed science, to the study of matter, I can tell you as a result of my research about atoms this much: There is no matter as such. All matter originates and exists only by virtue of a force which brings the particle of an atom to vibration and holds this most minute solar system of the atom together. We must assume behind this force the existence of a conscious and intelligent mind. This mind is the matrix of all matter".

THEREFORE, THAT WHICH WAS FOUND TO HAVE A LIMIT/END, WE KNOW THAT IT MUST HAVE HAD A FIRST BEGINNING WHICH HAD NO BEGINNING BEFORE IT, AND A STARTING WITH NO STARTING BEFORE IT. AND WHEN WE CONSIDER THE FINITE CHARACTER OF ALL THE BEGINNINGS FOUND IN THE WORLD, WE MUST CONCLUDE THAT THEY HAD A FIRST BEGINNING WITH NO BEGINNING BEFORE IT AND A FIRST STARTING WITH NO START BEFORE IT, SINCE THERE CANNOT BE AN INFINITE CHAIN OF BEGINNINGS.

Tov Halevanon commentary: This means to say that anything which has a limit/end (i.e. is finite), must also have a beginning, i.e. a start [of its existence], because something which has no end [to its existence] is only that which is infinite from all perspectives (i.e. no finiteness whatsoever). This matter also applies to [finite] things which do not actually exist together simultaneously, but rather follow each other, when this one comes [to exist], the other ceases [to exist] (such as living things where offsprings outlive parents) - that it is impossible for this to go on countlessly in endless stages until one can say that they have no first beginning, because then even the thing that is here in the present would not exist, similar to the familiar saying among the philosophers: "if the first did not exist, the last (present) would not exist", which means to say, if there was not a first beginning to the thing, then it would be impossible for the thing to exist in the present also.

(Translator: This means if you have something non-eternal in the present, you cannot explain its existence by saying that it was the effect of something else non-eternal (its "cause"), and that also was the effect of something else-non eternal (its "cause"), etc. endlessly, in an infinite regress, because this is an attempt to get something from nothing.

Fallacy of Infinite Regress of Causes
Infinite regress of causes is sometimes invoked to negate the need for a first eternal cause.

So instead of saying the universe is eternal or that it was created by something eternal, we can simply say that the universe existed and evolved from one form to another, in an infinite chain of non-eternal forms. An analogy for this: if we want to explain the existence of a chicken in the present, then instead of saying the chicken lineage had a first beginning, we can simply say that there was infinite regress of chicken/egg/chicken/egg etc. infinitely back, without beginning, where the chicken/egg/etc. regress is an analogy for the various forms of the universe.

Hence there is no need for anything eternal and the universe simply existed and evolved from one form to another, in an infinite chain of non-eternal forms. This is known as infinite regress of [non-eternal] causes.

However this is logically incoherent.
If we think of causes and effects as links in a chain, then consider that every link in the chain depends on the previous link. hence, the chain as a whole depends on something which does not even exist.

As an illustration, consider a chain hanging down from above almost touching the floor.
One asks, what is the chain fastened to?
Answer: The next link.
And what is that fastened to?
Answer: The one before that.
And that one?
Answer: The next one before, and so on...

I think it can be seen evidently that it doesn't matter whether there are a million or infinite links - there is nothing to hold up the chain. Without some tangible, real support the chain cannot hold *even if it is infinitely long.*

So too here, if you don't have something eternal, then a chain of non-eternal links will not help to explain the existence of something in the present, even if it is infinitely long.

Furthermore, the result of an infinite regress is indeterminable unless there is some eternal source.
As an illustration consider a square room with mirrored walls reflecting an image of a human being in an infinite regress simulation.
If there is no source, i.e. a real human being then the picture being reflected infinitely is indeterminable. Why should it be a human face, or a chicken, or whatever?

The only possible solution would be if there is no picture in the mirrors.

So too here, unless there is "something" eternal, nothing would exist in the present. **The infinite regress is just an attempt to push off the same problem indefinitely, never solving it.**

Some want to answer this problem by saying: If history goes back ad infinitum, then there are certain causal chains involving objects of a certain kind that go back ad infinitum also. Hence, we might say that the fact that the objects in this causal chain are chickens, as opposed to fish or frogs, is just the way things happen to be. Indeed, something just happening to be the case is roughly what we take to be the condition sufficient for a state of affairs to be contingent as opposed to necessary, and the fact that there are chickens is taken to be a contingent fact.

To this we reply, that it is possible to imagine in one's mind infinite reflections of chickens in the mirrors without the existence of a source, i.e. a real chicken but the power of imagination deceives. The mind can also imagine and suppose things which are impossible in actuality. In practice, you must have something real otherwise nothing will show up in the mirrors. Trying to make the problem disappear into infinity is an illusion of the imagination.

(In the above mirror analogy, we simulated the two types of "things" in existence. One, a thing which is possessed of its own intrinsic cause (not caused by something else). Two, a thing which is dependent for its existence upon extrinsic causes (other things). There is no intermediate alternative between the two types of things. In the mirror system, the reflections appearing in the mirrors are all of the second type since their existence depends on either a previous reflection or on the human being in the room. The human being in the room is the intrinsic primary cause, since his appearance does not depend on the reflections in the mirrors. From this analogy it should be evident that a system cannot be comprised of only the second type of causes, since it as a whole would be dependent on something indeterminate (and which does not even exist!). Rather, there must be some kind of source (i.e. an intrinsic cause, something real) for the reflections otherwise nothing would exist.

To Summarize: The infinite regress is fallacious reasoning. Essentially, it attempts to account for a phenomenon in terms of the very phenomenon that it is supposed to explain. This creates an endless repetitive argument that actually explains nothing. *Manoach Halevavos:* (later) Anything that we see that must be the effect of a cause and that its existence is impossible without a cause (i.e. that it is not eternal) it must be that either (1) its cause is eternal or (2) that its cause is the effect of another cause, and that one to another, and so forth until you reach a first cause which is eternal. Because if this were not so, then the whole thing would collapse. Because since we see the effect [in the present] cannot exist without a cause, how can its cause in turn possibly exist without some firm origin which everything depends on. This is just like one who ties one rope to another and another to another in order to hang a weight on its end. It cannot work unless the other end is firmly attached to a ceiling. This is self-evident.)

SECOND PROOF THAT BEGINNINGS/CAUSES ARE FINITE IN NUMBER

(*Manoach Halevavos*: This is a second proof. The first proof relied on "self-evident" truths, namely, that it is evident that there is a limit to the number of beginnings... Now he will bring a second way in the form of a logical proof which demonstrates that the universe has a finite number of beginnings.

FURTHERMORE, IT IS EVIDENT THAT ANYTHING WHICH HAS PARTS MUST HAVE A WHOLE, SINCE A WHOLE IS MERELY THE SUM OF ITS PARTS. THEREFORE, IT IS NOT POSSIBLE FOR SOMETHING INFINITE TO BE COMPRISED OF PARTS, BECAUSE A PART, BY DEFINITION, IS AN AMOUNT SEPARATED FROM ANOTHER AMOUNT (where a small part is separated from the whole - *ML*), AND THROUGH THE PART THE WHOLE IS MEASURED, AS EUCLIDES MENTIONED IN THE FIFTH TREATISE OF HIS BOOK OF MEASURES.

(*Tov Halevanon commentary*: If we have before us many things together, then the nature which each part has on its own, will also be contained in the combined whole since the whole is the sum of its parts, and through the part we measure the whole, namely how many parts are in the whole, and since each part is finite then it must be that the combined whole is also finite. This is a clear proof that it is impossible for many combined [finite] measures together to be infinite.) (Translator: i.e. you cannot have something of infinite character from infinite finites of non-infinite character (except in the imaginary world of mathematics), since infinity is not a sum of parts but rather a special "unbounded" character. this will be explained.)

IF WE CONSIDER IN OUR THOUGHTS SOMETHING WHICH IS INFINITE IN ACTUALITY, AND WE TAKE A PART FROM IT, THE REMAINDER WILL UNDOUBTEDLY BE LESS THAN WHAT IT WAS BEFORE. AND IF THE REMAINDER IS ALSO INFINITE, THEN ONE INFINITE WILL BE GREATER THAN ANOTHER INFINITE, WHICH IS IMPOSSIBLE.

(Translator: In mathematics it is possible for an infinity to be comprised of a set of units such as the infinite set of all positive integers $S=\{1,2,3,...\}$ You can take out/exclude a finite subset so that $S'= S - \{4,5,6\}$ and S' remains an infinite set. The two infinities can even be substracted to result in a finite set, so that $S - S' = \{4,5,6\}$ with cardinality of 3. Likewise one infinity can be bigger than another infinity, for example the infinite set of all rational numbers is one infinite power bigger than the infinite set of all integers since between any two integers there are infinite rational numbers.

Hence the author's statement "one infinite will be greater than another infinite, which is impossible" is incorrect. Some scientists such as Stephen Hawking have claimed to refute this statement with such mathematical proofs.

However, on closer look, the author guarded from this in saying "something which is infinite in *actuality*", which the Marpe Lenefesh commentary explains:

"This means that the thing to consider is infinite in *actuality*, but for something which is not actually infinite but just theoretically infinite, that the mind imagines something infinite - from this one cannot bring a refutation, because the power of imagination deceives, and one can picture and think in his imagination also on impossible things. The Kuzari says in treatise 5 section 18: "it is within the power of the mind to consider thousands, and thousands of thousands multiplied over endlessly, this is in potential, but for this to come to the realm of actuality - no", see there."
(End of Marpe Lenefesh commentary)

Hence some things are possible in the realm of mathematics, but are nevertheless impossible in reality. This is because mathematics is pure [human] logic and logic is not truth. Logic is merely a tool which we use to investigate topics, but anything it has to say on the subject is from premises which we supply. So what is logically possible depends on the premises we adopt. If, for example, we start with the premise that we have an infinite set of numbers, then mathematics can take this and work with it logically, despite that the premise may be impossible in actuality.

In reality, you cannot have an infinite quantity because *infinity is not a number*. It's not like it is somewhere on the number line. When you start walking now, you will walk 1 mile, 2 miles, 3 miles, and so on further, *but you'll never reach the point that you've actually walked infinity miles*. You cannot think of infinity as the amount of a set of items. You cannot have infinity apples - in reality, that is. Therefore, you cannot think of decreasing and increasing that "amount".

Hence, **infinity is a description not a number**. Infinity describes a thing as having no end, no limit, no boundary or edge, it literally goes on forever, ad infinitum. Because infinity is not a number, large numbers are no 'nearer' to infinity than small numbers. Number 1 trillion for example is no nearer to infinity than number 1, because the two, numbers and infinity, are in no way related. *It is then impossible to approach infinity, a thing is either infinite and immeasurable, or finite and measurable, it cannot be part way towards infinity.*

Hence, if you try to treat an infinity as a set of finites and try to manipulate it like removing or adding a part from it, you will be trapped with contradictions.

Even in the world of mathematics, you can sometimes run into trouble if you treat infinity as a number.
For example consider the infinite sum: $S = 1 + 2 + 4 + 8 + 16...$
Now multiply both sides by 2 so that $2S = 2 + 4 + 8 + 16... = S-1$ (since it is equivalent to S without the 1)
Subtract both sides by S, and $S = -1$ which is an absurd conclusion indeed.

Another simpler example: infinity + 1 is still infinity since you can't make it any larger.
Therefore infinity + 1 = infinity
and we subtract infinity from both sides proving 1 = 0

Another example, consider if space were infinite. If we draw a number line and label it 0,1,2...Infinity
Drawing a line from 1 to the end = Infinity

Drawing a line from 2 to the end = Infinity
Substracting both lengths, you get 1=0, since the first line is 1 greater than the second.

Another example, consider an infinite amount of apples. Removing an apple should not decrease the amount, since infinity cannot be decreased. If so, I can remove many apples and create a new infinity from the first. Then, do the same with the second infinity and create a third infinity, and so forth infinitely, which seems absurd.

Nevertheless even though infinity is not considered a "real" number, it is a useful concept to help conceptualize certain otherwise impossible mathematical operations. For example, 1 divided by 0 is technically undefined because you can't divide something into no segments. However, this case comes up frequently when dealing with many math forms, so the concept of infinity is useful. As you divide 1 by smaller and smaller numbers, the result is a larger and larger number. Dividing 1 into any real number of segments will yield some real amount in each segment. But you can get zero in each segment if you have an unreal infinity of segments. So, technically you would say that 1/0 is undefined, but it "approaches" infinity. Returning to the above example of apples, mathematically, you can make many infinities out of a single infinity. Mathematically, 2 times infinity is just infinity. All the contradictions go away once you realize infinity is not a real number.

Hence, it is not possible to have an infinity of anything finite in the real world. And even if we were to suppose for argument's sake that there are in fact infinity apples in the universe, this is not a property of the apples rather it is a property of the single entity called "the universe" which itself is inherently infinite; i.e. it's not that you have infinity apples but rather you have a higher entity called the universe which may or may not have apples. The description "infinity" applies to the universe not to the apples. The apples' infinity is not their own. It is granted to them by the higher non-finite entity which has them, namely the single infinite universe which may or may not have apples.

It comes out of this that the only place we can find an actual infinity is in the framework of existence which you exist inside of (in our case - space). If one tries to apply infinity to anything else, he will be trapped with contradictions. I think this is the author's intent in saying: "since it is impossible for man to fathom the limits of that which is without beginning". i.e. That which is without beginning (eternal) is the ultimate framework of existence - the root framework, the Framework of all frameworks. This "Framework" is also fundamentally different than other frameworks since the existence and the framework are one and the same, unlike us for example, where the existence (body) is separate from the "framework" (space) it exists inside of. Hence, the Eternal cannot be grasped in any way. It is a completely different "type" of existence than anything we are familiar with. There is an interesting analogy brought by Rabbi Nechemia Coopersmith in an article which illustrates this distinction. Here is an excerpt:

There is a scene in Kurt Vonnegut's novel, "Breakfast of Champions", The main character, Kilgore Trout, is having a drink in a bar, minding his own business. Suddenly he senses an awesome presence about to enter the bar. He breaks out into a cold sweat. Who walks in?

Kurt Vonnegut. When the author of the book steps into the novel to visit his character, Kilgore's perception of his world turns upside down. He realizes that he does not exist independently. Rather, every moment of his life requires a new stroke of the author's pen. Without the author, he ceases to exist.

He also realizes that his universe exists only in the mind of the author, and that beyond his ephemeral world there is a higher dimension -- the realm of Kurt Vonnegut - that is more real than his own. (End quote)

With this introduction we will hopefully understand the commentaries better:

Author's words: *"If we consider in our thoughts something which is infinite in actuality, and we take a part from it, the remainder will undoubtedly be less than what it was before. And if the remainder is also infinite, then one infinite will be greater than another infinite, which is impossible"*

Marpe Lenefesh commentary: "If we were able to take out a finite part from something infinite then perforce it must be composed of two opposite characters - finite and infinite, and this is an impossibility..."

Tov Halevanon: i.e. before we took a part from it undoubtedly it was greater than it is now. And since it is now also infinite therefore it must be equal to what it was before we took out the part since anything infinite cannot be made less (i.e. $X - 1 = X$ which is impossible for any number.)

and earlier:
Tov Halevanon: If we have before us many things together, then the nature which each part has on its own, will also be contained in the combined whole since the whole is the sum of its parts, and through the part we measure the whole, namely how many parts are in the whole, and since each part is finite then it must be that the combined whole is also finite. This is a clear proof that it is impossible for many combined [finite]

measures together to be infinite. (i.e. something of infinite character cannot be comprised of infinite finites of non-infinite character, rather only something intrinsically infinite can have infinite character.)

Along the same lines, you cannot have an infinite number of finite causes. Since each causation unit is finite, namely, that it is non-eternal, therefore, it must be the effect of another causation unit. And since the second causation unit is also finite since it too is non-eternal, therefore it too must be the effect of another causation unit. For finite causation units this cannot go on and on endlessly of the same repetitive argument - because it is viewed from a primate concept of "infinity" as a sum of "infinite" "finites". Rather, there must be an eternal Entity which is *intrinsically* infinite. The Infinity of the Creator BB"H is not at all of the same "type" of the poor and primitive "infinity" of the above far-fetched causation-argument. His Infinite-true-Infinity so to speak is different in essence of all "types" of humanly-thought-of "infinites". He is The First Cause which is inherently infinite, i.e. eternal and without beginning, H-shem, blessed be He.)

ALTERNATIVELY, IF THE REMAINDER (OF THE WHOLE) IS NOW FINITE, AND WE PUT BACK THE PART THAT WE TOOK AWAY - THEN THE WHOLE WILL BE FINITE (since both are finite - *ML*), BUT IT WAS ORIGINALLY INFINITE, IF SO THE SAME THING IS FINITE AND INFINITE WHICH IS A CONTRADICTION AND IMPOSSIBLE. AND THEREFORE, IT IS IMPOSSIBLE TO TAKE OUT A PART FROM SOMETHING WHICH IS INFINITE, SINCE WHATEVER IS COMPRISED OF PARTS IS UNDOUBTEDLY FINITE.

NOW OF ALL THINGS THAT HAVE EVER EXISTED IN THE WORLD, IF WE TAKE OUT A PART OF THIS TOTAL NUMBER, SUCH AS ALL THE INDIVIDUAL THINGS THAT CAME INTO EXISTENCE (since both are finite - *ML*) FROM THE DAYS OF NOAH TO THE DAYS OF MOSHE. THE TOTAL NUMBER OF INDIVIDUAL THINGS OF THIS PART IS FINITE, THEREFORE THE WHOLE TOGETHER IS ALSO FINITE. AND SINCE THE WHOLE OF THIS WORLD IS FINITE IN THE NUMBER OF ITS INDIVIDUAL THINGS, IT MUST ALSO BE THAT THE NUMBER OF ITS BEGINNINGS (CAUSES) IS ALSO FINITE, AND PERFORCE THIS WORLD HAS A FIRST CAUSE WHICH HAD NO PREVIOUS CAUSE, AND IT IS NECESSARY BECAUSE OF THIS, THAT THE BEGINNINGS REACH AN END (to the Source of their beginning, namely, the Creator, as he will explain next chapter - *ML*).

(Translator: The Manoach Halevavos commentary writes that this last analogy is not correct for this proof. See there. He concludes that really this whole lengthy proof is not necessary, since if a thing cannot make itself, then it is obvious that there must be an Eternal Creator which created the world from nothing [since as we will see, an eternal universe is not possible]. On the other hand, the Pas Lechem commentary learns that this last analogy is going on "time". That time itself can be divided and quantified hence it cannot be infinite and eternal.

Translator: Perhaps the author's intent is to refute the views of some religions, especially eastern ones, which are of the view that the way things are is the way they've always been. What comes around goes around. Nothing ever changes - just like there are human beings now, so too there always were. Hence, by demonstrating that infinity cannot be comprised of a sum of finites, then this view is incorrect.)

some interesting points:
Manoach Halevavos commentary: One cannot refute from the years of G-d, namely that He and His years are infinite (i.e. we see that an actual infinity can be quantified and comprised of a set of units, since G-d's existence can go back infinitely in time yet every year is finite. ANSWER: no), because there (in the realm of G-d), there is no separation or division - everything is one "entity", and it is incorrect to call some of His years a "part", because they cannot be divided in actuality but rather only in thought...furthermore time does not relate to Him, and He is not subject to it, and time does not even apply to Him because time is a creation. This is well-explained in the Moray part 2 intro 15,26.

(Translator: If you ask, we see in mathematics an infinite number of points between 1 and 2 therefore it is possible for something infinite to have parts. Answer: each point is not a part since it is defined as infinitely small. So really this is circular logic. A point is just a convenient hypothetical mathematical abstraction, and since it is defined as zero width you cannot look at it as a "part".

If one also tries to refute from "space" saying: "perhaps space can stretch infinitely yet I occupy a finite space, therefore something infinite can indeed have a part". One could answer this by saying: 'I occupy a finite space' is from the human perspective - a decidely finite perspective, not from the 'infinite perspective'. Your perception of something called 'finite space' is simply because you are finite and have no other way of experiencing Space. But that has no bearing on the true nature of space.

Alternatively, space is not really infinite but is some kind of finite sphere to contain space/time, as we see from Einstein's general relativity theory that space/time can "curve". Or from black holes, that intense gravity can cause the "fabric" of space/time to go haywire. Therefore space/time is some kind of finite character "fabric" which only appears infinite because we are inside it.

If one tries to refute saying, if G-d is infinite and the universe and its parts occupies His "space", then the universe is a part of G-d, so to speak. Therefore, something infinite can have a part. Answer: As an analogy, picture in your mind an orange fruit of shiny blue color. This orange has an existence at some level in your mind through you as long as you continue picturing it in your mind. Hence, you are the source of the orange and the orange in no way takes up any of the space in your plane of existence. So too, G-d who is the Creator of all and everything exists because of Him. His "thoughts" are continuously giving existence to the universe (as brought down in the book Tanya Shaar Yichud v'Emuna ch. 7: "G-d's Thought and Knowledge of all created beings encompasses each and every creature, for this is its very life-force and that which grants it existence from absolute nothingness."). The universe can even be infinitely big and this still in no way take up any "space" in G-d's realm since His infinity is on a higher degree plane of existence.

According to this, it is theoretically possible to have more than one thing which is infinite as long as they are on different "levels" of existence. That way a lower existence infinity does not limit a higher existence infinity in any way. Hence, G-d is the highest existence since everything depends on His existence but not vice versa, therefore His infinity is an absolute infinity while any other infinity is a "relative" infinity since its existence depends on His higher existence, of this kind of absolute infinity - there can only be One.

I asked a great Torah scholar and gifted kabalist in Jerusalem about the infinities mentioned in this chapter and he wrote me back that: this does not refer to what you think or interpret infinity. It refers to that which is really truly absolutely and ultimately infinite. In mathematics there are different levels of mathematical infinity such as countable infinity vs. uncountable infinity or density of the natural rational numbers to the irrational numbers, or rational vs. transcendental numbers. Infinites are distinguished between themselves (in true manner/level/standards) only if the power of one is infinitely stronger than the other one. For example, the infinite set of all irrational numbers is one level infinitely bigger than the set of all rational numbers (since there are infinite irrational numbers between any two rational numbers), and two levels bigger than the set of all integers (since there are an infinite number of rational numbers between any two integers). Here too there are quite a few principal and intrinsic levels of "infinity", similar to what and how it is described in Chassidut, such as infinite-light, infinite (luminary), infinite all-able. These are intrinsic levels of infinity and some are infinitely bigger (or smaller) from each (and from this it is also in math and HKB"H is infinite infinities "greater" than any type or

level or class or magnitude of "infinity" - so to speak). These are part of the
intrinsic meditations of the Shema and Barush-shem verses (something
which is impossible to do here and now [i.e. it must be learned in person]) -
sensing the infinitely bigger/smaller levels of infinity - how they are in
comparison one to another - this is the practical exercise of yichuda-ila'ah
and yichuda-tata'ah and their mutual simultaneous existence - this IS the
ONLY meaning of KNOWING H-shem.

Not so clear exactly what he meant. We see from his words though that
there can be more than one thing which is truly infinite. The explanation
must be as above, that it refers to different levels of existence which G-d
created in the chain of worlds until our finite character world. Afterwards, I
asked him whether space is finite or infinite and he said: "space is not and
cannot be infinite." I asked for an explanation and he said: "If (physical)
space would be "infinite" it will "compete" so to speak with the Infinite
BB"H...The only levels which are truly infinite are the realms of HBB"H
(G-d) Himself so to speak - so called "olamot-ha'ein-sof" - all the levels of
Elokut (G-dliness) which are truly Infinite in some aspect - as "light" or
(going higher) as "luminary" or as "ability"/"yecholet" etc. - many different
levels and sublevels of distinction in G-dliness - all truly Infinite only on
different levels of Infinity as we already communicated about. Of course
HBB"H can do "whatever" He wishes - but here - He determined the
borders of expressions of what Infinity is and what are the true Infinites
that are "His" levels so to speak and what are the limited realms, realities,
and worlds." (End quote)

Another time, I asked him to explain the practical exercise of yichuda-ila'ah
and yichuda-tata'ah. Here is an excerpt of his reply:

(1) in Kriat-Shma shacharit and arvit at the end of the shma verse think for
some time (still with eyes closed and hand over eyes) the thought: how the
entire Creation (creations worlds etc.) - all are total nothingness zero and
annihilated dust in comparison to His Infinity (yichuda-ila'ah). Make this as
REAL as you can while thinking very quietly and "softly" about it.

(2) Then say the verse of "baruch-shem"... - at its end - think for some time
more (all still in the same position) how the entire Infinity of HBB"H - the
ONE you just thought of at the end of the shma - "that-one" - is now as if
being entirely "squeezed" into each and every infinitely small element of
Creation (yichuda-tata'ah). (This is the opposite of the first yichud - infinity
of HBB"H is also [simultaneously] in each and every zero size element of
Creation - even if "zero" in "size" - the biggest "topological" paradox -
intrinsic part of His true infinity.)

(Translator: I asked him, "how can His entire Infinity be squeezed into each

and every element simultaneously? Isn't that a case of 1+1=1?" He
answered me that you cannot say "part" of G-d is in this element and
another "part" is in another element ch'v, since G-d is not comprised of
parts (as before, since an actual infinity is a special "infinite character", not
a sum of finite character parts). Rather all of His infinity is simultaneously
in each and every element no matter how small, and it's not a contradiction
since infinity plus infinity equals infinity.

The main point to get out if this, I think is not that G-d is "inside" this or
inside that the way we commonly understand "inside", since G-d is beyond
all and transcends all (i.e. G-d is the "place" of the universe and not the
opposite). He exists in a different way than we do. Rather, the main
awareness to build in this meditation is that G-d is fully "with" you and has
His full attention on you, despite that you and everyone else in the universe,
and even the universe itself is totally insignificant relative to His infinite
existence and despite that He also has His full attention on everyone else
and everything else simultaneously.

(3) Then - during Tefilah (Amidah) - think the same thought in the
following manner - EVERY time there is Shem-Havayah in the brachot of
the Amidah except in the last signing verse of "baruch-atah"... - except in
the "ending" verses - every time you run into Shem-Havayah - stop for 10
seconds and think again about the yichuda-ila'ah as at the end of the shema-
verse - and every time you say the word (the one after "baruch") "atah" in
the last lines/signatures/endings of the brachot of the Amidah - stop also for
10 seconds - and think the same thought of yichuda-tata'ah as at the end of
the "baruch-shem" verse above... End Quote. He told me that this exercise
is merely a tiny drop in the ocean and even less - since it is only a basic
"first" idea. Note that the book "Tanya" seems to exhort on doing these
types of meditations. See there Shaar Yichud v'Emuna chapter 7. Also
worth seeing is the book Jewish Meditation by Rabbi Aryeh Kaplan page
113 for some powerful meditations in the Amida. Keep in mind that these
practices are NOT generally endorsed by most Rabbis and can make a
person "strange" if he does them too much. I included it mainly due to its
relevance to this gate.

Here's an interesting excerpt from Shaarei Kedusha by Rabbi Chaim Vital
Part 4 which seems similar to the above:
"(R.Chaim will now quote a book:) In the book Meiras Einayim
(enlightening of the eyes), parshat Ekev, on the verse 'and to cling to Him':
"I, Yitzchak the small one, son of Shmuel from Ako says, that whether for
special individuals (yechidim) or for the general public, that whoever wants
to know the secret of the connecting of his soul on high, and the clinging of
his thought to G-d on high, in order that he acquires with that constant and
uninterrupted thought, the Olam Haba (World to Come), and that G-d will
be with him in this world and in Olam Haba, he should picture in front of
his eyes the letters of G-d's primary Name (Yud-Heh-Vav-Heh), blessed be

He, as if they are written in front of him on a book in ashuris script (sefer Torah hebrew), and every letter should be large in his eyes without limit. This means that when you put the letters of the primary Name in front of your eyes, the eyes of your imagination should be on them (i.e. picture them), and the thought of your mind and your heart on the "Ein Sof" (infinite), everything simultaneously, the seeing and the thought - both of them together. And this is the secret meaning of the true clinging mentioned in the Torah "and to cling to Him" (Deut. 30:4), or "And in Him you shall cling (Deut. 10:20), or "And you who cling to G-d" (Deut. 4:4).) End Quote. Translator: Perhaps this exercise is comparable to the above, if instead of thinking of the two simultaneously, one switches back and forth between the two - not as a real meditation, but as a "light" thought whenever one's mind is free. Warning: Frequently practicing these exercises without being sufficiently spiritually ready may damage a person or make him "strange". See the book "Path of the Just" by Rabbi Luzzato for the correct order of ascent up the rungs of the spiritual ladder.

PROOF OF THIRD PREMISE

The demonstration of the third premise: Anything composite is evidently composed of more than one thing, and these things which it is composed of must precede it by nature. Likewise, whatever assembled the compound must also precede it by nature and by time.

(*Tov Halevanon*: The composite thing occurs in one of two ways, (1) either its parts precede it also in time, such as water and flour, whereby the water precedes the dough in time, and they also precede it by nature, namely that the water and the flour can exist independently without the existence of the dough, while the existence of the dough cannot exist without the existence of the water and the flour. (2) Or, the parts do not precede the composite [in time], such as the composite of a living man, for example, [1] the physical body and [2] the "life spirit" in a man, even though both were created simultaneously, nevertheless they precede the formation of man by nature, since the formation of these parts does not need the existence of man but the existence of man needs them. Therefore the author only wrote that the parts precede the composite by nature, while the composer precedes the composite by time and by nature)

Translator: If you ask, are elementary subatomic particles composite? Answer: They can be converted to radiation whose energy can be combined and divided, hence it is in a sense plural and composite. (Also, in kabala anything physical is viewed as a composite of physical and spiritual forces).

In later chapters the author will demonstrate that ultimately, everything is inherently composite in some sense. The only exception is that which is

Infinite in all respects.

The *kadmon* (that which always existed), is that which has no cause, and that which has no cause has no beginning, and that which has no beginning has no limit/end (as before). Consequently, that which has a beginning is not *kadmon*, and anything which is not *kadmon* is *mechudash* (created, brought into existence from nothing), since there is no third term that can be between eternal and created which is neither eternal nor created. If so, anything which is composite is not eternal, and therefore must have been created. Since the third premise has been demonstrated, all three premises have been established.

Summary of the Three Premises:

First Premise - a thing cannot make itself. If there is no framework for existence, i.e. no spacetime, no laws of physics, absolutely nothing whatsoever, then a thing cannot just pop into existence.

Second Premise: You cannot have an infinite regress of non-eternal beginnings.
This means if you have something non-eternal in the present, you cannot explain its existence by saying that it was the effect of something else non-eternal (its "cause"), and that also was the effect of something else-non eternal (its "cause"), etc. endlessly, because this is an attempt to get something from nothing.

Similarly, if you have something non-eternal in the present, it can be the cause for something else which is also non-eternal, and it could be again the cause for something else which is non-eternal, but it can never be the cause for something which is eternal and it cannot last forever - such cause and effect chains will always and must reach an end to it, otherwise - it will also be an attempt to create "something" (i.e. "infinite","eternal") out of "nothing" (i.e. "finite","non-eternal").

From these 2 premises, there must be something eternal (and ONLY ONE such "thing" as we will see)

Third Premise - Anything composite cannot be eternal. Later chapters will show that everything with any kind of finiteness is inherently composite, which rules out anything physical or more than one eternal being. End of Summary.

Note: that there are ways to attack the premises found in this gate such as that the notion of time did not exist before the Big Bang and therefore, the concept of cause/effect may be obscure (we will discuss this). Philosophers even propose avoiding the problem of an infinite cause/effect regression chain using a cycle of causes, where A=>B=>C=>A, and the like, including potentially complicated networks of mutual-causation, or they propose that really an infinite regress of causes is indeed possible or even an uncaused event is possible, since the whole problem is a paradox anyways. After all, the two premises: (1) a thing cannot make itself (i.e. everything must have a cause), and (2) there cannot be an infinite regress of causes are conflicting statements. The only way to resolve the two is if there exists something Eternal. Since they prefer not to acknowledge this, therefore, they propose, that human logic itself is questionable as to its reliability due to the flaws in our assumed premises of what is logical. Hence, according to them, we cannot rule out infinite regress or uncaused events, etc. even though these things do not seem rational.

This approach is not an attempt to answer what *must be* but rather to escape into endless and inconclusive speculation as to what *might* otherwise be. Indeed, the oracle at Delphi said that Socrates was the wisest man in Athens simply because he realized that he knew nothing. For without acknowledging the inevitable (G-d) one is doomed to run around in circles exchanging one theory with giant holes for another.

Translator; Some other evidence of G-d's existence:
INTELLIGENT DESIGN - Our universe seems to be extremely fine-tuned to allow for the existence of life. Furthermore, modern advances in microbiology have provided materials for a new and enormously powerful argument to design. By observing diverse life forms we can know that the Eternal Source is not some kind of natural phenomenon, but rather is an intelligent Thinker of awesome wisdom, awesome power, and awesome ability.

HASHGACHAH PRATIS (Divine providence) - Everyday stories from life; both from the lives of others (who one knows and trusts) and from one's own life. If a person pays close attention to what happens around him, he cannot help but note the Hand of G-d in so many events in our lives. There is no need to elaborate here.

PRAYER - If a person prays to G-d regularly, he will see G-d answer him. That does not mean that every prayer is answered, but it does mean that if we turn to G-d regularly, we see totally unexpected turns of events that can only be attributed to prayer. This can be seen (sometimes even more vividly) with regard to the prayers of others as well.
The prayer of a Tzibur (congregation) carries more weight that that of a Yachid (individual), and its effects are equally more evident.

PROPHECY - Even today, the power of prophecy can be seen when pondering the Torah's promises (can a nation exiled from its homeland and splintered into a dozen minor ethnic groups for 2,000 years, have the ability and resolve to return en masse to their homeland and become a universally recognized world power?).

Perhaps closer to home, those who have had the merit and opportunity of meeting with the Tzadikim (righteous Sages) of the generation know that even today, we can find shadows of "prophecy".

This category includes the infinite wisdom in the Torah, which is evident to all who study it in depth.

*** Chapter 6 ***

The application of the previous premises we mentioned to demonstrate the existence of the Creator, is as follows.

When we contemplate on this world, we find it is composite and compound. There is no part of it that does not have the character of composition and coordination. For to our senses and intellect it appears like a built and furnished house, whereby all its needs are prepared. The sky above like a roof, the land below like a carpet, the stars in their array like candles. All the objects gathered in it like treasures - everything has its need (every land has things needed for the needs of the people of that land - *TL*). Man is like the master of the house who uses all that is in it. The various types of plants are prepared for his benefit; the various kinds of animals serve his use, as David said: "You have made man to have dominion over the works of Your hands; You have put all things under his feet; All sheep and oxen, and the beasts of the field; The birds of the air, and the fish of the sea, and whatsoever passes through the paths of the seas" (Ps. 8:7).

(*Kuzari* 5:10   Even though we don't know what benefit can be derived from most of the creations, just like we don't know the purpose of all the parts of a ship and consider some unnecessary, while the maker of the ship understands them. Likewise, we would not know the purpose of many of our organs and bones if they were detached in separate pieces and placed before us, even though we use them, and it is clear to us that if one of them were missing, our actions would be lacking and we would be in need of it, so too every part of the world is known and counted by their Creator, and there is nothing to add or to diminish.

Tov Halevanon: There are no plants created for nothing. Every one is for man's need, whether for his food, his animals' food or for healing purposes [or clothing material, etc], likewise for animals, or for the benefit of their skin or for various types of healing.

Translator: If you ask - what possible benefit can there be for creatures long extinct such as the dinosaurs? Answer: the purpose of creation is human free will. Hence, it is necessary that there be room for a naturalistic explanation for everything, including life. This is why we have evidence in nature of common ancestry (evolution), or that the world appears billions of years old as a result of some cosmological accident, etc. Likewise, today we have things which don't seem to be of use to man, such as mosquitos, deep-sea creatures, or a vast universe. It's all necessary to make an environment where human free will can function. Furthermore, another purpose of nature is to teach us about G-d as mentioned in chapter 1 of Gate 2. The vast variety of creatures, teaches us about His vast wisdom. The vastness of the universe teaches us about His almighty power, how He moves these huges galaxies, etc. Hopefully with these lessons, man will learn to feel humble..

And the order of the sunrise and sunset - to establish the daytime and nighttime, and the rising and lowering of the sun to establish the heat and the cold, the summer and the winter, for the matters of the seasons and their benefits, and their continuous changing according to this order without interruption as written "Who commands the sun, and it rises not; and seals up the stars." (Iyov 9:7), and "You make darkness, and it is night" (Ps. 104:20).

And the orbits of the planets, with their various movements and periods, and the stars and constellations who follow precise movements and exact order, without straying and without changing, and the purpose of everything is for the benefit of mankind, as Solomon said: "To every thing there is a season, and a time to every purpose under the heaven" (Eccles. 3:11), and "also He has set the world in men's hearts" (Eccles. 3:1).

And everything, whether in part or as a whole, can be observed to be composite and compound. When we examine a plant or a live creature, we find them composed of the four elements - fire, air, water, and earth, which are separate and different.

(*Tov Halevanon* - This we can observe after burning something, the fire can be seen, the air which is the smoke rises, the moisture in the smoke is the element of water, and the ashes are the element of earth)

Excerpt from Morey Nevuchim 3:14 (Rambam's Guide for the Perplexed): "Do not ask me to reconcile all matters of astronomy that they (the Sages) stated about astronomy with the actual reality, for the science of those days was deficient, and they did not speak out of traditions from the prophets regarding these matters. Rather, because they were the wise of that period in these matters or because they heard them from the wise of that period." i.e. the Rambam is telling you not to try to reconcile his approaches with our conventional scientific understanding. Like the Sages, he was basing his teachings on the knowledge of the philosophers and mathematicians of the time period in question. (from: judaism.stackexchange.com/questions

/29886)

Also, Rabbi Avraham Kook notes (regarding evolution and the age of the universe) that some scientific ideas are intentionally kept hidden, as the world may not be ready for them, either psychologically or morally: "G-d limits revelations, even from the most brilliant and holiest prophets, according to the ability of that generation to absorb the information. For every idea and concept, there is significance to the hour of its disclosure. For example, if knowledge of the rotation of the Earth on its axis and around the sun had been revealed to primitive man, his courage and initiative may have been severely retarded by fear of falling. Why attempt to build tall buildings on top of an immense ball turning and whizzing through space at high velocity? Only after a certain intellectual maturity, and scientific understanding about gravity and other compensating forces, was humanity ready for this knowledge." from: ravkookTorah.org/NOAH60.htm

(*Translator's note*: (Note that our "fire" is not the same as the element of fire as will be explained.) In Midrashic literature, the world is viewed as being constructed of four basic elements: earth, water, air and fire (Bamidbar Raba end of 14:12; Zohar 1:27a, 2:23b-24b; Tikunei Zohar intro; Sefer Yetzirah Ch. 3; Ramban Bereishit 1:1; Etz Chaim kitzur aby'a ch.10 and many others). Some mistakenly attribute this system to Aristotle, but we know this is incorrect since they are mentioned in the Sefer Yetzira which is attributed to Abraham who lived well before him. The Sefer Yetzira was reportedly used by master Kabalists to create life forms. According to the Talmud (sanhedrin 65b,67b), the Rabbis of the Talmudic era used its system to miraculously create a calf every friday and eat it on the Sabbath (sanhedrin 65b,67b). Mystics assert that the Biblical patriarch Abraham used the same method to create the calf prepared for the three angels who foretold Sarah's pregnancy in the Biblical account at Genesis 18:7 (Chesed L'Avraham Mein Chamishi). All the miraculous creations attributed to other rabbis of the Talmudic era are ascribed by Rabbinic commentators to the use of this book.

The earth, water, air, fire, system is aligned with and incorporates the physical as well as the spiritual roots of this world, while modern science's system, which combines everything with E=mc2 describes only the physical side of reality. This is good for engineering purposes but it is merely the tail of the elephant of what constitutes reality.

The spiritual side of reality cannot be detected by physical instruments. This is because they are driven not by physical forces but by spiritual forces, namely, virtue and morality or their opposite, both of which have no place in the scientific paradigm. In many places throughout the book, the

author hints at these forces such as in Gate #8: "And when you do this with a faithful heart and a pure soul, your mind will become illuminated... A new, strange, supernal sense will arouse in you, unfamiliar to you of all the senses you are used to knowing..". I have personally met some rare individuals in Jerusalem with varying degrees of such "sixth sense", best not to elaborate... Generally, these people shun publicity at all cost and certainly never advertise. Those who "advertise" are always charlatans or worse. For the skeptics out there, I refer you to the words of the famous Kabalist Rabbi Yaakov Hillel, who is considered the expert on the subject in the Jewish world. He even wrote a book against such things called "Faith and Folly". Nevertheless, even he concedes that such things do exist. Here is an excerpt of his words from an audio lecture he gave: http://audio.ohr.edu/track/id=521
(at 46:01) "sometimes some of these people seem to have some sort of power of intuition. they can be quite prophetic. impressively. they can know hidden things. sometimes I've checked it out and I found out they have a well organized system of obtaining information (i.e. they are charlatans) ... but others really have this type of power... (skipping to 51:18) we should not be impressed when we see someone who knows hidden things...there are these types of things. It exists. but that's not what impresses us."

In the purely physical plane (the realm of science), the four elements parallel the four primary states of matter - solid, liquid, gas, plasma (some say energy). Further still, they parallel the four dimensions of space-time (space=3+time=1), four fundamental forces in physics (gravitational, electromagnetical, strong nuclear, weak nuclear), four main particles (proton, neutron, electron, photon, all governed by the four fundamental mathematical operations +-x/).

Interestingly, Dr. Michael Denton points out in his excellent book "Nature's Destiny" several examples of the number four appearing throughout molecular biology. In page 192 there he writes: "we have also seen that because of the natural twist in the DNA double helix, protein recognition motifs such as the alpha helix can only feel about 4 bases in the DNA double helix. It has often been said that G-d is a mathematician; on the evidence of molecular biology we might add that He is keen on the number four".

Likewise, in the life plane, they parallel the four types of life forms - inanimate (earth), plant (water), animal (air), human (fire). For in truth, the underlying reality is not atoms and subatomic particles as scientists believe, but rather - life. Life is the underlying reality. It is manifest to different degrees in this world, namely, the four degrees mentioned above. The lowest being inanimate objects where it is concealed to the utmost degree.

As we go up to plants, the hand of G-d begins to be noticeable as the machine analogy breaks down. Something else is manifest there beyond the molecules. It grows and builds itself autonomously. Order seems to prevail over disorder. There is a creative Power manifest. Further up, we find consciousness in animals, a higher form of life and further still free will and morality in humans. In all these things, the machine analogy breaks down... G-d is life in its most true form, most real form - eternal life. He is the source of all life.

In the human lower soul, they parallel the four traits which must be rectified before connection with higher spiritual forces is possible - sadness (earth), lust for indulgence (water), useless speech (air), arrogance/anger (fire). Ascending higher to the higher soul, they represent the four levels of soul - nefesh (earth), ruach (water), neshama (air), chaya (fire). These are rooted in the four spiritual worlds which in turn are rooted in the four levels of Torah interpretation and ultimately in the four letter Tetragramaton Name of G-d, who continuously gives life and sustains all of creation. (see the book Shaarei Kedusha for more details).

THE MYSTICAL FIRE
Translator: In truth, the fire that we know is not the element of fire in its pure form. The only place where this special, elemental fire manifested in the physical universe was on the altar of the first temple in Jerusalem, as the Maharsha comments on Yoma 21b "because it (the fire on the altar) was the elemental fire, unlike our fire which is a composite of other elements, hence it can be extinguished by the other elements, such as water. This is what the Talmud means "the fire of the altar was never extinguished by rain", this is because there was mixed with it, the higher form of fire, the elemental fire. And that which the Torah says (Lev. 6:6) "Fire shall be kept burning upon the altar continually; it shall not go out" (which implies that it is possible to extinguish) - This refers to the second kind of fire, namely "our fire" which the Kohen brought wood, since it was a commandment to bring fire from below." End quote. Hence, the fire on the altar contained both types of fire. One, our fire which the Kohen kindled with wood and two, a higher form of fire, the elemental fire. The elemental fire cannot be extinguished through "physical" water. Hence, despite that the altar was outdoors and exposed to rain, snow, and the strongest winds of the Jerusalem winter, the weather was incapable of extinguishing the fire on the altar.

The Talmud says there (Yoma 21b) that this kind of fire did not produce smoke, and it consumed water just like it consumed dry things. The fire consumed at a supernatural speed thousands of sacrifices each day, since behold, King Salomon alone brought 1000 burnt offerings every day despite that the area of the fire was only a few square meters and despite that only two logs of wood were added to the daily arrangement each day (Yoma 39a). Hence, it consumed the flesh and bones of entire animals at a miraculous rate.

The Talmud in (Yoma 21b) discusses the different types of fire:

> The Master said: 'And the [smoke arising from the] pile of wood on the altar'. [Question] But was there smoke arising from the pile of wood? Has it not been taught: Five things were reported about the fire of the pile of wood: It was lying like a lion, it was bright like the sun, its flame was of solid substance, it devoured wet things like dry things, and it caused no smoke to arise from it? [Answer] What we said [about the smoke] referred to the wood from outside [i.e. our type of wood-kindled fire mixed inside]. For it has been taught: And the sons of Aaron the priest shall put fire upon the altar - although the fire comes down from heaven, it is a mitzva to bring fire from outside too.
>
> 'Lying like a lion'. But has it not been taught: R. Hanina, deputy high priest, said: I myself have seen it and it was lying like a dog? - This is no contradiction: The first statement refers to the first Temple, the second to the second Temple. But was the fire present at the second Temple? - Surely R. Samuel b. Inia said: What is the meaning of the scriptural verse: And I will take pleasure in it [we-ikabed] and I will be glorified? The traditional reading is 'we-ikabedah', then why is the [letter] 'he' omitted [in the text]? To indicate that in five things the first Temple differed from the second: in the ark, the ark-cover, the Cherubim, the fire, the Shechinah, the Holy Spirit [of Prophecy], and the Urim-we-Thummim [the Oracle Plate]? - I will tell you, They were present, but they were not as helpful [as before, i.e. the fire consumed at a much slower rate].
>
> Our Rabbis taught: There are six different kinds of fire: (1) Fire which consumes but does not drink; (2) fire which drinks but does not eat; (3) fire which consumes and drinks; (4) fire which consumes dry matter as well as wet matter (water); (5) fire which pushes fire away; (6) fire which consumes fire.
> (1) 'Fire which consumes but does not drink': that is our fire [since water extinguishes it];
> (2) 'which drinks but does not eat': the fever of the sick;
> (3) 'consumes and drinks': that of Elijah, for it is written: And it consumed up the water that was in the trench;
> (4) 'consumes dry as well as wet matter': the fire of the pile of wood [on the altar of the temple];
> (5) 'fire which pushes other fire away': that of Gabriel (the Midrash explains that when Abraham was hurled in a fiery furnace, the angel Gabriel came, whereby the fire was repelled out of the furnace and burned everyone in its outside vicinity);

(6) 'fire which consumes fire': that of the Shechinah (divine presence), for a Master said: He put forth His finger among them and burned them (the angels, which are made of a kind of spiritual fire, who advised against creating man). [It is stated above], 'But the smoke arising from the pile of wood, even all the winds of the world could not move it from its place'.

Some other sources on this subject:
Ramchal - *Mevo L'Sefer Haklalim*:

The philosophers and scientists can grasp only the external surface of the world, namely, the physical world, according to what appears to their physical eyes. However, this is merely the outermost garment of the spiritual roots, namely, the sefiros who govern the world and are the innermost spirituality inside the physical... Just like the form of man alludes to the entire system of Divine governance, so too it is alluded from all the parts of nature, and every creation is an expression of one detail of His governance...

And on this are based most of the sayings of the Sages which refer to the Creation and to all matters of the world, whether in heaven or on earth and all of their derivatives, this is also a broad and important subject.

When our Sages instruct us on matters of nature and of this world, they are referring to its inner aspect - not on its external garment. Therefore, sometimes in their words we find things which appear strange, and which appear to be clearly false from what we perceive with our senses. But the truth is that they are speaking according to the true governance which is hidden from human eyes, which they received from the prophets and from the holy Torah...

Sefer HaBris *(Maamar 5 ch.3)*

"the early philosophers agreed with the view of the Kabalists regarding the four elements fire, wind, water, earth..... The later philosophers then rose up to completely destroy the view of the early philosophers and denied it saying it is not so. This is their way, one builds and another destroys, one dreams and another interprets... Some completely denied the matter of physical and form, and slashed mercilessly, others denied the four elements, others still held there are 3 elements... either way all of the later philosophers held there is no element of fire... and after time, they agreed that there is fire in the depths of the earth...and this view is supported by the volcanos in Italy and other places.... The bottom line is that all of their views are completely unreliable... and we have already received a tradition that there indeed exists four elements fire, wind, air, water like the view of the ancient ones, and that they are joined from physical and form, because thus wrote the man of G-d, Rabbi Chaim Vital zt'l in Etz Chaim (shaar kitzur aby'a ch.10), and his words are living, enduring, and faithful forever and ever.

If you ask: "if this four element system is superior why were the ancients so ignorant technology wise. Modern science has brought us far superior advances in medicine, and technology etc.?" The answer seems to be that G-d withheld the discovery of technology for so long to protect man from destroying himself, like a child who is given a toy plastic hammer instead of a real metal hammer so that he won't hurt himself. Man is much too dangerous to be given access to nuclear weapons. Technology may seem good to us now, but after 50 or 100 years we may look back and see that it was not a good thing - it can really bring TREMENDOUS destruction. As to why G-d allowed it in our times, this is because we are near the end of days, as we can see the prophecies of the end of days being fulfilled before our eyes as the Jewish people return to their homeland and many other signs. The Zohar (commenting on Bereshit 7:11) actually predicted that technological advancement will start in the year 5600, as a precursor and preparation for the Messianic Era (read about it here dafyomireview.com/430). However, all this requires many introductions to explain properly.. Another possible explanation as to why technology was withheld is that it is necessary to maintain free will. Advances in microbiology are increasingly unraveling the inner workings of cells and this is leading to a new and enormously powerful argument to design. Scientists are backing themselves further and further into a corner for the more wisdom they discover, the harder it becomes to attribute it all to chance, and to unguided natural processes. Perhaps this is the intent of the Zohar's prediction.

(back to the book)
We do not have the capability to join the four elements, in the natural way we find them compounded in nature because they are different and even repel each other. If we attempt to artificially combine them, the result rapidly changes and disintegrates, while the synthesis brought about through nature is complete and endures until the (appointed) time of its end.

Some of the philosophers thought that the planets, stars, supernal Ishim (type of spiritual beings - *PL*) are from the element of fire (this was the accepted scientific view among most in his time - *TL*), and similar to this David said: "Who makes winds His messengers; Flames of fire His ministers" (Ps. 104:4), and this is a support for this view, and that they are not of a fifth element (quintessence) as Aristotle held.

(And since there is a proof from reason and scripture that they are from the

element of fire, it is no longer necessary to bring a proof that they are not
eternal - *TL*)

Since all existing things that we find are from the elements, and composed
of them, and we know that they were not combined on their own, and by
their inherent nature do not join together because of their repelling
characteristics, it is clear to us that something else must have joined them
and bound them, and fused them together against their nature, by force -
this is their Creator, who joined them and ordained their union.

If we investigate the four elements, we will find them to be composed of
Matter *(chomer)* and Form *(tzura)* which are the Essence *(etzem)* and
Incident *(mikre)*.

(*Marpe Lenefesh*: There was already much discussion from the early Sages,
the philosophers, and receivers of the true tradition on the subject of
"physical and form", as you can see in the Moray, the Kuzari book, the
Raavad's introduction to the book of Yetzira, and the Ramban's
commentary on the verse: "And the earth was without form, and void"
(Gen. 1:2), see them. The summary of what comes out of all of them is as
follows: When G-d wished to create the world, He first created a primordial
physical without form (energy?), similar to clay in the hands of a potter, or
raw metal which the metal smith uses to make various objects of different
forms, but of the same material. So too regarding the four elements, before
each one received the form visible to us, it was first composed of the
primordial substance, which is called by the Greeks, "hiyuli", and in the
kabalistic books, "nefesh yesodot", since the form requires the underlying
physical, without which it cannot hold its form, and the substance is the
essence of the thing while the form is the incident *(mikre)*, because
sometimes it is embodied in this form and sometimes in another. The
physical and the form of the four elements always existed simultaneously,
because their existence preceded that of all the creations, and from them all
creations were composed...now you will understand well the author's
coming words)

The [formless] Matter of the elements is the primordial matter, which is the
root of the four elements, the physical or "hiyuli" of them.

(For other creations, their physical is a combination of the four elements,
but the physical of the four elements is the primordial physical which has
no underlying physical before it, it is the root of the four elements, and it is
simple, not composite - *PL*)

Translator: Ultimately, later on we will see that everything is in some sense composite (except the underlying essence of all - G-d)

Their Form is the primordial form which comprises all forms, and which is the root of all forms, whether essence or incident such as heat (which is essence in fire but incident in other things - *ML*), cold, wetness, dryness, heaviness, lightness, movement, rest, etc.

[To summarize], combination and union are apparent throughout the world, as a whole and in all of its parts, in its roots and in its branches, in that which is simple (i.e. even in the four elements which are a union of only two things, namely the primordial matter and the Form - *ML*) and in that which is complex, in that which is above and in that which is below. Therefore, based on our previous premises, it follows that the world is entirely *mechudash* (created), since it has been clarified that whatever is composite must have been brought into existence. Therefore it is proper for us to conclude that the world is *mechudash*, and since this is so, and that it is not possible for something to make itself, therefore it must be that there was a Maker who started it and brought it into existence.

(*Marpe Lenefesh*: And even the supernal realms (angels, mystical worlds) are also composite from the four spiritual elements. They are composed from the four letters of the tetragrammaton (YHVH, G-d's primary Name as He manifests Himself to His creations), which is the source of the four spiritual and the four physical elements, and there is nothing whether in the upper realms or in our world which is not composed from the four letters of the tetragrammaton, and the Ein Sof ("light" of G-d) which dons them, as written in Shaarei Kedusha part 3 gate 1, and the Alshich on parsha Bereishis, see there)

And because we have demonstrated that it is not possible for there to be an infinite chain of causes, it must be that there was a first Cause without a previous cause and a Beginning without a previous beginning - and He is the one who formed it and brought it into existence from nothing, not with the help of anything nor for anything.

(*Marpe Lenefesh*: that there was nothing forcing Him to create the world, neither was it for His benefit, but rather, He created everything to bestow good to another, like the nature of the good to bestow good. For, we saw that of everything He created, it is only that which is needed for man and not more. While according to G-d's infinite power and ability, this entire world is as nothing. For He bestows good on everything according to what it is capable of receiving)

As the verse says on this matter: "I am the L-ord that makes all things; that stretches forth the heavens alone; that spreads abroad the earth by Myself" (Isaiah 44:24), and "He stretches out the north over the empty place, and suspends the earth over nothing" (Iyov 26:7). He is the Creator, Whom we have investigated and sought with our reasoning and intellect. He is the *Kadmon* (Eternal) which there is no beginning to His beginning, and the First, whose eternity is endless, as written: "I am first and I am last" (Isaiah 44:6), and "Who has performed and done it, calling the generations from the beginning? I the L-ord, the first, and with the last, I am He" (Isaiah 41:4).

There are some people who claim that the world came into being by chance, without a Creator who created it and without a Maker who formed it. It is amazing to me how a rational, healthy human being could entertain such a notion. If such a person heard someone else saying the same thing about a water wheel, which turns to irrigate part of a field or a garden, saying that it came to be without a craftsman who designed it and toiled to assemble it and placed each part for a useful purpose - the hearer would be greatly amazed on him, consider him a complete fool, and be swift to call him a liar and reject his words. And since he would reject such a notion for a mere simple, insignificant water wheel, which requires but little ingenuity and which rectifies but a small portion of the earth - how could he permit himself to entertain such a notion for the entire universe which encompasses the earth and everything in it, and which exhibits a wisdom that no rational human intellect is capable of fathoming, and which is prepared for the benefit of the whole earth and everything on it. How could one claim that it came to be without purposeful intent and thought of a capable wise Being?

It is evident to us that for things which come about without the intent of an intender (i.e. an intelligence) - none of them will display any trace of wisdom or ability. Behold and see, that if a man suddenly pours ink on clean paper, it would be impossible for there to be drawn on it orderly writing and legible lines like it would be with a pen, and if a man brought before us orderly writing from what cannot be written without use of a pen, and he would say that ink was spilled on paper, and the form of the writing happened on its own, we would be quick to call him a liar to his face. For we would feel certain that it could not have happened without an intelligent person's intent.

Since this appears impossible to our eyes for mere symbols (the alphabet) whose form is merely conventional, how could one entertain the notion for something whose engineering is far more fine, and whose formation is infinitely more fine, deep and beyond our comprehension, to say that it is without intent of an Intender, and without the wisdom of a wise and powerful Being.

What we have brought to establish the existence of the Creator from the aspect of His deeds should be enough for anyone who is intelligent and admits the truth, and it is a sufficient refutation to the group of kadmut, who claim the world is *kadmon* (always existed), and to disprove their claims. Know it well!

Translator: - If you ask, if so what brought G-d into existence? Why is He the exception to this rule? Answer: G-d is eternal. You cannot ask what brought the eternal into existence. All these author things cannot be eternal as the author will explain the things which disqualify something from being possibly eternal. This will leave out everything except the true Unity.

If you ask, "hasn't Darwin's theory of evolution refuted the argument by design?" Answer: not in the least. If you look closely at the evidence, you will see that none of them ever address this point. Everything they bring is for side issues, such as proving common ancestry through DNA similarities or the like and then extrapolating to this point. But as for random processes making new engineering of non-trivial complexity - there is always a trick to their words. If you can't see the trick in an example they bring or theorize, email me and I'll show you.

(Final words from *Marpe Lenefesh* commentary: In the Moreh Nevuchim (Rambam's Guide for the Perplexed) Chapter 13: "I say that any work done with intent must have a purpose for which it was done... and likewise it is clear that the thing which was made with intent is *mechudash* (created) after there was not... And Aristotle already clarified that the plants were created for the creatures, and likewise for other things, each one for the other, and all the more so for the limbs of the creatures. Know that this existence of plan and purpose in natural matters brought the philosophers to believe in a beginning beyond nature... Know that the greatest proof to the chidush of the world, for one who admits the truth, is from the natural world around us, since all of them have a purpose and that each one is for the other - this is a proof on intent from an Intender, and intent which is carried out..." End of the Rambam's words.
I wrote this because even though the Rambam greatly engaged in debating and refuting all the different viewpoints, whether for *kadmon* (eternal existence of the world) whether for creation, as you can see in that entire book, this is what he found most proper in his eyes from all the proofs, and he brought it as his final words. In truth, it is a foundation and root.

Therefore, the author (of this book) also built all of his building on it, since they are things which can be [tangibly] grasped intellectually - but to delve deeper in these matters is extremely dangerous, as the Rambam wrote in the Moreh part 2 chapter 16: "When it became clear to me [that arguments can be made against each of the proofs that Aristotle brought to show that the world was eternal (and not created), and therefore] the question of whether the world is kadmon (eternally extant) or created remains unresolved [through philosophical proofs], I chose to resolve the question based on the prophecy of the prophets, since prophecy is able to clarify matters that are beyond the power of the intellect to resolve and even those who believe that the world is eternal do not deny the existence of prophecy....", see there.

And in part 2 chapter 17, he brought a very powerful analogy against the heretics who believe in kadmut (eternal existence of the world), and he said that all of their proofs and logic are only from the nature which exists in the world after the Creator has already created them in perfect form from all angles as they are now. But how can we possibly bring a proof from this as to how it was before it was created and called to existence from nothing: "the analogy of this is to a child who was born in a deserted island, and then his mother died, and this orphan never saw a female. When he grew up and matured intellectually, he asked his father how a man was formed. His father answered him 'each person among us, came to be and was formed in the belly of a female, who is of our kind, like us, of such and such form, and the man was in her belly, small, and his body was closed. And he grew there slowly, slowly, for fixed months until the time he was forced to go out from her belly through an opening which opened for him. Afterwards he grew until he became mature in his limbs, senses, and intellect, as you see now.'

The orphan started to deny all of this, and built proofs against all these true things, saying that "they are impossible and are lies, because how is it conceivable that a live man can breathe through his nostrils inside a container which is closed on all sides, and it appears impossible that one can live for any time without breathing, or if one cannot excrete the waste of his food, he will die a painful death, and how could his mouth be shut and his navel open, and his eyes closed and his limbs constricted together for such a long time, and when he comes out of there, all of his limbs and his eyes should be intact". This is a clear proof that the formation of man could not have occurred in this way, even though it is truly so.

He ends off: "contemplate this analogy and test it, and you will find the two matters to be identical, and that we are of these who pursue Moshe Rabeinu, peace be unto him, and Avraham our forefather. We believe the world came to be in such and such a way, and it was such and such, and it was created such and such, and afterwards Aristotle came to refute our words, and he brought proofs from the laws of this nature, which are complete and with us, here in the present, but which are not comparable to what existed at the time of creation, for this was after absolute non-existence..."

He then finishes: "and you must be careful in this matter as it is a great protective wall, which I have built around the Torah.. to protect from the stones of all who hurl at it", until here is the Rambam, see also what is written in the introduction of the book "Haemunot". Note it well!)

(*Translator:* Rabbi Dovid Gotlieb has a nice lecture on the Rambam's analogy. see www.audio.ohr.edu/track/id=2006)

*** CHAPTER 7 ***

The demonstration of the Creator is one is as follows. Since it has been clarified to us, through logical proofs, that the world has a Creator, it is incumbent on us to investigate on Him, whether He is one or more than one and we will demonstrate the truth of His unity from seven arguments.

FIRST ARGUMENT FOR THE UNITY OF G-D

The first, from our examination of the causes of existent things. When we investigate on them, we find that causes are always fewer than their effects, namely, the higher up one ascends into the chain of causes, the fewer the number of causes, and the more and more one ascends this chain, the fewer and fewer will be their number until eventually one reaches one Cause, which is the Cause of all causes.

The fuller explanation of this: Individual things (Ishim) that exist are countless. When we investigate the kinds (minim), which comprise them, we will find their number to be fewer than the individuals under them, because each kind includes many individuals, and they are not countless. And when we categorize the kinds into (broader category) "types" (sugim) which includes the kinds, we will find the number of types to be fewer than the number of kinds, since each type includes many kinds, and the more one ascends the fewer the number, until one reaches the primary types.

(Translator: The commentaries will now bring a lot of background information which will be useful throughout.)

(*Tov Halevanon:* Every thing and every creature by itself is called an "individual" (Ish), such as one man or one living thing like a horse or mule or a grass or a tree. The term "kind" (min) refers to a group of individuals such as the species of man or the species of horses. The term "group" (geder) refers to something which includes many "kinds" such as "living creature", which includes the species of man and all the various living things (animals, birds, fish, etc). The term "type" (sug) is more general, as you would say the term "growing (thing)" includes all the trees and plants and all the living creatures. There is a higher "type", namely "composite" (murkav of the elements) which includes inanimate objects like stones, metals, and all growing (living things). There is another type even more inclusive, such as the term "physical" (geshem), which also includes the four elements, but which only includes physical things, until the term "essence" (etzem), which includes every existing thing, whether physical or spiritual. This is the type which is over and above (most general) and is called the supernal type.

Pas Lechem: If I were to properly explain the following matter, our discussion would become very lengthy. One who wishes to know should get a hold of the book "Ruach Chen" and the book "Milot Higayon"; there he can quench his thirst.

Tov Halevanon: The intent of the author is to ascend to the first cause, therefore I did not need to explain here the matters of Mikre (incident).

The philosopher (Aristotle) already said that the general types are ten: Etzem, Kama, Eich, Mitztaref, Ana, Matay, Matzav, Kinyan, Poel, and Nifal. (explanation in below commentaries)

MIKRE (incidental/accidental properties) VS. ETZEM (essence)
Pas Lechem: In order to understand the following things, you need to know that all the philosophers agreed that everything that exists in the world is composed of Etzem (essence) and Mikre (incident). The Etzem is the essence of the thing, which never changes as long as the thing exists, through it we are able to know what it is and what is its essence.

Tov Halevanon: (from beginning of Chapter 8) Mikre is something which is not essential for the thing and it can exist without it, sometimes it is attached to it and sometimes not, while something which is in its essence is found on it always.
Translator: For example, hotness is something found in hot water as Mikre (incidental property), but in fire it is essence, since you can remove the hotness from water without destroying the water but you cannot remove the hotness from fire without destroying the fire.

(*Pas Lechem*:
The Mikre (incident) is that which could happen or occur to the Etzem (essence), sometimes like this and sometimes like that. The Etzem is always one thing while the Mikre divides into nine parts through which all things are included. They are upper types... Rabbi Yaakov the son of the Chacham Tzvi wrote that they correspond to the "ten sayings" (through which the world was created as brought in Pirkei Avot) and the "ten sefirot" (in kabala), and he explained them there one by one, examine there (Lechem Shamayim Ch.2 Chagiga). Perhaps they (the gentile philosophers) found them from an early book of one of our Sages, and stole and denied and put it in their bags as they did for other wisdoms they ruled over and called it on their names, as written in the Kuzari book (maamar sheni ot 1).

(THE 9 ATTRIBUTES OF MIKRE (incidental properties, non-essence)

Kama: This is when you describe a thing by its measure, namely, when you wish to label it by its measure and you call it "the long" or "the short", "the tall" or the "low height". This is an internal measure. An external measure is for example when you say "the one" or "the two", or "the three".

Eich: This is when you describe and label something by one of its physical or nonphysical properties, for example, you describe it "the white" or "the black", or "the solid" or "the liquid". (not sure what he means by nonphysical - translator).

Mitztaref: When you describe this thing and label it relative to something else and through this label, both are described, such as when you describe this one as a "father" or a "master". From this label we know for certain that he has a son or a servant, since there is no father without a son and no master without a servant..

Ana: This is when you describe something and give a sign by its place. For example: Mr. X who lives in house Y or in city Z.

Matay: Describing and labeling a thing by a known time, for example, Mr. X born at date and time Y.

Matzav: Describing something through its situation, for example "the sitting" or "the lying down" or "falling on his face".

Kinyan: Describing a thing by the possessions it acquired for itself, for example "he is wearing X clothing" or "with hair X", as long as it is not separated from it, it can be described through this

Poel and Nifal: All the books have these two in reverse order.. this refers to describing the Etzem (essence) by one of the changes in it, or that it divests itself of one form and dons another, such as earth which changed to a mouse (through food, etc ingested by its mother), or through an incident that it's measure changes, that it was small and grew, or that it was white and darkened.

Nifal: That you describe the "doer" through changes which occurred to the thing "done unto". Because everything "done unto" has an external "doer" which causes it these changes. For example, that you say that from the tree was "done" a chair, the changes to the etzem of the tree happened indirectly and the craftsman who caused the changes is the one who did them.

Likewise for something which existed in potential and went out to actual, and changed from potential to actual - there must have been an external "doer" which brought out this potential to actual.

For the rest of their details, divisions, and explanations, see the Moreh and the "Ruach Chen" chapter 10, and the other books dealing with them. The summary of all of them is what I wrote, and this is enough to understand the author's words)

The causes of these ten general types are five: Motion and the four elements - Fire, Air, Water, and Earth. (since without motion nothing can come to be or change - *PL*).

The causes of the four elements are found to be two: Matter (chomer) and Form (tzura), and if we further examine on the cause of these two, undoubtedly it will be less than them. This (cause) is the will of the Creator, and there is no number less than two but one, if so, the Creator is one.

And likewise David, peace be unto him, said: "Yours, O L-ord, is the kingdom and You are exalted as head over all" (Chronicles 29:11), which means that G-d is exalted above all that is exalted, lofty above all that is lofty. He is the First of all beginnings and the Cause of all causes.

THE SECOND ARGUMENT FOR THE UNITY OF G-D

The second argument is drawn from the perspective of the signs of wisdom manifested in the universe, whether above or below, in the inanimate, plants, and animals on it.

When we contemplate the world, it will become apparent that - it is the design of one Thinker, and the work of one Creator. We find its roots and foundations to be similar in its derivatives and uniform in its parts. The signs of wisdom manifested in the smallest of the creatures as well as the biggest testify that they are the work of one wise Creator. If this world had more than one Creator, the form of wisdom would exhibit different forms in the different parts of the world, and vary in its general character and divisions.

Pas Lechem : Even though the creatures are different in size, they are very similar in the amount of the Creator's wisdom exhibited by them. Just like the elephant and the camel have a mouth, legs, and a belly to receive food, so too for the mosquito and the moth.

Marpe Lenefesh: Each Creator would have created different creatures which are not at all similar to the creatures of the other, and each Creators' works would have demonstrated a different form of wisdom, so that all can recognize that it is from a different Creator. But now that we see that they are all similar to each other - it must be that one Wisdom made all of them. Translator: All known living things are closely related. For example, they all, share a similar DNA system. Likewise, even the simplest bacteria are enormously complex and are given the poor scientists quite a run for their money. For the more they study, the more and deeper the complexity they

confront (even for the "simplest" bacteria), and the more they are baffled
by the divine wisdom before them.

Furthermore, we find that it is interdependent for its maintenance and
welfare, no part is completed without the help of another part, like the links
in a coat of armor, the parts of a bed, the limbs of the human body, or other
things which have interdependent parts for their functioning.

(*Marpe Lenefesh*: Every creation in the world depends on something else
for its existence and welfare, plants and anything which comes from the
ground needs water, and animals need both, and man needs all of them...)

Can you see that the moon and the planets need the light of the sun, and the
earth needs the sky and the water, and that the animals need each other, and
some species feed on other species, such as predatory birds, fish, and
beasts of the forest all need each other? And Man's need for everything,
and the rectification of everything through man (man gives a higher
purpose to everything). Countries, towns, sciences and trades are
interdependent (each country has special resources/skills unique to it - *TL*).

And the Divine wisdom appears in the tiny creatures as well as the large
ones, because the wisdom manifested in the formation of an elephant,
despite its huge body, is no more wondrous than the wisdom manifested in
the formation of a tiny ant. On the contrary, the smaller the creature the
more wisdom and power it appears to reflect, and the more it testifies to
the wondrous ability of the Creator. (since its tiny limbs and sinews are
more amazing due their small size than they are in the big creatures - *TL*)

This teaches that they are all the design of one Designer and Creator, since
they are similar and alike in furthering and completing the natural order
and maintenance of the world in all of its parts. If there were more than
one Creator, the form of wisdom exhibited would be different in some of
its parts, and things would not be interdependent. Since the world, despite
its being different in its roots and foundations, it is equal in its derivatives
and compounds, one can see that its Creator who put it together, its
Governor, and Designer is one.

A philosopher once said: "no part of what G-d created is more wondrous
than another part". Which means the wisdom in a tiny creature of this
world is similar and equal to that in a large one, as David, peace be unto
him, said: "O L-ord, how manifold are Your works! with wisdom have You
made them all: the earth is full of Your possessions" (Ps. 104:24), and "O

L-ord, how great are Your works! Your thoughts are exceedingly deep"
(Ps. 92:6).

(Translator: Even in the tiniest segment of the inanimate world, there is an
infinite character of wisdom as the Nobel prize winning physicist Richard
Feynman said (from his book: *The Character of Physical Law* - Chapter 2 -
the relation of mathematics to physics):
"It always bothers me that according to the laws as we understand them
today, it takes a computing machine an infinite number of logical
operations to figure out what goes on in no matter how tiny a region of
space, and no matter how tiny a region of time. How can all that be going
on in that tiny space? Why should it take an infinite amount of logic to
figure out what one tiny piece of space/time is going to do? So I have often
made the hypothesis ultimately physics will not require a mathematical
statement, that in the end the machinery will be revealed and the laws will
turn out to be simple, like the chequer board with all its apparent
complexities. But this is just speculation." End quote. (Hence, in truth, the
scientists don't grasp ANYTHING fully, because who can understand the
work of G-d? If this is so for even the tiniest speck of empty space. How
much more so, for an electron, or beyond to living organism, whose design
is perfectly coordinated from the atomic level up. Go and see how scientists
worldwide are dumbfounded at fully understanding even the simplest
viruses which are far less complex than cells.

(*Michtav M'Eliyahu vol 3, pg.167*: "The scientists rely solely on what is
detectable by the physical senses. Through this [scientific method] does
one save himself from error or, on the contrary, he will fall in greater and
more extreme error? Let us imagine: if a man receives letters from
unknown people who come from different places. From one place, all the
letters come written with green ink (since green ink is common there).
From the second place, all the letters come in black ink. The letters are
different in content. Those written with green ink are all full of nonsense
and foolish matters. While those written with black ink are all words of
wondrous wisdom.

An intelligent person will realize that the writers of the letters with wisdom
are wise men. While the writers of the nonsense are fools. But a scientist
will come and say: "I cannot say on the writers of the letters. For I cannot
actually see them, much less can I say anything on their thoughts since it is
concealed in their brains. Therefore, if I investigate their wisdom according
to the content of the letters, this is not the scientific way. Rather, I am
forced to examine their difference based on physical evidence that I can
detect. Through this clear evidence, I will resolve the solution. Based on
the evidence, I will hypothesize that the green ink is the cause of the
foolishness in the letters from one place, while the black ink is the cause of

the wise words from the letters of the other place.

So too, for the matters of our world. If we don't give thought to the inner side of the matter which is grasped by the heart (intuition), inside our soul, and we restrict our sight only to the superficial appearance of things, we will certainly not at all draw closer to the truth... we must look with an inner eye and look at the matter from all perspectives.

THE THIRD ARGUMENT

(*Tov Halevanon*: The scientist/rational investigator, from the role he assumes as rational investigator, it is his way to believe only that which he has clarified through logical proofs. While the "believer", who believes that which has not been clarified to himself through logical proofs, has already gone out of the role of "scientist/investigator" and has no business debating with them. And now that we are here today, and we have permitted ourselves to delve in the sea of rational investigation in order to clarify through logic the existence of G-d, to affix faith in Him in our hearts, in addition to the faithful tradition of our Torah. We have already attained an understanding of a logical proof of this, through which, out of love for Him, we can fix in our hearts.)

The third argument, from the chidush (non-eternal nature) which applies to the entire universe. Since our previous proofs demonstrated that the world is created (see chapters 5-6), it follows from this that it must therefore have had a Creator. For it is impossible for something to come into existence by itself. And when we see that a thing exists, and we are certain that at some time it did not exist - we will know through the testimony of a sound intellect that something other than itself created it, brought it into being, and formed it. (The intellect convinces our minds and testifies to us that it must be so, it is not possible in any way that there is not a Creator who created all that exists - *TL*)

Since we have established that the world has a Creator who created it and brought it into existence - we need not deliberate whether He is more or less than one since it is impossible for the existence of the world without at least one Creator. And if it were possible to conceive that the world could have come into existence with less than one Creator, we would consider this. But since we cannot conceive that something less than one can bring anything into existence, we conclude that the Creator must be one. Because in the case of things which were established through logical proofs, and the proof of their existence is impossible to deny - we do not need to assume more than what is necessary to account for the phenomena which the proof demonstrates.

> (*Pas Lechem*: Since the logical proofs necessitate the existence of one Creator, why and from where do we need to consider that He is more than one, since this logical proof on the existence of the Creator is completed and suffices also without more than one.
>
> *Tov Halevanon*: It is not proper for one to look to the ends of the earth, and consider more than what the proof requires him to believe in order to resolve the difficulties raised in his rational inquiry.

The analogy of this: When we see a letter of uniform handwriting and style (that the handwriting style and the spacing between letters and words is uniform from beginning to end - *PL*), it will immediately occur to us that one person wrote and composed it because it is not possible that there was not at least one person. If it were possible that it could have been written with less than one person, we would consider this possibility. And even though it is possible that it was written by more than one person, it is not proper to consider this unless there is evidence which testifies to this, such as different handwriting style in part of the letter or the like.

> (*Marpe Lenefesh*: If you see discrepancies in handwriting style, then you can say that perhaps two people wrote it due to the variation and the non-uniformity of the handwriting. But all the time that you don't see any irregularity or non-uniformity, what pushes you to say that perhaps two people wrote it? - on the contrary, the fact that there is no irregularity testifies that one person wrote the entire letter.)

Since this is so (that we do not need to consider more than one Creator - *PL*), it is not necessary to know Him face to face, if this is not possible (just like it is not necessary to know the writer face to face in order to determine whether the letter was written by him alone or with someone else - *PL*), and it will suffice for us to see the letter, accepting as proof the writer's acts, namely, the form of the writing, instead of seeing the writer himself. From this, we will know with certainty that there exists a writer, who knows how to write and is capable of writing, who wrote this letter.

He did not partner with someone else in writing it. This we can see from its orderly form and uniform handwriting, since the work of two makers varies. It is not uniform and orderly in one manner, and it changes in quality and character.

> (*Tov Halevanon*: Therefore when we see a legal document (in court), orderly and of uniform handwriting, behold there is a strong likelihood that

only one writer wrote it, and we will judge the case assuming so. And if someone claims that it is the work of two scribes, the burden of proof will be on that person. And even though this is not a complete proof, nevertheless it is sufficient proof. Because it is not proper for us to ask a man to bring proofs and verify strange and remote possibilities, but rather only for normal and regular cases. The author will soon bring clearer arguments. He also brought this argument in order to strengthen the matter, like the usual way of investigators/philosophers.)

Similarly we will say regarding the Creator, since the signs of wisdom in His creations are similar and uniform, we must conclude that one Creator created them, and that without Him they could not have come into existence, although the Creator is not something that can be perceived either in Etzem (essence) or Mikre (incident). And since He cannot be seen, it is impossible to find Him and know Him except through the proofs and observations of His handiworks which point to Him. Then will our belief stand firm that He exists and that He is One, that He is Kadmon (eternal), who was and will be, the First and the Last, Mighty, Wise, Living.

(*Pas Lechem*: He began with the title: "Mighty" because according to our understanding, He existed before everything, since immediately after we grasp that there exists a Creator who created the world from nothing, we will immediately recognize His Might, namely, the act of creating something from nothing... After this, when we reflect on the details of creation, and we study them and their parts - we will see signs of His wisdom and we will know that He is wise. Afterwards, we contemplate His providence in governing the world, we will know that He is living and among us always. Understand that all of these descriptions are obligatory and follow one after the other, with the creation of the world as their first source.)

Since He is not among the things which can be seen, the proofs regarding Him will stand for us in place of seeing Him.

(*Pas Lechem*: That the rational proofs stood for us to bring us to believe in His existence, as if we had grasped what He is and as if we had seen Him... Perforce, we are forced to suffice with our limited grasp, by accepting the logical proofs instead of actually seeing Him because He is not among the things which can be seen.

Therefore, it is necessary for us to conclude that one Creator created the world, because the existence of created things is impossible without Him. The assumption of more than one God is superfluous and unnecessary.

Therefore, one who claims this - his claim cannot be considered legitimate unless he brings a sound logical proof other than that which we have brought. But it is impossible to establish such a proof, since two sound logical proofs do not contradict each other (and we already brought sound proofs that He is one - *PL*).

All the evidence thus testifies on His unity, and negates the attributing to Him of any plurality, association or similarity, as G-d Himself declares: "Is there a god besides me?" (Isaiah 44:8), and "I am the First and I am the Last" (ibid 44:6), and "My hand has laid the foundations of the earth, and My right hand has spread out the heavens" (Isaiah 48:13), and "a just G-d and a Savior; there is none besides Me" (Isaiah 45:21).

(*Manoach Halevavot*: Since G-d is not visible, He wanted His handiworks to testify on His existence and wisdom. It is the way of a craftsman to desire that it be known that the craft was made by him. Therefore perforce He is one, because less than one is impossible and for more than one, the proofs don't hold, and all the evidence testifies only on one Creator..

Pas Lechem: "Plurality" refers to another of similar essence. "Association" refers to associating another in His deeds. "Similarity" refers to His deeds, namely, that none can make other deeds similar to His.

Translator: If you ask: I read on the news that scientists have created new living bacteria in the laboratory. Answer: if you research the claim, you will see that the scientists merely modified a living bacteria and then hoped it survived. Alternatively, their new "bacteria" does not grow and reproduce autonomously like actual living things. For to implement the latter is enormously complicated, requiring many systems such as energy, information, growth, import/export, transport, regulation, timing, etc. etc. We are nowhere near getting anywhere close to even making a blueprint for such a device. Way too many reactions and no known prototype other than the cell itself.

Just briefly, to get a feel for what even the "simplest" bacteria needs to do, let us consider the basic autonomous cell whose only task is to reproduce and synthesize the parts it needs from raw materials.

1. Information System - to build something which can reproduce and synthesize its own parts from raw materials requires a coordinated series of steps. Chemicals cannot do this. On their own, they just combine chaotically or crystallize into regular patterns such as in snowflakes. Hence, there must be information (ex. RNA or the like) storing the instructions to orchestrate the assembly.

2. Energy System - information by itself is useless. To implement the instructions requires energy. A system that cannot generate or source energy just drifts chaotically or crystallizes into simple forms, forced to follow the path of least resistance. Hence, a system of producing or sourcing energy is necessary along with subsystems of distribution and management of that energy so that it goes to the proper place.

3. Copy System - in order to reproduce itself, the device must be able to implement the instructions of the information system using the energy system. This includes the ability to rebuild all critical infrastructure such as the information and energy systems and even the copy system itself.

4. Growth System - Without a growth system, the device will reduce itself every time it reproduces and vanish to zero-size after a few generations. This growth system necessitates subsystems of ingestion of materials from the outside world, processing of those materials, and assembling those materials into the necessary parts.This alone is a formidable chemical factory.

5. Transportation System - the materials must be moved to the proper places. Hence, a transportation system is needed for transporting raw materials and products from one place to another within the cell. Likewise, a system for managing the in-coming of raw materials and out-going of waste materials of all these chemical reactions.

6. Timing System - the growth system must also be coordinated with the reproduction system. Otherwise, if the reproduction occurs faster than the growth, it will reduce size faster than it grows and vanish after a few generations. Hence, a timing or feedback mechanism is needed.

7. Communication System - signalling is needed to coordinate all the tasks so that they all work together. The reproduction system won't work without coordination with the growth and power systems. Likewise, the power system by itself is useless without the growth and reproduction systems. Only when all the systems and "circuitry" are in place and the power is turned on is there hope for the various interdependent tasks to start working together. Otherwise, it is like turning on a computer which has no interconnections between the power supply, CPU, memory, hard drive, video, operating system, etc - nothing to write home about.

Hence the "simple" task of reproducing and synthesizing parts is by no means simple. A cell is a marvelous entity no less mind-boggling than a full fledged organism. And this is just for the basic cell. Furthermore, all of this complexity is just for the basic cell. Consider for instance, all the processes that need to occur in the human egg cell after fertilization. It magnifies its size in only a few weeks or months thousand-folds and more. It self-organizes into some trillion specialized cells. What system known in reality is able to do so, only with mother's food and air digested and moved through the blood? Nothing like it even a tiny bit 1000 times exists anywhere ever. Such brilliant ability to magnify a structure by such an enormous factor, such sophistication and wisdom of creation - all autonomously in the womb.

REFUTATION OF ARGUMENT TO DESIGN
Parenthetically, one may come across "refutations" of the Argument from Design by the atheists/anti-theists out there along the lines of the following:

Things that look designed must have a designer - but designers look designed too. And designers are more improbable than the things they design. Hence, this premise is false.
As an illustration, my coffee mug looks designed, so it must have a designer. That designer was a production line, which is more improbable than the mug. A factory production line looks designed, so it must have had a designer. The designer was a team of human beings, which is more improbable than the production line. Human beings look designed, so they must have had a designer. That designer was G-d, which is more improbable than humans. G-d is the termination point of this regress, because nothing can be more improbable than G-d because G-d is Infinitely Improbable. Since G-d is Infinitely Improbable, He is impossible and does not exist. Therefore, the original premise of the argument is false.

Answer: This argument is based on ignorance regarding what eternal implies. You cannot ask what designed something Eternal. By definition the Eternal always existed. The argument from design only applies to something we see cannot be eternal. If we see some intelligent design and we also know that it cannot be eternal, then we can reasonably conclude that it must have had a designer.

Human beings cannot be eternal (since they are composite, finite, etc.) therefore they must have had a designer. But G-d is eternal so we cannot ask what designed Him. We can say that we don't understand how something can be eternal. That's valid and correct, and it stems from our inability to understand and relate to the Eternal because we are non-eternal. On this, Maimonides wrote, "if I could understood Him, I would be Him". In truth though, when you think about it, the mystery is not "how can the eternal exist?", but rather "how can the non-eternal exist?".
To summarize, one cannot ask "what brought G-d into existence?" for in truth He is existence/reality itself as explained next argument...

THE FOURTH ARGUMENT

(*Translator*: Important Note. In this argument, we are talking about spiritual matters which are exceedingly deep. You can't think on them the same way you think on physical things. The author already warned in chapter 2 that only a select few can grasp these very subtle arguments. commentaries to follow!)

The fourth argument: We will say to anyone who thinks the Creator is more than one as follows. It must be that the essence of all these (supposed creators) is either one or not one.

If you say, that in essence they are one, if so, they are one thing, and the Creator is not more than one. (since certainly for the Etzem of one thing it is not applicable to attribute plurality - *PL*)

If you say that each one of them is, in essence, different from the other, it must therefore be there is some distinction between them due to their difference and non-similarity. If so, whatever is distinct is limited/bound. And whatever is limited/bound is finite. And whatever is finite is composite - and whatever is composite was brought into existence, and whatever is brought into existence must have a Creator.

Therefore, one who thinks the Creator is more than one must also assume that this creator was brought into existence. We already demonstrated, however, that the Creator is Kadmon (without beginning), and that He is the Cause of causes and the Beginning of all beginnings. Therefore, He must be one and as the verse says "You are the L-ord, You alone" (Nechemia 9:6). (end of proof)

> *some commentaries*
> (*Tov Halevanon*: there is a consensus that mikre (incident properties) do not apply to spiritual matters, (the nine attributes of mikre brought earlier): "Eich", "Kama" (brought earlier in this chapter), etc., because it is not relevant to speak of movement, place, or situation. Hence for spiritual things the only difference is in their Etzem/essence).
> "whatever is distinct is limited/bound" - i.e. any difference is a border. For once there is a difference between two things, namely, that one has something that is not in the other, this difference limits it in that it does not attain the matter in the other thing.
> "whatever is finite is composite" - i.e. you cannot have finiteness in something, namely, that its matter is different (less) than the other thing,

unless it is the effect of some cause. And an effect is a composite of two matters. Firstly, its own existence. Secondly, from the aspect of its cause. Therefore, it is necessarily mechudash (non-eternal).

Manoach Halevavos: The explanation of "limited/bound" is as follows. The matter of "limiting" something is to limit/bind it into its "type" and "difference". For example, a human being is a "living creature" that is "speaking". "Living creature" is its type which includes human beings, animals, and other living creatures, while "speaking" differentiates him from the animals and other living creatures. Hence, a man is necessarily composite of two things, namely, "type" and "difference". This is what he meant by "whatever is distinct is limited/bound", i.e. anything separated out of a group must have some matter which is "different" between it and what it was separated from which distinguishes it. And anything distinguished between itself and something else must be similar to it in some respect, namely, the "type" which included them together... "whatever is finite is composite", i.e. since it has a "type" which includes it and a "border", namely, its "difference", if so, it is composite of "type" and "difference"... (see there)... This matter is exceedingly deep.

He brings the Moray Nevuchim Part 2, ch.2. which the Shem Tov Commentary there explains: "if there were two creators, then there would necessarily be some matter which they would share in common in their both being "creators". Because if we say there are here two human beings, it is necessary that these two human beings share in common the matter of "being human", and it must also be that there is some matter for which they are separated from each other. Because if they were not separated, then they would not be two. And if there is in each one something which is not in the other, then each one is a composite of two things (since each one has what it is in common with the other and what separates it from the other. [note that these are deep spiritual ideas and should not be looked at in physical ways.], and neither one can be the First Cause nor of necessary existence. Therefore, each one is subject to causes (i.e. is an effect of a cause)...)

Pas Lechem: If the Creator is more than one, it must be that each part (supposed creator) has its own etzem (essence) by itself. If so, we must say that there is a separation between them, namely, some boundary which separates between their etzem since they are split...if so, since there is a boundary between them which separates them, and behold, each one is limited, since each one does not spread out infinitely, since that would leave no existence for the second. Therefore each has an end and a limit, if so, each has the attribute of extent and spreading out since behold its limit is the extent of its spreading out, and anything which has the attribute of extent and spreading out can receive divisioning (i.e. it is not of infinite character), and whatever can receive divisioning is composed of parts, and anything composite must be brought into existence, as we clarified earlier, that the parts precede it. And anything brought into existence has a Creator since a thing cannot make itself..

Marpe Lenefesh: ... Here is a quote from the Rambam (Yesodei Torah 1:7): "This G-d is one. He is not two or more, but one... If there were many gods, they would have body and form, because like entities are separated from each other only through the circumstances associated with body and form. Were the Creator to have body and form, He would have limitation and finiteness, because it is impossible for a body not to be limited. And any entity which itself is limited and defined [possesses] only limited and defined power. Since our G-d, blessed be He, possesses unlimited power, as evidenced by the continuous motion of the spheres, we see that His power is not the power of a body. Since He is not a body, the circumstances associated with bodies that produce divisioning and separation are not relevant to Him. Therefore, it is impossible for Him to be anything other than one. The knowledge of this concept fulfills a positive commandment, as [implied by Deuteronomy 6:4]: [Hear, Israel,] The L-ord is our G-d, The L-ord is one." End quote.

(*Translator*: I had some email correspondence with a great Chasidish Torah scholar/teacher which sheds light on this exceedingly deep subject. Since this is an important part, I am including the transcript of our correspondence (Disclaimer: I cannot defend or guarantee the accuracy of his answers. Also note that he often puts words in quotes "like" "this" because he is careful not to utter or write any words which he deems are not completely true):

[QUESTION:] the Shaar Yichud of Chovot Halevavot says that whatever is not totally infinite must be composite and hence mechudash (created/not eternal). Cannot understand clearly why. can you please explain?

[ANSWER:] (filled in)
(*Rabbi F.*) Something which is not totally infinite has to have some kind of a border or limitation like beginning, end, etc.

As such it has a "measurement" of some sort and "size" and "dimensions" also of some sort.

As such - it has to be composite - at least from what it "is" and its "borders" of limitations/definitions/descriptions etc.

And as such - it has to be a result of a previous "something" that either "made" it or "shaped" it or "defined" it - something which CAUSED its "borders" to be what they are.

And if so - there has to be a point of "time" where it did not "exist" and then started to exist by the "definitions" of its "borders"/"limitations" and alike - i.e. not "everlasting" and "infinite" - but "mechudash" - something that showed up somewhere along the time axis as "new" (HKB"H (G-d) never showed up on the time axis C"V as "new" that wasn't there beforehand.).

End of "proof."

[QUESTION:] trying to understand this. but what it "is" and its "borders" seems to be within itself, no?

for example, a square has its area, and its borders (perimiter). but both are within the area of the square, so there is no real distinction between inside the square and its borders. so how is this a composite of itself and its borders?

[ANSWER:] (filled in)
(Me:) trying to understand this. but what it "is" and its "borders" seems to be within itself, no?

(Rabbi F.) that is the entire point (!) - for something truly Infinite - you are right - for something which is not - these are 2 different things - that is the whole point.

(Me:) for example, a square has its area, and its borders (perimiter). but both are within the area of the square, so there is no real distinction between inside the square and its borders. so how is this a composite of itself and its borders.

(Rabbi F.) a square is a very general definition. There is infinite (really) number of possible squares. The specific borders derive the specific square. The "border" and "limit" the general concept into its specific measure. The "concept" and its "borders" are 2 separate entities.

[QUESTION:]
just to make sure I understand what you're saying, it sounds like anything finite is composite in that it was preceded by the framework which set its borders.

So it is not really composite by itself, just that it must be preceded by the framework which limits it, hence it cannot be eternal.

If so, it is composite in the sense that it needs a framework, not that it itself is composite in its constitution. For example, matter needs space, so space must precede matter. Is this correct?

[ANSWER:] (filled in)
(Me:) It sounds like anything finite is composite in that it was preceded by the framework which set its borders.

(Rabbi F.) yes.

(Me:) So it is not really composite by itself, just that it must be preceded by the framework which limits it hence it cannot be eternal.

(Rabbi F.) not exactly - once it is set with its borders - it is also "composite" by itself as well - it is intrinsic part of its "innate" "nature" - a "being" WITH "borders."

(Me:) if so, it is composite in the sense that it needs a framework, not that it itself is composite in its constitution. For example, matter needs space, so space must precede matter.

(Rabbi F.) correct in principle - WITH the correction above - matter is (obviously) composite in its "constitution."

(Me:) is this correct?

(Rabbi F.) now it is :)

[QUESTION:]
(I wrote earlier:) it sounds like anything finite is composite in that it was preceded by the framework which set its borders. (And you responded: "yes". kind of like saying an idea must be preceded by its inventor since the idea's existence depends on the inventor.)

so HBB"H is the framework of existence, or more precisely, existence itself, correct? (Hence, it is not relevant to ask "what created Him?" since He Himself is existence.)

If so, then why must He be infinite? Perhaps He is just infinite only in the sense that there is no existence besides Him. But perhaps existence itself is finite. Hence, HBB"H is everything, but everything is not necessarily infinite.
Like space. Space holds everything physical but it is not infinite (as he explained earlier and which I quoted in chapter 5).

[ANSWER:] (filled in)

(Me:) so HBBH is the framework of existence, or more precisely, existence itself, correct? (Hence, it is not relevant to ask "what created Him?" since He Himself is existence.)

(Rabbi F.) yes - HE is the existence - HE is the framework - and HE is the borders.

(Me:) if so, then why must He be infinite?

(Rabbi F.) because there is ONLY ONE TRUE MEANING of INFINITY - and this IS HE - so HE has to be INFINITE.

(Me:) Perhaps He is just infinite only in the sense that there is no existence besides Him.

(Rabbi F.) that is a built-in-contradiction!! "Infinite" in only "one" sense - or even in huge finite number of senses - is already a limitation that limits HIS TRUE INFINITY (which is in INFINITE ("number" of) senses).

(Me:) But perhaps existence itself is finite.

(Rabbi F.) existence of the creating is finite - HIS existence is INFINITE in ALL INFINITE ("number of") senses.

(Me:) Hence, HBB"H is everything,

(Rabbi F.) true.

(Me:) but everything is not necessarily infinite.

(Rabbi F.) if the line above is correct (and it is) - then this one cannot be correct.
"Everything" is INFINITE in HIS senses of "Everything" - the "everything" we know - even all the worlds etc. - it is NOT HIS EVERYTHING.

(Me:) Like space. Space holds everything physical but it is not infinite.

(Rabbi F.) NO - in this "comparison" the "container" and the "content" are both finite.
HBB"H as the "container" is INFINITE and the "CONTENT" (the worlds and the creations in them) IS finite.

[QUESTION:]

have been thinking alot about this border thing, and even asked around but
nobody seems to know.

1. This whole idea that whatever is finite is intrinsically composite as a
"being with borders".

normally the word "composite" is used to say something is made up of two
or more constituents. This "border" is not a "constituent" but sounds more
like a conceptual idea.

Electrons or quarks for example, have no internal structure and are
basically point-particles so they cannot have any kind of physical border
encircling them. so what is their border? is it something tangible or is it just
a concept?

For example two electrons are identical in every respect. the only
difference between the two is that this one is not that one. is this what you
mean by border?

Basically, I'm just having a very hard time understanding what this
"border" is and how it is considered a "constituent" to make the thing a
"composite".

[ANSWER:] (filled in)
(Me:) have been thinking alot about this border thing, and even asked
around but nobody seems to know.
1. This whole idea that whatever is finite is intrinsically composite as a
"being with borders". Normally the word "composite" is used to say
something is made up of two or more constituents. This "border" is not a
"constituent" but sounds more like a conceptual idea.

(Rabbi F.) correct - in a way - because truly - even an "idea" - IS a
SPECIFIC "something" - "knowing" "something" is ALREADY "fitting" it
into "frames" of words thoughts or anything that the soul uses in order to
RELATE to "it."
So REALLY - the existence of a "border" and ANY type or sort - IS
already 100% classified as "composite."

(Me:) Electrons
(Rabbi F.) not a good example - see further here. :)
(Me:) or quarks
(Rabbi F.) same comment.
(Me:) [Electrons] for example, have no internal structure and are basically
point-particles so they cannot have any kind of physical border encircling
them. so what is their border?

(Rabbi F.) they have numerous REAL borders - momentum - speed - position - energy - spin - color - charge - mass - weight - SO many parameters (and more) that border them to be each one what they are!

(Me:) is it something tangible or is it just a concept?

(Rabbi F.) VERY tangible! - how else would you be able to write me this email (one out of "trillion" examples of how and where the knowledge of their borders (= and their characteristics) is known used and applied)?!

(Me:) for example two electrons are identical

(Rabbi F.) no.

(Me:) in every respect.

(Rabbi F.) no. see above

(Me:) the only difference between the two is that this one is not that one.

(Rabbi F.) no. see (again?) above

(Me:) is this what you mean by border?

(Rabbi F.) ANY level, type, sort, meaning, or aspect of "definition" your mind uses in order to relate to "something" (and watch the 5 words precisely chosen paralleling the 5 levels of kotz-Y-K-V-K).

(Me:) basically, I'm just having a very hard time understanding what this "border" is and how it is considered a "constituent" to make the thing a "composite".

(Rabbi F.) now hopefully less hard time and IY"H even EASY times!

(Me:) 2. I hear what you mean, that HBB"H is infinite and the creation is finite.

but how would you then define infinite?

(Rabbi F.) INFINITE is ONLY HBB"H - this is the ONLY "definition" that one can apply with our limited finite language and minds.
EVERYTHING else that uses this term is to start with a "loan" - we "borrow" this word from HIM (with his generosity) for essentially EVERY single FINITE concept - such a "built-in" contradiction - the reason you on

your own is able with a blink of an eye to dismiss the stupidities of the goyim as you do it so well below (and so did the KUZARI king! What a SMART guy he was!).

(comment: As a crude analogy, a video game has certain characters, each one having certain properties, abilities, or position on the screen, etc. These things must have been set by a computer programmer. They cannot just exist eternally, without beginning.

Hence, the only thing that can be Eternal (without beginning) is that which has no properties or limitations in any way. It is completely infinite and boundless in all respects. It has no parts or boundaries. This is a completely different "kind" of existence than anything we are familiar with. Anything else which has some sort of limitation or property cannot be eternal.)

[QUESTION:]
why can't we say the infinite framework is eternal and also the finite "squares" inside it are also eternal.

[ANSWER:]
If you have a square - it has boundaries - correct?

If the square is infinite - does it have boundaries?

Of course not it is - infinite.

If the square is at any possible size - but finite - it had boundaries - that define it - yes - of-course!

If it is finite - it has boundaries - if it is not finite - infinite - it has NO boundaries.

Obviously - square - is merely a - mashal (analogy) to everything - NOT - just - a "square".

It therefore seen - proven - to ANYONE who just has a minimal common-logical sense - that - the BOUNDARIES are always - GREATER - LARGER - BIGGER - BROADER - than - what's in them - in any number of dimensions! - even in math - in abstract structures and so-called by their spaces - their bounded spaces etc - ALWAYS - the boundaries - contain the space-volume-structure-etc!

Hence - there is no way for anything to be greater than its boundaries!

If HAVAYAH-EINSOF has boundaries even one - it means - the boundary - is coming - from something - greater - bigger!

Therefore - its uniqueness - is limited - finite - enabling-permitting empty spaces or existence of another G-d - G-D-FORBID!

[QUESTION:]
Just a question about how "anything which is finite (i.e. is not everything) must be preceded by the framework of its existence."

Physicists claim, there's no space or time before the supposed "Big Bang" so finite and infinite does not apply. How does one answer this?

Also, there was no time before the supposed "Big Bang" so there is no notion of "before and after". How can one answer this?

Can we say that "precede" means its existence depends on the framework, hence the framework "precedes" it in some non-time sense?

[ANSWER:] (filled in)
*(Me:)*Just a question about how "anything which is finite (i.e. is not everything) must be preceded by the framework of its existence." *(Rabbi F.)* who "gave" it its "definitions" (name, title, descriptions, borders etc.)? This source is the framework which preceded its existence. *(Me:)*Physicists claim, there's no space or time before the supposed "Big Bang" so finite and infinite does not apply. How does one answer this?

(Rabbi F.) First - to *start with* - what you write is about a reality as perceived and described by the Torah - so it is obvious that you are coming from somewhere *very* different and that has its own world-perspectives and teachings - so you do not *really* owe anyone any "explanation" - you are not there to "excuse" yourself - as if what you write about and the "big-bang" are "equivalent" in their level of legitimacy.

Second - the "big-bang" is a theory where one of its assumptions is based on a certain and specific "narrow-minded" behavior of time - namely - *linearly.* The theory "insists" - on inserting a non-linear process in it - while keeping the time-ticks linearly - "squeezing" different amounts of events into the same "ticks" of time. The more you go "back" - the more you need to squeeze into smaller and smaller segments of time. It is inevitable - that there is a point of *singularity* where there are infinite amounts of "events" in zero amount of time! In equivalent words ("inversion" of the space-time coordinates) - it is like saying that there are finite amount of events within infinite time - precisely the concept of Creation. So how do they go around it - simply - they IGNORE the existence of the singularity - they have NO explanation for it WHATSOEVER except TOTALLY WILD and CRAZY ideas - ideas that they CANNOT EVER check OR prove - they get away from the singularity by "inventing" more and more of those crazy ideas - sounding so "beautiful" and "inspiring" ("free leap of the vacuum" "quantum leap" "strings and sheets" and so many others - totally far-fetched and assumptions - just in order to justify their ideas of the expanding universe - deceiving everyone that they "know" everything that happened after it began (which is also ALL FULL of assumptions and a composite structure of pieces of theories that have NO (!) continuity (!) between them - only MORE assumptions) - and no matter how close you can get to the singularity - you can never "reach" it - and they make you "believe" that because they *supposedly* "traced" everything back to the first 10^{-35} of the "first second" or so (and that process itself is FULL of assumptions and holes) - then it means they "know" "everything" - where EVERY child that knows basics of math will tell you that no matter how "short" and "tiny" the time-interval - you can dissect it "infinite" amount of times and still remain with something finite. Even though it is small, but still there is infinite "ROOM" there for Infinite amounts of events - but they make you "believe" (and "suppress" by this the REAL problem) that if you are "SO" close - it must be that you actually "know" everything - while the truth is that this is NOT the case - they can't really hide the singularity and the fact that it IS their main unresolved problem.

(comment: i.e. no matter how close you are to the big bang, you are still infinitely far from explaining what happened at point zero.)

*(Me:)*Also, there was no time before the supposed "Big Bang" so there is no notion of "before and after". How can one answer this?

(Rabbi F.) there was time - "order of times" - no time in the sense of ticks we know now - but there was "order-of-times/events."
Namely, *sequence* of events did take place - even *before* the "time" when time as we know it began to "tick." This sequence of events (which are various type of process in the Infinite BB"H like the emanations of higher realms and even prior to it - definitions of certain borders levels etc. as part of certain levels of Infinity where elements of "measurements" of some sort were already part of it as preparation for the lower worlds etc. - these will also exist and take place *after* the end of the "ticking" era that we know from our *limited* borders of sensation and connection with Divinity.

We are in the "midst" of a limited era in which the borders and limitations are maximized. And part of it is the existence of the sensation of the "ticking" of time - [which is] one "certain" type of "time-sensation." But there are more types of time - like above - sequence of events priorities first and last order of things etc. - which are different types of time - something the "science" obviously does not include in its "definitions" and is using just *one* type of time as if it is the only type of time. All the other types of time are not limited to the physical existences and the "ticking"-type-of-time. They are all Infinite in nature (and from them descended the very limited and specific type of *our* "ticking"-time). Science "insists" on and can deal only with the "ticking"-time - and even that, it knows how to deal with it *only* in a *linear* manner - one of the causes for its false description of the "universe" - its size and its date etc.

Trying to argue with them *from* their own limited system is like trying to explain to a creation that lives on a curved surface which is extremely small relative to the curvature and thinks and even measures its world as flat - even though it isn't. Only from a hugely bigger "astronomical" perspectives is when you can see that the curvature actually is the true description.

In a way - phenomenon related to the theory of relativity in very high speed did to our concept of time a similar change in terms of *high* speeds - *much* higher than the speeds we live in and experience - speeds that do not exist in daily life (except the light) that for many years were counted as "infinite." When these speeds were acknowledged as "high but finite" instead of "infinite" - countless realizations of the curved behavior of time and space were revealed to the human mind to see that our reality is not at all linear - it is only a good linear approximation for very very low speeds.

And yet - for all practical senses and even when knowing all these facts - for essentially almost all humans - these curved behavior of space and time are all totally foreign and unaccepted as if it is a fantasy mamash.

The same idea but different is true regarding the nature of time as "ticking" being part of much broader concepts of time which are different in nature - and only in very very "low" "speeds" of time (i.e. "ticking") - it appears as the "only" type of time. However - if time were to "tick" faster than we are used to - *much, much* faster - our consciousness will be open to naturally see the broader meaning of time and its INFINITE "curve" and nature - something that the limited concepts of it, including accepting its pace of ticking as "constant" "eternal" and "axiomatic" by the limited scientists - are merely "linear" approximation of the actual truth.

(Me:) Can we say that "precede" means its existence depends on the framework, hence the framework "precedes" it in some non-time sense?

(Rabbi F.) I believe that the above "teaching" covers *and* explains the meaning of the "yes" to this question. Good for you to think in this manner!
END OF THREAD

In a separate correspondence, a friend of mine asked him the question: "How can I remember (or even better -- be naturally motivated) to ask G-d for help throughout the day?", he answered:

(Rabbi F.) with the thought that HE is the ONLY ONE, that is the ONE and ONLY - i.e. there are those that are only one of them (like people - each one there is only one) - namely - there are those that are one but not the only one because there are others that are also people - but HBB"H is not only ONE - but he is truly the ONE and ONLY ONE - NOTHING like it exists. This is why HIS "existence" as the Sages call it is INTRINSICALLY NOT as all other existences - that HIS PRESENCE is NOT like any other presence - and therefore HIS EXISTING PRESENCE is ALWAYS there to speak ask and communicate - in INFINITE (!) ways and forms that are ALWAYS available to one that seeks it truly with his kavanah and knowledge of HIS BEING as the ONLY BEING.
END OF ANSWER

With these introductions, we will understand the following passage in the Tanya (Likutei Amarim ch.22): "However, The nature of G-d is not like that of a creature of flesh and blood. When a man utters a word, the breath/sound emitted in speaking is something that can be sensed and perceived as a thing apart, separated from its source... But with the Holy One, blessed be He, His speech is not, separated from His blessed Self, for there is nothing outside of Him, and there is no place devoid of Him. Therefore, His blessed speech is not like our speech."
Back to the Shaar Yichud...

THE FIFTH ARGUMENT

The fifth argument, from the concepts of plurality and unity as follows. In his book, Euclides defined unity as: "Unity is that property through which we say of any thing that is one". This means that by nature, unity precedes the individual thing, just as we say that heat precedes a hot object. If there were no "unity", we could not say of anything that it is one.

(Marpe Lenefesh: If we see some unity and we call it "one", it must be that there is something else which exists whose unity is absolute, and from which stems this characteristic to also call the thing we see as a "unity", as we say on an object which is now hot, that there must be something intrinsically hot (fire/energy) from which it received its warmth, and that we also call "hot", as he will explain later)

The idea which we need to form in our mind of unity is of oneness that is complete, a uniqueness, that is absolutely devoid of composition (that we cannot join anything to this unity - *ML*) or resemblance (there is nothing similar to Him - *ML*). Free, in every respect of plurality or number, that is neither associated with anything nor dissociated from anything.

> (*Pas Lechem*: since association or dissociation only applies to things with some form of similarity, but He is the singular Unity which has no resemblance in any form whatsoever.
>
> *Marpe Lenefesh*: No "number" means the concept of numbers does not apply to this unity, since it is absolute unity which has nothing after it. But if we describe Him as "one", we would be standing by Him since "Ein Od Milvado" (there is nothing besides Him), because if there were other things like this, we would be able to count them, hence the true Unity has no number. The idea of plurality is the opposite of this...)

The idea of plurality is that of a sum of unities. Plurality therefore cannot precede unity of which it has been formed. If we conceive something plural with our intellect or perceive it through our senses, we will know with certainty that unity preceded it, just like when counting things, the number one precedes the rest of the numbers. Whoever thinks the Creator is more than one, must therefore nevertheless concede that there was a preceding unity, just as the numeral one precedes the other numbers, and just like the notion of unity precedes that of plurality. Hence, the Creator is absolutely One, and Eternal (Kadmon), and none is Eternal but He as written: "Before Me no G-d was formed, nor shall any be after Me" (Isaiah 43:10).

> (*Tov Halevanon*: The number one precedes all of them since, for two things, there is something which precedes them by nature, namely, unity. And that which is Eternal (without beginning) cannot have any matter whatsoever preceding it.

THE SIXTH ARGUMENT

The sixth argument, from the Mikre (incidental) properties that attach to everything that is plural. Plurality is an incidental property ascribed to the Etzem (essence), and comes under the category of "Kamus" (quantity). Since He is the Creator of essence and incident, none of these attributes can be ascribed to His glorious Being. For, it having been clearly demonstrated through scripture and reason that the Creator is above and beyond all comparison with, and similarity to, any of His creations, and seeing that plurality which adheres to the essence of anything that is plural is an incidental property - this property cannot be fittingly ascribed to the

Creator's glorious Essence. And if He cannot be described as plural, He must certainly be One because there is nothing in between the two possibilities, as Chana said: "There is none holy as the L-ord: for there is none beside You" (Shmuel I 2:2).

THE SEVENTH ARGUMENT:

If the Creator were more than one, then either each one of these hypothetical creators is capable of creating the universe by itself or could not have done so without the help of the other.

If any one of them is capable - the other Creator is superfluous, since the first is capable without him and does not need (the help) of the other. (and since he is not needed, and there is no evidence for more than one Creator, why should we be in doubt or be concerned for his existence? - *PL*)

And if the creation of the world cannot be completed without their partnering together, then no single one of them had full and complete strength and capacity. Each lacked the necessary power and ability and was weak. What is weak is finite in strength and essence. What is finite is bound. Whatever is bound - is composite. Whatever is composite has been brought into existence, and anything brought into existence must have some one who brought it into existence (a Creator).

Hence, what is weak (finite) cannot possibly be Eternal since the Eternal does not fall short in any respect nor stands in need of another's help. Therefore, the Creator is not more than One.

(*Tov Halevanon*: This proof was similar to the fourth proof, except that there he built the proof from the matter of difference or boundary that must exist between them. There, he did not get into the matter of finiteness but instead came from the aspect of difference and border. Here he started from the argument of finiteness, namely that its power must be finite, and then ended with the argument of border - because it's all the same thing. (i.e. its a different way of saying the same thing). He repeated it [differently] to strengthen it and impress it in the mind of the reader.

If it were possible for the Creator to be more than one, it would also be possible that there would be disagreement between them in the creation of the world and that the matter would not have been completed. Since we find that all of this world follows one order, and a uniform movement for all of its parts, which does not change over generations nor does it seem to change in the nature of its conduct, therefore, we know that its Creator and Ruler is One, and that none besides Him alters His work or changes His rule, as scripture says: *"And who, as I do, shall call, and shall proclaim it, and set it in order for Me" (Isaiah 44:7)*, and David said: *"Forever, O L-ord, your word is stands fast in heaven; Your faithfulness is unto all generations: You have established the earth, and it abides" (Ps. 119:89-90)*

The Creator's perfect governance which we observe in His creatures (also indicate His unity - Rabbi Hyamson). For government can be perfect and abidingly consistent, smoothly in one way only when there is a single individual making decisions and conducting the matter, as in the king ruling a country or in the soul controlling the body.

Thus Aristotle said in his book on the subject of unity: "it is not good to have many heads, but rather to have only one head". So too Solomon said: "For the transgression of a land many are the princes thereof" (Mishlei 28:2).

> *Pas Lechem*: That when the people are rebelling and sinning to G-d, G-d will appoint on them multiple rulers, and automatically the governance will fail and the country will fall apart and be ruined...as in the second temple era where the governance fell in the hands of 3 strong rulers...as mentioned in the book of Josephus until the land became corrupted and destroyed through them.
>
> If we had evidence of any disagreement in the creation or conduct (ex. laws of physics change sometimes) of the world, it would be possible to suspect that perhaps there is a second G-d...

What we brought here should be enough for the understanding person (and not stubborn to hang on to wings of stubbornness and far off, stretches of the imagination answers - *TL*), and this should suffice to answer the believers of dual gods or the trinity gods of the Christians, and others. For when we establish the unity of the Creator of the world, all those who claim that He is plural will be automatically refuted (since in clarifying the unity there are no difficulties and no far off answers - *TL*). Note it well.

*** CHAPTER 8 ***

The distinction between true (absolute) unity and conventional unity is as follows.

> *Tov Halevanon - "conventional"* (lit. passing) - that this term is said in passing only, without intent of its precise meaning.

The term "one" is derived from the concept of "unity". The term is used in two senses. One of them is mikri (incidental), which is the conventional unity. While the second is in essence and enduring - this is true (absolute) unity.

> *Tov Halevanon* - For example, one man does not have absolute "unity" due to his being joined and composite of many parts. But he has some unity relative to two people
>
> *Tov Halevanon - Mikre* (incidental) is something which is not essential for the thing and it can exist without it, sometimes it is attached to it and sometimes not, while something which is in its essence is found on it always.

Incidental unity subdivides into two divisions. In one of these the character of multitude, collectivity, and aggregation is apparent in it, such as one genus which includes many species or like one species which includes many individuals, and like one man which is comprised of many parts or one army which includes many men.

Or like we say one Hin (measure), one Rova (measure) or one liter (ex. of rice or water) which contain smaller measures, each of which is also called "one" (even though each smaller measure can be broken down further - *TL*). Every one of these things we mentioned are called "one" conventionally, because the things included under the one name are alike. Every one of them may also be called "plural" since it includes many things which when separated and isolated will each be called "one". Unity in all these manners we mentioned is *Mikre* (incidental). Each is a unit from one perspective and plural from another aspect. (The term "absolute unity" does not apply to it since from one perspective it is correct to refer to it as plural - *PL*)

The second division of incidental unity is the unity attributed to a single individual, who though seemingly not plural and not a collection of several things, yet is essentially plural, - being composed of matter and form, essence and incident, susceptible to "creation" and "destruction", division and combination, separation and association, change and variation. (see commentaries)

Plurality must be attributed to anything for which any of these things we mentioned applies to, for they are contradictory to unity. Unity ascribed to anything essentially plural and variable in any way is undoubtedly *Mikre* (an incidental property) (not in its essence - *PL*). It is unity conventionally, but not in a true sense. Strive to understand this.

> *Pas Lechem "it is susceptible to creation and destruction"* - if so it changes from one form to another since it goes through many forms in its formation and likewise in its destruction until it ceases completely, as is known. Its formation is not completed suddenly in one instant. Likewise, its destruction does not occur suddenly without stages, one form to another. Hence, it is correct to ascribe to it plurality, since it necessarily has a "beis-kibul" (ability to receive) all of its potential stages. understand this.
> *"division and combination"* - i.e. that the thing can be divided. Hence, one can divide it or leave it as is in its assembled state. This is from the aspect of itself.
> *"separation and association"* - is from the aspect of relative to something else. That it can be separated from it by distance or associated with it by being in close proximity...

True (absolute) unity is also of two kinds. The first in abstract thought and the second in actual reality.

The abstract thought version is numerical unity, namely, the root and beginning of all numbers. It is the sign and symbol of a beginning unprecedented by any other beginning. For every true beginning is termed "One", as for example: *"And there was evening and there was morning, one day" (Gen. 1:5)*. Instead of saying "the first day", the verse uses the term "one (day)", because the term "one" refers to any beginning unprecedented by any other beginning. When repeated, it is called "the second", and when repeated again - "the third", and so on until the number "ten", "a hundred", "a thousand", which are also units of new series, and so on to infinity.

> (*Pas Lechem*: In his fine words, he incidentally answered the question of Rashi in Genesis 1:5, who asked: "according to the order of creation, the verse should have said 'first day', but according to the author's words, the

intent of the verse was to teach on absolute creation, which was the beginning of everything, including time...

"the first abstract and the second actual" - the first is unity grasped conceptually in the mind, not associated with any real object. The second is unity on something which actually exists. This only applies to the Creator, as he will explain.

"numerical unity, namely the root and beginning of all numbers" - "one" is the root of all counts since every count is comprised of a sum of ones. Hence, "one" is the root and foundation on which one builds a counting. It is also the beginning of the count for it is impossible for a counting not to start with one.

Tov Halevanon: The "one" with which we count some number is itself not really a number, because a "number" is basically: the grouping together of matters. And also, "one" never makes plurality, as you say "one multiplied by one", "one multiplied by two", everything remains unchanged, unlike the number two and above which always multiplies over, since two multiplied by two is four, two by three is six, and similarly for all numbers. Therefore "one" is only the foundation of numbers and the sign of beginning....there is nothing truly one besides G-d, if so, perhaps this term was borrowed to refer to a beginning without prior beginning. Likewise the Midrash Bereishis Raba says: "the verse did not say 'the first day', but rather 'day one', to teach on the unity of G-d")

Therefore the definition of number is that it is a sum of units. The reason I called it "abstract thought" is because the notion of number is not perceived by the physical senses. Rather, it is grasped only in thought. It is the "numbered" object (ex. eggs, nuts - *PL*) alone which is perceptible to the five senses or by some of them.

Pas Lechem: *"perceptible to the five senses or by some of them"* - some things are perceptible to all the senses. For example, a goat has an appearance perceived by the sense of sight, a sound perceived by hearing, a taste, when eating its meat, an odor by the sense of smell, and a texture to the sense of touch. Some things are perceived only by some senses such as an apple which is not perceived by the sense of hearing. A rock is perceived only by sight and touch.

The second kind of true unity exists actually. It is that which is neither plural nor susceptible to change or variation, is not described by any of the corporeal attributes, is not subject to "creation" (rather He is Kadmon/without beginning - *TL*), destruction or end. Does not move (from place to place - *TL*) or waver (this refers to any change whether in *Etzem*/essence or *Mikre*/incident - *TL*), does not resemble anything nor does anything resemble it, and is not associated with anything. It is from all possible perspectives - true Unity and the root of everything plural. For as we already pointed out, unity is the cause of plurality.

> (*Pas Lechem*: "nor susceptible to change or variation" - it is not correct to ascribe to the true unity any change from one form to another, nor is it correct to ascribe variation to say it is the opposite of something else... a rock for example, cannot be termed "speaking" nor can it be termed "mute". So too, for the true Unity, it is incorrect to associate it with anything nor to say it is the opposite of something.
>
> "not described by any corporeal attribute" - such as anger, mercy, etc. whatever is said of Him is only metaphorical, as is known.
>
> *destruction or end* - he added "end" because there exists some things which don't become destroyed but they end, such as a specific time. It is incorrect to say that time was destroyed, but rather to say it was completed and ended.
>
> "It is, from all possible perspectives - true Unity" - i.e. from all possible perspectives of plurality that we turn to, we find Him completely devoid of it.
>
> *Tov Halevanon*: "does not resemble anything" - That He has no comparison whatsoever to any of His creations. For example, for one grain of sand versus the universe and everything in it, even though this is extremely tiny and this is extremely big, nevertheless there is a comparison between the two and a shared characteristic...and the difference between them is only in size, but relative to Him, one cannot make any comparison by any trait or measure, just like one cannot compare a voice to a picture)

The true unity has neither beginning nor finiteness because anything which has a beginning or finiteness necessarily must be subject to origination and destruction. And anything subject to these is also subject to change, and change is inconsistent with Unity. Hence, it would be more than one since it had existed as one thing and then changed into a different thing, and this necessarily implies plurality.

> (*Tov Halevanon*: A thing which changes must have two powers, namely, the power that it is now, and the power for that which it has the potential to become, and this contradicts unity.

Pas Lechem: Anything which changes must have had plurality in its first state, because it had two powers, one: what it was, and two, the beginning [potential] for the second existence which it changed into, and it is so that the philosophers agree that anything which changes had the potential for change inside it from the beginning, since if this is not so, from where did it come out afterwards to actuality? because that which is not in potential will never go out to actual. The commentators already expounded this from the verse "the day of death from the day of birth" (Eccles. 7:1). If so, behold, it has two powers, namely the previous entity and the beginning for the second entity, and it is not one.. Understand this.)

Similarity is also an incidental property (mikre) in anything which is similar (to something else), and whatever has an incidental property is plural. But absolute unity, in its glorious essence, is not subject to any incidental properties whatsoever in any respect.

Pas Lechem: *"similarity"* - A comparison term which is ascribed to the bearer of that comparison, that it is called "similar" to - it is *Mikre*, because it is attached to the *Etzem* (essence) of the bearer of that term.
"whatever has an incidental property is plural" - since behold it has essence and incident (2 things).

Tov Halevanon: If we say, for example, that Reuven is similar to Shimon, this comparison that we are comparing Reuven with is an "incident" that occurred to Reuven, that he is similar in that respect... Anything which has *Mikre* is considered more than something else, because *Mikre* is something which is added to the *Etzem* (essence) of that thing.

If one will claim that the quality of "unity" is itself an incidental property in the Absolutely One.

Tov Halevanon: It is possible to ask - How can we say on G-d that He is the absolute unity. Behold, this is also *Mikre*, it is a type of numerical property which is also ascribed to physical things. i.e. they are ascribed the incidental property of number, namely the number one, two, etc. If so, the true unity is also an incidental property and something additional attributed to His essence, and this is also plurality.

We will answer this as follows: The ascribing of true unity is intended to express the exclusion of multitude and plurality. When we describe Him as One, we mean only the negation of any multitude or plurality. But the true Unity, cannot be described by any attribute that would connote in His glorious essence any plurality, change, or variation. With this we have completed our words, regarding the true unity and the relative unity. Note it well.

> *Pas Lechem*: We are not ascribing to Him unity, just negating the opposite, namely plurality. Likewise, the intent for any "attributes" we ascribe to Him such as "Living", "Wise", "Powerful" is only to negate the opposite.

*** CHAPTER 9 ***

Tov Halevanon: he will now clarify that the Creator is the true Unity, in addition to what he clarified in chapter 7 that the creator is one)

The proof that the Creator is the true (absolute) Unity and that there is no true Unity besides Him is as follows.

Any composite thing only comes completely into existence when the parts of which it is comprised join together and unite. The association (of the parts) is the unity.

And likewise, the existence of something composite is not possible without the (possibility of - *TL*) dividing (or disintegrating) the parts of which it is comprised, since composition necessarily implies more than one part. The divisioning of the parts is plurality.

And since the signs of composition, synthesis, and arrangement are found in the universe as a whole as well as in its details and parts, in its roots and derivatives, it is necessarily subject to synthesis and division, and must contain the basic principles of Unity and Plurality.

And since, in essence, Unity precedes Plurality, just like the number one precedes the other numbers, it follows that the First cause of everything that is plural, which was at the head of all beginnings is itself not plural since all things plural are preceded by unity.

(*Tov Halevanon:* - The head of all beginnings cannot possibly be plural, since if it were plural, then unity must have preceded it, and we already said that He is the head of all beginnings.

And since causes must reach a limit at their beginning, and it is not possible for a thing to make itself, therefore it is impossible for the cause of unity and plurality to itself be of unity and plurality like them (since that would necessitate another unity that preceded it - *TL*)

And since the First Cause of the creations cannot itself be plural nor a combination of plurality and unity, it must necessarily be that the Cause is a true (absolute) Unity.

(*Manoach Halevavos*: It is not possible for the cause of unity and plurality to be unity and plurality like them since anything which has unity and plurality, namely, unity from one side and plurality from the other - is composite, and every composite is mechudash (created) and necessitates another maker since a thing cannot make itself)

And we have already demonstrated that the more one ascends the succession of causes, the fewer the causes will be until eventually the root of all numbers is reached - this is the true Unity, and this true Unity is the Creator.

(the following is another proof - *TL*)
Furthermore, it is known that anything which is found in something as an incidental property must also exist in something else as its true essence and cannot be separated from that (something else) without destroying it. For example, hotness, an incidental property of hot water, is the permanent essence in fire. Or, moistness, an incidental property in various objects, is permanent essence in water.

(*Marpe Lenefesh*: hotness can only leave the fire if the fire is completely destroyed because it is in its essence whereas for hot water, even if the hotness leaves the water, the water remains in existence because the hotness was in the water only as an incidental property)

And it is known that anything which is found in an object as an incidental property, that object must have received the incidental property from something else for which that incidental property is in its essence, such as hotness in hot water which is incidental in the water. It was given to the water from fire whose hotness is in its essence or some other energy source. And when we see moisture in moist things as an incidental property, we know that it was transferred to them from water whose wetness is in its essence. Similarly for all things, if we examine their matters.

Pas Lechem: Any quality that we find in a subject as an incidental property, namely, that it is not a quality in its essence but rather only an incidental property attached to it, we will know for certain that this quality must be found in another subject as a true name reflecting its essence. Since the quality is "essence" in that thing its name is called on it in truth, not as a borrowed, passing term. Therefore, it is called its true name.

He brought as an example, hotness in hot water, that even if we never saw fire but only saw hot water and we know that hotness is not an "essence" property in water and is just acquired and attached to it from outside - from this we would understand that there must exist something for which hotness is a quality in its essence and from there the water acquired this property as an incidental property, namely, from fire (note: one can heat water without fire, for example through friction or radiation. I think he means here the foundation of fire which is general manifested energy)

Through this principle we can direct our words to the matter of unity. Since unity is found in every created thing as an incidental property, as we introduced, it necessarily follows that it must be a true and permanent essence in the Cause of all created things, and from it all created things derived the matter of unity as an incidental property, as we explained.

When we investigated the matter of true (absolute) unity among the created things, we did not find it to be absolute or permanent in any of them. If we try to apply it to any of the sugim (types, i.e. broad category such as animals), minim (kinds, categories of a type such as horses), ishim (individuals, subcategories of kinds such as one individual horse), Etzemim (essence of things), (mikre) incidental properties, planets, stars, spiritual bodies (angels, he called them "bodies" since they are also of limited power - *PL*), numbers, numbered objects, (to summarize) anything which is finite and limited, and we try to call it one, and try to ascribe the term "unity" to it - this we cannot correctly do to call it "one" except in a passing (relative) sense. For each of them comprises things which are collectively called "one" due to their similarity and joining together in one respect.

But essentially, each of them is plural, being subject to multitude and change, division and separation, association and dissociation, increase and diminishment, motion and rest, appearance and form, and other incidental properties, whether specific to it or general that belongs to every creation.

(*Pas Lechem*: For example, appearance, form and change is specific to physical things of our world and do not apply to spiritual creations in the (higher) spiritual worlds... However the general incidental property of plurality and finiteness applies to all things except G-d.

Absolute Unity is not found nor truly ascribed in any created thing. And since unity exists among the created things as an incidental property, while all the evidence points to the Creator being One, we will deduce with certainty that the relative unity that we ascribed to any of the created things emanates from the true (absolute) One. And this true (absolute) unity can only be ascribed to the Creator of all. He is the true One. There is no true (absolute) Unity besides Him.

All the implications of absolute Unity we have mentioned befit Him alone. All the matters of plurality, incidental properties, change, motion, comparison, or any qualities which is not consistent with true Unity cannot be ascribed to Him, as David said: "Many, O L-ord my G-d, are Your wonderful works and Your thoughts towards us, there is no comparison to You" (Ps. 40:6), and "To whom then will you liken G-d? Or what likeness will you compare unto Him?" (Isaiah 40:18), and "Among the gods (angels) there is none like unto You, O L-rd; neither are there any works like unto Your works" (Ps. 86:8).

It has been clarified and demonstrated that the Creator of the world is the true Unity and that there is no other true Unity besides Him. For anything which is ascribed the term "one" besides the Creator, is a unity from one aspect but plural from another aspect. But the Creator is one from every respect as we explained. What we have brought in this matter should be sufficient for the intelligent person.

*** CHAPTER 10 ***

> (*Tov Halevanon*: After he brought proofs that G-d is the true Unity, he returns to clarify that G-d has no plurality from the view of the attributes of praise and good traits with which we praise G-d and which are found in scripture...)

(Translator: Rabbi Moses Hyamson's translation was heavily consulted here and in the previous few chapters due to the difficult language) Regarding the Divine attributes, whether known from reason or from scripture, which are ascribed to the Creator - the intentions in them are numerous according to the numerous creations and the kindnesses bestowed on them.

They (the Divine attributes) divide into two divisions: Essential (in essence) and Active (i.e. from His deeds).

> (*Marpe Lenefesh*: Some attributes are in Him as etzem (essence), even if He did not create the world, while others we call Him due to His deeds)

The reason we call them Essential (in essence) is because they are permanent traits of G-d, belonging to Him before the creations were created, and after their creation these attributes continue to apply to Him and to His glorious essence.

These attributes are three:
1. That He (permanently) exists
2. That He is One
3. That He is Eternal, without beginning.

> (*Pas Lechem*: Even after the creation no existing thing can be associated with Him in these three attributes...they can be ascribed exclusively to His glorious essence, unlike the "Active" attributes that the creations can associate with them a bit, as will be explained, and as the Sages say (Shabbat 133b): "cling to His ways, just like He is merciful so too be merciful, just like He is gracious, so too be gracious, etc.")

We ascribe to Him these three attributes and speak of them in order to indicate His Being and true existence, to call attention to His glory, to make human beings understand that they have a Creator whom they are under duty to serve (as to the question of why should we serve Him if He lacks nothing and needs nothing, this will be explained in gates 2 and 3).

We must ascribe to Him "existence", for His existence is demonstrated by proofs based on the evidence of His handiworks, as written: *"Lift up your eyes on high, and behold who has created these things? He that brings out their host by number: He calls them all by name. By the greatness of His might, and for He is strong in power; not one fails" (Isaiah 40:26).*

We must necessarily ascribe existence to Him because it is a principle accepted by our reason that for something which is non-existent no action or result can come. Since His works and creations are manifest, His existence is equally manifest to our intellect.

We ascribe to Him Eternity (no beginning), because rational arguments have demonstrated that the world must have a First (cause) which had no previous cause before it and a Beginning which had no prior beginning. It has been demonstrated that the number of causes cannot be infinite. It logically follows, that the Creator is the First Beginning before whom there is no Beginning, and this is what is meant by His Eternity, as written: *"From everlasting to everlasting, You are G-d" (Ps. 90:2)*, and *"before Me there was no god formed, neither shall any be after Me" (Isaiah 43:10).*

Regarding declaring of Him that He is One, we have already sufficiently demonstrated this by well known arguments and it has been established by clear evidence, that true Unity is inseparable from His glorious essence. This unity implies absence of plurality in His Being, the absence of change, transformation, incident, origin or destruction, joining or removal, comparison or association or any other properties of things that are plural.

It is necessary for you to understand that these attributes do not imply any kind of change in His glorious essence, but only to denote a negation of their opposite. What the attribution of them should convey in our minds is that the Creator of the world is neither plural, nor non-existent, nor created (which are the opposites of unity, existence, and Eternity - *PL*)

Likewise it is necessary for you to understand that each one of these three attributes we mentioned implies the other two, when we analyze them. The explanation of this is as follows:
When true Unity is the inseparable and permanent property of a thing, that thing must necessarily also be Eternally Existing (without beginning), since that which is non-existent cannot be ascribed neither unity nor

plurality. Hence if true (absolute) Unity is the attribute of any thing and essentially belongs to it, it logically follows that the attribute of Existence with its implications also belongs to it. It must also be Eternal (eternally existing) because true (absolute) unity neither comes into existence nor passes out of existence, neither changes nor is transformed. Hence, it must be Eternal, for it has no beginning (and no end, for what has no beginning is endless - Rabbi Hyamson). Hence, that which the matter of true Unity belongs has also the attributes of Existence and Eternity.

So too, we say that the attribute of permanent Existence, attributed to a thing, implies the attribution to it of absolute Unity and Eternity (without beginning).

> (*Manoach Halevavos*: "permanent existence" - this he derived earlier from the premises in chapter 5 that the world must have a Creator, for the number of beginnings cannot be infinite, and that a thing cannot make itself, hence the Creator's existence must be a permanent existence. For otherwise, how could He come to exist after He did not exist since a thing cannot make itself?)

It implies absolute Unity since that which permanently Exists could not have come into existence from nothing, and cannot pass from the state of existence into that of non-existence. Such a thing is not plural since that which is plural is not permanently existent, as it must have been preceded by Unity. Therefore, that which exists permanently is not plural, and is accordingly, One.

The attribute of Eternity (without beginning) also belongs to it, since that which exists permanently has neither beginning nor end, and is accordingly Eternal.

So too, we assert that the attribute of Eternity, belonging to any Being, also implies in that Being, the attributes of absolute Unity and permanent existence.

It implies Unity, since that which is Eternal has no beginning, and that which has no beginning is not plural, since all things plural have a beginning, namely, a (parent) unity. Therefore, that which is plural is not Eternal, and that which is Eternal can only be One. Therefore, the attribute of absolute Unity is implied in the attribute of Eternity.

Likewise, the attribute of existence is implied in that of Eternity. For the non-existent cannot be described as either Eternal or created.

We have clarified that these three attributes are one in meaning and imply the same thing. They do not imply any change in the Creator's glorious essence, nor do they imply any incidental property or plurality in His being, because all that we are to understand by them is that the Creator is neither non-existent, nor created, nor plural. If we could express His being in a single word which would denote all three of these attributes as they are understood by the intellect so that these three attributes would arise in our mind when the one word was used, we would use that word to express it. But since we do not find such a word in any of the spoken languages which would designate the true conception of G-d, we are forced to express it with more than one word.

This plurality in the Creator's attributes does not, however, exist in His glorious essence but is due to inadequacy of language on the part of the speaker to express the conception in one term. You must understand that, regarding the Creator, there is none like Him, and whatever attributes we speak of regarding Him, you are to infer from them the denial of their opposite. As Aristotle said "negating attributes of G-d gives a truer conception of Him than affirming attributes". For all affirmative attributes ascribed to G-d must necessarily ascribe properties of Etzem (essence) or Mikre (incidental properties), and He who created etzem and mikre has not the properties of His creatures in His glorious essence. But the denial of such properties to Him is undoubtedly true and appropriate to Him. For He is above all attributes and forms, similarity or comparison. Therefore, you must understand from these attributes that they refer to the negation of their opposites.

(*Marpe Lenefesh*: It is better to negate ascribing to the Creator attributes which are lackings on Him. For example, it is more correct to say that the Creator is not plural, not non-existent, not created, which are opposites, and which are more true than saying and affirming on Him that He is the "true Unity", "permanently existing", "eternal", because we are not capable of understanding what is true Unity,...)

THE ACTIVE ATTRIBUTES

The active attributes of G-d are those which we speak of the Creator with reference to His works. It is possible, when speaking of them, to associate Him with some of His creations. We were permitted, however, to ascribe these attributes to Him because of the forced necessity to acquaint ourselves with, and realize His existence, in order that we assume on ourselves the duty of His service.

We have already found that the Torah and the books of the Prophets extensively use these active attributes, as also in the Psalms of prophets and saints. They are used in two manners:

One, attributes which denote physical form such as in the verse "So G-d created man in His own image, in the image of G-d, He created man" (Gen. 1:27), "for G-d made man in His image" (Gen. 9:6), "by the word of G-d" (Numbers 9:18), "I, even My hands, have stretched out the heavens" (Isaiah 45:12), "in the ears of G-d" (Numbers 11:1), "under His feet" (Ex. 24:10), "the arm of G-d" (Isaiah 51:9), "who has not taken My soul in vain" (Ps. 24:4), "in the eyes of G-d" (Gen. 6:8), "G-d said in His heart" (Gen. 8:21), and other similar verses regarding physical limbs.

Two, attributes which denote bodily movements and actions, as written: "and G-d smelled the pleasing aroma" (Gen. 8:21), "And the L-ord saw...and the L-ord regretted" (Gen. 6:5-6), "and G-d came down" (Gen. 11:5), "and G-d remembered" (ibid 8:1), "and G-d heard" (Numbers 11:1), "Then the L-ord awakened as one out of sleep," (Ps. 78:65), and many more activities of human beings like these attributed to Him.

Our Rabbis, when expounding the scriptures, paraphrased the expressions used for this class attributes and were careful to render them in an honorable way, and ascribed them all to the "glory of the Creator". For example, the verse "behold G-d stood over him" (Gen. 28:13), they rendered - "the glory of G-d was present with him"; "and G-d saw" (ibid 6:5), they rendered - "it was revealed before G-d"; "and G-d came down" (ibid 11:5)- "the glory of G-d was revealed"; "and G-d went up" (ibid 35:13) - "the glory of G-d departed from him".

They rendered everything in a reverential way, and avoided attributing them to the Creator in order not to ascribe to Him any kind of physicality or incidental property.

The great master, Rabeinu Saadia, already expounded sufficiently at length on this in the Sefer Emunot Vedeot, in his commentary on parsha Bereishis, parsha Vaera, and in Sefer Yetzira, and we do not need to repeat his explanations in this book. What we are all agreed upon is that necessity forced us to ascribe physicality and to speak of Him with the attributes of

His creations in order that human beings can have some way to grasp the existence of the Creator. The books of the prophets connoted Him with corporeal terms because these are closer to our mind and understanding.

If they had spoken of Him in a more accurate fashion, using words and matters connoting spiritual things, we would not have understood neither the words nor the matters, and it would have been impossible for us to worship something which we do not know, since it is not possible to worship an unknown. Therefore it was necessary that the words and concepts be according to the understanding ability of the listener so that the matter will first be grasped in the listener's mind in an understandable, corporeal sense from the concrete terms. Afterwards, we will enlighten him and explain to him that all this was only metaphorical, to bring the matter close and that the true matter is too fine, too sublime, too exalted, and too remote from the ability and powers of our mind to grasp. The wise thinker will endeavor to remove the husk of the terms and their corporeality and will ascend in his mind step by step until he will reach the true intended meaning according to the power and ability of his mind to grasp.

The foolish and simple person will conceive the Creator in accordance with the literal sense of the metaphor, and if he assumes the service of His Creator, and he endeavors to labor for His glory, he has in his simpleness and lack of understanding, a great valid excuse because a man is held accountable for his thoughts and deeds only according to his ability, intelligence, understanding, strength, and material means. But if the foolish is capable of learning wisdom and he neglects it - he will be held accountable for it and punished for his lacking and refraining from study.

If the scriptures had employed more accurate, truer terminology, then nobody would have understood it except the wise, understanding reader and most of mankind would have been left without religion and without Torah (guidance) due to their limited intellect and weak understanding in spiritual matters. But the word which may be understood in a material sense will not damage the understanding person because he recognizes its real meaning, and it is at the same time beneficial to the simple person so that it will fix in his heart and mind that there is a Creator which it is his duty to serve.

This is similar to a man who came to visit a friend who was of the wealthy class. His wealthy host felt a duty to provide his friend with a meal and also food for the animals which he brought with him. The wealthy man sent to him an abundant quantity of barley for his animals and a small quantity of food fitting for him but only enough for his need.

So too, the scriptures and the books of the pious abundantly employed material analogies when referring to the attributes of the Creator according to the understanding of the masses and according to the common language which the masses converse. Therefore, when referring to this, our Rabbis said "the Torah speaks like the common language of men" (Bava Metzia 31b). And the scriptures gave few hints of spiritual matters which are intelligible only to the (few) wise and understanding men.

In this way, even though all people have different views of G-d's glorious essence, nevertheless, all people are equal with regard to knowing the existence of the Creator (and that it is one's duty to serve Him - *ML*).

Likewise we will say for all subtle matters found in the Torah such as the reward in the next world or its punishment.

(*Tov Halevanon*: Since the good reward cannot be understood by a foolish or a simple person. The crude cannot understand spiritual pleasure, only physical pleasures, and likewise only physical punishments. Therefore, the scriptures speak only of physical reward and punishment, and limited in few places of spiritual reward and punishment)

And likewise we will say for the clarification of the inner wisdom (the duties of the heart) which was our intention to clarify in this book. The Torah was very brief in expounding their matters, relying on the intelligent men. The Torah only hinted at it to arouse one on it, such as mentioned in the Introduction of this book, so that anyone who is able to enquire and investigate them will be aroused to do so until he has understood and mastered them as written: "those who seek G-d will understand all things" (Mishlei 28:5).

(*Manoach Halevavos*: For spiritual matters, the Torah gave few hints because this is only for the wise, and the truly wise have a single, common viewpoint, and all of them grasp exactly the same matter with only these few hints, according to what is fitting and possible for them, because the false and erroneous ways are numerous but there is only one way of truth.)

The prophet (Moshe Rabeinu) has already warned us against thinking that G-d has a form or likeness as written "Take therefore good heed unto yourselves; for you saw no manner of form on the day that the L-ord spoke unto you in Horeb (Sinai) out of the midst of the fire" (Deut. 4:15), and "And the L-ord spoke unto you out of the midst of the fire: you heard the voice of the words, but saw no form; only you heard a voice" (ibid 4:12). When saying "take good heed", he warned us in our minds and thoughts to not represent the Creator under any form (tavnis) or to conceive Him under the likeness (demus) of anything or any comparison (dimyon) since your eyes never perceived any form or likeness when He spoke to you.

> (*Pas Lechem*: "Tavnis" is the form. It is called "tavnis", derived from the (similar Hebrew letters of the) word "binyan" (building), since the form is like a building, built from the assembly of specific parts according to a determined amount. This term is used for living creatures such as "tavnis of all fish" (Deut. 4:18), since they are built and synthesized from different organs/parts. And they are of form. This term is also used in buildings such as "tavnis heychal" (the form of the inner temple), unlike fire or wind where the term "tavnis" is not relevant to them since they don't have a specific form. It is only correct to employ for them the term "demus" (likeness), since they are grasped in likeness by a mirror. But G-d is beyond any form or likeness...and for other types of physical characteristics such as sleep, laughter, joy, sadness, or the like he said "dimyon" (comparison), that would make comparable through these acts to His creations. Understand this.)

And it is written "To whom will you liken to G-d? What likeness will you compare to Him?" (Isaiah 40:18), and "to Whom will you liken Me that I will be equal to, says the Holy One" (ibid 40:25)

> (*Pas Lechem*: Behold not only is it beyond the power of man to conceive in Him a likeness but even G-d testifies on Himself that He has no connection whatsoever to any kind of likeness.)

And it is written: "For who in the heaven can be compared unto the L-ord?" (Ps. 89:7), and "Among the mighty ones there is none like You, O L-ord" (Ps. 86:8), and many more like this.

Since it is impossible to form a representation of Him with the intellect or picture Him with the imagination, we find that Scripture ascribes most of its praises to the "Name" of G-d (and not to His essence - *PL*), as written: "And they shall bless Your glorious Name" (Nehemiah 9:5), and "that you may fear this glorious and revered Name" (Deut. 28:58), and "Let them praise Your Name, great and revered" (Ps. 99:3), and "of My Name he was afraid" (Malachi 2:5), and "But unto you that fear My Name shall the sun of righteousness arise with healing in its wings" (Malachi 3:20), and "Sing unto G-d, sing praises to His Name, extol Him that rides upon the skies, whose Name is the L-ord" (Ps. 68:5).

All this is in order to honor and exalt His glorious essence because, besides clarifying that He exists, it is impossible for us to clarify in our minds anything about His Being except for His great Name.

> (*Pas Lechem*: Which the Torah has taught us that He is called by this Name... it teaches on the "revelation of His glory".
>
> *Marpe Lenefesh*: This is the "shem hameforash", the "shem haetzem" (name of essence), "this is My Name forever" (Ex. 3:15). This name was not known, rather G-d revealed it to the prophets. All the other names are taken from the honoring (titles) of humans and all of them have an explanation and definition, such as "Adon-ay" which is like "Adoney Yosef" (the masters of Yosef), and the judges are called "Elohim", etc. unlike the "Shem Hameforash" as the Kuzari extensively wrote about (Maamar 4 ot 1-3).
>
> Tov HaLevanon - His true name, as He is. What we are not capable of uttering in its true way (Translator: perhaps he means the 72 letter name uttered by the Kohen Gadol on Yom Kipur)

But as for His glorious essence and His true nature - there is no picture or likeness that we can grasp in our minds. Therefore, His Name is frequently changed in the Torah and likewise in the books of the prophets.

Because we cannot understand anything about Him except for His Name and that He exists. His glorious Name is also associated with heaven and earth and the Spirits, as Abraham said: "And I will make you swear by the L-ord, the G-d of heaven and the G-d of the earth" (Gen. 24:3), and Yonah said: "I fear the L-ord, the G-d of heaven" (1:9), and Moshe said: "the G-d of the spirit of all flesh" (Numbers 27:16). And the verse proclaims: "Behold, I am the L-ord, the G-d of all flesh" (Yirmiya 32:27).

> (*Tov Halevanon*: (His Name is changed in the Torah) such as the name "Yud-Hey-Vuv-Hey" which teaches that He was, is, and always will be. Or the name "Adon-ay" which teaches that He is master over the creations, or the name "Elo-him" - that He is powerful and all-capable, or the name "Sha-day" - that He is "meshaded" the marachos. The verse adds "of heaven and earth" to teach that we do not completely understand His true Name but rather we see Him according to what we understand through His existence and deeds)

The reason for this is that He is known to us in the way possible through the traditions of our forefathers from whom we have inherited the knowledge of His ways, as written "For I have known him (Abraham), to the end that he may command his children and his household after him, that they may keep the way of the L-ord, to do righteousness and justice" (Gen. 18:19).

Perhaps, G-d revealed Himself to them because they were the only ones in their generation who took on to serve Him since the people of their generation worshipped other "gods" (idols, sun, moon, money, etc.)

Similarly we will explain for His being called (in scripture) "the G-d of the Hebrews" (Ex. 3:18), "the G-d of Yisrael" (Gen. 33:20), as the verse says "not like these is the portion of Yaakov for He is the Creator of all" (Yirmiya 10:16).

> (*Pas Lechem*: i.e. the verse has called G-d "the portion of Yaakov", also for this reason - since G-d chose Yaakov for His portion, namely, to perform His service)

And David said: "O L-ord, the portion of mine inheritance and of my cup" (Ps. 16:5). And if we were able to grasp His true nature, He would not be known to us through other things.

> (*Tov Halevanon*: His Divinity would not be a term described through our forefathers, heaven and earth, or "spirit of all flesh".)

Since it is not possible for our intellects to grasp His true nature, when referring to His glorious essence the scripture describes Him as the G-d of the choicest of His creations, rational or otherwise. Therefore, when Moshe Rabeinu asked G-d "when the Israelites ask me what is His name, what should I answer them?", G-d answered him: "so shall you say to the descendants of Israel: 'Ehe-ye' sent me to you'". And since G-d knew that the Israelites would not understand the true nature of this name (Ehe-ye), He added an explanation and said: "thus should you say to the Israelites: "The L-ord, the G-d of your forefathers, the G-d of Abraham, the G-d of Isaac, and the G-d of Jacob sent me to you, this... (Ex. 3:15)".

G-d's intent (to Moshe) in this was that if the people did not understand these words and their implications through intellectual reason, then tell them that I am known by them through the tradition they received from their ancestors. The Creator did not establish any other way to know Him except through these two ways, namely, (1) that which intellectual reason testifies through the evidence of His deeds which are visible in His creations, (2) and that of ancestral tradition, as scripture says: "Which wise men have told from their fathers, and have not hid it" (Iyov 15:18).

And since our perception of all existing things is through one of three ways:
1. Physical perception, such as through sight, hearing, taste, smell, or touch.
2. Through our reason, by which the existence of something is demonstrated from its indications and effects, until the reality of its existence and nature are established to us as if we perceived it with our physical senses.

> (*Marpe Lenefesh*: see end of chapter 6, the example of finding a letter with orderly style and uniform handwriting which demonstrates that there exists a man who knows how to write who wrote this letter, even though we never saw him. Hence, the handwriting is proof on him as if we saw him with our senses. So too for other similar things.)

This is called in the book of proverbs "understanding and intellectual discipline" (Mishlei 1:2-3).

> (*Manoach Halevavos*: The habitual practice, that a man habituates himself to understand the ways of proofs, and the premises and logical relationships to understand the intellectual things. And since a man must discipline himself for some time to understand the depth of the things difficult for him, until he is habituated in them - therefore it is called "intellectual discipline")

3. True reports and reliable tradition.

Since it is not possible for us to perceive the Creator through our senses, we can only know Him through true reports or from proofs on Him based on the evidence of His deeds.

> (*Marpe Lenefesh*: - the Kuzari wrote (Maamar 1 Ot 25): "it is the duty of the entire congregation of Israel to believe all that is written in the Torah, since it has been clarified to them that great assembly (at Mount Sinai) with their own eyes, and afterwards the ensuing tradition which is considered as if one saw it with his own eyes.

And since the proofs drawn from the evidence of His deeds in the creations are established and greatly numerous, therefore the attributes ascribed to

Him because of them are also numerous.

The saints and the prophets described His attributes in different ways. Moshe Rabeinu said "The Rock, His work is perfect, for all His ways are justice" (Deut. 32:4), and he also said: "He is G-d of gods, and L-ord of lords, the great G-d, the mighty, and the awesome" (Deut. 10:17), and also "He exacts justice for the fatherless and the widow" (Deut. 10:18). And G-d Himself described His own attributes as written: "And the L-ord passed by before him, and proclaimed: 'The L-ord, the L-ord, G-d, merciful and gracious, long-suffering, and abundant in goodness and truth, keeping mercy unto the thousandth generation, forgiving iniquity and transgression and sin, etc.'" (Ex. 34:6).

> (*Tov Halevanon*: All of these different attributes is because we are not capable of reaching even the tiniest part of praise that is befitting to Him.
>
> *Marpe Lenefesh*: We are not capable of understanding even one of His praises. For example, when we praise Him with the praise "righteous judge", "merciful", "gracious", - who is capable of knowing or making known how He is a righteous judge? Sometimes He decrees on this man poverty, destitution, and sufferings, and everything was just, while other times such a person lacks no good. Likewise for merciful and gracious or the like. Therefore any praise we say of Him due to the signs of His wisdom and deeds is not even a drop in the ocean compared to what is befitting Him.)

(That G-d possesses) these attributes we see from the evidence of His deeds towards His creations and also from the wisdom and power which His deeds reflect. And if we investigate this matter with our intellect and understanding, we will fail to grasp the smallest of the smallest of part of His attributes, as David said: "Many, O L-ord my G-d, are Your wonderful works which You have done, and Your thoughts which are toward us..." (Ps. 40:6), and "Who can utter the mighty acts of the L-ord? who can show forth all his praise?" (Ps. 106:2), and "And blessed be Your glorious name, which is exalted above all blessing and praise" (Nehemiah 9:5). And the Sages said in the Talmud (Berachos 33b):

A certain person led the prayer service before Rabbi Chanina and said: "the great, the mighty, the awesome, the powerful, the glorious, the potent, the feared, the strong, the powerful, the certain, and the esteemed G-d!". R' Chanina waited until he finished. When he finished, R' Chanina said to him: "did you complete all the praises of your Master? What need is there for all of this? even us, these three praises that we say (in the daily prayers), if not for the fact that Moshe Rabeinu said it in the Torah (Deut. 10:17), and the men of the great assembly came and established it in prayer, we wouldn't be able to say them! And you say all these praises and continue? It is analogous to a king of flesh and blood who had thousands upon thousands of golden coins, and they would praise him for possessing silver coins, isn't this a disgrace to him"?

And "to You silence is praise" (Ps. 65:2), to which our teachers said: "the best potion is silence, the more you praise a flawless pearl, the more you depreciate it" (Megila 18a).

Therefore, you should exert your mind until you know the Creator through the evidences of His works and not strive to know Him in His glorious essence. For He is exceedingly close to you from the side of His deeds but infinitely remote in any representation of His essence or comparison with it. As already stated, we will never be able to find Him in this way. When you arrive at the stage where you abandon (trying to find Him) through your thoughts and senses because He cannot be grasped in this way, and you instead find Him in the evidence of His deeds, as though He were inseparable from you - this is the pinnacle of knowledge of Him which the prophet exhorts us on in saying "Know therefore this day, and consider it in your heart, that the L-ord He is G-d in heaven above, and upon the earth beneath. there is none else" (Deut. 4:39).

One of the Sages said: "the more one increases knowledge of the Creator, the more one is awe-struck with regard to His nature" (realizes how little he understands of Him - *TL*).

Others said: "the truly wise person in the knowledge of G-d realizes his ignorance regarding His glorious essence while the ignorant person thinks that he understands G-d's glorious essence." (his understanding of G-d is in the way of materializing or through form or likeness - *TL*).

One of the Sages was asked on the Creator: "what is He?". He answered: "One G-d". The asker then asked: "What is He like?". He answered "A great King". He then asked: "Where is He?" He answered: "in the mind".

Tov Halevanon: i.e. the mind's eye, He cannot be found in any place. Only through reason we know His existence, that at least He exists

The asker: "I did not ask you on this"

Tov Halevanon: i.e. I did not mean to ask on existence in the mind, namely, intellectually where is He. Rather I meant, concretely - where is He in space?

The sage answered: "You asked me on attributes which apply to created things, not to the Creator. And the attributes which can be ascribed to the Creator, I replied to you, (and even these (i.e. one G-d, great King, that He dwells secretly in the hidden realm of intellect, are not befitting Him and - *ML*) the reason we ascribe them to Him is) because otherwise it would be impossible for us to know Him.

It is said of one of the Sages who would say in his prayer: "My G-d, where can I find You, yet where can I not find You. You are hidden and invisible yet everything is filled with You, similar to the verse "Do I not fill heaven and earth says the L-ord" (Yirmiya 23:24).

Tov Halevanon: He is not localized in any place whatsoever, but from the side of spiritual life force of everything created, it is clear to us that nothing is devoid of Him.

The pinnacle of knowing Him is to reach the stage where you admit and believe that you are completely ignorant of the truth of His glorious essence.

Pas Lechem: that you admit this before Him, and believe in your heart that this is truly so, and not like one who praises flesh and blood who says praises but His heart does not believe in them.

If you form in your mind a picture or representation of the Creator, strive to investigate His Being.

Tov Halevanon: through the proofs which demonstrate that the Creator is exalted above any likeness or form and that they are merely Mikre (incidental properties) of His creations.

Then you will clarify His existence.

Pas Lechem: you will clarify that His existence is hidden and beyond any comparison.

And you will reject any type of likeness of Him, until you will find Him only through the way of reasoning.

(*Pas Lechem*: "way of reasoning" - this refers to His deeds which are

| proofs to us of His existence.

The analogy of this:
We realize the truth of existence of the soul without perceiving of it any form or likeness, or appearance or smell, even though its effects are visible and its acts are recognizable in us.

Tov Halevanon: The soul does not occupy any "place", even though it fills the body, it has no physical place. And that which the Sages say that the soul dwells in the heart or the brain, this only refers to the beginning of its influence. But certainly it does not dwell there in space..

Likewise the intellect whose effects and signs are evident and noticeable, yet the intellect has no form or likeness, nor can we compare it in our thoughts.

Marpe Lenefesh: - through the intellect we think and understand things, yet we don't understand what it is.

And all the more so - the Creator of everything, which there is none like Him. And a philosopher said: "if our efforts to fully know the soul are vain, all the more so for the matter of the Creator".

Since we have reached until here in our discussion, it is not necessary to proceed further.

(*Marpe Lenefesh*: - Likewise the Kuzari wrote several times - that distant proofs and logical explanations cause a man to stray and bring him to apikorsut (heresy), and he extensively wrote on this throughout his just book. And his opinion throughout the book is that a man should be simple with G-d (Deut. 18:13) without investigations and proofs, see there)

The reason being, that it is our duty to be in fear and awe, and to guard from it, as some of the Sages said: "that which is beyond you, do not expound, that which is hidden from you, do not investigate. That which is permitted to you - contemplate. Do not have any business with hidden things" (Ben Sira in Megila 13a).

And our Sages said: "whoever is not concerned for the honor of his Creator it is better for him had he not been created" (Chagiga 11b). And they expounded on the verse "Shall it be told him that I speak? if a man speaks, surely he shall be swallowed up" (Iyov 37:20) - Whoever comes to speak the might of G-d will be destroyed (Talmud Yerushalmi Berachos 9a). And the verse says: "And he struck the men of Beth Shemesh, because they had looked into the ark of the L-ord" (Shmuel 6:19) (who stared at it with coarse hearts, without due awe- PL), and "It is the glory of G-d to conceal a thing" (Mishlei 25:2), which means to conceal His secret from men who are not wise (since due to their weak intellect there will remain nothing left for them to believe in - *TL*), and "the secret of G-d is with them that fear Him" (Ps. 25:14).

Furthermore regarding the physical senses we mentioned and the mental faculties, namely, memory, thought, imagination, counsel/will, recognition, which all refer to one power, namely, the mind which gives them the ability to apprehend things.

THE PHYSICAL SENSES

Each one of the (physical) senses has a distinct ability to perceive certain types of sensations which the other senses lack. For example, form and color can only be perceived by the sense of sight. Voices and music can only be perceived by the sense of hearing. Scent and various odors - only by the sense of smell. Various tastable things - only by the sense of taste. Hot and cold and many matters of quality - by the sense of touch.

Each sense has a power to perceive its relevant sensation to a definite extent, beyond which it is incapable of perceiving further. For example, sight has the ability to perceive something close by, and the further away one goes, the weaker its ability to apprehend it, until eventually it ceases to apprehend it completely. Likewise for the sense of hearing, and also for the other senses.

And it is impossible to grasp a sensation without the appropriate sense designated for it. One who strives to grasp it with a different sense will fail to accomplish his desire. For example, one who strives to grasp a melody with the sense of sight or visible things with the sense of smell or taste with the sense of touch - he will not be able to find them or grasp them, despite that they exist, because one is trying to perceive them without the limbs designated for perceiving these sensations.

Likewise we will say for the mental faculties we mentioned. Each one of them has a distinct power to perceive a specific thing which the others cannot, and a limit to which it can grasp no further, as we mentioned for the physical senses.

Likewise we will say for the mind (in total) which grasps intellectual things by itself or through proofs. For things that are close to it, it will grasp its truth directly through itself, while for things which are remote and hidden, it will grasp it through building proofs which point to it.

And since the Creator is infinitely remote and hidden for us from the side of His glorious essence, the intellect can grasp only that He exists. (since neither the physical nor the mental senses have any path or approach to build any proofs on Him - *TL*)

And if it strives to grasp His glorious essence or to imagine Him - even His existence will be hidden to it (and one will think that He does not exist - *TL*), because it strove to grasp something beyond its ability, as we mentioned for trying to grasp a sensation with the wrong sense.

Therefore, we must seek the existence of G-d through the evidence of His deeds in the creations - and these will be proofs on Him for us. And when His existence is established for us in this way, we must then cease and not seek to liken Him in our thoughts or to try to represent or figure Him in our imagination, or attempt to apprehend His glorious essence. For, if we do this, thinking we will understand Him more closely - even the realization of His existence will disappear from us, because anything we imagine in our minds will be other than Him. And scripture says: "Have you found honey? eat only as much as is sufficient for you, lest you be filled with it, and vomit it" (Mishlei 25:16).

> (*Tov Halevanon*: This verse is an analogy on the study of the hidden, that one should learn or examine only until the limit he is capable of grasping, since otherwise he will vomit even that which he learned and no emuna (faith) will be left in him.)

I saw fitting to try to bring the matter close to you using two illustrations.

The First of the two will demonstrate that each physical sense perceives its class of sensations and then it reaches its limit whereby the next physical sense picks up where it left off. And afterwards, it will also reach its limit and the next sense will start, and so on for all the senses. When they all reach their limit of perception, the intellect will then start to perceive what is in its power to apprehend. This will be demonstrated by means of one object.

Imagine that a stone was thrown far away. It makes a whistling/crashing noise and strikes a man. The man perceived with his sense of sight the appearance of the stone and its form. Then he perceives with his sense of hearing the whistling/crashing noise, then he perceives with his sense of touch the coldness and hardness of it. Afterwards, the physical senses cease to apprehend any more of the stone. Then the intellect perceives that the stone must have had a thrower who threw it, since it is clear to it that the stone did not move from its place by itself.

That which is normally perceived through the physical senses cannot be apprehended by the intellect without the physical senses. And all the more so, that which is normally perceived by the intellect cannot be perceived by the physical senses.

> *Marpe Lenefesh*: He is now giving a reason why the intellect did not perceive the matter from beginning to end. He says: it is impossible for the intellect to perceive that which is perceived by the physical senses, namely, the noise and the touch. If he did not see the rock, hear the noise, or feel the strike, the intellect would not have known whether or not there was any stone which produced a noise or struck. Likewise for other similar things. From there he will make a kal v'chomer (major to minor logical inference) - if the intellect cannot perceive that which is normally perceived with physical senses, all the more so that it is impossible for the physical senses to perceive what is normally perceived by the intellect (since the intellect is on a higher plane.

The second illustration will demonstrate that for spiritual matters, once we are convinced of their existence, it is not proper to investigate their nature because this approach only ruins our intellect. This is like one who tries to understand the sun from observing its light, radiance, shine, and its power to dissipate darkness. If he accepts its existence, he will benefit from it, use its light, and attain all that he seeks from it (and will know for certain that the sun exists - TL). But one who strives to study its roundness and focuses his eyes to stare at it - his eyes will dim and (eventually) their sight will be lost and he will not benefit from the sun. (not even from its light - TL).

The same thing will happen to us. If we study the existence of the Creator from the evidence of His signs in the creations, the wisdom manifested in them, His power shown in all His creations - we will think and we will understand His nature. Then our minds will be illuminated with knowledge of Him and we will attain all that is possible for us to attain, as written "I am the L-ord your G-d who teaches you for your benefit, who leads you by the way that you should go" (Isaiah 48:17).

But if we exert our minds to understand the matter of His glorious essence, and to try to liken or represent Him in our minds - we will ruin/diminish our intellect and understanding, and we will not grasp even what was known to us, as would happen to our eyes if we stared at the sun. We must be careful in this matter, and remember it when we investigate on the matter of the existence of G-d.

(*Marpe Lenefesh*: - As we find recorded in books, that most of the early philosophers became insane. And we see even in our generation - those groups which go after their opinions and investigations, either they became crazy or they go out to evil ways... Perhaps this explains: "Ben Zoma looked and was damaged, and Acher went out to evil ways" (Chagiga 14b regarding the 4 great Sages who entered Paradise upstairs using holy names). One must be careful and guard to not represent G-d with any likeness or form, G-d forbid. We must remember this in our investigations in this gate when examining the matter of the existence of the Creator. We must also guard to not represent Him or ascribe to Him any kind of physical form. Likewise, the Moray (Rambam's Guide for the Perplexed Part 1 ch.35) wrote: "just like it is necessary for the masses to realize and the young ones to be taught that G-d is one, and that one must not serve other than Him. So too, it is necessary to educate them in this in the way of tradition that G-d does not have a body and that there is absolutely no comparison in any way whatsoever between Him and His creations." He then ends off with "even though they don't understand the reasons for the matter and don't know the logical proofs which establish the matter in the mind, just like you are not obligated to teach him by proofs that G-d exists. Rather, let them accept everything in the way of tradition, and afterwards when they grow, the matter will be explained to them stage by stage according to their intellectual ability", see there for more details)

Likewise, we must be careful regarding His attributes, whether those which describe His glorious essence or those the prophets ascribe to Him - not to take them literally or according to what would seem in a physical sense.

(*Pas Lechem*: In scripture there are verses with expressions of His glorious essence which are said in first person form such as "See now that I, I am He, and there is no god with Me" (Deut. 32:39), while other expressions which the prophets speak in third person)

Rather, we must know clearly that they are in a metaphorical and incidental sense according to what we are capable of grasping with our powers of recognition, understanding, and intellect, due to our crucial need to know Him and His loftiness. But He is infinitely greater and loftier above all of this, and like the verse says "Blessed be Your glorious Name, that is exalted above all blessing and praise" (Nehemiah 9:5).

One of the philosophers said: "He whose mind is too weak to understand the matter of divesting (he cannot strip off the physical from the terms which connote abstract spiritual matters - *ML*), he holds fast to the terms in the Divinely given scriptures, and does not realize that the terms in scripture are adapted to the intelligence of those to whom they were addressed, not according to (the intelligence) of the One who addressed them. Rather they are like the whistling call to a herd of cattle at the time of water drinking, which brings them to drink far more effectively than clear and accurate words."

When you master this level of the Unity in your intellect and understanding, devote your soul to the Creator, strive to grasp His existence from (observing) His wisdom, His power, His grace, His mercy, and His abundant providence over His creations. Become pleasing to Him by doing His will. Then you will be among the seekers of G-d (and it is written: "those who seek G-d will understand all" (Mishlei 28:5) - *ML*), and then you will receive from Him the help and strength to understand Him, and to know His true nature, as David said: "The secret of the L-ord is with them that fear Him; and He will show them His covenant" (Ps. 25:14). I will clarify for you some illustrations in the second gate of this book. When you practice them, and go in their path, the matter will be easier for you with G-d's help.

THINGS DETRIMENTAL

The things detrimental to the (wholehearted acceptance of G-d's) unity are numerous. Among them, to association of other beings with the Creator. This occurs in several ways.

Among them, believing in multiple gods, worshipping forms, the sun, moon, constellations, fire, plants, animals.

(Manoach Halevavos - That one serves them, by associating them with G-d, even though one knows that the stars and idols are themselves not divine, and intends only to draw down their spiritual powers, and even though one thinks this will be pleasing to G-d that one serves His creations)

Among them, ascribing physicality to the Creator, while understanding the true intent of scripture.

Among them, hidden association, namely trying to find favor with other people with regard to religious matters. This occurs in several ways. I will clarify them in the fifth gate of this book, with G-d's help.

> (*Marpe Lenefesh*: - "hidden" in that other people do not know his intent, that he associates something else with G-d, namely that he serves G-d with fraudulent intent, but "visibly" he appears as if he is serving G-d alone...)

Among them, turning (excessively) to the physical pleasures. This is subtle association - that a man associates the service of his lusts with the service of the Creator. And the verse says: "There shall not be in you a strange god", to which our Rabbis expound: "what is the 'strange god' which is in the body of a man? - This is the evil inclination" (Talmud Shabbos 105b).

> (*Marpe Lenefesh*: - When a man turns to the physical pleasures, he will not stop nor rest day and night, and all of his aspirations will be to fulfill his desires. And all of his acts are not l'shem shamayim (for G-d), because he will always look first - whether he will receive benefit from it. If yes, then he will do it. But if not, he will drop it all)

Perhaps the simple and foolish person, when he reads this book and considers what we wrote in this gate will say to himself: "will the matter of unity of G-d be unknown to anyone who reads even one page of the Torah whereby this author needs to stir us and instruct us it?"

I will answer this as the wise man answered: "Answer a fool according to his folly" (Mishlei 26:5). For one who asks this is too weak of understanding to grasp the extent of a universal topic which is addressed to different classes of people. Such a universal topic is grasped differently depending on whether the person understood much of it or little of it, and whether he is of strong intellect or of weak intellect.

> (*Tov Halevanon*: so too, for one who claims to have understood the matter of unity by learning one page this is because his understanding is weak and he does not benefit from the matters of the Unity hinted at in the Torah. His benefit is like the benefit of a blind man from the light of the sun, as will be explained.)

The analogy to this - the benefit of the light of the sun which is universal to all men. We find this benefit divides into three classes:
The first class: Those whose eyes are healthy and free from all diseases. They benefit from the sun, use its light, and attain all types of benefit from it.

The second class: The totally blind, whose eyesight is completely lost. The light of the sun does not damage nor benefit them. Their benefit from it is through other people (who guide them).

The third class: People whose eyes are too weak to tolerate the light of the sun, and the sun's light will damage them if they don't avoid it. If they hasten to heal their eyes with medications, potions, and therapeutic diets, and at the same time are careful not to expose their eyes to the light of the sun - it is possible that they will become healthy and they will benefit from the sun which was previously damaging to them. But if they delay healing their eyes, they will quickly lose their eyesight completely and belong to the class of the totally blind.

Similarly, the classes of understanding G-d's unity taught in the Torah divides into three classes. The matter is taught to all rational beings, just like the light of the sun is available to all seeing beings.

The first class: Men of clear intellect and pure understanding.

The second class: Men whose intellect is completely too weak to understand anything of what is written in the Torah.

The third class: Men whose intellect is too weak to grasp what the first class is able to grasp but they have sufficient intelligence to comprehend most of the near and easy matters.

The first class, namely, the men of complete intellect, free from all detriment. When they put to heart to understand what they encountered in the Torah on the matter of the Unity, they will understand it, and its matter will enter their heart through their powerful understanding and pure intellect. They are of those who don't need this book, except to remind them of what has escaped their attention.

(*Marpe Lenefesh*: - Certainly they don't need to plumb in-depth to bring proofs on the Unity of G-d, since none of this is hidden to them due to their powerful intellect and understanding. Also, every man, especially those who study the Torah, need that there should be before them a "book of remembrance" of mussar and yira, especially this book, so that one can rebuke and reprimand himself always from within the book, lest and perhaps one goes out from the bounds of the service of G-d, without realizing. Therefore it is necessary to consider and examine one's acts always. Because the yetzer (evil inclination) is close by, and does not leave a person who does any good thing until he has enticed him to abandon it, like the author wrote in the fifth gate...as the maggid (angel) prescribed to the Beis Yosef (to study daily from the Chovos Halevavos to subjugate the yetzer)...and in my book "HaZechiros", I elaborated a bit also from other early books on the greatness of the obligation on every Jew to always toil in books of yira and mussar, and especially Torah scholars, since the greater a man, the greater is his yetzer.)

The second class do not know G-d's Torah, all the more so the matter of Unity in it. They hear its teaching but do not comprehend its matter. They will have neither benefit nor damage from this book.

The third class who understand the matter of the Unity mentioned in G-d's Torah with some understanding, but they don't have the intellectual power to understand its matter and realize its true meaning. If a teacher instructs them and makes them understand its matter through the way of true proofs and sound intellectual reasoning - its meaning will become clear to them, and its secret will be revealed to them, and they will reach the level of the first class.

But if they shirk from investigating and are lazy in examining in that which will strengthen their understanding and sharpen their intellect they will sink to the level of the foolish.

To those of this class, this book will be of great and comprehensive benefit, because they are capable of investigating. It will benefit them just like potions benefit those with weak eyesight, who hope to be healed by their application.

Scripture already compared the foolish man - to a blind man, wisdom - to light, and foolishness - to darkness, in saying: "Then I saw that wisdom excels folly, as far as light excels darkness" (Eccles. 2:13), and "The wise man's eyes are in his head; but the fool walks in darkness" (Eccles. 2:14), and "Hear, you deaf; and look, you blind, that you may see" (Isaiah 42:18).

(*Pas Lechem*: The wise man is he who sees the future consequences. When he stands at the beginning of a matter, he contemplates and thinks about what will happen at the end of it. Unlike the fool, who is like one who walks in darkness who does not see what is ahead of him)

And they compared wisdom and mussar - to a tree of life (which a man eats from and lives forever - *PL*), as written: "It is a tree of life to them that lay hold upon it" (Mishlei 3:18), and "For they are life unto those that find them" (Mishlei 4:22).

(*Tov Halevanon*: Not only does wisdom benefit to heal the eyes of the intellect but rather it is an elixir of life to the entire body and the soul)

May the Almighty teach us the way to the knowledge Him, direct us to His service, and bestow on us His grace, in His mercy and compassion. Amen.

*** TRANSLATOR'S SUMMARY ***

The following is a brief summary of the logical proof of the existence of G-d from the Shaar Yichud according to the translator's limited understanding. Note that it is impossible to arrive at a water-tight mathematical type proof as the author wrote in his introduction to this book:

> I propose to take the most direct (easiest) method of arousing, teaching, and instructing, using language clear, direct, and familiar, so that my words will be more easily understood. I will refrain from deep language, unusual terms, and the arguments in the way of "defeat" (nitzuach), which the logicians call in arabic "Algidal", and likewise for remote inquiries which cannot be resolved in this work, for I only brought such arguments as are satisfactory and convincing according to the methods proper to the science of theology.
>
> As the philosopher said "it is not proper to seek of every inquiry a conclusion in the way of mofet (irrefutable proof), since not every topic in rational inquiry can be demonstrated to this extent. Likewise, we should not be satisfied in the science of nature with the method of 'sufficient' (since a full "raya" proof can be achieved there through experiment). Nor in the science of theology should we strive to apprehend with the senses or draw comparisons with physical phenomena."
>
> (*Tov Halevanon commentary*: "defeat" (nitzuach) - It is known that the science of logic divides into three methods nitzuach (defeat), raya (proof), and mofet (definitive proof). Nitzuach (defeat) is when one cannot decide on either of the two views definitively, only that one view has more and stronger questions and claims which can be raised against it than the other view. The view which has fewer and weaker questions against it will prevail over the other view, and it is proper to follow that view even though it may also have some questions which can be raised. The "proof" (raya) is where one view has many questions and claims which can be raised against it while the other view has no claims against it.
>
> Certainly, it is proper to uphold it. This is better than nitzuach (defeat). Because here there are no claims and questions against it from the aspect of rational inquiry, but nevertheless, perhaps his inquiry was somehow flawed [for example, due to lacking certain information]. The "mofet" (definitive proof) is that which is impossible to refute, in almost any way whatsoever, similar to the miracles of the prophets which were openly visible to the senses [at that time]. Behold, science is divided into three divisions:

theology, nature, mathematics. It is known that for most of the science of theology, it is impossible to bring a "raya" (proof), and all the more so, a mofet (definitive proof).

For due to the enormous depth and awesomeness of this science, and the limitations of human intellect, it is almost impossible to establish a clear view which is without any doubts. But they can be clarified in the way of Nitzuach (defeat), and a few of its topics through "raya" (proof) which are close to being mofet (definitive proof). For the science of nature, on the other hand, which is not as deep, one can explain much of it in the way of raya (proof), and some even from mofet (definitive proof). But the science of limudit which is the science of mathematics and geometry, all of its matters are clarified through mofet (definitive proof). This is what the author wrote that not all rational inquiry is found as mofet (definitive proof), but as nitzuach (defeat) or rayah (proof).)

(*Pas Lechem* commentary: for it is impossible to explain things in theology using our physical senses or to explain it through a familiar analogy, because it is exalted above and beyond all senses and comparison. It has no connection whatsoever with these things.)

Let us begin. By understanding the (theological) proof that G-d must exist, we will automatically get an introduction to G-d. Although it is impossible for us to understand Him directly nevertheless we can at least understand to some small extent what He is not.

Now, the logical proof of G-d is based on three premises
1. A thing cannot make itself.
2. causal chains cannot be infinite in number.
3. Anything composite is not eternally existing.

Regarding the first premise: It is self-evident that something which is totally non-existent cannot do anything. And if it does something, then it is already existing.

If you ask, physicists find particles (quantum fluctuations) which appear and disappear in empty space. Answer: as explained in chapter 5, the particles do not pop out of nowhere. They are consequences and properties of a pre-existing space-time medium governed by pre-existing laws of quantum mechanics. Thus, there are not at all coming from absolutely nothing. See there for more.

Regarding the second premise, causal chains cannot be infinite in number. This means you cannot explain the existence of an egg by saying there is an infinite regress of chicken-egg, chicken-egg, and so on, endlessly.

Another analogy, if we have a room of parallel mirrors with infinite reflections of a human face. You can't reasonably explain the existence of the faces in the mirror by saying there is no source face and they are all just reflections of each other. In reality, there must exist a source, a real human face otherwise nothing would be reflected in the mirrors.

Hence according to these two premises, to explain the effect of the existence of the universe requires us to conclude that something exists which is eternal (without beginning). Now, the question is what can be eternal?

The third premise states that anything composite cannot be eternal (without beginning). The eternal by definition cannot have anything preceding it. So for example, "dough" needs flour and water to exist, hence "dough" cannot be eternal since its existence depends on the pre-existence of flour and water.

What about something like an electron or a photon or even spacetime? These things are composite in a subtler sense. They are composites of themselves and their "boundaries/limitations/properties". For example, an electron has position, spin, charge, mass, momentum, energy, etc. Therefore it is a composite of itself and whatever boundaries, limitations or properties were set on it. Hence it is a composite of two matters - 1) its own existence and 2) from the aspect of that which it must have a cause which set its boundaries/properties/limitations. i.e., it has to be a result of a previous "something" that either "made" it or "shaped" it or "defined" it - something which CAUSED its borders/properties, etc. to be what they are.

For example, a video game has certain characters, each one having certain properties, abilities, or position on the screen, etc. These things must have been set by a computer programmer. They cannot just exist eternally, without beginning.

Hence, the only thing that can be Eternal (without beginning) is that which has no properties or limitations in any way. It is completely infinite and boundless in all respects. It has no parts or boundaries. This is a completely different "kind" of existence than anything we are familiar with. Anything else which has some sort of limitation or property cannot be eternal.

This automatically rules out anything physical or more than one Eternal (since then each supposed Eternal would be limited in some sense and therefore automatically could not be eternal) and leaves only the One G-d. He is One in an absolute sense.

Obviously, we have no way whatsoever of comprehending such an infinite existence, but we can know for sure that the Eternal must exist otherwise we would not be here. By studying the world with this outlook, we can learn about the Eternal.

Once this is clear, it follows that prophecy is necessary for Him to tell us what this is all about and this leads us to the first and foremost book on prophecy - the torah. (see torah authenticity at dafyomireview.com/430 for much more on this).

Here's a quote from the Pas Lechem commentary in ch.7 which summarizes this.

> He began with the title: "powerful" because according to our understanding, He existed before everything, since immediately after we grasp that there exists a Creator who created the world from nothing, we will immediately recognize His power, namely, the act of creating something from nothing...After this, when we reflect on the details of creation, and we study them and their parts - we will see signs of His wisdom and we will know that He is wise. Afterwards, we contemplate His providence in governing the world, we will know that He is living and among us always. Understand that all of these descriptions are obligatory and follow one after the other, with the creation of the world as their first source.

To summarize, G-d is the "muchrach hametziut" (the necessary existence), and that which is the necessary existence IS the Existence itself. He is so intensely One that really there is nothing besides Him.

*** Shaar HaBechina - Gate of Reflection ***

from Chovot Halevavot - Duties of the Heart

by Rabeinu Bahya ibn Paquda zt'l

original english translation by Rabbi Moses Hyamson, former chief Rabbi
of British Empire, New York, 1925
OCR scanned with permission from http://www.hebrewbooks.org/3186
(now public domain)
*new revision including select classic commentaries translated by Rabbi
Yosef Sebag*

* Introduction

* Chapter 1 - What is the examination

* Chapter 2 - Is examination a duty or not

* Chapter 3 - Its various modes

* Chapter 4 - the diverse marks of divine wisdom in created things which
we should examine

* Chapter 5 - Which of these is closest to us and should receive more
attention

* Chapter 6 - factors that are detrimental to examination

*** Shaar HaBechina - Gate of Reflection ***

On the examination of created things and G-d's abounding goodness towards them.

INTRODUCTION.

> (*Rabbi YS*: note that this gate has many commentaries due to its being densely packed with hidden meaning. I tried to include only those that seemed to me essential for understanding the author's intent.
>
> *Matanas Chelko*: the custom practiced in the yeshiva world is not to study the Shaar Yichud (Gate#1). And even though, there is no doubt whatsoever that all of what he says there is absolute truth, nevertheless, his words are of philosophical inquiry and this inherently leads to many questions in the mind of the person studying them, and not every person is capable of fully understanding them. It is possible therefore that one could remain with unresolved questions, or at least with doubts, that would not have occurred to him had he not studied this work. Therefore, it is customary to walk simply and accept as a given, simple faith that the Creator is One. And the explanation of One is that there is no power in the world besides Him, no place in the world devoid of Him, and nothing in the world without Him. These things are above the powers of our minds to grasp.

The author says: Since we began in the previous treatise, with the various ways in which the Unity of G-d can be demonstrated so that it shall be wholeheartedly acknowledged, and we found that the examination of the wisdom manifested in the universe is the nearest way to clarify His existence and the clearest path to know His reality. [Therefore] we deem it our duty to deal with this theme, so that to each treatise, the one most nearly resembling it should be joined, and each topic should be followed by the most appropriate topic - this being among the subjects which we have to deal with in regard to the Almighty's service, the purpose for which we were created, as the wise man said (Kohelet 3:14) *"And G-d has so made it that man should fear before Him"*.

> (*Pas Lechem*: *"nearest way...the clearest path"* - ... nearest in that it does not require many logical constructs and preliminary introductions like the other ways [such as philosophical inquiry]. Clearest in that it is a well-trodden path by many people, and a well-trodden path is free from stumbling blocks, mishaps, and errors. In other ways of inquiry, a man is not assured against mishaps and mistakes in treading them, as in truth,

there are many, many casualties strewn along the path of philosophical inquiry unlike the path of examination [of G-d's wisdom], which none grow weary or stumble in it.

Rabbi YS: If you ask, if so why do so many modern scientists err and do not ascribe the wisdom in the universe to G-d? Answer: The role of the scientist is to consider only naturalistic, materialistic explanations. This is his job as a scientist. Hence, he is not allowed to consider supernatural explanations (such as G-d) despite that ultimately there is no other way to explain much of what we see around us as explained in this gate.

Matanas Chelko: *"And G-d has so made it that man should fear before Him"* - i.e. not only certain specific deeds of G-d bring a man to fear (reverence), but rather everything - everything that G-d has made is in order to bring one to fear. This is the purpose of everything that G-d has created. In truth, the author writes this at the beginning of the introduction to this book... "who created all that is found as a sign of His Unity, who formed beings to serve as witnesses of His power and brought things into existence to testify to His wisdom and great benevolence"...

First we have to note that though the benefits G-d bestows upon His creatures are all-embracing, as Scripture says *"The L-ord is good to all"* (Tehilim 145:9), nevertheless, the majority of mankind are too blind to recognize these benefits or comprehend their high excellence, and they do not think over their matters due to three reasons.

(*Matanas Chelko*: "all-embracing" - i.e. all without exception. This is the contemplation here - that G-d is good to all. Not only human beings, but even to animals.

Pas Lechem: *"(1) too blind to recognize .. (2) comprehend .. (3) think over"* - He specified three terms corresponding to the three types of blindness which tends to affect human beings. (1) Benefits which one does not recognize at all and which one is completely ignorant of - on this he wrote *"too blind to recognize"*. (2) Benefits which he realizes a bit, but he does not contemplate them to *"comprehend their high excellence"* and goodness. (3) Thirdly, and this is worse than the first two, that some benefits seem at first impression to be bad, and they require to deeply *"think over"* to recognize their benefit and understand the good concealed in them. On those like this it is written, "the wicked do not understand, but the thinkers will understand" (Yirmiya 12:10), and the wise man said "he who thinks on the matter will find good" (Mishlei 16:20) i.e. he who is not satisfied with the first impression that appears to him but instead applies his intellect and understanding on it - "will find good", i.e. after thinking it through he will find the thing to be good, unlike the superficial appearance which deemed it evil. He will now explain that these three types of blindness are due to three reasons and that each reason is a cause for one of the above three types of blindness. I will explain each of them, G-d willing, after his words.)

1. One of these reasons: their absorption in matters of this world and its pleasures, their lusting for what they will not attain of it, their neglect to look onto the benefits G-d bestows upon them because their hearts are preoccupied with what they hope for, of satisfying their lusts and fulfilling their wishes. For whatever level they have attained of it, they proceed to seek what is higher than it, and strive for what is after it. The many benefits bestowed on them are, in their view, but few. The great gifts already given to them, they deem small. Until they consider any advantage possessed by another person as if it was taken away from them, and when others attain some benefits, it is as if evil befell them. They do not understand the works of G-d who bestows good to them, as Scripture says (Tehilim 10:4) *"The wicked, in his high arrogance, does not enquire. G-d is not in any of his thoughts"*.

(*Pas Lechem*: *"their absorption in (1) matters of this world and (2) its pleasures"* - Two terms corresponding to love of "useful" things and love of "enjoyable" things. For in saying (1) [their absorption in] *"matters of this world"*, the author's intent is on the way of most people, that most of their occupation and most of their time is squandered in fulfilling their lust for "useful" things such as building houses, making garments, and amassing possessions. The author called this "matters" [of this world], since "matters" (inyan) connotes "conduct" [in Hebrew] as Rashi explained on the verse "but to the sinner He has given a matter to gather and to accumulate" (Kohelet 2:26), and "it is an evil matter [that G-d has given to human beings with which to occupy themselves]" (Kohelet 1:13). (2) On the second term *"its pleasures"*, the author's intent is on love of "enjoyable" things such as eating, drinking, marital relations where the [following] term "lusting" applies primarily to this type.
"lusting for what they will not attain of it" - i.e. they constantly lust to attain more worldly lusts that they have not yet attained in the past. One can also render this as referring to the future, i.e. even for something which is beyond their ability to ever attain, and certainly they will never attain it, nevertheless they strive full strength to attain it. Hence, their heart is forever absorbed in a prolonged longing which never ceases.
"of satisfying their lusts and fulfilling their wishes" - here too, the author's intent is for the two kinds [of love] as above, since for love of "enjoyable things", which a person, by nature, is enthusiastic about fulfilling, it is proper to use the term *"satisfying their lusts"*, while for love of "useful" things, it is proper to use the term *"fulfilling their wishes"*.
"seek what is higher than it, and strive for what is after it" - Two terms. (1)

"higher than it" refers to increasing the same kind [of worldly thing], such as regarding wealth, where our Sages said "he who has 100 coins wants 200 coins" (Kohelet Raba 1:13). (2) The second term, *"strive for what is after it"* refers to a stage of a different kind which normally follows his current stage. For example, honor seeking normally follows after wealth seeking. Hence, he who has attained the stage of wealth, now strives to attain honor. Therefore, he used the term *"strive"* which connotes great exertion since it is a different stage [and a new beginning] which he has no momentum in and, as is known, (Rashi Shemot 19:5) "all beginnings are difficult".

Tov Halevanon: *"any advantage possessed by another person as if it was taken away from them"* - It is human nature for one to think that all the good he sees by his fellow is stolen from him and that G-d created the entire universe for his honor only (i.e. selfishness - each person tends to think that he is the center of the universe.)

Pas Lechem: The hunger of lust intensifies so much in them until they will desire everything for themselves, and they will imagine that they deserve everything that is in other peoples' hands and imagine that it is as if other people plundered them and stole from them.
"(1) any advantage possessed by another person as if it was taken away from them...and (2) when others attain some benefits, it is as if evil befell them" - immediately when someone else attains some benefit, their heart will be disturbed and will be bitter on this, as if some evil befell them because good that reaches others is evil to them. The first expression above (1) refers to benefits already in other peoples' possession, and they hope for and long for it, like a man who hopes for and waits to recapture that which was stolen from him. The second expression (2) refers to the initial time when the good reached the other person's hands, they are disturbed and feel bad, since the primary pain of feeling a bad thing is in the beginning of it.

"They do not understand the works of G-d who bestows good to them" - they do not understand that these benefits are the works of G-d, and since they come from Him, and His hand distributed them, there is no room for jealousy, and there is no avail to excessive hishtadlut (striving, since it is all G-d's decree what each person will attain as explained in gate 4).

"The wicked, in his high arrogance, does not enquire" - due to his arrogance, he does not examine the cause of his benefits to know their Source, because G-d is not in any of his thoughts. Alternatively, due to his arrogance, he thinks he deserves everything. Therefore, he is not content with what he has and seeks what he did not yet attain.

Tov Halevanon: He thinks that the benefits which he is proud of are not from G-d, because he thinks G-d does not exist. Alternatively, he thinks G-d does not help him. Alternatively, due to his arrogance, he thinks he deserves those benefits more than the other person, therefore he thinks that benefit is evil and therefore it must be that G-d did not bestow it. Therefore, he does not pray to G-d to thank Him for his own benefits.)

2. The second reason is that human beings when they come into this world are like foolish beasts and a donkey's colt (without any intellect whatsoever and no sense of good and evil - *ML*), as scripture says (Iyov 11:12) *"Like a wild donkey's colt is man when born"*. They grow up with an abundance of continuous and recurring Divine favors which they experience constantly, and to which they become so used to and familiar with that they come to regard these as intrinsic parts of their being, not to be removed or separated from themselves during the whole of their lives. Though their intelligence develops and their mental faculties become strong they (remain ignorant and - *PL*) foolishly ignore the benefits the Creator has bestowed on them and do not consider the obligation of gratitude for Divine beneficence, for they are unaware of the immense degree of the benefit, and of the infinite greatness of the Benefactor who bestowed it upon them.

(*Matanas Chelko*: "donkey's colt" - i.e. a person comes to this world without any intellect like a newborn donkey. He may also remain like this and grow up like this, until he becomes a big and strong adult donkey. For this one must study books of Mussar (torah ethics) so that this does not happen to him and he does not remain thus. For this is the work placed on him - to change himself from a wild donkey to a human being.

Pas Lechem: *"continuous and recurring Divine favors"* - on constant favors such as life and health, he wrote *"continuous"*, while for favors which come and go over time, he wrote *"recurring"*.
"they become so used to and familiar with" - on the constant favors, he wrote *"used to"*, while for those that come and go, he wrote *"familiar with"* since even though they are not so used to them, nevertheless, these are familiar to them and ingrained in their imagination due to their recurring many times.
"not to be (1) removed or (2) separated from themselves" - There are two ways a man can lose his benefits. Either (1) they can be removed from him and cease to exist such as in the death of his children or the burning down of his possessions. Or, (2) they can be separated from him and transferred to someone else.. In truth, they are different calamities. The first case is difficult in that there is no hope left for reattaining this thing which no longer exists unlike something which still exists but is in someone else's possession where one still sits and hopes perhaps it will someday return to

him. On the other hand, the second case also has a harsher evil since (Shir 8:6) "Jealousy [is] cruel as the grave", that a man sees his hard earned work in someone else's hands, as written (Yeshaya 1:6) "your land, strangers devour it in your presence".

Matanas Chelko: In truth, this is the reason our sages instituted so many morning blessings on each matter, such as pokeach ivrim (granting eyesight), zokef kefufim (straightens the bent), mitzadei gaver (directs feet), etc. All this is to bring one to recognize that all that he has is a gift from G-d. We mistakenly think we deserve these things. But in truth it is not so. Just because we had these things yesterday, does not necessitate or establish that we will merit these things also today. When we encounter someone who has no eyes to see with, or not feet to walk with, G-d forbid, we think to ourselves "oy to that person, but this is not my lot." This is not true! We are also like these people r"l. Only that G-d in His kindness bestows on us limbs and senses at all times. In the blessing of the Shema we say that G-d every day continuously renews (recreates) the universe. This means, every day He gives anew. Hence, in truth, a person has nothing - no eyes, no hands, and no feet - only that G-d, in His kindness and benevolence, renews and regives him these things anew every day. Therefore the proper outlook on these senses and limbs should be from the perspective that one feels that he was lacking them and then afterwards receives them. In this way, he will undoubtedly thank G-d for His kindness and benevolence.)

In this respect, they resemble an infant, found in the desert by a kind hearted man. The man had pity on the infant, brought it into his home, raised it, fed it, clothed it, and generously provided all that was good for it until it grew up and understood the ways of the many benefits it had received.

(*Pas Lechem*: "understood the ways of the many benefits" - the author precisely chose the term "the ways", which means, that the infant was ignorant and did not understand from which ways his benefits came from and what chain of causes bring him the benefits. He only experienced the end benefits and its enjoyments. Unlike, when he grew up and understood the ways of his benefits and the chain of causes which bring them to him. Understand this.)

Afterwards the [same] kind hearted man heard about a man who fell in the hands of his enemy who for a long time treated him with utmost cruelty, starved, and kept naked. The prisoner's suffering aroused the kind hearted man's pity. He appeased the enemy (with words - *PL*) until the enemy freed the prisoner and forgave his debt. The benevolent man brought the man into his home and benefited him to a lesser extent than that which he bestowed on the infant. Yet, the man recognized the good more and was more thankful than the infant who grew up with them. The reason is because he went from a situation of destitution and suffering to one of goodness and tranquility while his mental faculties were mature. Therefore, he fully recognized the goodness and the kindness of his benefactor. But the infant did not realize the great extent of the goodness even after his perception and understanding had matured because he was used to them since his childhood.

No person with intelligence will doubt that the kindness to the child was wider in scope and more clearly recognizable, and that consequently there was in its case a greater obligation of constant gratitude and praise to the benefactor.

> (*Marpe Lenefesh*: Since if the kind hearted man did not take the infant into his home, it would have died there. But for the prisoner, it is possible that he would have found a way to save himself from his enemy through some strategy. If so, the former should have been more grateful and praised the benefactor more than the prisoner. But he did not do so. The reason being that he is used to the benefits from childhood and thinks that this is normal and that he deserves it. Thus it is so with most human beings, who behave like this infant.)

This is similar to what scripture says (Hosea 11:3) *"And I carried Ephraim (from Egypt - ML), taking them in my arms, but they knew not that I healed them."* (they did not want to know - *ML*)

> (*Matanas Chelko*: they did not know that this was for their healing. Furthermore, they did not even realize that they were sick people in need of healing. All this is due to habit.
>
> Hence the first reason we do not recognize the great divine benefits is because of lackings in the middos (good traits). Firstly, lusts - that we always desire more. Secondly, due to the bad things which befall us, we are not able to contemplate the divine benefits [in them] due to jealousy of others. Hence, the first reason is lacking in the middos (good traits), for even lacking in middos hinders emuna (faith) and consequently, service of G-d.
>
> The second reason is habit. Even if no bad things or sufferings ever befell him throughout his life, and his lot in life was solely to receive good benefits, and even if he is always saying "thank G-d for all the good things", nevertheless he will not be so affected and will not be so moved by it. For being affected and moved by benefits comes only when a man feels

he is totally lacking and that he needs help, support, and kindliness [of another] - like that child who needed so much help and kindliness. but when one recognizes this with a full and mature intellect - then it is possible that he will be touched by all the beneficence G-d has bestowed on him.

3. The third reason is that human beings are struck in this world with various mishaps and damages to their bodies and possessions and they do not understand the ways in which these misfortunes are a means to benefit them, nor the benefits of trial and suffering, as Scripture says *"Happy is the man whom You, O L-ord, chastens and teaches out of Your Law"* (Tehilim 94:12).

(*Pas Lechem*: *"(1) benefit them, and the benefits of (2) trial and (3) suffering"* - Three terms. The tribulations that G-d brings on a man fall into three categories. Either G-d's intention is that this bad thing will result in benefit for them in this world, such as the sale and imprisonment of Joseph, which eventually caused him to become king [of Egypt]. Some tribulations He intends for the benefit of trial, namely, that the person tested comes to recognize his level. It is very beneficial for them to strengthen themselves and bring out their potential to actuality, as explained in the Sages regarding the trials of the righteous, especially on the binding of Isaac.. On this he wrote *"benefits of trial"*. Or G-d's intent is for the benefit of suffering, namely, to bring him suffering in this world in order to save him from fury and wrath (of the evil forces created by his sins) in the world of retribution.

Tov Halevanon: *"trial"* - as written "He fed you in the wilderness with manna, which your fathers knew not, that He might humble you, and that He might test you, to do you good in the end" (Devarim 8:16). *"suffering"* - to humble his pride and submit his high heartedness.

Marpe Lenefesh: One should always think that everything G-d does is for the good, and all the bad things are actually good for him. Either they are for the benefits of trial, namely, that G-d tests the righteous to increase their reward. These are the yesurim shel ahava (chastisements of love) or they are in the way of punishment, and his sins are forgiven through them, as written in Gate 8 accounting #27, see there.

Matanas Chelko: a person should know and understand that G-d is bestowing good to him by bringing suffering on him. G-d's wish in this is that the person will listen to the voice of the sufferings and from them he will learn to improve his ways. He should feel great joy when he hears the mussar (ethics) of G-d.

They forget that they themselves and all they have are benefits which the Creator in His generosity and loving-kindness has bestowed on them, and that He decreed on them justly in accordance with His wisdom. They are resentful when His judgment is visited upon them and they do not praise Him when His mercy and loving-kindness are manifested to them.

(*Pas Lechem*: They resent the things which appear bad, even though in truth, concealed inside them, G-d's intent is for the greatest possible good for them. This leads them to not praise G-d even for the good which manifests openly towards them. Alternatively, even when the thing which appeared bad was visibly seen to result in good, nevertheless they still don't praise Him..

Matanas Chelko: This is another point - they forget that all the good they attained was pure generosity and loving-kindness. For in truth, they deserve nothing whatsoever; i.e. it is not that G-d is not bestowing [good] on them now as He used to do, but rather it is all pure generosity and loving-kindness. The analogy of this is to a fundraiser who collects money for a torah institution. A certain donor who he meets usually gives 1000 dollars but this time gave only 500 dollars. Is this not also charity and kindness?... so too G-d sometimes gives 1000 and sometimes only 500.. Nevertheless, it is all generosity and kindness. Only that sometimes G-d bestows a greater amount than other times. One must realize that the Creator has precise reasons why sometimes He bestows much and sometimes less..)

Their foolishness leads them to deny the benefits and the Benefactor. Their folly may even bring many of them to speculate that they know better concerning G-d's work and the various creations which He created for their well-being.

(*Marpe Lenefesh*: Like the Moray Nevuchim writes in part 3 ch.12 on the grumbling of a certain philosopher that the bad things in the world are more numerous than the good, etc. The Rambam answered there at length. The summary of his words is that most of the bad things which befall a man are due to his own bad choices, such as due to a bad way of living in eating, drinking, [excessive] marital relations, or that he pursues things which are not necessary for him. Through this, he falls into mishaps and troubles, and he then complains about G-d's traits. But if he had subsisted with the necessary only, he would have been spared from all these troubles, because the minimum necessary is easily obtained and is assured for every human being. see there and Gate 8 accounting #22 for similar to this..

Pas Lechem: "G-d's work" refers to general things in the world such as extreme heat, or extreme cold, which a person's soul hates, and the fools speculate that their absence would be better than their existence. Alternatively, it refers to G-d's providence with which He guides the world... and in truth, most people are resentful in seeing bad things happening to good people or vice versa, and these fools think that if the world's conduct was in their hands, it would be better and more orderly than it is now.

"the various creations which He created for their well-being" - this refers to damaging creatures and poisonous plants, and the like, where, in truth, everything was created perfectly for the well-being of mankind.

Tov Halevanon: Since they don't realize that G-d intends good for them, and that He brings these troubles to benefit them in their final end, they may stumble into evil in trying to remove these troubles, until they will say that evil is more prevalent than good, and thus G-d created the world, so man will toil and suffer, and that bad things happen randomly through "nature".

Matanas Chelko: He thinks that if he were G-d, he would do things differently. For example, if a bad dog bit him, he would say "I would not have created bad dogs. But in truth, even bad dogs have a purpose in this world, namely, to inflict suffering on him so that he will learn its lesson. Likewise regarding G-d's conduct, he thinks that if he were G-d, he would not act in this or that way. All this is foolishness for he does not understand in the least the many considerations of the Creator as to why He does this. On this the Talmud says (Bava Kama 38a): "Rav Shmuel bar Yehuda's daughter died. The [Babylonian] Rabbis said to Rabbi Ula 'let us go console Rav Shmuel bar Yehuda'. Rabbi Ula refused to go with them saying 'why should I join the consolations of Babylonians which is blasphemous, for behold they say 'what can we do?', which implies that if it were possible to do something to annul G-d's decree they would have done so." End quote. Hence, one who goes to a mourner and says "what can we do?", this implies "if I were the Master of the world, I would not have done like this." This is blasphemy and heretical towards G-d [as Rashi explains there]. For behold, G-d does what He deems to be the best possible way. Rather one should say something good to console the mourner as the Talmud continues. see there. Hence, one must have complete faith that all that G-d does is for the good. And even if one cannot recognize or see the good in what has occurred, he should nevertheless believe that it is good. This reason impedes one's ability to examine the beneficence of the Creator more than the previous two reasons. For on the first two, one can overpower them, unlike this reason which depends on faith.)

In this regard, how like are they to blinded people who were admitted into an institution specially built for them and furnished with everything needed for their comfort. Every single thing was in its right place and arranged for their advantage in the way that might best serve the specific purpose of improving their condition. Useful healing potions had also been provided and a skilled physician appointed to heal them by the application of these potions so that their sight may be restored. They however neglected to toil in the healing of their eyes and did not heed the directions of the physicians who sought to cure them (for they sought only leisure there - *MC*).

They wandered about aimlessly in the institution, miserable because of their blindness. Often as they were walking, they would stumble over objects that had been placed there for their benefit, and fall down on their faces. Some were bruised, others suffered broken limbs. Their pains and injuries increased and multiplied. Then they burst forth in complaints against the owner and the builder of the home, condemned his work, charged him with falling short in the fulfillment of his duty and condemned him as a bad manager. They persuaded themselves that his aim and purpose had not been to do them good and show them kindness, but to cause them pain and injury. This attitude of mind caused them at last to deny his goodness and kindliness, even as the wise man said (Koheles 10:3) *"Yea also, when a fool walks by the way, his understanding fails him and he declares to everyone that he is a fool"*. (i.e. he tells others that they are fools, but he does not realize that he himself is a fool. Alternatively, he calls everything foolishness even though it is good and done with wisdom. - *MH*)

(*Pas Lechem*: *"falling short"* - this refers to one who performs some undertaking in a lazy manner, without proper attention. Then the resulting work does not succeed perfectly. Therefore, he is called *"falling short"*, that he reduces the matter from its perfection, and something which is lacking, not only is it not useful, but sometimes it is even harmful.

Pas Lechem: Now that the author has finished presenting the three reasons, you, intelligent reader, put your attention to what I have made known to you - to clarify how they correspond to the three types of blindness mentioned earlier.
(1) For corresponding to the first cause, namely, their great absorption in matters of this world and the endless clamor of its waves of pleasures which do not allow quietude of the imaginations of his heart, behold, for a man caught in this, certainly there is no hope whatsoever that on his own, he will stir himself to recognize the beneficence of the Creator, and praise Him on them. Because, from where will this recognition come? Since his heart is preoccupied with too many things until there is no room left to think of anything else. Combine this, with his imagining always that he is

lacking much, and whatever he has is worth nothing to him. Either way, there is way that his heart will come to recognize G-d's beneficence. On this he wrote earlier *"the majority of mankind are too blind to recognize these benefits"*. He wrote *"blind"* without qualification, in that they do not recognize them at all.

(2) Corresponding to the second cause, namely, being greatly habituated in them from childhood, behold, it is known that habit alone cannot by itself annul and desensitize a person from feeling something. If someone strikes him with a stick every day for several years, he will also feel the latest one, only that his fear of the feeling will not be so great, like someone who never experienced it. Hence, habit alone is not enough to block out the recognition completely. Likewise for the good, due to being habituated in them he does not recognize them properly, relative to their high excellence. On this he wrote: *"or comprehend their high excellence"*.

(3) Corresponding to the third cause, namely, that a man is bitter and complains on many of the matters that are actually good for him due to their appearing bad on the surface, without contemplation. On this he wrote *"they do not think over their matters"*, as explained earlier. Think and contemplate this for I have been brief.)

Since this is so, men of wisdom and knowledge have deemed it their duty to arouse those who did not understand the Creator's beneficence and instruct human beings to realize through their own intellect the high degree (of this good -PL). For many benefits fail to be enjoyed altogether or their enjoyment is marred because they are not realized and their high degree is not known. But when the attention of the beneficiaries is called to their high degree and what had been hidden from them is revealed to them, they will offer, in more abundant measure, laudation and thanksgiving to their divine Benefactor, and so will have pleasure and happiness in their life here and receive their good reward in the hereafter.

(*Pas Lechem*: *"to realize through their own intellect"* - i.e. the sages do not fulfill their duty in informing the people the high degree of the good by simply informing them so that the people will accept it with faith. Rather, it is their duty to teach them through rational inquiry until they understand it on their own.

Matanas Chelko: "instruct human beings to realize" - The author asserts here that not only is it a duty to inquire of all of the Creator's beneficences in the world, but it is also a duty for one who has attained some wisdom in this and recognizes it - to teach others on these matters. For example, if he hears his friend complaining or condemning, he should tell him: "why are you complaining to G-d? Don't you realize He did everything for your benefit?"

It appears the source of this is from the Sifri. The Rambam brings this Sifri in explaining the Mitzva (precept) of Love of G-d (Sefer Hamitzvot positive commandment #3): "this miztva includes calling all people to G-d's service and believing in Him. As an analogy, when one loves a human being, he will praise him to others and seek that others also love him. So too, when one truly loves G-d according to how much he grasped of His truth, behold undoubtedly you will seek out and call out to the deniers and fools to come to realize the truth which you yourself have come to realize...")

The wise man already said on this subject: *"The words of the wise are like goads; and like nails, firmly fixed, are the compilers (Baale Asufoth)"* (Koheles 12:11). The words of the wise are compared by the sage to goads, because they arouse and stir up; they are also compared to nails firmly fixed, because they (the wise men -TL) fix wisdom in their hearts always, and their wisdom endures in them.

The phrase "Baale Asufoth" means, according to the commentators, compilers of books. The term *"Divre"* in the first half of the verse also applies to its second half; which should be rendered: *"and like firmly fixed nails are the words of compilers"*. For books authored on the branches of wisdom endure, their benefit is without interruption (for all generations) and therefore they are compared to nails firmly fixed.

(*Marpe Lenefesh*: Even though the sages do not stir a person to the good, behold, there are books of wisdom and understanding available, and whoever wants to learn and stir himself, let him come and learn. For without toiling in books of mussar (ethics), a man does not fulfill his duty.

Matanas Chelko: "goads" - this is the tool which is used to steer and guide the ox when it plows so that it goes in a straight line. So too, the Sages guide and steer human beings and stir them to go in the just path and to recognize the beneficence of the Creator... By studying their books, a man will come to recognize the beneficence of G-d and will overpower the three reasons mentioned earlier which impede this.

We must now discuss six topics on the subject of examination (of created things)

1. What is to be understood by the examination and its true meaning?

2. Is examination of created thing a duty or not?

3. What are the various ways in which it is to be conducted?

4. How many are the diverse marks of divine wisdom in created things which we should examine?

5. Which one of these is closest to us and should receive more attention than the rest?

6. The factors that are detrimental to the examination and its results.

CHAPTER 1

What is the examination? Contemplating the marks of the Creator's wisdom manifested in the created things and evaluating these marks according to (the utmost of -ML) one's mental capacity.

(*Tov Halevanon*: "*according to one's mental capacity*" - because certainly, no man is capable of understanding G-d's wisdom fully. Only that it is one's duty to recognize a bit according to his mental capacity.)

For [divine] wisdom, though varied in its manifestations in created things, is fundamentally and essentially one - just as the sun is one body, while the appearance of its rays when passing through glasses that are white, dark, red or green, varies and assumes respectively the color of each medium, and just as water with which a park is sprinkled assumes the color of the blooms on which it falls.

(*Tov Halevanon*: The difference in wisdom is not from differences in the Maker but from differences in the receiver of the wisdom.
Pas Lechem: His intent in this analogy is so that one will not claim: "since we see the marks of wisdom are diverse in the creations, and what appears in this one does not appear in that one, if so, each one must originate from a different source of wisdom... Therefore, since there are so many sources of wisdom, why should I waste my time endlessly examining each one. For certainly many of them are beyond me, and from where will I know how to approach each one? To this, he answered that it is a mistake. Since in truth, even though the marks of wisdom appear different, they are all from one Source, and only one power is needed to recognize them all. Hence, the author continues: "therefore, contemplate...")

Therefore, contemplate G-d's creations, from the smallest of them to the largest, and reflect on those matters which are at present hidden from you; and, with the help of the Almighty, you will find that they are as I have told you. And because these marks of divine wisdom vary in created things, it is our duty to contemplate them and think on them until the whole matter becomes established in our souls and abides in our consciousness.

(*Pas Lechem*: "*you will find that they are as I have told you*" - You will find that I was right - that all the marks of wisdom manifested in them stem from one root.
Manoach Halevavos: From every creature one can see the wisdom of G-d, thereby, clarifying His Unity, for the wisdom is fundamentally and

essentially one.

Marpe Lenefesh: If you find something which you do not know its benefit and its reason, then when you reflect and examine well all things, you will find that all were done with awesome wisdom, and there is nothing which does not have a purpose and a benefit.

Rabbi YS: Even in the tiniest speck of the inanimate world, there are marks of the infinite divine wisdom as the Nobel prize winning physicist Richard Feynman noted (from his book: The Character of Physical Law - Chapter 2 - the relation of mathematics to physics): "It always bothers me that according to the laws as we understand them today, it takes a computing machine an infinite number of logical operations to figure out what goes on in no matter how tiny a region of space, and no matter how tiny a region of time. How can all that be going on in that tiny space? Why should it take an infinite amount of logic to figure out what one tiny piece of space/time is going to do? So I have often made the hypothesis ultimately physics will not require a mathematical statement, that in the end the machinery will be revealed and the laws will turn out to be simple, like the chequer board with all its apparent complexities. But this is just speculation." End Quote.

Pas Lechem: Corresponding to *"contemplate them"*, he wrote: *"established in our minds"*, i.e. to delve so deeply until one grasps the matter clearly, then his mind will be established and accept the matter without the gnawing of doubt.
Corresponding to *"think on them"* he wrote *"abides in our consciousness"* - that one thinks on them for such a long time, until he is assured it abides by him, and will not be easily forgotten.)

If these marks [of divine wisdom] were the same in all created things, no man would have any doubt in them [that they all stem from one Source]. The wise and the fool would be equal in their recognition. The reason (why the creations are not the same -ML) being that when one and the same thing is always being produced in the same way, it is clear that the maker is not a voluntary agent but a force acting according to the nature imposed upon it - compelling it to act in a definite way which it has no power to alter, just like fire whose sole function is to burn, or water whose nature is to cool. But one who has the power to do as his will prompts him will act in various ways at various times.

(*Pas Lechem*: *"wise and the fool"* - The fool is one who does not realize the qualities of wisdom, and does not want to strain his mind to toil in it. He is satisfied with the first impression. Hence, the author wrote that the wise and the fool would be equal in their recognition. Because the fool also understands things that are common and familiar, and due to repetition he understands certain things without needing to think over and contemplate. Hence, if everything were the same, he would know the hidden from the revealed.)

Since the Creator has free will in whatever He does, is not forced, needs nothing and is not forced by any nature, therefore He created things diverse, according as His wisdom each time dictated; so that the variety shall point to His unity and His free-will in whatever He does, as it is said *"Whatsoever the L-ord pleased, has He done in heaven and on earth"* (Tehilim 135:6).

(*Manoach Halevavos*: i.e. since they are similar in one respect and different in another, they point to His unity. See also my explanation in Gate 1 ch.7 argument 2.

Pas Lechem: *"has free will, not forced, etc."* His intent in this is that something which is bound to a nature such as inanimate objects, always do the same thing. But something which acts by will and desire, namely, a human being, which possesses free will - he will have different actions, but not at the same time, rather according to his needs of the time. And the Creator is not bound by any "nature", ch'v, nor is he forced, nor needs anything. The latter two terms "not forced" and "needs nothing" the author wrote to contrast with man. Because a man is sometimes "forced" in his actions, to avoid harm, or he needs to bring some benefit. Therefore, though, he acts with free will and desire, one cannot truly call him as doing with "free will", except in a borrowed sense since necessity may prevent him in this. Hence, the term "free will" correctly applies only to G-d, since His will is free of any form of need or necessity, and all the more so of any "nature".

Marpe Lenefesh: *"shall point to His unity"* - it is a clear proof and plain evidence that G-d is alone in His world... All the creations, generally and specifically - all of them guard their post (for example, the planets are forced to revolve around the sun according to His physical law). This points that they are all forced by one Master, and all are under His domain and power.

Matanas Chelko: [If He did not create things diverse] we would think that G-d is like some kind of machine (natural phenomena) which can only do one thing. Even though one would be amazed at such a machine just like we are impressed at various machines such as a machine which manufactures paper. Though we may not know how it manufacturers the paper, nevertheless, when we observe it, we are impressed at the engineering wisdom inside it. However, since we see that it can only make one thing, namely, paper, the engineering wisdom inside it is not so impressive to our eyes. We deem that the wisdom is not so great... So too, we would think the same of G-d, that He is forced and limited to this wisdom only and that He is not all-wise and all-powerful... But when we see such a multitude of types of flowers, trees, etc., even though we have no need for all these types, and likewise for all the different varieties in plants, animals, and humans - all this teaches on the wisdom of the Creator. For if there were not such a multitude, a man would not contemplate and come to recognize His great wisdom.

G-d alone knows if it is on this account only that all creatures have not been made in one form and likeness; rationally it would seem that this is the purpose of the variety in the marks of wisdom exhibited in created things. But the Creator's wisdom is too exalted for us. What we have just mentioned is only one out of many other reasons to the knowledge of which we have not attained. Complete wisdom belongs to G-d alone, and there is no power beside Him.

(*Matanas Chelko*: Summary - One is under duty to contemplate the wisdom of the Creator. The first amazement should be at the endless multitude of types of things and endless wisdom exhibited in the natural world. From this we see so many signs of wisdom in the world [such as animals, foods, flowers, trees, human beings.] All this proves and demonstrates to us also on His power and ability, that He is not forced by anything and does as He wishes.

YS: We have prepared a collection of amazing creatures at dafyomireview.com/427

CHAPTER 2

Is it our duty to study created things or not? We reply that the examination of created things and deducing from them the wisdom of the Creator is a duty which can be demonstrated from Reason, Scripture, and Tradition (the oral torah).

From Reason: For our reason bears witness that a rational creature's superiority over an irrational one consists in the former's superior ability to perceive, understand and acquire knowledge of the marks of wisdom found throughout the universe, as Scripture said *"Who teaches us more than the beasts of the field, and makes us wiser than the fowls of heaven"* (Job 35:11).

And when a man thinks of, and reflects upon, these foundations of wisdom and examines its marks in the universe, his superiority over the animals rises in proportion to his understanding. But if he neglects to observe and reflect, he is not equal to the beast, but inferior to it, as Scripture said *"The ox knows his owner, and the donkey his master's crib, but Israel does not know, my people do not consider"* (Yeshaya 1:3).

(*Tov Halevanon*: Even though the animals of the land and the birds of the sky also possess signs of intelligence and amazing things, as known to the studiers of nature, nevertheless, this is set in them only according to their survival needs (it is a "practical intelligence" only), unlike the superiority of human beings whose wisdom is encompassing, allowing him to understand the secret of other creations, in order to understand through this the will of G-d, and His wisdom.

Matanas Chelko: The human being is superior to the animal due to his intellect, namely, that man is able to contemplate wisdom, to make calculations, and draw conclusions. This is his superiority. Besides this, "a man's superiority over an animal is nothing".
"Who teaches us more.." - he did not bring this verse as a proof to the duty of examination but rather to show that the intellect is man's superiority over the animals.

When a man loses his intellect (becomes insane), he becomes worse than an animal. He can damage himself and others and come to corrupt and destroy. This one can also realize by contemplating the world, for everything has its place. And when it does not use its special abilities properly - it has no place in the world. Regarding this, there is no difference between one who does not use the intellect G-d has graced him with and one who has become insane. Both are worse than the animal. Though, one who does not use his intellect to contemplate and understand is not as wild as one who has become insane, nevertheless, regarding the damage he has caused, they are both equal, for both are inferior to the animal.

From Scripture: The same can be demonstrated from Scriptures, as it is said, *"Lift up your eyes on high and behold, who created these?"* (Yeshaya 40:26). And again *"When I behold Your heavens, the work of Your fingers, the moon and the stars, which You have established"* (Tehilim 8:4). Scripture also said *"Have you not known? have you not heard? has it not been told you from the beginning? [have you not understood from the foundations of the earth?]"* (Yeshaya 40:21) Further *"Hear O deaf, look O blind, that you may see (the wisdom of the Creator - PL)"* (Yeshaya 42:18); *"Better to go to the house of mourning than to go to the house of feasting, since that is the end of all men, and the living will take it to his heart"* (Koheles 7:2); *"The wise man, his eyes are in his head; but the fool walks in darkness"* (Koheles 2:14). *"But the path of the righteous is as the light of dawn that shines more till the day is perfect. The way of the wicked is as darkness; they know not at what they stumble"* (Mishlei 4:18-19).

(*Tov Halevanon*: The righteous go in the proper light, i.e. they follow the light of their intellects and gaze with wisdom to examine which path is the proper path so that they do not stumble [in the wrong path].

Pas Lechem: *"and the living will take it to his heart"* - Even though death is something everybody knows, since behold, it is the normal way of the world. Nevertheless, it requires contemplation and putting to heart on the sign of wisdom which is manifested in it, as our Sages expounded on the verse *"behold it was good"* - this refers to death (Midrash Bereishis Raba 9:5).

Tov Halevanon: *"and the living will take it to his heart"* - i.e. while a man is still alive, he must investigate the purpose of man and his end.)

From Tradition: The sages said (Sabbath 75a) "He who is capable of calculating the courses of the stars and planets and does not do so - of such a one, Scripture said (Yeshaya 5:12) 'And the harp, and the lyre, the timbrel, and flute, and wine, are in their feasts: but they regard not the work of the L-ord, nor do they contemplate the work of His hands'". And they say further (Sabbath 75a) "From where do we know that it is a duty to calculate the courses of the stars and planets?" Because it is said (Devarim

4:6) 'Observe therefore and do them, for this is your wisdom and understanding in the sight of the nations that, when they hear all these statutes, they shall say: 'Surely this great nation is a wise and understanding people'. This verse refers to the duty of making astronomical calculations."

Further they said (Pirkei Avos 2:1) "Consider the loss from doing a mitzvah (precept) against its reward and the gain from doing a sin against the loss it involves".

(*Marpe Lenefesh*: this is a general proof that a man must not be like a wild horse without understanding, rather he must consider and examine all of his actions always.)

And they further said (Eruvin 100b) "If the Torah had not been given to the Jews, we could have learned decency from the cat, chastity from the dove, etiquette from the rooster and honesty from the ant" (hence it is our duty to examine the creations - *TL*).

(*Pas Lechem*: The cat covers his excrement. The dove does not exchange his mate. The rooster appeases the hen before mating. The ant does not steal the food particle that his fellow ant acquired.)

Thus far it has been demonstrated that it is a duty to examine created things and draw the deductions from the marks of Divine Wisdom exhibited in them. Note it well!

CHAPTER 3

How are the several ways of examination to be conducted?

Examination of created things means a close study of the elements of which the Universe is composed; the products that result from the combination of these elements; the character of the constituents of each composite; the ways in which it is useful; the marks of wisdom exhibited in its production, form and shape, and in the purpose for which it was created; the beautiful spirituality of this world; its causes and effects; and the complete perfection for which it was created; to know its contents - spiritual and physical, rational and irrational, the immobile and the mobile (solid and fluid), minerals and plants; its higher and lower parts; and to realize that the Creator created the Universe in a perfect and orderly combination - each of its parts distinctly recognizable, - so that it hints and teaches on the Creator, as a work points to the workman, or a house indicates the builder.

(*Pas Lechem*: *"the marks of wisdom exhibited in its production"* - i.e. the beginning of its existence, while it is forming, such as in living things, some species gestate and give birth, others lay eggs, and by plants, this species grows by itself, another through a seed planted. Similarly, there are many many differences in the formation of creatures.
"its causes and effects" - i.e. to know and understand the cause and effect in each thing, that through this thing it is completed and endures, as you will find in living things, that animals need plants, plants need water and soil. Hence, plants are a cause for the animals, that it becomes complete and enduring in the world. Likewise for all creations - all have a cause which completes it... and to reflect and understand the purpose of all creations, why they were all created and what benefit they have. When one looks and thinks on this, he will see and discern that everything was created for man, as he wrote in the first gate...

Marpe Lenefesh: G-d made the universe so that all who behold it will recognize and know that a wise, mighty, and capable One, of which there is none like Him, created it just like a building teaches on the wisdom and ability of the builder. So too, we can deduce from the world and everything in it on the Creator even though we cannot grasp His essence as explained in Gate 1.

Pas Lechem: *"so that it hints and teaches on the Creator"* - *"hints"* refers to a general vague teaching whose explanation is not clear, such as "He winks with his eyes" (Mishlei 6:13). *"teaches"*, however, refers to a clear teaching which explains the thing. Behold, on the surface examination and first impression on the general existence of the universe - immediately, it teaches on the existence of the Creator who created it because a thing cannot create itself, as explained in gate 1, just like a handiwork reveals the existence of the craftsman who made it. However, it is an encrypted teaching, only hinting, since it does not explain His intent, wisdom, and ability. However, after much contemplation on the details of the creations and their connected purpose - it will teach us clearly and explain to us His intent, wisdom, and ability to do as He wishes, just like the existence of a building teaches on the existence of its builder, which certainly also teaches on the builder's intent, wisdom, and ability. Unlike a general vague deed, as before, (that creation alone does not show all this). And this is what he wrote: *"as a work points to the workman, or a house indicates the builder"*. "The work" corresponds to the "hint" (general vague teaching of creation), while the "house" corresponds to the "clear teaching" on His will, wisdom, and ability. Understand this.

Matanas Chelko: those who believe that the world simply popped into existence by itself without a Creator is not only a heretic but also a big fool. (note: I think the Rav is not referring to the average scientist who was trained in this way of thinking since his youth and is not to blame, but rather to the leaders, the innovators, the militant atheists who are constantly pushing this outlook on humanity.)

For if a person would come and try to convince him that this table assembled itself on its own, he would consider it an insult that the person considers him so foolish and of crooked intellect that he thinks he can convince him of this. In truth, the heretic is not so because he concluded these things (that there is no Creator) in his mind and thoughts, but rather because he concluded this in his heart. For if he admits that this world has a Creator, he would then be under duty to assume His service. Therefore, these people look for and invent all sorts of rationalizations and excuses in order to assert that the universe created itself. And it is all for the purpose of exempting themselves from the service of G-d. They say these crazy things only out of great necessity. For when a man is cornered and has no choice, he will then say or do something foolish. So too here, it is only out of great necessity that they claim the world simply came into existence by itself. So too, for those who accept their theories and fool themselves into believing that it is true. For behold, from the universe itself it is possible to see that there is a Creator.

Behold in science, the more wisdom they discover, the more heretical they become. While for the believer it is the opposite, that their faith becomes strengthened. The reason is that the outlook and attitude of the scientists is "kochi v'otzem yadi" (it is our strength and ingenuity that has accomplished this for us). Therefore, the result is that the more the scientist discovers, the more he will feel he has done more (become more proud). But the believer knows that every new thing he discovers in the world is another strong proof of the Creator...

It is proper that you should know that the whole world (even inanimate things - *TL*) is synthesized of the physical and the spiritual, so intimately mixed and fused, that each of them sustains the other, like body and soul in living creatures.

(*Pas Lechem*: *"like body and soul (nefesh) in living creatures"* - the soul prolongs and sustains the body. When the soul leaves the body, the body immediately inanimates and decomposes ("life" ceases). Likewise, the body sustains the animal soul in animals, and when the animal soul leaves the animal's body, it (the animal soul) ceases and nullifies. Likewise, for the nefesh tzomachat (plant soul) in plants. For the nefesh medaberet (human soul) we can say the same regarding its existing in this physical world, because immediately after the human soul leaves the body, it returns to its place in the higher worlds [as written (Eccl. 12:7) "Then shall the dust return to the earth as it was: and the spirit shall return unto G-d who gave it."].
Translator: see Gate 1 ch.5 where we showed that living creatures which can grow and reproduce are simply too complicated for any kind of purely physical machine.)

The marks of wisdom exhibited in all of this are of three kinds.

(1) Those of the first kind are clear and apparent, and do not escape the notice even of the fool, and of course not of the thinking person. An example is the [relative] movement of the sun above the earth to illuminate the habitable portion of the globe, to benefit the creatures that live there; as Scripture said (Tehilim 104:22-24) *"The sun arises, they assemble and crouch in their dens. Man goes forth unto his work and to his labor until the evening. How manifold are Your works, O L-ord! With wisdom have You made them all. The earth is full of Your possessions".*

(2) The second kind consists of marks of wisdom, whose benefit and necessity is hidden from most people and known only to the intelligent person who comprehends that they are right. Such as death, the fate that overtakes all flesh and which is necessary for the welfare of the world. As our sages expounded the verse: (Bereishis 1:31) " 'And G-d saw everything that He had made, and behold it was very good'. 'Behold it was very good' - this refers to death." (Bereishis Raba 9:5). So, too, the wise king said

"wherefore I praised the dead which are already dead more than the living which are yet alive" (Koheles 4:2).

> (*Tov Halevanon*: Even though death appears to be something very bad for that individual creature, but when one reflects on the collective good, one will realize and understand that this is how it must be according to the physical nature of the world, and without this evil, the world could not endure due to the coming generations, for it is impossible for one thing to arise without the loss of something which preceded it.
>
> *Marpe Lenefesh*: Without death, the human race could not endure for several reasons. Without death, why should a man work endlessly under the sun? When would he take his reward? Since in truth, the good of this world, is not really good and likewise for the bad. The wicked person would not fear death and would always remain in his wickedness. [With death,] the righteous man will receive his reward there according to his deeds... and there are other good reasons for death which we cannot comprehend...
>
> *Matanas Chelko*: Without death, we would lose this final source of fear of heaven... For when a person remembers the [coming of the] day of his death, he can defeat his base nature and evil inclination. For he reflects how through death, he will go on to a new world, and that he must prepare for this. Therefore death is necessarily very good. Hence, by understanding this, he will recognize how death is a divine benefit to man. Through it he can attain fear of heaven and fulfill his purpose of service in this world, thereby acquiring his portion in the Olam Haba (afterlife).

(3) The third kind consists of marks of wisdom that are partly obscure and partly clear. The man endowed with but little mental power will not recognize them unless he ponders them and studies them in minute detail. An example is the changes that take place in the year, its four seasons etc.

> (*Tov Halevanon*: From warm to cold, from summer to winter. It appears that the warm is better, but after examination, one will realize that each one has a specific benefit.
>
> *Matanas Chelko*: Why we need four seasons, and why is it not enough for less than four. There is amazing wisdom in this to those who know - what each season brings, such as snow in winter, falling of leaves in autumn. Much contemplation is necessary - and to learn from someone who has a mesora (torah tradition) in this subject in order to fully understand it.

The wise and intelligent man will choose from the world for study its fine and spiritual elements; use them as a ladder by which to obtain proofs of the existence of the Creator of all, to Whose service he will then cling to according to his heartfelt recognition of the greatness and exaltedness of the Creator, and his realization of the Almighty's gracious benevolence to all of His creations and that G-d has graciously bestowed abundant benefits to him, and has elevated him (above the animals, etc.) while he had done nothing nor possessed any moral quality that would entitle him to deserve any divine reward.

(*Marpe Lenefesh*: "study its fine and spiritual elements...obtain proofs" - i.e. he will not look solely at the physical side of things, so one should not think man was created for physical things such as eating and other needs. Because then it would not be necessary for each creature to have some fine and spiritual elements. Rather the spiritual in each thing is a clear proof on the blessed Creator, as is evident to one who reflects on this. When a person habituates himself in everything he looks at and in every creature he sees, he will be able to see the work of G-d for it is awesome, and through this he will be able to fulfill the verse: "I have set G-d before me always" (Tehilim 16:8). When he habituates in this, the awe and fear of G-d will enter his heart and "he will then cling to the service of G-d".
Pas Lechem: The wise man will put his attention to know the fine and spiritual side of the world... He will set them as a ladder in intellectual investigation to ascend higher and higher. And the purpose of all this - so that he attains understanding into the greatness and exaltedness of the blessed Creator and clings to His service. The intensity of his clinging will be according to the intensity of the picture in his heart of the greatness and exaltedness of the Creator, and according to how much he recognizes the marks of G-d's benevolence to His creations... i.e. to first contemplate G-d's collective benevolence towards all of His creations and afterwards to contemplate the special favor G-d has shown specifically to him [*Rabbi YS*: such as making him a human being instead of a frog]

Matanas Chelko: the wise man understands that the purpose of this world is not just for his pleasure, but rather it is in order to understand and find the Creator through the manifested wisdom therein. This outlook applies to all physical matters of this world - that one uses them as a ladder, to bring proofs on the Creator. For through every thing, it is possible to see the greatness of the Creator, and through this he will come to thank Him, as the author will explain.
"to Whose service he will then cling" - A man's service towards G-d depends on the degree to which he recognizes the greatness and exaltedness of the Creator."
"and that G-d has graciously bestowed abundant benefits to him" - For even before a man has done anything whatsoever, he already received many benefits from G-d. Through this, he will obligate himself to recognize the

| good (be grateful) and to try to make a return through his service.

Afterwards, he will select for himself, of the material things, only those that promote his physical benefit and material well-being, but only to the extent needful and sufficient. He will abandon the rest, of the superfluities and worldly desires which turn the heart away from G-d. He will rather busy himself with working for his final home, the place to which he will go after his death. The world and its possessions, he will regard as a means of providing for his appointed day, his latter end. He will take of this world only what can accompany him on his journey.

Matanas Chelko: This is along what is written in chapter 1 of the Mesilas Yesharim: "the primary purpose of a man's existence in this world is solely the fulfilling of commandments, the serving of G-d and the withstanding of trials, and that the world's pleasures should serve only the purpose of aiding and assisting him, by way of providing him with the contentment and peace of mind requisite for the freeing of his heart for the service which is placed upon him" End quote. Hence, this world is built in such a way that a person is required to partake of a certain measure of physical pleasures and tranquility. It is permitted and even a duty to do so according to how much he needs for his particular makeup. One who abstains from physical pleasures and through this he has no peace of mind to serve G-d - this is false religiosity (frumkeit b'alma). And the opposite, one who excesses in worldly pleasures and seeks the superfluous or seeks to indulge in physical pleasures - he is not on the right path and it is forbidden to go in this course. The balance in this is very fine. Every person must carefully weigh himself and estimate himself according to his own particular physical and mental makeup what he truly needs to help and aid him so that he has the proper contentment and peace of mind in order that his mind is free to serve G-d. These are permitted and even an obligation. Conversely, those pleasures which distract and obstruct a person from the service of G-d are forbidden.

But a person ignorant of the ways of the world and of its evidences of divine wisdom, regards it as his everlasting home and fixed abode. He busies himself with it strenuously, sets all his heart and concentrates all his energies upon it, thinking that he is rapidly furthering his own interests and does not realize that the fruits of his toil and the superfluity that he has gathered will go to others possibly during his lifetime and undoubtedly after his death. And thus he totally neglects his interests hereafter.

(*Marpe Lenefesh*: This world and all of its possessions was created only so that a human being will prepare in it his provisions for the Olam Haba (afterlife). Because there is his true home and residence. While here, he is like a visitor who stopped by temporarily. "This world is like a hallway to the Olam Haba..." (Avos 4:16), "today to do them and tomorrow to receive their reward" (Eruvin 22a). Therefore, one should take from this world only what will be good for him in the afterlife, and not more. But the fool, who does not understand what G-d asks of him, and why he came to this world and in this body, and thinks that here is his home and residence, and that he will be here forever. Therefore, he works only for worldly matters and completely forgets his final end.

Matanas Chelko: "a person ignorant of the ways of the world and of its evidences of divine wisdom" - He does not contemplate them. He does not see the divine wisdom. He does not feel all the good he received and does not long to make a return.

How analogous these types are to two brothers who inherited from their father a piece of land that needed cultivation. They divided it between themselves. Neither of them possessed anything else. One of them was sensible and industrious; the other was the opposite (foolish and lazy - *PL*).

The sensible brother realized that if he occupied himself solely with his plot of land, this would prevent him from earning his livelihood and attaining his immediate needs. So he hired himself out as a day-laborer in a field belonging to another person and was thus able to subsist on the wages he received. After he had finished his daily task he worked an hour every evening in his own field industriously and zealously. When he had saved enough out of his wages to keep him for one or more days, he stopped working for others and labored on his property with the utmost energy and zeal. In this course he persevered until his plot was in a proper state of cultivation. When the harvest time came he gathered the products of his field and orchard, stored them and had sufficient produce to support himself for the next year. Then he cultivated his land as he desired and planted more trees until it not only produced enough for his maintenance, but yielded a surplus with which he bought additional land.

The foolish brother, recognizing that working on his land alone would prevent him from earning a living, neglected his property completely, hired himself out to others as a field-laborer, spent the whole of the wages he received and saved nothing. Whenever he had enough left of his earnings to provide him with food for a single day, he turned it into a day of rest, idleness and amusement, never giving a thought to his property. The hours during which he was free on the days when he worked, he spent in the bath. His land remained waste and yielded nothing. It was all covered with thorns and thistles. Its fences were broken. Its trees were swept away by a flood (which entered through the breaches in the stone fence - *ML*). It was in the condition described by the wise man in the text (Mishlei 24:30-31) *"I passed by the field of the slothful and by the vineyard of the man void of understanding and behold, it was all overgrown with thorns; nettles had covered the face thereof, and the stone wall thereof was broken down."*

(*Pas Lechem*: *"a day of rest, idleness and amusement"* - Three disgraces each worse than the other. The first person who hates hard work, and after a bit of strain, already wants to rest. He does not realize that a "man was born to toil" (Iyov 5:7),and according to the greatness of the purpose will be the greatness of the necessary strain to attain it, as written "[he saw that the rest (in the afterlife) was good, and the land that it was pleasant;] and bowed his shoulder to bear" (Bereishis 49:15). Worse than this person, is a lazy man who loves idleness, and does not desire any work, as written "A sluggard buries his hand in the dish; he will not even bring it back to his mouth" (Mishlei 19:24). Even worse than both of these, some people hate idleness and are energetic. However, all of their toil is in futilities and foolishness, such as playing with dice or the like. Hence, this person sometimes makes "a day of rest", to rest from the feeling of strain of the previous days. Sometimes, even though he does not feel any strain in his body, he desires idleness, and sometime he made that day a day of amusement, to amuse himself with futile toil.)

The intelligent reader who reflects intently upon this parable will draw from it the lesson as to his final end, which is his true home, and he will work on it with all his might. While for his earthly needs, he will work as one does for others, in moderation and only to the extent absolutely necessary. The fool, however, acts oppositely in two ways. His interests here on earth he pursues with zeal and diligence while for his welfare in the hereafter he utterly ignores; even as the wise man said, when he observed the fool (Mishlei 24.32), *"Then I saw and considered it well. I looked upon it and drew lessons* (to the matter of the soul - *TL*)".

(*Tov Halevanon*: *"will draw from it the lesson as to his final end"* - For his land refers to his neshama (soul), which G-d gave to him "to work it and to guard it" (Bereishis 2:15) in purity, to succeed in planting and bearing fruit in the vineyard of G-d, until the time it is called back. The intelligent man sees that if he spends all of his time working only for his soul, he will not be able to earn a living to provide for his body, and like our sages said: "all torah study without working for a livelihood will in the end be neglected" (Avot 2:3). Therefore, he sees proper to hire himself out to some work, or some business dealing with faith, in order to sustain himself. But when he is free from this work, he returns diligently to torah study and service of G-d until he reaches the level of Tzadik (righteous). Then G-d will direct special attention on him to give him abundance and to bless his handiwork, as scripture says: "I never saw a righteous forsaken" (Tehilim 37:25), until he increases strength and pure hands to honor G-d with his money (give charity etc), and to ascend his soul from level to level until he merits the Olam Haba, eternal rewards, and a higher soul. But the fool does not work on his soul. Rather, he only endeavors to make profit, to serve his body, and to amass the superfluous and the pleasures of the masses, and he abandons his soul barren and to waste. Unseeded, it will not sprout, nor receive on it any shefa (spiritual light) or divine clinging until it will no longer be capable even to return to its source due to having defiled itself. Rather, to the sheol (Gehinom) he will descend, and the underworld will blanket over him. On him it is written (Yeshaya 3:9) "Woe unto their soul! for they have brought evil unto themselves".

Marpe Lenefesh: Gan Eden is a person's true home. In this world, he is like a visitor who camped for a temporary stay. Only that he needs room and board, and must therefore prepare his livelihood. But he must not abandon his plot of land in Olam Haba (the afterlife) by ignoring cultivating it lest it become a barren wasteland...)

Chapter 4

How many are the marks of divine wisdom in created things which we can examine?

To this we reply that even though there are many kinds of created things and each kind has many constituents, the cornerstones of wisdom found in them are seven classes.

One of these is the mark of wisdom apparent in the primary and fundamental elements of the universe. The Earth, we observe is at the center; close to it and above it is water; close to the water is the atmosphere; above all is fire in a just and unchanging balance and measure. Everyone of these elements maintains its proper position appointed for it. The ocean bed, with the waters imprisoned therein, stays in its place and does not pass beyond its boundaries despite the roaring of the waves and the raging of the winds, as it is written *"And I prescribed for it My decree, and set bars and doors; and said: 'Thus far you shall come, but no further, and here shall your proud waves be stayed'"*(Iyov 38:9-11).

> (*Tov Halevanon*: *"The Earth, we observe is at the center"* - the earth and everything in it, is suspended in space by the word of G-d, and its inhabitants dwell all around its surface, and despite that it is a globe, no one falls from it, even though it would seem that those living on the opposite half, who stand opposite us, should fall off. It appears to each of the inhabitants that they are standing on top of the earth, and the heavens are above them. This is an unbelievable wonder of the wisdom of the Creator. [*Rabbi YS*: learn to appreciate gravity!])

Concerning the stability of heaven and earth, Scripture said (Ps. 119:89-91) *"Forever, O L-ord, Your word stands fast in heaven, Your faithfulness is unto all generations; You have established the earth and it stands. They stand this day according to Your ordinances; for all things are Your servants"*. David also dwelt on this theme in his Psalm (104) beginning *"O my soul, bless the L-ord. [He dons light like a garment, spreads the heavens like a curtain]"*.

> (*Tov Halevanon*: *"Forever, O L-ord, Your word stands fast in heaven"* - The word of G-d and the power of His deeds are always in the celestial spheres and all of their hosts - this is what perpetuates their existence, similar to the verse: "You give life to all of them" (Nechemia 9:6). If G-d were to

withhold His hashpaa (influence) from them, they would immediately
cease to exist.
"Your faithfulness is unto all generations" - G-d's kindness is faithfully on
all the creatures of the earth.
"They stand this day according to Your ordinances" - i.e. the continuous
existence of all the creations is due to Your constant ordinance and
command.
"for all things are Your servants" - none of them exist through "nature",
rather it is G-d who grants them existence continuously.
"O my soul, bless the L-ord..." the entire Psalm is in the present tense, i.e.
G-d does this always, as David ends off "but if You turn away Your face,
they shall vanish". All this teaches that G-d's power never ceases to sustain
all.
Pas Lechem: The psalm describes how the creations guard the [physical]
laws of G-d and never deviate from their purpose.)

The second cornerstone is the mark of wisdom apparent in the human
species, - a universe on a small scale that completes the ordered series of
creation, and constitutes its crowning beauty, glory and perfection. David,
peace be on him, referred to Man when he acclaimed *"O Eternal, our
L-ord, how glorious is Your Name in all the earth."* (Tehilim 8:1).

(*Marpe Lenefesh*: Through man all of what G-d created is completed and
perfected for everything was created for the benefit of man and to serve
him, and man is in this world, like the owner of the house.)

The third cornerstone is the mark of wisdom apparent in the formation of
the individual human being, - his physical structure the faculties of his
nefesh (lower soul) and the light of reason with which the Creator has
distinguished him and thus given him superiority over other living
creatures that are irrational.

Man resembles the large universe, being like it fundamentally and in its
original elements. To this Job refers when he said (Job 10:10-12) *"Have
You not poured me out as milk and curdled me like cheese? With skin and
flesh have You clothed me, and with bones and sinews have You knit me
together? Life and favor have You granted me, And Your providence has
preserved my spirit".*

(*Tov Halevanon*: *"faculties of his nefesh (lower soul)"* - the feeling soul
from which arise the five senses, and also the power of imagination, and
the power of awareness, and other bodily powers. [PL - such as the power
of growth, reproduction, etc. The Kabalists counted 70 powers.]
"the light of reason" - this is the neshama (higher soul). Through it man

was distinguished from the animals, since they also possess faculties of nefesh.

Manoach Halevavos: *"Your providence has preserved my spirit"* - i.e. the binding of the neshama (soul) and ruach (spirit) with the body. This is an amazing thing, it is unimaginable, and impossible were it not for the command of G-d, and His decree.)

The fourth cornerstone is the mark of wisdom manifested in other species of living creatures, from the least to the greatest. Those that fly or swim or creep or move on four feet, with their various forms, traits, uses, benefits, and purpose in the world. This is mentioned in the speech in which the Creator rebuked Job in order to arouse him to his duty (Job 38:41) *"who provides for the raven his prey?, etc."* and the further references (Job 39) to various species of animals that live in the deserts and the seas.

(*Pas Lechem*: *"forms, traits, uses, benefits, and purpose"* - Each creature reflects a particular part of wisdom. The terms *"forms"* refers to external appearance. *"Traits"* refers to the special traits of creatures, such as bravery of heart to the lion, brazenness to the leopard, anger to the bear, and the wise king attributed zeal to the ant, and similarly for others. The term *"uses"*: that man uses each one for a particular use. Such as the ox for plowing, the horse for riding, the donkey for carrying, the camel and elephant for travel in deserts/jungles. *"Benefits"* that man benefits something from each one, such as cattle and sheep for their meat or milk. Wild animals for their skins. These are uses for enjoyment. But some creatures provide man with *"purposeful"* uses such as the crab and the eggs of the "kastor" which are needed for medicinal purposes, and many many more examples, as known by those who study [natural] medicine. Likewise, many others are needed for different benefits.
"the speech in which the Creator rebuked Job in order to arouse him to his duty" - to arouse his heart to reflect on the greatness of the Creator and His wisdom. Then automatically, he will realize his lowliness relative to Him, and will close his mouth.

Marpe Lenefesh: Rabeinu Tam writes in the sefer hayashar shaar 13 that it is proper to recite that speech in Job [ch.38])

The fifth is the mark of wisdom displayed in plants and other natural products (ex. minerals) that have been provided for the improvement of the human race, because of their usefulness to man in various ways, according to their natures, constitutions and powers. The ancients already expounded this subject in their works, according to their conceptions. Thus it is said (Melachim 5:13) *"And he (Solomon) spoke of trees from the cedar that is*

*in Lebanon even unto the hyssop that springs out of the wall: he spoke also
of beasts, and fowl, and of creeping things and of fishes".*

(*Tov Halevanon*: *"And he (Solomon) spoke of trees"* he revealed the benefit
of each plant and explained for which use it was created)

The sixth is the mark of wisdom discernible in the sciences, arts and crafts
which the Creator, blessed be He, provided for man, to contribute to his
improvement, to enable him to obtain a livelihood and gain other benefits
of a general and particular character. To this mark of divine wisdom
Scripture refers in the texts (Job 38:36) *"Who has put wisdom in the inward
parts? Or who has given understanding to the mind?"* and again (Prov.
2:6) *"For the L-ord gives wisdom; out of His mouth comes knowledge and
discernment".*

(*Marpe Lenefesh*: *"of a general and particular character"* - that all human
beings need that trade such as plowing and sowing, or the like, while some
trades are only for some people such as gold and silver smiths, which are
needed only by the wealthy..
"who has given understanding to the mind" - who has given wisdom to man
and set understanding in his mind to think thoughts and do all the works
and deeds which man does?

Rabbi YS: If you ask, why did G-d conceal modern science from man for
thousands of years? Modern technology is far superior to the animal labor
of old. Answer: I would suggest that the animal labor way is necessary long
term because it limits man's destructive ability. Modern science may seem
good now, but in 50 or 100 years from now we will see in retrospect that it
was not a good thing - it can really bring tremendous destruction. For
mankind to survive in equilibrium long term, the destructive potential of
the wicked must be restrained. As to why G-d has granted it in our era,
perhaps because we are near the final showdown as described in scripture.
Another possible explanation is that it is necessary to maintain free will.
Advances in microbiology are increasingly unraveling the inner workings
of cells and this is leading to a new and enormously powerful argument to
design. Scientists are backing themselves further and further into a corner
for the more they discover the harder it becomes to attribute it all to chance.
It is, after all, a tremendous feat to produce a contraption which will grow
and reproduce itself autonomously. see my treatise on evolution at
dafyomireview.com/421 for much more on this.)

The seventh is the mark of wisdom exhibited in the appointment of the
Torah and its statutes, to teach us how to serve the Creator and secure for
one who diligently lives according to their dictates, immediate happiness

here, and reward in the hereafter, as it is written (Is.55:2-3) *"Hearken diligently unto me, and eat ye that which is good (in this world - MH) and let your soul delight itself in pleasantness (in the next world - MH). Incline your ear and come to Me; Hear and your soul shall live."* To this should be added the customs by which the government of other nations is regulated together with their useful features. For those nations, these customs take the place of the Torah - but only in secular matters.

(*Marpe Lenefesh*: G-d set His torah among us so that we may properly know what to do and how to conduct ourselves in this world. Through the torah, we may know how to do G-d's will. Without it, a man is like a fool, walking in darkness. Not only that, but through the torah one also attains the pleasures of this world as explained in parsha Bechukotai: "if you will walk in My statutes, I will give..." (Vayikra 26:3) and many similar verses.

"To this should be added the customs by which the government of other nations is regulated.." - the explanation is like the Chacham, author of Sefer Ikarim, that whatever is found in something incidentally must be found in something else as essence. For example, hotness is found in hot water as an incidental property, therefore it must be found somewhere else as essence, namely, fire. (hotness is an essence property of fire since you cannot remove it without destroying the fire), and the water acquired this property incidentally. Likewise, if a real man did not exist, you would not find forms or statues of man. Likewise, if there did not exist a true divine religion/law, there would not exist other forms of religion/law....)

It has been stated that the relation of nature to the Torah is that of a servant to his master. The forces of nature in the universe operate in harmony with the teaching of the torah, as it is said (Shemot 23:25) *"And you shall serve the L-ord your G-d, and He will bless your bread and your water; and I will take away sickness from your midst"*. And again, (ibid. 15:26) *"If you will diligently hearken to the voice of the L-ord your G-d, and will do that which is right in His sight and will give ear to His commandments and keep all His statutes, none of the diseases which I have brought upon the Egyptians will I bring upon you, for I am the L-ord that heals you"*, and many other passages like this.

(*Marpe Lenefesh*: Even though it appears that the world acts independently according to natural laws, in truth nature is under rule of the torah, i.e. those who fulfill the torah. They can rule over nature as they wish as a master can rule over his slave (subject to certain limitations by G-d). This is not something supernatural because G-d, who created the universe and the laws of nature - He Himself gave us the torah, and He decreed on all of His creations that they be under the rule of those who fulfill the torah.. And as the verses in the torah teach...)

Some are of the opinion that when the wise man said (Mishlei 9:1) *"Wisdom has built her house; she has hewn out her seven pillars"*, he had in mind the seven cornerstones which we have mentioned.

Chapter 5

Which class [of Evidences of Divine Wisdom] is nearest to us, so that it is our duty to examine it more? To this we reply that, while the close study of each and everyone of the [seven] classes previously enumerated is necessary and obligatory more [than it seems at first sight - PL], the evidence of divine wisdom which is nearest and clearest to us is that manifested in the human species, a microcosm of the universe, the closest cause (ultimate purpose) to the existence of the larger world.

(*Pas Lechem*: *"nearest and clearest"* - nearest in proximity because why should a man go out to find other creatures and approach them to observe and contemplate them? Is not man in close proximity to himself? Furthermore, knowledge of himself is clearer to man than knowledge of other creatures.
"the closest cause to the existence of the larger world" - As our sages said on the verse "this is all of man" (Koheles 12:13) - that the entire world was created for this. The author called man the *"closest cause"*, since G-d created many worlds, which emerge and chain out one from the other. And this [physical] world, which is perceptible to us, is the end of the chain. Hence, it arouses through a long series of causes. However, since man is the ultimate purpose - he is the closest cause of all of them, since "the end of action is first in thought". And immediately when G-d thought to create man, He also thought about the creation of our world, and subsequently, the causes through which our [physical] world can come to existence. Understand this.)

Hence, it is our duty to study the beginning of a human being, his birth, the compositions of his parts, the joining together of his limbs, the purpose of each limb/organ and the necessity which caused his being made in its present form. Next, we should study man's advantages, his various temperaments, the faculties of his nefesh (lower soul), the light of his intellect, his qualities - those that are essential and those that are incidental; his lusts, and the ultimate purpose of his being (for what purpose was he created - *PL*). When we have arrived at an understanding of the matters noted in regard to man, much of the mystery of this universe will become clear to us, since the one resembles the other.

(*Pas Lechem*: *"man's advantages"* - instincts the Creator set for his benefit, such as arousing compassion for him in the heart of his parents, lack of intellect and perception in his early years, benefits of crying in his babyhood, and other matters as will be explained.

"his temperaments" - such as pride, humility, anger, contentment, or the like.

"faculties of his nefesh" - such as memory, thought, and also others enumerated such as sustenance, growth, reproduction, and the like, as will be explained.

"his lusts" - such as eating, drinking, relations.)

And thus some sages declared that philosophy is man's knowledge of himself, which means, knowledge of what we have mentioned regarding the human being, so that through the evidence of divine wisdom displayed in himself, he will become cognizant of the Creator (and His wisdom and ability - *ML*); as Job said (Job 19:26) *"From my flesh, I see G-d"*.

(*Marpe Lenefesh*: *"philosophy"* - i.e. general wisdom, because all the wisdoms and all the rational investigations are given the general term "philosophy". And the author says that the general principle of wisdom is only man's knowing himself.

Tov Halevanon: the "Aruch" explained that in Greek language, "philosopher" means "one who loves wisdom". The term "philosophy" is derived from the term "philosopher".)

Since this is so, it is proper that we should call a bit of attention to each of the topics noted in regard to man, in order to arouse the negligent person to what it is his duty to always have in mind; and thus he will be induced to investigate further into matters that I have not mentioned. And then, realizing the abundance of G-d's loving kindness and goodness toward him, he will be filled with the spirit of humility and submission towards the Creator, and his gratitude towards his Maker will abound, as David, peace be upon him, said: *"I will give thanks to You for I am fearfully and wonderfully made; wonderful are Your works; and that, my soul knows right well. My frame was not hidden from You, when I was made in secret, and wrought (with flesh and sinews - ML) in the lowest parts of the earth (i.e. the womb - TL). My unformed substance Your eyes did see; and in Your book were they all written, in the days when they would be fashioned, while as yet there was none of them."* (Tehilim 119:14-16)

(*Pas Lechem*: *"in order to arouse the negligent person"* - He who is by nature lazy and negligent, we must arouse his heart and make him understand *"what it is his duty"*.

"he will be induced to investigate further" - after he investigates these matters and his palate will taste the taste of understanding and its delectable sweetness, this will induce him to desire more, and to investigate further on his own even on what we did not mention.)

The first topic to which it is right that you direct your attention is the origin of a human being and the earliest processes of his development. You will then see that it is the divine loving-kindness that has brought him into existence out of nothing. The fundamental elements of the world, out of which he is formed, pass into the vegetable state which becomes nourishment and changes into seed and blood. This is transformed into general life which finally assumes the form and nature of a human being - living, rational and mortal - who travels through life, experiencing changes and metamorphoses and continually varied conditions and circumstances that are connected according to a properly thought out and coordinated plan.

> (*Tov Halevanon*: all the changes and variations of circumstances are according to a properly thought out plan to benefit him in his final end and to complete his tikun (rectification/mission) in this world)

When you will contemplate this and will see the evidence of the Creator's goodness, wisdom and power manifested in everything, consider and reflect upon the visible constituents of man's being, namely his body and his soul. You will observe that his body is composed of various elements with dissimilar qualities. These the Creator put together by His Almighty power, combined by His wisdom, and formed out of them a stable organism which in appearance has the character of unity but his body is composed of various elements with diverse natures. To this human body, G-d has joined a spiritual and intangible essence akin to the spirituality of the higher beings (angels). This essence is his soul, bound up in him with the body by means adapted to serve both these extremes. These means are the Ruach Chaim (spirit of life), natural heat (life force), the blood, the veins, nerves, and arteries. To protect and guard them against injuries, G-d has provided flesh, bones, sinews, skin, hair and nails. All these are shields and defenses to ward off injuries.

> (*Pas Lechem*: "*the visible constituents of man's being, namely his body and his soul*" - a human being is a composite of many things, only that these two things, the body and the soul, are the roots which include generally the entire structure... He called them "visible" because the particular parts are hidden, such as in the body, the intestines, small veins, biles, etc. or, in the soul, the hidden powers inside it. However, the general structure of body and soul are visible, i.e. generally perceptible. The body is perceptible to the eyesight, and the soul is perceptible in the intellect, in that the body can feel and move when the soul is inside it, and the opposite when the soul leaves it.
>
> Rabbi YS: The soul animates the body to life. Life is not just a physical

process. Likewise all life forms, even bacteria, have a spiritual component which animates it. It is simply beyond the ability of any kind of physical machine, which necessarily functions in a direct manner, namely, one thing reacts which causes another to react, etc. motorically - to grow and reproduce as we explained in Gate 1 ch.5 . Too many things need to happen simultaneously, see there.

Marpe Lenefesh: *"G-d has joined a spiritual and intangible essence"* - A complete independent spiritual creature, with 248 limbs and 365 sinews just like the body (see Shaarei Kedusha 1:1), and it is intangible and invisible to the physical eye, like the higher beings, namely, the spiritual melachim (angels).

Tov Halevanon: *"This essence is his soul, bound up in him with the body by means"* - Behold, the physical and the spiritual are opposites of each other, only that they are joined through intermediate means suited to receive both of them. The Ruach Chaim (spirit of life), which is the nefesh bahamit (lower soul) is bound to the spiritual, namely, the neshama (higher soul), and it is also bound to the natural heat (life force), and the natural heat is bound to the blood, and the blood to the sinews, and the sinews to the bones.)

After this, reflect on the favor shown by the Creator in His providential guidance of man.
At the beginning of a human being's existence, the Creator appointed the mother's body to serve as a crib for the fetus so that it might abide in a safe place, a strongly guarded fortress, as it were, where no hand can touch it, where it cannot be affected by heat or cold, but is shielded and sheltered and where its food is ready for it. Here it continues to grow and develop, even becomes capable of moving and turning, and receives its nourishment without any effort or exertion. This nourishment is provided for it in a place where no one else can in any way reach it, and is increased as the fetus develops until a definite period.

Then it goes out from its mother's belly through a narrow track without any contrivance or help on its part, but solely by the power of the wise, merciful and gracious One who shows compassion to His creatures; as He said to Job (39:1-2) *"Do you know the time when the wild goats of the rock-bring forth? Or can you mark when the hinds do calve? Can you number the months that they fulfill? Or do you know the time when they bring forth?"*

(*Pas Lechem*: *"wise, merciful, and gracious One"* - G-d is merciful towards him that he not be injured in going through a narrow track, and in His wisdom, He made the birth canal widen and expand then to make for him a secure exit path.)

Afterwards, the infant emerges into this world - all its senses, except those of touch and taste, being weak - the Creator provides for it food from its mother's breast. The blood which had been its nourishment before it was born, is now converted into milk in the mother's breast, pleasant and sweet, flowing like a gushing spring whenever needed. The milk is not so abundant that it might become burdensome on the mother and drip out without suction (thereby going to waste - *ML*), nor so scarce as to tire the child when taking the breast.

Divine grace is also manifested in His having made the orifice of the nipple like the eye of a needle, not so wide that the milk would run out without suction, in which case the child might be choked while being suckled, nor so narrow that the infant would have to exert itself in drawing its nourishment.

Afterwards, the infant's physical faculties grow stronger, so that it is able to distinguish sights and sounds. G-d inspires the parents' hearts with kindness, love and compassion for their offspring, so that raising it is not overly burdensome to them. They are more sensitive to its needs in regard to food and drink than to their own requirements. All the labor and trouble involved in bringing it up, bathing and dressing it, gently leading it, and warding off everything harmful, even against its will, is of little account in their sight.

(*Marpe Lenefesh*: "G-d inspires the parents' hearts with kindness" - G-d implanted in human nature that the infant finds favor in his parents' eyes. Without this, no kids would ever be raised [properly].

Tov Halevanon: "They are more sensitive to its needs" - the parents feel the infants pain and exertion more than they feel their own pain.

Pas Lechem: "warding off everything harmful, even against its will" - For behold, the infant is foolish, and tends to pursue even harmful activities, such as to hold a razor with his hand, or grasp a burning stick, or instigate a dangerous dog, or the like. When the parents remove him from these things, he screams and cries, and anguishes his parents with his screams.)

Afterwards, the offspring passes from infancy to childhood. His parents do not tire of him nor become angry at his numerous needs and little recognition of the burden which they bear in caring and providing for him. On the contrary, the concern they feel on his behalf increases until he reaches adolescence, when he has already learned to speak correctly and properly, and his physical senses and mental faculties have become strong enough to acquire wisdom and knowledge. Then he apprehends some physical phenomena with his senses, and some intellectual ideas with his mental faculties, as the wise King said (Prov. 2:6) *"For the L-ord gives wisdom: out of His mouth comes knowledge and discernment."*

(*Pas Lechem*: *"little recognition of the burden"* - when the receiver of benefit knows and recognizes the good that another is bestowing on him, and he also recognizes the exertion that the person is exerting himself for him and he appreciates it - through this the benefactor feels some contentment and consolation from his toil. But this is not the case by the child.)

Among the many benefits to a human being is that during his childhood he is not a thinker and is unable to distinguish good from evil. For had he, while growing up, been endowed with a ripe intellect and mature powers of perception and had he been able to discern the superiority of adults, in their ability to manage for themselves, move freely and keep clean, and realized the opposite case presented by his condition in all these respects, he would have died of worry and sorrow.

(*Pas Lechem*: *"he is not a thinker and is unable to distinguish good from evil"* - He has no knowledge, neither from intellect, nor from recognition. For the power of recognition is something independent of the intellect, and even other creatures (i.e. animals) have the power of recognition despite that they have no intellect.
"manage for themselves" - The adults are able to manage their needs, and do not depend on the management of another unlike him whose management is not according to his will.
"move freely" - unlike him that due to his weakness all his movements are sluggish.
"and keep clean" - while he, due to his weak ability to hold in, is forced to roll in his own excrement and urine, and dirty himself with filth.
"he would have died of worry and sorrow" - worry on each detail of his lackings, and general sorrow on his lowly situation.)

Remarkable too it is that crying, according to what learned physicians state, is beneficial to an infant. For in the brains of infants there is a humor (mucous), which, if it remained there undischarged, would produce evil results. Weeping dissolves this humor and drains it away from the brain, and thus the infants are saved from its injurious effects.

The Creator's abounding grace to man is also manifested in that the new teeth come out singly, one after another, and so the gradual falling out of the old teeth during the process of replacement does not interfere with his ability to chew.

Later on he is subjected to illnesses and meets with painful incidents so that he recognizes the world, and that its nature is not concealed from him. Thus he is put on his guard against trusting in this world thereby permitting his lusts to rule over him, in which case he would become like the animals that neither think nor understand; as it is written *"Be ye not as the horse or as the mule which have no understanding"* (Tehilim 32:9).

> (*Tov Halevanon*: *"illnesses"* - such as chicken pox and measles. *"painful incidents"* - many weaknesses come in the boyhood years. PL - accidents such as stepping on a metal nail.
> *"Be ye not as the horse or as the mule"* - they need to be leashed and muzzled, so too man. The painful incidents humble his lusts.
> *"so that he recognizes the world"* - how a person's situation can change swiftly from contentment to pain so that he realizes not to trust in it and its tranquility - rather to always be afraid and to seek refuge in G-d's shadow.
>
> *Marpe Lenefesh*: If a human being had only constant good in this world, he would forget and not recall the matters of his final end, and he would trust (hope) in this world and follow the musings of his heart and his lusts for all of his days. Therefore, it was among the divine plan to send him sometimes bad illnesses, even during his youth in order that he recognize and know that there is no complete good in this world. And even if he is in a very good situation, the bad illnesses can come and ruin his joy, so that he won't trust in this world.)

One should then consider and reflect upon the usefulness of the limbs and organs and the ways of his rectification through them - the hands serving for taking and giving; the feet for walking the eyes for seeing; the ears for hearing; the nose for smelling; the tongue for speaking; the mouth for eating; the teeth for chewing; the stomach for digestion; the liver for purifying the food; the tubes for removing superfluities; the bowels for retention. The heart is the sanctuary of the natural heat and the well-spring of life. The brain is the seat of the spiritual faculties, the well-spring of sensation, and the root from which the nerves begin.

The womb (in a woman) serves to preserve and develop the seed. And so it is with the rest of the bodily organs. They all have their specific functions, of which more are unknown than are known to us.

> (*Pas Lechem*: *"the usefulness of the limbs... the ways of his rectification from them"* - some of the limbs are crucial for preserving his body while some were created so that his body will be in a better way, as the scholars wrote regarding the doubling of the limbs of senses (2 eyes, 2 ears, etc.). For the first kind, he wrote "the usefulness", while for the second kind, he used the term "rectification". Understand this.
>
> *Marpe Lenefesh*: *"The heart is the sanctuary of the natural heat"* - in the heart all the blood of the body is drawn through. The nefesh chiyuni (lower soul) is bound to the heart, like a flame to a candle as I quoted earlier the words of the Kuzari, see there. [*Rabbi YS*: and likewise, the neshama (higher soul) is bound to the brain like a flame to a candle wick])

So too, one who reflects on these matters will take notice of the natural processes by which the nourishment received by the body is apportioned to every one of its parts. These marks of wisdom observed by him will stir him to thank His Creator and praise Him for them, as David said *"All my bones shall cry out: 'O G-d, who is like You' "* (Tehilim 35:10). Thus the food passes into the stomach through a tube that is utterly straight, without bend or twist. This tube is called the esophagus. The stomach grinds the food more thoroughly than the teeth had already done Then the nutriment is carried into the liver through fine intermediate veins which connect these two organs (bile ducts), and serve as a strainer for the food, permitting nothing coarse to pass through to the liver. The liver metabolizes the nutrient it receives into the blood which it distributes all over the body, sending the vital fluid to all parts of the body through conduits formed for this purpose, and resembling water-pipes.

The waste substances that are left are eliminated through canals specifically adapted to that purpose. What belongs to the green gall goes to the gall bladder. What belongs to the black gall goes to the milt (spleen); other substances and fluids are sent to the lungs. The refuse of the blood passes into the bladder.

Reflect, my brother, on the wisdom of the Creator manifested in the formation of your body; how He set those organs in their right places; to receive the waste substances, so that they should not spread in the body, and cause it to become sick.

Then consider the formation of the vocal organs, and instruments of speech. The trachea, hollow for the production of sound; the tongue, lips, and teeth serving for the clear enunciation of consonants and vowels. These organs have other uses also. The air enters the lungs through the trachea; the tongue is the organ which enables one to taste things, and aids also in the moving around of the solid and liquid food. The teeth serve to chew solid food. The lips enable one to retain liquids in the mouth, and swallow the quantity desired, and only when one wishes to do so. In regard to the other organs, the uses of some are known to us while others are unknown.

Then, my brother, reflect on the four bodily faculties with their respective functions: (1) the drawing faculty by which food is received and carried into the stomach; (2) the faculty of retention by which food is retained in the body till nature has done her work on it; (3) the digestive faculty which digests the food, extracts the finer elements, separates it from the useless refuse, and distributes the former to all parts of the body; (4) the excretory faculty which ejects the refuse that remains after the digestive processes have taken from the food all that the body needs.

> (*Pas Lechem*: *"carried into the stomach"* - we cannot say it is simply gravity, since the food would then easily get delayed or stuck in the esophagus, and certainly, when a person is lying down or on his side, whereby the stomach and the esophagus would in be of equal height. Hence, it is clear that there is a faculty (muscles) specially made for this, to draw the food and pull it to the stomach.)

Observe how all these faculties have definite functions, whose purpose it is to promote physical well-being. It is just like a King's court where there are servants and officers appointed over the royal household. One of them is charged with the duty of supplying the servants' need and delivering these to the king's steward. The second official has to receive the necessaries brought in by the first, and place them in the store-room, until they are prepared. The business of the third official is to prepare the stores and, after rendering them fit for use, distribute them among the servants. The task of the fourth servant is to sweep and cleanse the palace of all dirt and refuse, which he has to remove.

> (*Marpe Lenefesh*: *"like a King's court"* - the body is like the king's court and the king which dwells there is the Sechel (mind). All the limbs and organs are like servants of the court. There are officers appointed to provide food for them so that they can minister to the king, i.e. the intellect. Hence, it is no wonder that a human being is called a "miniature world", for his inner workings is like the entire world.)

Tov Halevanon: *"there are servants and officers"* - this corresponds to the four powers in the stomach he mentioned. The servants are the organs/limbs and sinews, veins, etc. generally and specifically. On them are four officials which are: drawing, retention, digestion, excretion.
"One of them is charged with the duty of supplying the servants' need and delivering these to the king's steward" - i.e. the man in totality is the king over the body's limbs/organs. The official who receives all income from the king designated for the needs of the servants and deposits them to the steward who collects all goods for this purpose. This official is the power of "drawing" and the steward refers to the stomach, where all food and drink descend there. The second official refers to the power of "retention", just like the treasurer of a king manages the property of the king and distributes meat, bread, and wine, or the like according to the needs of each one of the king's servants. The third official corresponds to the power of digestion, while the fourth refers to excretion.)

Afterwards, reflect on the faculties of the soul and their place among the benefits bestowed on man - the faculties of thought and memory, the power of forgetting, the feeling of shame, the faculties of understanding and speech. Picture to yourself, what would a man's condition be if even one of these were lacking. Take memory, for instance. How much loss a person would suffer in all his affairs if he were unable to remember what he owned and what he owed; what he had taken and what he had given; what he had seen or heard, what he had said and what had been said to him; if he could not remember the one who had done a benefit to him and the one who had brought him harm; the one who had rendered him a service, or inflicted upon him an injury. Such a person would not recognize a road even if he had frequently traversed it, nor remember any wisdom though he had studied it all his lifetime. Past experience would not be of any benefit to him. He would not weigh any matter by what had happened in the past. Nor could he estimate future events by what was taking place in the present. Such a person would be almost entirely outside the class of human beings (without memory, he would be like an animal - *ML*).

Among the benefits of forgetting: Were it not for the ability to forget no man would ever be free from sorrow (such as due to death of loved ones - *PL*). No joyous occasion would dispel his sadness. The events that should bring him joy would give him no pleasure, when he recalled the troubles of life. Even from the realization of his hopes he could not hope to derive rest and peace of mind. He would never refrain from grieving. Thus you see how memory and forgetfulness, different and contrary to each other as they are, are both benefits bestowed upon man, and each of them has its uses.

(*Tov Halevanon*: *"forgetting"* - i.e. that the matter dissipates from his mind, and it is not constantly held at attention in his thoughts. It remains only as long as he wants to remember it.)

Afterwards, reflect on the feeling of shame with which man alone has been endowed. How high is its value! How numerous are its uses and advantages. Were it not for this feeling, men would not show hospitality to strangers. They would not keep their promises, grant favors, show kindness, nor abstain from evil in any way. Many precepts of the Torah are fulfilled only out of shame. A large number of people would not honor their parent if it were not for shame, and certainly would fail to show courtesy to others. They would not restore a lost article to its owner, nor refrain from any transgression. For whoever commits any of the disgraceful acts which we have mentioned, does so only when he has cast off the garment of shame. As Scripture said: *"Yea they are not at all ashamed, neither know they how to blush"* (Yirmiyahu 6:15), and *"The sinner knows no shame"* (Tzefania 3:5).

(*Pas Lechem*: *"shame with which man alone has been endowed"* - unlike the other characteristics which are also found in the animals such as memory, forgetting, anger, as mentioned in the books of the scholars. *"Many precepts of the Torah are fulfilled only out of shame"* - i.e. come and see how powerful this trait is, since behold it stops a man from evil more than the commandments of the torah. And if you ask, "even though this trait is implanted in human beings, nevertheless there are still evil doers. Hence, that which stops them [from evil] is not shame." To this he answered, that whoever you see doing one of these things, know that it is due to their divesting themselves from the garment of shame out of their evil choice as written...

Marpe Lenefesh: And likewise our sages said (Pirkei Avot ch.5): "a shamed face person is destined for Gan Eden (paradise)", and (Nedarim 20a) "whoever has shamefacedness will not sin swiftly"...)

It is a great amazement that G-d has implanted man with shame in the presence of other human beings due to the advantages we mentioned and others we did not mention, and yet G-d did not implant man with shame in the presence of his Creator who observes him continually. The reason for this is so that a human being would not be forced in the service of G-d whereby its reward would not be deserved (since man would have no free will in this - PL). It is, however, our duty to feel shame in the presence of the Creator, as a result of reflection, realization of the service we owe to

Him, and our consciousness that He observes every thing that we do openly or secretly; as Scripture said *"Be ashamed and humiliated of your ways, O House of Israel"* (Yechezkel 36:32).

(*Pas Lechem*: This is a great amazement at first thought, but with a bit of reflection the answer is nearby...

Marpe Lenefesh: ...the reason is so that man would not be forced in his actions. For a man would never sin if he reflects that the great King, the holy One, blessed be He, stands over him and observes his deeds, as written in the Shulchan Aruch Orach Chaim Siman 1, see there. Hence, if it were naturally so that a man were ashamed before his Creator, just like he is before human beings, he would be forced, and would not be deserving of any divine reward. And in truth, "everything is in G-d's hands except the fear of G-d" (Berachos 33b), so that there would be room for reward and punishment for his free will.

Pas Lechem: *"it is our duty to feel shame...as a result of reflection"* - i.e. general reflection, which is the subject matter of this gate, namely, a man's examination of the marks of wisdom manifested in the creations. Through them he will grasp the greatness of the Creator.

"realization of the service we owe to Him" - through this one will reflect on how much he is falling short in G-d's service [and be ashamed].

"Be ashamed and humiliated of your ways" - two expressions corresponding to falling short in avoiding evil and in doing good.)

The abounding goodness of G-d to us is manifested in, the capacities of thought and perception with which he has uniquely endowed us and distinguished us from other living creatures. The value of these faculties in the care of our bodies and ordering of our activities is known to all, with the exception of those who have suffered a loss of these faculties due to brain damage.

The (good - *ML*) traits which we can attain through the understanding are many. Through the understanding we know that we have a Creator, wise, everlasting, [absolutely] One, who has existed from all eternity; infinite in power, unbound to time and space; exalted above the qualities of His creatures and beyond the conception of all existing beings; merciful, gracious and beneficent; resembling nothing nor does anything resemble Him.

(*Marpe Lenefesh*: *"unbound to time and space"* - God is not bound to time, all of the past and the future are before Him simultaneously as something in the present. For time is His creation. He was, is, and always will be. And even though we are not capable of understanding this, the verse already says: "For as the heavens are higher than the earth, so are My ways higher than your ways, and My thoughts than your thoughts" (Yeshaya 55:9), as the Rambam wrote on the mishna in Rosh Hashana "all are examined in one sweeping look", see there amazing words, and the book Shomer Emunim [Kadmon] spoke of this at length.

"and space" - as the Midrash (Bereishis Raba 68:9) expounded the verse "place is by Me" Shemos 33:21.

Matanas Chelko: it is obvious that all of these traits are nothing whatsoever relative to what G-d truly is. However, all of what we understand and grasp of the Creator is through our intellect. This is the quality of the human over the animal. And even though animals have some spiritual connection to the Creator, nevertheless the connection between man and G-d is through the intellect. Therefore it is incumbent on a man to contemplate on this great gift from G-d.

It is through the understanding that we realize the Creator's wisdom, power and mercy, of which the universe provides clear evidence. It is the understanding which shows us that we ought to serve Him, because service is rightly due to Him (on account of His greatness and exaltedness - *ML*), and because of His beneficence, bestowed upon all universally and on each one specifically. Through the understanding we are confirmed in our faith in the truth of the Book of G-d's Law given to Moses, His prophet, peace be upon him. Because of a human being's faculty of reason and perception, he is an accountable creature whom his Creator will hold to a strict reckoning (in the future - *MH*). A person who has lost his understanding, loses all the excellencies of a human being and is exempt from the mitzvot (precepts), and (receives no - *ML*) reward and punishment.

(*Tov Halevanon*: *"to a strict reckoning"* - he whose understanding is greater, G-d holds him to a stricter reckoning, because he understands more to guard from sin.
Pas Lechem: This is the purpose of man - to receive the reward of his deeds, and this is impossible without a reckoning.)

Among the benefits of the understanding: through understanding man obtains his knowledge of all things perceived by the senses or apprehended by the intellect (common sense - *MC*).

By the understanding he discovers aspects of visible objects, unrevealed to the physical senses, as for instance, the movement of the shadow (on a sun-dial), or the action of a single drop of water on the hard rock.

(*Tov Halevanon*: it appears to the eye, that the shadow is something "tangible", since it moves from place to place. But with the understanding, he understands that the shadow is not, rather it is due to an obstruction between the rays of the sun and the place of the shadow... Likewise, it appears impossible that a single drop of water, small and weak, can carve a hole in a hard rock. But we can see that if this happens continuously for a long time, on a hard rock, a hole is carved out. The understanding grasps that the drop caused this hole. Because each time the drop fell on the rock, it carved out a tiny amount which the senses cannot detect until many drops like this combine their effects.)

By the understanding man distinguishes between truth and falsehood, between excess and deficiency, between good and evil, between the praiseworthy and the disgraceful, between the necessary, the possible and the impossible.

(*Pas Lechem*: A man needs to be complete in three areas, deot (outlook/thought), midot (character traits), and in peulot (deeds). Corresponding to "deot", he wrote *"truth and falsehood"*, for example, the belief in the Unity of G-d is truth, while ascribing plurality to Him is a falsehood, and similarly for all other contemplations in chakira (inquiry). Likewise for *"excess and deficiency"* - just like G-d is exalted beyond all praise, while the opposite for flesh and blood which is much deficient in praises.

Corresponding to peulot ("deeds"), he wrote *"good and evil"*, namely that doing kindness and justness is good, while corruption and oppression is evil.

Corresponding to the "midot" (character traits) he wrote *"the laudable and despicable"*. For instance humility is a praiseworthy trait while arrogance is disgraceful.

"the necessary, the possible and the impossible" - this refers to the two extremes and the middle way. "Necessary" is what the understanding obligates that it should be this way. While "impossible" is the opposite. The "possible", which is the middle way between the necessary and the impossible.)

By his understanding, man makes other living creatures work for his benefits and pleasures (such as the horse to ride on, the donkey to carry loads, or sheep and cattle for food and clothing - *ML*). By the use of this faculty, he recognizes the position of the planets (PL), determines their distances and their movements in their orbits, comprehends the relations and comparisons treated in the sciences of mathematics and engineering, the figures and modes of demonstration [syllogisms] set forth in logic, and other sciences and arts too numerous to mention.

So too, all the other faculties of man, if you study them, you will find, display the utmost perfection and are of the utmost benefit to him, as we have shown, regarding the understanding.

(*Pas Lechem*: such as anger and tranquility, generosity and stinginess - all are for man's benefit, for each one has a time and place.
Marpe Lenefesh: All the traits in man are designed in the utmost perfect and beneficial way, provided that man uses his understanding in them. But if he does not use his understanding, then he cannot rectify any trait or any deed properly.)

Afterwards, reflect further on the benefits G-d has bestowed on man by the gift of speech and the orderly arrangement of words, whereby he gives expression to what is in his mind and soul and understands the conditions of others. The tongue is the heart's pen and the mind's messenger. Without speech, there would be no social relations between one person and another; a human being would be an animal. Through speech, the superiority of an individual among his fellows becomes apparent. The pacts between man and his fellow are made through speech, and likewise between G-d and His servants. By means of speech, a man turns away from his perverseness and seeks forgiveness for his iniquities. Speech is the greatest evidence of a man's nobility or ignobility. Man, it has been said, is heart and tongue. And this completes the definition of a human being. For a human being is defined as a "living, speaking, mortal creature" and by speech, he is differentiated from the brute animals (who are defined as "living, mortal creatures" [not "speaking"], hence speech alone differentiates man from them - *PL*).

Then consider the advantages derived from written characters and the art of writing. By their aid, the deeds and affairs of those who have passed away and of those who are still existing are recorded for the benefit of those who will come after them; communications reach the absent, and information is received concerning those far away and concerning relatives in another country; and it is possible that the receipt of this information may save their lives or deliver them from misfortune and mishaps. By this means, knowledge of the sciences is preserved in books; dispersed thoughts are gathered together. Men write down their dealings with each other in commercial transactions, in loans, purchases, marriages, divorces. The subject is too wide to be dealt with completely.

Among the completing benefits bestowed on man is that he has been provided with hands and fingers, with which he can draw, write, embroider, kindle fire and perform other acts and fine operations that are beyond the capacity of other living creatures, because these are not needed by them.

> (*Pas Lechem*: *"Among the completing benefits..."* - this is one of the things which demonstrates that G-d's will is that man's good should be to the utmost extent, i.e. that he should be lacking nothing that could possibly be beneficial to him.)

I assert that there is not one of these organs the uses of which I have mentioned that does not show to one who reflects on them marks of divine wisdom in its structure, form and combination with other organs. They display strong evidence and clear proof of the Creator's mercy towards us. Galen, in numerous treatises, has expounded the functions of the bodily organs. Were we to do so in the case of one of these, we would depart from our goal of conciseness. What we have brought with G-d's help, is sufficient to arouse any one to whom the Creator will teach (arouse his heart to - *PL*) the way of His salvation.

> (*Pas Lechem*: *"clear proof of the Creator's mercy towards us"* - since behold, our eyes can see that everything was designed in the most perfect and most beneficial possible way for man.)

STUDY OF NATURE

The study of the other species of living creatures, their habits and their sustenance will not be concealed by one who observes them and reflects upon the marks of divine wisdom manifest in them. Hence, the scriptures repeatedly refer to them when mentioning G-d's wonders: *"Who provides for the raven his prey when his young ones cry unto G-d"* (Job 38:41), and *"He gives to the beast his food, and to the young ravens which cry"* (Tehilim 147:9). There are many other similar passages.

And so too, when one studies the course of the heavenly spheres, distinguished by their various movements and the individual luminaries all contributing to the order of the Universe - he will see in them evidences of power and wisdom, such as the human mind cannot grasp and would become weary in attempting to describe. As David, peace be upon him, said, *"The heavens declare the glory of G-d, and the firmament show forth His handiwork"* (Tehilim 19:2), and *"When I behold Your heavens, the work of Your fingers, the moon and the stars which You have established"* (Tehilim 8:4) .

It is a wonder that among all the great works of the Creator, which the human eye beholds, the heavens are always present For wherever on earth a man stands, he sees above his head a hemisphere of firmament encompassing the earth. And when he contemplates it thoughtfully, he will realize that the One who created it by His Will is infinite in power, wisdom and greatness.

For the sight of any example of architecture of the ancients arouses in us wonder at their ability to make anything like it, and indicates to us the physical strength and fine souls of those who constructed a strong fortress for themselves. Now if such very small and petty work that transcends our capacity by only little, looms so large in our sight, how exceedingly indeed should we marvel at the infinite greatness of Him who created the heavens and the earth and all that therein is, without effort or exertion, labor or fatigue, out of nothing, with [the aid of] nothing, solely by His will and wish. As it is said *"By the word of the L-ord were the heavens made; and all the host of them by the breath of His mouth"* (Tehilim 33:6).

(*Pas Lechem*: *"solely by His will and wish"* - this is to exclude the view of those who believe in the "necessity" of creation, y"sh. See Morey Nevuchim II ch.13-15, that they ascribe the creation to G-d as a kind of "necessity", like a shadow to a pillar, without will.)

Among the benefits bestowed upon man, the following is to be noted. When you contemplate the marks of divine wisdom in created things, you will find that, besides testifying to the divinity and might of the Creator they all without exception are in various ways useful to man and contribute to his improvement. Only that some of these uses are evident, while others are obscure. Take light and darkness for instance. The benefits of light are obvious and evident, but those of darkness are hidden. For human beings are weary in the dark; their activities and movements are interrupted at its arrival. But were it not for the darkness of night, the bodies of most living beings would be worn out by their incessant toil and protracted movements. Through the recurrence of night, one interval of time is separated from another. It gives knowledge of periods which would otherwise be unknown, (e.g. counting days and weeks;) and makes known the respective length or brevity of human lives.

If time were uniform (i.e. without alternation of day and night,) there would be no commandments for special seasons, such as Sabbaths, festivals or fasts; no appointments could be made for a definite date; most of the sciences related to time would be unknown. Even food would not be perfectly digested by any living creature (sleep aids digestion - *TL*).

As man however needs light at night to do some of his work, and to nurse the sick, the Creator has provided him with a substitute in the light of fire which he can kindle at any time and extinguish whenever he pleases.

Wondrous too it is that the hue of the sky belongs to the colors that strengthen the sight, For it inclines to black which has the special quality of gathering together and strengthening the light that enters the eyes Had the color of the sky been white, it would have injured the eyes of living creatures and weakened them. Similarly, other marks of wisdom are exhibited by other created things.

Out of G-d's abounding goodness to mankind, He put the fear of man into other creatures that are dangerous, as it is said (Bereishis 9:2) *"And the fear of you and the dread of you shall be upon every beast of the earth,"* so that an infant is secure against hurt by a cat or rat or similar creature, while a grown-up man, after death, is not safe from their attacks; even as our sages said: "A living child, a day old, need not be guarded against rats; Og, [the giant] king of Bashan, dead, needs such protection."

(*Tov Halevanon*: *"He put the fear of man"* - this is due to the spiritual powers in man... [*Rabbi YS*: this fear has been dulled due to the diminishing spiritual level of man])

What you should also realize is the exalted [or mysterious] property in all things created - the higher and the lower, from the smallest to the greatest - by which the entire universe is ordered and perfected, and which is not apprehended by the physical senses. This is the quality of motion (change), inherent in everything composite. None of the bodily senses can grasp it, but the intellect grasps it by inference from the moving/changing object which the senses detect. Had there been no motion, not one of existing things would have been brought into complete being, nor could any of them suffer destruction. A philosopher said that the majority of physical things are in a state of motion.

(*Pas Lechem*: His intent is on "coming to be" and "ceasing to be" (havaya v'hefsed), whereas a thing moves and changes from one stage to another until its form ceases to exist. This "changing" he called "motion".
"the intellect grasps it by inference" - i.e. the essence of change is grasped by us through the thing changing, namely, that we saw it at first in one state, and now we see it in a different state. Besides this, we have no knowledge of what "change" is in of itself. Likewise, for time. For time and

change are two sides of the same coin, and both are intangible to us. This matter is exceedingly deep and impossible to grasp for one who is not accustomed to thinking on these things.

Manoach Halevavos: One can explain this to refer to two forms of "motion": 1. Physical motion that is not perceptible to the senses. Such as the movement of the sun [i.e. rotation of the earth]. Only that we see the sun here, and after some time, there. This is what he meant, *"but the intellect grasps it by inference from the moving/changing object"*... 2. All change is called "motion". For example, growth in a plant. It is not perceptible to the senses, but at first the plant was tiny and after some time it is large. Because in that time, it grew slowly (i.e. soil, minerals and water moved and combined - *TL*). This kind of change applies to all things composite and assembled [i.e. everything except for G-d as explained in Gate 1])

When you will understand the mystery of motion, comprehend its true essence and spiritual character, realize that it is one of the marvels of divine wisdom and recognize in it the Creator's abundant compassion towards His creatures, it will become clear to you that all your movements are tied to the Creator's desire, guidance and will, whether these movements be great or small, visible or invisible, with one exception only, namely those movements that He has left to your free will, in the choice of good or evil.

(*Tov Halevanon*: *"all your movements are tied to the Creator's desire"* - the "Moray Nevuchim" Part 1 ch.72 writes that all "motion" found in the world, ultimately started from the tenuat hagalgal (movement in the mystical worlds). For certainly, all the movements and changes of living creatures which are not related to the commandments of G-d are due only to "movements" in the time and circumstances. Hence, the creature depends on the "movement". Likewise, when a living creature moves to seek food, this is due to hunger, whereby the previous food has now been digested and consumed, and this is also a "movement". Likewise, any human desire, or wish comes due to something else which aroused him on this. Hence, everything depends on the "movement". Ultimately, the root of all movements is tied to the "galgal elyon" (upper mystical worlds), which changes the times and circumstances - and the "movement" of the galgal elyon is tied to the Creator's desire. Understand this. Hence, remember that every turn which you turn to is tied to the wish of the Creator, except for matters of good and evil.

Marpe Lenefesh: This power that a man possesses, whereby he "moves" - it is a spiritual power, and certainly the spiritual is tied to something else spiritual, namely, the will of G-d. Through changes, G-d directs a man any way He wishes, like an animal's leash in the hand of the herdsman. Thus, we are in G-d's hands. In all of our movements, big or small, visible or invisible - everything is in His hand and His power.

Rabbi YS: Even though we have free will, G-d has total control over our lives. An analogy is playing chess with a chess grandmaster. Even though you have free choice, nevertheless he can manipulate you any way he wishes. And how much more so, when the Grandmaster knows your thoughts and every move you will ever make.)

And when this will have become clear to you, watch yourself in every movement that you make. Be ever conscious of the bond by which the Creator has attached you to Him; always feel abashed in His presence; fear Him; submit to His judgment; accept His decrees. And so you will attain His favor, and your final end will be good, as it is said (Tehilim 32:10) *"... But he that trusts in the L-ord, will be surrounded by kindness."*

(*Pas Lechem*: *"feel abashed in His presence; fear Him"* - for things which a man knows and senses are disgraceful, namely, what the Understanding obligates, he wrote *"feel abashed"*. While for the received commandments [whose moral wrongness is not detectable by the Understanding], he wrote *"fear Him"*.

Matanas Chelko: "the bond" - In the book Chochma U'Mussar, it is explained from the first Mishna in Tractate Shabbat how through a mere, small turning of the hand (with warning) one can incur a Biblical capital offence of transgressing the Sabbath thereby forfeiting his life. But if he did not turn his hand and instead the other person took the object from him, he is exempt from a painful execution. Hence, a man is bound by his movements. For every one of his movements, he is bound to the Creator, that it be according to His will. This is what follows from this Gate to the next gate (Gate of Service of G-d). The explanation is that if a man does something contrary to the will of G-d, then he is employing the power which the Creator has bestowed on him to do against His will. This feeling is what brings a person to assume the duty of serving G-d. Not that serving G-d is a [forced] obligation, but rather it is a responsibility. For to use the powers of the Creator which He has given you and to do against His will - this is ingratitude. It is literally no different than one who G-d gave rocks to use for a good purpose and he turns around and throws them at Him... see the Tomer Devorah ch.1)... And when a person transgresses G-d's will, not only does G-d not remove His life-force from this person, but He also continues to bestow it on him.. Contemplate the ingratitude in this, and the corresponding duty and responsibility one has to serve G-d.

Marpe Lenefesh: "And when this will have become clear to you" - hence, it is proper that in all your movements, you will remember and check yourself, and think to yourself what you will do with this movement so that it will not be against the will of G-d, since you are tied to Him and He has the ability to change it. If you do thus, that all your deeds will be l'shem shamayim (for G-d), and you feel abashed always before Him, since behold, He is always with you in all your deeds then you will...
"*submit to His judgment*" - i.e. trust in Him, that everything that He does to you is certainly good.
"*accept His decrees*" - that you are content with whatever He decrees on you.
"*And so you will attain His favor*" - there is no greater good thing, namely, that G-d finds favor in us and in our deeds. This is the purpose of this world and the next as the author wrote in the introduction.)

In regard to secular matters, it is proper that you should always look to the final outcome of hard experiences. You will discover the surprising fact that many seemingly adverse events turn out in the end to be to our advantage, and vice versa. A story is told of a company of travelers who lay down near a wall to rest overnight. A dog, passing by, wetted one of them. The man awoke and got up to wash off the uncleanliness. After he had gone some distance from his fellows, the wall fell down on his companions and killed them, while he alone escaped. Events frequently happen in similar fashion and vice versa.

Matanas Chelko: The Rambam wrote (Berachos 9:5): "that which the sages said just like one must bless on the good [he should bless on the bad], this means to accept the bad with joy and a good heart and to subdue his anger. He should be just as glad when he blesses "dayin haemes" (on the bad) as when he blesses hatov v'hametic (on the good). End quote. It would seem to us that this matter depends on the degree of one's faith that G-d does only what is good for him. But the Rambam does not continue like this. He continues: "this is a principle of reason to those who understand. And even if the verse did not tell us, for we see many times that certain things appear good in the beginning but turn out in the end to be great calamities. Therefore, it is not proper for the understanding person to be upset when a great calamity befalls him because he does not know what its end will be. Likewise, the sages forbade one to be excessive in joy and laughter. Rather, let his joy be in spiritual deeds, namely righteousness, and to pursue that." End quote This is also the author's intent here. For since G-d runs the world entirely, according to the final end purpose, it is not proper to praise the good, or despise the bad done to him. But rather, to wait patiently to see what will be the end of the matter.

One of the most important subjects on which you should reflect is the wonderful gift of G-d to living creatures and plants - the rain, which besides falling in its due season, descends in showers when needed. As Scripture said, (Yirmiya 14:22) *"Are there any among the vanities of the nations that can cause rain? or can the heavens give showers? are You not He, O L-ord our G-d? therefore we will hope unto You: for You have made all these things"* (Yirmiya 5:24) *"Neither say they in their heart: Let us now fear the L-ord, our G-d, that gives rain, both the former and the latter, in due season; that reserves for us the appointed weeks of the harvest."* The importance of the rain, you will find also emphasized in the text (Job 5:9-11) *"Who does great things and unsearchable; marvelous things without number: Who gives rain upon the earth and sends water upon the fields; so that He sets upon high those that are low, and those that mourn are exalted to safety."*

How astonishing too is the growth of foods from seeds. A single grain that has been saved from mishaps, produces a thousand grains and more. It has even been stated that out of one grain of wheat, as many as three hundred ears will spring up, each containing over twenty grains. We also come across gigantic trees whose roots have sprung out of a single seed or a single shoot and have increased many times as much as those mentioned. Praised be the All-Wise and Gracious One who brings into existence such vast effects from causes so small and weak, as Scripture said (Shmuel 2:3) *"And by Him actions are weighed."* The foods assigned to different living creatures are too numerous to specify. The wise man, when he reflects on them and understands their causes, will recognize the supreme wisdom of the Creator's plan. Concerning these things David said (Tehilim 124:27-28) *"All of them wait for You, that You may give them their food in due time. You give it unto them they gather it; You open Your hand, they are satisfied with good"*. He says further (Tehilim 145:16) *"You open Your hand, and satisfy every living thing with favor"*. I will clarify this topic further in the "Gate of Trust" with G-d's help.

(*Marpe Lenefesh*: *"A single grain that has been saved from mishaps produces a thousand grains and more"* - this is a wonder and a great benefit. Were it not for this, that the land would produce such great amounts, how would human beings attain their sustenance? And their toil would be for nothing.
Tov Halevanon: *"mishaps"* refers to our sins which diminish the good.)

The greatest of the benefits that the Creator has bestowed upon man and the strongest proof of His existence is the Torah that was delivered to

Moses, His prophet, peace be upon him, and the manifestation of [supernatural] signs by him - changes in the normal natural phenomena, and exhibition of awe-inspiring miracles to bring faith in the Creator, blessed be He, and in His prophet; as it is said (Shemot 14:31) *"And Israel saw the great work which the L-ord wrought upon the Egyptians, and the people: feared the L-ord, and they believed in the L-ord and in Moses, His servant. (Deut. 4:35-36) "*Unto you it was shown, that you may know that the L-ord, He is G-d; there is none else beside Him. Out of Heaven He made you to hear His voice, that He might instruct you; and upon earth He made you to see His great fire; and you did hear His words out of the midst of the fire."

> (*Marpe Lenefesh*: *"strongest proof"* - ...that all these miracles were done before millions of people, and no nation can refute this to us due to its being so openly well known... The "Kuzari" book expounded on this at length, and it is the central theme of the book from beginning to end. see there.
>
> *Matanas Chelko*: "the greatest of the benefits..." - i.e. even without the giving of the torah, and even without the exodus from Egypt, we would need to believe in G-d. Namely, we would need to delve into all this on our own in the way our forefather Abraham did. Hence, it is among the benefits of G-d to have given us the torah and done for us miracles in Egypt, for through both there is strong proof of the truth of Judaism.

If any one seeks evidence at the present day similar to those just mentioned, let him look with candid eyes at our position among the nations since the Exile began and our orderly condition in their midst, notwithstanding that we do not agree with them in belief or practice - of which disagreement they are aware. Observe that even so, our financial situation is close to theirs, and perhaps even better than theirs. You will see that an average person among them must toil more for his livelihood than an average or even a below-average among us. This is like our Creator promised us: *"And yet for all that, when they are in the land of their enemies, I will not reject them neither will I abhor them, utterly to destroy them and to break my covenant with them for I am the L-ord their G-d"* (Vayikra 26:44), and *"For we are bondmen; yet our G-d has not forsaken us in our bondage"* (Ezra 9:9). *"If it had not been the L-ord who was for us, let Israel now say, if it had not been the L-ord who was for us, when men rose up against us, then they had swallowed us up alive, when their wrath was kindled against us"* (Tehilim 124:1), and the rest of the Psalm. In the Gate of the "Service of G-d", I will expand on the exceeding favor G-d has bestowed upon us in His Torah which he gave to us.

(*Matanas Chelko*: "If it had not been the L-ord who was for us.. when men rose up against us, then they had swallowed us up alive" - Not only by the tradition do we have proofs for these things, but also even in our time we can see the truth of this with our own eyes. The survival of one sheep among 70 wolves (see Midrash Raba Esther ch.10). This is the greatest miracle, no less than the exodus from Egypt. A sheep is a weak, helpless creature, and it is among 70 wolves who want and are able to rip apart and annihilate that sheep. Furthermore, the nations know full well that we do not accept their belief and practices. Nevertheless, even though we suffer from them every generation, we are always saved by miracles in every generation. Furthermore, we even live among them, side by side, year after year. This is the fulfillment of the prophetic verse written 3000 years ago, "and even though they shall be in the land of their enemies..." (end of Lev.) That G-d promised to save us from their hands.

Likewise, the Torah is still among us, despite decrees and persecutions forbidding torah study and burning the torah, periods when the gentiles forbade us to educate our children in torah, even so He promised us "and when many disasters and calamities come on them... it will not be forgotten by their descendants" (Deut. 31:21). It remained intact among us through miracles.

Hence we do not need to contemplate on the great miracles of the Exodus, in order to examine and demonstrate G-d's goodness and infinite power For behold, we have a faithful witness which cannot be denied - our survival during this exile among the nations. It is proper to quote the holy words of Rabbi Yaakov Emden (sidur beit kel):

"Who is so blind as to not see the divine providence below, that His eyes are on them always. How could the denier of providence not be ashamed and stand disgraced? He who examines our unique situation and standing in the world. We the exiled nation, a dispersed sheep. After all the troubles and shifts for two thousands years. No nation in the world is as pursued as us. How great have been our troubles! How powerful have been those who lifted their heads against us from our earliest beginnings - to exterminate us, root us out, and eradicate us, due to their intense hatred which stems from jealousy. They have brought on us great sufferings but were never able to triumph over us, to eliminate us and destroy us. All these ancient, powerful nations - have gone by, their strength has withered, their protection has eroded - but we who cling to G-d are all alive today (Deut. 4:4). We have not lost in this long, intense exile even a single letter or vowel of the written Torah. The words of the Sages (oral law) endured. The hand of time did not prevail over us, they were not able to prevail over us. What will the sharp philosopher answer to this? Can the hand of chance do all this? I swear by my soul, for when contemplating these things, they are greater in my eyes than all the great open miracles G-d has performed for our forefathers in Egypt, the Sinai Desert, and in the land of Israel. (the author wrote that the miracle of our survival in this exile is equal to the miracles of Egypt, but Rabbi Yaakov Emden holds that it is an even greater miracle) The longer the exile, the more the miracle is confirmed, and G-d's strength and power becomes apparent. For the prophets already saw the exile's intensity, complaining and moaning on its amazing protracted length before it happened. Behold, none of their words fell to the ground (failed to happen)..." End quote

As Moshe Rabeinu told us from the outset that such and such as trouble would befall us, and thus it happened. Likewise, for all of our exile - the prophets already predicted what will happen. For all the persecutions and pursuits that befell us, such as the holocaust, it is all spelled out in the verses of the Torah which speak on those times... Can we not see these things with our own eyes?! Behold, only by examining and contemplating is it possible to see them. Without contemplating them, we remain totally blind.

What you should also attentively consider and examine is the fact that despite the wide diversity of dispositions among human beings there is whole-hearted agreement among them in the appointment of one of their number to rule over them (a king); they assume the option to serve him, and render him obedience in all that he commands and charges them. He on his part protects them, treats them with sympathy, judges their causes righteously, governs them for their common good, so that their interests shall not suffer and no enemy prevail against them. If every individual only cared for himself and only troubled to ward off hurt from his own person, men would never agree or build a tower or wall, and their common interests would be unprotected. This also is to be noted that the ruler himself observes the statutes, governs his people in accordance with righteous judgments and in good and upright ways, and overall is a servant of the law and observes righteousness. So conducting himself, his dominion will be established and his sovereignty endure, as it is said (Mishlei 20:28) *"Mercy and Truth preserve the king."* Our sages also have said "Pray for the welfare of the government; since if not for the fear thereof, men would swallow each other alive" (Pirkei Avot 3:2).

(*Marpe Lenefesh*: i.e. G-d puts in the heart of the king to govern his kingdom with righteousness and justice, and to punish the wicked, and to benefit the good so that his rule will endure and so that he does the will of G-d..

Matanas Chelko: it is human nature that each person wants only what is good for him. Each person looks at things with a different outlook and thinks that his way of looking at things is right and correct. Nevertheless, they come to an agreement on one view and to one leader. This is one of the wonders of the Creator.

Another subject that you need to examine, and understand from it marks of the divine wisdom and beneficence, is the agreement of human beings to buy and sell goods for gold and silver which, through G-d's mercy they endeavor to accumulate and thus improve their positions, though their actual needs cannot be satisfied with gold or silver. For when any one is afflicted with hunger and thirst through want of food or lack of water, an abundance of gold and silver will not avail him or cure his lacking. And if any one suffers pain in any of his limbs, he will not be cured by silver and gold; for while other minerals are largely used for medicinal purposes, this is less so in the case of gold or silver.

(*Matanas Chelko*: in truth it is strange and unusual that a person will desire something he cannot use...

Pas Lechem: That which human beings tend to yearn for and endeavor to amass gold and silver - this is a nature implanted in them by G-d in order promote their welfare. The proof is that they themselves are of little use, since they have no food or thirst value, therefore it must be that it is an implanted nature that man loves them without a reason.

Tov Halevanon. It is a nature implanted in man to pursue business dealings and to hoard money in order to give to he who is good before G-d and to strengthen society.

A wondrous evidence of wisdom is also that, while a few individuals possess large amounts of these precious metals, the majority of mankind have but little of them. If all human beings possessed them in abundance they could not use them as a medium for obtaining what they desire (they would be worthless, like rocks - *ML*). Some people have much and others have little. They are precious from one point view and of little account from another, because intrinsically they are useless. This too is within the plan of the Creator's supreme wisdom.

(*Pas Lechem*: "*the plan of the Creator's supreme wisdom*" - since most of the testing of man which demonstrates his free will, whether he chooses good or evil - is through them. For money pulls from one side and pushes from another. Understand this. [*Rabbi YS*: this will be explained in the Gate of Trust.]

Tov Halevanon: When the thing to buy with them is not available, they are useless, as written regarding a famine: (Yechezkel 7:19) "they will cast

| their silver to the street and their gold will be worthless...")

Then consider carefully the things on which depend the life of human beings and continuance of their normal state and condition until the end of their lives. You will find that all things are more or less plentiful in proportion to the need for them. Whatever is greatly needed is readily at hand. Whatever, on the other hand can be dispensed with, or one can for a time do without, is scarcer and harder to obtain.

For example, the air that is breathed - since one cannot possibly exist without air for any length of time, the Creator has so provided, that at no time and in no place shall a human being be deprived of it. And since human beings, while also needing water, can exist without it for a longer period than they can without air, the Creator distributed it over the entire surface of the earth, collecting it however in particular places to which creatures go and from which they are not excluded. But such places where water is collected are not found everywhere as is the case with air. Water has to be bought with money by some people. This is not the case with air. Water is more readily obtained by some than by others, air exists for all and is obtained by all equally and in the same way.

Food is also a necessity from which however we can abstain and for which we can find a substitute for a longer time than is possible in regard to air or water. Hence food is scarcer and harder to procure than water. But normally it is abundant and human beings are not deprived of it altogether.

So too with regard to garments of skin, wool and vegetable fiber. Substitutes for some of these can be more easily obtained than in the case of food; and clothes take time to make up, the reason being that for a short period a person can dispense with a new supply of clothing, and content himself with a scanty wardrobe for a longer period than he can with a small supply of food.

But precious stones, gold and silver and other minerals are essentially little needed. Their occasional use is due to convention. Hence a smaller quantity of these minerals is found among a multitude of human beings than of the food possessed by a single individual. The reason is, as we have stated, that a human being can do without these things.

| (*Rabbi YS*: as to why G-d did not make everything readily available, this is to provide a framework for testing man's free will as will be explained in the Gate of Trust.)

Praised be the All-Wise and Compassionate Creator who shows mercy to His servants towards whom He directs His beneficent regard for all that is for their improvement. Even as He said to Yona (4:10), *"you have had pity on the gourd, for which you have not labored, neither made it to grow, which came up in a night, and perished in a night; and should not I have pity on Nineveh, that great city...?"* And David said *"The L-ord is good to all and His mercies are upon all His creatures."*

Chapter 6

Regarding the factors detrimental to the examination and the things it depends on, I would say that all the factors noted in the first treatise as detrimental to the study of the Unity of G-d are equally injurious to the study of His works.

(*Marpe Lenefesh*: *"the factors noted in the first treatise"* - since one who does not believe in the One Master of the universe, that He alone created all these things, certainly such a person cannot discern the benevolences of the Creator, and to thank Him for them, etc., since for such a person, there is nothing fitting to serve, "the fool says in his heart, 'There is no G-d'" (Tehilim 53:2). But if he would examine with an open eye, on the greatness of the Creator, and His wisdom and providence - he would believe in the Master of the world, and that inevitably, He alone created all this, as explained there. Hence, this depends on that.)

In addition, there are the three factors mentioned at the beginning of this treatise. Another detrimental factor is the arrogant attitude towards the Creator's favors which the simple fool thinks are his due, and yet more beside. He does not examine these favors nor recognize any obligation on his own part to render praise and thanks to the Creator for them. Of such a person, the wise man said (Mishlei 16:5) *"Every one that is proud in heart is an abomination to the L-ord."*

(*Pas Lechem*: *"arrogant attitude towards the Creator's favors"* - The author spoke on the three detrimental factors at the beginning of this gate. There, however, he focused on the great toil, etc. which distracts a person, while now, he is adding the detriment due to arrogance.

Tov Halevanon: This is one who has a proud spirit, the entire world and everything in it is not enough for him.

Matanas Chelko: "the three factors" - (1) that man always chases after the vanities of this world, and lusts to obtain more than what he has. Due to this, he does not contemplate what he has. (2) That he is used to these benefits, and therefore does not contemplate them. (3) Man is not happy with his lot and does not accept everything with the proper faith. This certainly is detrimental to contemplating the beneficence and kindness of the Creator. A person should be happy with his portion so that he recognizes that hidden inside everything is only the goodness and kindness of G-d. Hence, it is necessary to strengthen oneself in these things so as not to ruin this awareness and contemplation.)

The things that the examination depends on:

(*Marpe Lenefesh*: i.e. there are some things which depend and are related to the examination, and it is proper to mention them.)

Among them, that a person understands the benefits he receives from G-d and will assume the obligation of serving Him because of them.

(*Marpe Lenefesh*: Because for what purpose, should a person examine and know the greatness and goodness of G-d without assuming His service, as our sages said (Berachot 17a): "the purpose of wisdom is repentance and good deeds")

Among them, that one will constantly recall the marks of divine wisdom and will never cease to think of them and investigate them-both those that can be apprehended by the senses and those comprehended only by the intellect. And so he will discover every day a new mark of divine wisdom, as David said (Ps. 19.3) *"Day unto day utters speech."*

(*Pas Lechem*: "constantly recall...never cease to think" - to keep in mind what he has grasped and to inquire on what he does not yet know of them.

Marpe Lenefesh: To not cease to think all the time, every second, and everything that he beholds of G-d's creations, whether it is big or small, and especially on his own self, how G-d guides him in all matters. If a person puts his mind to all these things mentioned earlier, certainly, he will see new marks of the Creator every day and every hour. See also Gate 8 ch.3 #23

Matanas Chelko: i.e. there is an additional benefit and result (from the examination), namely, that through this, a man will come to constantly contemplate the marks of divine wisdom. He will come to recognize always that everything is goodness and kindness from G-d. Hence, the Gate of Examination has no limit and no end. It continues and intensifies in awareness and grasp. Every day, a person needs to contemplate on a new good and a new greatness of the Creator.)

You should know that what I have called your attention to in this treatise, is but a small portion of the vast knowledge concerning the mysteries of wisdom you can acquire by your own understanding-mysteries which will be revealed to you if you purify your heart and refine your soul. When you have attained in these matters the utmost knowledge of which you are capable, you should realize that all this knowledge which you have acquired of the Creator's wisdom and power, as manifested in this universe, is as nothing compared to His real power and wisdom. For what is manifested is only that which is needed for a human being, not according to the true extent of His power, for it is infinite. Hence you should think of the awe-inspiring nature of G-d and His infinite might as they essentially are, not as you with your limited intelligence can perceive them.

> (*Pas Lechem*: *"purify your heart"* - that one's heart is simple, without ulterior motives or pretentiousness, while *"refine your soul"* refers to refining the soul through deeds, either by doing good, or refraining from evil.
>
> *Matanas Chelko*: i.e. a person must stand in awe and fear before the greatness of G-d. However, it is difficult to do so since it is impossible to attain a clear conception. Hence one must contemplate the following analogy.

Imagine rather that your condition here on earth is like that of a child born in a prison pit belonging to a king. The king took pity on the infant and ordered that it should be provided with everything good for it and needed for its well-being until it grew up and attained mature intelligence. But the child had knowledge of nothing except the prison and its contents. A royal officer of the king (Moses) visited the lad regularly, brought him all necessaries-light, food, drink, clothing; and informed him that he was a servant of the king, and that the prison and all it contained as well as the food brought him, belonged to the king; and that therefore he was under an obligation to thank his royal benefactor and laud him.

The lad replied, "I praise the owner of this prison who has accepted me as his servant, singled me out with all of his good and placed his eye and heart on me."

> (*Pas Lechem*: *"eye and heart"* - a caretaker must first see what is lacking in his subject, and afterwards put to heart how to fill his lacking.)

Said the officer, "Do not say so lest you sin. For the royal domain does not consist of this prison alone; but his widely extended lands immeasurably exceed its limited area. Nor are you his only servant, for his subjects are countless. And the benefactions and kindnesses you have received are insignificant compared to those he has bestowed on others. The care that he has taken of you is as nothing compared to the care of others."

(*Pas Lechem*: and in truth, one must also praise G-d also on the beneficence He bestows on others, as our sages said in the blessing of *"haTov vehaMetiv"* [Who is good, and bestows good].)

"I know nothing of what you mention", the lad replied. "As to the king, I can only understand what I have myself experienced of his goodness and dominion." The officer then said to the lad: "Say, I praise the exalted sovereign to whose dominion there are no bounds and whose goodness and kindness are without limit. Among his countless hosts, I am of no account, and in the greatness of his might my affairs are as naught.'"

The lad now obtained some understanding - such as he had never had before - of what the king was, and thus his respect for the sovereign's exalted state increased. Reverence for the ruler penetrated his consciousness. Owing to the lad's realization of the king's high position and his own utter insignificance, the royal goodness and benefits extended to him as well as the gifts bestowed upon him were magnified in his eyes.

And you my brother, put your heart to this parable when you behold the vast universe that encompasses the earth. What happens in a small area on earth we cannot understand. How much less can we understand the whole of the earth and how much more so for what is beyond this universe (the mystical worlds).

Consider, brother, this parable. Study it thoroughly, and then think of the Creator as He is, and His goodness and loving-kindness with which He has favored you will be more appreciated by you. From among all His creatures, He has taken special notice of you for your benefit.

(*Pas Lechem*: i.e. even though He has countless creatures like you, nevertheless, He put His eye on you with hashgacha pratis [special providence]

Matanas Chelko: We are living in the microcosm of our tiny physical world. In truth, there are countless other worlds which the Creator sustains and presides over. Above all this, is His essence which we have no grasp of whatsoever.

Look to His Scriptures, His commandments and statutes with a broad vision. Consider the great awe and respect you feel towards any man who has acquired more worldly good than you have. For the higher his position is compared with yours, and the less he stands in need of you, the more will you esteem his greatness and his beneficence; the more will you respect his commandments and prohibitions; the more energetically will you strive and labor in his affairs. Think and reflect and you will find with G-d's help.

> (*Marpe Lenefesh*: put to heart how you humble yourself before a rich person who has more than you, and all the more so if he is beneficent towards you, the favor will be great in your eyes, and you will revere him and esteem him since he does not need you, and you need him, and his status is higher than yours. Likewise, you run to do the command of this rich person according to how much he is important in your eyes.
> *"the more energetically will you strive"* - i.e. strive and labor to do His service with all of your might.

May the Almighty set us among those who are in His service and who realize His goodness, mercies and kindnesses. AMEN.

> (*Matanas Chelko*: Rabeinu finishes with an additional point. We must realize that G-d grants us the powers and merit to realize His goodness. This is as we conclude every prayer service "Aleinu Leshabeach...", i.e. that we must also be grateful for the ability and merit to be able to recognize the King and all of His goodness and kindness on us.

*** Shaar Avodas HaElokim - Gate of Service of G-d ***

from Chovos Halevavos - Duties of the Heart

by Rabeinu Bahya ibn Paquda zt'l

original english translation by Rabbi Moses Hyamson, former chief Rabbi of British Empire, New York, 1925
OCR scanned with permission from http://www.hebrewbooks.org/3186
(now public domain)
new revision including select classic commentaries translated by Rabbi Yosef Sebag

----

*** Introduction ***

On the service of G-d, expounding various grounds for the obligation to assume the service of G-d, blessed be He.

Having, in the previous treatises, expounded the obligation of wholeheartedly acknowledging the unity of G-d and the obligation of examining the various modes of His benefits to mankind, we have next to indicate what a human being's conduct should be, once the foregoing has become clear to him - and that is to assume the obligation of the service of G-d, as reason would require from a beneficiary to his benefactor.

It is proper to open this treatise with an exposition of the various kinds of benefits human beings render each other, and the corresponding obligations of gratitude. We shall then ascend to the consideration of what we owe to the exalted Creator in praise and thanksgiving for His abounding kindness and great goodness to us.

> (*Marpe Lenefesh*: i.e. once all this has become clear to a person, namely, that there is a G-d above and below and He alone created everything, and it has also become clear how much abounding beneficence He has bestowed on us, as written in the previous two gates - the consequence of this is that a human being is under duty to assume on himself the yoke of the service of G-d.)

We assert, as a truth generally recognized, that if anyone benefits us, we are under an obligation of gratitude to him in accordance with his intent to help us. Even if he actually falls short, owing to some mishap which prevents his benefiting us, we are still bound to be grateful to him, since we are convinced that he has a benevolent disposition towards us and his intention is to be of benefit to us. On the other hand, should we obtain any benefit through one who had no such intention, the duties of gratitude to that person would cease and we are under no such obligation.

> (*Pas Lechem*: "he has a (1) benevolent disposition towards us and (2) his intention is to be of benefit" - these are two different modes, for it is possible to find someone who loves his friend and has a benevolent disposition towards him, but nevertheless never has intent to try to actually benefit him, whether due to laziness or due to inability. Likewise, it is possible to find someone who has intent to be of actual benefit to his fellow, but not because he has a benevolent disposition towards him, but rather due to some outside interest, either to appear noble, or to annoy his

enemy who desires evil for that fellow... Hence, the author wrote two expression: *"benevolent disposition"* and *"intent to benefit"*. Or perhaps the intent is for positive benefit and saving from harm.

Marpe Lenefesh: [According to reason] everything goes after the intent. If he benefits him without outside interest, even though sometimes he falls short and is prevented from this due to some incident or mischance, nevertheless - we are under duty to thank him for his good intention and faithful heart.)

When we consider the benefits human beings render each other, we find that these fall into five classes:
(1) a father's beneficence to his child;
(2) a master's to his servant;
(3) a wealthy man's beneficence to the poor for the sake of heavenly reward;
(4) the beneficence rendered by human beings to each other in order to gain a good name, honor and worldly reward;
(5) the powerful man's beneficence to the weak, induced by pity for the latter and sympathy with his condition.

(*Pas Lechem*: When the powerful man sees the pain of the weak, then his heart is moved by the latter's pain. And even when he no longer sees him, nevertheless, whenever he remembers him, he feels pain at his plight and bad lot.

Tov Halevanon: The powerful man is pained by him and feels the wretchedness of this weak person and that he has no helper.)

Let us now consider the motive in each of the classes mentioned:
Is it disinterested, the sole aim being to help the beneficiary, or is it not so? First, a father's beneficence to his child: It is obvious that the father's motive in this is to further his own interest. For the child is a part of the father, whose chief hope is centered in his offspring. Do you not observe that in regard to its food, drink, clothing and in warding off all hurt from it, a father is more sensitive about his child than about himself? To secure ease for it, the burden of toil and weariness is lightly borne by him, the feelings of tenderness and pity for their offspring being naturally implanted in parents.

(*Pas Lechem*: "whose chief hope is centered in his offspring" - he hopes to receive from his offspring a future and a hope, either by having a name and a remnant in the world through his offspring, something human beings naturally long for. Or, he hopes through torah law, that "a son brings merit to his father" (Sanhedrin 104a), for "the crown of elders is grandchildren" (Mishlei 17:6). He first mentioned the reason that the child is a branch of his tree, and it is a logical reason that the Understanding obligates a bit. Afterwards, he brought the second reason of "natural instinct" - that even if it were without any logical reason, for natural love is without any reason.)

Nevertheless, the Torah and reason impose upon children the duty of serving, honoring and revering their parents, as Scripture says: *"Ye shall, everyone, revere his father and his mother"* (Vayikra 19:3); *"Hear, O my son, the instruction of your father and forsake not the law of your mother"* (Mishlei 1:8) ; further, *"A son honors his father, and a servant his master"* (Malachi 1:6). (And these duties are enjoined) despite that the father is impelled by a natural instinct and the benefaction comes from G-d, while the parent is only the agent (i.e. G-d provides the benefits He decreed for the child through the father - *TL*).

(*Pas Lechem*: *"Ye shall, everyone, revere his father and his mother"* - the author did not bring the commandment "honor your father and your mother" (Levit. 20:12) from the Ten Commandments. The reason being that his intent is to demonstrate that the torah commanded this from the perspective of human understanding not as a statute (without reason) like other statutes of the torah (such as shatnez or milk and meat). In the Ten Commandments, it says "honor your father... in order that you lengthen your days". Once the torah designated reward as such, the status of the commandment appears to be as a Biblical precept (i.e. not a precept derived from reason). But in the verse, "Ye shall, everyone, revere his father and his mother", there it reveals that the torah obligates this from the side of Reason. Hence, the torah wrote the mother first, since she toiled more in his upbringing. And on "honor", he brought the verse "A son honors his father, and a servant his master", which clearly shows from the language of the verse that the intent is from Reason, since it was not stated as a command but rather in a language of "custom of the world", as a natural duty derived from common sense...[see there for more].)

The kindness of a master to his servant: It is obvious that the master's intent is to improve his property by an outlay of capital, since he needs his servant's work, and his motive in this is to further his own interest. Nevertheless, the Creator, blessed be He, imposes upon the servant the duties of service and gratitude, as it is said, *"A son honors his father and a servant his master"* (Malachi 1:6).

(*Pas Lechem*: It appears the author's intent is to bring a proof from this verse that the servant is under duty to show gratitude to his master. The reason being that it is learned out from the verse's context of a son's honor for his father. If so what "honor" is a servant obligated in besides his service? Thanking him verbally.)

The rich man's beneficence to the poor man for the sake of a heavenly reward: He is like a merchant who acquires a great and enduring pleasure which he will enjoy at the end of a definite time by means of a small, perishable and inconsiderable gift which he makes immediately. So the rich man only intends to win glory for his soul at the close of his earthly existence by the benefaction which G-d entrusted to him, in order to bestow it upon anyone who will be worthy of it. Yet it is generally recognized that it is proper to thank and laud a benefactor. Even though the latter's motive was to gain spiritual glory hereafter, gratitude is, nevertheless, due to him, as Job said: *"[because I delivered the poor who cried for help, and the fatherless who had none to help him;] the blessing of him that was ready to perish came upon me"* (Job 29:13); and further, *"did not his heart bless me, when he warmed himself with the fleece of my sheep?"* (Job 31:20).

(*Marpe Lenefesh*: *"for the sake of a heavenly reward"* - i.e. even if his intent is for heavenly reward [which is the highest of the ulterior motives], nevertheless, he is like a merchant who purchases merchandise with little money with intent that he will profit afterwards with this merchandise a lot of money. So too, for one who gives charity to receive heavenly reward With the small donation he gives to the poor person, he intends to acquire a great and enduring pleasure, namely, the afterlife.

"the benefaction which G-d entrusted to him" - Certainly the extra benefits a person has in his possession which are beyond his needs are only like a deposit by him, and he is like a manager and dispenser of it, to give them to those who are worthy of receiving it, as Rabbi Moshe Alshich expounded on the verse: "that your brother may live with you" (Vayikra 25:36), i.e. the life of your brother, i.e. his sustenance, is with you and by you. For G-d wants to bring merit to the wealthy person through the mitzvah of charity...)

Kindness men show each other for the sake of praise, honor and worldly rewards: This is as if one were to deposit an article in another's care or entrust him with money, because of the depositor's apprehension that he may need it later on.

(*Pas Lechem*: He fears that if it remains in his hand, perhaps it will be lost through some mishap, and it will not be his at a time of need.)

Although, in benefiting another person, the aim is to further his own interests, the benefactor is nevertheless entitled to praise and gratitude for his kindness, as the wise king said, *"Many beseech the generous man, and everyone is a friend to him that gives gifts"* (Mishlei 19:6) ; and he also said, *"A man's gift makes room for him and brings him before great men"* (Mishlei 18:16).

> (*Pas Lechem*: *"praise and gratitude"* - [Regarding gratitude] "many beseech the generous man" - Even though this verse makes no mention of praise, nevertheless, since the way of the world is to beseech a generous man, if so, reason obligates that when one beseeches him and he accedes to your request that you must thank him for it.
> [Regarding praise] - *"A man's gift makes room for him and brings him before great men"* - it appears from this verse that his giving acquires for him nobility, hence the receiver must praise him.)

The kindness of one who has compassion on a poor man in pain: The benefactor's motive is to get rid of his own distress that results from depression and grief for the one he pities. He is like one who cures a pain which has attacked him by means of the bounties that G-d bestowed upon him. Nevertheless, he is not to be left without praise, as Job said, *"Could I see any perish for want of clothing or any poor without covering? Did not his heart bless me, when he warmed himself with the fleece of my sheep?"* (Job 31:19-20).

> (*Pas Lechem*: *"nevertheless, he is not to be left without praise"* - the author's intent in using this expression is that for this category, Reason has the tendency to deem him least worthy of praise than all the previous categories, because here the benefactor is acting to relieve an immediate pain he has. Unlike the previous cases, where the benefactor's benefit was not immediately felt and apparent. Even so, he is not to be left without any praise.
>
> *Tov Halevanon*: *"Could I see any perish for want of clothing or any poor without covering?"* - even though the author already brought a proof from Job previously on someone giving charity to receive heavenly reward (and here he is bringing a proof for one who acts out of pity). [Answer:] There he brought a proof from the verse "The blessing of him that was ready to perish came upon me", namely that it is proper for the blessing of the poor to come on him as a reward for the mitzvah (good deed) he did, since certainly, he also had intent for heavenly reward in giving charity to the poor in the case when he did not feel his pain. For a man is not so moved to feel pity in giving food to a poor person because the suffering of hunger is not so visible to the eye. Whereas here, the verse is speaking of a case where a person is distressed and feels pain on seeing the poor man perishing without any clothing, and the eye sees his predicament, naked

| and destitute.)

From what has here been advanced, it is clear that anyone who bestows benefits on others has first his own interest in mind - either to secure an honorable distinction in this world or hereafter, or relieve himself of pain, or improve his material possessions. Yet all these considerations do not absolve the beneficiaries of their duty of praising, thanking, respecting and loving their benefactors and making them some return. And this, despite that the benefit was only loaned to the benefactors (since everything belongs to G-d as written "gold and silver is Mine" Chagai 2:8 - *PL*); that they were compelled to dispense it, as we have pointed out; and that their beneficence is not permanent, their generosity not prolonged, and their benevolence is mixed with the intent either to further their own interest or to ward off harm. If so, how much more then does a human being owe service, praise and gratitude to Him who created the benefit and the benefactor, whose beneficence is unlimited, permanent, perpetual, without any motive of self-interest, or purpose of warding off injury, but only an expression of grace and loving-kindness emanating from Him towards all human beings.

(*Pas Lechem*: *"and their benevolence is mixed"* - it seems that this is the same as what he wrote before "that they were compelled to dispense it", but in truth, they are two categories. Because in the latter he was referring to their free choice - that their free choice is not completely free since necessity compels them, either due to natural instinct or worldly necessity. On the other hand, this case [that *"their benevolence is mixed"*] means, even if we you were to suppose they had free will (and nothing compelled them) and we will say that they are being benevolent in this, nevertheless, it is not true benevolence since certainly, "their benevolence is mixed, etc.".

Tov Halevanon: *"who created the benefit and the benefactor"* - since all good that manifests in the world comes from G-d's decree [as will be explained in the Gate of Trust])

We should furthermore come to understand that any human being who renders a kindness to another in any of the modes above specified is not superior to the person whom he benefits, except in some incidental detail, while in their humanity and essence (i.e. body and soul - *PL*) they are alike and akin to one another, in substance and form, in physical construct and figure (or mentality - Gen. 1:27) in their natures and in a larger part of what happens to them. Nevertheless the beneficiary, as we have set forth, is under an obligation of service to his benefactor.

And if we thought that the beneficiary was extremely defective and imperfect in his physical conformation, figure and appearance [we would conclude that], the obligation of service on his part would be so much the greater. So also, if we should deem the benefactor the best and most perfect of all beings, while the beneficiary was the most defective of all things and the weakest of all creatures, reason would require that the service to the benefactor should be increased to an infinite degree.

Following this analogy, when we investigate, through reason, the relation of the Creator, blessed be He, to human beings, we will find that the Creator, blessed be He, is infinitely exalted and glorified above everything existing, above all that can be apprehended by the senses or conceived by the intellect as has been expounded in the first treatise of this book; and that a human being, in comparison with other species of animals, is the most defective and weakest of them all.

This can be demonstrated in three respects:
(1) In respect to his infancy and early childhood: For we find that other species of living creatures are stronger than he is, better able to endure pain and move independently, and do not trouble their parents in their period of growth to the same extent as a human being does.

(2) In respect to the filth and foulness within the human body and the similar appearances on the skin when one has neglected to wash and cleanse himself for a length of time, as also in respect to the state of the body after death-the discharge of a human corpse being more nauseating than that of the carcasses of other creatures, and a human being's excrement more offensive than that of other creatures. Likewise for his other waste matter (such as waste from the nose or ears - *PL*).

(*Marpe Lenefesh*: *"and the similar appearances on the skin"* - i.e. it is similar to the filth and foulness inside the body if he does not wash himself for a long time, such as skin diseases, or the like, unlike the animals even if they don't bathe.)

(3) In respect to a human being's incompetence when, due to a brain injury, he loses the rational faculty which G-d bestowed upon him and which constitutes his superiority to the other creatures that are irrational. For at such times he is stupider and more senseless than other animals. He may inflict serious injuries on himself and even kill himself. Most animals, too, we find, possess an apprehension of what will be to their advantage, and show an ingenuity in obtaining their food, while many intellectual men fall

short in this regard, not to speak of one who has lost his intellect.

(*Marpe Lenefesh*: *"due to a brain injury"* - hence, he lost his ability to reason, then he is "stupider and more senseless", like the way of the crazy people. For then he is worse than an animal, because despite that an animal does not have an intellect, nevertheless, it does not act crazily. Sometimes he inflicts on himself serious injury or even kills himself, unlike the animals who recognize what will be to their advantage and show ingenuity in obtaining their food such as the spider's web or the honeycomb of the bee, or the like, something which many wise men cannot do like them.)

When we comprehend in our thoughts on the greatness of the Creator, exalted be He, on His infinite might, wisdom and wealth [i.e. resources]; and then turn our attention to a man's weakness and deficiency, in that he never attains perfection; when we consider his poverty and lack of what he needs to supply his wants and then investigate the numerous benefits and favors which the Creator has bestowed on him; when we reflect that the Creator has created man as he is with deficiencies in his very being - poor and needing for his development all necessities which he can only obtain by exerting himself - this too stems from the Creator's mercy to him, so that he may know himself, examine all his conditions and cleave, under all circumstances, to the service of G-d, and so receive for it the reward of the world to come, for the attainment of which he was created, as we have already set forth in the second treatise of this book - how much indeed then does a human being owe to the blessed Creator, in service, thanksgiving and continuous praise, in view of the demonstration already given of the obligation of praise and gratitude that human beings owe to each other for favors rendered them.

(*Tov Halevanon*: *"has created man with deficiencies"* - even this that He created man lacking everything, poor and destitute - this is out of mercy for man, in order that he examine his matters and sees his lacking, and that he has no other option than to lift his eyes to his Father in heaven.

Pas Lechem: i.e. everything that G-d does with man - it is all for man's good and due to G-d's compassion for him. Whether that which man is born lacking everything, or whether that which he is forced to toil and exert himself for all of his needs and for his livelihood.

Tov Halevanon: *"so that he may examine all his conditions"* - i.e. his intellect will push him to assume the service of G-d after he examines all these things.

Pas Lechem: *"and cleave to the service of G-d"* - in everything man does, big or small, G-d is with him, and he can examine through it the kindness of G-d. Hence, after he realizes and it is clear to him that it is all from G-d, and no created being can advise any plan or exercise any control except through G-d's permission - if so, he will place his trust firmly in G-d [and cleave to His service].

"under all circumstances" - whether G-d benefited him or harmed him, as written: "all the ways of G-d are kindness and truth" (Tehilim 25:10), as will be explained in the Gate of Trust.

"receive the reward of the world to come, the attainment of which he was created" - i.e. for this man was created - to cleave to the service of G-d and receive his reward in the next world.)

Should anyone be so foolish as to contest this obligation of a human being towards the Creator - when he examines and closely studies the subject, and acknowledges the truth to himself, the sleeper will surely awake, the negligent will be aroused, the ignorant will investigate, the intelligent will understand, the demonstration of the obligatory character of the service of G-d, through the clear proofs (from reason - *PL*), well known testimony (from scripture - *PL*), and true signs (miracles of the Exodus from Egypt - *ML*); as the prophet, peace be unto him, said concerning one who neglects to reflect upon the obligation of the service of G-d, *"Do you thus repay the L-ord, O foolish and unwise people? [is not he your Father that has acquired you? has He not made you, and established you?]"* (Devarim 32:6).

Thus the obligation to assume the service of G-d, incumbent on human beings in view of the continuous benefits He bestows on them, has been demonstrated.

In dealing with the subject-matter of this treatise, we have now to expound ten topics:

(1) the necessity of arousing men to G-d's service, and the methods to be employed to this end;
(2) the need for each of these methods;
(3) definition of the service (of G-d); its divisions and degrees;
(4) the form which the Torah takes to arouse us; its divisions; and the excellencies which men attain through knowledge of the Torah and comprehension of its contents;
(5) the way in which the exercise of our reasoning faculties prompts us in this regard, set forth in the form of questions and answers;
(6) the various classes of obligations to the service of G-d, corresponding

to the various kinds of benefits received, and their divisions;

(7) exposition of the minimum of service which the recipient of any benefit owes to the benefactor;

(8) the difference in the views of the learned in regard to (the problem of) necessity and (divine) justice, and which of these views is nearer the truth;

(9) the mystery of the purpose for which the human species was created on earth, concisely set forth;

(10) an account of the use we should make of all our capacities, each in its right place.

(*Tov Halevanon*: *"the minimum of service"* - i.e. the least and minimum service of G-d which a person does not fulfill his obligation less than this.)

CHAPTER I.

Arousing man to G-d's service and its various branches are necessary on the following grounds. The understanding and the faculty of perception both instruct on human beings the duty of serving G-d. But between the time when the benefits that man receives and the time when he has sufficient intelligence to realize the services he should render in return for them, a long period intervenes. Hence, it is a duty to arouse human beings to their obligations of deeds and inward faith which make the service of G-d complete, so that a human being should not be without religion up to the time when his mental powers have become fully developed.

(*Tov Halevanon*: From the time a human being is born, the beneficence that G-d bestows on him is apparent, but the time when he will be able to comprehend this good through intellectual inquiry is only after he has matured and is able to grasp intellectual things, to understand wisdom, to examine the greatness of the Creator and His benevolence towards him... [*Rabbi YS*: in our era of ketchup and hotdogs, the time when a person thinks on these things starts much later in life if at all]

Marpe Lenefesh: Hence it is proper and a duty to teach him the path he should walk, and the deeds he should do - to stir him and stand him on the true faith from his early years so that he does not walk without religion and without good deeds for a long time. For otherwise it is possible that he will become ingrained in this like a wild horse.)

(now he will explain the 2 divisions of this arousing:)
This calling attention is twofold.
(1) One of them is inherent in the understanding, implanted in the human faculty of cognition, innate from the beginning of his existence.

(*Marpe Lenefesh*: It is in human nature, for every person with intelligence, that just like he knows and can discern between good and evil, so too he knows that it is proper to humble himself before his Benefactor.)

(2) The other is acquired through instruction, namely, the torah, which the prophet conveys to human beings, so as to teach them the mode of service which it is their duty to render to the Creator, blessed be He.

(*Marpe Lenefesh*: There is something additional which arouses him, namely, what he hears and learns from other people, i.e. what we heard from Moshe Rabeinu, peace be unto him, the master of all prophets - how we should serve G-d.)

CHAPTER 2

Both methods (understanding and torah - *TL*) of calling attention to the service of G-d are necessary because the innate urge of the understanding is weak in three respects; and we are therefore under duty to strengthen it by religious instruction.

First, man is made up of diverse entities, natures conflicting and mutually antagonistic. These entities are his soul and his body.

(*Marpe Lenefesh*: "natures conflicting" (literally: overpowering each other) - the nature of the body is to be drawn after the physical, while the nature of the soul is to be drawn after the spiritual. Each tries to overcome the other and wants to conquer the other, that it will be drawn after it, because each one needs the help of the other.
"*[natures] mutually antagonistic*" (literally: essences which are enhanced in conflicting ways) - this yearns for physical delights and is enhanced by them, while this yearns for spiritual yearnings and is enhanced by them. Hence, they are enhanced in conflicting ways.)

The Creator has implanted in his soul qualities and forces which make him yearn for things, the use of which will promote his physical well-being, so that he will develop vigor to populate the earth, in order that the race may continue while individuals perish. This quality is the desire for bodily pleasures common to all living creatures that propagate their species.

(*Tov Halevanon*: i.e. to build, to plant, in all types of acts and works of his, which deplete his strength. And even though there is foolishness in this, that he strains himself for a world which is not his, and it should be enough that he troubles himself only for things that endure for the duration of his lifetime. Nevertheless, it is a nature, which the Creator implanted in the hearts of human beings which is necessary for the propagation of the human race, for without this, the world would be desolate.
"*common to all living creatures*" - even other creatures have a nature to amass and hoard more than their needs as we see by the bees and its honey, and other living creatures.
Alternative interpretation:
Marpe Lenefesh: without the lust for physical pleasures man would not procreate and the human race would become extinct.
"*The Creator has implanted in his soul*" - the Rambam writes in the Shemonei Perakim that: "even though the nefesh (human soul) is essentially one (i.e. not physically divisible. This is why it is invisible),

nevertheless it has 5 "powers", namely, sustenance which allows [the organism] to grow (i.e. an underlying spiritual power which drives and animates the biological cells), feeling, imagination, awareness, and intellect. The intellect is the primary essence while the other powers are implanted by the Creator in order to guide the body, for without this, the body could not endure..." the Rambam ends off there: "and if a man uses all his powers except for the intellect, then it is all for nothing. And this is what scripture says: (Mishlei 19:2) "Also, that the soul be without knowledge is not good; and he that hastens with his feet sins".

Rabbi YS: The book Shaarei Kedusha explains that life forms (plants, animals, humans) are a composite of physical and spiritual "souls" of varying degrees and powers. It is simply too complicated for any kind of purely physical machine to (1) grow and (2) reproduce. Physical machines necessarily function in a direct manner, namely, one thing reacts, which causes another to react, etc. motorically. With this limitation it is impossible to build the above. Likewise for things like consciousness. Therefore, it is necessary for a spiritual component to be added to life forms which animates the body and drives the countless simultaneous processes. The soul is able to integrate all these aspects because its essence is not physical and its knowledge is unbound to physical matter and existence. See Gate 1 ch.5 for more.)

The Creator has also engrafted in the human soul other qualities and forces, which, if he uses them, will make him loathe his position in this world and yearn to separate himself from it. This is the desire for perfect wisdom.

(*Marpe Lenefesh*: This is the intellect and understanding, through them he will yearn for lofty spiritual things, not for the body and its pleasures, and he will desire to part from the body and this world, because it yearns for its root [in the higher worlds] as the nature of all things is to yearn for its root.)

Since, however, bodily pleasures come to a man's soul first, already in early youth, and the attachment to them is, from the outset, strong, great and extremely urgent, the desire for sensual pleasure overcomes his other faculties, until it overpowered the intellect, for the sake of which man was created. And so his spiritual sight fails and the indications of his desirable qualities disappear.

(*Marpe Lenefesh*: Hence, the lusts overpowered the intellect, for the intellect is likened to a poor youth [in scripture as in "better a poor and wise child than an old and foolish king who no longer knows to receive admonition" (Koheles 4:13)"], while the lusts, which are the yetzer hara (evil inclination) is a foolish elder, since he came before the yetzer tov [good inclination which starts to come after 13 years of age].)

Man therefore needs external means, by the aid of which he may resist his despicable instinct - the lust for animal enjoyments - and vitalize the marks of his noblest endowment - the intellect. These aids are the contents of the Torah, whereby G-d, through His messengers and prophets, taught His creatures the way to serve Him.

(*Pas Lechem*: *"vitalize the marks of his noblest endowment"* - i.e. to bring out from potential to actual. He used the term *"vitalize"* (literally: bring to life) since a trait which exists in potential only, is without movement, like a dead thing. But when he takes it out to actual, it moves like a living thing.)

Secondly, the intellect is a spiritual entity, originating in the higher, spiritual world. It is a stranger in this world of gross material bodies. Sensual lust in man is the product of natural forces and of a combination of his physical elements. Its foundation is in this world, its root in this abode. Food gives it strength. Physical pleasures add to its vigor, while the intellect, because it is a stranger here, stands without support or ally, and all are against it. Hence it follows that it must become weak and that it needs an external means to repel the mighty power of lust and overcome it. The Torah is the remedy for such spiritual maladies and moral diseases.

(*Marpe Lenefesh*: *"the intellect is a spiritual entity"* - As written, "And He breathed into man the soul of life" (Bereishis 2:7), this is the soul which originates from the higher spiritual worlds. And it includes within it all the levels of the spiritual worlds. It has 248 spiritual limbs and 365 spiritual sinews. Therefore, the body was also created in this form, as a tailor who makes a garment like the measure of the man. The body which is physical matter from the ground, is mixed and synthesized from the four elements and their spiritual components. This is called the "foundation soul" (nefesh yesodit). On this, the intellect, or "neshama" abides. The intellect does not benefit from physical pleasures, therefore it has no support or ally in this world, and all of the worldly pleasures are against it. This nefesh (foundation soul) is called the "nefesh bahamit" (animal soul), and it is an intermediary between the physical body and the soul (intellect), as is well explained in the book "Shaarei Kedusha" (essential reading) and in the book of Moshe Alshich.

Rabbi YS: the following commentary is not so clear to me, but since he ended off: "understand all this", I tried to translate it anyways.
Pas Lechem: *"Sensual lust in man is the product of natural forces and of a combination of his physical elements"* - *"natural forces"* is general

[physical] human nature. Afterwards he wrote: *"combination of his physical elements"*. Hence, the foundation of lust is in this world. Therefore, he continued *"Its foundation is in this world"*. He added *"its root in this abode"*, because the foundation of something is that which that something is built upon. This corresponds to the *"general [physical] human nature"*, because on top of the necessary needs [of food, etc.] of human nature, lust builds a desire for the superfluous. Hence, to lust, the natural needs are at the level of "foundation". He wrote *"root of its abode"*, a term connotating "dwelling place", corresponding to *"combination of his physical elements"*. Since in them is the power of lust and there is its dwelling place. He used the term "root" because the power of lust which is in potential, is the root of the [active] movements of lust which go out from potential to actual. Understand all this.

"food gives it strength" - corresponding to the potential, while *"Physical pleasures add to its vigor"* refers to the actual pleasure a man enjoys. This pleasure strengthens the power of desire, namely, lust in its actual state, which then strengthens and vigorates [more] to attain its desires.)

The Torah therefore prohibits many kinds of food, clothing, sexual relations, certain acquisitions and practices, all of which strengthen sensual lust; it also exhorts us to use those means which resist lust and are its opposite. These are prayer, fasting, charity-giving, [acts of] kindness; by which the intellectual faculties are revived and man is aided in this world and for the world to come, as David said. *"Your word is a lamp to my feet (in this world - MH) and a light to my path (in the next world - MH)"* (Tehilim 119:105) ; *"For the commandment is a lamp and the torah is light"* (Mishlei 6:23) ; *"I saw that wisdom is preferable to folly as light is preferable to darkness"* (Koheles 2:13).

(*Pas Lechem*: *"Prayer"* is opposite to the lust for unbridledness (hefker), wildness, and prikas ol (removal of the yoke of G-d's law) which is found among immoral people, as written "the vile person says 'there is no G-d'" (Tehilim 14:1). *"Fasting"* is opposite lust for food. *"Charity-giving"* is opposite the lust for amassing possessions. *"Kindness"* is the opposite of jealousy and love of harming other people (i.e. cruelty), as written "For they cannot sleep unless they are doing evil, and they are robbed of their sleep unless they cause someone to stumble" (Mishlei 4:16).

Marpe Lenefesh: *"For the commandment is a lamp and the torah is light"* - like a candle which dispels darkness and then one can see what to do, so too the torah enlightens a man, and then he will be able to use his understanding, and not be blinded [by the lusts].)

Third, the sensual desire, constantly employed in feeding the body, never ceases working by day or night (in eating, drinking, or sleeping - *TL*). The intellect, on the other hand, is only called into activity to help one gratify his passions. Now it is well known that physical faculties which are constantly exercised in accordance with their nature, improve and become more efficient, while those that are less frequently used deteriorate and become inefficient. It logically follows therefore that the sensual desire would become stronger because it is continually exercised, while the intellectual faculty would weaken, because it is so seldom used, and so little for its proper purpose.

Hence it was necessary for there to exist something, whose true (proper) use would not involve man's physical organs nor the animalistic lusts, but only the exercise of his intellect, freed from the predominance of lusts. This aid is the Torah, the study of which will make the intellect stronger, purer, and more luminous and will drive away from man the folly that masters his soul and prevents him from seeing things as they really are and placing them in their proper relations. As the Psalmist said, *"The law of the L-ord is perfect, restoring the soul; the testimony of the L-ord is faithful, making wise the simple; the ordinances of the L-ord are right, rejoicing the heart; the commandment of the L-ord is pure, enlightening the eyes"* (Ps. 19:8-9).

(*Pas Lechem*: there needs to exist something which will be an aid to the intellect, that this thing can only be employed by an intellect saved from the overpowering of lust - this is the torah. For the torah cannot be employed (studied) unless one throws off of himself all the vanities of this world, at least for that study time period.
[*Rabbi YS*: since he has no hope for monetary profit nor any physical indulgence etc. from torah study. Unlike intellectual study of science or other subjects where he may have hope to get money or honor, etc. Sometimes these subjects may even give intellectual pleasure but they don't carry any moral responsibility. Unlike the torah whose study makes demands on how one should lead his life. One who desires to be morally "free" and follow his lusts, will find nothing but guilt feelings in the study of torah.]

"whose true (proper) use" - i.e. the true use, since actually, some employ the crown of torah also for physical things and make it into a spade with which to dig. [a reference to Pirkei Avot 4:7]

"(1) The law of the L-ord is perfect, restoring the soul; (2) the testimony of the L-ord is faithful, making wise the simple; (3) the ordinances of the L-ord are right, rejoicing the heart; (4) the commandment of the L-ord is

pure, enlightening the eyes" - four terms corresponding to the four things
he mentioned above [(1)stronger, (2) purer, (3) more luminous...(4) seeing
things as they really are"].

"restoring the soul" - corresponding to *"the study of which will make the
intellect stronger"*, for the term 'restoring the soul' teaches on this.

"making wise the simple" - corresponding to *"purer"*, that the intellect will
be pure through torah study from the impurities of simpletonness.

"rejoicing the heart" - corresponding to *"more luminous"* since joy is the
spreading out of the inner power towards the outside, as known. This is
called "zohar" in Hebrew, as written "And they that are wise shall shine as
the brightness (zohar) of the firmament" (Daniel 12:3).

"enlightening the eyes" - corresponding to *"will drive away from man the
folly"*. Since the fool walks in darkness, and there is no blindness like the
overpowering of foolishness, as he wrote *"and prevents him from seeing
things as they really are"*.)

From what has been said, it is clearly established how necessary it is that a
human being should be aroused to the service of G-d by the Torah, which
includes rational precepts as well as those accepted on authority
(prophecy), so that through these we may rise to the service of G-d which,
our reason demonstrates, is man's duty and the main purpose for which the
human species has been called into existence in this world.

CHAPTER 3

Definition of the Service of G-d; explanation of its parts; the merits of each of these parts.

Service may be defined as a beneficiary's submission to his benefactor, expressed in rendering good that is within his power to the latter in return for the favor received (i.e. all that is in his power to render - *ML*) . This submission is of two kinds. The first is submission induced by fear, hope, necessity or compulsion. The second is submission arising from a sense of duty, from the conviction that it is right to aggrandize and exalt the person to whom submission is rendered.

> (*Marpe Lenefesh*: "*fear, hope, necessity or compulsion*" - that he submits due to fear of punishment. "*hope*" that he hopes for and waits for good reward. Hence, he submits out of necessity and compulsion.
> "*the second*" - that it is a duty and the understanding dictates that it is right and proper to submit to this benefactor even without any fear and compulsion.
>
> *Tov Halevanon*: "*fear, hope, necessity or compulsion*" - i.e. that this submission comes from fear of hope, which means something which will come in the future, namely, reward and punishment. It pains him that instead of reward, he will get punishment. These things submit him out of necessity and compulsion when he contemplates the contrast, i.e. receiving reward versus receiving punishment instead.)

Of the first kind is that submission to G-d which has been induced by an external stimulus (the torah), as we have mentioned, and the obligation of which arises from hope of reward or fear of punishment in this world and the next (since the torah is built on the foundation of reward and punishment - *ML*). But the second kind is the submission which arises from an inward urge in the intellect (conscience), innate in the nature of a human being in whom body and soul are joined together.

> (*Tov Halevanon*: because the soul is joined to the body, i.e. the intellect in the soul causes submission of the body. [*Rabbi YS*: like the rider on a horse])

Both kinds of submission are praiseworthy and lead to salvation in the life hereafter, the world of eternal rest. But one of these leads to the other and is a step by which we ascend to it. The former is the submission induced by the study of the Torah. The [latter] submission which is induced by the urge of the understanding and based on rational demonstrations, is nearer to G-d and more acceptable on seven grounds:

(*Tov Halevanon*: *"one of these leads to the other"* - i.e. submission due to fear of punishment and hope for reward induced by the torah leads to the submission induced by the understanding. Because before a person will be straight in his intellectual perception, he was not able to resist the lusts which naturally overpowered his intellect, as the author mentioned last chapter. Only when he has submitted his lusts using the torah way (of fear and hope), then this will cause him to ascend to the submission induced by the intellect. Hence it is like a ladder to it.)

(1) First, For the service (of G-d) induced by the study of the Torah, it may be that the person will be l'shem shamayim (devoted to G-d alone). It may, however, be hypocritical; the aim may possibly be to obtain praise for it and honor among one's fellow-men, since this kind of service is rooted in, and founded on, hope (of reward) and fear (of punishment). But the service of G-d induced by the intellectual urge is wholly and solely devoted to G-d. No hypocrisy is mingled with it, nor any false pretense for the sake of self-glorification, since this service is not founded on hope or fear, but is based on wisdom and knowledge of what service a created being owes to its Creator.

(*Marpe Lenefesh*: i.e. not that he will certainly always serve out of hypocrisy, only that we find it is so for most people who serve G-d only due to the stimulus of the torah - that their intent is for honor and praise of other people, since the torah is built on the foundation of reward [and punishment], as written many times "if you will listen to My commandments...I will send the rain in its time" (Devarim 11:13-14), and "if you will walk in My statutes..." (Vayikra 26:3), and many curses and punishments if they will not listen. All these things apply to the body. And all the time a person's heart is not perfect with G-d, to serve Him for His sake and His greatness, and the person serves only due to the study of torah, then he will also serve sometimes for honor and praise of other people, since his primary intent is for his own benefit. He will think to himself "what's the difference between receiving benefits from G-d and benefits from human beings?", because he is primarily seeking his own glory. But if he serves G-d from inducement of the understanding, namely, what a created being is obligated to his Creator, if so, certainly he is not serving out of expectation of any reward from his Master. As to why the torah is built on the foundation of reward and punishment, this will be explained soon.

Pas Lechem: Since all of his drive is due to desire for reward and personal benefit or the opposite, namely, to flee from punishment. If so, when the opportunity comes for some potential good in this world such as reward from people or praise from them, his heart will turn to this, since who cares whether it is reward in this world or in the next? This is unlike the inducement from the understanding, however, whose aim is not for any hope of personal gain whatsoever.

Tov Halevanon: Hence, it is possible that he will combine his fear of punishment and hope for reward from G-d with the fear and hope from human beings since he is habituated in this.)

(2) Secondly, service of G-d induced by the Torah is only rendered as the result of hope of reward or fear of punishment; but the service urged by the understanding comes from volunteering of the soul and and its desire to strive with all its might to serve its G-d for His own sake after knowledge and comprehension (of G-d and His greatness and exaltedness - *ML*). For the soul will not freely give all it has, unless it is convinced that what it receives in exchange is greater than what it gives, and this [reward] is that G-d is pleased with it.

(*Rabbi YS*: Many commentaries here. Each one adds something important. It seems to me the Lev Tov rendering is closest to the text. Decide for yourself.

Lev Tov: The service of G-d which is a result of being stirred by the torah, since it springs from hope for reward and/or fear of punishment, a man does not do it with all his strength and ability. But the service of G-d which is a result of being stirred by the understanding, it can only spring from volunteering of the soul, after knowledge and understanding of the greatness and exaltedness of G-d - out of good will to endeavor with all of its strength, and with great enthusiasm in the service of G-d for His own sake. The reason being that the soul does not volunteer to serve G-d unless it is first convinced that the exchange it will receive for the service, namely, that G-d will be pleased with it, is greater than the service. And the soul will not attain this goal unless it gives itself over to serve G-d with all of its ability and strength. [*Rabbi YS*: i.e. since G-d is pleased only when someone does all that is in his ability to do. The proof is that G-d does not abundantly help a person until the person does everything in his power to do as the Vilna Gaon explained here: dafyomireview.com/276]

Tov Halevanon: i.e. if the soul does something not motivated by reward and punishment, but rather only by willing generosity, such as in the case where a man gives a gift to his friend due to love that he feels towards him, not because he fears him or hopes for some reward in exchange - certainly this is because the contentment he feels that the receiver favorably accepts his gift weighs as much or more than the gift he donated. So too, one who serves G-d out of love, that which G-d desires in his service is [the reward] he receives in exchange for it, and the person who serves thus chooses this exchange more than the toil of his service. (hence he is primarily motivated to please G-d not for self serving reward and punishment - Rabbi YS)

Manoach Halevavos: the difference between this case and the first case is that in the first case he pointed out the difference from the aspect of hypocrisy, not from the aspect of strengthening and zeal in the service with all of one's heart and ability. In this second case, he wrote that one who serves from the inducement of the understanding strengthens himself with all of his heart, because he grasps with his intellect that reward and punishment naturally follow the soul (since the favor of G-d is the reward in the afterlife as explained in Gate 4 - Rabbi YS). But one who serves only due to the stimulus of the torah, knows only what is written in the torah, which promised on reward and punishment. But he does not understand that this follows from logic and necessity. Therefore, he is only a "hoper" that the promise will be kept. Therefore his strengthening is not so intense. *"For the soul will not freely give all it has etc."* - For example, if one volunteered to donate tzedaka (charity) with money he has. He will not do so unless he is convinced that the reward he will receive in exchange for the deed is greater, and that he will receive more benefit in this than the benefit he would have received if he held on to his money and did not give tzedaka. Apply this example to all others deeds. So too here, the soul will not give all it has (of its powers, efforts) unless it is convinced, etc.

Marpe Lenefesh: i.e. if a person did not learn the torah and the rewards and punishments mentioned there, he would not, on his own, be stirred to serve and fulfill the commandments written in the torah. Rather, only after he hopes for reward and fears from the punishment. And after he has been stimulated by the torah, and reached the level that he is not serving in order to get reward as mentioned in #1. This is the difference between the first and this second case. In this second case, he is on a higher level than the first. But if he served G-d through inducement of the understanding, he does not need to be stirred by reward and punishment. Rather, he volunteers on his own and willingly endeavors with all his might in the service of G-d with great enthusiasm.

But this only occurs, *"after knowledge and comprehension"* - *"knowledge"* of G-d and His greatness and exaltedness; and *"comprehension"* that it is fitting to serve G-d, and that man is lacking everything while G-d rules over everything, and the other things which arouse a person to serve G-d, as the author mentioned in Gate 10 ch.3, see there. This knowledge and comprehension is a prerequisite, for without it, the soul will never come to this level, to serve G-d out of love and generous willingness. Nevertheless, even with this knowledge and comprehension, the soul will not freely volunteer all it has, unless it is convinced that what it receives in exchange is greater than what it gives, namely, that it recognizes that through this, it will attain that the Creator will be pleased with it and love it, like a father is pleased with his [righteous] son, as the author wrote in the end of the introduction, namely, that the greatest possible good attainable is that G-d is pleased with him, and likewise for the converse [the greatest evil is that he kindled G-d's wrath due to his sins]. see there. And this is the main thing of all, to strive that G-d be pleased with him, not that one's intent is to receive any reward, but only to do G-d's will. To understand this fully, it is proper to cite the words of Rabeinu Tam in Sefer Yashar shaar 5: "after we have reached the ultimate purpose.. there is no greater attainment than the Creator's love for a person. For in this love, all good reward is included..." see there powerful words.)

Third, the service due to the urge of the Torah is manifested in external good deeds rather than in inward thoughts and feelings, hidden in the heart. But in the service induced by the understanding, that which is hidden in the heart, namely, the duties of the heart, is many times as much as what is seen in the external activity of the bodily limbs.

(*Pas Lechem*: *"service due to the urge of the Torah is manifested in external good deeds"* - since his motive is on the reward. If so, his intent is only in fulfilling his obligation in the external act. But his heart is not so complete, for if it were possible for him to attain the reward without the deeds, he would prefer that.

Tov Halevanon: i.e. for good deeds which are induced by the torah and their cause is hope for reward or fear of punishment, the picture in the man's mind of reward and punishment will only be of a physical character, related to his body, just like he feels now (since he is superficial), and so too will be his service. But he whose service is induced by the understanding and by love, this [reward and punishment] is pictured by him spiritually. Therefore, all of his service is from his spiritual side. Understand this.)

Fourth, the service induced by the Torah is to be regarded as a path to the service prompted by the understanding. The former is like seed planted in the ground. The study of the Torah is as cultivation is to the soil - ploughing and clearing it. The aid that comes from G-d is like the rain that waters the field. And the fruit that is produced and brought forth is what establishes in the heart - the service of G-d for His sake only, and not prompted by hope (of reward) or fear (of punishment). So our wise men have exhorted us, "Be not like servants who minister to their master upon the condition of receiving a reward . . . and let the fear of Heaven be upon you." (Ethics of the Fathers 1:3).

> (*Marpe Lenefesh*: This is the purpose of all his toil, which he ploughed, and soughed, etc. so that it produces good, blessed fruits. So too, the main thing, and ultimate purpose of all the torah study and service is - the service of G-d for His sake alone, not for any reward or punishment, even in the afterlife. This kind of service is the main purpose of everything.
>
> *Tov Halevanon*: The torah is like an opening and a path to the service prompted by the understanding. The fear/submission placed in a man's heart induced by reward and punishment is like a seed which is planted. A man's heart is like the field. The torah is like the working of the land, namely, plowing, for the torah teaches the heart which matters bring punishment and which bring reward.
> *"the aid that comes from G-d"* - who breaks his physical lusts (food, drink, rest, etc.) which are contrary to the torah, is like the rain.
> *"And the fruit that is produced"* - i.e. after it grew successfully and bore fruit, then the service will be established in his heart out of love, not out of reward and punishment alone. Therefore, now, the service induced by the understanding is greater than the service induced by fear (reward and punishment) just like the produce of a field exceeds the seeds planted.)

Fifth, the commandments of the Torah are limited. They are a known number, 613 precepts. But the duties imposed by the understanding are almost countless, for a person daily increases his knowledge of them; and the more his faculty of perception develops and the more he comprehends G-d's beneficences, mighty power and sovereignty, the more will a man submit and humble himself before Him. Hence you find that David (peace be upon him), besought G-d to arouse him to the knowledge of these duties and remove the curtain of folly from his eyes; as it is said, *"Open my eyes that I may gaze at the wonders of Your Torah"* (Tehilim 119:18); *"Teach me, O L-ord, the way of Your statutes..."* (ibid. 119:33); *"Incline my heart unto Your testimonies, and not to covetousness"* (ibid. 119:36). Furthermore it is said *"To all perfection have I seen an end; but Your commandment is exceedingly broad"* (ibid. 119:96); that is to say, our obligation of service to You for Your continual benefits to us is without limit because there is no limit to the varieties of Your favors to us.

It is also related of some ascetics that they spent the whole of their lives in repentance. Each day they were moved to renewed repentance, because every day their recognition of G-d's greatness increased, and they realized how much they had fallen short in the fulfillment of their obligation of service in the past, as David said, *"Day communicates knowledge unto day"* (Ps. 19:2). Furthermore, it is said, *"Streams of water run down mine eyes, because they kept not Your laws."* (Ps. 119:136).

(*Pas Lechem*: *"Streams of water"* - *"streams"*, the term connotes wellsprings, which have no end to their water.)

Sixth, the service instructed by the Torah is within the range of a human being's capacity. Provided he is intent upon it and sets about it, it is not withheld from any one who seeks to fulfill it. But the service prompted by the understanding can only be performed with great strength and with the help of G-d, since human power is insufficient to attain it. Hence you find that David repeatedly imploring G-d in Psalm 119 to give him this aid.

(*Tov Halevanon*: *"with great strength"* - if so, it is more acceptable to G-d, as our Sages said: "according to the difficulty is the reward" (Pirkei Avot ch. 5). *"and with the help of G-d"* - And that which G-d helps on it is an indication that certainly it is more precious in His eyes, and more important before Him.

Marpe Lenefesh: *"with great strength"* - Because the main thing of all the service is - that a man be complete and right with G-d always, in his inner being and outer being, when he lies down and when he gets up, and that all the actions he does, even matters of his body and all his needs - that they all be devoted to G-d, as David said: "I have placed G-d before me always" (Tehilim 16:8). And this is something beyond the power of a man to attain unless G-d helps him. It comes only after one does all that is in his power to do, and afterwards to increase this in zeal and exertion - then G-d will help him to attain what is beyond his ability, etc. See later in Gate 8 accounting #23 all these words well explained.)

Seventh, when service is only derived from the Torah, a person can never be sure that he will not stumble. For in that kind of service, the force of evil passion is always lurking in ambush, waiting for the time when he will neglect it. But when the service is prompted by the understanding, a man can be sure that he will not stumble and sin, for the soul is attracted to service of G-d only after physical lust has been slayed (overcome) and the intellect has obtained the victory over it, and controls it according to his will and desire. Hence, this type of service affords a guarantee against stumbling, and one who has attained it, is guarded from sin, as Scripture says, *"There shall no evil happen to the righteous"* (Mishlei 12:21).

> (*Marpe Lenefesh*: i.e. when he is not learning torah or praying, then the power of lust strengthens over him when he is engaged in matters of the body.
>
> *Pas Lechem*: perhaps some periods he will weaken in the service, and then the power of lust will strengthen against him to ensnare him.
>
> *Manoach Halevavos*: "*after physical lust has been slayed (hemyas)*" - "*hemyas*" connotes moaning. that the body howls and screams on the deprivation of its lusts. Some books have the text "*hamis*" (slayed) which connotes death. That text is correct.
>
> *Rabbi YS*: "*the force of evil passion is always lurking in ambush*" - this is the yetzer hara (evil inclination) which is lust. See Vilna Gaon commentary on Esther 1:1)

It is necessary, however, that I should expound some of the advantages of instruction in the Torah, as these occur to me. The grounds that necessitate the urge of the Torah to service of G-d are also seven.

> (*Marpe Lenefesh*: The inducing by the torah is also necessary. Even though the inducing by the understanding is more acceptable to G-d, but without Torah a man will never get to this.)

First, man is composed of soul and body. Among his tendencies there are some that tempt him to surrender himself to physical pleasures, indulge in lowly desires, and break the restraining bonds of the understanding. There are also other tendencies that will make him abhor this world and renounce society, because of reverses that he has sustained and continued troubles and sorrows that have befallen him, and so he would turn to the higher spiritual life.

> (*Marpe Lenefesh*: When a man is calm and contemplates the swift changing of matters in this world, that each day brings greater troubles than the previous one, and the never ending grievings - through this he desires to tend towards the next world and he abhors this world altogether.)

Neither of these plans is praiseworthy. The latter (if generally followed) would bring about destruction of the societal order. The former would lead to his ruin in this world and in the next. The exalted Creator, in His compassion and infinite goodness to man, favored him with a means by which he may improve his condition and direct aright his ways, leading to happiness here and hereafter. This means, which points out the middle road between the understanding and physical desire, is the Torah which is faithful, preserves righteousness outwardly and inwardly, keeps man away from his lusts in this world and reserves for him his reward at his latter end, as Scripture says, *"Incline your ear and hear the words of the wise ... or it is a pleasant thing if you keep them within you . . . That your trust may be in the L-ord, I have made known to you this day . . . Have not I written to you excellent things in counsels and knowledge, That I might make you know the certainty of the words of truth; that you might answer the words of truth to them that send unto you"* (Mishlei 22:17-21).

Second, the inducing by the understanding does not lead to the recognition of active obligations in the service of G-d such as prayer, fasting, tzedaka (charity), maaser (tithing), acts of kindliness. Nor does one attain knowledge of the types of punishments incurred by one who is negligent in the service (such as Gehinom and Kaf Hakela hinted in the words of the prophets - *TL*). In all this, there is need of a framework and a boundary in the way set forth by the Torah and the prophet's instruction, so that by their combination (the urge of Torah and of the Understanding - *TL*) the Divine purpose may be explained in orderly fashion - that purpose being the service of G-d, exalted be He, as it is said, *"And G-d made it, so that man should fear before Him"* (Koheles 3:14) ; that is to say, G-d gave us a law to teach us His service.

(*Tov Halevanon*: Without the torah, the intellect does not understand the benefit of prayer. Because G-d will not change nor be affected by his prayer. And if the man is not worthy of the good [that he is praying for], due to his [insufficient] deeds, how can he possibly entice G-d with his words, and ask before Him to grant him his request? And if he is worthy of the good due to his deeds, certainly G-d will not corrupt justice, and will not withhold support to a righteous man. But from the torah, we see that the forefathers and the prophets (who were exceedingly righteous) were answered in their prayers. And we were commanded on it, and it is a positive Biblical commandment according to that view, as the Talmud (Taanit 5a) expounds on the verse "to serve Him with all your heart": "what service is with the heart? This is prayer". And even though our understanding falls short of being able to grasp its full matter, just like the understanding does not understand other precepts in the torah. Likewise, for the fast which we fast on Yom Kippur which atones for all our sins. And for Tzedaka (charity) as a certain heretic asked Rabbi Akiva (Bava Basra 10a): "if your G-d loves poor people, why doesn't he support them?", etc. until he brought the verse: "Is it not to share your bread with the hungry...[Then shall your light break forth as the morning]" (Yeshaya 58:7), see there. Likewise, tithes and acts of kindliness is because of this. And even though there are many other matters which the understanding cannot grasp, the author took as examples primary pillars that the world almost stands on.

Manoach Halevavos: If we were not commanded in prayer by the torah and the Rabbinical decrees, we would not know through our understanding what would be the order of the tefila, shacharit (morning), mincha (afternoon), and arvit (evening), and the other times. And even prayer itself, the understanding does not dictate that we should pray to G-d, because the understanding obligates that G-d gives to each creature and each thing in the world the portion fitting for it. And if it is not fitting for it, prayer should not help in this. Furthermore, according to the divine wisdom (Kabala), and the Moray Nevuchim wrote on this (Part 1 ch.5), that G-d does not "change". Hence, the whole matter of prayer seems to the understanding as if there is "change" in G-d, similar to a request which a man begs before a flesh and blood king, to arouse favor and pity in the heart of the king. All this does not apply by G-d. Therefore, he wrote that if the torah did not command this, and that we did not see from the torah that prayer does help, regarding the prayer of Avraham, Yitzchak, Yaakov, Moshe, and others, and that our Sages did not institute its order, we would not know at all through the understanding neither its order not its matter. The reason we have been commanded in it is hidden, it is among the hidden precepts of the torah. It has great benefits to arouse a person to awareness of G-d's existence, and His almighty power, and that it is proper to serve Him, and many other fundamentals and good traits which are aroused through prayer. In kabala it is known that by a hitorerut (stimulus) from below, one causes a hitorerut (stimulus) above (i.e. that G-d made the world in such a way that man's actions have repercussions in the mystical worlds which in turn affects this world. see the book Shaarei Kedusha for more details.) This is sufficient for the wise person.)

Third, the intellectual urge cannot include equally all who are under the obligation of service, because some human beings are of limited intelligence, while some are superior in understanding. But the urge of the Torah applies equally to all who have reached the status subjecting them to this service (i.e. us Jews - PL), even though they vary in their understanding of it, as we have noted at the close of the first treatise of this book.

(*Pas Lechem*: *"some are of limited intelligence, while some are superior in understanding* (literally: recognition)" - limited intelligence applies to many people. While *"superior in recognition"* is a different aspect, namely, since one person may recognize the nature of the world and its creatures more than his fellow, and he may have superior ability to contemplate them than his fellow despite that his fellow may have a stronger intellect.)

It sometimes also happens that an individual falls short in some duties and exceeds in others. The intellectual stimulus varies in different individuals in accordance with their capacity of recognition. But the urge of the Torah is not subject to variation. Its form is the same for the child, the youth, one advanced in years and the old man, the wise and the foolish, even though the resulting practice varies in different classes of individuals. And so Scripture says in regard to the all encompassing character of the instruction of the Torah for all the people, *"Gather the people together, men and women, and children, and the stranger that is within your gate, (that they may hear and that they may learn and fear the L-ord your G-d . . .)"* (Devarim 31:12). Further, it is said, *". . . you shall read this law before all Israel in their hearing."* (Devarim 31:11).

(*Marpe Lenefesh*: Even though we find that through the stimulus of the torah, some people do alot while others do few commandments of G-d despite that they were all equally commanded. The reason is because this one's understanding is strong and he does the commandments of G-d with zeal and with simcha (joy) without diminishing, while this one's understanding is weak and he does not understand how to do the commandments of G-d. Therefore, he does them sluggishly and sometimes not at all. All this is due to the understanding, but the torah itself does not change, rather it commands everyone equally to do the service of G-d and each one does according to his understanding and recognition. But if there were only the urge of the understanding, without the torah, most people would remain ignorant, without any service of G-d.)

Fourth, it is recognized that the obligations of human beings to render service are proportionate to the degrees of benefits bestowed upon them. In every period there have been events which occasioned one people to be singled out from all other peoples for special benefits that G-d bestowed on it. It follows that individuals belonging to that people are on that account under special obligation to render additional service to the Creator beyond that required of other peoples. There is no way of determining by the intellect alone what this service should be. Thus G-d chose us from among other nations by bringing us out of the land of Egypt, dividing the Red Sea and bestowing other benefits subsequently, too well known to be mentioned. Furthermore, the exalted Creator specially distinguished us from all other nations by designating us for the service for which we are under an obligation of gratitude to Him; and, in return for our acceptance of this service, He has assured us a reward in this world and in the next, - an abundance of grace and goodness, emanating from Him, that is indescribable. All this can only be clearly made known to us by the Torah, as Scripture says, *"You have seen what I did unto the Egyptians and how I bore you on eagles' wings, and brought you unto Myself. Now, therefore, if you will obey My voice indeed, and keep My covenant, (then you shall be a treasure unto Me above all people) and you shall be unto Me a kingdom of priests and a holy nation"* (Ex. 19:4-6).

Fifth, the stimulus of the Torah is a preparation for, and introduction to that of the Understanding, the reason being that a man in his youth needs training and guidance, and restraint from yielding to his passions, until the time comes when his understanding has become strong and firm. So, too some women and frivolous (superficial) men do not follow the intellectual lead, because its control over them is weak and loose. This condition made it necessary to provide guidance of a medium character which they can endure and which will not be impossible for them to stand. Hence, the instructions of the Torah revolve around hope and fear - the poles of its axis.

Whoever does not fall short in fulfilling the obligations of this service (who diligently performs the torah commandments according to his ability - *TL*) belongs to the class of the pure pious ones and is worthy of reward in this world and in the next. But one who rises from this stage to the service of G-d, induced by reason, reaches the degree of the prophets and the elect of the Supreme - the saints (whose reward is infinitely great - *ML*). His reward here on earth is joy in the sweetness of the service of the L-ord, as the prophet said, *"Your words were found, and I did eat them; and Your word was unto me the joy and rejoicing of my heart; for I am called by Your name, O L-ord G-d of hosts"* (Jeremiah 15-16); furthermore, *"The righteous shall be glad in the L-ord and trust in Him; and all the upright in heart shall glory"* (Ps. 64:11) ; furthermore, *"light is sown for the righteous, and joy for the upright in heart"* (Ps. 97:11). His reward in the world to come will consist in his attaining the highest illumination which we are unable to describe or picture, as it is said, *"If you will walk in My ways and if you will keep My charge... I will give you a place to walk among these that stand by"* (Zachariah 3:7); further, *"How great is Your goodness which You have laid up for them that fear You, which You have done for them that trust in You before the children of men"* (Ps. 31:20). Furthermore, *"Eye has not seen, O G-d, beside You, what He will do for one that waits for Him"* (Isaiah 64:3).

Sixth, the Torah includes matters, the obligation of which reason cannot explain, namely, the received commandments (such as shatnez, milk and meat, or the like which reason does not prescribe or reject - *TL*) and the general principles, of the roots of rational precepts. This is because the people to whom the Torah was given were at that period in such a condition that animal lusts dominated them and they were too weak in their knowledge and perceptive faculties to understand many of the rational precepts. The Torah, therefore, used one method only for both the rational precepts and the received commandments. The people were stimulated in the same way in regard to both classes of duties. An individual whose understanding and perception are strong, will exert himself and undertake the obligation of fulfilling them on both grounds that they are rational and received. And one whose intellect is too weak to perceive their rational ground will accept them because the Torah exhorts him, and will treat them as received precepts. Thus all classes will be benefited, as it is said, *"Its ways are ways of pleasantness, and all its paths are peace"* (Mishlei 3:17).

(*Marpe Lenefesh*: the torah included together the received commandments, i.e. the statutes such as the red heifer, shatnez, pork meat, and the like, which reason does not obligate them at all. Likewise the torah clarified general principles and roots of the rational precepts such as the existence of the Creator, His Unity and eternity, love and reverence [of Him], even though these things can be deduced by reason, nevertheless the torah did not refrain from mentioning them because a person whose understanding is not complete due to overpowering of the lusts as was the case at the time of the giving of the torah. Otherwise, they would not seek them because they require some introductions. Therefore, the torah included them in general principles.

Tov Halevanon: *"Its ways are ways of pleasantness"* - the ways of commandments in it are ways of pleasantness, many of them are explained by reason; *"and all its paths are peaceful"* - even he who lacks understanding will be rectified through it, and will complete the service of G-d in fulfilling it, for it is complete. No instruction is lacking in it, even those which depend on the understanding.)

Seventh, we come to the Torah through a human intermediary (Moses) by whom were shown signs and miracles equally perceived by all the people with their senses, the evidence of which they could not deny. Hence, the message which he brought with him in the name of G-d was demonstrated to them through the senses as well as the intellect. The demonstration through the senses was an addition to the intellectual stimulus which human beings naturally possess.

Whoever considers G-d's bounties, bestowed upon him, which are in common with all other human beings, will faithfully accept the obligation of the service of G-d in the ways indicated by his intellect. Whoever reflects on the Creator's special bounties to him by which his nation has been distinguished from other nations, will faithfully accept the special obligation to obey the precepts that are binding on his people, on the authority of the Torah (i.e. the received commandments in the torah) and which are not binding on other peoples (except the 7 commandments of Bnei Noach).

And when one considers G-d's bounties to him, by which his tribe has been distinguished from the remaining tribes of his people, such as, priesthood (for a Kohen) or the Levitical degree (for a Levi), he will faithfully accept the obligation to fulfill precepts by which G-d has distinguished his tribe. Hence you find twenty four priestly ordinances corresponding to twenty-four special benefits which the Creator bestowed upon the priests. These are the twenty-four priestly dues.

Analogously, any individual whom G-d has distinguished by special favors beyond those enjoyed by other human beings, should undertake a special service not incumbent on them, striving at the same time, according to his capacity and perception, to fulfill the duties in the obligation of which he is included with them and thanking G-d, blessed be He, for the benevolence with which G-d specially favored him. Thus will he insure its continuance and increase, and will also receive his reward in the world to come.

A person should not behave like the one of whom it is said, *"And silver I gave her in abundance and gold which they prepared for Baal (idols)"* (Hosea 2:10). One who falls short in the special service which he has to render for the bounty with which he has been specially favored, will be induced to fall short in the service specially incumbent upon his tribe and afterwards in that incumbent upon his people, and at last he will renounce the Torah altogether. Not accepting the Torah, he will not even accept the obligation of the precepts that reason dictates. (as the sages said (Avot 4:2): "sin leads to more sin" - *TL*)

And when he does not accept the obligations dictated by the understanding with which he is endowed, and its rebuke, he loses the character of a rational creature; and the cattle understand how to improve their condition better than he does, as it is said, *"The ox knows his owner, and the donkey his master's trough; but Israel does not know; My people does not consider"* (Isaiah 1:3). Such a person's fate will be like that of one, concerning whom it is said, *"But the wicked shall perish; and the enemies of the L-ord shall be as the fat of lambs, they shall be consumed; into smoke shall they be utterly consumed"* (Psalm 37:20).

(*Tov Halevanon*: i.e. woe to him for bringing evil on his soul, since he is left with neither torah, nor rational precepts, and he is analogous to the animals of the field, and even worse than them. For then, his soul is singed by matters of the body and its lusts until when the body dies, nothing will be left for it. Rather, his soul will separate and be destroyed like his body and go up like smoke, similar to what our sages said (Rosh Hashana 17a): "their souls are burned and its 'ashes' scattered under the feet of the righteous".

CHAPTER 4

It is now proper for us to explain the form in which the Torah urges one to the service of G-d, and its divisions; the various levels attained by those who study the Torah, their characters, their faith in the Torah and their acceptance of it.

(*Marpe Lenefesh*: "*its divisions*" - Even though the torah appears to have 613 commandments, and likewise many commandments of the understanding, but the thinking person will categorize them all into only 2 categories - good and evil, namely, the positive commandments and the negative commandments, as he will explain.
"*various levels*" - there are 10 levels of those who study the torah, as will be explained. That this person learns and toils like this, and another person like that.
"*their faith and acceptance of it*" - since this person believes in the torah like this and that person like that, their acceptance, i.e. fulfillment of the torah varies, namely, this person fulfills the torah more than that one as will be explained.)

I assert that the urge of the Torah is a revelation from G-d, through the medium of a certain individual who, among them, was good in G-d's eyes, a revelation which makes known to human beings the service to be rendered by them to Him, so that, out of His kindness, generosity, and goodness, He may bestow upon them, for their acceptance of it, a reward in this world and in the world to come.

(*Manoach Halevavos*: "*who, among them, was good in G-d's eyes*" - i.e. G-d chose in that man (Moshe Rabeinu) because he behaved better in G-d's eyes than other human beings, namely, he served G-d more than other human beings.

Tov Halevanon: He was complete with all qualities and traits which bring a person to Ruach Hakodesh (enlightenment) and prophecy, as they said in Sotah (end of mishna ch.9). Fear brings to purity, etc. [*Rabbi YS*: see the book "Path of the Just" for the road map to these levels.]
"*kindness, generosity, and goodness*" - i.e. the purpose of creating the human race in this world, is only in order to bestow on man kindness, generosity, and goodness - the eternal life of the next world.

Pas Lechem: "*out of His kindness, generosity, and goodness* - "kindness" from the aspect of the receiver who was not deserving of this. "*Generosity*" from the aspect of the Giver who receives no good whatsoever from this. It is only out of His generosity of heart. Or the opposite. *"goodness"* because it is the nature of the Good to bestow good.)

The Torah divides human actions into three classes: (1) those that are commanded (positive commandments - *ML*), (2) prohibited (negative commandments - *ML*) and (3) permitted (not a commandments and not a sin - *ML*).

POSITIVE COMMANDMENTS

These commanded fall into two divisions.
(1) One of these consists of duties of the heart. These, which are grounded in genuine faith are: acceptance of the Unity of G-d; being whole-heartedly with Him, trusting in Him, surrendering to Him, accepting His decrees, believing in His prophets and in His law, revering Him, keeping His commandments, meditating on His wondrous deeds, examining His beneficence and many more duties of the same character too numerous to set forth in detail.

(*Pas Lechem*: *"whole-heartedly with Him"* - not to suspect Him.
"trusting in Him" - for all his needs.
"surrendering to Him" - in a general way, to unload all one's ways on Him, and surrender all one's guidance to His hand, yisborach. [*Rabbi YS*: Gate 4 will discuss this at length]
"accepting His decrees" - after the act (of surrendering to Him), to accept with joy and a good heart all that G-d sends his way, as the Sages said (Berachos 54a): "a man is under obligation to bless [on the bad just like on the good]")

(2) The second, those duties that involve devotion of the heart together with physical activities, such as consistency in speech and thought, reading and studying the book of the Torah; praying, fasting, giving tzedaka (charity); rest from labor on Sabbaths and Festivals, building a Tabernacle (Sukkah), taking the Lulav (palm-branch, and the three other plants on the festival of Sukkot); wearing Tzitzit, and similar precepts.

(*Marpe Lenefesh*: *"consistency in speech and thought"* - when he recites the Shema Yisrael, and declares that G-d is One, that the heart (mind) should be with him, i.e. that he understands what he is saying - that G-d's Unity is not like other unities which are also called "one" as explained in Gate 1.

Marpe Lenefesh: *"reading and studying, fasting, giving tzedaka, rest from labor, etc."* - all these things need intent of the heart, that in them, his heart

| needs to be l'shem shamayim (devoted to G-d).)

NEGATIVE COMMANDMENTS

Prohibitions also fall into two divisions.

(1) One division consists of duties of the heart. (2) The other comprises active duties.

Prohibitions in the category of duties of the heart are, for example, associating with G-d either secretly or by flattery, loving to do that which G-d has forbidden; pride, haughtiness, arrogance contempt for human beings, mocking the prophets and the messages they utter which come from G-d; abhorring good and those who do good; finding pleasure in evil doers; jealousy, covetousness, desiring to hurt human beings (that he feels pleasure when evil befalls others. alternatively, he enjoys doing bad to others - *PL*); resentment at the Creator's decrees (when suffering befalls him - *TL*), and many sentiments and emotions of a similar character.

| (*Tov Halevanon*: "associating with G-d either secretly or by flattery" - such as one who serves G-d outwardly, but also has intent in this so that other people will praise and honor him. Hence, he associates in his worship, [two motives: devotion to] G-d and benefit from human beings. Likewise, one who flatters other people in matters of religious worship because he fears them - this person also associates fear of G-d with fear of flesh and blood... "loving to do that which G-d has forbidden" - that he lusts in his heart to do what the torah prohibits.

| *Marpe Lenefesh*: he longs constantly to do sins, even though he doesn't actually do them.

| *Pas Lechem*: "pride, haughtiness, arrogance" - 3 terms corresponding to the 3 levels mentioned in Yirmiya (9:22), which are wisdom, might, and wealth. i.e. pride in wisdom, haughtiness in might, and arrogance in wealth. "contempt for human beings" - this is also due to arrogance, that other people are worth nothing in his eyes.)

The following are examples of prohibitions of actions: revealed association of anyone with G-d, false swearing, lying, tale bearing, eating forbidden food, forbidden relations, bloodshed, and many offenses of similar character.

| (*Pas Lechem*: "revealed association of anyone with G-d" - this is idol worship.

[alternatively]
Tov Halevanon: he transgresses the commandments of G-d openly due to
fear of human beings or love of them.)

PERMITTED THINGS

Things permissible also fall into three divisions, namely, the sufficient, the
excessive and the deficient. The sufficient is that which is indispensable
for preservation of the body or management of one's affairs, in food and
drink, clothing and covering; necessary speech in conducting one's
business, activities and commercial transactions; all kinds of physical
movements and their proper employment to the extent needed for the
proper maintenance of one's welfare, as Scripture says, *"Good is a man
who is gracious and lends; he measures his affairs with measure?"*
(Tehilim 112:5).

(*Manoach Halevavos*: he measures and weighs all his affairs with justness)

The second division applies to cases where one crosses the border of the
sufficient to the domain of the superfluous which one has no need for, such
as excess in food and drink, against which the sage warned us when he
said, *"Be not among winebibbers; among gluttonous eaters of meat"*
(Mishlei 23:20). So, too, extravagance in personal adornment, dress,
luxurious homes, and superfluity in speech, in regard to which there is no
assurance that one will not stumble because of them, as the wise man said,
"In the multitude of words there lacks not sin" (Mishlei 10:19).
Furthermore, excess in sexual relations, concerning which the sage said, *".
. .He that keeps company with harlots destroys his substance"* (Mishlei
29:3), and *"do not give your strength to women"* (Mishlei 31:3). It is also
said concerning kings, *"Neither shall he multiply wives unto himself"*
(Devarim 17:17).

Striving for large possessions and accumulation of money, of which it is
said, *"Labor not to be rich, cease from your own wisdom"* (Mishlei 23:4).
Concerning the king, it is said, *"Neither shall he greatly multiply to himself
silver and gold"* (Devarim 17:17). All these superfluous things we
mentioned which are for the improvement and enjoyment of the body
transform in the end to evil because they mislead one to that which the
Creator warned us against, and forbade (as written: *"But Jeshurun grew fat,
and kicked: you are grown fat, you are grown thick, you are covered with
fatness; then he forsook G-d who made him, and lightly esteemed the Rock
of his salvation"* (Devarim 32:15).

(*Tov Halevanon*: *"do not give your strength to women"* - for the semen is the life of the body, as the Rambam wrote in Deos 4:19.
"Labor not to be rich, cease from your own wisdom" - *"Labor not to be rich"* - lest you become satiated and rebel against your Maker. *"cease from your own wisdom"* - do not say "I will not allow my heart to stray due to wealth".)

The third division in the use of things permitted is the deficient.

(*Tov Halevanon*: i.e. that the torah commanded us to separate ourselves from what is permitted to us, as a fence, or in the way of asceticism. *Marpe Lenefesh*: See Gate 8, end of chapter 3. These things are more explained there.)

This is the case when a person denies himself what is sufficient in food and drink, clothing, sexual relations, speech, sleep, or in the occupation by which he will obtain what he needs for his maintenance in food and other requisites. Deficiency falls into two subdivisions. It may be motivated by piety or by worldly considerations.

If the motive is a pious one, proceeding from a longing for nearer and closer communion with G-d by asceticism (to break one's lusts - *TL*), it is laudable and will be rewarded, as the sage said, *"The heart of the wise is in the house of mourning; but the heart of fools is in the house of merrymaking"* (Koheles 7:4).

(*Tov Halevanon*: *"The heart of the wise is in the house of mourning"* - his heart is broken and he always worries on the day of his death. *"but the heart of fools is in the house of merrymaking"* - always joyful and good spirited on account of his bodily pleasures, similar to the verse (Yeshaya 22:13) "eat and drink for tomorrow we will die".)

If the motive is worldly, namely, to increase his money, or be praised as one who abstains from what is permitted and takes from the world less than he needs in food, it is reprehensible, for a person who acts thus departs from the path of the middle way, and robs his body of its needs. All this comes from excessive love of this world, in reference to which a sage said, "He who separates himself from the world, out of love for the world, is like one who would extinguish a flame with straw."

(*Tov Halevanon*: On the contrary he will come to love the world even more, because he abstains himself from small worldly benefits in order to attain greater worldly benefits.

Lev Tov: One who tries to extinguish a fire with straw, it appears at first as if he extinguished the fire by covering it with straw. But soon he will discover that one the contrary, he increased and strengthened the fire. So too, one who abstains from this world out of love of this world, it appears as if he separates from pleasures and lusts and comes closer to the spiritual, but in reality, he attains the opposite - he sinks deeper in the lusts and pleasures of this world.)

But to be sparing in speech and in sleep is praiseworthy; in speech, because in the end silence is better, as the wise man said, *"Be not rash with your mouth, and let not your heart be hasty to utter anything before G-d; for G-d is in heaven and you are on earth; therefore let your words be few"* (Koheles 5:1).

(*Tov Halevanon*: As he wrote earlier in chapter 2, "Secondly, the intellect is a spiritual entity, originating in the higher, spiritual world. It is a stranger in this world of gross material bodies. Sensual lust in man is the product of natural forces and of a combination of his physical elements. Its foundation is in this world, its root in this abode." Hence it is natural that the intellect becomes weak against the power of lust. This is what is written *"G-d is in heaven"*, and if so, the soul within you is like a stranger among the bodily lusts since *"you are on earth, therefore let your words be few"*. Because it is likely that you will allow your mouth to sin and be drawn in your words after the body.)

Similarly, in regard to sleep, it is said, *"Yet a little sleep, a little slumber, a little folding of the hands to sleep. [So shall your poverty come as a traveler, and your want as an armed man (who arrives suddenly)]"* (Mishlei 6:10).

In what has been mentioned, it has thus been demonstrated that all human activities belong either to those (1) commanded, (2) forbidden or (3) [permitted which is] sufficient. For whatever is not in the category of [permitted which is] "sufficient", and is either superfluous or deficient, must necessarily belong to the category of what is commanded, if done for the sake of G-d; or it belongs to the category of the forbidden, if it is not done for His sake.

(*Rabbi YS*: i.e. among the 3 categories of permitted activities mentioned earlier, namely, the sufficient, the excessive and the deficient, the latter two, do not really belong to the category of permitted things. They belong either to the category of positive commandments or negative commandments depending on whether they were done for the sake of G-d or not.

Sometimes it is a mitzvah to go into the domain of the excessive. For example, if one is by his mother and it would please her if he ate everything on the plate.)

Enquiring more closely into what is "sufficient", for example, in obtaining a livelihood, we find this too in a commandment, set forth in the account of Creation, *"And G-d blessed them, and G-d said unto them: 'Be fruitful and multiply, fill the land and conquer it.'"* (Genesis 1:28). And it continues, *"Behold, I have given you every herb bearing seed, which is upon the face of all the earth [.. to you it shall be for food]"* (ibid. 1:29). Hence, to seek a sufficiency in food belongs to the class of the commanded.

(*Lev Tov*: to do acts which are necessary to obtain one's food is a commandment. Just like "be fruitful and multiply" is a commandment, so too "conquer it" and the next "I have given you every herb bearing seed..[for food]" are also commandments.
Rabbi YS: i.e. to obtain one's livelihood is also in the category of "commandments". Hence, all human activities belong either to those commanded or those forbidden. Not 3 categories (commanded, forbidden, and sufficient) as stated earlier.)

This being the case, it has been demonstrated that all human activities are either in the category of what is commanded or in the category of what is prohibited. If what is done is in the category of the commanded, it is a good deed. If one is able to do it but neglects his obligation, he falls short in his duty. So, too, if one does one of the things that are prohibited, he is a sinner (he will be punished - *ML*). If he abstains from doing it, he is a righteous man (he will receive reward - *TL*), provided that he abstains out of fear of G-d, as Scripture says, *"They also do no iniquity. They walk in His ways."* (Tehilim 119:3). (i.e. one who refrains from iniquity is as if he walks in the way of G-d - *TL*)

And so, if one does one of the things permitted, in the right and proper way, he is righteous, as the Psalmist said, *"A good man is gracious and lends; he conducts his affairs with measure"* (Tehilim 112:5). If he, however, exceeds and goes beyond what is sufficient, he falls short in his duty, because this will mislead him to what G-d warned against. So, too, if he denies himself what is sufficient when he is in a position to obtain it, his aim being to train himself in the service of G-d and to reign over his lusts, so as to come nearer to G-d or separate himself from this world and direct his attentions to the better world hereafter, he is righteous and his conduct is good. But if he does this not for the sake of G-d, he falls short in the fulfillment of his duty, and his conduct is reprehensible.

Hence, human actions fall into the categories of good and bad. The intelligent person is one who weighs his actions before he does them, as is here set forth, examines them carefully with his mind and recognition, chooses what is good among them and abandons what is not good, as David, peace be unto him, said: *"I thought on my ways and turned my feet unto Your testimonies. I made haste and did not delay to keep Your commandments"* (Tehilim 119:59-60).

> (*Marpe Lenefesh*: i.e. who is considered intelligent and righteous in all his deeds? He who makes it a habit and second nature in this - that he does nothing in this world, whether in religious or secular deeds, until he first ponders in his mind what he is about to do. If it appears something good will come out of it, he does it. If not, he will abandon it. This general principle includes the entire service of G-d.
> *"I thought on my ways"* - Through my thinking and putting to heart, all of my ways, what will be their end, through this - *"I turned my feet unto Your testimonies".*)

That this division of deeds into good and evil is correct is proved in the wise man's statement: *"For G-d will bring every deed into judgment with every secret thing, whether it be good or evil"* (Koheles 12:14). The sage thus places all actions under two categories, good and bad; this coinciding with what we call praiseworthy and reprehensible.

> (*Tov Halevanon*: *"whether it be good or evil"* (Koheles 12:14) - whether he benefited himself with superfluous pleasures, or whether he refrained himself and afflicted himself not for the sake of G-d - G-d will bring him to judgment)

Hence it has been demonstrated that all human actions fall into only the two categories of the torah, namely, commandments and prohibitions.

THE TEN CLASSES OF TORAH UNDERSTANDING

And since the Torah consists of words and matters, individuals, in respect to their understanding of its wisdom, fall into ten graded classes.

> (*Marpe Lenefesh*: So that a man will know on which level he is holding, and will strive to ascend from level to the next level, as he concludes in the end.)

The beginner's class consists of those who have learnt the Torah (five books of Moses) and the rest of the Scriptures and are satisfied with their ability to read the text without any understanding of the contents. They do not know the meaning of the words nor have they any acquaintance with the grammar of the language. They are akin to a donkey laden with books.

(*Marpe Lenefesh*: *"who have learnt the torah, etc."* from their youth, and even when they get older, they do not change from this path. They are satisfied like this, and they don't know nor understand what they are saying such as those who read shnayim mikra, without understanding anything. Likewise, their prayers are like this.)

The second class consists of those who have tried to learn to read correctly, pay heed to the vowels and specially concentrate their attention on the right position of the accent. They [may be said to] belong to the class of Punctuators and Massorites.

(*Marpe Lenefesh*: People who sought to study their reading, so that their tongue does not mispronounce, that they recite Hebrew with proper vowelization and taamim (cantilation notes), but they don't understand the contents like those who read the torah merely by way of grammar. They do not understand anything.)

The third class consists of those who have noted the insufficiency of the previous classes and have striven to know the principles of punctuation and musical accentuation (neginoth). They have in addition sought to acquire knowledge of the correct use of the language and its grammar, nouns and verbs, modifying parts of speech (prepositions, conjunctions and adverbs) absolute and construct forms (of nouns and adjectives) ; use of the future to express the past and of the infinitive to express the imperative; the various classes of verbs: complete (all three letters sounded), defective (one letter omitted), silent (one or two letters not sounded), duplicate (verbs with the second and third letters the same) ; the apparent and the hidden. (i.e. Closed and open syllables; the former ending in a consonant, the latter in a vowel sound.)

(*Marpe Lenefesh*: they sought the reason why this word is voweled like this and that one like that. For example yira versus yerae (same word different vowels) - that the meaning of this is not like the meaning of that.)

The fourth class consists of those individuals who have advanced beyond the preceding classes in their ability to explain words of doubtful meaning in the Holy Scriptures, and in their understanding of the plain sense of the text. They have also investigated the figurative and the literal meaning of words in the Hebrew language; homonyms and synonyms; derivative nouns (derived from other words), primary nouns, foreign nouns; and so with adjectives and verbs.

(*Marpe Lenefesh*: They also learned the grammar of Hebrew, since without clear understanding of hebrew grammar, a person cannot lift his hand anywhere in the torah as is known and evident. Only that a person should not waste all of his time in these matters, and refrain from learning other things which his soul needs. Many authors have already warned at length against this practice.)

The fifth class consists of those who have advanced beyond the preceding classes in their knowledge of the subject-matter of the Holy Scriptures, have sought to understand its fundamental principles and have endeavored to investigate the metaphorical sense and the true meaning of its contents with regard, for instance, to the anthropomorphic expressions in the Bible. They are those who attempt to explain the Scriptures of G-d according to the plain meaning without relying on the received Tradition (Oral Torah).

(*Marpe Lenefesh*: Up until [and including] now, he is speaking about people who try to explain the Torah using only grammar. They explain the matter, but according to their understanding and desire (the plain meaning - TL). They are not interested in the explanations of our Sages of blessed memory, as received by the Tradition. These are the Sadducees and Karaites.)

The sixth class consists of those who rely on the ancient Tradition as contained in the Mishnah, so that they have attained knowledge of some of the duties, commandments and laws of the torah without studying the Talmud.

The seventh class comprises those who have added to what we have just mentioned an intense study of the Talmud and devoted themselves to a knowledge of its text, reading its decisions without attempting to answer its questions and clearing up its difficulties.

The eighth class consists of those who were not satisfied with the knowledge of the Torah, which had been sufficient for the previous class, but exerted themselves to comprehend the words of the Talmudic sages, resolve the doubtful points and elucidate the obscurities, with the purpose of winning a name and glory. But they ignore the duties of the heart. They pay no attention to what would be detrimental to their religious and moral activities. They spend their days in the study of singular deductions from the legal principles and of what is strange and difficult in the final decisions; they cite the conflicting views of the Talmudic authorities on novel points of law while they neglect topics which they have no permission to do - topics that affect their spiritual interests which it is their duty to investigate, such as the truth of the prophet's signs and of tradition, and the modes by which it can be demonstrated; the obligation which the Creator has imposed upon us to bring proofs with our reasoning faculties of His existence and to serve Him with a perfect heart, and many similar points that can be intellectually understood and which I will explain in this treatise.

> (*Marpe Lenefesh*: i.e. since they don't learn any books on yira and mussar (ethical books), certainly all of their learning is only to show off their brilliance and breadth of knowledge to the masses, "to acquire a name"... and even though they toiled in the torah to the best that a human being is capable, nevertheless, they are still on the outside, since they are not learning l'shem shamayim (for G-d alone), rather only to "win a name, etc." for themselves. However, they are near to the exalted level if they will just open their eyes on their ways, and from lo lishma (undevoted), they can come to lishma (devoted). Let one put this to heart so as not to inherit a double Gehinom as our sages said in Yoma 72b.)

The ninth class consists of those who have exerted themselves to know the duties of the heart as well as the active duties and also what is detrimental to right conduct; who understand the plain sense of the Holy Scriptures as well as their inner meaning, and have arrived at a conviction of the truth of tradition, based on Scripture and on reason; have arranged the laws into an orderly system, divided the practical duties in accordance with circumstances of time and place, as a result of their understanding of the fundamental principles of the Pentateuch; scrupulously observe the duties and exhort others (to do likewise); cherish truth inwardly and outwardly, and follow it wherever it may lead them. They are the Talmudic teachers and the Geonim who continued their predecessors' customs.

The tenth class consists of those who received the wisdom of the Torah from the prophets, with all its interpretations and detailed results of fundamental principles. They are the men of the Great Assembly and their successors (the Tanaim) who received the traditions from them, the authorities named in the Mishnah and Beraithoth (additional teachings and views not incorporated in the Mishnah) as set forth in the Ethics of the Fathers: "Moshe received the Law from Sinai and delivered it to Yehoshua; Yehoshua to the elders; the elders to the prophets; the prophets to the men of the Great Assembly; the men of the Great Assembly to Shimon the Just; Shimon the Just to Antigonos; Antigonos to Joseph son of Joezer and Yosi son of Jochanan the Jerusalemite; they delivered it Joshua, son of Perachiah and Nittai the Arbelite; they delivered it to Judah son of Tabbai and Shimon son of Shetach; they delivered it to Shemaiah and Avtalion; from them it passed to Shammai and Hillel; from them to Rabban Yochanan ben Zakai; from him to Rabbi Eliezer, Rabbi Yehoshua, Rabbi Gamaliel, Rabbi Elazer ben Arach, Rabbi Yosef the Priest: and Shimon, son of Nathanel; from them it passed to Rabbi Akiba, Rabbi Elazar ben Azariah, Rabbi Tarfon, Rabbi Shimon ben Gamaliel; from them to Rabbi Meir, Rabbi Judah, Rabbi Yosi, Rabbi Shimon [bar Yochai], Rabbi Judah the Prince". The last is our sainted teacher who gathered together the dicta of the Mishnah, arranged them in order, divided them into chapters and compiled them in a work. This compilation is the essential element of the whole tradition on which we rely in our Torah.

TEN CLASSES OF FAITH IN THE TORAH

(*Marpe Lenefesh*: Now, he will explain that there are different classes of faith in the torah, and due to this, their corresponding undertaking of the service of G-d will likewise be different.)

The outlooks of those who owe allegiance to the Torah fall into ten classes of varying degrees in their faith and in their acceptance of the service of G-d.

Of the lowest degree are those who are misled by foolishness and the overwhelming force of evil passions to reject the Torah which they consider to be similar to the laws by which other peoples are guided and the simple kept in check. This attitude results from the powerful hold that sensual lust has obtained over their understanding, and from their gross nature; they do not submit to the yoke of the Torah, nor will they be bound by the restraints of reason, due to their longing for unrestrained license. Of people of this sort the sage says, *"A fool has no delight in understanding but only that his heart may discover itself (follow its impulses)"* (Mishlei 18:2).

(*Marpe Lenefesh*: Due to foolishness and worldly lusts, they found excuses to shed the yoke of torah, and they think that the torah is similar to the laws and customs which come from gentile kings - without reason, and only the fools will believe them and fulfill them. Likewise, they say that there is no reward and punishment in the torah (in the afterlife).

Pas Lechem: "the simple kept in check" - i.e. like the methods the gentile leaders employ to lead their nations, or like those the intelligent people lead the fools.

Tov Halevanon: the Rabbis made up laws and customs so that human society can endure.)

Of the second degree are those who cannot deny the signs and wonders that were manifested by the prophets, because of their publicity, but they doubt the truthfulness of the Torah, and express views that approach those of the foregoing class, namely, that G-d only wished to point out to His creatures a way by which they would improve their condition in this world, and therefore stirred the prophet (Moses) to guide them with statutes that they needed, and granted him signs and wonders, so that they should listen to his words and accept his ordinances. The members of this second class do not believe in reward and punishment (in the afterlife - *TL*).

(*Pas Lechem*: *"do not believe in reward and punishment"* - Since according to their views G-d's intent in giving the torah was only for their welfare in this world. Hence, there is no punishment for one who rebels against it, only ruining of his worldly affairs.

Marpe Lenefesh: *"who cannot deny the signs"* - since the great signs and wonders performed by the prophets are so familiar and well known, and certainly the signs were from G-d, but the matter of prophecy itself they deny, believing it is inconceivable that G-d will speak with a human being. For speech is physical while G-d is exalted and above all physicality, as this view is mentioned in the Kuzari book. Hence, they claim that the torah is not from G-d. G-d's intent was only that people should conduct themselves justly in this world, that their matter should not be unrestrained. Therefore, G-d stirred the prophet to guide them in the right way, according to how he wants. G-d made signs and miracles so that they will listen to the prophet's words and commands. They also do not believe in reward and punishment like the first class.

Rabbi YS: In ancient times, the Exodus from Egypt and the miracles of the ten plagues, etc. were known more as a historical fact than as belief. This is because they were closer to it in time. Historical facts are very difficult if not impossible to establish since they need a consensus from everyone simultaneously. An example of a historical fact today, would be the Spanish Inquisition or the conquests of Napoleon, something no one doubts due to their being so well known and familiar. And even today, the Torah remains the most popular book of all time. Likewise, no other book has been translated into so many languages.)

I will give here briefly the answers to these views by refutation and also alternatively by agreement, (for argument's sake).

By refutation: The Creator is too exalted to alter the course of nature for the sake of one who resorts to falsehood in regard to Him and utters in His name things which He had not said, even if that person aims, by means of these falsehoods about G-d, to direct people in the right way. For the vision of the truth manifested to the prophet is not more wondrous or harder to apprehend than a change in the order of nature that takes place for the prophet's sake.

> (*Marpe Lenefesh*: It is inconceivable that G-d would make signs and miracles for one who will say falsehood in His Name, i.e. that the person will utter in G-d's name, that G-d commanded him on everything in the torah. And according to their view, the prophet (Moses) made up on his own the entire torah. How could G-d change the natural order for him if he were a liar? If you say, G-d changed the natural order for the prophet so that he will be able to direct the people to the way of G-d. This is also inconceivable since why wouldn't G-d Himself command as to how to do His will? For certainly the vision of prophecy to the prophet, to command him on words of the torah is no more wondrous and no more difficult before G-d than performing miracles. If G-d wants to change the natural order for the prophet why would He not command him also. Is one more difficult than the other? Is G-d's power lacking? Rather, certainly G-d spoke the words of torah to the prophet. See also Kuzari maamar 1 siman 89)

By agreement (for argument's sake): If it were clearly demonstrated by an irrefutable proof that the fact was as these people say (that the Torah was not revealed to the prophet, but was the prophet's own invention), it would even then be right to follow him, for the exalted Creator would not change the order of nature and manifest a wonder through one who does not know the good and right way. And if the exalted Creator has chosen one to teach us the good and right way and guide us, after wondrous signs had been manifested by him, he is sufficiently worthy that we should rely upon him in our behavior and way of life. Seeing that we owe this to a king or governor, even if he is not endowed with wisdom, as it is said, *"O, my son, fear the L-ord and the king"* (Mishlei 24:21), how much more is this our duty toward one through whom a wonder has been shown. Thus, from both points of view, we are under an obligation to accept the Torah. Concerning people of this class, the wise man says, *"O, ye simple, understand wisdom: and ye fools, be of an understanding heart"* (Mishlei 8:5).

> (*Tov Halevanon*: *"fear the L-ord and the king"* - Just like you fear G-d, so

too you are under duty to fear the king which G-d has appointed, in His place on the actions of human beings.

Marpe Lenefesh: And likewise, one who has demonstrated miracles, that you can see tangibly that he is a messenger of G-d, how much more so that you are under duty to abide by his commands.)

Of the third degree are those who are convinced of the truthfulness of the Torah but think that it was given as a favor of G-d, to direct aright His creations and guide them exclusively in this world, but not for the sake of reward in the world hereafter. Their reason for this view is that in the prophetical books, reward and punishment in this world are frequently mentioned but there is no mention of retribution in the next world. Our teacher, Saadyah, in his commentary on the weekly portion Behukothai (Vayikra, Chapters 26 and 27) expounded on this topic and clearly demonstrated the nullity of the views expressed by these people. (see also the Gate of Trust ch.4 for sufficient answers to this view - *ML*)

The prophetical books contain clear indications of reward and punishment in the world to come. The following are examples: *"For G-d shall bring every work into judgment, with every secret thing, whether it be good or evil"* (Koheles 12:14) (a reference to the Judgment Day when G-d will stand every human being to be judged - *TL*). *"And you shall tread down the wicked; for they shall be ashes under the sole of your feet"* (Malachi 3:21). *"[behold a day is coming, it burns as a furnace and all the wicked shall be as stubble...] then shall you return and discern between the righteous and the wicked, between him that serves G-d and him that serves Him not."* (Malachi 3:18). *"And they shall go forth and look upon the carcasses of the men that have transgressed against Me; for their worm shall not die. neither shall their fire be quenched, and they shall be an eternal abhorrence unto all flesh"* (Yeshaya 66:24). *"How great is Your goodness, which You have laid up for them that fear You, which You have wrought for them that trust in You before the children of men"* (Tehilim 31:20). *"Thus says the L-ord of Hosts, if you will walk in My ways . . .I will give you places to walk among these that stand'"* (Zach. 3:7). *"Eye has not seen, O G-d, beside You, what He had prepared for him that waits for Him"* (Yeshaya 64:3). *"And many of them that sleep in the dust of the earth shall awake, some to everlasting life, and some to shame and everlasting contempt"* (Daniel 12:2). *"Your righteousness shall go before you; the glory of the L-ord shall be your reward"* (Yeshaya 58:8). And there are many passages to the same effect, too numerous to mention.

Of the fourth degree are those in whose consciousness the genuineness of the Torah and the truthfulness of reward and punishment in the world to come are firmly established. But their disposition inclines them to love of the world and its lusts; and they use the practices of the service of G-d as snares with which to obtain worldly advantages. They accept the Torah outwardly but not inwardly, with their tongues and not with their hearts. Of such people it is said, *"One speaks peaceably to his neighbor with his mouth, but in his heart he waits in ambush for him"* (Yirmiya 9:7). Further, *"With mouth and lips, they honor Me; but their heart is far from Me"* (Yeshaya 29:13).

(*Marpe Lenefesh*: Due to their great lust for worldly enjoyment they undertake the religious service as a snare to trap this world. They are not able to attain their lusts due to their weakness and poorness. Therefore, they pretend to be pious and ascetics and wear garments of torah scholars so that others will believe in them, give them gifts, and deposit their money by them [for safekeeping]. They are hypocrites to people and to G-d. In the Gate of Abstinence ch.4 the author concludes regarding them that they are the worse class of all human beings.)

Of the fifth degree are those who are convinced on all the points we have mentioned in regard to the Torah and of the truth of reward and punishment in the world to come. But their disposition inclines them to love of the world; they indeed accept the Torah; but in their acceptance their intent is to obtain reward from G-d as well as praise and honor from human beings. This is one of the branches of hypocrisy, namely, the concealed joint worship [of G-d and something else].

(*Tov Halevanon*: He serves concealed idolatry, namely, he joins the service of G-d with the service of praise and honor, only that it is concealed and other people cannot detect that he serves G-d jointly.
[i.e. he is worshipping G-d and praise of human beings. He has two masters not one - RYS].

Pas Lechem: *"joint worship"* i.e. with idolatry since he worships himself not his Creator. He is called concealed in that his intent is not visible to everyone.)

Of the sixth degree are those who in their religious practice aim at a reward from the Creator solely in this world, because of their love for it, and because they prefer its delights. They do not comprehend the reward hereafter and its bliss.

(*Marpe Lenefesh*: These people are worshipping only l'shem shamayim (solely to G-d). But their intent is for worldly reward because they do not understand the bliss of the afterlife.

Tov Halevanon: They do not yearn for the bliss of the afterlife, hence they are not able to break their lusts for the reward of the afterlife because they don't understand its bliss, even though they know that there is reward in the afterlife. The reason being, because they love this world very much.
Rabbi YS: i.e. since they love this world so much, they don't strive to understand the bliss of the afterlife. Perhaps because they know that to work for the bliss of the afterlife, they would need to break their lusts and distance themselves from physical enjoyments.)

Of the seventh degree are those who are convinced of all that we have mentioned. But their motive in the service of G-d is the expectation of reward in this world and in the world to come. They have no conception whatever of service of the Almighty for His own sake, to magnify, honor and exalt Him, as alone befits the worship of Him. Of these, our wise men have said, "Be not like servants who serve the master upon the condition of receiving a reward; but be like servants who serve the master without any condition of receiving a reward; and let the fear of Heaven be upon you" (Ethics of the Fathers: 1:3).

(*Marpe Lenefesh*: They are still outside [the goal] since they hope for reward in their service. If not for hope of reward, they would not be doing the service of G-d. And in truth, it is proper to serve Him for His own sake, etc.)

Of the eighth degree are those who are convinced of all that has been mentioned, but they accept the service of G-d out of fear of His punishment in this world and the next. We have already pointed out how reprehensible these two views are (in chapter 3 where he disgraced those who serve out of reward and punishment alone - *MH*)

(*Marpe Lenefesh*: They are not concerned about the reward, but they are serving G-d out of fear of punishment of this world or the next. From our words, one can see the difference between each of the degrees, which are going up in ascending order, from the lowly to the lofty, so that a man will know how to ascend from level to level, as the author ends off. See the [book] Shl"Habris and you will understand all these levels.)

Of the ninth degree are those who believe in the Torah and in reward and punishment in both worlds. In serving G-d, their intent is to do so for His Name's sake and in the way befitting Him alone, but they are not careful to avoid whatever is detrimental to this service, and when detriments have

caused injury they do not know from where the trouble came. This is
suggested in the verse: *"Dead flies make the apothecary's oil to ferment
and send forth a foul odor; so a little folly outweighs the rarest wisdom
and honor"* (Koheles 10:1). Further, *"One sinner destroys much good"*
(ibid. 9:18).

> (*Tov Halevanon*: each one of the dead flies will spoil and bring up bubbles
> in the [perfumed] oil until eventually the oil exudes a foul odor. This
> analogy is to arrogance and pride which bubble inside him and produce hot
> air until it eventually spoils his service and piety.
> *"a little folly spoils the rarest wisdom"* - a little folly is heavy and
> outweighs all the wisdom and exalted states in him and drives them out.
>
> *Marpe Lenefesh*: He wrote later in Gate 5 that every good thing has
> corresponding bad things which ruin it. These are the musings of the evil
> inclination which desires to topple him from this world and the next. See
> there. Therefore one should study all the things detrimental to avoid them
> and only then he will be able to do good. See there at length.)

One of the pious once said to his disciples, "If you would be absolutely
free of sins, I would be anxious about you and fear something worse than
sins." They said to him: "What is worse than sins?" He replied:
"Haughtiness and pride," as Scripture says, *"An abomination unto the
L-ord is everyone that is proud in heart"* (Mishlei 16:5).

> (*Marpe Lenefesh*: If you did not learn torah nor do mitzvot and good deeds,
> you would have nothing to be proud about. Through good deeds one comes
> to arrogance. Furthermore, a person is embarrassed to do sins, but one who
> is arrogant becomes increasing more and more without realizing it.
> Furthermore, when one commits a sin, he will rouse himself to repent for it.
> But if he does not do sins and is proud of this, he does not arouse himself to
> repent [for his pride], therefore pride is the worst sin (LT).
>
> *Pas Lechem*: Certainly arrogance is the greatest detriment of all. And in
> truth, he does not know from where the loss came, because a person does
> not become haughty unless he first imagines that he deserves to be proud.
> Therefore, he will not find any sins he committed.)

The tenth degree, those people for who it has become clear to them the
truth of the Torah and all the rewards and punishments which they will
incur on account of it in both worlds, and who have become aroused out of
their neglect [of it]. Their hearts have seen what they owe to their Creator
in return for His great benevolence and loving kindness towards them.
They do not fix their hearts on reward or punishment, but hasten to fulfill

the service of G-d for His Name's sake, to aggrandize and exalt Him with longing and wholehearted devotion, because they know Him and recognize His matter.

(*Pas Lechem*: they know His greatness and exaltedness and recognize the matter of His conduct with His creations.
Lev Tov: They know His greatness and exaltedness and recognize His wisdom and goodness.

Marpe Lenefesh: "*have become aroused out of their neglect*" - If they neglected to do some good thing or [neglected] not to do some [bad thing], immediately they aroused themselves and stood up against their evil inclination, so that the Yetzer (evil inclination) has no opening to strengthen himself over them.

Rabbi YS: Rabbi Eliya Lopian zt'l would compare the evil inclination to a fly. If you shoo it from here it returns on a different place. Only when one has no pus anywhere will the fly leave you alone. So too only when one does not give in to it in the least will the evil inclination leave a person to search for better spoils. [Artscroll Reb Elyah])

This is the highest degree to be attained by the men of the Torah. This is the degree that was attained by the prophets and chasidim (pious ones) who devoted themselves to G-d, made a covenant with Him, were always communing with Him, accepted His ruling, gave up to Him themselves, their children, their possessions, and firmly kept their faith in all that they undertook, even to the surrender of their lives. Concerning these, Scripture says, "*Gather My saints together unto Me; those that have made a covenant with Me by sacrifice*" (Tehilim 50:5).

(*Pas Lechem*: "*gave up to Him their lives, their children, their possessions*" - i.e. they resolved that their lives, children, and possessions - all belong to G-d, and they are prepared to return it to Him if need be to do His will. After this, he wrote that just like they resolved and accepted this on themselves, so too they fulfilled it when the time came and they firmly kept their faith.)

This is the form of the inducing of the Torah in urging the service of G-d, and these are the degrees of those men of wisdom who devote themselves to the study of the holy books of the Torah and the excellencies of those who believe in it. It is possible that there may be other degrees among men of understanding in the Torah, other than those that we have set forth. But we only mentioned those degrees that are found among the large majority of the people. Still, the list of degrees that we have given will be of use to one who seeks the right way, for, when he finds in this list a degree to which he is near, he will know what is the next higher degree and will strive to rise to it, then notes the distance between the degree that he has attained and the highest of the degrees, and strives to ascend to it gradually, one degree after another-he will find the ascent easier to accomplish.

(*Pas Lechem*: He will know the next higher degree, i.e. next higher rung. And since one needs to ascend to the top rung, he wrote *"then notes the distance between the degree that he has attained and the highest of the degrees"*, so that he will strive to ascend from level to level until he reaches the highest.

Rabbi YS: The tenth level is the goal. Perhaps, the other levels are ordered according to their distance from the goal not according to moral superiority. Hence, the commentary wrote in the fourth level: "they are the worse class of human beings".)

CHAPTER 5

(*Marpe Lenefesh*: until now, he explained the urge of the torah. Now he will explain what is the urge of the understanding.)

It is now proper for us to proceed to explain the mode in which the intellect urges us to the service of G-d in the form of questions and answers - this method being most suitable to a clear presentation of the topic we are investigating.

(*Pas Lechem*: The role-playing through questions and answers, as if two people are debating, one asking and the other answering, is a deep method of clarifying a topic, to one who contemplates it. Because the way of the questioner is to strive to ask a powerful, wise question, and the Sages say (Mivchar hapeninim 1:3) "the question of the wise man is half of the wisdom". While the way of the answerer is to strive to heal the illness of the questioner by refuting it to the best of his ability. [*Rabbi YS*: the Talmud is built on this method of question and answer])

We will assert that the urge of the intellect means that G-d reminds a human being through his intellect, of his duty to know Him, and to become cognizant of the marks of His divine wisdom. This call of G-d comes to one who has taken the Torah as the light of his path, attained intellectual maturity and capacity for clear perception, yearns to gain the Almighty's favor and rise to the spiritual heights of the saints, and turns his heart away from worldly cares and anxieties.

(*Marpe Lenefesh*: "*G-d reminds a human being*" - When G-d reminds a man and stirs him so he does not fall into the trap of forgetfulness and sinks into the abyss of lusts. G-d warns him through his intellect and neshama (soul) which is called the "yetzer tov" (good inclination).
"*comes to one who has taken the Torah...*" - i.e. after he conducts all his affairs in line with the torah, and does not veer neither right nor left as G-d commanded Moses. Then he can ascend higher and higher to the intellectual urge. Because, without torah, he is a fool who walks in darkness. He is entrenched in bodily lusts and erroneous outlooks, as the author wrote in chapter 2.)

The things through which a person will experience the intellectual urge are as follows: that a person should come to realize what the Creator has implanted in the human mind, namely: [that it is proper - LT] to esteem truth and detest falsehood, [it is proper - LT] to choose righteousness and avoid injustice. [It is proper - LT] to repay benefactors with good deeds and express gratitude to them, and to punish the wicked and condemn them. [It is proper - LT] to keep at peace with all human beings and act beneficently towards them, estimate good deeds [in comparison] with the resulting praise, righteous deeds with their reward, wrongdoings with their punishment, the superiority of one reward over another, the severity of one punishment compared with another and forgiveness of transgressors when they truly repent.

(*Marpe Lenefesh*: When does a man experience the intellectual urge? He answered, when he comes to realize the just and true outlooks which a straight intellect obligates, namely, that it is proper to esteem truth and detest falsehood, etc.

Rabbi YS: "*what the Creator has implanted in the human mind*" - i.e. G-d has implanted the voice of conscience in the human mind so that he can recognize the truth if he truly seeks it.

Lev Tov: "*to punish the wicked and condemn them*" - even though the torah forbade us to do this, as written: "do not take revenge nor bear a grudge" (Vayikra 19:18), nevertheless, a man must know that Reason dictates that it is proper to pay back evil with evil. And if a person pays back the Creator with evil despite the great benefits G-d has bestowed on him, it is proper that G-d pays him back evil accordingly. Through this, one will refrain from transgressing G-d's will out of fear of punishment.)

After these concepts have been clearly established in a man's soul through his reasoning ability and power of perception, his intellect will have become sound and his perception strong. And when G-d will remind him of the way of His goodness, that person will arouse his mind and soul to appreciate G-d's kindnesses to him, and his recognition of them will become stronger. And when he will attempt to recount them and realize them with his understanding and will find himself unable to do so, because of their universality, multitude, continuity and permanence, he will make demands upon his soul in regard to his duty of gratitude towards benefactors, as pointed out to him by his intellect, and his duty to act righteously. He will then resolve to make a return to the exalted G-d for the multitude of benefits he has received from Him.

(*Marpe Lenefesh*: "*when G-d will remind him*" - i.e. G-d will place in his heart good thoughts, and stirs him to choose for himself the proper path which will be good for him in both worlds.
"*that person will arouse his mind and soul*" - then he will start to consider

and think by himself on how many benefits G-d has bestowed on him. *"and his recognition of them will become stronger"* - he will see to it to recognize them meticulously, and not forget even one of them - that they be like Totafot (tefilin) between his eyes, the great favors which G-d did with him every day, at all times.)

And when he perceives with his mind's eye that he does not have the ability to do so, for the Creator has no need of him, then he will feel the obligation to humble himself and become conscious of his lowliness and insignificance, and he will then insist of his understanding concerning what he has to do, that it may be possible for him to approach and draw near to G-d in order that communion with Him may serve as a substitute for the return due to G-d, and his understanding will aid him to the right path in this regard.

(*Tov Halevanon*: *"he does not have the ability to do so"* - i.e. that it is impossible for a created being to benefit the Creator, and especially since the Creator, who is absolutely perfect in every way, does not need anything.

Marpe Lenefesh: Even if he had the ability to repay the benefit, he will understand and realize that the Creator does not need him or his benefits.

Pas Lechem: *"to humble himself"* - with acts which demonstrate lowliness such as fasts, sackcloth, and ashes, as written "have you seen how Achav has humbled himself before Me" (Melachim 21:24).
"and become conscious of his lowliness and insignificance" - in his thoughts. *"lowliness"* from the perspective of himself, to regard oneself as lowly which is the opposite of arrogance. *"Insignificant"* forbearing and humble before others..

Marpe Lenefesh: *"to humble himself..."* - to say to oneself, "what am I and what significance am I that You have brought me until here? You have bestowed on me these tremendous favors and I am not capable of repaying You in the least, as the pious king (David) said (Divrei Hayamim 17:16): "Who am I, O L-ord G-d, and what is my house, that you have brought me this far?" Examine the whole matter there and you will be inspired.)

THE DELIBERATION BETWEEN THE UNDERSTANDING AND THE SOUL

(*Tov Halevanon*: Now he will begin to explain the urge of the understanding in the way of questions and answers; How the understanding induces the service of G-d out of love, over the service induced by fear of punishment, whose source is in the nefesh, which feels reward and punishment and is from the aspect of good and evil. The understanding argues with its own source, namely, the aspect of truth and falsehood - to establish the nefesh in the service which is induced from the Understanding.

Manoach Halevavos: The "understanding" refers to the neshama (higher soul). The "soul" (nefesh) refers to the life spirit (lower soul, animal soul).

Marpe Lenefesh: The soul (nefesh) is the life spirit, through it the body lives and is maintained. The Creator has implanted in it lusts for all bodily things. It is called the "nefesh bahamit" (animal soul), for an animal also lusts for things which furthers its body. But the superiority of a human being lies in his intellect, which is like the king over the body, to guide everything in the just way and to yearn for spiritual things. See the Shemonei Perakim of the Rambam ch.1 and what I quoted from the book Shaarei Kedusha later on.)

It (the Understanding) will say to his soul (nefesh):
Is it clear to you and firmly fixed in your mind that you are pledged (i.e. under debt - *ML*) to your Creator for His goodness and belong to Him because of the multitude of His kindness and His great favors?
The Soul (nefesh): Yes. (it is true what you say - *TL*)

(*Pas Lechem*: "*you are pledged... and belong to Him*" - As is the nature of the world. The poor debtor will first give his property as a pledge to his rich creditor because it is hard for him to sell it, and he hopes that maybe he will earn some money afterwards and redeem it back. Afterwards, when he sees that he needs more money, and borrows more until the debt becomes greater than the value of the pledge and the pledge then belongs to the creditor. So too here, at first he is obligated only a little to his Creator. As time goes on, his debt increases until even his life belongs to the Creator. "*kindness and favors*" - on the benefits which He bestowed on you and the favors which he saved you from troubles.)

The Understanding: Is it your intention to repay a portion of what you owe to the Creator?
The Soul: Yes.

(*Pas Lechem*: "*a portion*" - i.e. even though you are not able to fully repay any of them, you can nevertheless pay some of them according to your ability.)

The Understanding: How is this possible when your longing for this is so weak. Only a person who longs for health will put up with the bitterness of a medicine; but one who does not long for health will not submit to bearing the severity of the treatment.

(*Marpe Lenefesh*: How can you say that your intention is to repay a portion, etc. while you do not long and yearn for this with a tremendous desire. Your words contradict your heart.)

The Soul: My yearning is strong and my pain is great, to repay as much as I can of what I owe to my G-d; therefore continue to exhort me (and teach me how and what to repay Him - *LT*).

(*Pas Lechem*: My yearning is strong for the future and my pain is great for the past, that I was lazy in this. Alternatively, my pain is great due to my ignorance how and what to repay for I did not have a mentor until now.)

The Understanding: If you are telling the truth in what you are saying, the treatment may possibly be successful in your case. But if it is not the truth, why should you deceive yourself? For a sick person who lies to his physician only cheats himself, wastes the physician's efforts and aggravates his sickness (for it is the way of medicines to harm those who are not suited to them as the Rambam wrote - *PL*).

The Soul: And how can it be determined whether my longing (to repay the Creator - *LT*) is strong or weak.

(*Tov Halevanon*: i.e. how can I know whether the longing in me is true or false?)

The Understanding: If your longing stems from a clear realization how great is your debt to repay G-d, how little it is in your power to fulfill it and that your neglect of it is your downfall, while your striving to fulfill it is your salvation and life - your longing is genuine and your want is urgent; if not, it is false.

(*Marpe Lenefesh*: Know and understand that all the time that you are lax and negligent to long for this, namely, that you do not know and contemplate always "when will the time come that I can do something to fulfill the will of G-d?", and that through this will be your salvation in this world and life in the next world - then you are still on the outside. But if not, know that this is a true longing.

LONGING VS WANTING
Pas Lechem: "your longing is genuine and your want is urgent" - "your longing is genuine" i.e. it is powerful and enduring and therefore indirectly,

you will swiftly reach your want. This is the meaning of *"your want is urgent"*. "longing" and "want" are two separate things. It is possible to have "longing" without "want" or vice versa. The term "longing" applies to strong yearning in the nefesh (soul), to cling to that which it deems cherishable while the mental imagery of that thing is in its thoughts. Hence, it works in a kind of natural way. Nevertheless, perhaps he will not "want" that thing due to some impediment. For example, consider a person who feels extremely hungry on a fast day. It is correct to say that his nefesh (soul) longs for food but nevertheless he does not want the food. Because the term "want" applies to will by cognitive choice. It is possible also to find "want" without "longing". For example, if a man takes a bitter potion for healing purposes. He "wants" it by necessity but his nature does not "long" for this. It is known that in all human powers, there are varying degrees, higher and lower. Likewise for "longing". There is a strong longing, and there is a stronger longing. However, there is no such thing as an utterly lax longing, since if it is lax, it is not at all a "longing" (by definition). Through this presentation, you will understand all of the author's words regarding longing and want. Understand this.)

The Soul: My want was never other than lax, and my longing was always false, from the time when my only inducements (to the service of G-d) were the records of former ages that have passed away up to the time when the truth of what you have stated has become rationally clear to me, first through the exhortation of the Torah, and later by rational demonstration, so that my longing now is genuine and my want is clear.

(*Tov Halevanon*: i.e. even though the stories in the torah and the prophets induced me to the ways of G-d, nevertheless, my longing was lax and false. Unlike now when it has become clear to me through the method of wisdom (rational enquiry).

Pas Lechem: *"my want was lax"* - the term lax applies correctly to "want", but not to "longing", as [I explained] before. Therefore, he used the term "false", which connotes ceasing, for it is possible for a man to long for something and afterwards his yearning cools down, hence his longing is [retroactively] proved false.
"my want is clear": i.e. strong. He used the term "clear" because what causes a want to become lax is the mixtures of impurities of outside interests which conflict with that want. This is like the mixture of impurities in a man's blood which conflicts with the natural health and weakens his strength. But when the "want" strengthens, this indicates that the impurities have shed and it is now clear [pure].)

The Understanding: If what you say is true, then prepare yourself to bear the pain of the treatment, and endure the bitter taste of the medicine and its unpleasantness, after you will have first given up the bad diet to which you were accustomed.

> (*Marpe Lenefesh*: For the physician will not give the treatment to the patient as long as the patient is continuing to eat the bad foods which the illnesses stem from. He then says that the bad foods to the soul are the bad traits which divide into two categories.)

The Soul: What is the bad diet to which I was accustomed ?
The Understanding: It is the bad disposition (trait) which has mastered you from your beginning and the forces which have maintained it, from the earliest years of your growth.

> (*Pas Lechem*: *"from your beginning"* - the beginning of your existence. From the beginning of the formation of the body, the soul was joined to it. Regarding the "forces", he wrote *"earliest years of your growth"* since these are the superfluous things which he has accustomed himself in when he has attained some understanding. Hence, he did not write "beginning" regarding these since one is not in control of his ways while in his mother's belly.
>
> *Marpe Lenefesh*: If you wish to understand why he refers to bad traits as bad food, and why the healing of bad traits is not part of the healing regimen itself, see the words of a holy man, the man of G-d, our teacher, Rabbi Chaim Vital in his book "Shaarei Kedusha". There he explains this matter at length as he received it from his teacher, the Arizal, through the divine presence which rested on him... The summary of what he says is that good and bad traits in a human being stem from the nefesh bahamit (lower soul). The body is comprised of the four elements of the world and their spiritual counterparts, which are material and form. Therefore, all the traits fall into two main divisions which in turn subdivide into two subdivisions: "arrogance", from the element of fire (*Rabbi YS*: see Gate 1 ch.6 for an explanation of the four elements system of classification. Modern science combined everything with E=mc2 because it ignores the spiritual side of reality). [Excessive] speech, whether good or bad springs from the element of air. Lust for physical pleasures springs from the element of water, sadness and laziness from the element of earth. From their opposites spring the good traits in a human being. The 613 commandments correspond to the 613 spiritual limbs of the soul which are enclothed inside the nefesh bahamit which in turn is enclothed in the 613 physical limbs of the body. Therefore, the body is not able to work and fulfill the 613 commandments if the soul is ill with the sickness of these bad traits, just like if the body were ill. Therefore, the traits were not included in the 613 commandments.

It comes out that bad traits are more severe than fulfillment of the commandments themselves, since then the body and soul are not capable of fulfilling any commandment properly. Therefore, the bad traits are like bad food to a sick body - all the medications in the world (i.e. the commandments) will be of no avail as long as he continues with the bad food. See there at length the words of the wise man and you will understand it well.)

The Soul: What disposition is this, and what are the forces that maintain it? The Understanding: The reprehensible dispositions in you are many. But the root and stock from which they spring are two. One of them is love of physical pleasures - eating, drinking, marital relations and other bodily needs. This disposition you have acquired from your bad neighbor, the body.
The second disposition is love of domination and superiority - pride, haughtiness, jealousy. This brings you to refrain from making a return to your Benefactor. This disposition you have acquired from your associates, among whom you have grown up, namely, your siblings and [other] relatives.

The Soul: What are the forces that I need to keep far from me? The Understanding: The forces that maintain the former evil disposition are superfluity in eating, drinking, dress, sleep, rest, tranquility and other similar things. The forces that uphold the latter evil disposition are superfluity of speech, excessive socializing, approval seeking [of human beings], love of praise and honor, jealousy of others because of their material possessions, even if what they possess consists only of sheer necessaries; contemptuousness, picking on the faults of others, and so forth. If what you have said of your strong desire and yearning to make a return for the benefits G-d has bestowed upon you is true, keep far from you, with all your strength, the forces and dispositions that I have mentioned to you, and I will then bring you to the first gate leading to recovery.

(*Pas Lechem*: *"rest"* - from physically toiling with one's limbs. *"tranquility"* means tranquility of heart from the toil of thoughts.

Tov Halevanon: *"tranquility"* - a mind tranquil and quiet from the worries of the service of G-d.

Manoach Halevavos: *"jealousy of others"* - i.e. jealousy of them because they acquired worldly possessions, and things necessary for their livelihood. Alternatively, due to great jealousy, he comes to steal forcefully what is in their hands.

"contemptuousness" - due to his great pride and arrogance, he desires to denigrate other people and recall their faults.

Pas Lechem: *"keep far from you, with all your strength, the forces and dispositions"* - he first mentioned the "forces" which are the causes which maintain the dispositions. One must first remove the cause for when the cause is removed, the effect (i.e. the bad dispositions) will also be removed. *Translator*: see Gate #9 chapter 5 for a detailed regimen by the author for conquering one's lusts for excessive things.)

The Soul: To renounce these faults would be very hard for me, on account of the long time that I have been habituated to them; therefore be kind enough to show me in what way I can do so more easily.

The Understanding: Surely you know that a sensible man will consent to the cutting off of one piece of flesh or to the loss of one of his limbs, if it is attacked by some disease which he fears will spread and affect the remaining limbs, as soon as he considers the difference between the two states and realizes the inequality of the two evils. So, too, if you wish that the separation which is so hard should seem easy to you, concentrate your mind and employ your intelligence in weighing the good you will derive from the separation and the evil which will befall you if you continue your association with it; and then separation from your reprehensible disposition, which seems so hard, will be easy.

(*Pas Lechem*: *"cutting off of one piece of flesh or to the loss of one of his limbs"* - i.e. when flesh is cut off and it eventually heals, there is no recognizable loss. The entire suffering was the pain of the cutting it (and its healing), therefore he used the term *"cutting off"*. But for a limb, where the loss is also in lost functionality he used the phrase *"and its loss"*.

Tov Halevanon: *"concentrate your mind..."* - i.e. which is the worse evil, to lose one limb or to die altogether?

Pas Lechem: *"concentrate your mind..."* - At first one must picture in his mind the two extremes, and afterwards to employ one's faculty of contemplation to weigh the difference between them.)

The Soul: What is the good that separation from it will bring me, and what is the evil that will befall me if I continue to keep it?

The Understanding: The good will consist in your spiritual tranquility and relief from the darkness of this gloomy world, the pleasures of which are mixed with grief, while its lusts soon cease; also, that your strengthened power of perception will finally lead you to realize your destiny in the place of your rest (the life hereafter) and that therefore you should busy yourself and be concerned about it. This is one of the gates on which depend your salvation and your life.

(*Tov Halevanon*: *"the pleasures are mixed with griefs"* - there is no pleasure in this world which is complete, without worries. They inevitably become increasingly mixed with worries. A human being always longs for what is more. What he possesses is as nothing compared to his heart's desire to obtain more than this, as our Sages said (Koheles Raba 13:1) "no man ever dies having obtained [even] half of his desire". Hence, his desire and grief in what he lacks is greater than what he has obtained.

"its lusts soon cease" - the pleasures of this world and its enjoyments. A man desires and lusts for some matter which he is not able to obtain. And when he does obtain the thing he desired, the thing transforms to being loathsome in his eyes and his lust for it then becomes heavy on him. Understand this.

"your strengthened power of perception" - this is the good that you will obtain when you separate [from the lusts] - you will perceive what awaits you in your final end - a pleasure without interruption and without worry. The good that awaits you when separating from the lusts and physical enjoyments of this world is that this will bring you to understand "your strengthened power of perception", i.e. great recognition and intent on your final abode, i.e. after death. When you see just how great your power of perception has been magnified after you have renounced the worldly lusts, all the more so, after death when the body has become completely separated from you.

Marpe Lenefesh: your perception, namely, your thoughts will be primarily on the next world, for there is your true home, and there you will rest and be tranquil.)

The evil [resulting from not renouncing your bad tendencies] is recurrence of your anxiety, multiplication of your grief, continuance of your mourning at the non-fulfillment of your desires in this world which, if they were satisfied, would only bring you something that is vain, without permanence or continuance, and which will undoubtedly pass to someone else; so that nothing will remain to you of this world nor will you secure the world hereafter; and, what is more obvious, you will not fulfill your wishes, however long you strive for them.

The Soul: I understand what you have said. I hope that the separation which previously was so hard will now become easier for me. Continue now to lead me to the second part of the healing methods which will teach me what I desire to learn of the service of G-d.

(*Lev Tov*: Now the understanding will start to teach the soul what it needs to do to become closer to G-d and to find favor in His eyes. As an introduction, he explains that the foundation of the service of G-d is that a man relates towards G-d, who is above him and benefits him, in the same way that he expects from his slave who is inferior in status and benefits from him.)

The Understanding: The ruling principle and sum of the matter is that you assume towards Him who is above you all those obligations which you would desire should be assumed towards yourself by one beneath you-presupposing that relations in both cases are equal. What seems to you good and what displeases you as evil in the conduct of the latter, do and refrain from doing, towards the former.

The Soul: Be more explicit.
The Understanding: Think of the benefits bestowed by G-d that you share with others, and of those benefits with which you are specially favored. Then imagine that you have bestowed similar favors on your slave whom you acquired by purchase; and the kind of behavior on his part towards you that would be pleasing to you, undertake to show to your Creator, and what seems to you evil, on his part, you too must regard as evil on your part to your Creator.

(*Marpe Lenefesh*: i.e. the root of the matter and general principle how it is fitting to serve G-d - take a proof from your own self. If you own a slave and the slave receives benefits from you (room and board, etc.), you want that this slave will honor you and serve you with all types of service, as he will explain. So too, it is proper to take on yourself all kinds of slavehood and service towards Him, since He is your superior, the Master of all, and you receive countless benefits from Him.

Tov Halevanon: "presupposing that relations in both cases are equal" - i.e. not that they are really equal, but rather, according to the extent and quality of the benefits bestowed on man by G-d relative to the extent and quality of the benefits bestowed on a master to his slave. So too, should be the corresponding greater service of a man to G-d relative to the service of a slave to his master.)

The Soul: I have understood in general what you have just said. But kindly explain all this to me in detail.
The Understanding: The duties of good conduct of any servant towards his master, who bestowed upon him even a tiny portion of the bounties your Creator has bestowed upon you, consist in honoring the master in word and

deed, in faithfulness to him, exerting himself in his master's affairs, openly and inwardly, and showing reverence and fear when standing in his presence. As a pious man said, "Do not rebel against your master when he observes you."

(*Pas Lechem*: *"faithfulness to him, exerting himself"* - i.e. faithful in his matters and exerting himself in them. The author's intent in these two terms is to divide the matters of slavehood into two divisions, namely, duties of the heart and duties of the limbs. On the duties of the heart he wrote *"faithfulness"* while on the duties of the limbs he wrote *"and exerts himself"*.

"reverence and fear" - fear due to picturing his ability to punish those who transgress his will, even though, G-d is beyond any representation of the mind, nevertheless, He is close from the aspect of His providence. Therefore, he wrote *"reverence and fear"*. Reverence from far and fear from close.

Marpe Lenefesh: *"Do not rebel against your master when he sees you."* - therefore David said "I have set G-d before me always" (Tehilim 16:8), in order not to transgress before Him.)

Among these duties are also included that he should be humble and submissive to his master, in his visible behavior and innermost secret thoughts; that he should conduct himself with humility before him, in his attire and habits.

Marpe Lenefesh: A slave should not dress up before his master in honorable clothing like free men, unless it is for his master's honor. He should also not act important in his traits, for example, to not become angry before his master even on someone who it is proper to get angry on. Likewise, he should not machria his words (affirm his opinion as if you are equal to him), as the Sages wrote regarding honoring one's father Kidushin 31b.

That he should honor and exalt him, in his speech and thought, that he should praise and laud him by day and by night; that he should recall his good deeds privately and publicly; recount his praises according to what befits him; run to do his service joyously and goodheartedly out of love that he will find favor in his master's eyes (i.e. because he loves and wants that he will find favor in his eyes - *PL*); strive to draw nearer in his behavior to his master's will; ever beseech his master to be pleased with him and forgive him; to love him; to be afraid that he may be falling short in doing what he had been commanded;

(*Pas Lechem*: *"be afraid"* - literally "be afraid that he WILL BE falling short" - that perhaps he is falling short in his commandments. He wrote "will be" in the future tense, i.e. he is afraid perhaps it will become known to him on the day of reckoning that he had fallen short. Alternatively, as our Sages said that a righteous man is afraid on future sins. Alternatively, the author's intent is that he pictures "fear" to himself when preparing for some act of service that perhaps he will fall short in it.)

That he should heed the master's command, keep far from that against which the master had warned him, think of the many iniquities which he has committed in the past, appreciate the benefits he has received on account of their great number and importance and diminish the value of what he has done in comparison with what he should have done; that he should regard his efforts as petty, compared with what is befitting him.

(*Tov Halevanon*: In every act of his [master's] service, he should not credit himself with good, rather he should think that this service is very petty compared to the service he is obligated to his master. i.e. that [generally] his service be petty in his eyes relative to what he is obligated to his master.)

He should admit his own insignificance compared to the greatness of his master. He should bow to him frequently, in deep humility and lowliness. He should put his trust in his master for all his needs and be satisfied with whatever position his master assigns him to. If the master provides for him fully, he should thank and praise him. If the master leaves him hungry, he should accept and bear his condition patiently. He should never suspect the master of unfairness in his judgment of him, nor charge him with perverseness in his decree. He should be contented with what the master favors him with, and justify the master when he has punished him.

(*Pas Lechem*: *"he should accept and bear his condition patiently"* - *"accept"* favorably [the hard condition the master subjected him to] at the beginning and bear the condition throughout its duration, without trying to remove it from himself through human strategies [rather to beseech only his master - Rabbi YS].
"never suspect the master of unfairness in his judgment" - on the small portion the master has allotted him for his needs while his eyes see much greater good that the master has allotted to others. He should not suspect that there was favoritism...
"nor charge him with perverseness in his decree" - if the master decreed some bad for him, he will not ascribe perverseness to the master. We find these two divisions in parsha Haazinu (Devarim 32:4) "The Rock, His work

is perfect, For all His ways are just", corresponding to G-d's allotting of benefits. The verse continues: "A G-d of faithfulness and without injustice, Righteous and upright is He", corresponding to the decrees of bad. Afterwards, he explains his words *"He should be contented with what the master favors him with"* corresponds to the first division. *"and justify the master when he has punished him"* - corresponds to the second division.)

Other things which are proper on his part: that in every movement of his limbs and in all his traits, he should exhibit evidence of his servitude and of his master's ownership.

(*Pas Lechem*: How he is the property of his master. [*Rabbi YS*: such as wearing a kippa on the head or tzitzit, tefilin, Brit Mila])

He should ponder only on remembrance of his master.

(*Pas Lechem*: in all of his thinking, one will find that his mouth expresses remembrance of his master.)

Look nowhere else than to the master's ways.

(*Pas Lechem*: To learn for himself the ways of his master, as written (Devarim 28:9): "you shall walk in His ways")

Listen only to his master's words, eat only the food that his master provides for him, think only of his master's greatness, render no service except to please his master.

(*Pas Lechem*: All of the service he renders to his master has no other aim than to find favor with him.)

Rejoice only in serving his master.

(*Pas Lechem*: To not be joyful of any thing in the world whatsoever except in performing the service of his Creator.)

Seek only his master's will.

(*Pas Lechem*: *"a seeker"* refers to one who exerts himself on something to attain it. He wrote that the slave will not exert great exertion on anything in the world except for attaining the favor of his master.)

Hasten only on his master's errands, abstain only from whatever might be against the master's will.

(*Pas Lechem*: *"abstain"* - [the literal translation is "stand"]. The intent of using the word "stand" is that he "stops"... i.e. that he will not fear and halt from doing anything in the world when he senses that it is harmful like he panics, trembles and halts from some matter when he senses that he is rebelling against his Creator in that matter.)

Stay nowhere except in his master's house, remain ever faithful to him alone.

(*Pas Lechem*: For any matter in the world, he will not consider it so much to be steadfastly strong in it and so that he won't slip in it, except for his faithfulness to his master - he will strengthen himself with all of his might in it so that his heels will not slip.)

Only read his books, wear only the garment of reverence for his master.

(*Pas Lechem*: He compared the fear of G-d to a garment that a person wears to cover and hide his naked parts. So too, the fear of G-d will cover the disgrace of lowly traits in man's potential so that they don't come out to actual.)

Sleep only on the couch of love for him, keeping ever in his mind the master's likeness.

(*Pas Lechem*: One who is very much beloved to someone, due to that person's great love, his picture will cleave to his heart. And the picture which clings to his heart becomes manifested and pictured before him always as if it were placed before him. This is the pshat (plain meaning) of the verse (Tehilim 16:8) "I have set G-d before me always".)

Awaking with the sweetness in thinking of him.

(*Pas Lechem*: When something is beloved and precious to a man, it is the first of all his thoughts. Immediately when he wakes up, it precedes other thoughts in entering his mind.)

Finding no pleasure except in being with him, fleeing from naught except disobedience to him, never mourning except when his master is angry [on him - PL], feeling no fear except fear of his master, hoping for naught but his master's kindness, never angry except at that which his master obliges him to be so. He will only be pleased with one who does his master's will; take nothing but with his master's permission; only give to one to whom his master orders him to give.

And so with all his movements. He will not move a foot, nor raise an eyelid except to fulfill his master's will.

The habits that are bad in a servant are the opposite of those that are good in his master's sight. When these good habits are reversed, they are easily recognized.

> (*Pas Lechem*: in all matters, one can know and recognize the unknown side from the known side which is its opposite. For example, a poor man can picture the goodness of being wealthy through his recognition of the sufferings of poverty which is its opposite. On this, they wrote "knowledge of the opposites is one". The intent here is that once we have clarified the conducts which are good in the eyes of the master, indirectly we also know that the opposite conducts of the slave are bad in his eyes. And one must renounce the bad and adopt the good.)

I have assembled for you a sufficient number of examples to indicate to you the rest of the duties and their opposites. And as the conduct of servants, regarded by their masters as good is as we have described it, and you know how insignificant is the kindness of masters to their servants, how much more in reduplicated measure to what we have mentioned do you owe in service to the blessed G-d in return to Him for the multitude of bounties He has bestowed upon you.

CHAPTER 6

The Soul: I have understood what you have stated and your explanation is sufficient. Now explain to me the various aspects of favors for which I am under an obligation of increased service to the blessed G-d.

(*Tov Halevanon*: increased service [in return] for the specific benefits to me which is in addition to the service which all human beings are obligated in)

The Understanding: The obligation of increased service incumbent on human beings varies according to the benefits - general and specific - bestowed on them. These benefits fall into four divisions.

The first is the universal goodness of G-d which embraces all mankind, in having brought human creatures into existence when previously they were naught; in keeping them in life and bestowing on them bounties which we have cited in the second treatise of this work. They are accordingly under a universal obligation of service to the blessed Creator. This consists of obedience to all the rational laws observed by Adam, Enoch, Noah and his sons, Job and his companions, up to the days of our teacher Moses, peace be upon him. If one adheres to all these laws for the sake of G-d's service, the Almighty will bestow on him favors beyond those enjoyed by other men, and give him a higher degree in this existence and a great reward in the World to Come, as was the case with Abraham, to whom G-d said, "Do not fear, Abraham; I am your shield (in this world - *PL*); your reward is exceedingly great (in the next world - *PL*)" (Bereishis 15:1). But one who rebels against G-d, despite His beneficence, will fall from the degree of rational beings and their excellencies, sink to the low condition of irrational creatures and share the fate of the beasts of the earth, as it is said: *"And the enemies of the L-ord shall be as the fat lambs (they shall be consumed; into smoke shall they be consumed)"* (Tehilim 37:20). And in the next world they will be sentenced to an evil of which there is none greater, as it is said: *"As to your spirit - fire shall devour you"* (Yeshaya 33:11).

(*Pas Lechem*: "share the fate of the beasts of the earth" - his matter will be like the animals. i.e. even though you may see him at a time of success, nevertheless, they are being well fed and fattened up to prepare them for slaughter.

Marpe Lenefesh: "an evil of which there is none greater" - for just like we understand that the good of the next world is unimaginable and incomparable. So too, we can imagine that its evil also is incomparable. For, if even in this world there are many troubles and evils, and sufferings - all the more so for one who has incurred the wrath of the great King, the King of kings, the holy One BB"H. How many great evils will befall him of which there are none worse.)

The second division consists of G-d's special goodness to one people among the peoples, one nation among the nations, as for example, the favors He showed the children of Israel, in taking them out of Egypt and bringing them to the land of Canaan. Thus He put them under an obligation of service, additional to the universal service which we have mentioned. This consists in obedience to the authoritative commandments (Divine precepts received by Moses, the reason of which is not clear), after He had exhorted them and aroused them concerning the rational moral duties (which reason can deduce such as honor your mother and father, don't steal, etc).

(*Marpe Lenefesh*: "authoritative commandments" - (literally "heard" commandments) these are the statutes which were made known by "hearing" (prophecy). This is what the verse says (Devarim 16:12) "And you shall remember that you were a slave in Egypt: and you shall observe and do these statutes". This verse was said regarding the holiday of Shavuot to teach that only the "statutes" (Chukim-commandments without rational explanation) were new in the giving of the Torah.)

Whoever assumed the service for the glory of G-d was favored by the Almighty with special bounties, for which he was under an obligation of additional service beside the service due from his nation and the rest of his tribe, as Moses said: *"Whoever is on the L-ord's side? Let him come unto me. And all the descendants of Levi gathered themselves together unto him"* (Shemot 32:26). G-d showed them additional favor and then chose from among them Aaron and his sons to minister to His glory. He charged the Levites with special precepts in addition to those he gave to the rest of the nation, and promised them a great reward in the life hereafter. But whoever of them rebels against the exalted Creator, will fall from both these degrees of excellence and be punished in both worlds; as the wise man says: *"But it shall not be well with the wicked, neither shall he prolong his days"* (Koheles. 8:13).

(*Tov Halevanon*: "whoever assumed the service for the glory of G-d" - i.e. even the commandments which the intellect obligates, if he assumes them also because G-d commanded them in addition to because the intellect obligates them - his reward is greater, similar to what our Sages said (Avoda Zara 3a) "one who is commanded and does is greater than one who is not commanded and does...", and even greater is one who fulfills G-d's torah because they are G-d's commandments and dedicates his life on this as we find by the tribe of Levi.

Marpe Lenefesh: "whoever assumed the service for the glory of G-d" - i.e. both torahs, the authoritative precepts and those which the intellect obligates - if he assumed them for G-d's glory alone, not for his own needs, and therefore, he fulfills them with all his heart and soul, as the Levites did, to endanger their lives in order to exact revenge on the sinners [of the golden calf].)

The third division is the special goodness of G-d to a certain family among the families of the nations, such as the appointment of the priesthood and the Levites, as also the succession of sovereignty conferred upon the house of David. In return for this, He charged them with additional duties, of which those assigned to the priests and Levites are known and clearly set forth in the book of G-d's law, the Pentateuch. The specific law applying to the House of David is thus set forth: *"O house of David, thus says the L-ord, execute judgment in the morning; and deliver him that is spoiled out of the hand of the oppressor"* (Jeremiah 21:12). One who completely fulfills these duties, because he loves to please G-d, will be singled out by the Almighty for happiness here and a great reward hereafter. He will be a distinguished nobleman or a teacher of righteousness, as the Scripture says concerning Pinchas, *"Then stood up Pinchas and executed judgment and the plague was stayed. And that was counted unto him for righteousness unto all generations for evermore"* (Ps. 106:30-31). Further, *"But the priests, the Levites, the sons of Zadok that kept the charge of My sanctuary...[They shall come near to Me to minister unto Me]"* (Ezek. 44:15). But whoever among them rebels against G-d falls from those highest degrees in this world, and will suffer severe pain in the world to come, as you know from what befell Korach and his company.

(*Tov Halevanon*: "But whoever among them rebels against G-d" - i.e. of the family which G-d has bestowed special goodness above the rest of the nation, and it was proper for them to increase service for this. But instead, on the contrary, they rebelled against G-d, their punishment will be greater.

Pas Lechem: i.e. the special goodness itself was the source of their rebellion like Korach and his company that through his wealth and distinguished lineage, he rose up against Moses.)

The fourth division is G-d's goodness to an individual, by which he has been singled out from the rest of his family and people and other rational beings, as for instance, one chosen to be either a distinguished prophet, a leader appointed to govern a nation or a Sage whose spirit G-d has awakened and endowed with wisdom, understanding, counsel and similar qualities. For every one of these bounties, he is under the obligation of additional service of G-d. He who performs this service in full measure unto him will these gifts - general and special - be continued in this world, and G-d will increase his power over them and understanding of them, as it is said, *"The L-ord has sworn unto David in truth-he will not depart from it, of the fruit of your body, I will set upon your throne. If your children will keep My covenant and My testimony that I shall teach them, their children shall also sit upon your throne for evermore"* (Ps. 132:11-12). The reward in the world hereafter is indicated in the following verse: *"unless I had believed to see the goodness of the L-ord in the land of the living"* (Ps. 27:13).

But whoever [among these who] rebels against G-d, despite the beneficence which G-d has specially bestowed upon him, will fall from all these degrees, and the Creator will hold him more strictly to account in this world, as it is said, *"... this is it that the L-ord spoke, saying, I will be sanctified in them that come near Me, and before all the people I will be glorified. And Aaron held his peace"* (Lev. 10:3); furthermore, *"You only have I known of all the families of the earth; therefore I will punish you for all your iniquities"* (Amos 3:2). His punishment in the next world will be more severe, as it is said: *"For Tophet (Gehinom) is ordained of old; yea, for the king it is prepared; He has made it deep and large. He makes great with fire and wood. The breath of G-d kindles it, like a torrent of brimstone"* (Isaiah 30:33).

> (*Pas Lechem*: *"for the king it is prepared"* - i.e. that the Gehinom's fire was made deeper and wider for the king than the rest of the wicked individuals like him of his nation. Because since he was the king, singled out for benefits, his sin is exceedingly great. Therefore, his downfall and punishment will be greater for his wickedness.)

According to the above four divisions, human beings are under obligations to serve G-d. Whenever G-d increases His beneficence to an individual, that individual is under an obligation to render additional service for it. This is illustrated by the following examples. It is a duty to tithe produce, as it is written, "You shall tithe all the yield of your seed that comes from the field year by year" (Deut. 14:22). One to whom G-d has given one hundred kur of produce is obliged to give ten kur; one to whom G-d has only given ten kur has to give one kur. If the former were to separate nine and a half kur and the latter were to separate one kur, the former would be punished, while the latter would receive a reward.

> (*Marpe Lenefesh*: "it is a duty to tithe" - it is written in the Shl"a and the book "Kenei Chachma", that this is not only for produce, but rather for all good a person receives, he is under duty to tithe it. And from all profit that G-d bestows on a man, he is obligated to give one tenth to the poor. Since, behold, the forefathers took on themselves to do this as written: "he (Abraham) gave him one tenth of everything" (Bereishis 14:20) and "of all that you give me I will give a full tenth to you" (ibid 28:22), and "put Me to the test, says the L-ord of hosts, if I will not open the windows of heaven for you and pour down for you a blessing until there is no more need" (Malachi 3:10). Since this mitzvah is lax in our times, it is proper to remind and make known its importance. Here is an excerpt from the book "Yesh Nochalim" (ch.2 ot 30) and the Sefer Chareidim siman 144: "woe to those who refrain from giving their maaser, for in the end nothing will remain in their hands except the one tenth. This is something tangibly visible for in the places where people were careful to take maaser properly, they became wealthy and their wealth stayed by them until they bequeathed it to their children. While in those places where people were not careful in this, they lost their wealth through some calamity and bequeath nothing to their children see there and the book Kenei Chachma at length.)

So, too, if a man has no son, the obligation of circumcising and teaching his son Torah does not apply to him. If a person is lame, the duty of going to Jerusalem for the three festivals is not obligatory for him. When a person is sick, the precepts which he is unable to fulfill are not binding upon him. Analogously, if a person has been singled out by the Creator for special beneficence, he is under an obligation to increased service for it.

Hence, the saints in ancient times, when some good fortune happened to them, were troubled in two respects: First, that they should not fall short in the complete fulfillment of the service and gratitude they owed for this good fortune and that it should not turn into evil for them, as our ancestor Jacob said, "I have diminished from all the mercies, and truth which You have shown unto Your servant" (Gen. 32:11); secondly, that it should not be the Creator's reward for their service, and thus their reward in the world to come would be diminished, as the ancients explained the text, "And repays them that hate Him to their face to destroy them (in the afterlife)" (Deut. 7:10). This will suffice on this theme.

The Soul: I have understood all that you have mentioned. But I do not feel myself able to repay the Creator with services in return for His bounties, not even for those all men enjoy, much less for those with which He has specially favored me. And when it is my wish and desire to fulfill the service which it is my duty to render for them, before I have even completed forming the resolution, the hope of a future reward enters my thoughts.

> (*Tov Halevanon*: i.e. when I wish to serve G-d for the good He has bestowed on me, immediately, I start to think that I will do this service and repay G-d so that He will bestow on me additional future benefits as reward for this repayment.
>
> *Pas Lechem*: Immediately, it enters my mind that my aim and intent in doing this deed, is in order to receive potential reward in the future due to this act of service.)

And so it is with my gratitude to G-d; when I thank Him, I thank Him for His great goodness to me in words but my thought and intent is the wish that the reward may be continued and increased. I am not like the one who renounced all expectation of an increase of the reward or its continuance. And if I behave in this way in my service and gratitude to G-d, with so little of clear intent to fulfill my obligations for His universal goodness, how will I ever be able to fulfill the rest of the service I owe to Him for bounties with which He has specially favored me? I therefore need that you should teach me the minimum of service that it is my duty to render for these favors, so that I may be worthy of their continuance.

> (*Marpe Lenefesh*: It would be proper for my intent in my service and rendering of thanks to make my heart renounce future benefits. Namely, that even though G-d will not give me anything, nevertheless, I am under obligation to render thanks for the past. Because all the while that my intent is to increase benefits, I am like one who serves in order to receive reward, thereby doing it only for my own honor.
>
> *Pas Lechem*: "*I thank Him for His great goodness to me in words but my thought and intent*" - in my words, one can hear only thanks on the past which He already bestowed. This is proper. However, I recognize my lacking - that my main thought and intent in the thanking is to seek the continuance of this good, i.e. that this good will continue and maybe even that it will increase more.
>
> "*I am not like the one who renounced..*" - in truth, a man needs to direct his mind to make his heart abandon the desire for increased or continuance of

good as before. Then his heart will be perfect in intent of thanking only for the past. Behold, he first said *"continue and increase"* and afterwards said *"increase and continue"*, since in both instances he spoke in the way of "not only this but also this" (lo zu afzu). Understand this.

Tov Halevanon: *"with so little of clear intent to fulfill my obligations"* - i.e. what causes me these thoughts is because it appears to my eyes that His benefits to me do not obligate so much service and I can discharge my duty with just a little bit of service.

Pas Lechem: *"therefore teach me the minimum of service"* - teach me a minimum amount whereby I would be fulfilling my duty and this would be considered an acceptable service. Because if you load on me a great amount of service, perhaps it will be too much for me and I will not be able to bear it. But if this is a small amount, I will be assured that I will be able to endure it.)

The Understanding: Your complaint of your scanty devotion in the service of G-d and ingratitude to Him and that the words of your mouth are [hypocritically] those of one who expresses thankfulness, while your purpose is that of a requester, and the wish in your heart is for an increase in the bounty and its continuance - all this is due to three dispositions:

The first is your excessive self-love, and desire to draw for yourself enjoyable things. You do not move a step to the service of the Almighty or for any other purpose without the motive to enjoy pleasures. I have already recommended as the beginning of my course of treatment that you should strive with all your might to keep this evil disposition far from you, and then I may hold out the best of hopes for you.

(*Tov Halevanon*: you forget to thank on the past good for you are constantly preoccupied in seeking future pleasures.

Pas Lechem: you do not take any step in the service of G-d nor help any human being unless you hope to gain some personal benefit from it.

Marpe Lenefesh: you love yourself, i.e. your body, namely, you pursue pleasures, to seek enjoyments in everything. Whether you are working for the next world or for this world, your intent is to have immediate pleasure from this... and (Pirkei Avot) "lust ,etc drive a person out of the world")

The second is that you do not realize the Creator's kindness to you and imagine that you will not obtain His bounty except through your supplication for it, whereas G-d has been good to you in what you know

and in what you do not know, and when you supplicate Him, you do not
consider Who has done all this for you from the beginning. If you would
put away from yourself this idea, your service would be wholly devotional,
your thanksgiving to Him would express your inward feelings (i.e.
wholehearted - *TL*), and your hopes to Him [of benefits] would then be
worthier and more justified.

(*Marpe Lenefesh*: You [mistakenly] think that if you supplicate for
something then you will obtain it but if not, then you won't. You do not
consider that G-d has already bestowed many benefits on you which you do
not even think about or know about. If one would reflect on this frequently,
he would not associate his thoughts in his service or in his prayers on
receiving reward...
alternatively,
Tov Halevanon: *"except through your supplication for it"* - of that which
your heart desires and seeks from G-d, that which appears good to your
eyes and your outlook.
"and in what you do not know" - i.e. even though it appears to your eyes
that the Creator has not benefited you because you do not understand the
good He has done to you in refraining from fulfilling your heart's requests.
This is for your ultimate benefit, which you will obtain in your final end.
The Creator knows that this request [of yours] will have a bad ending.
"who has done all this for you from the beginning" - all these benefits
without your requesting them, and likewise He refrained from granting
your requests in order to benefit you in the future.
"your service would be wholly devotional" - to unload all your needs on
G-d, and thinking that all that He has done to you - it is all for your benefit
according to the decree of His divine wisdom. This is like the saying of one
of our Sages (Taanis 21a) "this is also for the best" and (Berachos 60b) "all
that the Merciful One does, is for the best".)

The third reason is that you neither know yourself nor how to conduct
yourself. You deem yourself deserving of the greatest benefits and you
never cease beseeching G-d for them. And when you obtain any of them,
your mind yearns for something higher. You do not, however, realize that
the exalted Creator deserves the greatest service on your part. When you
render any service, you regard it as a favor granted by you to Him, though
you realize that for all your needs you are dependent on Him and that He
has no need of you.

(*Tov Halevanon*: *"you neither know yourself nor how to conduct yourself"* -
i.e. you do not realize how little is your understanding and how petty are
your merits, and what [little] benefits you actually deserve for your wisdom
(torah study) and deeds.

Marpe Lenefesh: you do not put to heart from whence you came and who you are. You are a petty creature, worm and maggot in your life and in your death. You constantly need the kindness of the Creator while He does not need you or your service.)

If you were to uncover (remove) this blinding folly, study the matter with open eyes and realize that the Creator who created you thinks of you and knows what is good for you and what is not good, better than you do, you would be contented with whatever benefits He bestows upon you, and would render great thanks to Him for them with a perfect heart. Then you would not rest your hope on what disturbs you, and keeps you from recognizing the bounties that you have gotten and from discharging the obligations that you owe to G-d for them.

(*Marpe Lenefesh*: "remove this blinding folly" - that you come to know and understand this, that you do not deserve any good while the Creator deserves the greatest service on your part due to His great favors to you. "thinks of you and knows what is good for you..." - and also you consider that the Creator thinks on you. It appears to me that this point is against the second disposition.
"you would be contented with whatever benefits He bestows upon you" - whether good or bad, little or much - you would greatly thank Him for them and not put your mind to your benefit and gain in all that you do. This point is against the first disposition.)

And it is impossible that you should not attain what you are fit for, when it will become due to you by reason of your service, and not merely because you hope for it and fix your mind on it.

(*Marpe Lenefesh*: if you would remove and divest yourself of these three dispositions certainly you will attain all good things fitting for you due to your service and you would not need to fix your mind and hope on this.

Pas Lechem: "fit for..due to you" - "fit" from your side, that you are more fitting and prepared to receive the good when you understand His kindness. "due to you" - from His side, from the side of His trait of goodness which necessitates bestowing to those worthy of the good.)

CHAPTER 7

In regard to your question as to what is the minimum service of G-d, below which, a person would not be discharging his duty, and which is requisite for the continuance of the Divine bounty, there are ten matters, as follows:

> (*Marpe Lenefesh*: "*In regard to your question*" - of how can I conduct myself in the service of G-d in the minimum way, and even though one is not able to do more, nevertheless this small amount should be with kavana (proper intent). The Understanding answered that there are ten matters which one must conduct himself in. This is the minimum of all levels of service [of G-d] and every human being is capable of fulfilling it.
>
> *Tov Halevanon*: "*which is requisite for the continuance of the Divine bounty*" - i.e. through this service, G-d will not remove His kindness and truth from him.)

(1) One should not use the Divine bounty (G-d's favor) as a means to rebel against G-d.

> (*Tov Halevanon*: to not make the good which the Creator has bestowed on him into a destructive tool to sin with, such as a wise man with his wisdom or a rich man with his wealth. Likewise, not to rebel against his Maker due to the great favors similar to (Devarim 32:15) "But Jeshurun grew fat, and kicked [...then he forsook G-d who made him, and lightly esteemed the Rock of his salvation]")

(2) One should verbally declare G-d's bounty always and also abundantly thank and praise Him in his heart for it, in harmony with his utterances.

> (*Marpe Lenefesh*: to always verbally recall the favors which G-d has bestowed on him.)

(3) The bounty should not seem to him insignificant and small.

> (*Pas Lechem*: "*insignificant*" in quality. "*small*" in quantity.
> *Marpe Lenefesh*: the bounty of G-d should not be insignificant and small in his eyes. Rather, it should be big, important, and cherished.)

(4) He should not ascribe it to anyone beside G-d; and, if it comes through an intermediary (such as another human being or the like - *TL*), he should not thank the intermediary and fail to thank the Creator for it.

(*Marpe Lenefesh*: to not ascribe the good to other people who benefit him and thank only the person because the person is just an intermediary between him and G-d, which G-d has made into an agent. It is proper to thank the human being for his good heartedness and because G-d has brought good through him [since G-d brings good through the meritorious]. But the main thing is to thank G-d because He is the primary Benefactor, and the good comes from Him alone as will be explained in the Gate of Trust.)

(5) He should not pride himself of it, nor think that he obtained it by his own strength and wisdom or by what is fitting for it.

(*Pas Lechem*: that he prides himself that he possesses what is fitting for obtaining that thing therefore he obtained it. i.e. if it is something which needs to be obtained through strength, he will pride himself in his strength and say that his might and strength obtained for him this thing. If it is something obtained through plan and strategy, he will pride himself in his wisdom and say that it is due to his wisdom. Similarly for other things. alternatively,
Marpe Lenefesh: To not pride oneself in them and think "my power and the might of my hand have achieved all these things for me" (Devarim 8:17), or that he says that he is worthy of this due to his good deeds. In truth, all the bounties are a kindness of G-d for a man is not worthy of this as will be explained.)

(6) It should not enter his mind that he can secure its continuance by his striving, and will lose it if he neglects the effort.

(*Marpe Lenefesh*: He should not think that this good will continue only if he exerts himself with all his strength to amass it and guard it but if he neglects it, he will lose it.

Tov Halevanon: if he engages in that good and in its continuance, it will continue by him, but if he abandons exerting himself in it and seeking after it, it will leave him. Rather, he should believe that its continuance depends on the will of G-d and His decree.)

(7) He should not despise one who lacks the bounty and regard himself as better before G-d than that person, since it may be that G-d is trying him in order to expose the evil hidden in his nature, so that his good fortune is actually leading him astray, while everyone who lacks this good fortune is better before G-d than he is.

(*Marpe Lenefesh*: that he should not despise the poor man and think that he is better before G-d than the poor man since he has received many bounties. This is not a proof because perhaps your heart was evil before G-d and other people did not know about it. Therefore, G-d gave you much good and this good will entice you to do bad things in public view. But if G-d had not done this, there would have eventually been a chilul Ha-shem (desecration of G-d's Name). (see next commentary).

Pas Lechem: through this good, his evil thoughts and interior will be exposed. For example, a person whose heart desires illicit relations and he prolongs desiring them and has no fear of G-d before himself. The only thing holding him back from actualizing his desires is that he is poor and lowly, and lacks the means to pay the prostitute. His evil heart is hidden from other people. But when he attains wealth, his evil interior will be exposed, and the Sages said (Yoma 86): "It is proper to publicize the identity of Chanafim (hypocrites) to prevent Chilul Hash-m" [which would result from people learning from the actions of these evildoers posing as Tzadikim and also from people questioning the punishment which comes to them])

(8) His heart should be wholly with G-d in devotion and humility, and if he is not more active in his service than he had formerly been, and does not increase his gratitude and thankfulness, he should at least continue to maintain his standard. In his service he should endeavor to direct his heart to G-d, and prosperity should not cause him to diminish his former [pious] practices, nor disturb him in the effort to increase his devotion to G-d.

(*Pas Lechem*: "he should endeavor to direct his heart to G-d" - that at least for the little service which he is upholding until now, his heart should be with proper intent in it.)

(9) His attention should always be directed to one beneath him in material well-being, not to the one who is above him in this respect. So, too, his gaze should always be fixed on one more zealous in the service of G-d than he is, so that he will strive to rise to the latter's degree; and not on one who is less zealous, so that he may not become proud of his piety and negligent in his duties.

(*Tov Halevanon*: He should estimate himself compared to other people whose bounties are less than his, thereby seeing the kindness of G-d towards him, instead of being jealous of those who have more bounties than him.

Pas Lechem: "proud of his piety and negligent in his duties" - two bad things will befall him by this. One, by seeing his fellow who is more negligent in the service than him, he will become proud in his heart and will say to himself that he is better than them. Two, through this, sometimes when he feels laziness, he will also become lax in his duties saying to himself "it's enough for me to be like him".)

(10) The protracted period during which the Creator overlooks his sins and restrains His anger should not entice him into thinking that he is safe from the Divine wrath, and so may rebel against the Almighty.

(*Pas Lechem*: i.e. this is part of the test and the system of free will granted to man so that it will seem to a man as if he is safe from Divine retribution, therefore his heart entices him to rebel against G-d. But if G-d did not delay the retribution, then a man would greatly fear at all times that the evil inclination is enticing him to sin due to the punishment immediately incurred from a sin and its swift execution. Hence, he would have been forced to guard from sin and would have been without free will.)

For individuals, concerning whom reports have reached us from ancient times, as well as some also among our contemporaries, who were favored by G-d with various bounties and departed from the service of G-d and rebelled against Him, stumbled only because of the erroneous views which I have mentioned to you. This is also clearly set forth in the books of the prophets in every generation. All these faults are detrimental to the service of G-d which we endeavor to expound in this third treatise.

Yet, whoever cannot increase his service of G-d, but is able to undertake what I have set forth for the sake of G-d, will be worthy of a continuance of the good [portion] which has been specially allotted to him. And if this is withdrawn from him, it will be for one of two reasons: either to erase some previous sin or bestow on him in the life hereafter with a reward greater, more precious than, and much exceeding that of which he has been deprived here.

(*Marpe Lenefesh*: For *"G-d does not come with complaints [unreasonable demands] on His creations"* (Avodah Zara 3) but nevertheless a man can take on himself these ten matters mentioned.
"will be worthy of a continuance of the good" - as if to say "I guarantee on this that no damages shall strike his material possessions and he will succeed in all of his ways."
"And if this is withdrawn from him" - i.e. even if sometimes one who fulfills all these ten things, and nevertheless G-d withdraws the bounties from him and his situation reverses, and he is struck with poverty or some other troubles, he should not feel bad because "all that G-d does is for the good". Either through this, G-d will erase his sins in this world, so that they

are not prepared for him in the next world, because there the justice is extremely harsh. Or it is to increase his reward, as the Sages said regarding "chastisements of love" (Berachot 5a), for certainly one hour of the bliss of the afterlife is better than all the life and pleasures of this world. Hence, either way it is good for him...)

CHAPTER 8

The Soul: You have occupied yourself with my treatment and helped my recovery. You have clarified for me, acted generously, and with your luminous mind supervised my treatment and dispelled the darkness of folly that enveloped me. But of the factors that are detrimental to the service of G-d, one still clings to me. If you will relieve me of the pain it causes me and remove the worry it occasions me, I will be delivered from my worst suffering, and will be near a cure of all my afflictions.

(*Pas Lechem*: *"treatment ... recovery"* - *"treatment"* refers to the early stage of healing, before the [physician's] work is finished, while *"recovery"* refers to after the work has been finished. Alternatively, the author's intent is that *"treatment"* refers to internal illnesses while *"recovery"* refers to external wounds. Because a man has internal illnesses in his soul, namely, in matters of emunot v'deot (faiths and outlooks), and external wounds attributed to the soul, namely, [bad] physical deeds.

"relieve me of the pain...remove the worry" - this is the extra [pain] of the wise man over the fool. The fool is compared to an animal, without understanding, which was struck with some pain or illness. It has only the suffering of the sensation of feeling the pain or the illness. This is unlike the wise man, which besides the pain also has the worry of what will be the outcome of this pain or illness, and how much will it pain him before it leaves. This is the meaning of "more understanding more pain" (Eccles. 1:18). Therefore, he specified these two distinctions.

"I will be delivered from my worst suffering" - I will consider it that I have been saved from the worst of all illnesses.

"and will be near a cure of all my afflictions" - for this illness is the root and cause of all illnesses. And when one removes the cause, the effect is automatically removed.)

The Understanding: What is it that troubles you, as you say?
The Soul: I have found in [the sacred] books in reference to the topic of necessity and fate, divine authority and will, that all things created mineral, vegetable, animal and rational being - are in the power of G-d, as it is said: *"Whatsoever the L-ord pleases, that He does, in heaven and on earth"* (Ps. 135:6). Further, *"The L-ord kills, and makes alive: He brings down to the grave and brings up again; the L-ord makes poor and makes rich; He brings low and lifts up"* (I Sam. 2:6-7). *"Who is he that says and it comes to pass, when the L-ord commands it not? Out of the mouth of the most High, proceeds not good and evil?"* (Lament. 3:37). *"I form the light and*

create the darkness: I make peace and create evil" (Isaiah 45:7). "Except the L-ord build the house, they labor in vain that build it; except the L-ord keep the city, the watchman wakes but in vain" (Ps. 127:1). "Vain it is for you to rise up early, to sit up late, to eat the bread of sorrows; for so He gives His beloved sleep" (Ps. 127:2).

(Tov Halevanon: "Whatsoever the L-ord pleases, that He does, in heaven and on earth" - all the changes in the elements and their synthesis occur by the will of G-d.

"The L-ord kills, and makes alive" - hence, life and death of living things also depend on the will of G-d.

"the L-ord makes poor and makes rich, etc." - hence, even the "incidents" on human beings and their benefits depend on Him.

"Who is he that says and it comes to pass, when the L-ord commands it not?" - this includes generally all the events and matters which occur to human beings - it is all from the command of G-d.

"Out of the mouth of the most High, proceeds not good and evil?" - i.e. who is the rational person which can claim that something can happen in the world which G-d did not ordain? i.e. that G-d did not decree that it shall be so.

"Vain it is for you to rise up early, to sit up late, to eat the bread of sorrows" - i.e. the workers will rise up early in vain to their work, and even so, at night they will eat their bread in sorrow.

"for so He gives His beloved sleep" - to those who deprive themselves of sleep to toil in torah, the Holy One will give them their livelihood in abundance. From here, we see that G-d rewards human beings according to their good deeds.)

There are many passages to the same effect, all of which indicate that the Creator formed man and other living creatures to fill the world. When they move, they are moved by His permission, His power and His ability. When they rest, it is because He ordains that they shall rest, as it is said, "When He gives quietness, who then can make trouble?" (Job 34:29). "You hide Your face; they are troubled. You take away their breath; they die and return to their dust" (Ps. 104:29). And all the sayings of the ancients in every book indisputably agree in this.

(Tov Halevanon: "the Creator formed man and other living creatures to fill the world" - to guide the world according to His wish, they are all forced according to His decree.

"they are moved by His permission, His power and His ability" - on those which move by will, namely, animals and humans, the author wrote "permission", i.e. that they take permission from Him to do according to their will. The intent of this is that G-d's will is the underlying force which moves and stirs their will. On the growing things (plants, bacteria, etc. which grow without will), he wrote *"His power"*. On the inanimate things where movement is contrary to its nature, since the nature of inanimate objects is to rest and be still, and G-d moves mountains with His might and shakes the ground from its place, it is proper to use the term *"ability"*, as it demonstrates His ability and might.)

We find, however, in the book of the Torah a contrary view, namely, that a human being's visible acts are in his own power. He can choose then as he pleases. They are effected by his choice and free will and he is accordingly liable to reward or punishment for service and transgression respectively, as it is said, *"See, I have set before you this day life and good, and death and evil"* (Deut. 30:15). *". . . therefore choose life"* (Deut. 30:19). *"Through your hands this has come"* (Malachi 1:9). *"For according to a man's act, He requites him"* (Job 34:11). *"A man's folly perverts his way"* (Prov. 19:3). Everything in our religious literature, whether it be instruction, precept or moral exhortation, demonstrates this view. And whatever is there set forth concerning reward for service, and punishment for transgression, indicates that a human being's acts are left to himself and that the Divine glory does not interfere in his prosperity or in his ill-fortune, in his righteous deeds or in his perversities.

(*Pas Lechem*: *"a contrary view"* - since one cannot instruct, command, or rebuke, one who is forced in his deeds.)

This is hard for me to grasp, and to reconcile the contradiction of these two views is exceedingly difficult. If there is a remedy for this difficulty which troubles me sorely, may G-d relieve me through your aid.

The Understanding: The difficulty you state of reconciling these two contending conceptions, found in the books, is no greater than that of solving the contradiction found in observing life's actual experiences. For we see that a human being's activities are sometimes in accordance with his thoughts and desires and sometimes they are against his wish and intent.

These differences show you that the exalted Creator has control over a human being and that the latter is bound by the Almighty who permits him to do only what He wishes and prevents him from doing what He does not wish. This is also apparent in the function of speech, hearing and sight. And, on the other hand, I see that reward and punishment come to a human being; that he is rewarded and punished according to his deeds and movements either in serving G-d or rebelling against Him.

(*Marpe Lenefesh*: You wonder at the contradictions in scripture on this matter, but you do not wonder that you can see this tangibly by mere observation that these two things contradict each other.

Sometimes, a man is able to accomplish all that his heart wishes and no one can hold him back. While for some matters and some times, he cannot perform things the way he wishes, and many times things happen against his wishes. From this you can see and observe that man is under the chains of G-d, and G-d has total control over him like the pottery in the hands of the potter. If G-d wants, He will grant him the ability of free will and sometimes, G-d holds back and blocks his free will if He does not want this thing [*Rabbi YS*: G-d will put thoughts/decisions in his mind].

Pas Lechem: "*a human being's activities are sometimes in accordance with his thoughts and desires and sometimes they are against his wish and intent*" - sometimes things turn out like his thoughts and desires while other times, they turn out against his wish and intent. Behold the author changed the terms. He first said "*thoughts and desires*", that it turned out perfectly according to what he wished from the beginning, and so he may pride himself and consider himself a wise man, who sees the long term consequences and predicts the future, and it all turned out perfectly according to his best wish. Then the author wrote the extreme opposite "*against his wish and intent*" - that it did not at all turn out as he intended, and the result is completely against his wish. Understand this.

Translator: perhaps the author refers to periods of time, i.e. some periods of time a person has one success after another, while other periods it is the opposite.)

Controversies have long raged among the learned as to the modes of reconciling the issue between necessity and righteousness (divine decree vs free will).

(*Pas Lechem*: he called free will "righteousness" because it is through free will that a man can be called righteous. Unlike if his actions were through "necessity" [i.e. divine decree])

Some say that all human activities proceed according to man's will, capacity and strength; that G-d has left the conduct of these affairs in a man's own hands, and given him control over them. And since the Divine glory does not interfere in these, therefore a human being is liable to reward and punishment for them.

(*Tov Halevanon*: the Moray Nevuchim mentions this view in part 3 ch.17 in the name of the group of Metozla which are non-Jews who maintain that the acts of G-d follow His trait of wisdom while the bad we see follow His trait of kindness only that we do not understand His ways of beneficence. Likewise, the good we see by the wicked is really bad according to the divine decree. They maintained that the primary reward and punishment is in the next world....)

Others ascribe all human actions, like everything else, to the Creator, blessed be He, and say that every movement in the universe from that of a rational being to that of an inorganic body, is in the control of the Creator, takes place by His decree and compulsion, and which cannot be varied by as much as a hair's-breadth, neither more nor less.

When, against this view, the justice of reward and punishment was questioned, they replied, "We have no knowledge on the subject of reward and punishment; we do not know its form nor the way it is enforced. G-d, however, is righteous and will not do any iniquity. He is faithful in awarding recompense and retribution as He appointed them, and will not depart from His rules. Our minds are too feeble to grasp His infinite wisdom. His righteousness is too apparent, His loving kindness too evident, that we should cast suspicion on His decisions, and there is no G-d beside Him.

(*Tov Halevanon*: the Moray Nevuchim also mentions this view in part 3 ch.17 in the name of the group of Ashria which are arabs... they hold that even though man is forced in all his deeds, nevertheless, G-d gave man the torah to command them despite that man does not have the ability to fulfill it and it is possible that G-d commanded us on the impossible... and according to this view, it is possible, that one who fulfills the commandments will be punished, while one who transgresses them will be rewarded. This is indeed a disgraceful view.)

Some find it possible to accept both principles - necessity and righteousness. They say that one who goes deeply into these subjects will not escape sin and will stumble, in whichever way he apprehends them. They therefore assert that the proper course to follow is to act on the principle of one who believes that actions are left to a human being's free will, who will therefore be rewarded or punished for them, and that we should strive for all that will avail us with the Creator in both worlds. At the same time, we ought to trust in G-d with the trust of one, fully convinced that all things and movements, together with their advantageous and injurious results happen by the decree of the Eternal, under His authority and according to His sentence, and that G-d has a victorious claim upon us while we have no claim upon Him.

Of all the views that we have mentioned this is the nearest approach to the way of salvation. For honestly and in truth, we must confess our ignorance on this topic which refers to the wisdom of the Creator, because our knowledge is too weak, and our comprehension too limited. This ignorance is one of the various forms of divine beneficence; it is for our good that knowledge is hidden from us. If there had been any advantage to us in understanding this mystery, the Creator would have revealed it to us.

(*Tov Halevanon*: i.e. that the reward comes from good deeds, and punishment from committing bad deeds and rebelling against G-d. This is contrary to the view of the Ashria who maintains the reward and punishment is only from the will of G-d [*Rabbi YS*: since according to them a human being is always forced by the will of G-d].

"in both worlds" - i.e. even though we see a wicked person prosper in his wickedness while a righteous man is destroyed in his righteousness, it should not be difficult to us, since we believe that the primary reward and punishment is in the next world.

[Overview of the book of Job:]

"at the same time...all things.. happen by the decree of the Eternal" - like the second view. And that nothing is hidden from G-d as Elihu said: "For His eyes are upon the ways of man, and He sees all man's steps; There is no darkness, nor shadow of death, where the workers of iniquity may hide themselves" (Job 34:21-22). And this is what took Job out of the trap of his error, that due to the question of necessity versus righteousness, and pre-knowledge versus free will, he almost turned the plate upside down, to claim that G-d left the universe and does not supervise over this world. The view of Eliphaz HaTemani is the view of our torah, only that he did not know how to answer these questions. Therefore, he steadfastly maintained that it is impossible for man to be punished unless he sinned. The view of Bildad HaShuchi is the view of the Metozla we mentioned. The view of Tzofat HaNaami is the view of the Ashrias. Job debated with them until Elihu enlightened the eyes of all of them and answered them like the author mentioned, as I will explain. (see also Moray Nevuchim Part 3 ch.23).

"G-d has a victorious claim upon us while we have no claim upon Him" - i.e. the human mind has no ability whatsoever to forward a claim against G-d. Because His scope of vision is not like ours, His guidance of His creatures is not like the guidance we utilize for ourselves, His wisdom is not like ours, and there is no comparison whatsoever between them... and as scripture says "For as the heavens are higher than the earth, so are My ways higher than your ways, and My thoughts than your thoughts" Isaiah 55:9)

A close analogy we can observe in the case of a person with weak eyes, who cannot enjoy the light of the sun without putting on a thin veil to protect his eyes. The more the eyes are impaired, the thicker the veil which he needs to aid his sight. When the impairment lessens, a thinner veil is suitable for him.

(*Tov Halevanon*: so too due to our weak power of apprehension, G-d placed a veil, i.e. the secret, between our understanding and the wisdom behind His providence so it may be easier for us to approach His service. And the more our intellect strengthens, the more we will understand this secret.)

Furthermore, we note in regard to a large number of physical occupations, that if we did not behold them with our own eyes, and only knew of them by report, we would right away declare the reporter a liar. Take for instance, the astrolabe (a measuring instrument formerly used by astronomers). If we had never seen this instrument with our eyes but someone had told us of its form and appearance and what can be apprehended by its use concerning the movements of the spheres, the positions of the stars, the precise determination of each of the seasons, the distances between stars and many other facts that would otherwise be unknown to us, we would have no clear conception of it, nor could we form a picture of it in our minds.

The same is the case with a thing we are more familiar with, which belongs to tools which many men use - the fulcrum scale.
[*Rabbi YS*: a scale like: -|-^-----|- where one side is longer than the other.]

For were it not that we apprehended it with our sense of sight, we could not possibly deem it conceivable that one could truly weigh with a balance scale one of whose parts is longer than the other. And what is still more surprising is that on this balance and by means of a single stone, many objects, varying in weight, can be weighed, some of these weighing more, others weighing less than the single stone.

A thing that people use still more is the upper millstone which the water causes to revolve regularly by a slight contrivance. When we cast a small stone into a swift current of flowing water, it does not stay on the surface for a single moment, but sinks to the bottom, while the millstone is many times heavier than the stone and the force of the water by which the mill is set in motion is much less than that of the current. If any one had told us this and we had not seen it with our own eyes, we would have quickly denied and rejected his statement.

All this is because we know so little of the secrets of nature and because our faculties are too limited to recognize the fundamentals of created things and their results, their natural constitution and special forces. Since a person is so ignorant, as we have shown, in regard to a familiar thing which he constantly handles, it is not surprising that he does not comprehend the divine decree and the righteousness of the exalted Creator's judgments, these being hidden and infinitely exalted beyond all that we have stated.

On a similar topic, David, peace be upon him, said, *"L-ord, my heart is not haughty, nor did I lift up my eyes . . ."* (Ps. 131:1). And he adds in the next verse, in regard to submission to G-d, *"Surely I have stilled and quieted my soul, like a weaned child with his mother; my soul is with me like a weaned child"* (Ps. 131:2).

(*Pas Lechem*: Behold even though the author seemingly brought this verse incidentally, come and see, and be amazed, how each verse of this Psalm corresponds one-to-one to each of the points raised by the author:
"L-ord, my heart is not haughty" - to attribute the free will to myself, and to think that my choice is released and depends only on my free will. G-d forbid, I do not hold this arrogant view.
"nor did I lift up my eyes" - i.e. likewise, G-d forbid, for me to lift up my eyes to heaven, and to attribute all of my actions and movements to You, and claim that I am forced in them. Hence, I do not hold of either extreme view.
"Nor do I involve myself in great matters, Or in things too high for me" - Likewise, I know that I am incapable of distinguishing between "necessity and righteousness". These are the words of the author for "one who goes deeply into these subjects will not escape sin and will stumble". He wrote *"great matters"* corresponding to their magnitude. And *"too high for me"* corresponding to the concealment of their essence.
"Surely I have stilled and quieted my soul" - i.e. you know and can testify that I indeed conducted myself like this.
"stilled and quieted" - *"stilled"* means strengthened myself such as "I stilled myself until the morning" (Isaiah 38:13). i.e. I took on myself to hold on to both views - in some of them I strengthened myself and told myself "See now that I, even I, am he, and there is no G-d with me" (Deut. 32:39), for G-d left the free will in my hands. Namely, in matters of [doing good] deeds. As the author wrote earlier "the proper course to follow is to act on the principle of one who believes [that actions are left to a human being's free will, who will therefore be rewarded or punished for them]". While in other matters I *"quieted my soul"* anticipating G-d's will, namely in matters of Bitachon (trust in G-d). As the author wrote "At the same time, we ought to trust in G-d with the trust of one, fully convinced [that all things and

movements, together with their advantageous and injurious results happen by the decree of the Eternal]". This is the meaning of the term *"quieted"*, and this term is used in scripture regarding Bitachon (trust) such as "wait quietly for the salvation of the L-ord" (Eicha 3:26) and "Wait for the L-ord and hope for Him" (Ps. 37:7).

Afterwards, he clarified his words in saying *"like a weaned child with his mother"*, that in being on his mother's breast, he is entirely dependant on her will. But after he has been weaned, his matters are dependant on both his will and her will. Namely, to fulfill his needs, he must engage himself to walk with his feet to the place of food and to take it with his hand and place it in his mouth, and likewise to put on clothing. But he is still lacking the ability to obtain his needs independently . Therefore, he must place his trust in his mother, that she will provide for him. This is the meaning [of the double expression]: *"like a weaned child with his mother; my soul is with me like a weaned child"*. Namely, that for matters of bitachon *"like a weaned child with his mother"*, while for others, namely doing good deeds, *"my soul is with me like a weaned child"*, that it depends on me. The Psalm ends with bitachon (Trust) which is the foundation of Judaism, and its perfection, saying "Let Israel hope in the L-ord from this time forth and forever".)

CHAPTER IX.

The Soul: You have comforted me in having made me give up the hope of ever fathoming the mystery of this subject because of its subtlety and depth. But reveal to me the mystery of my existence in this world, its aim and purpose.

> (*Tov Halevanon*: even though you said it is impossible to fully understand this mystery, nevertheless, help me to understand a bit so that I may grasp some understanding of it. And just like your analogy of the sun, where if one's eyes are not so weak, it is enough for him a thin veil to protect his eyes. So too, perhaps I do not need to be completely ignorant of this knowledge.)

And give me, as well as you can and briefly, some approximate conception of necessity and righteousness, so that the same should not happen to me as happened to a king who, as I learned, did not appreciate the various aspects of his good fortune. The story is that in one of the Indian islands, there was a state, the citizens of which decided to appoint over them every year a stranger as a ruler; and when the year had elapsed, they would banish him and he would have to return to the status he had had before he had been appointed over them. Among those elected, one was a fool who knew nothing of their secret plans in regard to him. He accumulated much money, built palaces which he fortified, and sent nothing out of their country. On the contrary, whatever he had outside the state - his money, his wife and children, he brought into it. And when the year was ended, the citizens sent him out, stripped of all his possessions, and deprived of all that he had built or acquired before he entered office up to the time he relinquished it. And so when he left, he had nothing of what had belonged to him in the city and outside it. He grieved and regretted the trouble he had taken and the efforts he had expended on the edifices he had erected and the treasures he had accumulated and which now would go to another person.

Afterwards, the citizens decided to appoint as their ruler a stranger who was wise and understanding. After he had been appointed, he selected a person to whom he showed kindness and inquired of him the customs of the people and their laws which they had observed with reference to the one who had preceded him in office. The favorite revealed to the new ruler their secret plan and what they intended to do to him. When he learned this, his activities took a different turn to those of his predecessor. He strove and labored to take everything valuable in the country to the land where he had placed all his other treasures. He did not trust his subjects' exaltation of him nor the honor they showed him. During the whole time he stayed in their country, his mood was in between grief and joy. He was grieved that he would soon have to leave the people, and that the treasures he could bring out were in his estimation, so few. If he could have remained longer, he would have been able to bring out more. But he was glad that he would soon leave and be able to settle in the place where he had put his treasures and would be in a position to use and enjoy them in various ways, with a quiet mind, confident spirit and uninterruptedly.

And after his year was up, he was not troubled at leaving, but prepared for the event speedily, calmly and joyously, with approval of his work and diligence. He was going to great good fortune, honor and enduring joy. So he had happiness in both positions and attained his wishes in both places.

I fear, however, that what happened to the fool who wearied himself in both matters and lost out in both places, may happen to me. Since G-d has favored me in sending you to be my advisor, please instruct me and show me my position and tell me all you know in regard to the mystery of my being and the ways in which it should be improved.

(*Marpe Lenefesh*: This is a powerful parable on a human being, who is here now and tomorrow in the grave. Not only does he accumulate money and builds here as if he will live forever, but even what he has there, namely, the torah and mitzvot which he should have received reward for in the next world, he does them in order to receive reward in this world, namely, for honor and [worldly] benefits. Therefore, he received his reward for them in this world like he wished. And when he is lowered in the grave, he will be destitute here and with nothing in his hand for there. Then too the regret he will feel will be of no avail. But the wise king, when he realized the truth, did the opposite, etc. So too, a wise man, everything he does in this world, even for things of his body and benefit, which people deem valuable - he leaves them there, namely, he does everything l'shem shamayim (with wholehearted devotion to G-d). Hence, he will find his reward in the next world, and there he will delight in them. Therefore, he is always joyful, whether in this world or in the next.

Tov Halevanon: "*who wearied himself in both matters and lost out in both places*" - First that he wearied himself in hoarding money and to build buildings in that country which he left to another person. Two, his leaving the country naked and destitute, and his remaining days were impoverished and barren.

Pas Lechem: The fool who did not know their secret, did not eat well even in the time of his reign. Even at night, he did not rest because he was busy and troubled in the matters of the country, to build palaces and towers, and other fortifications. This is the way of kings, to engage heavily at first in fortifying the country so that he can sit afterwards in peace and quiet. Hence, the fool lost out in both places while the wise man reached his desire in both.)

The Understanding: In the parable you related, you have already given a picture of your state in this world and shown that your situation therein is like that of the kings you mentioned. You clearly realize that you are a stranger here and will soon depart from it. You should therefore act as the wise and understanding ruler did, so that the outcome in your case may be like his. Should you deviate from this course, my words will be of no use to you, my fine language will bring you no advantage.

The Soul: If I had no desire in the matter, I would not have troubled to investigate what is hidden from me in regard to my condition.

The Understanding: The mystery of your being is that the Creator created you out of naught, in common with all spiritual beings that He created; and His purpose is to exalt you and elevate you to the high degree of His treasured ones-the chosen and elect who are nearest to the light of His glory-for your good and as a kindness towards you. But you will only be worthy of this favor when three conditions have been fulfilled:

(*Marpe Lenefesh*: the soul is from the spiritual worlds. It's state was like that of angels (spiritual beings not destined to enter a physical body - Rabbi YS), before it came into this world. Only that they are forced in their deeds, and they stand always at the same level. They have neither reward nor punishment.

"His purpose is to exalt you" - i.e. G-d wanted to exalt the soul and elevate it to a greater level than even the angels. Hence, the author continued "nearest to the light of His glory". For the souls of tzadikim are mamash the [holy] chariot (see Ezekiel 1), and close to the Shechina (divine presence) as the Sages said (Bereishis Raba 47:6) "the forefathers are the chariot". And every human being can reach their level with his deeds. All this is accepted by all the kabalists - that the level of tzadikim is higher than the level of angels. Likewise, it is the view of the author, and the view of Rav Saadia Gaon... See also the end of Shaarei Kedusha and in the Shl"A.)

The first is the removal of the curtain of folly from yourself so that He may enlighten you with the gift of His knowledge.

> (*Tov Halevanon*: to remove from the nefesh bahamit (animal soul) in you the curtain of folly, namely, its animalistic lusts. So that G-d may enlighten you with His wisdom.
>
> *Marpe Lenefesh*: To not be foolish, as in: "Be you not as the horse, or as the mule, which have no understanding" (Ps. 32:9)
>
> *Pas Lechem*: "*enlighten you with the gift of His knowledge*" - He granted you of His knowledge, as our sages said: "[On seeing the Sages of Israel one should say: Blessed be He] who has imparted of His wisdom to them that fear Him" (Berachot 58a). Wisdom is called "light", for "the fool walks in darkness" (Eccl. 2:14), and "wisdom excels folly, as light excels darkness" (Eccl. 2:13). And since He granted of His wisdom to His people, He called them His "treasured people".)

The second is that you be tried and tested as to whether you will choose to serve Him or rebel against Him.

> (*Tov Halevanon*: through this you will be worthy of reward, in that you stood up against your evil inclination and chose good.
>
> *Pas Lechem*: "*tried and tested*" - it is known that the term "*trial*" is from the verse "lift up a banner over the peoples" (Isaiah 62:10). Because through trials the level of the tzadik is elevated. This is G-d's intended purpose in doing this. The term of the actual act of testing is called "*test*". The author first said "*tried*" because the thought preceded the act.
> *Rabbi YS*: i.e. G-d already knows what each person will do. The purpose of the trial is to elevate the person who passes it.)

The third is that He disciplines you in this world by your bearing the yoke of His service, in order to raise you to the degree of the higher beings who serve Him, of whom it is said, "*Bless the L-ord, ye His angels, ye mighty in strength, that fulfill His word*" (Ps. 103:20). All this could not have been possible if you remained in your former state.

> (*Marpe Lenefesh*: G-d sends sufferings and other trials on a man to demonstrate whether he will scorn them or receive them with love and serve G-d with whatever G-d sends his way. Like the forefathers, whose days were full of displacements and sufferings. And likewise, for the pure and straight of every generation, they are in a state of suffering due to this reason - in order to elevate them to a higher level than the angels which are called "*mighty in strength, etc.*" For if man had only good in this world, with what would he be worthy of all this greatness?

"All this could not have been possible if you remained in your former state" - when you were there, in the world of souls, [it was not possible] to do these three things to you.

Alternative explanation,
Tov Halevanon: *"He disciplines you in this world"* - by bearing hard labor, prepared for every human being, as written: "man was born to toil" (Job 5:7).
"by your bearing the yoke of His service" - to subdue your lusts so that you will be suited to take on the yoke of His service.
"ye mighty in strength" - who strongly and mightily serve Him.
"All this could not have been possible if you remained in your former state." - i.e. of utter nothingness.

Pas Lechem: *"by your bearing the yoke of His service"* - G-d's service in this world, is hard as stone and grueling work against the physical nature of man which tends towards physicality [*Rabbi YS*: since torah study has no physical benefit so the body resists it]. But the righteous man bears it. Through this, the righteous weaken the power of their physical side and purify their hearts. G-d refers to them as "pure of heart" (bar levav) just like the grain of wheat, after it has been purified from the waste of chaffs and husks through threshing is likewise called *"bar"*.)

Therefore the exalted Creator, by His wisdom, created for you this world with all that is therein - minerals, plants and living creatures, everything suitably arranged and properly administered - and all for your benefit (everything that was created in this world, it is all for man - *ML*). Out of the finest elements, He chose for you a palace similar to the world in its origin (the human body is a microcosm of the universe - *ML*), foundations, products and form. In this palace he set five gates opening to the external world, and appointed five trustworthy keepers of the gates. Those gates are the organs of the senses - eyes, ears, nose, tongue, hands. The gatekeepers are the five senses which employ these organs, namely, the sense of sight, the sense of hearing, the sense of smell, the sense of taste and the sense of touch, by means of which you are enabled to attain to the knowledge of all that can be useful to you in this world. He also prepared for you in this palace four degrees for the four rulers. These are the brain, the heart, the liver, and the testicles.

Furthermore, He placed four stores for four officers, namely, the faculty of ingestion, the faculty of retention, the faculty of digestion, the faculty of excretion. Their stores and offices are the two galls-black and green, the white lymphatic fluid and the blood.

Within and without this palace, He distributed servants to attend to it and take care of it. Those within are the intestines, veins, sinews, nerves and arteries; those outside are the hands, feet, tongue, teeth, nails and other similar parts.

He furthermore made for you connecting intermediaries between the spiritual and physical, namely, the blood, the natural heat and the life spirit (nefesh bahamit, the animal soul - *TL*). By His wisdom and power He joined you to this palace in a proper and well-ordered union, so that you might fulfill the three requisites which I mentioned to you.

(*Pas Lechem*: "well-ordered union" - i.e. these three intermediaries are intertwined so that through them the soul may be attached to the body. [*Rabbi YS*: for the soul cannot be attached to the body without an intermediary since the physical and the spiritual are total opposites, and cannot be joined, like fire and water and even more so.]
"*three requisites*" - he mentioned earlier. establishing the understanding, the test of free will, and the bearing of the yoke of the service.)

He provided you with two counselors. He appointed for them two scribes. He gave you servants and attendants for your needs in this world.

Of the two counselors the first is the Understanding which points out to you what the will of G-d is. The second counselor is your lust which entices and seduces you to do that which will arouse the anger of the L-ord, your G-d.

(*Marpe Lenefesh*: "two counselors" - the understanding and the lust. I term these the good inclination and the evil inclination. They are for your need, namely, so that you may have free will to follow whichever one you wish.

Pas Lechem "*entices and seduces... the L-ord your G-d*" - Behold the power of the yetzer (evil inclination) which brings a man's heart to sin is of two kinds. One, when a man is hesitant and not keen on doing a bad thing, whether due to fear of G-d or fear of something else. The yetzer comes cunningly and removes the fear from his heart, either by some rationalisation. Therefore he is called in this aspect "mesi" (enticing, literally "lift up") the heart of a man, which connotes lifting up, for he lifts up the man's hesitations.... The second aspect is that he intensifies his lust and warms his heart with imaginitive pictures of the pleasures of that act. Then he is called "seducer" (mesit)... (see there for more).... Now reader, the author ended with the words "*the anger of the L-ord, your G-d*". Certainly, he did not write two Names of G-d for nothing. They correspond to these two aspects. For the first aspect, where one removes the fear of G-d from his heart, he also arouses the wrath of the trait of mercy [the name "L-ord" corresponds to the trait of mercy]. But that which his heart turns towards superfluous lusts, there is room to have mercy on him and say that he is only entangled in the physical and he arouses only the wrath of the trait of justice [your G-d (Elokim) which corresponds to the trait of justice].)

Of the two scribes, one writes down your good deeds, whether done in private or in public, secretly or in the sight of all, through any of those already mentioned whom he placed at your disposition, the gate-keepers, officers, administrators, servants, counselors, attendants and sextons. The second scribe writes down the bad deeds in the same way as we have stated in regard to the good deeds.

(*Marpe Lenefesh*: Every thing that a man does creates something above (in the mystical worlds), whether good or bad, and it is very much as if he wrote it. It is known that a man creates with each deed either a kategor (prosecutor) or kanegor (defender). They [the prosecutors] stand and do not nullify until the man repents. Likewise, the sages said (Pirkei Avot 3:16): *"the shop stands open and the shopkeeper gives credit and the account book lies open and the hand writes..."*. And in the talmud (Taanit 11a) on the verse (Devarim 32:4) "righteous and just is He", the sages said (Taanit 11a): "When a man departs to his eternal home all his deeds are enumerated before him and he is told, 'Such and such a thing have you done, in such and such a place on that particular day'. And he replies, 'Yes'. Then they say to him. 'Sign' - And he signs, as it is written, "He seals up the hand of every man" (Job 37:7). And what is even more, he acknowledges the justice of the verdict and he says. 'You have judged me correctly'...")

The servitors and sextons are the soul's moods and qualities - cheerfulness, anxiety, gladness, joy and grief, memory and forgetfulness, wisdom and folly, courage and timidity, generosity and miserliness, righteousness and wickedness, bashfulness and arrogance, hope and apprehension, love and hate, pleasure and pain, pride and modesty, domination and submissiveness, and many similar dispositions which you use with your inner being.

The blessed Creator appointed these watchmen, leaders and administrators, servants, counselors, servitors and sextons, to listen to you and be ready to do your bidding, up to a definite period, except in certain matters which He explained to them when they were brought into association with you. Those are the matters wherein necessity and the divine decree prevail.

(*Tov Halevanon*: *"except in certain matters"* - i.e. sometimes all your powers are in G-d's hands. He will allow you to do certain things which He wishes and prevent you from doing things which He does not wish. Likewise, for your speech, sight, and other senses. Hence, sometimes G-d completely rules over a person and guides him against his will.

Pas Lechem: *"necessity and the divine decree"* - these servants are the matter of necessity stated regarding man, as you said "whatever G-d wants He does" (Tehilim 135:6), and other verses brought earlier. We asked how this can be reconciled with free will. However, in truth, man does act in accordance with his will and choice, and nevertheless it is correct to say that man's deeds are ascribed to G-d because G-d commanded man's servants to listen to his choice and do his bidding. This is the answer to the big question of the philosophers regarding free will - how is it possible for man's will to be left to his wish and to do things contrary to G-d's will? The answer to them is that this itself is G-d's will - that man be endowed with free will. Hence, it is incorrect to say this is against G-d's will.)

In other words, He gave you liberty to make use of all these aids for the improvement of your physical well-being and to do everything over which the Almighty gave you control and power, but only in certain ways and under certain conditions. These are comprised in the duties indicated by our natural Reason, or that are to be accepted on divine authority (torah), or that are permitted.

G-D'S MESSAGE TO ALL HUMAN BEINGS

And He said to you (i.e. G-d. He warned you before you came into this world, and likewise in this world through the Torah - *ML*): "Whatever I have put into your hands in this world and placed under your control, must not entice you, since none of them can contribute anything to your essential being nor take anything from it; nor will you obtain from any of them either pleasure or pain, for they are only things that incidentally affect your body, externally or inwardly. None of them is necessary for you. Their relation to you is that of the embryonic sack to the new-born baby or the egg-shell to the hatched chick.

(*Pas Lechem*: *"not entice you"* - to follow after them [the lusts].
Marpe Lenefesh: *"not entice you"* - know that all the pleasures you can possibly enjoy in this world - they are only to the body. Your soul has no pleasure or benefit whatsoever from them nor any pain in their absence.

Tov Halevanon: *"none of them can contribute anything to your essential*

being" - i.e. to the rectification of your soul and to your eternal reward.
"for they are only things that incidentally affect your body" - i.e. what
occurs when you eat and drink, namely, the production of blood, flesh, fat.
"None of them is necessary for you" - i.e. for what will be beneficial to you
in your final end.
"Their relation to you.." i.e. even though you are forced to engage in
matters to further your body's welfare, nevertheless, you have no benefit
whatsoever from the body and its powers in respect to your essential being.
The body is like the embryonic sack, or the egg-shell which is needed
incidentally while the embryo is not yet complete. So too your body is
needed only for the duration of your stay in this world so that you may
complete the matter of your soul.)

[G-d continues] "If you will understand and comprehend My intention
towards you (in sending you to this world - *TL*) and the benefit which I
have bestowed upon you, and you choose My service, and keep far from
rebelling against Me in the management of everything over which I have
given you control, I will raise you to the highest of the degrees attained by
My elect and favored ones. I will draw you closer to My mercy and love,
and enfold you with the radiance of My glory. But if you choose to rebel
against Me, I will punish you with a severe punishment and afflict you
with prolonged affliction."

(*Pas Lechem*: *"severe punishment...prolonged affliction"* - regarding bad
deeds, he wrote *"severe punishment"*. The intent is on the acts of
punishment which a man is actively punished by, just like he sinned with
actions, as written regarding sinners "for their worm shall never die, and
their fire shall not extinguish" (Isaiah 66:22). While on refraining from
doing good, he wrote *"prolonged affliction"*. The word *"affliction"*
connotes withholding something good and desirable such as the "afflictions
of Yom Kippur", which are all withholding of desirable things (such as
washing, eating, etc.) Likewise, in truth, on the wicked it is written there:
"behold My servants will eat and you will go hungry.." (Isaiah 65:13), and
"he will not see the good" (Jer. 29:32). Therefore he wrote regarding active
punishments "severe" and regarding afflictions "prolonged". For since, the
affliction is withholding of good, it is not proper to say "severe affliction".
For it is not correct to say this withholding is greater than that one. It is
only proper to use the term "prolonged", namely, that the affliction will be
for a long time. Furthermore, regarding the active punishment, which is
incurred for bad deeds, it is only for a limited time just like his bad deeds
were limited in time. On this it is written: "He does not maintain a dispute
continuously or remain angry for all time" (Ps. 103:9). But for the
affliction, which is withholding [good], it could be, G-d forbid, forever. For
just like he refrained from doing these good deeds, so too he will be

completely withheld from the good, and will never ever merit it. Hence, the intent in the word "prolonged" is on eternity, as they expounded the verse (Kidushin 39b):"you shall prolong your days" (Deut.22:7) - to the world which is eternally prolonged. Hence, it is correct to use specifically the term "severe" for this, and "prolonged" for that. Understand this.)

[G-d continues] "If you are ignorant of the modes in which you should use any of the things which pertain to your service of Me which I have appointed unto you as your duty and obligation, because you are too much occupied with your body and its concerns, with which I test you, I have appointed for you a counselor, wise and faithful. When you ask his advice, he will instruct you. If you ignore him he will arouse you. This counselor is the Understanding. Take counsel with him in all your affairs, for he will recommend you how to employ all your servitors who stand before you, in the right way of serving Me. The reprehensible qualities will be transformed into praiseworthy ones, even as does the wise physician, making use of injurious and even poisonous drugs for the benefit of the body."

(*Pas Lechem*: *"a counselor, wise and faithful"* - these are the two necessary conditions for a counselor whereby one can trust his counsel. One, that he is wise and knows what is good for the asker. Two, that he is faithful to him, and will not betray him by giving him bad advice.

Tov Halevanon: *"Take counsel with him in all your affairs"* - do not do anything before weighing the matter with your understanding, as the wise man said (Prov. 4:26): "Give careful thought to the paths for your feet".)

[G-d continues] "If you will continue to be of this mind, and strengthen your Understanding, and listen to his advice, the scribe who writes down good deeds will count all your permitted (neutral) movements among your good deeds to which they will be added, and all your servitors will help you in My service."

(*Marpe Lenefesh*: *"If you will continue to be of this mind"* - that all your deeds are l'shem shamayim (devoted to G-d). The scribe will count all your movements which are not a mitzvah such as eating, drinking, business dealings, and likewise all other bodily needs - they will be counted as good deeds and you will receive reward for them just like mitzvot since you did them l'shem shamayim (for serving G-d).

Tov Halevanon: since he is coming to purify himself, and sees his entire existence in this world in order to serve his Creator, behold, all the permitted pleasures he partakes of this world will also be counted for him as a mitzvah. For he is rectifying and strengthening his body for the service of the Creator. And likewise, the opposite, if he rebels against G-d with his faculties and chases after his heart's evil lusts, behold all his permitted pleasures will be added to his sins, in that he used his body to rebel the advice of G-d.)

[G-d continues] "But if you dismiss his advice and incline to the view of the second counselor who is in all respects his opponent, and use all the means placed at your disposal as he advises you, then your praiseworthy qualities will become reprehensible, even as the incompetent physician in his ignorance kills patients by his inexpert use of useful medicines. And the scribe, appointed to write down evil deeds will write, down all your permitted (neutral) movements and enter them in the record of your evil deeds, to which they will be added."

(*Marpe Lenefesh*: *"but if you dismiss his advice"* - you discard the advise of the Understanding and listen only to the advise of the lusts, which is the Satan, which is the yetzer hara (evil inclination), who is diametrically opposed to the Understanding.)

[G-d continues] "You will find that your aids, attendants and servitors and everyone with whom you come in contact, are agreeable and carry out your desire and thus you will have increased joy and gladness."

(*Tov Halevanon*: i.e. since you are coming to defile yourself, behold, all the powers and servants of your body will become habituated to lust for the lusts. And all your deeds will entice you to continue in the joy and gladness [in the lusts] they are used to. Day by day, they will lure you into sin, until your nature and body will tend towards and become ingrained to be disgusted by the service of G-d, and as the verse wrote: "Yeshurun became fat and kicked" (Deut. 32:15). And the sages said (Pirkei Avot 4:2): "sin brings more sin." Behold, he hinted here, that even though the free will is in a man's hands, nevertheless, there is an aspect of necessity and fate. For after, he chose for himself the path of righteousness, behold, all his actions and good deeds will pull his nature and force him towards the service of G-d, as the sages said "mitzvah brings more mitzvah". And the opposite, if in the beginning of his choice, he chose evil, behold, his sins will tend the powers and faculties in him toward animalistic pleasures, until they become habit and ingrained in him as second nature, and draw him by force towards more sin, as if he is forced into them.)

(That which I told you that the Creator will count all your permitted (neutral) acts either as good deeds or as bad deed, - *LT*) All this is in accordance with the justice of your Creator. Because, in your innermost thoughts and secret aims and purposes, you chose either to rebel against Him rather than serve Him, or serve Him rather than rebel against Him.

> (*Lev Tov*: Hence you channel your permitted (neutral) acts towards the aim which you chose for yourself.)

For what is open and revealed in you and what is concealed in you, are equally known to Him. He will requite you for all that His omniscience observes in you, though it remain hidden from human beings. For do you not see that a human judge decides according to what has been established before him as fact, whether on the evidence of witnesses or by his own senses. If what was in the mind could be established for him, he would also take that into account in his decision. Since the blessed Creator knows everything equally well, it follows that He judges according to His knowledge, as it is said: *"The secret things belong to the L-ord, our G-d"* (Deut. 29:28).

And when the Creator wishes to arouse you and admonish you, He charges one of the servitors to leave your service; and one or two of your limbs or all of them sicken and become painful for a definite time. If you awake and return to Him, He charges that servitor to return to your service. He heals your body, and it resumes its former function, as it is said: *"Fools, because of their transgression, and because of their iniquities, are afflicted. Their soul abhors all manner of food until they reach the gates of death; Then they cry unto the L-ord in their troubles... He sends His word and heals them"* (Ps. 107:17-20).

And when the days of your trial in this world are ended, the exalted Creator commands all those we have mentioned - gates, gate-keepers, servants and servitors - to depart from you and the bonds and connections between you and your body are severed, and you return to your first state. Your body has no movement and no feeling. It also returns to its first state, as the sage said: *"Dust will return to the earth as it was: and the spirit will return to G-d who gave it"* (Eccles. 12:7) : And then you will be shown the account-books, the record of your deeds and thoughts and what you had chosen and troubled yourself with in your earthly existence; and in accordance with this, will be your requital.

On all this, the Almighty, through His messengers and prophets and His faithful law, has exhorted and warned you, as the sage said: *"Incline your ear, and hear the words of the wise; put to heart my knowledge; . . . for it is pleasant if you keep them within you . . . Have I not written for you excellent things in counsels and knowledge, that I might make you know the certainty of the words of truth, that you might answer words of truth to them that send unto you"* (Prov. 22:17-21).

(*Lev Tov*: *"Incline your ears"* - hearken well.

"and hear the words of the wise" - who teach you My torah, and take on yourself lovingly the yoke of torah and mitzvot.

"put to heart my knowledge" - put to heart that My intent in this is for your benefit, to test you, purify you, and prepare you, so that you will be able to ascend to the highest degree possible.

"for it is pleasant" - it will be blissful for you in the next world.

"if you keep them within you" - when you conduct yourself according to the torah in all your matters of this world.

"Have I not written for you excellent things (literally: triple things)" - see, I have exhorted you through the torah, prophets, and holy writings "in counsels and knowledge".

"that I might make you know the certainty of the words of truth" - the absolute truth of why you came to this world, and what you are supposed to do here. So that you don't come to the world of truth empty handed and shame faced trying to justify yourself with hollow claims. Rather, when you must come give a reckoning before the King of kings,

"that you might answer words of truth to them that send unto you" - you will be able to answer that you fulfilled the mission for which you were sent to this world.

Tov Halevanon: what also comes out of this entire discussion of the Understanding is that even though the existence of man is primarily out of necessity and divine decree, according to what G-d implanted in him of powers and dispositions and to whether they will tend towards the good traits or the bad traits due to each person's particular nature, nevertheless, each person has been granted the ability to choose through his understanding and he can transform his traits from bad to good or vice versa. He will continue this theme in the next chapter. Know it well. For it is all precious words, and it includes all that the great and faithful thinkers deeply inquired into of the matter of necessity and righteousness, and foreknowledge versus free will, and everything that follows from this.)

CHAPTER 10

The Soul: I have comprehended your statement and paid attention to all that you have mentioned. And now I beseech your Honor to expound to me the occasions on which I should make use of my good and bad dispositions - each in such a way that there [in the next world - PL] I shall win praise and commendation for their proper employment.

> (*Marpe Lenefesh*: i.e. which occasions may I employ even bad traits, and even so I shall win praise for them in the next world.)

The Understanding: You possess many dispositions of which I shall briefly mention those that occur to me.

Among these there are two: joy and grief. They are opposites to one another. The proper occasion when joy is in place when you can trust that the pleasure will be everlasting without any mixture of grief, and uninterrupted by mishap. Then you may permit yourself the emotion of joy. The proper occasion for grief arises when something occurs to you that will cause you everlasting and unceasing pain, which you cannot remove nor separate from. Then you may permit yourself the emotion of grief and make use of it.

> (*Tov Halevanon*: "when you can trust that the pleasure" - i.e. the joy of doing a mitzvah, that we should know that through it, we will attain the delights of Olam Haba, a pleasure which is everlasting, without any mixture of grief. This is to exclude the pleasures of matters of this world which swiftly end and are mixed with grief.
> "for grief ... everlasting and unceasing pain" - If you see that your evil inclination overpowers you and you are not able to repel it, that is certainly a lasting pain. It is proper to feel grief. And all the more so, if you actually stumbled in deed - and to find solace in this through repentance.
>
> *Pas Lechem*: the intent is that a person should feel joy by remembering that through his service to the Creator, he is prepared and designated to "gaze at the delight of G-d" (Ps.27:4) and that "light is sown for the righteous" (Ps. 97:11), which is a constant and eternal pleasure which has no mixture of pain, unlike the worldly pleasures.
> "Then you may permit (literally 'release') yourself the emotion of joy" - He used the term "release" metaphorically, that this trait be restrained until you release it when you need it.

"cannot (1) remove nor (2) separate from" - a man can get rid of a trouble in two ways. Either he removes this pain from himself or he separates himself from that painful thing. For example, regarding a fire. He may have the ability to extinguish the fire or to run away from the flames. Hence he wrote here two expressions.

Marpe Lenefesh: If you do a mitzvah, which you trust that through it you may attain an enduring pleasure, namely, the reward of Olam Haba. Release this trait, i.e. to do the mitzvah with great joy as we wrote earlier in chapter 3. For otherwise [the wise man wrote:], "and of joy, what use is it?" (Eccl. 2:2). And the opposite, the proper place to use grief, i.e. sadness, is if an occasion happens that you are forced to commit a sin, that through this you will get enduring pain in Gehinom, it is permitted to use the trait of sadness. Likewise, for the death of righteous people or your relatives, it is permitted to mourn in sadness. But otherwise, sadness is a very bad trait as written in Shaarei Kedusha.

Lev Tov: i.e. a man should not be joyous except in the service of G-d and in fulfilling the torah and the mitzvot because then he is assured that the pleasure he will attain through this in the next world is eternal and will not be mixed with any sadness. But for every other pleasure, a man should not rejoice because it is liable to be mixed with pain and will inevitably cease. Likewise for the trait of sadness, a man should only be sad when he transgresses the will of G-d, because the pain that he will get for this will be everlasting and he will have no refuge from it.)

Among your traits there are other two - fear and hope. Fear is proper when you are in a situation which will lead to a painful situation that will not have a good end and which you have no strength or power to avert.

(*Marpe Lenefesh*: i.e. now you are engaged in some matter, and this matter is a path which leads to another matter which will have a bad ending that you cannot avert. Then, release the trait of fear. Hence, if this is not the case, do not fear and trust in G-d that He will do what is good for you.

Lev Tov: i.e. a man should not fear from what will happen to him in the future, except when he transgresses the will of G-d because then the outcome will be that he will suffer everlasting pain in the next world and his final end will not be good. But for everything else, he should not be afraid. Rather let him trust in G-d that He does only what is good for him. alternatively,
Tov Halevanon: i.e. to fear something which leads him to something eventually painful and which will not have a good end, and that he does not have the ability to avert that painful thing, even though right now it seems proper, as the wise man said: "there is a way that seems right unto a man,

but the end thereof are the ways of death" (Mishlei 16:25). Therefore, one must fear always [to be careful] that his deeds will not result in sin. This is to exclude matters of this world, whereby it is not permitted to fear events. Rather, trust in G-d. On this our sages said (Berachos 60a): "whoever fears is a sinner".

"which you have no strength or power to avert" - i.e. the pain of Olam Haba which is incurred due to sin, and which it is impossible to avert it in any way. [*Rabbi YS*: in Gate 4 he explains that if one did not repent before death, then it is impossible to avert the punishment for sins in the afterlife because the punishment is like a debt which one must pay.])

The occasion for hope arises when you busy yourself with the preliminaries that will bring you good and secure for you bliss with no hindrance to keep you from it, nothing that will separate you from it. And that is when you fulfill the duties which G-d commanded you and the result of which is good.

(*Tov Halevanon*: i.e. hope which is strength and trust - to busy himself in things whose end is the reward of Olam Haba, even though it appears to his eyes that these things will harm his secular affairs, let him hope to G-d that He will shield him.

Marpe Lenefesh: For example, to do your business dealings faithfully, i.e. according to the torah even though this may [seemingly] cause you losses, and trust in G-d that the end of this matter will be good in this world and in the next.)

There are two other emotions: courage and timidity. The right occasion for showing courage is when you meet the enemies of the L-ord, to wage war against them. [Courage is also in place,] to endure all distress and all trials in fulfilling the will of the exalted Creator and of His saints, as it is said: *"Yea, for Your sake are we killed, all the day long; we are accounted as sheep for the slaughter"* (Ps. 44:23). Further, *"Let the righteous smite me; it shall be a kindness; and let him reprove me"* (Ps. 141:5).

(*Pas Lechem*: "courage" - the intent is on courage of heart. While timidity refers to softness of heart.
"when you meet the enemies of the L-ord" - as David said [regarding Goliath]: "For who is this uncircumcised Philistine, that he should mock the armies of the living G-d?" And David put his life at risk, and strengthened his heart to wage war against him.
"bear all distress" - for the trait of forbearance requires courage of heart.
"all distress and all trials.." - bad things happen to a person sometimes to sadden him and make him suffer for his sins, as written (Eicha 1:16) "Look

and see if there is any sorrow like my sorrow..which the L-ord inflicted". And even if he is a tzadik (righteous person), he bears for his generation (to atone for them) like the prophet Yechezkel. Sometimes the intent is to test him.

Marpe Lenefesh: to be strong as a lion, to not transgress the will of G-d, even if this entails enduring many trials, distresses, and humiliations. Likewise, to fulfill the commandments of G-d and the commandments of His saints (the Rabbinical decrees), even though there are many obstructions against you - do not be swayed and endure their difficulties.)

The occasion for timidity arises when you meet those who love G-d, so that you fight neither them, nor those devoted to His service; and that you refrain from standing up against one who rebukes you for your good, as it is said: *"Because your heart was tender and you humbled yourself before the L-ord"* (II Kings 22:19).

(*Tov Halevanon*: i.e. even though you are in a stronger position than he who rebukes and humiliates you, nevertheless humble yourself before him since his intent is to benefit you.

Pas Lechem: *"you refrain (literally: delay) from standing up"* - he used the term *"delay"* since one needs only to delay and be patient. For due to surprise, and lack of deliberation and calmness, a man gets upset at one who rebukes him and stands up against him. But if he delays this, certainly, after time, he will understand that this is foolish and a great sin to pay them back evil for their good intent, and he will change his mind completely regarding standing up against him.)

Among your dispositions there are other two: shame and boldness. Shame is proper regarding rebelling against your Benefactor to His face while you are in His hands, using the good He bestows on you, and while He rebukes you by means of good or evil happenings; or by means of His prophets, as it is said, *"O, son of man, show the house to the house of Israel, that they may be ashamed of their iniquities"* (Ezek. 43:10); and further, *"O my G-d, I am ashamed and blush to lift up my face to You"* (Ezra 9:6).

(*Pas Lechem*: That you be ashamed to rebel against your Benefactor with the very same good that He is bestowing you - the wise man with his wisdom, the rich man with his wealth, the strong man with his strength. *"to His face"* - i.e. before Him, as in "a people who without ceasing provoke Me to anger to My face" (Isaiah 65:3). The author specified 3 aspects 1. to His face, 2. in His hands, 3. while He rebukes you. The first aspect is that he rebels against G-d with the good itself. On that he wrote *"to His face"*.

Secondly, that he knows that he is in G-d's hands, like pottery in the hands of the potter, who can do whatever he wants with it. How could he not be ashamed to rebel against G-d? Thirdly, that G-d already warned him. Therefore, he wrote *"while He rebukes you"*.

Alternative rendering:

Marpe Lenefesh: That you feel ashamed and humiliated when G-d removes the good which He bestowed on you until now. *"to His face, in His hands"* - i.e. even though your Benefactor is eternal and so are His benefits, therefore He has the ability to continue to bestow good to you, and even so, He retracts them from you and no longer wishes to bestow this good to you, then it is proper for you to feel ashamed before Him and to ask yourself why did G-d do this? It must be due to my sins. Then feel remorse and repent completely. And likewise be ashamed when He rebukes you either through good means, i.e. preachers who use good and nice words, or through bad means, namely, sufferings G-d sends on you which are usually measure for measure...)

Boldness is in place when one meets wicked people and transgressors and those who oppose the truth; and to exhort men to do kindness; and to warn people to avoid what is reprehensible. Boldness is proper to shame sinners and rebuke the small and the great, as it is said: *"I have set my face like a flint"* (Isaiah 50:7).

(*Pas Lechem*: *"wicked"* - these are the mufkarim ("free men" i.e. of religious duty) who are deliberate [in their wickedness].

"transgressors" - this refers to those who sin due to their lusts [ex. eats non-kosher meat to save money or out of lust for the food in that restaurant but if everything is equal, he will eat only kosher meat].

"those who oppose the truth" - even though one may not see them committing acts of sin, just that when one hears their words it becomes apparent that they oppose the main principles of the true faith - we must stand up against them.

"to exhort men to do kindness and to warn people to avoid what is reprehensible" - one must also use the trait of boldness and to strive to be a man - to exhort people to do kindness and warn them to refrain from reprehensible deeds. These last two are warnings for how to behave in the future. Afterwards he wrote: *"to shame sinners.."*, that it is proper after he has already warned them privately and they did not heed and they returned to their wickedness, one must rebuke them publicly, to curse them and shame them until they desist from their sins. Thus our sages learned from Nechemia (Moed Katan 16a).

Marpe Lenefesh: even though he wrote in Gate #5 that it is a ploy of the evil inclination to go and shame other people and that this is to induce arrogance, see there at length (ch.5). We must answer that here he is referring to thoroughly wicked people whose wickedness is well known. And likewise, if he is fitting for rebuking them and that his words are heeded. But there it refers to when he does this arrogantly, and also he does not know clearly their wickedness. It appears to me to make this distinction due to the different expressions used here and there.)

So, too, there are two traits - anger and satisfaction. Anger is in place when you see a departure from the way of truth and the rule of righteousness, when falsehood prevails over truth and those who follow it.

(*Pas Lechem*: when you see people turning away from the way of truth, namely, the way of the torah of truth. He wrote *"way of truth"* corresponding to the commandments between man and G-d and the *"rule of righteousness"* corresponding to those between man and his fellow. Behold, earlier regarding the trait of courage, he wrote "when you meet the enemies of the L-ord". There the intent was on the wicked who come to strike out at G-d's torah or His people, as written "For behold, Your enemies stir, and those who hate You raise their heads; Against Your people they plot cunningly, and they take counsel against Your protected ones; They said, 'Come, let us destroy them from [being] a nation, and the name of Israel will no longer be remembered.'" (Ps.83:35). There showing anger to them is not enough. Rather one must stand up against them and foil their plans, as written there. For this one needs courage, which is strength of heart, to be moser nefesh (self-sacrificing) in G-d's war, like David in the war against the Philistines, especially in the battle against Goliath, or like the Chashmonaim in the war against the Greeks. Here he is talking about individuals who are being wicked by themselves, and it is enough to show anger to them, to show them that you disapprove of their deeds, and that their deeds are evil in the eyes of G-d. Through this they will feel ashamed and perhaps they will repent.

Marpe Lenefesh: when people sway from the way of truth and when the falsehood strengthens over the truth. Likewise it is permitted to be angry at people of falsehood [who adopt the ways of falsehood].)

Satisfaction is proper when all things fall in their right direction, when everything is in its right place, always keeping, in regard to them, in the ways of truth.

(*Pas Lechem*: when he sees people acting properly, everything falling in its right direction and in its right place. These three expressions are opposite to the three he used earlier. Corresponding to *"rule of righteousness"*, he wrote *"all things fall in their right direction"*. Corresponding to *"when falsehood prevails over truth"*, he wrote: *"in its right place"*. Corresponding to *"when you see a departure from the way of truth"*, he wrote: *"always keeping the ways of truth".*

Marpe Lenefesh: When all things are done in the good and just way, and each and every person's direction and place will come in peace - this should be your desire and wish.)

So, too, there are two qualities - mercifulness and ruthlessness. The quality of mercy is to be shown to the needy, to the poor and the sick; to those who are leaving the world (ex. awaiting execution -PL); to one who does not realize what is good for him; to one who does not know how to guide himself; to the prisoner who is in the power of his enemy; to one who has lost a great benefit (such as a rich man losing his wealth); to one who regrets his iniquities; to one who weeps for his past sins, out of fear of Divine punishment.

(Pas Lechem : *"needy (dal), poor (ani)"* - the sages counted 7 expressions for the poor man (Vayikra Raba BeHar). Each one applies to a specific aspect. The term "dal" (needy) refers to one whose flesh is scant, with little fat, such as "Why are you becoming so thin, O' son of the king" (Samuel II 13:4). The term "ani" applies to his being submitted, such as "How long will you refuse to humble yourself before Me?" (Ex. 10:3).
"who does not know how to guide himself" - his understanding is not sufficient to guide him in the proper course whether in matters of this world or of the next.
"one who regrets his iniquities, one who weeps for his past sins out of fear.." - This expression is of the type: "not only this but also this". i.e. One who regrets his iniquities without being prompted by the [fear of] punishment - his regret is due to his sins only. After he repents, he regrets his bad deed of rebelling against G-d. Certainly it is proper to have pity on him. Not only that, but even one who weeps out of fear of punishment - it is also proper to have pity on him and to teach him the way of his rectification....)

Ruthlessness is in place in paying back the wicked and exacting vengeance on the corrupt, as Scripture says, *"neither shall you pity him, have mercy upon him, nor shield him"* (Deut. 13:9).

(*Pas Lechem*: *"paying back the wicked"* refers to those who are bad towards G-d. *"Exact vengeance on the corrupt"* refers to those who are bad to human beings, and who oppress them. Regarding the latter he used the term *"vengeance"* for them but not for those bad to G-d since the term *"vengeance"* is incorrect because if they acted wickedly, what [damage] did they do to G-d? And even though it is written in scripture sometimes, it is just a borrowed term.)

So with the two traits, pride and humility. Pride and haughtiness are in place when you meet those who deny G-d and turn away from Him. Do not humble yourself before such people nor show them deference, so as not to seem to justify them or even incline to their corrupt views; but release the trait of arrogance and pride, to indicate your opposition to their views and how little you agree with them, as you learn from the relation of Mordechai to Haman.

Humility is in place when you meet a man who is pious and pure, G-d-fearing, learned in the Torah and occupied in the service of G-d. So, too, if any one has shown you kindness and favor, you are under an obligation to make a return for it (in a humble demeanor - *TL*). And how much more so, if His benefactions are so great and weighty that you cannot make Him a return for them. Likewise, you should accept on yourself the justice administered to you by G-d [in acceptance of His judgment], as it is said, *"if their uncircumcised heart be humble and they accept their punishment then will I remember My covenant..."* (Lev. 26:41-42).

> (*Pas Lechem*: *"pious"* - in doing good. *"pure"* - pure and of clean hands from not doing bad. *"G-d fearing"* - that he places the fear of G-d opposite his face constantly. He preceded the fear of G-d to the torah wisdom as the mishna says "he whose fear of G-d precedes his wisdom [his wisdom endures]..." (Pirkei Avot 3:12). *"occupied in the service of G-d"* - generally, all his occupation is in the service of G-d. Even when he is doing his physical needs his intent is to serve G-d. However, it is not correct to call this "serving" hence he used the term *"occupied"*.
> *"accept on yourself the justice"* - i.e. that you accept the justice of the evil that befell you and receive it with love as an atonement for your sin.)

So with the two qualities, love and hate. Love is in place towards one who is in agreement with you in the service of G-d, and through whom you will secure abiding joy at the end of your earthly existence.

Hatred is proper against one who transgresses the will of G-d, stood up against men of truth and misled you to what angers your Creator, as it is said: *"They that forsake the law praise the wicked; but such as keep the law contend with them"* (Prov. 28:4).

> (*Pas Lechem*: Correspondingly, there are two reasons to hate the wicked. Either because they transgress the will of G-d, and hate Him. Or because joining their company is a substantial snare which can bring you to slip and stumble.
> *"stood up against the men of truth"* - i.e. if we see a man standing against

the men of truth, such as Korach and his company, even though we don't know his deeds, it is proper to hate him since he hates those G-d loves.)

So with the two traits, generosity and miserliness. The part of generosity is to assign to everything its proper place, and give to every good-charactered person of your money and of your wisdom, in a measure suitable to the recipient (and the donor - *TL*), as it is said: *"Withhold not good from them to whom it is due, when it is in the power of your hand to do it"* (Prov. 3:27); further, *"Let your fountains be dispersed abroad"* (Prov. 5:16).

(*Pas Lechem*: *"to assign to everything its proper place"* - to volunteer to put your attention to the conduct of your fellows, that their matters be in proper order.
"every good-character person" - since on the surface, we cannot know about someone whether he is truly G-d fearing. But if he is of good character, than we can assume he is also G-d fearing. And it is proper to grace him with money, if he needs, or to teach him wisdom. For it is not proper to teach wisdom (torah) to a student who is not worthy. As the sages said in several places such as Chulin 133a and Makot 10a)

Miserliness is in place towards the cruel and foolish and those who do not recognize themselves, nor the value of the beneficence bestowed on them, as it is said, *"He that reproves a scorner gets to himself shame: and he that rebukes a wicked man, it is a blemish to himself"* (Prov. 9:7). Our wise men say, *"He who does a favor to an ingrate is like a man who casts a stone to Markolis"* (A form of idol worship in ancient times).

(*Pas Lechem*: *"the cruel and foolish (enticed)"* - corresponding to generosity with your money, he wrote *"the cruel"*. Since they are cruel on others, why should one be generous towards them? Corresponding to wisdom he wrote the *"foolish"*, which are enticed by their evil inclination to distance themselves from wisdom.
"who do not recognize themselves" - their low worth. Therefore the beneficence of G-d is not big in their eyes. Alternatively, because they do not recognize the greatness of the good. All the more so for one who does not recognize either one, as he wrote in the introduction to the Gate of Examination.
"He that reproves a scorner gets to himself shame" - regarding stinginess with one's money, no proof is needed because since they are evil why should you give to them? Furthermore, you will be reducing what you have. This is unlike wisdom, which is similar to lighting a candle with a candle and the first candle does not lose anything, and maybe this wisdom will improve them. Therefore, he brought a proof from the verse that he is damaging himself. And regarding one who does not appreciate the good, he

brought the teaching of the sages *"He who does a favor to an ingrate..."*.

Marpe Lenefesh: so too one who teaches torah to a student who is not worthy, not only are you not doing a mitzvah, but you will also be punished for this. Because he will take the torah teachings and do all kinds of bad things with it, and like those apikorsim (heretics), and as the talmud says (Pesachim 49b) "those who learned torah and left it [hate the torah sages] more than all of them".)

And so with the two qualities - laziness and diligence. Laziness is proper in the gratification of physical desires, the pleasures of which pass away while nothing remains to him who indulges in them but shame in this world and punishment in the world to come.

(*Tov Halevanon*: i.e. when his soul is hungry for the forbidden food or forbidden relation, due to his lust, he will not yet understand the disgrace of this. But after he has done the deed, and his lust is gone, he will lie down in shame on his sin and his punishment is in the next world.)

Diligence is in place, in the spiritual pleasures and in doing deeds, with the intent to attain the favor of the blessed G-d, as David, peace be unto him, said: *"I made haste, and delayed not to keep Your commandments"* (Ps. 119:60).

(*Pas Lechem*: *"the spiritual pleasures"* - this is the pleasure of the wise in [the study of] wisdom, and their delighting in it. On actual good deeds, he wrote *"and in doing deeds"*.)

What I have expounded in this treatise should suffice for one who chooses the just way, seeks the truth for himself and desires wisdom for its own sake.

(*Tov Halevanon*: *"seeks the truth for himself"* - who does not fool himself with false claims.

Manoach Halevavos: *"desires wisdom for its own sake"* - like [the expression: "one who studies torah for its own sake", i.e. not to receive praise and honor of human beings.

Marpe Lenefesh: *"seeks the truth for himself"* - as in (Pirkei Avot 1:14) "if I am not for myself who is for me?" Why should a man oppress himself, for all that a man does, whether good or bad, is ultimately for himself.)

May G-d in His mercy lead us out (to the light of truth, i.e. - *ML*) to the paths of His service. AMEN.

*** Shaar Habitachon - Gate of Trust ***

*** Introduction ***

The author says: Since our previous treatise dealt with the duty to assume the service of G-d, I deemed proper to follow it with what is more necessary than all other things for one who serves G-d - placing one's trust in Him for all matters, the reason being the great benefits this yields both in religious and in secular matters.

The benefits in religious matters:
Among them, peace of mind, and trusting in G-d as a servant must trust in his master. Because if one does not place his trust in G-d, he will place his trust in something else. And whoever trusts in something other than G-d, the Al-mighty will remove His providence from such a person, and leave him in the hands of the one he trusted. And he will be as it was written: *"For My people have committed two evils; they have forsaken Me, the spring of living waters, to dig for themselves cisterns, broken cisterns that do not hold water"* (Yirmiya 2:13), *"They exchanged their Glory for the likeness of an ox eating grass"* (Tehilim 106:20), *"Blessed is the man who trusts in the L-ord; the L-ord shall be his refuge"* (Yirmiya 17:7), *"Praiseworthy is the man who made the L-ord his trust, and did not turn to the haughty and those who turn to falsehood."* (Tehilim 40:5), *"Cursed is the man who trusts in man, who makes flesh his strength and whose heart turns away from the L-ord"* (Yirmiya 17:5).

(*Matanas Chelko*: *"if one does not place his trust in G-d, he will place his trust in something else...they have forsaken Me"* - this is a great fundamental principle, namely, that every person trusts his life in something or someone. One who claims he does not trust in anything [unless he is 100% sure] is fooling himself. Since this is the way of the world. A man who purchases a loaf of bread from the baker trusts that no poison was placed there. If he takes his automobile to the mechanic for repair and afterwards drives it on the highway, he trusts that it was repaired properly. Likewise for trusting his life with the doctors and other similar matters. Hence, one who trusts in these things cannot say "I cannot trust in G-d until I fully understand everything and fully see everything". This is false! For behold, he trusts his life on many things and many human beings without fully knowing all that happened.)

If he places his trust in his wisdom and tactics, physical strength and industriousness - he will toil for nothing, his strength will weaken, and his tactics will fall short of accomplishing his desire, as written *"He traps the wise with their own cunning"* (Iyov 5:13) (that their tactics result in bad instead of good - *TL*), and *"I returned and saw under the sun, that the race does not belong to the swift, nor the battle to the mighty; neither do the wise have bread, [nor do the understanding have wealth, nor the knowledgeable favor, for time and chance happens to them all]"* (Koheles 9:11), and *"Young lions suffer want and are hungry, but those who seek the L-ord lack no good"* (Tehilim 34:11).

> (*Matanas Chelko*: *"whoever trusts in something other than G-d...the Almighty will leave him"* - i.e. that he places his trust (hope/peace of mind) on the country or on the alarm system in his home, or the like of the various cause and effect calculations. There are grounds for a claim against him for he does trust on things, just not on the Master of the world. His punishment is that G-d leaves him to "nature" and to the framework to which he placed his trust. Therefore, he is ruled over by that system of nature, with its many statistics of causes and effects. Hence, he who thinks his own strength and ingenuity earned for him all of his success, and he relies on this, G-d will leave him under that system of causes and effects. Through this, certainly he will eventually stumble and be lost. [because: "the race is not to the swift, nor the battle to the strong...."]

If he relies on his wealth, it will be removed from him and left to someone else as written *"He lies down rich, but there shall be nothing to gather; he opens his eyes, and his wealth is not"* (Iyov 27:19), *"Do not weary yourself to grow rich; cease from your own understanding."* (Mishlei 23:4), *"Should you blink your eyes at it, it is not here; for it will make wings for itself, like the eagle, and it will fly toward the heavens."* (Mishlei 23:5), *"so it is he who gathers riches but not by right; he shall leave them in the midst of his days, and at his end he stands dishonored"* (Yirmiya 17:11) (since if he placed all of his trust on his riches, certainly, he will not be clean from various forms of theft and dishonesty - *PL*)

Or, he will be prevented from its benefit as the wise man said *"the Almighty will not give him the ability to eat from it"* (Koheles 6:2), and it will be by him like a deposit that he guards from damages until it reaches someone worthy of it, as written *"[For to a man who is good in His sight, He has given wisdom and knowledge and joy,] but to the sinner He has given an occupation to gather and to accumulate, to give to him who is good in G-d's sight; this too is vanity and frustration."* (Koheles 2:26), and *"he will prepare, but a righteous man will wear them; and the pure shall divide the silver"* (Iyov 27:17). And it is possible that the money will be the cause of his destruction (*in this world*) and ultimate downfall (*in the afterlife*) as written *"There is a grievous evil that I saw under the sun; riches kept by their owner for his harm."* (Koheles 5:12).

(*Matanas Chelko*: A person thinks that if he attains great wealth, he will be free of worries. The truth is that it is not so. For example, a very wealthy man may be in constant worry and fear that his children will be kidnapped for ransom. Hence, his wealth has become the cause of his worry. For due to it, he is in fear of bad people. If he attains great wealth, he will see that he cannot trust in it and worries about potential mishaps. His days are squandered in worry and vexation. But he who trusts in G-d and prays to him at every step, and thanks Him for whatever he attains, then even if G-d bestows great wealth to him, he still stays with his trust and does not worry on account of his wealth. For, he never relied on himself, not before he became rich nor afterwards. While he who relies on his strength and ingenuity, and thinks the world works solely through causes and effects. Over time, he will be filled with worries and fears of many things. This itself is a punishment. It is possible also that he will be punished more severely than this, namely, that G-d will take away his wealth and he will not benefit from all his labor. Or even worse, that the wealth will be the cause of his evil as before (that his children are kidnapped for ransom or the like.)

Another benefit for the one who trusts in the Al-mighty, is that his trust will lead him to the following:
* to not serve other than G-d.
* to not hope in any man, nor expect from anyone (Micha 5:6).
* to not work to win their approval.
* to not flatter them.
* to not agree with them in what is not the service of G-d (ex. going to their time wasting parties - *PL*).
* to not be afraid of their matters.
* to not be afraid of disagreeing with them (of not conforming to their ways - *PL*; "to not be afraid if they quarrel with him and outcast him" - *ML*).
* to divest himself of the cloak of their favors and free himself from the burden of expressing gratitude to them, and from the obligation of paying back their favors (and therefore he will not need to flatter them, or join them in what is not the service of G-d - *TL*).

(*Marpe Lenefesh*: He endeavors and does everything he can to not need others and to not enclothe himself in the favors of others. For this would place him under an obligation to toil to express gratitude to them and to also make a return, as it is proper and obligatory to pay back a benefactor with good, as mentioned earlier in the beginning of the third gate. Rather, he desires that G-d alone be his benefactor and that he thanks only Him.)

* if he rebukes them, he will not be afraid of slighting them.
* he will not shy from humiliating them (so that his rebuke is effective - *PL*).
* he will not embellish their false ways (to them, but rather will denigrate it to them - *PL*)

As the prophet wrote: *"But the L-ord G-d helps me, therefore shall I not be confounded; therefore have I set my face like a flint, and I know that I shall not be ashamed"* (Yeshaya 50:7), *"Do not fear them or their words"* (Yechezkel 2:6), *"And you, son of man, fear them not, and fear not their words"* (Yechezkel 2:6), *"fear them not, neither shall you be intimidated by them"* (Yechezkel 3:9).

Another benefit: The trust in G-d will lead one to empty his mind from the distractions of the world, and to focus his heart to matters of service of G-d.

> (*Marpe Lenefesh*: This is because the chief cause of mental agitation and confusion which prevents a man from learning torah and devoting himself to religious service is - constant worry on his livelihood, how will he earn money and through what means. But one who trusts in G-d will diminish his worry in this and increase his worry for religious service. And he will have tranquility of heart like the Alchemist, and even more...)

And he will be similar in his peace of mind, tranquility of heart, and few financial worries to the alchemist, one who knows how to transform silver to gold and copper or tin to silver through skill and procedures.

> (*Pas Lechem*: the author used this trade as an example because many of the masses of his generation aspired to it, due to its making great wealth. Translator: In our times it is much easier to detect fake gold and so the trade has lost its appeal. Perhaps a modern day analogy of the alchemist would be one who owns a sophisticated counterfeit money machine.)

And the one who trusts in G-d will have the following 10 advantages over the alchemist:

(1) The alchemist requires special materials to perform his operation, without which he cannot do anything. These materials are not found at all times and in all places. But for one who trusts in G-d, his sustenance is assured and can come through any means of all the means of the world, as written *"[And He fed you with manna, which you knew not, neither did your fathers know]; That He might make known to you that man does not live by bread alone..."* (Devarim 8:3). For at no time and in no place are the

means of obtaining his livelihood withheld from him, as you know already from the story of Eliyahu and the ravens, or with the widow and the cakes and water (Melachim 17:9), or the story of Ovadia with the prophets, where he said *"I hid among the prophets of G-d, 100 men, 50 in each cave, and I fed them bread and water"* (Melachim 18:13) (i.e. Ovadia was a means to provide for the prophets - PL), and *"Young lions suffer want and are hungry, but those who seek the L-ord lack no good"* (Tehilim 34:11), and *"Fear the L-ord, His holy ones; for there is no want to those who fear Him"* (Tehilim 34:10).

(2) The alchemist must perform actions and follow procedures without which he cannot successfully complete his goal. It is even possible that the fumes and odors will cause his death, along with the long work and great effort with them day and night. But one who trusts in G-d is secure against mishaps, and his heart is assured against future (potential) bad things. Whatever comes to him from G-d, he will accept with joy and gladness and his livelihood comes to him peacefully, quietly, and happily, as written *"He causes me to lie down in green pastures; He leads me beside still waters"* (Tehilim 23:2).

(*Pas Lechem commentary*: "whatever comes to him from G-d gives him joy..." is an explanation of the previous statement "his heart is assured against bad things..." because certainly it cannot be taken literally, that for one who trusts in G-d, no bad things will ever happen to him. For what our eyes see contradicts this. Rather, after he trusts in G-d that He will not do to him anything that is not for his good, if so, "whatever comes to him from G-d, he will accept with joy and gladness", as the Talmud says in Berachot 54a. Therefore it is correct to say that no bad things ever happen to him.

Translator: Later on in Gate #8 he says: "And when you do this (spiritual accounting) with a faithful heart and a pure soul, your mind will become illuminated, and you will see the path to all of the exalted qualities... and you will reach the status of one treasured by G-d... You will not part from a permanent joy in this world and in the next..." see there.)

(3) The alchemist does not trust anyone with his secret due to fear for his life. But one who trusts G-d does not fear any man on account of his trust. On the contrary, it is a source of honor, as king David said: *"in G-d I trusted, I will not fear, what can a man do to me?"* (Tehilim 54:12).

(4) The alchemist must either prepare one large quantity of gold and silver for long term needs or must prepare small batches for short term needs. If he prepares a large quantity, all his days he will fear for his life that

perhaps all the gold and silver will be lost in any number of ways (and he will be left penniless), and his heart will never quiet, nor will his mind be at peace due to fear of the king and of the people (finding his big stash of gold).

If he makes small batches for short term use, it is possible that he will not successfully perform the procedure at a time of great need, due to a failure in one of the means.

> (*Matanas Chelko*: i.e. even if he is successful, he is in a constant state of worry. Likewise, in our times, we can observe that anyone who is successful in business is also worried about many factors - unless he trusts in G-d. Hence he is just like the Alchemist.)

But one who trusts in G-d, has strong peace of mind that G-d will provide for him at any time He wishes and in any place, just like He sustains the fetus in its mother's womb or the chick inside an egg, which has no opening to enter anything from the outside, and birds in the air, or fish in the sea, and the tiny ant despite its weakness, while the mighty lion some days cannot obtain food, as written *"Young lions suffer want and are hungry, but those who seek the L-ord lack no good"* (Tehilim 34:11). And *"The L-ord will not starve the soul of the righteous"* (Mishlei 10:3), and *"I have been young, and now am old; yet I have not seen the righteous forsaken, nor his seed begging bread"* (Tehilim 37:25).

> (*Translator*: "Young lions suffer want..." - notice dear reader that this verse was brought three times already. Perhaps, the intent is to teach one to repeat such verses to himself whenever he can as a way of working on trust.)

(5) The alchemist is under anxiety and fear of everyone, from the greatest to the lowest of people as a consequence of his work, but one who trusts in G-d will be revered by great men and honorable people, even animals and stones seek to do his will (i.e. do not harm him - TL) as written in the entire Psalm *"He who sits..."* (Tehilim 91), and *"In six troubles He will save you, and in the seventh no harm will touch you."* (Job 5:19), until the end of the matter.

(6) The alchemist is not immune from sickness and disease which hinders his joy in being wealthy, and prevents him from benefiting from what he has and enjoying what he has acquired. But one who trusts in G-d, is immune from sickness and disease except as an atonement or to increase his reward, as written *"Now youths shall become tired and weary, and young men shall stumble"* (Isaiah 40:30), *"those who hope in G-d will*

renew strength" (Isaiah 40:31), and *"for the arms of the wicked (who trust in their strength - TL) shall be broken, but the L-ord supports the righteous"* (Tehilim 37:17).

(7) It is possible that the alchemist will not be able to buy food with his gold and silver due to no food being available in the city at times, as written: *"they shall cast their money in the streets"* (Ezekiel 7:19), and *"neither silver nor gold will be able to save them"* (Tzefania 1:18). But for one who trusts in G-d, his sustenance will not be blocked at any time or in any place, as written: *"in famine He redeemed you from death"* (Job 5:20), and *"the L-ord is my shepherd, I shall not lack"* (Tehilim 23:1), and *"They will not be shamed in time of calamity, and in days of famine they shall still be satisfied"* (Tehilim 37:19).

(8) The alchemist does not linger in one place too long due to fear that his secret will be discovered. But one who trusts in G-d feels secure in his land and has peace of mind in his place, as written *"Trust in the L-ord and do good; dwell in the land and be nourished by faith"* (Tehilim 37:3), and *"The righteous shall inherit the land and dwell forever in it"* (Tehilim 37:29).

(9) The alchemist's skills will not accompany him in the afterlife. They may only provide him, in this world, security from poverty and from needing other people. But for one who trusts in G-d, the reward for his trust will accompany him in this world and in the next, as written *"Many are the pains of the wicked (in the afterlife - PL); but one who trusts in G-d will be surrounded by kindness"* (Tehilim 32:10), and *"how great is Your goodness that you hid away for those who fear You"* (Tehilim 31:20).

(*Tov Halevanon*: He will receive reward for his trust in G-d in the afterlife since placing one's trust in G-d is a big mitzvah, as written (Bereishit 15:10): *"And Avraham believed in the L-ord; and He counted it to him as a righteousness".*)

(10) If the alchemist's work is discovered, it will become a cause for his death, because his work runs contrary to the natural order, and the Director of the world will allow someone to kill him when he fails to hide his secret (G-d won't save him at a time of danger. Alternatively, G-d will cause him to be caught when his time has come - ML). But for one who trusts in G-d, when his trust becomes known, he will be held in high esteem and honored by the public. They will feel blessed to be near him or to see him, and his presence will bring good fortune to the city and shield the people from

troubles, as written: *"the righteous man is the foundation of the world"* (Mishlei 10:25), similar to Lot in Tzoar (Bereishit 19, who saved the city by his presence there - *TL*).

Among the benefits of trusting in G-d regarding religious matters: One who trusts in G-d, if he has wealth, will be quick to fulfill his monetary obligations to G-d and to men with a willing and generous spirit. If he does not have wealth, he will consider that lack of wealth to be among the favors of G-d to him, because he is exempt from the monetary obligations to G-d and men which wealth brings, and he is spared from the mental distraction of protecting and managing it, as one of the pious used to say: "may G-d save me from dispersion of the mind". They would ask him "what is dispersion of the mind?" He would answer: "to own property at the head of every river and the center of every town." And this is what our sages referred to in saying: *"the more possessions, the more worry"* (Avos 2:7), and they said: *"who is wealthy? He who is content with what he has"* (Avos 4:1).

One who trusts in G-d will receive the benefits of money, namely, his material needs, but without the mental distraction and constant worry of the wealthy, as the wise man said *"The sleep of the laborer is sweet, whether he eats little or much, but the satiety of the rich does not allow him to sleep"* (Koheles 5:11).

Another benefit, one who trusts in G-d will not diminish his trust on account of having much wealth because he does not rely on the money. He regards it as a deposit which he is ordered to use in specific ways, for specific matters and for a limited time. And if he stays wealthy for a long time, he will not become arrogant due to his wealth. He will not remind the poor person of his charity gifts since he was commanded to give to him, and he will not seek his gratitude and praises. Rather, he will thank his Creator who appointed him as a means for doing good to the poor person.

If his wealth is lost, he will not worry nor mourn his loss. Rather, he will thank his Creator for taking back His deposit, just like he thanked G-d when it was given to him. He will be happy with his portion, and will not seek to damage others (in order to gain benefit - *TL*). He will not covet other people's wealth as the wise man said *"A righteous man eats to sate his appetite, [but the stomach of the wicked shall feel want]."* (Mishlei 13:25).

(*Matanas Chelko*: This is analogous to a case of two poor neighbors. One

of whom had a rich relative who came to visit him and gave him a huge
donation of 1000 dollars and then left. Upon hearing about the donation,
the second neighbor begged his friend for 200 dollars but he refused. The
neighbor pleaded for 100 dollars and this time his friend painfully agreed.
But if from the beginning, the rich relative said to him, "I see you and your
neighbor are both in great poverty. Take 800 dollars for yourself and take
an additional 200 for your neighbor". Surely, he would have ran joyously to
his neighbor without sadness or heavy feeling. This is because he never felt
like the owner of that 200.. So too, one who has money beyond his needs
must feel that it is not only for himself but for distributing also to others.
Hence, one who trusts in G-d is always joyful in all situations for he knows
and feels this secret.

Benefits of trust in G-d for worldly matters:
* Peace of mind from the worries of this world.
* Peace from the frenzy and drive to pursue the lusts of this world.
* Feeling calm, secure, at peace in this world, as written *"blessed be the
man who trusts in G-d, and G-d shall be his refuge"* (Yirmiyahu 17:7), and
*"For he shall be like a tree planted by the water, that sends out its roots by
the stream. [It does not fear when heat comes; its leaves stay green. It has
no worries in a year of drought and shall not cease to bear fruit]"*
(Yirmiyahu 17:8).

Among them, peace of mind from the need to travel to faraway journeys,
which weakens the body, and hastens aging, as written *"my strength has
weakened from the journey, my life shortened"* (Tehilim 102:24).

It is said about a novice ascetic who travelled to a distant land in search of
a livelihood. He met one of the idolaters of the city where he arrived and
said to him: "how completely blind and ignorant you are to worship
idols!". The idolater asked him: "And what do you worship?". The ascetic
answered "I worship the Creator, the Omnipotent, the Sustainer of all, the
One, the Provider of all, which there is none like Him". The idolater
countered "your actions contradict your words!" The ascetic asked "How
so?", the idolater said "if what you say were true, He would have provided
a livelihood for you in your own city, just like He provided for you here,
and it would not have been necessary for you to trouble yourself to travel
to a faraway land like this." The ascetic, unable to answer, returned to his
city and reassumed his asceticism from that time on, and never again left
his city (for his livelihood).

Another benefit, peace of mind and body, due to sparing oneself from pursuing grueling jobs, and wearying occupations, avoiding work of kings - mingling in their culture and dealing with their corrupt servants.

But one who trusts G-d, selects among the different occupations one which is easy on his body, allows him to earn a good reputation, does not consume his mind, and is best suited for fulfilling his torah obligations and the principles of his faith. Because the choice of occupation will neither increase nor decrease the income he will earn unless G-d decreed so, as it says *"For it is not from the east nor from the west, neither from the desert does elevation come. But G-d judges; He lowers this one and elevates that one."* (Tehilim 75:7), and *"He causes me to lie down in green pastures; He leads me beside still waters"* (Tehilim 23:2).

Another benefit, minimal aggravation in one's business dealings. If one's merchandise does not sell, or if he is unable to collect his debts, or if he is struck by illness, [he will not worry] because he knows that the Creator is in charge of his life and knows best what is good for him, as written *"Only to G-d should you hope, my soul, for my hope is from Him"* (Tehilim 62:6).

Another benefit, joy in whatever happens to him, even if it is something difficult and against his nature. Because he trusts that G-d will do only what is good for him in all matters, just like a mother has compassion on her baby in washing it, diapering it, and harnessing or unharnessing it against its will, as David said: *"Surely I have behaved and quieted myself, as a child that is weaned of his mother: my soul is even as a weaned child"* (Tehilim 131:2).

> (*Matanas Chelko*: This is the essence of trust - to feel like a baby in the hands of its mother. One should contemplate this matter of bathing the baby. The mother needs to do all sorts of things in order to cleanse it. And even though the baby does not sense the good in these things, nevertheless, the mother must do them since she knows it is for the baby's benefit. This is the conduct of G-d towards us, like a mother with her baby. All that He does and metes out to us is only for our good.

Since I have clarified the benefits of trust in G-d for religious and secular matters, I will now clarify seven topics on the matter of trust:

THE SEVEN CHAPTERS OF THE GATE OF TRUST
(1) What is trust.
(2) The criteria for trusting someone.
(3) The prerequisites to trusting in G-d.

(4) When trust applies and when it does not.

(5) The difference between one who trusts in G-d in earning a livelihood and one who does not.

(6) Obligation to refute those who promote delaying the service of G-d until reaching sufficient material prosperity.

(7) Things that damage one's trust in G-d, and a summary of the matter of trust.

*** CHAPTER 1 ***

What is trust?
Peace of mind of the one who trusts. That one relies in his heart that the one he trusts in will do what is good and proper for him on the matter he has trusted him with according to his ability and his understanding of what will further his good.

But the main factor which leads one to trust in the one trusted, and without which trust cannot exist, is for one's heart to be confident that the one trusted will keep his word and will do what he pledged, and that he will also think to do what is good for him even on what he did not pledge out of pure generosity and kindness (this will be explained).

*** CHAPTER 2 ***

- The criteria for trusting someone

CRITERIA FOR TRUSTING ONESELF IN ANOTHER
There are seven factors which make it possible for one to trust in another:
(1) Compassion, pity and love. When a man knows that his friend has compassion and pity for him, he will trust in him and be at peace with regard to troubling him with all of his matters.

(2) To know that his friend, besides loving him, is not forgetful or lazy in taking care of his needs. Rather, he knows that his friend is active and resolved to do it. Because if all of this is not clear, one's trust in him will not be complete, since one knows of his forgetfulness and laziness in attending to his needs.
But, when the one he trusts combines these two traits, great compassion for him and full attendance to his matters, he will trust in him without a doubt.

(3) He is strong. He will not be defeated in whatever he desires, and nothing can prevent him from doing the request of the one who trusts him. Because if he is weak, one cannot fully trust in him, even though it is clear that he is compassionate and active, due to the many occasions in which he failed doing things. When one combines these three traits, trusting in him will be more fitting.

(4) That the one he trusts knows what is beneficial for him, both for his inner and outer life and also that none of the ways which benefit him or further his welfare are hidden to him. Because, if he does not know all of this, one will not be at peace in entrusting himself to him. But if he combines the knowledge of the ways which are beneficial to him, the ability to implement them, great attendance to them, and compassion for him, his trust will certainly be strengthened.

(5) That the one he trusts is under the exclusive care of him from the beginning of his existence, his development, babyhood, childhood, youth, adulthood, old age until the end of his days (i.e. that no one else has ever done to him any good except the one he trusts - *ML*). And when all this is clear to the truster, he is obligated to be at peace on his friend, and to rely on him, because of the many past benefits he already received from his

friend and the constant favors he still presently receives. And this will obligate strengthening one's trust in him. (since he has been continuously benevolent to him from then until now, certainly he will not abandon him until his final end - *PL*.)

(6) All matters of the truster are entirely in the hands of the one he trusts, and no one else can hurt him, help him, benefit him, or protect him from harm, as a slave chained down in a prison is entirely in the hands of his master. If the truster were in the hands of the one he trusts in this manner, it would be more fitting to trust in him.

> (*Pas Lechem*: The fifth condition was that no one else ever benefited him. This sixth condition refers to ability - that the ability to benefit or harm him is only in his friend's hands. No one else has any ability to benefit or harm him... since this is the case, his heart will not look towards trusting others and he will place all of his trust on his friend.)

(7) That the person he trusts is absolutely generous and kind (i.e. the most possible extreme of generosity and kindness - *TL*) to those deserving and to those who are not deserving, and that his generosity and kindness is continuous, never ending and without interruption.

> (*Marpe Lenefesh commentary*: Otherwise, he will abandon hope from the favors of G-d, since he is in doubt whether he is worthy of them, and his trust in G-d will diminish. And through this, he will distance from G-d and His torah. Rather, let him reflect that G-d is benevolent to the good and the bad, as written: "His mercy is on all of His creations" (Tehilim 145:9). And through this, he will come closer to G-d and repent and he will become worthy of the good.)

Whoever combines these traits, in addition to all of the previous traits has completed all the conditions that deserve trust, and would obligate the person who knows this to trust in him, to be at peace internally and externally, in his heart and in his limbs, and to give himself up to him and accept his decrees and judge him favorably in all his judgments and actions. (to assume that certainly everything is good and even what seems bad is actually good - *ML*)

When we investigate these seven conditions, we will not find them at all in the created beings, but we find them all in the Creator. He is compassionate to His creations as written *"The L-ord is merciful and gracious"* (Tehilim 103:8), and *"Now should I not take pity on Nineveh, the great city"* (Yonah 4:11).

(*Pas Lechem*: One may think that He is only merciful on those who are already in pain, but not before this, and therefore trust in Him will not help to be saved from future troubles. Therefore, the author brought the second verse from Nineveh, where G-d had pity on them even before the troubles came and annulled the decree...)

And that He never neglects us, as written *"Behold the Guardian of Israel will neither slumber nor sleep"* (Tehilim 121:4), that He is all-wise and invincible as written *"He is wise in heart and mighty in strength; who hardened [his heart] against Him and remained unhurt?"* (Job 9:4), and *"Yours, O L-ord, are the greatness, and the power, and the glory, and the victory, and the majesty"* (Divrei Hayamim I 29:11) and *"The L-ord your G-d is in your midst - a Mighty One Who will save"* (Tzefania 3:17).

And that He alone is the one who guides a person from the beginning of his existence and development, as written *"is He not your Father who has acquired you? He has made you and established you."* (Devarim 32:6), and *"by You have I been upheld from birth: You are He that took me out of my mother's womb"* (Tehilim 71:6), and *"did You not pour me out like milk and curdle me like cheese?"* (Job 10:10), and the rest of the matter.

That one's benefit or harm is not in the hands of people but rather, only in the hands of the Creator, as written *"Who has commanded and it came to pass, unless the L-ord ordained it? Out of the mouth of G-d, evil and good do not go out* (of the boundary He has set - PL)?" (Eicha 3:37), and *"[All flesh is like grass, and all their kindness is as the flower of the field]; The grass shall dry out, the flower shall wilt, but the word of our G-d will stand forever"* (Isaiah 40:8), and *"...surely the people are like grass"* (Isaiah 40:7), and we have already explained this sufficiently in the third gate of this book.

(*Pas Lechem*: (summary) First verse shows that decrees of G-d, whether for good or for bad, do not go out of the boundaries He has decreed, rather as He decreed - so shall it be.
Second verse: Perhaps one will think that only the beginning of the matter is from G-d, but it will not endure unless a man completes it and perpetuates it, therefore - "the grass shall dry out", i.e. every man, just like his existence is ephemeral, as he is like grass, which wilts and dies, so too the kindness man does is like a temporary flower, which passes but the "word of G-d will stand forever", i.e. just like He is eternal, so too His decrees and acts are eternal.)

That His generosity is universal and His kindness is all-embracing, as written *"The L-ord is good to all, and His mercies are on all His works"* (Tehilim 145:9) and *"Who gives food to all flesh, for His kindness endures forever"* (Tehilim 136:25), and *"You open Your hand and satisfy every living thing [with] will* (i.e. the good He bestows is not in a stingy way, according to basic need, but rather like His will - *PL*)" (Tehilim 145:16). But really, the intellect can infer that these 7 conditions exist in the Creator and not in the created beings (as he will explain next chapter - *TL*), and therefore I have brought these verses from scripture only as a remembrance.

> (*Pas Lechem*: i.e. my intent was not as a proof otherwise I would have brought more verses, but rather only as a remembrance, namely, when these verses are constantly on a person's mouth - he will remember the 7 factors through them.
>
> Translator: As the author wrote in the beginning of Gate #1: "that habitually having them on one's tongue always, brings one to *remembrance* of the heart...", see there)

When one clarifies this to himself, and his recognition in the true kindness of the Creator will be strong - he will place his trust in Him, give himself up completely to Him, and leave the guidance of his life to Him, never suspect Him in His judgments, nor be upset by what He has chosen for him, as David said (on the good - *TL*) *"I will lift up the cup of salvation and call upon the Name of the L-ord"* (Tehilim 116:13), and (on the bad - *TL*) *"I found trouble and sorrow and call upon the Name of the L-ord"* (Tehilim 116:3-4).

> (*Pas Lechem commentary*: He first stated two general phrases:
> (1) "he will place his trust in Him" - for providing his needs.
> (2) "give himself up completely to Him" - this refers to a general consent and acceptance that G-d will do with him as He wishes, even for what appears bad to him.
> Then he explained the two phrases:
> * "and leave the guidance of his life to Him" is an explanation of (1).
> * "never suspect Him in His judgments, nor be upset by what He has chosen for him" is an explanation of (2).
> This latter subdivides to:
> (a) "never suspect Him in His judgments" - if G-d sentences him to some bad trouble which is specific and short term.
> (b) "nor be upset by what He has chosen for him" - if G-d chooses for him a widespread life-long matter such as poverty or a bad wife, or the like.)

*** Chapter 3 ***

- the preliminaries to trusting in G-d -

The introductions which must be clearly understood and the truth of which must be realized in order that a person's trust in G-d will be complete are five.

> (*Pas Lechem*: When he understands them to their full depth and after this he verifies the truth of them in his heart to absolute truthfulness - then his trust in G-d will be complete)

FIRST INTRODUCTION TO BRING COMPLETE TRUST
To believe and clearly understand that all of the seven factors (in the previous chapter) which when combined make it possible to trust in someone apply to G-d. I have already mentioned them and commented on them from verses that occurred to me.
THE SEVEN FACTORS AS THEY APPLY TO G-D
One: the Creator is merciful on a man more than any other merciful being, and all mercy and compassion that a man is shown from anyone besides G-d is really derived from G-d's mercy and compassion, as the verse says *"He will give you compassion, and cause others to have compassion on you and multiply you"* (Devarim 13:18).

> (*Tov Halevanon*: i.e. even that which a person finds favor and compassion in the eyes of another human being - this is due to G-d's giving the person compassion on that human being towards him.
>
> *Matanas Chelko* - for example, a man walks on the street and sees a poor man. He feels compassion for him and gives him what he needs. From where did this compassion come from? From the Master of the world. On his own, the man would have kept walking and ignored the poor man. And even if he had stopped briefly and helped him a little bit, he would not have done so properly. But since G-d has compassion on the poor man, He imparts of His compassion on this man so that the man will feel compassion for the poor man. Hence, since the compassion stems from G-d, it is ascribed to G-d alone. This is the meaning of *"there is nothing but Him"* (Deut. 4:35), there is nothing in the world but G-d.

Two: none of the ways which benefit a man are unknown to the Creator. Logic necessitates this, since man is one of His handiworks. No one can know better than man's Maker the ways to further his making (i.e. biological conception in the womb - *PL*), and the ways of loss (where no conception will occur and the drop of human seed will be lost - *PL*), and the possible damages which can occur (in the development of the embryo in the womb during the time of pregnancy - *PL*), and the ways it (the born child during his growth and development - *PL*) can become sick and healed.

And this is also true for human makers (who know best what damages or benefits their inventions), although they do not really create anything new, but rather merely make a new form from existing raw materials, since to create a new form from nothing is impossible to man.

And all the more so, He who has called into existence from nothing the basic elements of man, his form, his anatomy, and the order of his synthesis (of body and soul - *PL*). Obviously, He is the wise One who undoubtedly knows which matters benefit or harm man in this world and in the next, as written *"I am the L-rd your G-d who teaches you for your benefit, who guides you in the proper path"* (Isaiah 48:17), and also *"G-d rebukes the ones He loves (to turn them to the proper path - TL), and like a father to a son He desires in"* (Mishlei 3:12).

Three: the Creator is the strongest of all the strong. His word reigns supreme and nothing can reverse His decree, as written *"Whatever G-d wants, He does"* (Tehilim 135:6), and *"so shall be My word that goes out from My mouth; it shall not return to Me empty, unless it has done what I desire"* (Isaiah 55:11).

Four: He watches over and directs the lives of all men, He does not abandon any of them (from bestowing good or benefiting them according to their needs - *PL*) nor neglects any of them (from saving them from damages - *PL*). None of their matters, small or great are hidden from Him, and no matter can distract Him from remembering another matter, as written: *"Why should you say, O Jacob, and speak, O Israel, 'My way has been hidden from the L-ord, and my judgment (i.e. my providence - TL) is passed over from my G-d'?"* (Isaiah 40:27), and *"Do you not know-if you have not heard-an everlasting G-d is the L-ord, the Creator of the ends of the world; He neither tires nor wearies; there is no fathoming His understanding* (i.e. on His providence of all the creations simultaneously - *TL*)" (Isaiah 40:28).

(*Pas Lechem*: That which the latter verse ascribes the creation specifically to "the ends of the world", this is to convey that G-d's power is infinite, therefore the nature of His handiworks also must be boundless and immeasurable, as in truth they are [physically boundless] among the spiritual creations (souls,etc). However, when G-d's divine wisdom ordained to call into existence a world of finite character, He constrained His power in His handiwork and held it at a certain amount. And this is an amazing feat to the thinking person, and this is what the verse alludes to in saying: "there is no fathoming His understanding")

Five: No created being can benefit or harm either itself or any other creature without the permission of the Creator.

(*Pas Lechem*: i.e. just like he cannot help himself, so too he cannot help others without the permission of the Creator.)

If a slave has more than one master, and each one has the power to help him, it is not possible for him to put his trust in only one of them, since he hopes to benefit from each master. And if one master can benefit him more than the others, he should trust proportionally more in him, even though he also trusts in the others. And if only one of the masters can benefit him or harm him, certainly he should put his trust only on that master, since he does not hope for benefit from the other masters. Similarly, when a human being will realize that no created being can benefit him or harm him without the permission of the Creator, he will stop being afraid of them or of hoping for anything from them, and he will place his trust in the Creator alone, as written: *"Put not your trust in princes, nor in mortal man who has no help"* (Tehilim 146:3).

(*Pas Lechem*: the expression "nor in mortal man who has no help" alludes to both points simultaneously. (1) That if the generous man helps him, the help is not ascribed to him but rather to the Creator, since he cannot help him without the permission of the Creator. (2) The expression "who has no help" also alludes to that which the generous man also cannot even help himself. Both interpretations are true and simultaneously intended.

Tov Halevanon: That a generous man cannot help due to his own power. Rather the help is from G-d and the man is just an agent, therefore it is more proper to trust in G-d.)

Six: That one is conscious of G-d's abundant goodness to man, and how He brought him into existence out of abundant and pure benevolence and kindness, without man being worthy of this, nor because G-d has any need for him. But rather only out of generosity, benevolence, and goodness, as we explained in the Gate of Examination in this book, and like King David said: *"Many, O L-ord my G-d, are Your wonderful works which You have done, and Your thoughts which are toward us: they cannot be reckoned up in order to You; if I would declare and speak of them, they are more than can be numbered"* (Tehilim 40:5).

(Translator: i.e. how do we know G-d brought man into existence out of pure benevolence and kindness? Because He does not need anything from man. This is logical because man is His creation and a creator does not need anything from His creation. As an illustration (heard from Rabbi Moshe Lazarus), close your eyes and think of a blue-colored orange fruit. You have just created that fruit in your mind. As long as you continue to think about it, it has a form of existence in your mind. Now, do you have any need for that orange? Of course not, it is just the opposite. The orange needs you for everything while you don't need it for anything. So too, we need G-d, not the other way around. His "thoughts" are continuously giving existence to the universe (as brought down in the book Tanya, Shaar Yichud v'Emuna ch. 7: "G-d's Thought and Knowledge of all created beings encompasses each and every creature. For this is its very life-force and that which grants it existence from absolute nothingness."). Therefore, since He has no need for us, granting us existence is a continuous act of pure benevolence and grace. Note that this is just an analogy, not to be taken too literally. For G-d is unknowable to us. Another reason, G-d is infinitely and absolutely perfect in every way. He cannot become any more perfect. Thus, He has no need for anything as explained in Gate 1.)

Seven: That one clearly realizes that all existing things in this world, whether purposeful or accidental have predetermined limits which cannot be increased or decreased from what the Creator has decreed, whether in amount, quality, time, or place. It cannot be numerous if the Creator decreed it few, nor few if the Creator decreed it numerous, nor come late if decreed to come early, nor come early if decreed to come late. And if something appears to be contrary to this, really, it was already pre-decreed with foresight, only that all decrees [are implemented through] causes and means, which in turn have causes and means.

(*Tov Halevanon commentary*: i.e. That incident did not happen by itself, even though this incident is caused by another incident, and the other incident itself is caused by another incident, and so forth until the first cause - all of them came through a decree from G-d. He coordinated all the incidents in a controlled way.

For example: A boat whose crew wanted to go out to sea at this time tomorrow, the Sultan then falsely accused the captain of the ship and delayed him for some time period. During that time period, wars broke out in the sea. When the boat finally set out to sea, the crew feared the wars and wanted to escape through a different route. The boat wound up broken by boulders which were along that route in the sea and the entire crew drowned. The sea then carried a floating case filled with treasures towards the shore. At the same time, the Sultan of a nearby city falsely accused a Tzadik (righteous person) who ran away to the sea shore. At that moment, the case appeared floating near the shore. The righteous man found it and was able to obtain his livelihood from it for the rest of his life.

Behold, this that the first Sultan falsely accused the captain was the beginning of the initial cause of providing for the livelihood of this Tzadik, since if the crew went out to sea earlier, before the wars broke out, they would not have turned towards the dangerous route which broke the ship. The second incident was the breaking out of the wars at that specific time. The third incident, that which the case was able to float on the sea. The fourth incident was that which the sea current pushed the case towards this side of the shore. The fifth, the accusing of the righteous man by the Sultan at that specific time. The sixth incident, that which was put in his heart the idea to run away. The seventh incident, that which he ran away at that specific time and to that specific place.

Behold, all these matters did not happen accidentally, rather, G-d in His wisdom, coordinated that everything happen in its time and place. And even the breaking out of the wars and the drowning of the crew - everything occurred by decrees of G-d, each with its own reason, just that He coordinated in His wisdom to complete all of His will and decrees simultaneously. Strive to understand this because it is deep and this is the author's intent.

... And the final incident (of providing for the tzadik) preceded everything and was the first cause of all the causes which followed (relative to this decree) until this cause of providing for the righteous man materialized. And even so, all the events which preceded this did not occur incidentally, namely, that they did not occur merely for this small first cause which was accomplished. Rather, all these chains of events which accomplished this first cause (of providing for the tzadik), were planned by G-d with foresight, and every incident had its own independent reason and decree. This is something which is beyond our finite minds to grasp, how it is possible that all of these things are coordinated in unison, and each one is not accidental. Rather, everything according to its decree, without one matter contradicting another, and like the verse says: "for the L-ord is a G-d of all-knowledge, and by Him actions are weighed" (Shmuel 2:3).

Likewise, for the development of later causes, for example: When we see a torrent of water which flooded all the inhabitants of a city. It appears that

due to the flood a single incident occurred to all those who were in that city. But this is not so, rather, there were other previous causes that occurred with G-d's coordination, so that all those who were decreed to die were assembled together in one place, due to many causes and chains of causes which preceded this cause of flooding, and everything occurring with G-d's foresight.
Translator: note that it was all planned with foresight from the creation of the world as explained in the story of R. Eleazar b. Pedat - Talmud Taanit 25a)

One who does not understand the matters of this world thinks that an immediate cause will force a change in matters, which in turn cause more changes (that present events constantly reshape the future). But really, a single cause is too weak to force a change by itself, as we see one grain of wheat can cause 300 ears of wheat to grow, which each contain 30 grains, so one grain would have produced around ten thousand grains. Can one hide the fact that one grain by itself is incapable of producing this amount? And likewise for other grains that one plants, and likewise we can say for a man or an animal from a drop of seed, or a huge fish from a tiny egg.

(*Lev Tov*: Rather, the true underlying power which causes the seeds to grow into ears of wheat is G-d's original decree from Genesis [that the seemingly biological life process driving the seed would unfold in this way]. And this pre-decree is what drives the matter to actuality through the available means.
Translator: Normally the effect does not exceed the capacities of the cause. Here it is clear that the effect (human being with spiritual soul) is beyond the powers of the cause (physical human seed).)

To busy oneself in trying to bring early what the Creator decreed would come later, or to try to delay what was decreed to come early, or to try to make numerous what was decreed to be few or to try to diminish what was decreed to be numerous in worldly possessions, unless it causes strengthening of G-d's service or accepting His torah (since on religious matters G-d does not decree on a man, rather the free will is in man's own hands, as will be explained - *ML*), - all this is due to (1) weakness in the recognition of G-d's all-knowing understanding (of us and our needs - *PL*), and (2) foolishness in failing to understand the benevolent character of G-d's conducts.

(*Pas Lechem*: i.e. that all of G-d's conducts with His creations is for their benefit. Through realizing these two points, there will be trust.

Translator: - The Madregos HaAdam wrote that one who worries and tries to earn more than what was decreed for him is like a man inside a moving train pushing the wall to make the train move faster.

The wise man has already hinted this when he said: *"everything has a time and moment under the heaven"* (Koheles 3:1), and afterwards he mentions 28 matters (corresponding to the 28 lunar positions which alludes to astrological fate - *TL*), as he says *"a time to be born, and a time to die.."*, until *"a time for war and a time for peace"*, and also: *"for time and fate will overtake them all"* (Koheles 9:11), and then he said: *"[If you see oppression of the poor, and deprivation of justice and righteousness in the province], wonder not about the matter, for the Highest over the high watches over them, and there are higher ones over them"* (Koheles 5:7). (that really it is not astrological "fate", but rather G-d is guiding everything behind the scenes through chains of causes according to His desire and decrees - *TL*)

(*Pas Lechem*: If you see oppression of the poor and deprivation of justice, etc., do not wonder, since certainly it has already been decreed on the wicked to get what they deserve, only that G-d will bring their retribution through chains of many causes (which are coordinated with everyone affected). Therefore, their retribution is delayed. But when the causes are finished, they will also be finished. This is what is meant by *"for the Highest over the high watches over them, and there are higher ones"*, to teach that thus Divine wisdom decided to implement the divine decrees through many causes...

Pas Lechem: (earlier) And if you ask: if it is so that everything was pre-decreed, if so, why does this not happen right away from the beginning, for example, for an almond, why does it start as a bud, then blossoms into a flower, then sprouts a shoot, then a hull, then an almond shell, etc., why didn't ripe almonds grow from the beginning, as we see them now? On this, he answered that this is what Divine wisdom decided - that everything be implemented through chains of many causes and means in a natural looking progression.

Translator's note: the reason G-d made the world in such a way that His decrees are hidden behind "nature" is so that man can have free will to choose between good and evil. Let us consider what would happen if G-d would manifest His presence on the sky in His full power and glory to hit with lightning bolts all those who commit evil deeds. In such a situation virtually all people would start to live in terror and in fear. No man would have the courage to do anything for doing of which would not receive a direct order from G-d. Science and technology would collapse, as no-one would have the courage to research, investigate, or to just speculate - as everyone would be scared that this may act against G-d's intentions. Social life would collapse as no one would utter a word out of terror of saying the wrong thing. Medicine would fall down as doctors would be scared to heal thus breaking G-d's wishes. Most would be too scared to lift a finger for fear of sin and deserving a punishment. People would then live like forced slaves and soon the entire population would die out. In order to avoid such consequences and provide an arena for free will, G-d introduced several prevention measures to His coexistence with people. Hence He almost never openly manifests Himself to living people. He always maintains people in ambiguity about His presence in order to maintain "free will" and the possibility of virtue. Therefore, everything that G-d does, He does in such a manner that it is ambiguous - i.e. that it can be explained in many different manners, etc., etc. (Jan pajak)

Note that this is only one aspect. There's a lot more to it than that. The primary reason (as heard from Rabbi Mordechai Kornfeld) is that it has lots in common with raising children (who is the better parent-the one standing ready with a stick and carrot, or the one hiding behind the door and letting his child grow?), coaching independence, and thus becoming akin to the Creator. The answer lies at the very root of the need for free will and the requisite amount of it, which is discussed by the Ramchal in Derech Hash-m (beginning of ch. 2 of the first section or so) and in Daas Tevunos (where he offers another, more familiar, explanation).

Related to this point, if G-d would manifest Himself openly to human beings, it would completely crush their egos. No man would be capable of thinking highly of himself due to perceiving just how utterly puny, weak, and insignificant he is compared to the infinite G-d. This realization would render him completely and absolutely humble and his divine service would be forced and meaningless.

Hence, it is necessary for free will that a natural order exists whose purpose is to provide a misleading appearance that the world carries itself. Therefore, when nature was created, with it came the loopholes for interpreting the world according to the atheistic views. It is essential for G-d's plan of human free will. For only in such a situation of free will can a person earn meaningful levels of righteousness and holiness. This is why the world appears billions of years old as a result of some cosmological accident, etc. etc. Likewise G-d created life forms in stages from simple to complex to make room for a naturalistic explanation, etc. etc. But the true truth seeker will see the marks of divine wisdom which are all around us and draw the correct conclusions, as explained in Gates 1 and 2.

Another reason is as the Ramchal writes (Daas Tevunos siman 40): "certainly G-d could have established the world through His omnipotent system, in such a way that everything would be totally incomprehensible to us, not before not after, without cause and effect. If He had done so, no one (atheist) would be able to open their mouths for we would not be able to understand anything whatsoever... but because He wanted us to understand a bit of His ways and attributes - on the contrary He very much wants us to exert ourselves on this..." end quote

Scientific progress has shown so far that the phenomena in the universe is understandable to man. Even the weirdest, most bizarre quantum mechanics, black holes, etc. can nevertheless be fit into human-made mathematical models that we can understand and use to make predictions. Albert Einstein said: "The most incomprehensible thing about the world is that it is comprehensible." This indicates that it is all for man. It is a kind of ladder to come to know a bit of G-d's wisdom and ways at our level.

The ways of judgments of the Creator are too deep, hidden and lofty for us to understand part of them, and all the more so to understand their general principles. And the verse already says: "As the heavens are higher than the earth, so are My ways higher than your ways and My thoughts [higher] than your thoughts" (Isaiah 55:9).

SECOND INTRODUCTION TO BRING COMPLETE TRUST
(2) To know and clearly realize that the Creator is watching him, and neither one's private or public conduct is hidden from Him, nor his innermost being or outer appearance. He also knows whether a man's trust in Him is with a sincere heart or not, as the verse says "G-d knows the thoughts of the heart, that they are vain" (Tehilim 94:11) and "Does not He that tests the heart understand it?" (Mishlei 24:12), and "You alone know the hearts of all men" (Melachim I 8:39).

When this is clearly realized by the one who trusts, it is not proper for him to claim with his lips that he trusts in G-d (in the daily prayers in many places - *ML*), without trusting in Him in his heart and thoughts, whereby he would be in the category of he of whom the verse says "with their mouths and their lips they honor Me, but their hearts are far from Me" (Isaiah 29:13).

(*Pas Lechem*: The reason the author counted this as one of the introductions/prerequisites to trust is only for the phrase: "He also knows whether a man's trust in Him is with a sincere heart or not", that through a man's remembering that G-d observes Him in all of his words and thoughts, he will also remember that included in this is G-d's observing whether or not his trust is sincere.

Marpe Lenefesh: When a man realizes that G-d knows the truth, whether what comes out of his lips is the same as what is in his heart, how could he then claim and say that he "truly trusts in G-d", when his heart is not with him. And then G-d will also remove His providence from him as mentioned in the beginning of the introduction to this gate ("..whoever trusts in something other than G-d, the Al-mighty will remove His providence from such a person..."), and then it will be a chillul H-ashem. And it is proper for us to put our eyes and hearts on the things which come out of our lips every day in our prayers, that we claim and say many times that we trust in Him and hope to Him, such as in Pesukei D'Zimra: "Nafshenu Chiksa L'H-ashem", "ki bshem kadsho batachnu", "yehi chasdecha..", and in Ahava Raba: "ki bshem kadshecha hagadol vehanora batachnu", and in the Shmonei Esrei "ve ten sachar tov lchol habotchim b'shimcha b'emes, vsim chelkenu imahem", "ki becha batachnu", and many others. It is proper for every man to put his eye and heart all of his days on the words of this gate, then "lo yevosh v'lo yikalem", not in this world and not in the next.

THIRD INTRODUCTION TO BRING COMPLETE TRUST
(3) That a person trusts in G-d alone for the things he is obligated to trust in (the things that one should not trust in G-d will be explained later), and not to associate Him with anyone else by trusting in Him and one of the created beings because then his trust in G-d will be invalidated in that he associated someone else with G-d. You know what was said about Asa, despite all of his piety, when he relied on the doctors, as written "during his illness, he did not seek help from G-d, but only in the doctors" (Divrei HaYamim II 16:12) (i.e. he did not also pray), and he was punished for this. And the verse says "Blessed is the man who trusts in the L-ord; the L-ord shall be his refuge" (Yirmiya 17:7).

And it is known that one who entrusts two or more men to do a task, the matter spoils. All the more so, for one who trusts in G-d and man, that his trust in G-d will be ruined (since he equated G-d with a created being, which is a great demeaning of G-d's greatness - TL).

(*Pas Lechem*: The talmud says (Eruvin 50a) "a pot of partners is neither hot nor cold", i.e. that for two people who are entrusted with a task, even though they are of approximately equal worth, nevertheless, each one is not pleased with your trust in him since you also charged the second person to head the task and trusted in him. All the more so that it is hard on G-d to be pleased when you equate a servant with his Master.

Translator: The Rayatz Rebbe would say "bitachon (trust) is when a person finds himself in the middle of the ocean with nothing, not even a piece of straw". i.e. this is how one should view his situation. Heard from D.L.Naiditch)

Furthermore, this will be the strongest factor for denying him the object of his trust, as written "cursed is the man who trusts in men,.. and turns his heart away from G-d" (Yirmiya 17:5).

(*Marpe Lenefesh*: Rather, let one reflect constantly that G-d is the Cause of all causes, and everyone and everything are merely His agents, as will be explained later on.)

FOURTH INTRODUCTION
That one is very careful and makes a great effort to fulfill what the Creator required of him in His service, to do his mitzvot and to guard oneself from what He has forbidden, just like he seeks that the Creator agrees to do with him in that which he trusts Him, as our sages said "make His will your will so that He will make your will His will, nullify your will to His will so that He will nullify the will of others to your will" (Avot 2:4).

(*Tov Halevanon*: i.e. nullify your taava (physical desires) so that they will not lead you to nullify a commandment of G-d, and separate from what is permitted to you, "so that He will nullify the will of others to your will", i.e. so that His providence on you will be greater than His providence on other people, and everyone in the world will yield for your sake, as the talmud says (Berachos 6b) "the whole world was created for his sake only".)

And the verse says "Trust in the L-ord and do good; so shall you dwell in the land, and verily you shall be fed" (Tehilim 37:3), and "G-d is good to those who hope in Him, to one who seeks Him" (Eicha 3:25).

But, If one trusts in G-d and rebels against Him, how foolish is he, how weak is his intellect and his understanding! For he can see in this world that if an employer appoints a man to do something or refrain from doing something and the man disobeys the instruction, this will be the strongest factor in the employer's refusing to fulfill his side of the deal. All the more so, for one who disobeys the commandments of G-d, for which G-d Himself testified that one who trusts in Him and disobeys Him will have his hopes foiled and his trust will be considered hypocritical.

Rather, he will be like that of who it is written "For what is the hope of the flatterer who deceives, when G-d casts off his soul? Will G-d listen to his cry when trouble comes on him?" (Job 27:8-9), and "Will you steal, murder, commit adultery, swear falsely, offer up to idols, and follow other gods that you know not. And will you come and stand before Me in this house, upon which My Name is called, and say, 'We are saved,' in order to commit all these abominations? Has this house upon which My name is called, become a den of thieves in your eyes? I, too, behold I have seen it, says the L-ord." (Yirmiyahu 7:9-11).

(*Marpe Lenefesh*: Even though G-d has compassion on all His creations, including the wicked, as he explained earlier, even so, for this, one should not think that G-d will forever tolerate him, and trust that G-d will continue bestowing good to him always despite his wickedness. And even though things are going well now, there is no escape from His judgments, and eventually, when He wishes, He will choose a time and place to collect His debt (of justice). Rather it is proper for a man to endeavor to fulfill all of G-d's commandments.

Matanas Chelko: Besides that one must realize that all powers are in G-d's hands, none can prevent Him from doing what He wishes, and further that G-d knows his thoughts, and it is impossible to trick Him. Hence, he cannot claim verbally that he trusts in G-d while he does not really trust Him in his inner being. Thirdly, that he should not associate anything or anyone else with G-d, as before. However, an extra condition is needed, namely, that this is in truth the will of G-d. For, one cannot place his trust in a strong person who can help him unless he knows that the person actually wants to help him. For example, if one tells a poor man: "such and such a person is a very rich man and is able to help you with all your needs. The poor man still should not place his trust in the rich man since he does not know whether the rich man actually wants to help him.

So too, by G-d, there is no doubt that He can perform signs and wonders for a person. But one cannot trust in this unless he knows that G-d truly wants to do so. The one and only way through which a person can know whether G-d wants to help and do for him is only if he himself does the will of G-d. Hence, necessarily, one of the pillars of trust is that he be a righteous person who does the will of G-d. And even though G-d also does the will of the wicked sometimes, nevertheless, they cannot trust in this because they cannot know for sure how long G-d will hold back retribution from them. Unlike the righteous, who can rest assured.
"make His will your will so that He will make your will His will" - the author is telling us that this mishna is the pillar of trust. He who wants to rest assured that G-d will do what he wants, let him do the will of G-d. Otherwise, how can he trust that G-d will do his wish? But if he exerts himself greatly to do the will of G-d, then he can hope and trust that G-d will likewise do his will... (Translator: see Gate 3 Chapter 7 where the author brings the minimum service whereby a person is assured of receiving continuous divine benefits.)
"Trust in the L-ord and do good; so shall you dwell in the land, and verily you shall be fed" - both things go together. If he wants to trust in G-d, he

must do good, as before. And that which the wicked can trust in G-d's trait of kindness and compassion, this is only temporarily. As the Marpe Lenefesh commentary wrote (see above). Hence, the wicked should not trust that G-d's compassion and kindness will continuously bestow on him forever. Rather, he can trust temporarily on G-d's trait of kindness and compassion, that G-d will withhold retribution from him and continue to bestow life to him. But he must repent in the end and he can never know for sure when the time will come that G-d will collect His debt [of justice]. On the other hand, one who does the will of G-d can place his trust in G-d. For through this he is assured that G-d wants to help him and do what's good for him since G-d already promised this.

"Will G-d hear his cry when trouble comes on him?" - hence G-d testified that he does not wish to help and aid a person who transgresses His word. One who thinks to himself that G-d will help him even if he does not fulfill what G-d commanded him to do - this is the greatest folly.

"Has this house upon which My name is called, become a den of thieves in your eyes?" - even though, of all places in the world, the Temple in Jerusalem is the place where prayers are most readily answered and for trusting in G-d, nevertheless, if it has become a den of thieves, already they should no longer trust in this, and they are not assured anymore that if they scream out in prayers that G-d will fulfill their request. (*translator*: for perhaps it is better for them to receive sufferings to atone for their evil deeds than to be saved)

Translator: nevertheless, one must know and trust that his repentance will always be accepted no matter how far he strayed and what he did etc. as the Marpe Lenefesh commentary explained earlier: "Otherwise, he will abandon hope from the favors of G-d, since he is in doubt whether he is worthy of them, and his trust in G-d will diminish. And through this, he will distance from G-d and His torah. Rather, let him reflect that G-d is benevolent to the good and the bad, as written: "His mercy is on all of His creations" (Tehilim 145:9). And through this, he will come closer to G-d and repent and he will become worthy of the good.")

FIFTH INTRODUCTION

A person should realize that every new thing that happens in this world after Genesis is completed in two ways:

First: By G-d's decree and His will that the matter should come into existence.

Secondly: Through intermediate causes and means - some near, some remote, some apparent, some hidden, all of which rush to bring into existence what was decreed, doing so with G-d's help.

(Ramchal: When a matter is decreed, a Bas Kol (Heavenly voice) is proclaimed throughout the mystical worlds which summons and gives the power to the appointed forces needed to carry out the matter.)

An illustration of the causes: Consider the act of drawing up water from the depths of the earth using a wheel system to which buckets are attached and which raises the water from the well. The buckets are the near cause. The remote cause is the man who harnessed an animal to the wheel and compels the animal to move in order to raise the water from the bottom of the well to the surface of the earth.

The intermediate means between the man and the buckets are: the animal, the mechanical contraption of interconnected wheels/gears which turn each other in series, and the rope. If a mishap were to occur to any one of the causes mentioned (i.e. the intermediate means or the near cause - TL), the intended purpose for which they were designed would not be accomplished.

And so it is for other things which come to existence. They cannot be produced by a man or anyone else, but rather, through the decree of G-d, and His preparing all the means through which the thing will be produced, as written *"And by Him, causes are counted"* (Shmuel I 2:3), and *"Who is great in counsel and mighty in carrying it out"* (Yirmiyahu 32:19), and *"it was a cause from G-d"* (Melachim I 12:15). And if the means are blocked, none of the actions which normally bring this matter into existence will succeed.

(*Pas Lechem*: i.e. by Him are all the number of means which cause each and every thing to occur. And if one of the means were missing the thing would not occur. And since it is not so clear from the first verse that He is the First cause which prepares the other causes, one might think that they are merely known to Him in number. Therefore the author brought the second verse "Who is great in counsel and Mighty in carrying it out", which teaches that He is the Master of all causes and the one who carries them out... And if one is still stubborn and wants to say that there is no proof from these two verses. They only teach that the causes are attributed to Him since He is the Creator of everything, therefore the author brought the third verse which teaches that the matter was from G-d with specific intent for that thing.

Matanas Chelko: even for making a loaf of bread, thousands of people are needed such as workers to plant, reap, mill, bake. And each stage requires machines built for sowing, reaping, etc. And the materials are transported through machines on roads and highways, etc. Hence even to make a piece of bread there are thousands of necessary details.. And even though we believe that G-d was behind everything, and that He can do it all without any intermediate means and can create ready to eat bread directly into our home, nevertheless, the author explains, that our eyes can see there is a nature and order that we must recognize and understand. Afterwards, he will explain why G-d wanted things to follow this order.)

When we examine the need for a man to pursue means and exert himself to complete his needs, we can see with our own eyes that for one who needs food and proper food is served before him, nevertheless if he does not exert himself to eat it by lifting the food to his mouth, chewing it, etc., he will not break his hunger. Likewise for someone thirsty, who needs water. And all the more so, if he has no food prepared, until he needs to exert himself through milling flour, kneading, baking, etc . And more so, if he needs to buy the food and prepare it. And even more still, if he has no money to buy them and will need even greater exertion to pursue means to earn the money or to sell the amount he needs from the objects he uses or his other possessions, or the like.

WHY MAN MUST WORK FOR A LIVELIHOOD
There are two reasons why the Creator obligated a man to pursue means and exert himself for his livelihood and other needs.

(*Tov Halevanon*: Man does not find his food readily like other living creatures which do not need to pursue causes and means.

Matanas Chelko: "*the Creator obligated a man...*" - "hishtadlus" (exertion) is an obligation! It is an obligation to exert oneself to provide for himself and his family. Likewise for all the other things which we are forced to enter into the system of causes and means. It is for two reasons...)

(1) Divine wisdom required the testing of man in the service of G-d or rebellion against Him. Therefore, G-d tests man with what demonstrates his choice in this - needs and lacking for external things such as food, drink, clothing, shelter, and marital relations. G-d commanded man to pursue and attain them through the available means in specific ways (according to the torah - *ML*) and at specific times.

(*Translator*: G-d knows already what each person will choose. The purpose of testing man is to give him an opportunity to elevate himself in the greatest possible way - by choosing good of his own free will, as explained in Gate 3)

What G-d has decreed that man will attain of them, man will attain fully after the completion of the prepared means.

That which has not been decreed that he will attain - he will not attain, and the necessary means will be withheld.

Through this process, his free choice of whether he served G-d or rebelled against Him will be demonstrated through his intention and choice, and the man will then deserve either reward or punishment, regardless whether or not he actually achieved his intentions.

> (*Pas Lechem*: the author said "through his intention and choice" because the status of the choice is according to the intention, namely, if he chooses good with bad intentions, such as choosing good with intent for flattery or boasting himself, or arrogance - he is evil. Likewise for the opposite, as our Sages taught us (Nazir 23b) from Yael)

(2) Secondly, if a man were not forced to exert himself in seeking a livelihood, he would kick (become defiant) and chase after sin, and he would ignore his debt of gratitude to G-d for His goodness to him. As written: *"And the harp, and the lyre, the timbrel, and flute, and wine, are in their feasts: but they regard not the work of the L-ord, neither consider the work of His hands"* (Isaiah 5:12), and *"But Yeshurun grew fat, and kicked: you are grown fat, you are grown thick, you are covered with fatness; then he forsook G-d who made him, and lightly esteemed the Rock of his salvation"* (Devarim 32:15). And the sages said *"it is good the study of torah with working for a livelihood because the toil in both removes thoughts of sin, and all torah study without work will in the end be abandoned and bring to sin"* (Avot 2:2). And all the more so for one who has no share in either torah or work, nor directs his attention to any of these pursuits.

> (*Pas Lechem*: From here we see that indulgence in physical pleasures makes a man's heart coarse, thereby causing him to refrain from doing the commandments.
>
> *Tov Halevanon*: If everything were prepared for man, he would be idle to chase after sin. Also his body's nature and physicality would tend to kick and be ungrateful for the favors of G-d due to the delight in his heart, since everything would be ready before him. He would think that he is deserving of all this and he would not realize that it is from G-d.
>
> *Marpe Lenefesh*: If everything were prepared and ready before a man, he would not have any free choice. And he would remain forever at the same level and he would not deserve any reward or punishment...

Matanas Chelko: In our times, people only want to work a little. Therefore, they lack the necessary exertion and they come to sin. The Creator's intent was that a man work so strenuously from morning until evening that when he returns to his home after a long day of work, he will not have strength to watch television. But, as we said, people do not tire themselves to this extent, so when they return home, they have strength remaining to sin and their evil inclination is still in its full power. The purpose of exertion is to weaken the evil inclination. This is what the sages said "it is good the study of torah with working for a livelihood because the toil in both removes thoughts of sin". In truth, if a man would exert himself in torah to such an extent that his evil inclination would be weakened, then he would have reached the intended purpose and would not need to also exert himself in earning a livelihood. But this path is only for special individuals. The vast majority need to exert themselves in both. Exertion in torah alone is not enough for them. However, the intent for both is the same, namely, that the exertion weakens his strength until he is no longer capable of sinning. Hence, the purpose is not simply to learn torah and work. For if these two do not weaken him to such an extent that he can no longer sin, then he will still come to sin. Rather, the aim is to toil and strain in torah and also in work until both exertions remove thoughts of sin.)

It was out of compassion for man that G-d has compelled him to be occupied with matters of this world and the next for all of his days, and so that he does not seek that which he does not need and which he cannot understand with his limited intellect, such as matters of what was before the creation and of the final end (since these things do not further his perfection and on the contrary - they damage him - *PL*), as the wise man said *"also the [toil of] the world He has set into their hearts, so that man should not seek the deed which G-d did, from beginning to end."* (Koheles 3:11).

WHEN G-D REMOVES THE BURDEN OF EARNING A LIVELIHOOD FROM A MAN

If a man strengthens himself in the service of G-d, resolves to fear Him, trusts in Him for his religious and secular matters, steers away from reprehensible things (such as anger or arrogance - *PL*), strives for the good midot (character traits), does not rebel in prosperity nor turn towards leisure, is not enticed by the evil inclination, nor seduced by the witchery of this world - the burden of exerting himself in the means to a livelihood will be removed from him, since the two reasons mentioned above no longer apply to him. Namely, to test him on his choice and to protect him from rebelling during prosperity. His livelihood will come to him without strain (of the heart - *PL*) or toil (of the limbs - *PL*), according to his needs, as written *"G-d will not bring hunger to the righteous"* (Mishlei 10:3).

(*Tov Halevanon*: "the witchery of this world" refers to the worldly pleasures which spellbind the eyes of the one who gazes at them until he thinks they are good for him but he does not realize their ultimate end.

Pas Lechem: "removes the burden.." - since he no longer needs to be tested because his heart has already strengthened in the service of G-d, and he is full of fear and trust of Him, and also he is not liable to rebel, so why should G-d trouble him further?

Matanas Chelko: This is another great principle. If a man thinks for whatever reason that he no longer needs to engage in the pursuit of a livelihood. This is only justified if he is clinging to G-d. Not because he merely trusts in G-d. Many people mistakenly think that the amount of hishtadlus (exertion for livelihood) is proportional to the amount of trust a person has. This is not correct. A man can have great trust but if he has not yet reached the level that he is straining himself as before or it is still necessary to test him whether or not he will do only the will of G-d, then even if he has much tranquility, he is still under obligation to exert himself in his livelihood....[see there at length]...In our times, if one learns in yeshiva or Kollel and has some sort of plan on how to support himself and his family - this is considered Torah study with work. For that which the sages said that one must combine torah and work, their intent was not that every person must specifically work but rather that he has some sort of plan... nevertheless he is lacking the second reason, namely, that one must strain himself until he has no strength left to come to sin. Therefore, he is under duty to strain himself in torah study to this extent.)

If one asks: Behold we see some tzadikim (very righteous people) which do not receive their livelihood except after hard and strenuous toil, while many transgressors are at ease, living a good, pleasant life?
We will say: The prophets and the chasidim (extremely pious) already investigated this matter. One of them said *"[Righteous are you, O L-rd, when I plead with You: yet let me talk with You of your judgments:] Why does the way of the wicked prosper? why are all they happy that deal very treacherously?"* (Yirmiyahu 12:1), and another *"Why do You show me iniquity and look upon mischief; and plunder and violence are before me; and the one who bears quarrel and strife endures?"* (Chavakuk 1:3), and *"for a wicked man surrounds the righteous; therefore, justice emerges perverted"* (Chavakuk 1:4), and *"Why should You be silent when a wicked man swallows up one more righteous than he?"* (Chavakuk 1:13), and another one said *"Behold these are wicked, yet they are tranquil in the world and have increased wealth."* (Tehilim 73:12), and *"But for naught I*

cleansed my heart and bathed my hands with cleanliness" (Tehilim 73:13), and another said *"And now we praise the bold transgressors, those who work wickedness are built up, they tempt G-d, and they have, nevertheless, escaped."* (Malachi 3:15), and many more like this.

But the prophet refrained from giving an answer because each specific case has its own particular reason (there is no general answer which includes everything - *TL*). Therefore Moshe Rabeinu commented on this in the torah saying: *"the hidden things belong to G-d"* (Devarim 29:28), and the wise man said in connection to this *"If you see the oppression of the poor, and perverting of justice and righteousness in a province, marvel not at the matter"* (Koheles 5:7), and the verse says: *"the Rock, His deeds are perfect for all His ways are justice"* (Devarim 32:4).
(i.e. ultimately, the matter is hidden and concealed by its nature and is beyond the powers of the human mind to grasp - *PL*)

WHY THE RIGHTEOUS SOMETIMES SUFFER

Nevertheless, I saw fitting to attempt to clarify this matter that should be to some extent satisfactory (so that it won't be so difficult - *TL*).
The possible reasons why a tzadik is prevented from obtaining his livelihood without effort and must instead exert himself for it and be tested by it is as follows.
1. A previous sin for which it is necessary to pay him for it, as written *"the tzadik will pay in the land"* (Mishlei 11:31).

> (*Marpe Lenefesh*: As the sages said (Kidushin 39b): "He whose merits outweighs his sins is punished (Rashi: in this world to cleanse him from his sins, so that he receives complete reward in the World to Come) and is as though he had burnt the whole Torah, not leaving even a single letter; while he whose sins outweighs his merits is rewarded (Rashi: to pay him the reward for his merits in this world so as to banish him in the World to Come) and is as though he had fulfilled the whole Torah, not omitting even a single letter!"
>
> *Translator*: and since the wicked man is unable to receive the reward of Olam Haba due to corrupting his soul too much, so might as well give him some good here - *Lev Eliyahu*.)

2. In the way of exchanging, to pay him more good in Olam Haba (the afterlife), as written *"to benefit you in your end"* (Devarim 8:16)

> (*Marpe Lenefesh*: These are "Yisurim shel Ahava" (chastening of love)

which are not due to sins, as the talmud says (Berachos 5a): "if he examined his deeds and did not find any sins let him be sure that these are Yisurim shel Ahava, as written (Mishlei 3:12): 'For whom G-d loves He chastens'", i.e. to increase his reward in Olam Haba more than his merits. *Pas Lechem*: To exchange for him a fleeting world for an eternal world.)

3. To demonstrate his good bearing and good acceptance of suffering in the service of G-d, so that others will learn from him, as you know from the matter of [the book of] Job.

(*Marpe Lenefesh*: That he receives everything with a good countenance, and he does not rebel in sufferings so that others will learn from him and see him and notice him and desire to serve G-d even though they don't have all their lusts, and even though they are in poverty, hardship or in painful sicknesses as we find with Job and many other sages, who were in suffering yet did not stop from torah and service, and as is known of Hillel who was extremely poor, and others who needed to labor for their livelihoods and nevertheless studied the torah.
Alternative explanation:
Pas Lechem: To show the world that the Tzadik bears the bad of this world, with good patience and a good countenance, and despite his suffering, he does not budge away from the service of his Creator in order to ease the bad. Unlike the wicked, that even for something he is forced to bear, he bears it with an angry heart, and therefore he throws off the yoke of service in order to ease his troubles.
Tov Halevanon: He bears his sufferings and is not begrudging towards G-d and accepts them with a good countenance)

4. Due to the wickedness of his generation, G-d tests him with poverty, hardship, or sickness to demonstrate/contrast his piety and service of G-d unlike them, as written *"Indeed, he bore our illnesses, and our pains he carried them"* (Isaiah 53:4).

(*Pas Lechem*: Here G-d knows that the people of his generation won't learn from him and they will get no benefit from this. Nevertheless, G-d tests him in order to demonstrate his level and worth and contrast it with them. That even though they are in enjoyment and he is in a life of suffering, they are ungrateful towards G-d while he is good with Him and serves Him in truth and wholeheartedly. The intent in this is so that they will acknowledge G-d's justice in the end of days when they will see the exceedingly great reward of the Tzadik. And like our sages said in Pirkei Avot 5:3, "Avraham was tested with ten trials..to show his high esteem."

Marpe Lenefesh: Due to the wickedness of the generation, sometimes G-d sends suffering to a Tzadik to atone for the sins of the generation (to avert disasters or the like), and without a doubt, his reward will not be withheld and the wicked will be paid what they deserve, as Rashi explained on the verse he cited)

5. Due to his not being sufficiently zealous in standing up for G-d, and exacting justice (i.e. protesting - *TL*) from men of his generation, as you know from the story of Eli and his sons, as the verse says *"And it will be that everyone who is left in your house, will come to prostrate himself before him for a silver piece and a morsel of bread"* (Shmuel 2:36).

(*Pas Lechem*: As the Talmud says (Shabbat 54b): "Whoever can forbid his household [to commit a sin] but does not, is seized (held accountable) for [the sins of] his household; [if he can forbid] the men of his city, he is seized for [the sins of] the men of his city; if the whole world, he is seized for [the sins of] the whole world")

Translator: There is another general purpose to suffering for everyone including children as explained in Gate 2 ch.5. Here is an excerpt:
Later on he is subjected to illnesses and meets with painful incidents so that he recognizes the world, and that its nature is not concealed from him. Thus he is put on his guard against trusting in this world thereby permitting his lusts to rule over him, in which case he would become like the animals that neither think nor understand; as it is written *"Be ye not as the horse or as the mule which have no understanding"* (Tehilim 32:9).
Tov Halevanon: "illnesses" - such as chicken pox and measles. *"painful incidents"* - many weaknesses come in the boyhood years. PL - accidents such as stepping on a metal nail.
"Be ye not as the horse or as the mule" - they need to be leashed and muzzled, so too man. The painful incidents humble his lusts.
"so that he recognizes the world" - how a person's situation can change swiftly from contentment to pain so that he realizes not to trust in it and its tranquility - rather to always be afraid and to seek refuge in G-d's shadow.

Marpe Lenefesh: If a human being had only constant good in this world, he would forget and not recall the matters of his final end, and he would trust (hope) in this world and follow the musings of his heart and his lusts for all of his days. Therefore, it was among the divine plan to send him sometimes bad illnesses, even during his youth in order that he recognize and know that there is no complete good in this world. And even if he is currently in a very good situation, the bad illnesses can come and ruin his joy, so that he won't trust in this world.
End Quote.
Another reason for suffering explained by the kabalists is to rectify something done in past lives. Most people are said to have lived previously in past lives (see shaar gilgulim). So for example, someone born into a life

of misery and suffering for no apparent reason whatsoever - this may be in order to rectify something from a past life. For example, the Zohar states that the Jewish slaves in Egypt who born and died doing hard labor slavery work for Pharaoh were reincarnations of the generation of the builders of the Tower of Bavel.)

WHY THE WICKED SOMETIMES PROSPER
Sometimes G-d sends good to the wicked for the following reasons:

1. A previous good deed he did, to pay him in this world, as written *"And He repays those He hates to their face, to destroy them"* (Devarim 7:10) which Onkelos renders: "He pays those He hates for their good deeds during their lives to destroy them".

2. As a temporary deposit, until G-d gives him a righteous son who is worthy of it, as written *"he prepares but the tzadik (righteous) will wear it"* (Job 27:17), and *"to the sinner He has given a preoccupation to gather and to accumulate, to give to him who is good in G-d's sight"* (Koheles 2:26).

3. Sometimes the money is the chief cause of his evil (in the next world) or death (in this world), as written *"There is a grievous evil that I saw under the sun; riches kept by their owner for his harm"* (Koheles 5:12) (such as Korach or Naval - *PL*).

4. Sometimes it is to give him time to repent and become worthy of it, as you know of the story of Menashe.

5. His father did good and it is fitting to benefit him in the merit of his father, as said to Yehu ben Nimshi *"four generations of your descendants will sit on the throne of Israel"* (Melachim II 10:30), and *"He who walks innocently is righteous; fortunate are his sons after him"* (Mishlei 20:7), and *"I was young, and have aged, and I have not seen a righteous man forsaken nor his descendants begging bread"* (Tehilim 37:25).

6. Sometimes it is to test those who are deceptive or have an evil interior. When they see the wicked prosper, they quickly stray from the service of G-d and hasten to win the favor of the wicked and to learn from their actions. In this way it will be clarified the pure men to G-d and it will be demonstrated who was faithful to G-d in bearing at a time when the wicked rule and persecute him. He will receive reward from the Creator for this, as you know of the story of Eliyahu and Isabel or Yirmiyahu and the kings of his generation.

(*Pas Lechem*: The intended purpose of all this was so that the pure men "will receive reward from the Creator for this".

Marpe Lenefesh: Through this it will be demonstrated who was of good, pure heart to G-d and faithful in His service. And even though the wicked were ruling over him and humiliating him, he bears everything and knows that their success is temporary and eventually G-d will collect His debt. And he doesn't learn from their ways and will receive reward for this. But if G-d were to punish the wicked immediately, and reward the righteous right away, there would be no room for free will (which was the purpose of creation), and everyone would hasten to do good and receive reward quickly and everyone would fear swift punishment.

CHOICE OF OCCUPATION:
Since it has been clarified the obligation for a man to pursue the means for a livelihood, now we will clarify that not every man is required to pursue every possible means.

The possible means are numerous. Some occupations are easy, requiring little strain such as shop keeping or light work with the hands such as sewing, writing, contracting businesses, hiring sharecroppers or workers, supervisors.

Some occupations require hard physical labor such as tanning, mining iron or copper, smelting metals, heavy transport, constant travel to faraway places, working and plowing land, or the like,

For one who is physically strong and intellectually weak, it is fitting to choose an occupation among those that require physical exertion according to what he can bear.
He who is physically weak but intellectually strong should not seek among those which tire the body but should instead tend towards those who are light on the body and that he will be able to sustain .

Every man has a preference for a particular work or business over others. G-d has already implanted in his nature a love and fondness for it, as He implanted in a cat's nature the hunting of mice, or the falcon to hunt smaller birds, the deer to trap snakes. Some birds hunt only fish, and likewise, each animal species has a liking and desire for particular plants or animals, which G-d has implanted to be the means for its sustenance, and the structure of its body and limbs is suited for that thing. The long bill and legs of a fish catching bird, or the strong teeth and claws of the lion, horns of the ox and ram (i.e. for defense - *TL*), while animals whose sustenance is from plants do not have the tools to hunt and kill.

Similarly you will find among human beings character traits and body structures suited for certain businesses or activity. One who finds his nature and personality attracted to a certain occupation, and his body is suited for it, that he will be able to bear its demands - he should pursue it, and make it his means of earning a livelihood, and he should bear its pleasures and pains, and not be upset when sometimes his income is withheld. Rather let him trust in G-d that He will support him all of his days.

> (*Pas Lechem*: For example, one for who the trait of compassion dominates him should distance from becoming a butcher. And likewise, the sages said: "a kapdan (irritable person) should not be a teacher" (Pirkei Avot 2:5), and similarly for other traits.)

INTENTIONS WHEN WORKING FOR A LIVELIHOOD

And he should have intention when his mind and body is occupied with one of the means of earning a living to fulfill the commandment of the Creator to pursue the means of the world, such as working the land, plowing and sowing it, as written: *"And G-d took the man and placed him in Gan Eden to work it and to guard it"* (Bereishit 2.15), and also to use other living creatures for his benefit and sustenance, and for building cities and preparing food, and to marry a woman and have relations to populate the world.

He will be rewarded for his intentions in heart and mind to serve G-d whether or not his desire is accomplished, as written: *"If you eat from the toil of your hands, you are praiseworthy, and it is good for you"* (Tehilim 128:2), and our sages of blessed memory said: *"Let all your actions be for the sake of Heaven (to serve G-d)"* (Avot 2:12).

In this way, his trust in G-d will be intact, undamaged by the toiling in the means to earn a livelihood, as long as his intention in heart and mind is for the sake of Heaven (to do the will of G-d that the world be populated and built up).

> (*Tov Halevanon*: It will not damage that which he is made idle from torah study and service of G-d since this too will be considered for him as righteousness and service.)

One should not think that his livelihood depends on particular means and that if these means fail, his livelihood will not come from a different means. Rather, trust in the Al-mighty, and know that all means are equal for Him. He can provide using whatever means and at any time and however He so wishes, as written: *"for with the L-ord there is no limitation to save with many or with few"* (Shmuel I 14:6), and *"But you must remember the L-ord your G-d, for it is He that gives you strength to make wealth, in order to establish His covenant which He swore to your forefathers, as it is this day."* (Devarim 8:18), and *"Not by might nor by power, but by My spirit, says the L-ord of Hosts"* (Zecharia 4:6).

*** Chapter 4 ***

- *When trust applies and when it does not*

The concerns for which the believer is obligated to put his trust in G-d are of two categories. (1) matters of this world, and (2), matters of Olam Haba (afterlife). Matters of this world subdivide to two divisions.

(1) matters of this world for the benefit of this world. (2) matters of this world for the benefit of Olam Haba (the afterlife).

The matters of this world for the benefit of this world subdivide to three parts:
(1) what is beneficial for the body only.
(2) what contributes to one's maintenance or enables one to gain wealth and various possessions.
(3) what is beneficial for [dealing with] one's household, wife and relatives, one's friends and enemies, and for those above and below him among the various classes of people.

Matters of this world for the benefit Olam Haba subdivide to two parts.
(1) Duties of the heart and limbs which relate to oneself only, and whose actions do not result in benefit or damage to others.
(2) Duties of the limbs which cannot be done without association with another person, where one of them is active and the other is passive. For example, giving charity, acts of kindness, teaching of wisdom, instructing others to do good or to refrain from evil.

Matters of the afterlife subdivide to two parts.
(1) The reward that is deserved.
(2) That which is a special kindness which the Creator bestows to the pious and to the prophets in Olam Haba.

THE 7 CATEGORIES TO TRUST IN
Thus all things for which one trusts in the Creator fall into 7 categories:
(1) matters of the body alone.
(2) matters of one's possessions and means of earning a livelihood.
(3) matters of one's wife, children, relatives, friends, and enemies [and for those above and below him].

(4) duties of the heart and limbs which only benefit or damage oneself.

(5) duties of the limbs which affect others as well, whether benefiting or harming.

(6) reward in the afterlife according to one's conduct in this world.

(7) reward in the afterlife from the Creator in the way of kindness on His treasured ones and those who love Him (i.e. to increase their reward due to their love and clinging to G-d - *TL*), as written: *"How great is Your goodness that You have hidden away for those who fear You; You have done for those who trust in You before the sons of men!"* (Tehilim 31:20)

Since I have explained the fundamental introductions (in chapter 3) which make it possible for one to place his trust in the Al-mighty, it is proper for me to follow them with an explanation of the proper way of trust in each of the seven categories, through which one should trust in G-d and in something besides Him.

(*Tov Halevanon*: i.e. To explain which is the proper way of trust, that can be called complete/flawless trust in G-d versus the trust which is mixed with trusting in something besides G-d such as one who trusts in G-d and also in some means, which would not be a proper and just trust.

Marpe Lenefesh: Namely, if he regards them as means between himself and G-d, and that they are merely agents from G-d as will be explained)

FIRST CATEGORY - MATTERS OF THE BODY ALONE

For the first category, matters of the body alone, these are: his life and death, his income for obtaining food, clothing and shelter, his health and illness, his traits. The proper way of trust in the A-lmighty for all of these matters is to submit oneself to the course the Creator has decreed for him in these matters, and to place one's trust in G-d and to know that none of these matters can come to be unless it was previously determined by G-d that this would be the most proper situation for his matter in this world and in Olam Haba (the afterlife), and ultimately the greatest good for him (even if right now it appears to his eye to be not good, certainly, it is the best thing for him for his ultimate end - *PL*), and that the Creator has exclusive, total control over all of these matters. In none of them can any created being advise any plan, or exercise any control except through His permission, decree, and judgment.

(*Pas Lechem*: (on the 3 terms: **permission, decree, judgment**) To not think that some human being's advice can possibly be beneficial unless it is through the permission and decree of the Creator. For example, regarding the healing of a sick person, the talmud expounds [on the verse Ex. 21:19]: "from this we learn that **permission** has been given to the physician to heal". The power in nature to heal through medicinal means is a permission of the Creator. This is a universal matter. And this is combined with the **decree** of G-d who decreed that this illness be healed through this specific doctor, as the talmud says (Avoda Zara 58a) "through such and such a doctor, using such and such a medicine". This is for the good category. On the bad category, if a man planned to harm him and succeeded, or that he led him in the bad path, and caused him to stumble, certainly, this **judgment** was sentenced by G-d, otherwise, he would not have succeeded.

Matanas Chelko: For all matters of this world, such as the things relevant to his body, home, or livelihood - everything was already pre-decreed by the Creator, and no man has any power or authority on these matters. This is one of the foundations of trust - that no man has any power in this. Therefore, there is no need to fear other people for none of them can benefit or harm him in any way.

And just like one's life and death, health and sickness, are not in the hands of others, so too, one's livelihood, clothing and other bodily needs are also not in their control.

With clear faith that his matters are given over to the decrees of the Creator, and that the Creator's choice for him is the best choice, it is also his duty to be engaged in means which appear to be beneficial to him and to choose what seems to be the best choice under the circumstances, and the Al-mighty will do according to what He has already pre-decreed.

(*Pas Lechem*: The author specifically stated the passive form of the verb "to be engaged" (in means...) instead of the active form "to engage" (in means...) since we are talking about a person who fully believes that all his movements are given over to the hands of the Creator, and if he does some thing, he is not doing it. Rather it is being done to him by G-d, like an ax in the hands of a woodchopper.

Translator: In Gate 3 chapter 8 the author explains this in more details and notes that it is beyond the ability of human understanding to grasp. see there with the commentaries essential reading.)

An example of this: Even though a human being's end and number of days are determined by the Creator's decree, nevertheless, it is a man's duty to pursue means to survive such as food and drink, clothing, and shelter according to his needs, and he must not leave this to the Al-mighty, and think: "if the Creator has pre-decreed that I will live, then my body will survive without food all the days of my life. Therefore, I will not trouble myself in seeking a livelihood and toiling in it".

Likewise, one should not put himself in danger while trusting on the decree of the Creator [that he will live a set time], drinking poisonous drink or going to battle lions or other dangerous animals without necessity, or to cast himself into the sea or into fire, or other similar things that a man is not sure of them and puts his life in danger. And the verse has already warned us in saying *"You shall not try the L-ord, your G-d"* (Devarim 6:16), because either one of two things will happen.

> (*Matanas Chelko*: "to battle lions or other dangerous animals without necessity" - the [extra] words "without necessity" come to hint that if one was attacked by a lion, he should not give up hope and think he has no chance of being saved. Rather, he should trust in G-d to save him, similar to what David did (Samuel 17:36-37).

Either he will die, and it will be considered as if he killed himself, and he will be held accountable for this just as if he had killed another man, despite that his death in this fashion was a decree of the Al-mighty and occurred with His permission.

> (*Tov Halevanon*: i.e. even though this person died through putting himself in danger and it was already predecreed by G-d that he would die through this danger and at that time. Nevertheless, he will be punished like one who murders another person, despite that the other person's death was predecreed. Even so, the murderer is guilty [since he had free will, and the decree of death could have been fulfilled through another way - Translator].)

And we have already been commanded not to murder another human being in any form from the verse: *"do not murder"* (Shmot 20:13). And the closer the murdered is to the murderer, the more the punishment should be severe, as written: *"on pursuing his brother with a sword, corrupting his mercy"* (Amos 1:11). And similarly the punishment for one who kills himself will undoubtedly be very great.

This is like a slave whose master commanded him to guard a place for a fixed time, and warned him not to leave the place until his messenger will come. When the slave saw that the messenger was late in coming, he abandoned his post, and the master became furious at him and punished him severely. Similarly, one who causes his own death (by doing dangerous things) moves out of the service of G-d and into rebellion against Him, by putting himself in mortal danger.

This is why you will find Shmuel say (to G-d): *And Shmuel said, 'How shall I go? For, if Saul hears, he will kill me.' And the L-ord said, "You shall take a heifer with you, and you shall say, 'I have come to slaughter (a sacrifice) to the L-ord.'"* (Shmuel I 16:2).

And this was not considered a lack of trust in the Al-mighty, and the answer from G-d to him shows that his zeal in this was appropriate (since G-d does not do public miracles without great necessity - *TL*), and G-d answered him: *"You shall take a heifer with you, and you shall say, 'I have come to bring an offering to the L-ord.'"* (Shmuel I 16:2). If this were considered a lack of trust G-d would have answered him: *"I cause death and grant life. I strike, and I heal"* (Devarim 32:39), or something similar, as He answered Moshe when Moshe claimed: *"But I am slow of speech and slow of tongue"* (Shmot 4:10), answering him *"Who has made a man's mouth? Who makes a man mute or deaf, seeing or blind"* (Shmot 4:11). And if Shmuel, with his perfect righteousness did not find it a light matter to put himself to a slight risk of danger, and even though he would be doing so by the command of G-d, as He commanded him *"Fill your horn with oil, and go, I shall send you to Yishai, the Bethlehemite, for I have seen for Myself a king among his sons"* (Shmuel I 16:1), all the more so for someone not commanded by G-d, that this would be considered reprehensible.

> (*Pas Lechem*: If you ask: "why was it considered a lacking by Moshe but not by Shmuel?". The answer is that Moshe was commanded "go and speak...", therefore certainly he will be granted the power of speech and he will be able to speak. Therefore [G-d rebuked him]: "Who has made a man's mouth?.." However, by Shmuel, his question was not against the command. It was possible for him to fulfill the command to anoint David and afterwards for Saul to kill him.)

(The second possibility) is that he will be saved by G-d's help. Then his merits will be annulled and he will lose his reward, as our sages said on this matter (Shabbat 32a): *"a man should never put himself in danger thinking that a miracle will be performed for him, because maybe no miracle will be done for him, and even if a miracle is done for him, his merits are reduced"*. And Yaakov our forefather said *"I am not worthy from all Your kindnesses"* (Bereishit 32:11), to which the Targum explains: *"my merits have diminished due to all of Your favors and kindnesses."*

PROPER TRUST IN MATTERS OF EARNING A LIVELIHOOD

What we have explained for matters of life and death, also applies to the duty to pursue means for health, food, clothing, shelter, good habits and distancing from their opposite - (he should engage in them) while firmly believing that the means to these things do not help at all in attaining them, without the decree of the Creator. Then, when a farmer must plow his field, clear it from weeds, sow it, and water it when rainwater is not available, let him trust in the Creator to make it fertile, and to protect it from plagues, to increase and to bless the crops. And it is not proper to leave the land unworked and unsowed and to trust G-d and rely on His decree that it will grow fruit without being sown first.

> *Matanas Chelko*: This is a powerful illustration from farmers.. For everyone can see that the farmer cannot claim it was all his own making. For even after all the work of plowing, sowing, etc., he must still rely on G-d for rain, and that the rain be not too much and not too little. This is a tremendous illustration on the ways of faith from which one can apply to all matters.

> *Translator*: Another illustration: The Jews in the Sinai desert received manna daily for 40 years. Based on a person's spiritual level, the manna would arrive daily either far away in the desert or directly at his doorstep. Thus even though the person was forced to exert himself to search in the desert, nevertheless, he knew that the portion he eventually found as well as the amount of exertion he had to do was pre-decreed for him from the beginning. So too, a person must exert himself according to what he needs. But at the same time, he must realize that the amount he eventually earns was designated for him by G-d from the beginning and that his exertion did not increase or decrease this amount.)

And likewise workers, merchants, and contractors are under a duty to pursue their livelihood while trusting in G-d that their livelihood is in His hands and under His control, that He guarantees to provide a man (as the verse "who gives sustenance to all flesh" - *PL*) and fully provides for him through whatever means He wishes. One should not think that the means can benefit or harm him in the least.

If one's livelihood comes through one of the means he worked on, it is proper for him not to trust in this source, rejoice in it, intensify in it, and turn his heart to it. For this will weaken his trust in the Al-mighty. It is improper to think that this source will be more beneficial to him than what was pre-decreed from the Creator. He should not rejoice for having pursued and engaged in it. Rather, he should thank the Creator who provided for him after his labor, and that He did not make his work and struggle result in nothing, as written: *"If you eat the toil of your hands, you are praiseworthy, and it is good for you"* (Tehilim 128:2).

> (*Matanas Chelko*: hence, the labor and the livelihood are two unconnected things. The labor is a kind of tax payment, and if through this he receives his livelihood and eats, he is also under duty to thank G-d for the food.
>
> *Translator*: I once asked a taxi driver in Israel if he makes good money driving. He corrected me saying "the taxi driving is my tikun (rectification), and the money is from G-d. The two are not connected. They're separate things.")

A pious man once said: "I am amazed of he who gives to another what the Creator decreed for the latter, and afterwards reminds the latter of the favor he did for him, and seeks to be thanked for this. And I am even more amazed by one who receives his livelihood from another who is forced to provide for him and then submits himself before him, pleases him and praises him."

> (*Marpe Lenefesh*: i.e. the recipient does not give praise and thanks to G-d who provided his livelihood through the donor, and appointed the donor as a caretaker of him. Rather, he submits only to the donor and flatters him as if the donor provided him of his own...and likewise he wrote later on "if only they realized that no human being has the power to give or prevent anything except to he who the Creator decreed - they would not hope to anyone other than Him, etc". And he wrote this again several times. This seems to be a contradiction (since the donor had free will whether or not to give to him). The answer to this is that the completion of something is not in man's hands. Rather, only the free will and resolve to do it [is in man's hands], and G-d is the one who brings all things to completion...
>
> Therefore this is the explanation here - a man is under duty to choose and resolve to separate from his money according to his generosity in order to give charity to the poor or to this poor man. And when the Creator desires to provide for this poor man through this donor, he arranges that they meet in one place so that this donor will give to this poor man, or sometimes to another according to His wisdom. Or if the man is not good before Him, G-d will make him stumble with bad people or other mishaps. But the main thing is that one tries to do the duty that is placed on him - to give charity and to do kindness. And if he is prevented, then he did his part and will receive full reward from G-d. Likewise for all mitzvot and all acts in the world as he will explain later on... And with this you will understand what

he wrote earlier in the beginning of chapter 3: "and all mercy and compassion that a man is shown from anyone besides G-d is really derived from G-d's mercy and compassion", see there. That G-d puts in the heart of this one to give to that one. With this introduction many difficult things are clear in the details of G-d's guidance of His world and through this you will understand most of this gate, with G-d's help.

Rabbi Yaakov Emden: Nevertheless, it is certainly a duty to thank and praise one's benefactor and not to think that one is exempt since the good came from G-d.... (see there in Masoret Yisrael edition for more)

Matanas Chelko: the recipient should not feel inferior and less thereby submitting himself towards the rich man and speak to him like a poor man...)

If one's livelihood fails to come through the means he has worked on, it is possible that the money allocated to him for the day has already reached his hands (and that he doesn't realize it - *PL*) or that it will come through other means.

However the case, it is proper for him to engage in the means of earning a livelihood and not to be lax in pursuing after them, provided they are suited to his traits and physical abilities, as I previously explained. And all the while, he should trust in G-d, that He will not abandon him (in providing his needs - *PL*), neglect him (regarding his physical health - *PL*), or ignore him (in whatever trouble befalls him - *PL*) as written *"The L-ord is good, a stronghold on a day of trouble and knows (Rashi - the needs of) those who trust in Him"* (Nachum 1:7)

(*Pas Lechem*: The first half of the verse teaches that G-d does not ignore his troubles while the second half includes the other two matters, that G-d does not abandon him nor neglect him)

PROPER TRUST IN MATTERS OF HEALTH AND SICKNESS

Similarly, we will say regarding health and sickness. A man is placed under a duty to trust in the Creator in this, while working on maintaining his health according to the means whose nature promotes this, and to fight sickness according to the customary ways, as the Creator commanded *"and he shall surely heal him"* (Shemot 21:19). All of this, without trusting in the means of health or illness that they could help or hurt without the permission of the Creator.

And when one puts his trust in the Creator, He will heal him with or without a means, as written: *"He sends His word and heals them"* (Tehilim 107:20).

> (*Pas Lechem*: From this verse we see that it is really His word, namely, His decree that heals - not the means.
>
> Translator: Rabbi Avigdor Miller would say that in ancient times bloodletting was a popular medical procedure. Today it is neither accepted nor effective. This does not mean that it was not effective back then. Actually it was. The science of the times had logical reasons why it should work, and people believed in those reasons. Therefore G-d healed them through the bloodletting. So too today, medical technology makes us believe certain medicines and medical procedures should work, and therefore G-d heals us through those.)

It is even possible that He will heal him through something that is normally very harmful, as you know from the story of Elisha and the bad water, that he healed their damaging properties with salt (Melachim II 2:19), and similarly *"And G-d showed him a tree and he tossed it into the waters [and the waters became sweet]"* (Shemot 15:25), And the Midrash Tanchuma there explains that this was a bitter, oleander tree. Another example, *"let him smear crushed figs on the boils, and he will heal"* (Isaiah 38:21) (and figs normally damage even healthy flesh - *PL*). And you already know of what happened to the pious king Asa when he trusted in the doctors, and removed his trust in G-d regarding his illness, the sharp rebuke he received for this (i.e. because he did not pray to be healed). And the verse says: *"For He brings pain and binds it; He wounds, and His hands heal."* (Job 5:18).

SECOND CATEGORY - POSSESSIONS AND MEANS OF EARNING A LIVELIHOOD

(Previously he spoke on trusting in the livelihood itself, that certainly it will come through whatever means employed. Now he will speak on proper trust when engaging in the means themselves. understand this. - *PL*) For the second category, the matters of man's possessions, means of financial gain in his various pursuits, whether in commerce, skilled trades, peddling, business management, official appointments, property rentals, banking, work of kings, treasurers, contracting, writing work, other types of work, going to faraway deserts and seas, and other similar things, from what people toil in to amass money, and increase the superfluous. The proper way of trust in the Al-mighty for this is to engage in the means which G-d has made available to him to the extent necessary for his maintenance and sufficient for his needs of this world (i.e. his minimum necessary needs only - *TL*).

And if the Creator will decree for him more than this, it will come to him without trouble or exertion, provided he trusts in the Al-mighty for it and does not excessively pursue the means nor inwardly trust in them in his heart.

And if the Creator has not decreed for him more than his sustenance, even if all those in heaven and earth were to try to increase it, they would not be capable by any way nor by any means. And when one trusts in G-d, he will find peace of mind and tranquility of spirit, confident that G-d will not give over his portion to someone else, nor send it to him earlier or later than the time He decreed for it.

> (*Pas Lechem*: A man's nature is to desire to indulge a bit in luxuries beyond his subsistence needs. Only that, he should not squander his time in occupying himself in this, since it is not essential. Rather, let one trust in G-d that he will find his desire also in this [i.e. in living at subsistence level], because "G-d will fulfill the desire of them that fear Him" Tehilim 119:15)

PROPER TRUST FOR THE WEALTHY

Sometimes the Creator directs the livelihood of many men through one man. This is in order to test that man whether he will serve G-d or rebel against Him. And G-d will place this to be among the man's most difficult tests and sources of temptation. For example, a king who provides for his army and servants, or princes, ministers of the king, important officials, all of who are surrounded with groups of their servants, attendants, officers, wives, and relatives. They (tend to) exert themselves to obtain money for those dependents through all types of means, regardless whether they are good or bad means.

> (*Pas Lechem*: the Creator will make this thing a strong means to test him. A man is tested in this more than any other test. Because the magnitude of a test is measured by the greatness of the temptation of the evil inclination, and certainly the temptation of the evil inclination in this is exceedingly strong, to close one's hand from providing for the poor and destitute, and to not be concerned about providing their needs, thereby diminishing his wealth, as written in Devarim 15:9: "Guard yourself lest there be in your heart". This is what he meant by "tests and sources of temptation". And likewise "wives and relatives" is referring to all men [i.e. every man is

master of his household and provides for his wife, children, elderly parents, etc.])

And the foolish among them will err on three fronts.

(1) In acquiring money, he will employ bad and degrading means to earn what the Creator has decreed he will earn. And if he had sought after his wealth with proper (honest) means, he would have reached his desire, and both his religious and secular affairs would have succeeded, and he would not have earned any less (money) from what the Creator had decreed for him.

(2) He thinks that all the money that reaches him is for his own support. He does not understand that the money consists of three parts: One part, for the food he needs for his own body alone, and this is something G-d assures to all living creatures to the end of its days. The second part, for the food of others, such as his wife, children, servants, employees, and the like. This (extra money) is not assured by G-d to all people (that his business will prosper to the extent that his wife and children won't themselves need to engage in some means - *PL*), but rather only to a select few, and under special conditions, and this opportunity presents itself at certain times but not at others, according to the rulings of the Creator's system of kindness and justice. Third, money to hold on to. This is money which has no benefit for the man. The man guards it and accumulates it until he bequeaths it to another or loses it. The foolish person thinks that all the money decreed for him by the Creator is for his own sustenance and physical maintenance, and so he eagerly pursues it and exerts much effort to acquire it; and it is possible that he is amassing wealth for his widow's next husband, his stepson, or for his greatest enemy.

(3) The third error is that he provides money to those (dependents) as the Creator decreed this would happen through him. But he reminds them of his favors as if he were the one who provided for them and did them a kindness. And he expects them to thank and praise him richly, and that they serve him due to them, and he becomes arrogant, haughty, and inflated of heart. He neglects to thank G-d for them (that G-d appointed him as a means to bestow good on others whereby he would be an agent for this and receive reward for it - *TL*). He thinks that if he did not give this money to them, it would remain by him, and that if he did not provide for them they would not have any money. But really, he is the poor man, who will toil for nothing in this world and will lose his reward in the next world.

(*Marpe Lenefesh*: One can explain this to also be referring to one who realizes that it is the decree of G-d that these be provided through him. But he thinks that if there were not a decree that he provide for the poor, the abundant money would remain by him. But he errs in his outlook, because a rich man is like a funnel. If it pours down below, then we pour more up above. But if it is clogged below, we stop pouring above.)

The wise man, however, conducts himself in these three ways according to what will be proper for his religious and secular pursuits.

(*Marpe Lenefesh*: i.e. he acquires money in good and honest ways, and he is not in a rush to become rich. If he does have wealth, he will distribute it to all those who it is fitting to distribute to. He is easy-going (vatran) with his money. If he gives he is not arrogant on account of this. He doesn't desire to be praised for it, and he praises and thanks G-d who appointed him as a caretaker of many people)

His trust in what is in G-d's hands is greater than his trust in what is in his own hands because he does not know if the money in his hand is meant for his own benefit or is merely placed in his care. And thus he will gain honor in this world and receive rich reward in Olam Haba (afterlife), as written in the Psalm (112) *"Haleluy-a praiseworthy is the man who fears G-d.."* until the end of it.

(*Matanas Chelko*: The author did not discuss how much money one should leave for himself and did not mention the Halachos (laws) we find in the Shulchan Aruch on this matter. In truth this is one of the greatest trials of a rich person. For he does not know exactly how much he must give to tzedaka and how much to keep for himself.... What the Sages said of the amount of chumash (one fifth), this was said regarding every person. For even one who is not rich can give this amount. Likewise, what they wrote "one who distributes his money should not distribute more than one fifth" (Kesuvos 50a) - this refers only to average people. But one who is very rich, certainly he was not given money so that it sits in the bank. But rather, to distribute it to the poor. The Gedolim have said that all the segulos of tzedaka such as "Tzedaka (charity) saves from death" or that it "atones for one's sins" - this is only after one has already given a fifth. For, a fifth is a duty placed on every person. Therefore, only that which one gives with mesirus nefesh (self-sacrifice) has these special merits and segulas. The amount to save in the bank for a time of need depends on each person and what is the proper amount according to the way of the world... [see there are length].

WHY THE MASSES ARE FORCED TO WORK ENORMOUSLY

There are some classes of people who busy themselves in acquiring money and amassing wealth only for the love of being honored by other people, and to make a name for themselves, and no amount of money is ever enough for them. This is due to their ignorance of what will bring real honor in this world and in the next. The reason they make this error is because they see the masses honoring the wealthy, but really, this honor is motivated by a desire for what they possess and to try to get some of what is in their hands.

(*Pas Lechem*: His intent is that there are two causes why the masses honor the wealthy. (1) Because they are hoping, seeking, and longing all of their days to attain that which will bring them wealth, and since these things are very important in their thoughts, they also regard the wealthy as important. (2) Because the masses hope to draw from their hands and benefit from them, therefore they flatter them. [likewise for other things which the masses admire such as popularity, power, etc - translator])

If the masses reflected and understood that the wealthy do not have the capability nor the power either to give or to hold back to someone except to whom the Creator decreed, they would not hope to anyone besides G-d.

(*Marpe Lenefesh*: If it was decreed for this person that his money will not come from that person, then that rich person does not have the ability to give to him. Even though man has free will, the completion is not in man's hands, as written earlier. Likewise, the rich man cannot prevent this, if the Creator decreed the money will be his. G-d will arrange that the rich man will lose the money, or some other means that will cause the money to reach the hands of that person.)

Nor would they find anyone worthy of honor except for he who the Creator has distinguished with praiseworthy qualities, for which he is worthy of the Creator's honor, as written *"Those who honor Me, I will honor"* (Shmuel I 2:30).

(*Pas Lechem*: i.e. he who is worthy of the Creator's honor due to his praiseworthy traits. And since man's worth is extremely puny to be conceivably worthy of the Creator's honor, he brought a proof from the verse: "Those who honor Me, I will honor". [note: simultaneously, the verse also teaches on what will bring true honor - *Translator*])

And because, in honoring the wealthy, the masses were foolish in the causes of real honor, the Creator added to their foolishness in the causes of their requests [for money] (that they constantly seek to become rich - *TL*).

And so they fell into great effort and tremendous toiling all of their days, while they abandoned that which is their duty to busy themselves with and to which they should hasten. Namely, fulfilling their duties to the Creator, and to thank Him for the good He bestows on them, whereby their desire (for honor - *TL*) would have undoubtedly been closer to them in this way, as written: *"long life is in its right, in its left wealth and honor"* (Mishlei 3:16), and *"wealth and honor is from You"* (Divrei Hayamim 29:12).

Among those who seek wealth, sometimes one reaches all his heart's desire through the means we mentioned (commerce, skilled trade, etc). For another it came through an inheritance or the like, and he thinks his wealth is due to the means, and without them, he would not have received anything, and he praises the means and not their Cause (i.e. the Creator who orchestrates all the means - *PL*).

How similar is he to a man in the desert, thirst weighing on him, who finds unclean water in a pit, and becomes full of joy. He quenches his thirst from them. And afterwards, he moves a bit further, and finds a well of pure water. He regrets on what he did previously, of drinking and quenching his thirst from the unpure water.

Similarly, for the man who became wealthy through a certain means. If this means would have failed, he would have attained it through other means, as we explained earlier and as the verse says: *"nothing can prevent G-d from saving, whether through many or through few"* (Shmuel I 14:6).

(*Pas Lechem*: If so, all of the bitter and wearying toil he exerted himself in this means was for nothing. For it could have come to him through a light and easy business. Alternative explanation:
Marpe Lenefesh: One who acquired wealth though distasteful means could have employed honest means and attained the same amount [of wealth].)

PROPER TRUST IN TIGHT FINANCIAL TIMES

And the proper way for one who trusts in G-d, when his livelihood is withheld for some day is to say in one's heart: "He who took me out (from the womb) to this world at a fixed time and moment, and did not take me out to it earlier or later, He is the One who is withholding my livelihood for a fixed time and a fixed day, because He knows what is good for me."

Likewise, when one's livelihood comes very exactly, no more than the amount for basic food, it is proper for him to reflect in his heart and tell himself: "He who prepared my sustenance at my mother's breast in my beginning, according to my need, and what was sufficient for me day by day, until He replaced it for me with something better, and (the milk's) coming exactly did not damage me at all. So too I will not at all be damaged now until the end of my days by His sending me my food in the limited, exact amount.

He will be rewarded for this, as the Creator told our ancestors in the (Sinai) desert, whose matter was in this way: *"The people shall go out each day and gather what they need for the day"* (Shemot 16:4), and *"go and call out to the ears of Jerusalem and say 'I remember for you the kindness of your youth, the love of your betrothal, when you followed Me in the wilderness, in a land that was not sown'"* (Yirmiyahu 2:2).

> (*Tov Halevanon*: The sages expounded on the reason - so that a man will always hope to G-d day by day that He will provide his daily bread [and his trust in Him will be strengthened])

Likewise, if one's livelihood comes through one means but not through any other means (that he would have preferred - *PL*), or from one place and not from any other place, or through one person and not through any other person, let one say in his heart: "He who created me in a certain form, shape, characteristic, and measure and not through any other, for my purpose and benefit, He has chosen that my livelihood come through ways suitable to my purpose and benefit, and not through any other ways." And, "He who brought me into this world at a fixed time, and through two specific people, and not through other people of the world, He has chosen for me my livelihood from a specific place and through a specific person, He made him the means to my livelihood for my benefit", as written *"G-d is righteous in all His ways"* (Tehilim 145:17).

THIRD CATEGORY - SOCIAL MATTERS

The explanation of the third category, matters of one's wife, children, household members, relatives, friends, enemies, acquaintances, those higher or lower than him among the various classes of people, the proper ways of trust in G-d is as follows. A man is necessarily in either one of two situations: either he is a stranger or he is among his family and relatives.

PROPER TRUST FOR ONE LIVING ALONE

If he is a stranger, let his companionship be with G-d during his time of loneliness, and trust in Him during his period of being a stranger. And let him contemplate that the soul is also a stranger in this world, and that all people are like strangers here, as the verse says: *"because you are strangers and temporary residents with Me"* (Vayikra 25:23). And let him reflect in his heart that all those who have relatives here, in a short time, will be left a solitary stranger. Neither relative nor son will be able to help him, and none of them will be with him (see Gate 8 ch.3 way #30 for more on this - Translator).

(*Marpe Lenefesh*: i.e. he should reflect in his heart that it is for his benefit that he has no relatives or friends that he can enjoy with, and it is good for him so that he makes his companionship with G-d and can places his trust in Him alone. For he has no one else to trust due to his being a stranger. Furthermore, all of us are strangers because the soul, which is of divine origin, is in this world like a stranger in a strange land. And in truth, the essence of man is his soul... and further in a short while he will leave this world, and certainly then he will lay there alone without relative or savior.

Tov Halevanon: One surrounded by family will benefit from this for only a short time. For either he will have a long life and will see the death of his children and relatives and will be left lonely and in painful solitude or if he will not live a long life, what need does he have for relatives? And this is worse than the first case.)

And afterwards, let him consider that as a stranger, he is freed from the heavy burden of maintaining relatives and fulfilling his duties towards them. He should consider this to be one of the kindnesses of the Creator towards him. For if he needed to pursue a livelihood for providing his material needs, his exertion would be lighter without a wife and children, and their absence is peace of mind for him and it is good. And if he is concerned about his interests (mitzvot) in the next world, his mind will undoubtedly be clearer and freer when he is alone.

And therefore the ascetics (pious) would leave their relatives and homes and go to the mountains, in order to focus their hearts in the service of G-d. Likewise, the prophets, during the era of prophecy, would leave their homes and live in solitude to fulfill their duties to the Creator. This is as you know from the story of Eliyahu's meeting with Elisha, which it is said of Elisha: *"twelve pairs of oxen were before him, and he was with the twelfth"* (Melachim I 19:19). And as soon as Eliyahu hinted to him a small hint (to come with him), he understood him and said *"Let me, please, kiss my father and my mother, and I will go with you"*, and afterwards, *"and he went after Eliyahu and ministered to him"*.

(*Tov Halevanon*: he left behind all of his work and separated from his mother, father, and all of his relatives and went after Eliyahu.

note: *"go to the mountains"* - such extreme asceticism is not in accordance with the teachings of Judaism and only sanctioned when practiced by such exceptional characters as Eliyahu the prophet - Rabbi Moses Hyamson zt'l [see also Gate#9])

It is said about one of the ascetics, who travelled to a country to teach its inhabitants the service of G-d. He found them all dressed in the same manner and adorned in the same way. Their graves were near their homes, and he did not see among them any women. He asked them about this and they answered him: "the reason we are all dressed alike is so that there's no noticeable difference between a rich man and a poor man and the rich man will not come to arrogance for his wealth, and the poor man will not be embarrassed of his poverty, and so that our matter above the earth should be in our eyes like our matter below the earth (i.e. in the grave where everyone is dressed the same way - *TL*). It is said of one of the kings that he would mix with his servants, and there was no noticeable difference between him and them, because he would conduct himself in the way of humility in his dress and adornments.

(Rav Yaakov Emden: i.e. the king would dress like them "so that his heart will not be haughty over his brothers" (Devarim 17:20). This is the way of the torah provided he does not become frivolous before them and that fear of him is over them.)

As to the reason why the graves of our dead are near our homes, they said, this is so that we encounter them and prepare ourselves for our deaths, and that we prepare our provisions for the afterlife. As to your noticing that we separated ourselves from women and children, know that we prepared for them a village near here. When one of us needs something from them, he goes to them and after obtaining his wants, returns to us. This we did because we saw how much distraction of the heart, great loss, and great exertion and strain there was when they were among us, and the great peace of mind from all of this, in separating from them, to focus on matters of the afterlife and to be repulsed by matters of this world. And their words found favor in the eyes of the ascetic, and he blessed them and commended them on their matters.

(*Pas Lechem*: He specified 4 points (distraction of the heart, great loss, great exertion and strain), the first two is the harm from desiring them, namely, when they are near, the eye sees them and the heart desires and he becomes always distracted from them, on this he wrote "distraction of the heart". And inevitably the constant desire will bring him to habitually have marital relations with them always. This causes great loss to a man's strength and health as the Rambam wrote in Hilchos Deos 4:19, on this he wrote "great loss". The latter two are the damages which come from providing for their needs (ex.big house). That when they are near, they persuade their husbands and act playfully and seek luxuries which brings to two harmful things. Namely, "great exertion" in exerting oneself to provide for their needs and "strain" of the mind in the mental distraction of providing their needs. And the Sages already said (Sotah 47a): "yetzer, child, and woman, let one's left hand push away while the right hand draws near".

Afterwards, he wrote: "to focus on matters of the afterlife and to be repulsed by matters of this world", because in distancing from them, the heart is free to think on matters of the afterlife, and also through being repulsed by this powerful lust, the heart of a man will habituate in being repulsed by the other lusts of this world.)

PROPER TRUST FOR ONE'S WIFE RELATIVES, FRIENDS, AND ENEMIES

If the one who trusts in G-d has a wife, relatives, friends, enemies, let him trust in G-d to be saved from them.

(*Tov Halevanon*: i.e. to be saved from their burdens, namely, all those things mentioned above that a stranger is saved from.

Marpe Lenefesh: To be saved from them by fulfilling his duties towards them.

Tov Halevanon: Here he added the term "enemies", something he did not mention earlier regarding the man who is solitary or a stranger, because this is the normal way of the world. Namely, that the solitary man or the stranger/foreigner due to his little worldly association and his low stature, has no enemies, unlike the man with a wife, sons, relatives, friends, who has much association in the world and develops enemies due to jealousy...)

He should strive to fulfill his duties to them (provide their necessities - *PL*), to do their wishes (to also provide them with a bit more than the necessities like the nature of the world - *PL*), to be wholehearted with them (to provide their needs willingly, not like one forced to do so - *PL*). He should refrain from causing any harm to them, try to promote what is good for them. He should deal faithfully towards them in all matters, and teach them the ways that will be beneficial for them in their religious matters and the secular ways [which will benefit them] in the service of the Creator, as written (Vayikra 19:18) *"you shall love your neighbor as yourself.."*, and *"do not hate your brother in your heart"* (ibid). Do not do this out of hope for future benefits from them or to pay them back for past benefits. Nor should you do this out of love of being honored or praised by them, or out of desire to rule over them - but rather with the sole motive to fulfill the commandment of the Creator, and to guard His covenant and precepts over them. (i.e. to see to it that they guard the covenant of G-d and His commandments - *TL*)

The person whose motive in fulfilling their wishes is one of the [reprehensible] motives we mentioned above, will not obtain what he wants from them in this world. He will weary himself for nothing, and will lose his reward in the afterlife (since his intent was not l'Shem Shamayim - *PL*). But if his sole motive is to serve G-d, the Al-mighty will help them to make a return to him in this world, and G-d will place his praise in their mouths and they will hold him in high esteem, and he will attain the great reward in Olam Haba (afterlife), as the Al-mighty said to Shlomo *"also what you did not ask, I will give you, also wealth and honor"* (Melachim 3:13).

(*Pas Lechem*. Corresponding to "do not do this out of hope for future benefits, etc.", he wrote: "the Al-mighty will help them to make a return to him".
Corresponding to "Nor should you do this out of love of being honored or praised by them", he wrote: "and G-d will place his praise in their mouths".
Corresponding to "(nor should you do this) out of desire to rule over them", he wrote: "and they will hold him in high esteem", that he will seem great and awe-inspiring in their eyes and automatically they will do whatever he says.
Therefore without intending to, indirectly, he attained all of their benefits in this world, similar to what our sages said (Nedarim 62a): "study the Torah out of love, and in the end, the honor will come". And his primary reward will be in Olam Haba)

PROPER TRUST FOR BENEFITING FROM OTHERS

But the ways of trust in G-d in dealing with those above him or below him in the various classes of men is as follows. The proper way to act when one needs to request some benefit of someone above or below him is to trust in G-d, and to consider them as means of obtaining what he needs, just like one makes the working and sowing of the land a means of obtaining his food. If G-d wishes to support him through it, He will make the seeds sprout, grow, and multiply, and one does not thank the land for this, but rather, he thanks the Creator alone. And if the Al-mighty will not desire to supply him through it, the land will not produce, or it will produce but be struck by damaging things, and one does not blame the land.

So too, when he seeks something from one of them, it should be equal in his eyes whether the person he asked is weak or strong, and he should trust in G-d for its completion.

> (*Pas Lechem*: i.e. that he does not trust more in his heart that his request will be completed if he had asked a strong person than if he had asked a weak person, since he believes that the man is only an intermediary and that G-d is the one actually doing it.)

And if it was completed through one of them, let him thank the Creator who fulfilled his desire, and thank the person through whom it was done for his good will towards him, and that the Creator brought his benefit through him. And it is known that the Creator does not bring good except through the tzadikim (righteous), and it is rare that He brings a loss through them, as the sages said *"merit occurs through the meritorious and guilt through the guilty"* (Bava Basra 119b), and the verse *"No wrong shall be caused for the righteous"* (Mishlei 12:21 - Rashi "No sin will chance before him inadvertently").

> (*Tov Halevanon*: i.e. perhaps you will say, if the matter is so (that G-d is doing it and the person is only an intermediary) why should I thank a person who benefits me, since he is forced by G-d and does good to me without choice due to the decree of G-d? (Answer:) you are obligated to thank him nevertheless since he is the one G-d chose to cause the good and G-d brings good through the righteous and faithful before Him...)

And if his request is not accomplished through them, one should not blame them, and not consider it due to their being lax in it. Rather he should thank the Al-mighty who chose what is best for him in this, and praise them according to his knowledge of their efforts to fulfill his will, even though the matter was not completed according to his will and their desire. Similarly, one should act with his acquaintances and friends, his business associates, employees and partners.

If someone higher or lower than himself requests from him to do something for them, he should wholeheartedly use every means to do it, and apply his mind to do the matter, provided one is capable of doing it and that the person who requested it is worthy that he exerts himself on his behalf (but if the person is wicked, refrain from it as he wrote in the end of gate #3 - *ML*). And after this, he should trust in the Al-mighty for its completion. If G-d completes it through him, and makes him the cause for benefiting another, he should thank G-d for this privilege. If G-d withholds this from him, and he is not capable of doing it, he should not blame himself, and he should inform the person that he was not lax in doing it, provided that he indeed exerted himself to do it.

PROPER TRUST FOR DEALING WITH ENEMIES

But for one's enemies, those jealous of him, those who seek to harm him, he should trust in G-d regarding their matters. He should bear their contempt, and should not treat them back in the same way.

> (*Marpe Lenefesh*: As the sages said (Yoma 23a see Rashi, Rosh Hashana 17a): "he who forgoes (overlooks) his honor when it is slighted will merit that all his transgressions be forgiven")

Rather he should pay them back with kindness, and to try to benefit them as much as he possibly can, and to remember in his heart that only G-d has the ability to benefit or harm him.

> (*Translator*: I once heard a lecture by Rabbi Nissan Kaplan of the Mir Yeshiva where he said that this method is one of the most powerful ways to work on trust. In order to internalize trust, one must do physical actions in this world, namely paying back evil with good. He says that getting into the habit of doing this, is one of the ways to build trust in the most effective way.
>
> Rabbi Avigdor Miller zt'l also says getting in the habit of always thanking G-d for the good and the bad also builds trust.

If his enemy becomes a means to harm him, he should judge them favorably and suspect that it is due to himself or his past deeds from his bad start in life towards G-d. He should plead to the Al-mighty and seek from Him to atone for his sins, and then his enemies will become his friends, as the wise man said *"when G-d is pleased with a man's way, even his enemies will make peace with him"* (Mishlei 16:7).

> (*Matanas Chelko*: the main trust in these matters is as the Chazon Ish wrote: "to abstain doing [bad] things to those who did bad to him" (Emuna U'Bitachon 2:2). For the primary denial of trust is to do [bad] against one who did bad to him or vexed him, as written in the Sefer Hachinuch

regarding the commandment not to exact revenge which is one of the roots of faith. Therefore, the author wrote that it is included in the commandment of "love your fellow as yourself". For denial of G-d is recognized and manifest when one exacts revenge on someone who did bad to him. He forgets the great principle of the Ramban (end of parsha Bo): "if he does G-d's commandments, G-d will reward him with success. But if he transgresses them, G-d will afflict him with punishments - everything is from divine decree."

Rabbi Yaakov Emden zt'l: This matter requires great investigation. We find many verses supporting this such as "Do not say: 'I will repay evil'; but wait on the L-ord, and He shall save you" (Mishlei 20:22), "If your enemy is hungry, give him bread to eat; and if he is thirsty, give him water to drink" (ibid 25:21). Likewise, we find by King David especially with Saul in the cave and with his garment, and like Saul said to him (Shmuel 24:19): "And you have shown today how you have dealt well with me, how the L-rd delivered me into your hand, and you did not kill me; For when a man finds his enemy, does he send him away safely? And may the L-rd repay you with goodness for what you have done to me on this day". And in Tehilim (35:13) "But as for me, when they (my enemies) were ill, my clothing was sackcloth", and (ibid 38:14) "Thus I was as a man that hears not, and in whose mouth are no reproofs (when others were mocking me)", and (ibid 37:7) "Be silent before the L-ord, and wait patiently for him: fret not yourself because of him who prospers in his way, because of the man who brings wicked devices to pass", and (ibid 62:5) "My soul, wait you only upon G-d; for my expectation is from Him", and many more like this.

On the other hand, we find many verses which contradict this, especially by King David for he sought to exact furious revenge from Naval merely for refraining from doing good to him. Likewise, he pleaded G-d to exact revenge on his enemies, as he said: (ibid 41:11) "be gracious to me and raise me up, so that I may repay them", and (ibid 28:4) "Give them according to their deeds and according to the evil of their endeavors", and he complained (119:84) "How many are Your servant's days? When will You execute justice upon my pursuers?", and many more like this. He even praised revenge in saying: (58:11) "The righteous shall rejoice when he sees the vengeance".

And his overlooking of Shimi in saying (Shmuel II 16:10) "G-d told him to curse" is not an indication since he was then in great troubles, and he humbled himself and accepted the humiliation as an atonement, thereby bearing the pain in exchange for the punishment fitting for him for the event with Batsheva. And in the end when Shimi sought forgiveness, it was fitting for him to pardon him due to the need of the time and also since one who admits and repents is treated with mercy (by G-d). Even so, David

guarded the matter and paid him back through his son Shlomo. And it does
not appear correct to say that whenever scripture praises revenge it is
referring to the gentile enemies of G-d and His people (who come to wage
war, etc.). Likewise, Yirmiyahu pleaded for revenge from the men of
Anatot, who were Kohanim of his own family, in saying (Yirmiyahu 15:15)
"avenge me of my persecutors; take me not away in your long-suffering".
We must answer all this by saying that everything varies according to the
severity of the matter and the greatness of the wrongdoing. (translator - and
the author here is speaking about most cases which are usually petty
matters)

Afterwards, he wrote: "He should plead to the Al-mighty and seek from
Him to atone for his sins", similar to what David did in the event with
Shimi. Then, "his enemies will become his friends" as what happened with
Yaakov and Eisav or the tribes with Yosef, and obviously with Shimi.

FOURTH CATEGORY - Duties of the heart and limbs which don't affect others

PROPER TRUST IN THE FREE WILL TO SERVE G-D

The explanation of the fourth category, matters of duties of the heart and of
the limbs which only benefit or harm oneself, for example, fasting,
praying, dwelling in a sukka, taking a lulav, wearing tzitzis, observing the
Sabbath and the holidays, refraining from sins. This category also includes
all of the duties of the heart since their performance does not affect others,
and their benefit or harm is limited only to oneself and is not shared by
others. I will explain the proper way of trust in the Al-mighty in all of
these, and I ask the Al-mighty to teach me the truth, in His mercy.

(*Pas Lechem*: In his examples, he first wrote "fasting" and "praying", since
these mitzvos are logical, and were practiced before the giving of the torah.
Adam also fasted and prayed for his sin. Afterwards, he gave the examples
of received mitzvot, and started with "sukka" since of all the mitzvot which
apply today, it is the reminder of the clouds of glory in the desert (i.e. the
Exodus from Egypt). He said lulav before tzitzis since it is preceded in the
torah... [see there for more details]

Matanas Chelko: "I ask the Al-mighty..." it seems from the author's words
that the following branch of trust is the most difficult to explain. Since we
don't find that he uttered a prayer like this anywhere else in the book when
explaining trust. Perhaps, it is because he is explaining the foundations of
free will.)

Any human action which is either service [of G-d] or sin can only take place if three factors occur. (1) the choice in heart and mind (i.e. a thought that it is fitting to do this thing - *ML*). (2) The intent and resolve to do what one chose. (3) The endeavoring to complete the act with one's physical limbs and to bring it into actuality.

[Of these three factors,] two are not beyond our control, namely, (1) the choice of service or sin and (2) intent and resolve to carry out the choice. For these, trusting in G-d would be a mistake and a foolishness, because the Creator left free choice in our hands whether to serve Him or rebel against Him, as written "...[life and death I have set before you] and you shall choose life" (Devarim 30:19).

(*Tov Halevanon*: If a man does not choose to pursue doing good and to refrain from sins, and instead trusts in G-d that He will prepare that good deeds will come his way and that G-d will distance from him the causes which lead to sins - this is a great mistake.)

But the bringing out of the act into actuality, He did not leave in our hands, but rather, made it depend on external means which sometimes are available and sometimes are not.

(*Tov Halevanon*: For example, fasting and prayer, perhaps his body will be too weak, or sukkah and lulav, perhaps he will not be able to obtain the sukkah wood or the lulav... Or to give charity, he needs to have money, and to encounter a proper poor man, etc. These external means are not in our free choice nor in the desire of G-d, but rather occur by encounter and opportunity. Only that for good deeds, there is a bit of siyata dishmaya (Divine assistance) as our sages taught (Shabbat 104a): "if one comes to purify himself, he is helped", but "if one comes to defile himself, he is given an opening" (ibid 104a), i.e. that the means are left to chance [Translator: not that G-d pushes him to defile himself but rather He withdraws His providence and leaves the person to chance as written in the introduction to this gate])

If in choosing to serve the Al-mighty, one would trust in Him and think to himself: "I will not choose the service of G-d nor attempt to do any part of it until He chooses what is good for me of it" - he has already strayed from the straight path, and slipped his feet away from the proper way. Because the Creator has already commanded us to choose in matters of His service, and to intend and make efforts towards it, with complete, wholehearted resolve for the sake of His great Name, and He has informed us that this is the proper way for our welfare in this world and in the next.

(Translator: His great Name refers to G-d as He manifests Himself to us. This is explained earlier in gate#1. We use the term "His Name" because G-d Himself is too beyond for us to even speak about.)

If the necessary means are available to us, so that we are capable of accomplishing the work in G-d's service which we chose to do, then we will receive the great reward for choosing it, for the intent and resolve to do it, and for completing the actions by our physical limbs. But if its accomplishment with the physical limbs is withheld from us, then we will receive reward for our choice and intent to do it, as we previously explained (in ch.3), and similarly for punishment of sins.

(*Tov Halevanon*: And if you ask, how can this be a mitzvah if there was no act done yet? For this he said that the completion of the act is not essential to the mitzvah. Even though the mitzvah is not accomplished, he will receive reward for the choice and resolve to do it. But if the act is completed, the reward is greater, and likewise for punishments of sins.)

The difference between the service of G-d and secular activities in this world, regarding trust in G-d, is as follows. For secular matters, it was not revealed to us which one of all the means is best and most beneficial for us nor the ways in which some course is more harmful and worse than other courses. We do not know which particular trade is best suited for us and most fitting for us in obtaining money, preserving health, and for general well-being. Nor do we know which business sector, which journey to undertake, or which other worldly endeavors will be successful if we engage in them.

Therefore, it follows that we must put our trust in the Al-mighty that He will help us choose and carry out what is the best choice for us, provided that we apply ourselves (in the means which are fitting to attain this thing - PL) and that we plead to Him to arouse in our hearts to make the good and proper choice for ourselves. (then after these two things we can have in our hearts the trust mentioned - PL)

(*Tov Halevanon*: Lest you ask: "if so, (that in the choice and resolve in the service of G-d, I must not trust in G-d) then also I must not trust in Him for matters of my livelihood. If so, why did the author say earlier that one should "submit himself to the course the Creator has decreed for him...". On this he answered, that there is a big difference between the two...

Marpe Lenefesh: He gave a reason for this difference, namely, "it was not revealed to us which means is best...", and we don't know what to do, whether engaging in this trade or that business will be best for us or maybe in something else. And as the sages said (Berachos 33b) "everything is in the hands of Heaven (G-d), except for fear of Heaven")

But the service of G-d is not like this, because G-d has already taught us the proper ways for it, commanded us to choose it, and gave us the ability to do it. If we then plead to Him in the choice we should make, and trust in Him that He will reveal to us what is good for us, we will be mistaken in our words (of prayer) and foolish in our trust. For He already taught us the proper way which will be good for us in this world and in the next, as written: *"G-d has commanded us to fulfill all of these statutes, to fear the L-ord, our G-d, for our good, all of our days"* (Devarim 6:24). And regarding the reward in Olam Haba *"we will be rewarded, if we are careful to observe"* (Devarim 6:25).

Furthermore, in secular matters, sometimes a good means changes to become a bad means and vice versa, while for service of G-d and transgression it is not so. Matters of good and evil do not switch positions and never change.

(*Marpe Lenefesh*: Furthermore, how can we charge our mind to choose this business or this trade? Many times we find one person becomes rich through this business or trade and it is good for him, while another person does not profit at all from it and it is bad for him. If so, there is no way for us to know, rather only that which G-d puts in our hearts [to choose] is for our good. We find many verses which teach this such as (Mishlei 19:21) "There are many plans in a man's heart but the counsel of the L-ord - that shall stand", and "A man's heart plans his way: but the L-ord directs his steps" (Mishlei 16:9), and "A man's steps are directed by the L-ord; how then can anyone understand his own way" (ibid 20:24), and many more verses. But the actions in the service of G-d that are good, namely, fulfilling the commandments - this is good forever and never changes. Likewise the negative commandments are always bad.
(another explanation)
Tov Halevanon: That even though it appears good, it is possible that in the end it will lead to destruction, and the opposite, what appears evil and bitter in one's eyes may turn out in the end to be a great salvation. And like our sages said (Berachos 54a): "a person should bless on the bad, like he blesses on the good...")

Hence, for religious acts, trust in G-d is proper only in the completion stage of the act. After choosing it wholeheartedly and faithfully and after the second stage of resolving and making efforts to do it with a pure heart, and with intent to do it for the sake of His great Name. With this, we are obligated to beseech Him to help us in it, and to teach us on it, as written: *"lead me in Your truth and teach me"* (Tehilim 25:5), and *"lead me in the path of Your commandments for I desired it"* (Tehilim 119:35), and *"I have chosen the way of truth, I have placed Your ordinances before me"* (Tehilim 119:30), and *"I have clung to Your testimonies; O L-ord; put me not to shame"* (Tehilim 119:31), and *"And take not the word of truth utterly out of my mouth; for I have hoped in Your judgments"* (Tehilim 119:43).

> (*Rabbi Yaakov Emden*: "we are obligated to beseech Him to help us in it" also against the Yetzer (evil inclination) since: "every day a person's evil inclination rises powerfully against him and seeks to slay him...Were it not for the Holy One blessed be He who helps him, a man would not be able [to contend] with it" (Kidushin 30b).
>
> *Pas Lechem*: "after choosing it" means: to make a strong decision in his mind to not budge from it.
> "wholeheartedly" means: not hesitantly.
> "faithfully" means: choosing to do it without outside interests.
> "with a pure heart" means: making efforts to do it without outside interests but rather "for the sake of His great Name".
>
> *Tov Halevanon*: "and with intent to do it for the sake of His great Name" - i.e. with all this, everything goes by the intent as our sages said (Nazir 23b): "a sin lishma (for the sake of G-d) is greater than a mitzvah that is not lishma.
> "to teach us on it" means to remove the veil of foolishness from our eyes and to strengthen our choice towards Him so that we may also know the ways of His service and by which way we should seek it.)

All these verses demonstrate that the psalmist's service of G-d was his own choice. He prayed to G-d for two things only:
(1) To wholly devote his heart and to strengthen his choice in the service of G-d by distancing the distractions of the world from his heart and eyes, as he said *"unite my heart to fear Your Name"* (ibid 86:11) and *"uncover my eyes that I may gaze at the wonders of Your torah"* (Tehilim 119:18), *"turn away my eyes from beholding vanity"* (ibid, 119:37), *"incline my heart towards Your torah and not to unjust gain"* (ibid, 119:36), and many more.

> (*Pas Lechem*: "To wholly devote his heart" means: that his thoughts be only in G-d's service, not in the vain worldly desires and to strengthen his choice that it be enduringly set and firmly established
>
> *Matanas Chelko*: "to strengthen his choice" - prayer is to strengthen one's choice, i.e. before the act is completed. For example, one who has decided

to go learn torah in the synagogue, it is possible that he will be met with many distractions along the way. He may see some event or hear something, or some idea enters his mind. Each of these can potentially change his plan or weaken his resolve so he does not learn properly. Therefore, one must pray even after the decision and resolve in order to strengthen one's choice against the distractions. This is the important principle Rabeinu is teaching us - the purpose of prayer for spiritual things is to strengthen one's will.)

(2) To strengthen him physically to be able to complete the acts of service of G-d. This is what is meant *"lead me in the path of Your commandments"* (119:35), *"support me and I will be saved"* (119:117), and many more like this. And I will explain in this gate which factors help and harm these things, and the proper path in it, with G-d's help.

Matanas Chelko: To summarize, in matters that one does not know the proper path, and with what should he engage in, he should trust in G-d and pray to G-d that He will put in his heart the will of what to do and how to do it. On the other hand, for things which he already knows are proper and that he should do them, such as the study of Torah and performance of commandments, it is not proper to beseech G-d to give him the will to do them. But one can beseech G-d to strengthen his will in them, remove the obstructions from doing them, and ask Him that he merits to accomplish his good choice to fulfill them.

A note on the matter of free will: Rabeinu (our teacher) included in his words the foundation of what is free will. Those who think free will means that a person can do what he wants - are mistaken. For behold, whether for physical or spiritual matters, one does not have the ability to do what he wants - for everything is done solely by divine decree. And even for doing a commandment or a sin - even though he wants to do it, it is possible that sometimes G-d will prevent him from doing it. Rather, free will means the will to do. A person has free will to choose what he wants to do. But to bring this thought to actuality is only in G-d's hands.

If we go deeper in this, we will see that in truth, even the will to do something is not "free will". For behold, even an animal has the will to do what it wants. The animal wants to eat, sleep, kick - and does it. So too, a man wants to eat, sleep, etc. and does it. If so, what is the difference between man and animal? The answer is that a man's free will is that he has the ability to refrain from doing what he wants.

This is the difference between man and animal. The animal cannot refrain from doing what it wants. That which its nature wants to do, it does. It does not have the power to refrain from doing what it wants. But a man has been granted the ability to refrain from doing what his nature wants to do. If an animal lusts for something, it does not have the ability to restrain itself from fulfilling this lust and will. A human being on the other hand, can lust for physical things. But he has the power to refrain from fulfilling that will and lust which his nature pushes him to do. This is true free will - to form in his being, through his intellect, the will and desire to overcome his natural desires.

The root of free will is fear of G-d. That which the torah says "you shall choose life" (Deut. 30:19), which implies man has free will, this refers to the free will to acquire fear of G-d. Namely, to form in his being the will to fulfill the will of G-d instead of pursuing the fulfillment of his natural will. This is free will. All the other things he does stem from the tendency of his nature, just like an animal. Hence, it is possible for a man to spend his entire life without ever using his free will even once! Because free will is that which a person creates and forms by himself through fear [of G-d], a new will to stand up against his animalistic and natural will, in order to fulfill the will of G-d. This is what our sages said (Berachos 33b): "everything is in the hands of Heaven except the fear of Heaven". For only through the power of fear of G-d that a person has can he overcome and stand up against what was already decreed from Heaven, namely, his natural will and powers.)

FIFTH CATEGORY - Duties of the limbs which affect others

The fifth category: physical duties which affect others whether beneficially or harmfully, such as giving charity, maaser (tithes), teaching wisdom, commanding others to do good, warning them against evil, returning loans on faith, keeping a secret, speaking well of others, good activities, honoring parents, bringing the wicked back to G-d, instructing/advising others what will be good for them, pitying the poor and treating them with mercy, patiently bearing their contempt when arousing them to the service G-d, inspiring them to hope for the reward [in doing good], and instilling in them fear of punishment [for doing bad].

The proper way of trust in G-d for these, is for one to keep in mind all these and similar acts, resolve and make efforts to practice them, according to what we previously explained in the fourth category. Namely, regarding the duty when choosing (in these things - PL) to have the sole intent of drawing near to G-d alone; not for acquiring a name or honor among human beings, nor out of hope to receive reward from them, nor to try to rule over them. And after one has done his utmost, he should trust in G-d in the completion of the acts which he undertook, according to what G-d wants from us (that we do His will, accordingly He will help us to complete what we undertook - *ML*).

In all of this, one should be careful to hide his deeds as much as possible from those who do not need to know. Because if it is kept hidden, the reward will be greater than if it becomes known. And that which he is unable to hide, let him remember the important general principle which we explained, namely, that neither benefit nor harm can come from the created things, except by permission of the Creator.

(*Pas Lechem*: If he cannot hide it and therefore, he is afraid lest the yetzer put in his heart ulterior motives, as before, then let him remember...

Manoach Halevavos: If he is unable to hide it, and he thinks he will be mocked by the mockers, or that he will be obstructed from completing it due to their hampering him, or that the poor man he benefits will receive shame, do not be concerned thereby refraining from the good deed. Rather "remember the important general principle...", and that it is not in the ability of others to obstruct him, or hamper him, and the mockery will not damage him. Likewise, the shame of the poor man will not harm him, with G-d's help.)

When the Creator completes a mitzvah (commandment) through him (that G-d benefits another person through him - *PL*), he should consider that this is a favor bestowed on him from the Creator. He should not rejoice if other people praise him for doing it, nor desire that they honor him for it. For this will bring him to become proud in his actions, and his purity of heart and motive towards G-d will be ruined, thereby his deeds will be spoiled and his reward for it will be lost. I will explain this later on in its proper Gate (in #6 the gate of submission - *PL*) with G-d's help.

(*Pas Lechem*: "his deeds will be spoiled" - G-d will not accept his deeds and also he will lose his reward.

Marpe Lenefesh: "his reward for it will be lost" since he had pleasure and praise for his deed, he already received his reward for this.)

SIXTH CATEGORY - reward in this world and the next

The explanation of the sixth category, regarding the reward in this world and the next which one merits for his good deeds in this world, is divided into two parts. (1) Sometimes for an act, the reward is given in this world only or it is given in the next world only. (2) Sometimes the reward is given in both worlds for one act.

This was not explained to us clearly. However, the Creator guaranteed to His people a general reward for general good behavior, but He did not specify the details of reward in this world for each act of service like He did regarding the punishments in this world for transgressions. For example, He specified which offences warrant capital punishment by stoning (i.e. falling from a height), burning, decapitation, or strangulation, or 40 lashes, death (through G-d's providence), premature death (karet), monetary fines - two, four or five fold, monetary damages by ox, pit, tooth, fire, damaging a man, embarrassing by seizing, slander, and other offences. But regarding the reward and punishment in the afterlife, the prophet [Moshe] did not explain anything for several reasons.

One of these is that the semblance of the soul without the body is foreign to us, and even less known is what the soul in that state would take pleasure in or suffer from. However, this was explained to one who understood such things, as G-d spoke to Yehoshua (the high priest) (who G-d granted special understanding into divine matters - *PL*) "I will give you a place to walk among these (angels) that stand" (Zecharia 3:7), and this was not referring to when the soul is joined to the body. But rather, was a hint to what would happen after death where the soul, in its simple, ethereal state, divested from and no longer using the body, resumes the form of the angels, after it had been purified and made radiant when its deeds were good in this world.

(*Pas Lechem*: "the soul in its simple, ethereal state":
"simple" - in that it is divested of the entanglement of its physicality.
"ethereal" - in that its essence is extremely sublime in spiritual constitution.
"after it had been purified and made radiant when its deeds were good in this world" - i.e. the soul will attain this through purifying itself in this world. He specified two terms "purified" and "made radiant" because there are two evils which the soul is susceptible to from the entanglement and sickness of physicality. One, that the physicality defiles it by causing it to do bad deeds and sins. Two, the defilement from the superfluous desires (for excessive food, speech, tranquility, etc. see Gate 3). Even though the latter does not cause "corrosion" on it as much as much as sins do, nevertheless, it will not escape from some defilement and filth which it absorbs from the physical...

Marpe Lenefesh: The above account of Yehoshua Kohen Gadol was entirely a spiritual vision, as it is written there: "And he showed me Yehoshua the high priest standing before the angel of the L-ord..."

Certainly those standing there are spiritual beings, and when he will "walk among them", certainly it means without a physical body.

Tov Halevanon: I will give you a place to walk among these (angels) that stand" - means that he will have kiyum (ability to exist) in the world of angels.)

Another reason is that the explanation of reward and punishment in the next world was received by the people from the prophets and can be derived by the wise (in every generation, in addition to the transmitted tradition - *PL*). And the explanation was left out of books just like much of the explanation of the positive and negative commandments were left out, relying on the transmission from the oral tradition.

(*Marpe Lenefesh*: The prophets would explain it to them by heart, just like most of the torah and the explanation of the commandments were transmitted orally by heart, due to many sound reasons.

Marpe Lenefesh: "can be derived by the wise" - since obviously the main reward and punishment is in the next world, since, behold, in this world life is short and its good does not last, and there is not one person in the world who is completely in enjoyment, without any sadness, worry, or fear to hinder his joy. If so, one who does the will of G-d in this world will certainly be rewarded according to His infinite ability and goodness, which cannot be imagined in this world, and certainly this is in the next world which is eternal and all good. See the Sefer Hayashar for a detailed explanation of this.)

Another reason is that the people were foolish and of little understanding (when they left Egypt) something which is not hard to see in the verses.

(*Pas Lechem*: Their foolishness was to such a great extent that it was not hard to see from what is written in the Torah, namely, their hearts' craving for the desires such as asking for meat and other complaints, and little understanding in fundamental matters of purpose, as we see from the incident of the golden calf or their complaints regarding the spies and the congregation of Korach.)

The Creator conducted Himself with them like a father who has mercy on his young son, when he wants to discipline him slowly and gently (so as not to overload him, so too the Creator did not want to inform them of the punishments in the afterlife which are very harsh - *PL*), as written *"Yisrael is a child, and I loved him"* (Hoshea 11:1). When a father wants to educate his young son in the wisdom with which he will attain exalted levels, and the youth is not capable of understanding them at that time, if he tries to induce him, saying "bear the hard discipline and the learning, in order that you later reach the great levels", the son would not have the patience to bear this, and would not listen to his father, because he does not understand them.

But if the father promised him with what is pleasurable right away, whether food and drink, fine clothing and a nice wagon, or the like, and warned him [that if he did not heed he would suffer] what will cause him immediate pain such as hunger, nakedness, spankings or the like, and gave him clear proofs and tangible evidence, so as to impress these promises and warnings in his son's mind and the truth of his statements, it will be easy for the son to bear the strain of the discipline and to endure its tedious work.

And when he becomes a young man and his intellect strengthens, he will understand the intent of the discipline he was put through (the exalted levels - *PL*) and turn towards them. He will think little of the sweetness of pleasures which he had earlier been so eager to run towards. This kind of education was a kindness toward him. (i.e. this conduct to motivate him initially through sweet things, etc. as before, was due to the father's mercy on him - *PL*)

(*Pas Lechem*: Two forms of strain are needed in the study of [torah] wisdom. One, that a person is required to be imprisoned in the prison of the study halls of wisdom. Namely, to be constantly entrenched at the feet of the sages, as the talmud says: "it (the torah) is not to be found among merchants and dealers" (Eruvin 55a), and likewise in Shabbos (120a) on the verse "I will not be a chovesh (binder up)" [the talmud expounds:] "I will not be of those who shut themselves up in the Beit Hamidrash (house of torah study)". Two, the strain of the learning itself, as the talmud says (Sanhedrin 26b): "why is the torah called tushia (in Isaiah 28:29)? Because it weakens the strength of man [through constant study]". Corresponding to these two the author used two expressions "(1) bear the hard discipline and (2) the learning", and correspondingly he wrote two expressions: "(1) the son would not have the patience to bear this, (2) and would not listen to his father", "because he does not understand them" - he does not understand the exalted levels which this will lead him to.
Afterwards he wrote: "it will be easy for the son to bear the strain of the discipline and to endure its tedious work" corresponding to these two.)

Similarly, the Creator encouraged his people with promises of rewards and threatened them with punishments that would come soon i.e. in this world -

PL. For He knew that after they would be strongly established in the service, their foolishness regarding reward and punishment here on earth would shed (i.e. that which they served primarily for reward in this world [would shed] - PL) and their intent in the service would be to Him, and they would direct their conduct for Him. And in this way, we can explain all of the physical forms ascribed to the Creator in scripture.

> (*Pas Lechem*: "and their intent in the service would be to Him" refers to the intent in each specific act, that they would direct their intent to G-d in every act that they do. And for the general conduct in the service he wrote: "they would direct their conduct towards Him", that all of their aspirations in their conduct would be to cling to Him.
>
> *Marpe Lenefesh*: that which scripture ascribes physical form to G-d, such as "the hand of G-d" (Shemos 9:3), "the eyes of G-d" (Devarim 11:12), is also for this reason - so that everyone will understand together, the wise man and the fool, that there is a Creator and Master, as explained at length in Gate #1 chapter 10)

Another reason, is that a man does not become worthy of the reward of Olam Haba (the next world) due to his good deeds alone (since the reward is infinitely great - *TL*). Rather he is deemed by G-d worthy of it due to two things besides his good deeds. (1) That he teaches other people the service of G-d, and guides them to do good, as written "they who bring merit to the public shall be as the stars forever" (Daniel 12:3). And also, "to them that rebuke shall be delight, and on them will come the blessing of the good" (Mishlei 24:25). And when the industrious man will combine the reward for those who he brought merit, with the reward for his own good deeds, and the reward for the faith in his heart and patient acceptance [of G-d's will] - he will be deemed by the Creator worthy of the reward of Olam Haba. (i.e. if he also brings merit to others in addition to his own piety, then certainly he is worthy of the reward, as written: "to them that rebuke shall be delight" - *ML*)

> (*Tov Halevanon*: (from Gate 8 ch.3) those who rebuke others on their wickedness, the delight of G-d and the blessing of G-d will come to them, and certainly for one who rebukes himself for his wickedness, his reward will be greater and more intense.
>
> *Matanas Chelko*: To merit entering the world to come, one must have earned the mitzva of bringing merit to the public. After he has merited to enter there, his state and level will be according to his specific service of G-d. But one who properly performed the commandments and became a

tzadik but did not bring any person to torah, he does not have the key to the world to come. (See there at length for an explanation. A summary is that one can be paid all his reward in this world for all commandments but not for sanctifying G-d's Name which comes through bringing others close to torah. see there.)

(2) The second factor is a kindness from the Al-mighty, and a generosity and goodness, as written *"to You, G-d, is kindness, for You pay a man according to his deeds"* (Tehilim 62:13) (i.e. even if one has only his own good deeds [and did not bring others to the good], G-d will bestow on him good reward in Olam Haba - *TL*).

The reason for this, is that even if a man's good deeds are numerous like the sand of the seashore, it would not weigh enough to cover even one favor the Creator has bestowed on him in this world. All the more so, if he has committed any sins. For if the Creator will hold a man strictly to account for his obligation of gratitude, all of his good deeds would be cancelled and wiped out by even the smallest favor the Creator has done for him, and that which the Creator owes him will not amount to anything. Hence, that which the Creator rewards a person for his good deeds is to be regarded as a Divine grace to him.

(*Tov Halevanon*: "it is a kindness of the Almighty" - i.e. to bestow good reward (Olam Haba) to a Tzadik (righteous man) due to his own good deeds alone, even if he does not teach others and rebukes them. Although, justice demands that a person be held accountable for the sin of his fellow since "all of Yisrael are arevim (responsible) for each other" (Shevuot 39a) for visible matters (provided one can effectively rebuke the other person) and also since we have been commanded to teach others and rebuke them as a positive commandment. Nevertheless, from the abundant kindness of G-d which has intensified on us, G-d does not withhold His reward in Olam Haba. Likewise, even if one teaches others and rebukes his fellow back to the good, it is still, [strictly speaking,] not enough to merit the reward of Olam Haba which is infinitely great, were it not for His kindness... Hence the torah and the prophets did not mention the rewards of Olam Haba in the section of the covenant and the rebuke (Parsha Bechukosai, Ki Tavo, Shema) since, according to justice, a man does not deserve this reward, and it is sufficient to give man reward in this world. Hence, the torah only mentioned what is proper according to justice. Similarly, our sages taught: "prophecy was asked 'what should be the punishment for the sinner?', It replied: 'the soul which sins shall die'. 'The torah was asked, etc.', it replied: 'let him bring an Asham (temple offering) and be atoned', G-d was asked, etc. He replied: 'let him come and do teshuva (repentance)'. Understand this. And since the torah did not mention the rewards, it likewise did not mention the punishments despite that it is a debt he must pay according to his sins.

Marpe Lenefesh: The Sh'la wrote (page 52b): "Consider an analogy of one who [severely] broke his leg or blinded an eye, and a great doctor came and through his great expertise, healed him for free, or even for pay. Wouldn't he love him greatly all of his days, and nothing the doctor asked of him would be difficult for him? Behold, G-d gave a person hands, feet - all of his limbs, and sustains him and watches over him, and gave him a soul so that he can come to immortality..." see there for more. And the author already wrote in Gate#2 ch.5 on some of the favors that G-d did to us from our first existence in this world until today. He who places them always before his eyes - then, his heart will become fiery (impassioned) towards G-d, yisborach.)

The punishment in both worlds, however, is through truth and justice, and it is a debt a man must pay. Yet here too the Creator's loving-kindness is extended to us in both worlds, as written *"to You, G-d, belongs loving-kindness"* (Tehilim 62:13), and *"the compassionate One will atone for sin, and will not destroy"* (Tehilim 78:38).

(*Tov Halevanon*: G-d's kindness here means that G-d waits for him always in this world and gives him time to repent, and if he repents, even if it is just before his death, G-d will exempt him from the punishments of Olam Haba (i.e. but if not, then no sins are overlooked and must be punished in order to pardon the person as will be explained later. - Translator)

Marpe Lenefesh: The kindness is that He pays man some punishment in this world with easy suffering (instead of paying him in the next world with far worse suffering), and also slowly, slowly one at a time, not in furious wrath, as written: "Only you did I love above all the families of the earth; therefore, I will punish you for all your iniquities" (Amos 3:2) as our sages expounded in Avoda Zara 4a. Otherwise [if one thinks G-d's kindness means He will overlook his sins], behold they said: "if a man says 'G-d will overlook my sins', his life will be overlooked", unless it is through [the system of] teshuva (repentance) and this is also a kindness.)

Another reason, is that good deeds are of two categories.
(1) Those concealed from others, and visible only to the Creator, like the duties of the heart, and other similar duties.
(2) Those visible in the limbs and not concealed from other creatures.
For the fulfillment of the visible duties of the limbs, the Creator rewards with visible reward of this world. While for fulfillment of concealed duties, He rewards with hidden reward, namely, in Olam Haba. Therefore, King

David, spoke of this with words which hint to this matter, as written *"how great is Your goodness which You hid away for those that fear You; [which you have done for them that take refuge in You before the sons of men]"* (Tehilim 31:20). And likewise, the way of punishments for hidden and revealed misdeeds, is similar to the way of reward.

(*Pas Lechem*: The above verse mentioned "fear" which is concealed in the heart of a person, and ascribed to it concealed reward [in future tense]. Afterwards, the verse continues that those who "take refuge" in Him, i.e. who cling to Him in acts which are visible before the eyes of "the sons of men", and on these G-d already payed the reward. Hence, "which you have done" is in past tense.)

The proof for this view is as follows. G-d has guaranteed to His people that for their visible service, He would give them visible and swift reward in this world. This is explained in parsha *Bechukosai* "If you will go in My ways.." (Vayikra 26), and likewise, for visible sins, visible and swift punishment in this world. This is because the masses understand only that which is visible (tangible), not that which is hidden - as written: *"the hidden things belong to G-d, but the revealed things belong to us and to our children, forever"* (Devarim 29:28). And the verse says *"if the people will turn their eyes away from the [evil] acts of this man and his family, I will turn My face (send punishment) to this man and his family"* (Vayikra 20:4). Hence, the reward and punishment for the fulfillment or transgression of the duties of the heart belongs to the Creator. Therefore, Scripture omitted an explanation of their reward and punishment in the next world. (see Tov Halevanon for more details)

Another reason why rewards and punishments mentioned in scripture are limited to those in this world only is because the prophet is addressing worldly people. On the other hand, since Yehoshua (kohen gadol) was in the mystical world of angels (i.e. his soul was divested of his body at that time and was in the spiritual world - *PL*), G-d told him, *"I will give you a place to walk among these (angels) that stand"* (Zecharia 3:7). The proper way of motivating with hope and fear should be in accord with the time and place. Understand this.

(*Marpe Lenefesh*: During the giving of the torah at Sinai, the Jewish people were in this world. Hence it is proper to inform them of the reward and punishments of this world, since a man does not fear that which is not tangible to him and that he does not understand.

Tov Halevanon: "the prophet is addressing worldly people" means according to their attachment to physicality and physical pleasures which their hearts constantly turn to and seek the good of their bodies and fear what is harmful to it, while the spiritual pleasure or pain which their soul will be subject to in the next world is worth nothing to them compared to the physical pleasure or pain [in this world]. This is like in the Kuzari 1:104 ..... Therefore, G-d mentioned the rewards and punishments in this world according to what they hope for, and fear from, while they are alive here, namely, while they are attached to the physicality of the body and standing in this lowly world. But Yehoshua Kohen Gadol was an exceedingly wise man, pure, and already divested of the desires of physicality and he elevated himself to the level of the spiritual. For him, the main reward was spiritual pleasure and he desired it even while still in this world, as explained in the wisdom of truth (Kabala). For this he wrote "Understand this". [i.e. the plain meaning as in Marpe Lenefesh, and the deeper meaning here. Both are correct.])

Another reason is that the purpose of reward in Olam Haba is essentially clinging to G-d, and drawing near to His supernal light, as written *"your righteousness will go before you, the glory of G-d shall gather you in"* (Isaiah 58:8), and *"the wise will shine like the radiance of the firmament"* (Daniel 12:3), and also, *"To bring back his soul from the pit (i.e. Gehinom see below Tov Halevanon), to be enlightened with the light of the living"* (Job 33:30). And no one can reach there except he who the Creator finds favor in, and the favor of the Creator is the root of the reward, as written *"his anger is but a moment, in His favor is life"* (Tehilim 30:6). And there are hints in Parsha Bechukosai that pleasing the Al-mighty [is the greatest reward], this is what is written *"My soul will not abhor you"* (Vayikra 26:11), and *"I will turn to you and be unto you a G-d and you will be unto Me a people"* (ibid, 26:9).

(*Tov Halevanon*: "the purpose of reward" - The intent of this answer is that the spiritual reward is only clinging with G-d, and we will attain this when we minimize tending towards the bodily desires and purify our souls by fulfilling His commandments, blessed be He. And then, our souls will be fitting and capable of clinging to the spirituality of G-d. And then G-d, in His kindness, will "conceal us in the shadow of His hand" (Isaiah 49:2), even though we are not deserving of this reward from [the merit] of our deeds, but rather by "His kindness which prevailed over us" (Tehilim 117:2). But when a man turns towards the physical desires in rebelling against the Divine wisdom, then his soul is stuck in the darkness of the physical, and it is impossible in any way to draw close to Him, blessed be He, except by its cleansing itself from its tuma (spiritual impurity), in purifying itself from its physicality in Gehinom, as known to the sages. And according to this, reward and punishment in Olam Haba is not according to judgment and justice, like the reward and punishment in this world. Rather, they follow (1) a kind of nature (i.e. purity from the bad effects of physicality) and (2) also a desire of G-d for those who fulfill His will, both of these two things simultaneously. This is the difference between this answer and the previous one "a man does not become worthy of the reward of Olam Haba due to his good deeds alone... but rather it is a kindness..." [previous answer focused only on (2)]. Understand this.)

TRUST IN THE REWARD AND PUNISHMENT

Trusting in G-d regarding the reward in this world and in the next, which He promised to the righteous man for his service, namely, that He will pay reward to one who is fitting for it, and mete out punishment to one who deserves it. This is incumbent on the believer, and is an essential part of perfect faith in G-d, as written, "and he believed G-d, and it was counted to him as a righteousness" (Bereishit 15:6), and "had I not believed to see the goodness of G-d in the land of the living" (Tehilim 27:13).

(*Tov Halevanon*: "that He will pay reward to one who is **fitting** for it" - One who has perfected his soul by purifying its physical and has become fitting to draw near to the spiritual light should trust that G-d will desire in Him, and will draw His kindness on him in the reward of Olam Haba, even though he does not deserve it due to his deeds.
"and mete out punishment to one who **deserves** it" - i.e. punishment comes on him through the aspect of justice and is a debt which he became obligated in [and must pay].)

It is not proper for one to trust in his own good deeds, and assure himself that he will receive reward in this world and the next due to his good deeds. Rather, he should strive and exert himself [to do good] and make efforts to thank G-d and be grateful for His constant kindnesses to him, and not be motivated by hope of future reward for his deeds. Rather he should trust in G-d and try his best to pay his debt of gratitude for His great favors towards him, as our sages have said *"Do not be like servants who serve their master on condition of receiving reward. Rather, be like servants who serve their master without the condition of receiving reward, and let the fear of Heaven be upon you"* (Pirkei Avot 1:3).

(*Matanas Chelko*: This matter is subtle. Even though one must know that he will receive reward in the next world, nevertheless, the cause of doing the commandment should not be the receiving of the reward. Rather, one should do them because G-d commanded it and even if one did not receive any reward, he would do them anyways. He does the truth because it is the truth... Only that in this knowledge that he will receive reward, he rejoices more in fulfilling the will of G-d. (see there for more)

Tov Halevanon: "and let the fear of Heaven be upon you" - i.e. don't think
that just like reward in the next world goes only by the grace and desire of
G-d, so too the punishments of Olam Haba are not according to his deeds
but only according to the desire of G-d... On this he wrote: "and let the fear
of Heaven be upon you", i.e. the fear of punishment from above should
nevertheless be upon you since punishment is according to Din (justice) in
this world and in the next - not from the aspect of "desire".

Translator: Nevertheless, the Ramchal explains that even punishment is
rooted in kindness, since the whole purpose of punishment is not as a
revenge but rather in order to be able to bestow the greatest good on the
person afterwards. G-d wants that the good a person receives in the afterlife
is earned by him for this is the greatest good. If it were merely a free gift,
then it would carry with it shame and would not be the greatest good. Thus
the attribute of justice was created to ensure this good is earned and that the
person's evil has a way of becoming pardoned.

Thus the attribute of justice does not have its own independent purpose.
Rather, it is merely a method of bringing out G-d's conduct of love to
actuality. Here is a quote from the Ramchal's book Daat Tevunot (siman
154): "the second examination through which we study the ways of divine
love is that through it itself stems the justice in all its general orders,
namely, kindness, justice, and mercy (Chesed, Din, v'Rachamim)". End
quote.

Likewise in Siman 138 there: "thus the mussar (sufferings) stems from
actual love. Hence, a revealed rebuke stems from hidden love. Two good
results come from this fundamental principle: 1) the mussar itself, even at
the time when it is meted out, is not done with furious cruelty, but with
great "sweetening" (mituk gadol) due to the hidden love which does not
allow the anger to rule and become cruel". End quote.

Likewise the Ramchal writes in Kalach Pitchei Chachma, petach #2:
The desire of the Creator is only [to bestow] good. It is impossible to say
that the Divine will desired that there could be other forces which can
prevent Him [from bestowing good] in any manner whatsoever. Because
the Divine will wants solely and exclusively to bestow good, [and if it were
the case that other forces could prevent this] then it would certainly not be
good that His goodness not be capable of spreading over His creations.

And if you ask: "[Perhaps] this is good, namely, the bestowing of good to
the righteous and the punishing of the wicked [is good]?"

Behold, it is written: "I will have mercy upon whom I will have mercy" (Shemot/Exodus 33:19), [which was expounded to mean:] "even though he does not deserve it" (Berachot 7a), and it is written: "[In those days, and in that time, says the L-ord,] the iniquity of Israel shall be sought for, and there shall be none; [and the sins of Judah, and they shall not be found: for I will pardon them whom I preserve]" - behold G-d desires to bestow good also to the wicked.

Perhaps you will ask: "But all this is only after the long exile and the receiving of their punishments?".

I will answer you: "on the contrary, this is a support. If so, behold, the Divine will coordinates the matters so that in the end, all will be meritorious (see Derech H-shem part 2 ch.2-4). This demonstrates that the Divine will is truly and solely to bestow good, only that it is necessary to go with each person according to his way. For the wicked it is necessary to punish them in order to pardon them afterwards. If the intent [in punishing the wicked] was to expel them, then they should have been completely banished - not that they be punished in order to make them meritorious afterwards. This is a clear proof, because behold the end of a matter reveals the intended purpose of all the parts of that matter. And the end of the matter for every human being, whether the righteous or the wicked [after they are rectified] is to bestow on them good. If so, the intended purpose is to bestow good on all. Hence, the Divine will is solely good. Therefore, nothing will endure except His good.

Now that we have reached this point, namely, that the Divine will is only to bestow good, it is necessary that the matters do not go on like this indefinitely. Explanation: if the Divine will did not abhor destroying the wicked, then we would say that punishment is not something evil, rather "Evil pursues sinners" (Mishlei 13:21), and this is the way it is. But since we have said that the way is not like this, but rather, it [the punishment] is in order to afterwards bestow good on him, if so the punishment is evil and must be temporary, not eternal so that the sinner can be released from it. And since it is evil - it is against the Divine will. However, since it is against the Divine will, just like for each person, it is impossible for it to be eternal, so too for the world in general it is impossible for the existence [of evil] to be eternal. (just like G-d wants to rectify every wicked person, so too He wants to rectify the entire world, and nullify the existence of evil. But He wants man to have a hand in this in the meantime..)...

Now let us see if punishment, which precedes the [good] end for the wicked is [in actuality] good or not. A thing whose final end is different than its beginning - its beginning and end are not of the same kind. The process which will act on the wicked will be different in the end from what it was in the beginning. If so, the beginning of this process and the end of it are not of the same kind. The end is good, and this was what the active [Divine] will wanted in the beginning. The means, i.e. that which is before the end is not of this kind. If so, then what preceded the end is not good, and was not the desire of the active will.

We will answer this: If so, why did it change? Rather, since it is impossible to reach the end without this. But if it were possible without this, it would not be proper for this means to exist. The summary of all this is that punishment is evil, and it is the opposite of the desire and intent of the Divine will, but its existence is necessary to be created in order to reach from it to the ultimate purpose. If it were possible without this, it would have been deemed better by the Divine will... [see there for more])

One of the pious said "if one takes strict account of what he is obligated to the Creator for His kindness to him, no man would ever be worthy of the reward of Olam Haba for his deeds. Rather it is only as a kindness of the Al-mighty, therefore do not trust in your deeds." And King David said of this: *"to You, G-d, is kindness, for You pay a man according to his deeds"* (Tehilim 62:13) (i.e. even the paying of a man for his deeds is only a kindness)

SEVENTH CATEGORY - trust in G-d for the special grace to His treasured ones

The seventh category - trust in regard to G-d's special grace to His elect and treasured ones on whom many favors which are indescribable will be bestowed upon in Olam Haba. The proper way of trust in G-d is as follows: To exert oneself in the means which bring one to the high levels of the pious who are worthy of this special grace from G-d. This entails conducting oneself in the ways of the ascetics who loath worldly pleasures, and to uproot from one's heart the love of them and desire for them and replace these with the love of the Creator, and to devote oneself to Him, to delight in Him, to be desolate/astonished from the world and its inhabitants (see commentary), and to follow the ways of the prophets and the pious, and to trust that the Al-mighty will show him favor as He will do with them in the afterlife.

(*Tov Halevanon*: To transform the love of this world and its great longing, which is the way of people to long greatly for matters of this world and its pleasures, and transform it with the love of G-d in this way of love [i.e. not to extinguish the normal great love of this world and its superfluous things, but rather to channel this love to the love of G-d].

Matanas Chelko: ...without a doubt, we are talking here about a very lofty spiritual level. Nevertheless, we must understand that whenever a man loves someone or something, it is impossible for him to have perfect and complete love of G-d and of Olam Haba. This is the author's intent here. If one does not loath this world, he cannot love G-d at this level. Likewise, if one has love for worldly pleasures and matters in his heart he cannot love Olam Haba perfectly. Therefore, to reach this level, it is necessary to remove all love of this world from his heart and to loathe it.

Marpe Lenefesh: "to be desolate from the world and its inhabitants" - to not have any contentment in joining in the company of people, rather to distance from their conversations and social gatherings. (see gate #8)

Pas Lechem: that the remembrance of the affairs of this world and the ways of its inhabitants be desolate and absent from his heart. Or, the intent is that one is astonished and wonders in his heart from the world and its inhabitants, how they busy themselves without a [true] purpose, and "follow the vanities, etc." (Melachim II 17:15) and to abhor their affairs, as in "I was appalled by the vision; it was beyond understanding" (Daniel 8:27).

Matanas Chelko: i.e. that he has no contentment or pleasure from this world or its inhabitants
"to trust G-d will show him favor in the afterlife" - "trust" means to trust in the kindness of G-d. For according to strict justice, there is no place for trust... nevertheless, there is a distinction between trust in worldly matters and trust in matters of the hereafter. For matters of this world, one can trust that G-d will do him favors even if he does not engage in the means of a livelihood, [for special scholars] such as Rabbi Shimon bar Yochai. But for matters of the next world it is impossible to trust in this manner. Because if one does not toil and do, if he does not love the next world and make it primary, but instead his love and desires are of this world, he cannot trust that G-d will grant the [bliss of the] afterlife to him as a kindness. It is impossible to attain the afterlife without hishtadlus (exertion). Only by exertion and strain in doing the will of G-d can one trust that he will receive good reward from the Creator in the afterlife. But without this, it is not trust but folly. This is what the author continues...

But one who trusts that G-d will thus favor him without the means of performing good deeds is a fool and a simpleton. He is like those of whom it is said "they act like Zimri and expect the reward of Pinchas" (Sota 22b). Some signs of those who have reached this high level are those who: (1) teach servants of G-d on the service (due to the love of G-d in all their being, they cannot hold themselves back from remaining silent on the falling short in the service of G-d in other people - *TL*), (2) demonstrating patient bearing and accepting in times of trial and difficulty, (3) regarding everything else as insignificant compared with the fulfillment of the commandments of G-d, as we see by the test of Avraham (Bereishit 22:1), or of Chananya, Mishael, and Azarya who were thrown in the fiery furnace (Daniel 3:13), or Daniel who was thrown in the lion's den (Daniel 6:13), or the 10 martyrs.

WHO IS WORTHY OF THE BLISS OF THE AFTERLIFE

Whoever chooses to die in the service of G-d, rather than rebel against Him; whoever chooses poverty rather than riches, sickness rather than health, suffering rather than tranquility, submits to the Creator's judgment, and desires in His decrees - such a person is worthy of the Divine grace of the Creator in the bliss of Olam Haba, of which it is written: *"That I may cause those that love Me to inherit substance; and I will fill their treasures"* (Mishlei 8:21), and *"no eye has ever seen, O G-d, beside You, what He has prepared for he that waits for Him"* (Isaiah 64:3), and *"How great is Your goodness that You have hidden away for those who fear You"* (Tehilim 31:20).

> (*Marpe Lenefesh*: The reason is that every mitzvah is not worthy of reward, as he wrote earlier in the sixth category, because as our sages said on: "Who has given Me anything beforehand, that I should repay him?" (Job 41:3) that first G-d bestowed all good to a person and afterwards man performs commandments to make a return. But one who offers his life and soul, and all that is his for G-d, out of love, then all the good of this world is worth nothing to him compared to his love of G-d. If so, how could he not be worthy of the good reward of the righteous and the just? This is clear.
>
> *Translator*: i.e. one who does not live for himself, but rather is "working" for G-d, then all the favors G-d does for him are "on the house" and in fact, even his mundane activities are considered as religious service as explained in Gate 3 chapter 9. See that entire gate at length with the commentaries for essential reading on properly understanding this gate.)

*** Chapter 5 ***

The differences between one who trusts in G-d and one who does not with regard to employing the means for earning a livelihood, I say, are seven:

> (*Marpe Lenefesh*: i.e. both are engaged in the means, whether in a handicraft or in a business, and even so, there is a big difference between them)

(1) One who trusts G-d accepts His judgment in all his matters, and thanks Him for good as well as for bad, as written: *"G-d gave, G-d took back, blessed be His Name"* (Job 1:21), and as written: *"of kindness and of judgment I will sing to You"* (Tehilim 101:1), which the sages explained: *"if kindness, I will sing, if justice I will sing"* (Berachos 60b) (Rashi: when You bestow kindness upon me, I will praise you [with the blessing:] "Blessed be He Who is good and does good", and when You perform judgment upon me, I will sing, "Blessed be the true Judge." In either case, to You, O Lord, I shall sing), and they also said: "a man is under duty to bless G-d on the bad (with joy - *ML*) just like he blesses on the good" (Berachos 54a).

But one who does not trust in the Al-mighty boasts on the good (saying "it is due to my might and ingenuity, etc" - *PL*) as written "For the wicked boasts of his heart's desire" (Tehilim 10:3), and he becomes angry on the bad as written "And the one who passes therein shall suffer hardships and hunger, and it shall come to pass,] that when he shall be hungry, he shall be enraged, and curse his king and his [idolatrous] god, and he will turn to Heaven" (Isaiah 8:21).

> (*Marpe Lenefesh*: He will curse them since he sees they are of no substance (ein bo mamash).
> Rashi: *"And the one who passes therein"* - in abandoning the Holy One, blessed be He and relying upon the kings of the nations.
> *"and he will turn to Heaven"*: to beseech the Holy One, blessed be He, but G-d will not heed, for the verdict will have been sealed.
>
> *Matanas Chelko*: one who trusts in G-d realizes that the results of all his efforts are only according to the will of G-d. Therefore, he thanks G-d whether he succeeds or not... but one who does not trust thinks that the exertion causes the success. And when he is not successful, he becomes angry at G-d or has some claims against Him [for not helping him].

In truth this is very strange, for if he has claims against G-d, then he recognizes that it is all from Him. Therefore, when he is successful why does he attribute this to his own strength and ingenuity? Why does he not also question G-d as to why he received such success?.. the answer is that he feels he is deserving of this success and is worthy of it. Only when bad things happen does he start to wonder what he did to deserve such bad things [why did G-d not help him] and he feels he did nothing wrong. All this stems from lack of trust. But one who trusts also wonders when he receives a great good that perhaps he does not deserve this, etc.)

(2) One who trusts in the Al-mighty has tranquility of spirit and a heart at ease regarding bad decrees, knowing that the Creator will arrange them for what is his good in this world and the next, as King David said *"my soul, wait you only on G-d; for my expectation is from Him"* (Tehilim 62:6). But one who does not trust in G-d, even when he is prosperous, is always pained and in a state of continual anxiety. He is saddened and grieving, because he is little satisfied with his situation, and yearns to augment, increase, and hoard in. And likewise in bad times because he is disgusted by it, and it is contrary to his desires, nature and traits. So too, the wise man said *"all the days of the poor are evil"* (Mishlei 15:15)

(*Matanas Chelko*: i.e. even if it is not good for him in this world, he knows and believes that it will be good for him in the next world. Therefore, he is not at all worried.

Tov Halevanon: *"all the days of the poor are evil"* - "poor" refers to one who is not content with what he has, as the sages said: "who is wealthy? One who is content with his portion." (Pirkei Avot)

Pas Lechem: *"yearns to **augment, increase,** and **hoard in**"* - corresponding to these three terms, he earlier wrote three terms denoting pain, namely:
(1) *"he is always pained"* - to **augment**. corresponding to love of pleasure, that whenever he is enjoying something, he is "pained" for augmenting the enjoyment from that thing.
(2) *state of continual anxiety* - to **increase**. corresponding to love of beneficial things, namely, money and possessions, he will "worry" always to increase his money
(3) *"saddened and grieving"* - to **hoard** in. corresponding to what he already possesses but which is spread out here and there and causes him mental distraction, he will be mourning to hoard it in. Likewise what his land produces and is outside in his field, he is saddened in that it is not assured from damages until he can bring it to his domain.
All this is during the times of prosperity. But during bad times, he is very pained and disturbed, *"because he is disgusted by it"* - corresponding to his

taava (love of pleasure), whereby a person is disturbed and repulsed by the matter, either:

(1) because of absence of luxuries, and on this he wrote: "it is contrary to his desires", or

(2) because of absence of necessary things, and this subdivides into two general categories:

(a) "nature": That the matter disturbs his nature. For example, one who is of cold nature (i.e. he needs to stay cool), he is disturbed by bearing things which are too warm or vice versa.

(b) "traits": That the matter disturbs his traits. For example, one who is hot-tempered is irritated by those who act brazenly against him. And the opposite, one who is of calm nature, is irritated by the company of the hot-tempered.

So too, the wise man said "all the days of the poor are evil": that one who is not a baal bitachon (firmly trusts in G-d), is always poor in his mind, as above)

(3) One who trusts in G-d, even while he is engaging in the means for earning a livelihood, his heart will not rely on the means. And he will not hope to receive profit or loss from them unless it is the will of G-d. Rather, he engages in them as part of his service of G-d who commanded us to occupy ourselves with the world, to maintain it and make it more habitable. If these means will yield him profit or help him avoid a loss, he will thank G-d alone for this, and he will not love and cherish the means more for this, nor will he rely more on them on account of this. Rather, his trust in G-d will be strengthened, and he will come to rely on Him and not the means. And if the means do not yield any benefit, he knows that his livelihood will come to him when G-d wants, and through whatever way He wants. Therefore, he will not reject the means because of this, nor abandon employing them, and thus he will serve his Creator (as above - TL).

But one who does not trust in G-d, engages in certain means because he places his trust in them, confident that they will yield him a profit and protect him against a loss. If they yield a profit, he will praise them and himself for his exertion in them and choosing them, and he will not try other means. But if they do not yield him a profit, he will abandon them and reject them, and lose interest in them, as written "Therefore he sacrifices to his net (through which he succeeded in his actions - TL), and he burns incense to his trawl, for through them he lives in luxury and enjoys the choicest food" (Chavakuk 1:16).

(*Matanas Chelko*: besides that he has no peace of mind in everything he does, he must also constantly change the means and strategies from one task or job to another. Through this he causes himself mental dispersion contrary to the peace of mind and tranquility of the one who trusts.

(4) One who trusts in G-d, if he has more money than he needs, he will spend it in a way which pleases the Creator (charity, etc.) with a generous spirit and a good heart, as written *"everything is Yours, and from Your hand we have given to You"* (Divrei Hayamim I 29:14). (since he knows and understands that everything is from G-d, and he is giving G-d of His money, certainly he will give with a generous spirit and a good heart - *PL*)

But one who does not trust in G-d, does not regard the entire world and everything in it as enough for his maintenance and sufficient for his needs. He is more concerned with saving his money than fulfilling his obligations to the Creator and to his fellow men, and he won't feel anything (of the causes which will suddenly strike his money - *PL*), until all of his money is lost and he is left destitute, as the wise man said: *"There is one that scatters, and yet increases; and there is one that withholds more than is right, but it leads to poverty"* (Mishlei 11:24).

(*Pas Lechem*: the intent of the verse is that even though both extremes are bad, because even excessive scattering (donating) is not proper, as the sages said in Ketuvot 50a, since sometimes one will become poor through this. Nevertheless, some do not become poor [by excessive donating], on the contrary he will increase from what he had, but "one that withholds more than is right" this leads only to poverty.

Matanas Chelko: the truster does not hold on to the extra money which remains after he has purchased his needs so that if, G-d forbid, he does not have enough money in the future, he will be able to sustain himself with this money. Rather, he gives it to others and spends it generously in the will of G-d, such as for tzedaka, or maaser. He knows that in truth everything is His. It all comes from Him, and G-d is fully capable of providing for him in the future for all of his needs. [i.e. he does not save beyond what is reasonable]

(5) One who trusts in G-d engages in a means of livelihood, in order to also prepare provisions for his end, and needs for his appointed home (in the afterlife). Only a means of livelihood which is clear to him that it is safe for fulfilling his torah study and fulfilling his religious service will he engage in it. But a livelihood which will bring any loss of torah observance or mislead him to rebel against G-d, he will not engage in, so as not to bring on himself spiritual sickness instead of healing.

(*Pas Lechem*: "to also prepare provisions for his end, and needs for his *appointed home*" - the word "provisions" applies to what a man will use on a journey, as written (in the exodus from Egypt) "nor had they prepared any provisions for themselves" (Shmos 12:39), or "Prepare provision for yourselves, [for in another three days you will cross this Jordan...]" (Joshua 1:11), and when the soul leaves this world until it reaches its place, it will need provisions, as Rabbi Ploni said (before dying) "the provisions are scanty and the road is long" (Kesuvos 67b). And when the soul arrives to its appointed place, it will be sustained there forever and ever with what it prepared here, and on this he wrote "needs for his appointed home")

But one who does not trust in the Al-mighty, trusts in the means, and relies on them, and he won't refrain himself from employing any of them. He will engage in good means as well as bad means (i.e. those permitted to him as well as those forbidden to him - *TL*), and he won't think about his final end, as the wise man said, *"the wise man fears and avoids evil"* (mishlei 14:16).

(*Matanas Chelko*: he is always mindful that all matters of this world are only means to reach in the future to the afterlife. Therefore, he is always thinking that he must prepare provisions for his afterlife.

Marpe Lenefesh: He will have provisions for the afterlife.

Translator: In his youth, the Novhardok Rabbi asked Rabbi Yisrael Salanter why he should learn torah, saying "but what will I live with?". To which Rabbi Yisrael countered: "but what will you die with?")

(6) The one who trusts in G-d is beloved by all classes of people, and they feel at ease with him, because they feel secure that he will not harm them, and their hearts are at peace with regard to him. They are not afraid of him that he will take their wives or their money (etc, as in the tenth commandment, do not covet your fellow's wife, etc - *PL*), and he also is not worried about them because he realizes that it is not in any created being's power or control to benefit or harm him. Therefore, he does not fear harm from them nor expects any benefit from them. And since he is assured from them and they are assured from him, he will love them and they will love him, as written: *"he who trusts in G-d will be surrounded by kindness"* (Tehilim 32:10).

But he who does not trust in G-d, has no [true] friend, because he is always coveting others, and jealous of them, and he thinks that any good that reaches others is a loss to him (as if it was in his hand and left from him to them - *PL*), and that their livelihood is taken from his own, and (1) any preventing of attaining his desires is caused by them, and that (2) others are capable of helping him to obtain his desires, and (3) if some harm comes to his money or his children, he will think they caused it, and (4) that they are capable of removing the harm and problems from him, and since his thinking is based on these principles he will [come to] despise them, slander them, curse them, and hate them. And he is the disgusting one in both worlds, regarded as a disgrace in both abodes as written: *"a crooked heart will not find good"* (Mishlei 17:20).

(*Pas Lechem*: He thinks *"any preventing of attaining his desires is caused by them"*, or he thinks that even though they did not cause him to be prevented from attaining his desires, but nevertheless, since it is in their ability to assist him to attain his desires and they don't assist him - he will hate them.

Pas Lechem: *"he will despise others, slander them, curse them, and hate them"* - He specified four types of denigration corresponding to these four previous divisions.
Corresponding to: (1) *"any preventing of attaining his desires is caused by them"*, he wrote: *"he will despise them"*.
Corresponding to: (2) that they don't want to assist him in attaining his desires, he wrote: *"slander them"*, since he is upset with them because of this and he speaks bad of them calling them midah sedom (selfish, refusing to help others), or the like.
Corresponding to: (3) *"if some harm comes to his money or his children, he will think they caused it"*, he wrote: *"he will curse them"*.
Corresponding to: (4) that they don't want to save him from his troubles, he wrote *"and hate them"*, since according to his view they hate him and rejoice on his troubles, therefore he also hates them.

Matanas Chelko: Trust is a foundation of all commandments between man and his fellow man. For perfection in fulfilling these commandments and in the commandment of "love your fellow..." comes through trust in G-d. The reason a man is not so much able to love his fellow is because when he sees that he is not succeeding as much as his fellow, he imagines that this is due to his fellow. But the truster realizes that it is all from G-d and His decrees. Through this he can feel only love for each and every person.... As we brought earlier from the Sefer Hachinuch (mitzva 241) on the commandment of not exacting revenge which is based on trust that everything occurs solely through the will of G-d, see there. But with this thought (of trust) it is impossible for him to hate his fellow or have complaints against him. Likewise for jealousy. It cannot occur in one who trusts in G-d. Hence, all matters of commandments between man and his

| fellow are rooted in the trait of trust.

(7) The one who trusts in G-d will not mourn if his requests are denied, or if he loses something he loves, and he will not hoard possessions nor be troubled by more than his day's needs (see below commentaries). He does not worry about what will be tomorrow since he does not know when his end will come. He therefore trusts in G-d to prolong his days, and provide his sustenance and needs during this time. He neither rejoices nor grieves about the future (i.e. he does not rejoice in hoping for a future good which is coming up and likewise, he does not grieve or worry on any future bad thing coming up - *PL*), as written *"do not delight in tomorrow because you don't know what today could bring"* (Mishlei 27:1), and Ben Sira said "do not anguish about the troubles of tomorrow because one doesn't know what today could bring, perhaps tomorrow he will be no more (i.e. perhaps you will not live to see tomorrow - *ML*), and he had anguished on a world that is not his" (Sanhedrin 100b).

Rather, his worry and mourning is on his lackings in the fulfillment of his obligations to G-d, and he tries to make up as much as he can of them, of his external (actions - *PL*) and internal duties (of the heart - *PL*). For he thinks of his death and the arrival of the day of in-gathering, and the fear that death may come suddenly increases his efforts and zeal to prepare provisions for his end, and he won't be concerned about preparing for this world. This is what our sages said "repent one day before your death" (Avos 2:10). They explained on this (Shabbat 153a): "repent today, perhaps you will die tomorrow, therefore let all your days be in repentance, as written 'at all times let your clothing be clean' " (Koheles 9:8).

(*Pas Lechem*: *"he thinks of his death and the arrival of the day of ingathering"* - "thinks of his death", the intent is on the death of the body and the nullification of his [worldly] desires. Thinking of "the arrival of the day of ingathering", the intent is on the ingathering of the soul to its place. Both contemplations are necessary because in remembering the death of the body, he will be repulsed by its desires, while by remembering the ingathering of the soul, he will worry on his sins, which prevent the ascent of the soul to its place.

Rabbi Yaakov Emden: *"nor be troubled by more than his day's needs"* - i.e. he does not ask of G-d more than his day's needs, as written: "[give me neither poverty nor riches,] but give me only my daily bread" (Mishlei 30:8). He will not trouble himself much for that which is not already arranged for him. For example, if he rents out things or works at a handicraft he will not worry about whether he will find a renter or a buyer tomorrow. Rather, he will trust that G-d will provide his daily bread, as written: "[Behold, I will rain bread from heaven for you;] and the people shall go out and gather a certain portion every day" (Shmos 16:4). And our sages said: "he who has what to eat today and asks 'what will I eat tomorrow?' is of those who are little in faith" (Sotah 48b).

However, one whose work is for a set duration and at a set period (of the year) such as farmers - certainly he must exert himself on the day and period (season of the year) which will be good for many days and for difficult times, as written: "he that gathers in summer is a wise son" (Mishlei 10:5), and he exhorted us to learn from the ant: "Go to the ant, you sluggard; consider her ways, and be wise...it stores its provisions in summer and gathers its food at harvest" (Mishlei 6:6), to learn from its ways and be wise to prepare during times available. And likewise, one who engages in business must journey to markets and fairs or the like. There is no prohibition to fill storehouses and to rely on them for years of famine, or to save cattle and properties from the extra that G-d has made available to him, so that it be ready for the time of need, and thus it is written in the torah: "But you must remember the L-rd your G-d, for it is He that gives you strength to make valor" (Devarim 8:18), which the Onkelos renders: "He gives you counsel to acquire wealth", and the wise man said: "The wealth of the rich is the city of his strength; the destruction of the poor is their poverty" (Mishlei 10:15), when it is wealth that was earned justly - take care of it, and do not kick at the blessing of G-d. Also, one is not obligated to scatter it all [to tzedaka, etc.], but rather through certain conditions. The intelligent person will arrange his matters according to the way of nature in accord with the will of G-d who arranged for him an order to seek his livelihood at certain times, with a perfect and faithful heart that trusts in G-d.

Matanas Chelko: *"nor be troubled by more than his day's needs"* - there is no doubt that the author is speaking about very lofty levels of trust, really (mamash) the greatest possible extreme of the trait - that one does not worry about tomorrow. Nevertheless, reason also necessitates that it be such. For when one contemplates on what happened yesterday and further back, he will see that he always had what to live on and what to eat, and everything was only through G-d. Then too, he had nothing for tomorrow. Therefore, even today he can also rely on G-d for tomorrow. But the imagination deceives him and tells him that it is not comparable for in those past times he certainly had enough for the next day. But in truth, it is not so. Therefore, one needs to work on feeling this level of trust and live in this way.

"since he does not know when his end will come" - this is a different point. The truster is not a dreamer. On the surface it seems that the wicked is more assured than the truster. For behold, the truster always worries that

perhaps he will die tomorrow, as Rabbi Eliezer told his disciples "repent today for tomorrow you may die" (Shab.153a) But the wicked does not live by this idea. But in truth, it is not so (that the wicked is more assured). For the end of every human being is death. This is not a thought of sadness. On the contrary, it is proper and beneficial. A man should constantly contemplate that he is given a fixed amount of time to live and work in this world. But the wicked does not contemplate this thought "to repent for perhaps he will die tomorrow". Rather, he trusts that certainly tomorrow and the day after he will still be among the living. This is a bit amazing for most people see through television, or the like, many murders, and that people do die, but they don't take to heart that it is possible they will also die like them. Rather, whenever they start to think about their deaths, they fall into great sadness. They feel so assured that they will be alive tomorrow and the day after that they don't even worry about this. It is known what the Chafetz Chaim said on how a man goes to a funeral and sees that people die, but does not reflect that perhaps he will also die tomorrow. Rather, he thinks that just like there is a "chevra kadisha" (funeral worker group), so too there is a "chevra of the dead", and he is not part of this group and is not counted among them. In truth, this is just repressing of the eye. For one must reflect on the time of his end in this world. This is not a matter of sadness [to avoid] but rather like a farmer working on his field who still has much work to do. If his friend tells him to finish everything quickly before nightfall for then he will not be able to work, certainly he will not answer him: "don't speak to me about night, for it is sad and dark". Likewise for death, which is the time of nightfall for a man. Therefore, one must and is under duty to reflect on his time for work in this world.)

But one who does not trust in G-d, mourns greatly the constant troubles of the world that befall him, that his wishes and the things he loves are taken away or denied from him (he worries constantly that these things will be lacking to him - *TL*). He tries to amass much wealth of this world, as if he were assured from passing on (that his situation passes from this world to the next - *TL*), and the fear of death has left him, as if his days are unlimited and his life will never end. He does not consider his end, occupied only with this world, unconcerned about his religious matters, making no provisions for the hereafter, and his eternal abode. His trust in prolonging his days in this world is a cause for his perpetual desire for his worldly affairs and for his little desire in matters of his final end.

(*Matanas Chelko*: "*his trust in prolonging his days...*" - in truth this is a great wonder. One who does not trust in G-d, trusts in only one thing - that he will not die and will live forever. For everything else he relies on his own strength and ingenuity, and that he has the power to decide and succeed. But regarding life and death, which everyone knows and recognizes that it is in G-d's hands - on this he trusts that he will live forever! This is what we wrote in the beginning of this gate, namely, that really every person trusts in something, and it is impossible to live otherwise. The difference is whether a person trusts in G-d, human beings, or in himself. For example, one who rides an airplane trusts in the mechanics that no failure will occur, and likewise on the pilot who knows how to drive the airplane. Likewise, he trusts that the baker did not put poison in the bread, and similarly for every thing. The reason is that this is the nature G-d implanted in man - to trust. For without this, it is impossible to live. One would be worried on every little thing, be it the baker or the workers, etc. [The proper way is that] in every thing it is proper to place one's trust in G-d (not the baker, etc.), but in things one does not know what will be, such as death, one must prepare for himself provisions for the journey.

When the preacher rebukes him or the teacher instructs him saying "how long will you avoid thinking about preparing provisions for your final journey and for matters of your eternal abode?"

He will answer "when I will have enough money for my needs and for the needs of my wife and children until the end of our days. Then I will have peace of mind from my worries of this world, and I will take time to pay my debts to the Creator, and will think about preparing provisions for my final end."

*** Chapter 6 ***

I saw proper to expose the foolishness and error in this way of thinking in 7 ways. I will reveal the greatness of their mistake, and if our words prolong, this is because there is much to shame and rebuke proponents of this outlook.

> (*Pas Lechem*: *"foolishness and error"* - Some of the matters he will bring demonstrate to the person that he is a complete fool, similar to one of the boorish people who have no human understanding. Other matters he will bring do not demonstrate his foolishness so much but rather show that he is mistaken, such as the fifth, sixth, and seventh.
>
> Afterwards, he wrote: "there is much to shame and rebuke..." corresponding to these two "foolishness and mistake", because a man is shamed when he is called a fool, and on the "mistake", he wrote "and rebuke", namely, to clarify his mistake to him.)

They are as "security pledge seekers", similar in their practice to merchants who sell goods on credit to someone he does not trust, and will demand a security pledge at the time of sale, because he minimally trusts his client or fears the client will not be able to pay him.

(1) The first of the possible ways to answer him: we tell him "You, the man who doubts the decree of the Creator, and doubts His [Almighty] power, you whose light of intellect has obscured, whose candle of understanding has extinguished due to being overwhelmed by the darkness of material desires. You deem proper to seek a security pledge from a client who has no dominion over you, and cannot give you orders. However, for a worker who seeks to be hired by an employer, it is not proper for him to seek a security pledge of his wages before he starts to work. All the more so, it is not proper for a slave to seek a security pledge of his food from his master before working for Him. And even more so, for a created being to seek a pledge from his Creator before fulfillment of the service he owes Him!

It is a wonder! For a slave to undertake service to his master with a precondition that the master pay him a wage after his service is completed would be regarded as a disgrace (since the owner boards, lodges, and clothes him and provides for all his needs - Rabbi Hyamson zt'l), as the sages said: *"be not like servants who serve their master on condition to receive reward, but rather like servants who serve their master even without condition of receiving reward"* (Pirkei Avot 1:3). And how much more so if he were so brazen as to demand a pledge for his maintenance from his master before he even starts working. On similar to this it is written: *"Is this how you repay the L-ord, you disgraceful, unwise people?! [Is He not your Father that has acquired you? has He not made you, and established you?]"* (Devarim 32:6).

(*Pas Lechem*: *"who doubts the decree of the Creator"* - you are of those of little faith, who doubt the decree of the Creator, i.e. who doubt whether or not all of a man's guidance and needs are governed exclusively by the decree of the Creator.

"and doubts His [Almighty] power" - you doubt His power, and the scope of His providence which spreads from the highest heavens (spiritual worlds) until the depths of our [physical] world, since the doubt on the providence [of G-d] in this world stems from their imagining and picturing the remoteness of the physical from His glorious holy place.

Marpe Lenefesh: *"whose light of intellect has obscured, whose candle of understanding has extinguished due to being overpowered by the darkness of material desires"* - i.e. since the darkness of his material desires has overpowered him, therefore "the light of intellect has obscured, and the candle of understanding has extinguished", to the extent that he does not understand even self-evident things which no man is capable of denying.

Tov Halevanon: *"even the work of a slave to a master on condition to be paid after the work is regarded as a disgrace"* - that which he does not know his owner (a reference to Isaiah 1:3 "The ox knows his owner...but Israel does not know"), who acquired him with his money on condition that he serve him. And all the more so, the Holy One, blessed be He, who is our Father, He acquired us, and it is proper for us to serve Him on account of the multitude of favors He has already bestowed on us, as the author wrote in the previous chapter.)

(2) One who takes a security pledge from a client receives a definite amount and his request is limited. But for the proponent of this thinking, there is no end to what he seeks. For he does not know how much money will suffice for his and his family's needs and luxuries for the rest of their lives. And even if he obtained money many times his needs, he would not be at peace, because the time of their end is hidden, and the number of their days is not known, and he is foolish in what he seeks because there is no end by him and no measure.

Pas Lechem: *"no end by him"* to the amount of his needs since he does not know how long he will live, and corresponding to the desire for luxuries, he wrote "no measure" since there is no measure for luxuries.

Translator: since he does not know his end, he imagines and conducts his life as if he will live forever as The Zohar wrote (Nasso 126):"A man walks in this world and he thinks that it will be his forever, and that he will remain in it for all time" (i.e. even though he knows intellectually that he will die, but he does not feel this at all).

(3) One who takes a security pledge from his fellow, only does so if there are no previous debts that he owes the fellow, and the fellow has no claims against him. Only then is he justified to request a pledge. But if he has outstanding debts to the fellow, and knows the fellow has legitimate claims against him, he has no business whatsoever in seeking a pledge, and it is not proper for him to accept it even if the fellow volunteered the pledge. All the more so, for the Creator who has such legitimate claims on man, so that if the service of all human beings who ever lived could be accumulated and credited to a single man, their total would not be sufficient return to cover the debt of gratitude that a man owes for even one of the benefits the Creator bestowed on him (such as bringing him to existence from nothingness).

(*Pas Lechem*: This is because the intent in the word "return" is: the receiving of a favor that the benefactor receives in return from the one who he benefited. But for G-d, it is completely not applicable to render to Him any favor from His creations. Therefore, it cannot be considered a "return".

Matanas Chelko: As written (Job 41:11) "Who has given Me anything beforehand, that I should repay him?", i.e. no man has ever done any commandment without having first received countless benefits from G-d. His life, possessions, and all matters - everything comes from G-d. The reason man cannot repay G-d is twofold. First, in truth, G-d does not get anything whatsoever from the fulfilling of His commandments. Hence, the fulfilling of a commandment cannot be considered a payment for all that one received. Secondly, all that a man does is worth less than a drop in the ocean in comparison with the gift of life which G-d has graced to man. All that man does - Shabbat, tefilin, talit, etc. is not payment for even one second of life.)

And how can this brazen faced person not be ashamed to ask from the Creator big favors on top of previous favors thereby increasing his debt to Him. (the man seeks from G-d more favors, and that they be bigger than the favors He bestowed on him until now - *PL*). And maybe he will not even be able to fulfill the service that he says he will do (after he acquires wealth) because his days will have passed and his end will have come.

> (*Pas Lechem*: *"his days will have passed and his end will have come"* - two expressions corresponding to two categories of a person's death. One, that the number of days allotted to him from the time of his birth have passed, as is known, that every person has a fixed number of days allotted to him. Two, due to a heavenly decree because of some sin for which he incurred a death sentence.)

One of the pious would say to people: "Gentlemen, is it conceivable that the Creator would demand payment today for debts that are not due until tomorrow? And likewise, would He demand payment today for debts that are not due until next year, or many years from now?"

They answered him, "How is it possible to claim from us payment of future debts when we don't even know if we will be living at the time when the debt is incurred? Rather, we are only bound to perform a definite service for a definite time and when the future comes, we will perform the service that is due then."

He would answer them: "So too, the Creator guarantees for you for every definite period its needed livelihood, and in return for this, you are indebted a great service (in that time period - *PL*). Just like He does not demand from you the special service before its appointed time, so too you should feel ashamed to ask for income before the time for it has arrived. Why do I see you seeking from Him income for several years in the future when you don't even know if you will live to reach those days? Furthermore, you ask Him to provide you with maintenance for a wife and children which you don't even have yet. You are not satisfied with the livelihood provided in the present and you seek to prepare money for needs and luxuries for future times that you are uncertain to reach and that are not assured to you. And, not only do you not render to Him service for the benefits you will receive in the future, but you don't even make an accounting with yourselves for the service to Him which you neglected to do in the past during which G-d has not neglected to provide for your livelihood in full."

(4) One who takes a security pledge from his fellow does so for one of three reasons: One, maybe the fellow will become poor and won't be able to pay him. Two, maybe the fellow will close his hand [refuse to pay] and

he may be unable to collect payment from him. Three, in case the fellow dies or won't be found.

The security pledge is like a medicine against these ailments that occur between people (i.e. if he takes a pledge he is immune from these ailments and worries - TL). But if men were assured of each other against these three mishaps, it would certainly be disgraceful to demand a security pledge. And the Creator for whom these three mishaps do not apply, how much more so is it a great disgrace to demand a security pledge from Him. And scripture already says: *"silver and gold is Mine"* (Chagai 2:8), and *"wealth and honor belong to You"* (Divrei Hayamim 29:12).

> (*Tov Halevanon*: It is not applicable to ask any kind of pledge from Him since everything is already by Him.
>
> *Pas Lechem*: The latter two reasons do not need a proof [from scripture], because who is so foolish as to not know that He is living and among us, and that He has no trace of dishonesty or stinginess, ch'v. But on the first reason, perhaps a person will think "from where will G-d pay me, since He does not make coins?" On this he brought the verse "silver and gold is Mine", that nevertheless He has full capacity to give to whomever He wishes
>
> *Matanas Chelko*: *"disgrace to demand a security pledge from Him"* - for G-d will not become poor or die. He can give whenever He wants. Only that a man doesn't believe in G-d and His ability. Therefore he seeks a pledge. But G-d already promised in His torah that human beings should do the commandments and He will support them all of their days.)

(5) One who obtains a security pledge from his fellow will be at peace with his pledge because he expects to collect from it and to derive benefit from it or its monetary value. But one who thinks that if the Creator will advance him future provisions he will have peace of mind regarding affairs of this world - his thinking is false and mistaken, because he cannot be sure the money will remain by him. It is possible that he will be struck by some mishap that parts him from the money, as written *"in mid-life he will lose it"* (Yirmiyahu 17:11).

And as for the claim that he will have peace of mind when he amasses wealth - this demonstrates falsehood and foolishness on his part. On the contrary this may well be the very cause that will cause him much mental pressure and anxiety as our sages said *"more possessions, more worries"* (Avot 2:7)..

(*Pas Lechem*: *"this demonstrates falsehood and foolishness"* - either he is mistaken in this, or he himself knows this and deceives with this excuse.

Marpe Lenefesh: Even though it is a mistake to demand a pledge from G-d for many reasons, nevertheless, if he were assured that the money (pledge) would stay by him and that he could do what he wants with it, his mistake would not be a falsehood. For example, suppose he took a pledge from someone who he did not realize that the man is an honorable and wealthy person. Even though he was mistaken in demanding a pledge, nevertheless, since he did not know the man, it is not falsehood, since nevertheless, he is assured by the pledge from many possible mishaps. But this that he took a pledge from G-d, not only was he mistaken in his outlook, but also his mistake will not yield any benefit. For he is still not assured that the money (pledge) will be by him at a needy time. Perhaps the money will be struck by a loss and nothing will remain or maybe he will die at midlife as [we see] happens every day. And even if we say that the wealth will stay by him, nevertheless it is uncertain whether he will serve G-d due to having wealth, because perhaps the money will bring him more mental pressure and anxiety than he had before he had it, since "more possessions, more worries")

(6) If one who takes a security pledge from his fellow were certain that the fellow would pay him before the due time, and would out of pure kindness compensate him with an amount twice as much as was due for his waiting time, he would not seek a security pledge under any circumstances. Now, the blessed Creator, of who it is known to us of His benevolent conduct towards us, and of His great past and present favors to us, and that He rewards acts of righteousness and service with reward that we cannot even imagine, as written: *"no eye had ever seen, O G-d, besides Yours, what He has prepared for those who wait (trust and hope - TL) to Him"* (Isaiah 64:3), certainly it is a great disgrace to ask for a security pledge.

(*Marpe Lenefesh*: *"reward that we cannot even imagine"* - that He bestows so much good reward for one mitzvah.
Pas Lechem: the hidden reward cannot be imagined by the human mind. All the more so, it cannot be described verbally.)

(7) One who takes a security pledge from his fellow, is only justified in doing so if he is able to supply him with the merchandise purchased for which he takes the pledge. But one who seeks a security pledge from the Creator, in seeking advance favors, is not capable of paying for them in services. He is not even certain of paying back what he owes from past debts, all the more so for paying what he owes for future favors. For the

righteous man cannot pay back the debts of gratitude of the Al-mighty on him except through the means of help which G-d renders him. And so, one of the pious in his praises of G-d said: "Even the thinking person who has knowledge of You, does not praise his own religious acts, but rather praises Your Name and mercy, for You have prepared his heart to know You. Through You (Your help - *ML*) the people of Israel will be found worthy and be praised saying: *"We praised [ourselves] with G-d all day long, and we will forever thank Your Name"* (Tehilim 44:9).

(*Marpe Lenefesh*: For example, if the lender takes a security pledge on condition that he will lend the borrower a 1000 gold coins. Then, if the lender has the 1000 gold coins available, he can take the security pledge. If he does not [have the 1000 gold coins available], then he cannot take it. And a man knows that he does not have the ability to pay G-d in [religious] services and righteousness corresponding to all the benefits he gets from G-d. And especially, if he pays back a little bit, it is through G-d's help, as our sages expounded (Midrash Vayikra Rabba 27:2) on the verse: "Who has given Me anything beforehand, that I should repay him?" (Job 41:3) - Who put up a mezuzah before I gave him a house? [Who built a Sukkah before I gave him a place upon which to build it? Who performed the mitzvah of tzitzis before I gave him clothing?], likewise, even one's wisdom and praises is from Him, blessed be He.

Matanas Chelko: even when a man praises G-d, the recognition itself that man has of G-d is from G-d, and the mouth with which he utters the praises is from G-d. Everything he does is using the tools which G-d has given him. This is what we say in the "Aleinu Leshabeach" prayer: "it is incumbent on us to praise the Master of the world... [and concludes] that we bow and praise the King of kings". What kind of praise is it to say that our portion is to praise Him? Rather, it is the exact same thing the author is saying; we are praising G-d for giving us the permission, ability, and opportunity to praise Him. Likewise, in the Modim prayer, it starts "we thank You..." and ends "on our thanking you"... The point is that a man does not do any "kindness" towards G-d. On the contrary, the kindness is from G-d who gave us the ability and possibility to come to the synagogue and pray to Him and praise Him. If one reflects on this, he will see it is the exact opposite of the outlook of the pledge-seeker who wants to receive everything before the service. But in truth, all the service they do - it is all from G-d.

*** Chapter 7 ***

Since we have completed in this gate, to the best of our ability, a fitting amount of discussion on the themes of trust, it is now proper to clarify the things detrimental to trust in the Al-mighty. I say that the detrimental things mentioned in the 3 preceding gates of this book are all likewise detrimental to trust [in G-d].

> (*Marpe Lenefesh*: i.e. the Unity - to believe in the Creator of the world, as explained there [in Gate #1], and likewise on the [Gate of] examination, to examine His creations, and to assume the service of the Creator, as is fitting to Him. Whoever is far from the things mentioned in those gates and fell into the things detrimental to them as was explained earlier - he undoubtedly does not trust in G-d.
>
> *Pas Lechem*: (from the introduction) On the other things of the inner duties such as placing one's trust in G-d, giving over oneself to Him, and devoting one's acts to Him, and the like, which stem from recognizing the greatness of G-d and of His beneficence.)

Additional things which cause a loss of trust:
(1) Ignorance with regard to the Creator and His good attributes. For one who does not realize the Creator's mercy towards His creations, His guidance, providence and rule over them, and that they are bound by His chains, under His total control - he will not be at peace (from mishaps - PL) and will not rely on Him (for providing his needs - PL).

> (*Marpe Lenefesh*: "*Ignorance with regard to the Creator*" - he does not realize that G-d is a great and awesome King and that His reign is over everything.
> "*and His good traits*" - how He guides His creations with kindness and mercy, and always gives them all their needs.
> "*that they are bound by His chains*" - all the creations are truly bound by Him, that everything is from Him, all things that a human being does is completely from Him, and there is nobody who can change anything, except for Yirat Shamayim (fear of G-d, i.e. moral choice) which G-d gave the free will in man's hands.
>
> *Pas Lechem*: (from the introduction) On the other things of the innner duties such as placing one's trust in G-d, giving over oneself to Him, and the like, *which stem from recognizing the greatness of G-d and of His beneficence*.)

(2) Another, ignorance of the Creator's commandments, namely His Torah, where He instructed us in it to rely on Him and trust in Him, as written: *"test Me in this..."* (Malachi 3:10), and *"trust in G-d forever"* (Isaiah 26:4).

> (*Tov Halevanon*: "to rely on Him and trust in Him" - in [performing] His service and guarding His commandments, and like our sages expounded: "take maaser so that you become rich", and [G-d] says: "test Me in this", i.e. in maaser, and likewise for all of the other mitzvot, and like the verse says (Tehilim 37:25): "yet I have not seen the righteous forsaken")

Another detriment to trust is to tend to rely on the means which one can see, without realizing that the nearer the causes are to the one affected by them, the less ability they have to help or harm him, and the further [up] they are, the stronger and the more power it has to help or harm him.

As an illustration, when a king decides to punish one of his servants, he commands his prime minister to take care of it, and the prime minister orders his chief of police, and the chief of police orders his sergeant, and the sergeant orders his officer, and the officer orders the policeman, and the policeman inflicts the punishment with the instruments (whip, stick, etc.) he has.

The instruments have the least capability of all of them to reduce or increase his suffering because they have no will of their own. The policeman has greater capability than the instruments (to reduce the number of whippings - *PL*). Likewise, the officer has greater capability than the policeman, and the sergeant than the officer, and the chief of police than the sergeant, and the prime minister than the chief of police, and the king more than all of them, because if he wants, he can pardon the man (from everything - *TL*).

As you can see, the weakness and strength of the agents to affect the person are according to their remoteness from him or nearness to him. And the exalted Creator, who is the First Cause and infinitely remote from those affected by Him, is the One who it is proper to trust and rely on because of His infinite power to help or harm, as we explained.

> (*Marpe Lenefesh*: the thing near to him from which his livelihood comes has less power to provide his livelihood than the thing remote from him, which is the cause of this [near] thing, and this remote thing to another more remote thing, etc. All these agents from the man on are called causes and means, and G-d is the Means of all the means and the Cause of all the

causes, and the man who receives from all the means is called "the affected". Understand this.)

The general principle in the matter of trust is that the degree of trust among those who trust in G-d increases according to the amount of knowledge of G-d, faith in His protection of them, and in His abundant providence to promote what is for their good.

(*Tov Halevanon*: "*increases according to the amount of knowledge of G-d*" - knowing and understanding the extent of His reign on each and every act and cause - that everything depends on Him, blessed be He. He will now bring an analogy to explain the matter.

Pas Lechem: The degree of level of trust among people, namely, the degree of trust which people differ in is "according to the amount of knowledge of G-d, etc."

Marpe Lenefesh: The proof of this is what he will mention shortly, that a baby at first trusts in his mother's breast, and afterwards on his mother, and afterwards on his father, and so on for the 10 levels he mentions. From this it is clear that the greater one's knowledge of G-d and of His providence on him, the more trust in G-d he will have.)

THE TEN LEVELS OF TRUST
(1) An infant, at the beginning of his existence, trusts in his mother's breast, as written: "*For You drew me from the womb; You made me trust on my mother's breasts*" (Tehilim 22:10).

(*Matanas Chelko*: i.e. if the baby could speak and one would ask it how it lives, it would respond "from my mother's breast", not "from my mother". In his eyes, the breast feeds and sustains him. This is the outlook of a baby. He cannot grasp more than this.

(2) When his perception strengthens, his trust moves to his mother, due to the great care she gives him, as written: "*I swear that I calmed and quieted my soul like a weaned child with his mother*" (Tehilim 131:2).

(*Matanas Chelko*: when he grows a bit and his intellect opens a bit more, he recognizes that he receives several benefits from his mother, such as washing him, clothing him, etc. Hence, now he realizes that his sustenance comes from his mother. It is proper to add here the following analogy from the trust of a child to his mother and father. When a child stands on a table or chair and his father asks him to jump to his hands and the child does so. Certainly, without strong trust in his father, that his father worries for him and loves him, he would never have jumped thereby placing himself in danger of falling to the floor. His trust in his father is so great that he jumps to his hands. Likewise, for a man's trust in G-d, he must jump into the hands of G-d and trust in Him that He cares for him and loves him just like a father's love for his child.

(3) When his understanding grows more, and he observes that his mother depends on his father, he moves his trust to his father due to the greater degree of protection he receives from him.

> (*Tov Halevanon*: the security and food which she bestows on him - everything depends on the gift from the hand of the father.
>
> *Marpe Lenefesh*: Even though his mother takes care of his needs, and not his father since he is not available, nevertheless, he recognizes his father's protection, that sometimes his father saves him from things which cause him pain.)

(4) When his body strengthens, and it becomes possible for him to earn for himself a livelihood through work or business, or the like, he moves his trust to his strength and resourcefulness, due to his ignorance that all the good that came before this was through the providence of G-d.

> (*Tov Halevanon*: he is still boorish and does not realize that wealth does not come from the trade itself, and all the livelihood he received until now was from G-d.)

It is said of one of the pious, whose neighbor was a swift scribe and would earn his livelihood through his scribal skills. One day he inquired to the scribe: "how are things?" He answered "good, as long as my hand is still in good shape." Then, that evening his hand was crushed, and he could not write with it for the rest of his life. This was his punishment from G-d, in that he placed his trust in his hand. (to atone for him. Note that he must have been at a very high level of piety, therefore G-d paid him in this world even for minute sins so as to spare him from any loss in the next world)

> (*Matanas Chelko*: "as long as my hand is still in good shape" - certainly it is permitted to speak like this. However, it all depends on one's intent. If he means "thank G-d, I still have the hand given to me to do my work", that he understands that the strength does not come from himself. Rather it is given to him by the grace of G-d, then his words are good and correct. However, it appears that the author's intent is that even words like this ascribe too much the ability and accomplishment to human power. If he thinks this is the way to his livelihood, that by G-d's giving him a hand, he is able to use

it to work and earn a livelihood for himself, this is already considered shituf (association), G-d and himself. Since, what comes out of his words is that his intent is if he did not have a hand, he would not be able to provide for himself. This is not correct. For G-d can provide for him through other means. True, right now G-d gave him a hand through which he is providing for himself, but true trust is to recognize that even without his hand, G-d can still provide for him through his feet, his head or any other way. Hence, whenever a person ascribes excessive power and ability in the means itself, he already diminishes thereby his trust in G-d.

Netziv commentary on Gen.40:23 - G-d punished Yosef for putting his trust in the Wine Master by causing the Wine Master to forget about Yosef for two years (Midrash, Genesis Rabba 89:3). From the fact that Yosef was punished for putting his trust in a person we learn about his greatness. The punishment indicates that Yosef had never before put his trust in man and was thus punished solely because he deviated from his high level of trust in G-d.

(5) If his livelihood comes through one of his fellow human beings, he will transfer his trust to them and rely on them.

(*Tov Halevanon*: The author returned to the previous matter, and said that there are those who do not rely on their own resourcefulness, and they recognize their own lackings. However, they trust in the salvation from human beings. He thinks that he does not need to trust in anything more, and even if he becomes disabled and unable to provide for himself, they will not abandon him.)

(6) But when his wisdom grows and he realizes their lacking and their need for the Creator, he will then move his trust to G-d, and rely on Him for things beyond his own control and which he cannot escape submitting to the decree of G-d. For example, the falling of rainwater on the crops, or (safely) travelling through the sea, or crossing a barren desert, or floods, outbreaks of a plague among the living, or the like among matters which human beings have no plan whatsoever, as written: *"In the time of their trouble they will cry out: 'arise and save us' "* (Yirmiyahu 2:27).

(7) If his knowledge of G-d strengthens more, he will put his trust in G-d in matters where he has some plan, such as avoiding earning a livelihood through dangerous means or exhausting occupations that wear down the body, and trusts in G-d that He will provide for him through a lighter occupation.

(8) If his knowledge of G-d strengthens more, he will put his trust in G-d

in all the means, whether difficult or easy, and while occupied in them, his intent will be directed to serve G-d and guard His commandments.

(*Tov Halevanon*: i.e. He will put to heart, that G-d has no limitations, and He can provide the livelihood of every person through any means. And that which he is occupied with a specific trade, this is in order to observe the service of G-d, which He commanded us to engage in matters that cause our livelihood to come, as the author wrote earlier [in chapter 4].)

(9) If his knowledge of G-d strengthens more regarding His mercy on the created beings, he will accept with heart and mind, outwardly and inwardly, the decrees of G-d. He will rejoice in whatever G-d does to him, be it death or life, poverty or wealth, health or sickness. He will not desire other than what G-d has chosen for him, and desire only what G-d has chosen for him.

(*Tov Halevanon*: i.e. he will acknowledge and bless G-d on the death of one of his relatives or children just like [he did] on their life, and likewise for poverty just like for wealth.)

He will give himself over to G-d, and surrender his body and soul over to His judgment. He will not prefer one matter over another and will not choose anything other than his current situation, as one who trusts in G-d said: "I never resolved to do a thing and desired something else".

(*Pas Lechem*: "*He will give himself over to G-d*" - regarding G-d's guidance of all of his needs.
"*surrender his body and soul over to His judgment*" - If some bad thing happens to him, he receives it and bears it with a good countenance.

Manoach Halevavos: He does not trust in one matter more than another. He does not think one matter is more profitable than another. All the causes and means are equal to him, because he realizes that they all depend on the will of G-d. Therefore, he trusts only in G-d. Because of this, when he resolves to do something, he does not desire something else.

Matanas Chelko: this is the level of a true "baal bitachon" (truster in G-d). He does not trust in any means (even though he engages in them). Rather, he knows and believes that everything comes only from G-d. This level brings one to accept everything G-d decrees on him in all matters of life.)

(10) When his knowledge of G-d strengthens more than this and he understands the true intent why he was created and brought to this fleeting world, and he recognizes the exaltedness of the eternal, next world, he will

think lightly of this world, and its means. With mind, soul, and body, he will flee from this world and surrender himself to the blessed Al-mighty, and delight in remembering Him in solitude. He will feel desolate when he is not (capable of - *MC*) meditating on His greatness.

> (*Matanas Chelko*: this is an additional level of intensity of recognition and trust. Not only does he trust in G-d's ability and providence, but this recognition has brought him to strengthen his trust in the will of G-d. Now, he recognizes full well why he came to this world - not in order to work and make money, but only in order to do the will of G-d.
>
> *Manoach Halevavos*: No thoughts come to his mind, except on the greatness of G-d. He is desolate and silent from other thoughts, and parts from them quickly if they enter his mind... He is astonished on those who do not contemplate. He thinks of the greatness of G-d always, and likewise he is amazed at himself if sometimes he does not meditate on the greatness of G-d, and he puts to heart that it is proper to think always of the greatness of G-d when sitting in his house, walking on the way, lying down, and rising up (a reference to the Shema).
>
> *Pas Lechem*: When he is in solitude, away from people, and nothing distracts his thoughts, he will greatly delight in this because then he can remember Him with a focused mind.)

If he is among a crowd of people, he will long for nothing else than to do His will, and yearn only to come near to Him. His joy in his love of G-d will distract him from the pleasures worldly people have for this world, and even from the joy of souls in the next world.

> (*Tov Halevanon*: His joy in love of G-d will distract him to such an extent that he will not be able to enter in his heart any joy of worldly people, namely, the worldly matters they rejoice in.
>
> *Marpe Lenefesh*: His joy in love of G-d is greater than the pleasure of the living in reaching their desires and even greater than the pleasures of the dead in the next world, as our sages said (Avot 4:17): "one hour of repentance and good deeds in this world is better than all of the life of the next world")

This is the highest of the levels of those who trust in G-d, reached by the prophets, pious ones, and treasured, pure men of G-d, and this is what the verse refers to in saying: *"Even [for] the way of Your judgments, O L-ord, have we hoped for You; for Your Name and for Your remembrance is the desire of [our] soul directed"* (Isaiah 26:8), and *"my soul thirsts to the Al-*

mighty, the living G-d; [when shall I come and appear before G-d?]"
(Tehilim 42:3).

These are the ten levels of trust which one cannot escape belonging to one of them. We find the matter of trust in scripture expressed in 10 synonyms corresponding to these 10 levels. They are:
Mivtach (trust), Mishan (support), Tikva (hope), Machse (protection), Tochelet (waiting), Chikui (expecting), Semicha (reliance), Sever (resting), Misad (confidence), and Chesel (assurance).

May G-d place us among those who trust in Him, who give themselves over to His judgment outwardly and inwardly, in His mercy, Amen.

The Gate of trust is Complete, to G-d the Last and the First.

> (*Translator*: some apt words from the introduction to the book "Path of the Just": "Therefore, the benefit to be gleaned from this book is not from a single reading... Rather the benefit derived [from this book] comes from review and diligent study..."
>
> *Rabbi Avigdor Miller zt'l*: When the Chovos Halevavos speaks about bitachon, trusting in Hakodosh Boruch Hu, as the most essential of all requirements of avodas Hash-em, he's talking there about a very high level of bitachon; he means complete confidence in Hakodosh Boruch Hu - trusting in Him constantly, continuously and implicitly. In order to be a noble servant of Hash-em, then this confidence, this bitachon in Hakodosh Boruch Hu, is the most necessary requirement. Of course, the bitachon in the sense that the Chovos Halevavos is describing there is a sublime achievement that's very difficult to attain. Anybody who thinks that this bitachon that the Chovos Halevavos demands from us is a pashuteh (simple) subject, that it can be transmitted in a few words, then he never really studied it. *It needs a lot of work - you're going to have to meditate on the ways of Hakodosh Boruch Hu for a long time until you become saturated with the consciousness of Hakodosh Boruch Hu; with the paramount awareness that everything is under His control and that everything that He does is for good.* (from Toras Avigdor, Parsha Bamidbar, Order and Tranquility).

Made in the USA
Las Vegas, NV
26 December 2023

83516281R00256